COLLECTED PAPERS

VOLUME THREE

Permission is gratefully acknowledged to the holders
of copyright to reprint these papers in a book form.

COLLECTED PAPERS

VOLUME THREE: POLITICAL ECONOMY

KENNETH E. BOULDING

LARRY D. SINGELL, EDITOR

COLORADO ASSOCIATED UNIVERSITY PRESS

BOULDER, COLORADO

COLORADO ASSOCIATED UNIVERSITY PRESS

BOULDER, COLORADO

Copyright © Kenneth E. Boulding 1973
Colorado Associated University Press
1424 Fifteenth Street
Boulder, Colorado 80302

Library of Congress Card Number 77-135288

ISBN 87081-046-4

CONTENTS

INTRODUCTION TO THE COLLECTED PAPERS OF KENNETH E. BOULDING

VOLUME III: POLITICAL ECONOMY

The papers in this volume were written for a variety of different occasions. And, while they possess many common themes and all deal with some aspect of the social system, almost the only feature which unites them is that they all are "applied" rather than "pure" social science.

About half of the papers deal with various segments of the social system. These include articles on agriculture (7 and 10), on corporations (8 and 11), a large number on education (21, 24, 27, 29, 30, 33 and 34), one paper on health services (17), one on religion (2), one on water resources (14) and five on the war industry (1, 16, 22, 26 and 32). Though these cover a fairly wide range of subjects, I make no pretense that they are definitive discussions of the subjects.

It is, perhaps, as interesting to note what subjects are missing from this group of papers as it is to note the subjects that are included, not only for the light it throws on my own deficiencies as a student of the social system, but also for knowledge on what subjects were salient and what were ignored by social scientists during this period.

There is very little, for instance, on financial institutions—banking, insurance, the stock market, international trade, etc. This is a field of great importance for economists, at least, and I find some need to explain why I did so little work on this subject. It is a vineyard where there is no lack of laborers, and I have always been attracted to areas which seem to be neglected. I must confess, also, that while I have found the theoretical problems connected with financial institutions of great interest, the organization and structural arrangements have been fairly stable during my professional life, at least in the capitalist world.

The international monetary system is an exception, perhaps, but the literature on it has been adequate for my purposes. Moreover, this subject is a little inaccessible to a student who is not a specialist. I certainly wish I knew more about the international monetary system, but I must confess I do not feel enormously deprived by my ignorance of it.

The labor movement and union organization is another area which is hardly represented in my published works, though this is a subject in which I have had a great deal of interest. I went to Iowa State College in 1943 at the invitation of T. W. Schultz, with the intention of becoming a labor economist, and I spent a whole year studying the labor movement. This experience had a profound effect on my subsequent intellectual interests. It persuaded me that economic models and abstractions were a rather small, though I still think essential, element in the study of any particular segment of the social system, and that, in particular, in order to study the labor movement one had to be a sociologist, anthropologist, and political scientist, as well as an economist. It was this experience which started me off in my interest in general social systems. I have written very little, however, on the labor movement itself, again perhaps because I felt I did not have much to add to the excellent descriptive literature in this field.

Another area which I have neglected is the study of the household and the economics and sociology of the family, still, perhaps, the largest single moderately homogeneous segment in any social system or economy.

The rest of the papers included in this volume—those that are "applied," but do not deal with segments of the social systems—can be divided into two main types: methodology and economic objectives.

Included among the group on methodology, systems, etc. are papers 3, 5, 6, 12, 18, 20, 28, 35, 36 and 37. These argue the need for a general social science, for an integrated view of the total earth system. Our present academic division of subject matter systems—such as the lithosphere, hydrosphere, atmosphere, biosphere and sociosphere—are all arbitrary, to some extent, and scholars in their separate disciplines too often forget that each arbitrary unit of study within the total earth system acts upon all others and is, in turn, acted upon by them. As a social scientist, of course, I have concentrated on the "sociosphere," the inputs, outputs, organizations, interactions, etc., of human beings. And while I am aware that the sociophere is embedded in a biosphere—as well as in the spheres of rocks, water and air—I make no claim to competence in these other fields.

The articles gathered under the general heading of economic objectives include a large number on economic progress or economic development (2, 4, 5, 12, 15, 19, 21, 23, 28, 29 and 38). There is one paper (13) on freedom as a goal of social organization. Unfortunately, there is nothing on justice in this volume (one is included in Volume IV). This is, perhaps, a reflection of the period in which these papers were written, but is, nonetheless, a serious deficiency. For with the approach of a stationary economic state—a "spaceship earth"—economic progress is no longer as important as it once was, though, of course, it remains enormously important for poor countries and the poor classes within wealthy countries.

In recent years, my interests have shifted toward "grants economics"and the integrative system. These are represented, however, only by papers 24 and 25.

A volume of articles on "Political Economy" cannot begin to exhaust the subject. Omissions are inevitable, for this collection is, after all, a record of what I have done, not what I have left undone. For these omissions, therefore, I must simply crave the reader's indulgence.

I would particularly like to thank Professor Larry Singell for the patience and hard work he has put into the editing of this volume. It has been a rewarding experience for me to work with him and I am most grateful for what he has done.

Kenneth E. Boulding

Boulder, Colorado, 1973

CAN WE CONTROL INFLATION IN A GARRISON STATE?

Social Action, 17, 3 (March, 1951): 3-24.

Can We Control Inflation In a Garrison State?

The rise in the cost of living above all previous records, and the prospect of a further rise have aroused most citizens to a tremendous interest in the problem of inflation. Indeed, inflation is likely to be the dominant economic problem of the coming generation, as deflation and unemployment were of the last.

Nature of Inflation

Inflation is a highly complex set of events and circumstances, and cannot be compassed in a single definition. Like most social problems that deeply beset us, this one cannot be explained in easy fashion with a few neat clichés. You will have to be willing to sweat out this issue with me. The principal characteristic of inflation is a rise in the general level of prices (including money wages as prices). Because all prices do not rise in the same proportion it is generally impossible to measure the rate or degree of inflation exactly. Nevertheless when the various indexes of prices, such as the wholesale price level or the cost-of-living index, more than double, as they have done in the past ten years, there can be no doubt in anyone's mind that inflation has been taking place. Another way of stating the same thing is to say that inflation is a decline in the purchasing power of the dollar; the dollar today will buy only about half as much as it did ten years ago.

Symptoms and the Disease

The rise in the general level of prices which is the usual measure of inflation is merely a symptom of the disease. It is, moreover, a symptom which may be suppressed for a time by price control and rationing, though it cannot be suppressed indefinitely. The price level alone, therefore, especially in short periods, will not tell us exactly how great is the inflationary pressure. The price level is the thermometer of inflation, but not the heat!

The "heat" of inflation is *the expenditure of money* in excess of the total value of things available for purchase at the *existing* price level. The total volume of money expenditure may increase for two reasons; either because of an increase in the total quantity of money, or because of an increase in what is called the "velocity of circulation." Even if the total quantity of money in the possession of the people does not change, the total volume spent may rise or fall simply because people are spending money "faster" than before. Small changes in the total money spent, and small changes in price levels may sometimes be accounted for by changes in the speed with which money "changes hands" or circulates. Large changes in the price level, however, such as we have experienced in the past ten years, are always a result of changes in the total quantity of money.

War and Inflation

Changes in the quantity of money sufficient to cause serious inflation are almost invariably the result of government deficits incurred as a result of war. The relationship is a direct one. A "cash deficit" of government means that the government is paying out to private citizens more money than it is taking in from them. The difference between what it pays out and what it takes in, in any period is the increase in the quantity of money in private accounts—private creation or destruction of money not being considered.

Thus if the government in any period takes in (from taxation and other sources) 100 million dollars out of the accounts of the people, and pays out (in wages, salaries, payments for purchases, interest, pensions, etc.) 120 million dollars, then there must have been an increase of 20 million dollars in the money holdings of the people. If government receipts come not only from taxes and the sales of goods but from the sale of government bonds, these bonds are also added to the assets of private citizens, and may represent a near-substitute for money and so add to the inflationary pressure. If government bonds are sold to banks the result is an increase in bank deposits (money) in private non-bank hands roughly equivalent to the amount of the bonds sold. This means a greater inflationary pressure than if the bonds had been sold to private persons.

Effects of Inflation

The more basic causes of inflation cannot be understood without a prior consideration of its *effects*. The most striking effect of inflation is the redistribution of income. Generally speaking those whose incomes or assets are fixed, or at least not easily adjustable, are made worse off by inflation; those whose incomes (profit) are derived from the ownership of "real" assets are made better off. Debtors are generally made better off by inflation, at the expense of creditors, for debt is almost always reckoned as a certain sum of dollars. Thus a farmer who has a mortgage of $10,000 on his farm can pay it off very easily if there is an inflation, for his money income rises along with the rise in prices, but the debt remains the same. Creditors and receivers of interest, on the other hand, find that they are worse off than before. They receive the same sum in dollars, but these dollars have smaller purchasing power.

The distribution of income is affected in similar ways, but in the opposite direction, by deflation. Creditors and the recipients of fixed money incomes, such as pensions and annuities, gain at the expense of the ordinary shareholder and businessman. The distributive effects of deflation, however, are further complicated by the fact that deflation usually gives rise to unemployment, which in itself creates a sharp shift in the distribution of income within classes between those who are employed, or whose resources are employed, and those who are unemployed.

Inflation, on the other hand, generally results in something approaching full employment, unless it leads into what is called "hyperinflation." This is a situation in which all faith in the stability of the purchasing power of money collapses, and the price level rises almost vertically—the kind of thing that happened in Germany after World War I and in Hungary after World War II. In hyperinflation the disorganization of all customary economic relationships may lead to unemployment;

normally, however, inflation and full employment are associated.

For this reason, among others, inflation is much more popular and over the long pull of history has been more frequent in its occurrence than deflation. Another, and less subtle reason, is that inflation has been an easy way out of the financial difficulties of sovereign states. When the state cannot raise enough money by taxation to pay for its extravagances, it inevitably finds it necessary to resort to some form of money-creation. Hence the history of almost all currencies has been a steady decline in the purchasing power of the unit. The United States in the past 150 years has been a remarkable exception to this rule.

"Need" Served by Inflation

Inflation—and also deflation—is not an arbitrary phenomenon which arises merely because of the whim of the state or the people. It is an expression of a deep-seated "need" of the economic system and has a "purpose" to accomplish. This "need" and "purpose" is not of course conscious—indeed it is generally quite unrecognized. Nevertheless we must ask what inflation is trying to bring about. Only by understanding this can we understand the fundamental conditions which give rise to it, and what must be done if it is to be stopped. Roughly speaking, inflation can be regarded as an attempt to check "overconsumption." Society cannot possibly consume *and* accumulate more than it produces. If, say, in a given year a closed society (*i.e.*, a society without imports or exports) produces 100 billion dollars worth of goods and consumes 80 billion dollars worth, there must be 20 billion dollars worth "left over" which is added to the total stock of goods. If now people's incomes and tastes are such that consumers are trying to consume 90 billion dollars worth, and households and business together are trying to accumulate a further 20 billions, the value of the total output must rise to 110 billion dollars. If the economy is at full employment so that there cannot be any increase in physical output, the only way in which this can be accomplished is through a rise in prices.

To put the matter in another way: What is "available" for households to purchase consists of the total output of goods, less what government and businesses take out of the "pot" for their own uses. If the total *value* of goods available for households at current prices is less than the amount of money which households wish to spend, there must be a rise in prices, in a free market, in order to "ration" the available goods. If prices under these circumstances are *prevented* from rising by price controls, "shortages" will develop; that is, at prevailing prices people will be willing to buy more than is available for purchase. Under these circumstances stocks of consumables will decline sharply. The shelves of the stores empty. Some form of rationing, whether an informal kind of the under-the-counter variety, or whether formal governmental rationing, must develop.

Object of Inflation

The *object* of inflation, therefore, whether it is overt or suppressed, is to reduce the consumption of the people, or to put it quite brutally, to reduce the general standard of living to what is "available." Inflation cuts the coat to fit the cloth. It is, however, a very ineffective instrument for this task. If we could have a rise in prices without any rise in money incomes, of course, consumption would be cut sharply and the object of the inflation achieved almost immediately. Unfortunately, however,

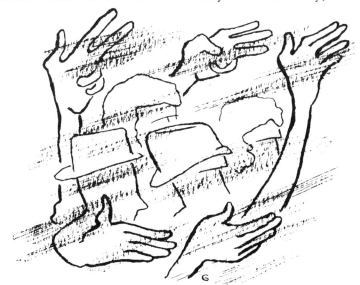

from the viewpoint of achieving a reduced level of living, as prices rise incomes rise too. This occurs because the incomes of most people depend on prices of some kind. Farm incomes, for instance, rise as the prices of agricultural commodities rise, and labor incomes rise as money wages rise. If everybody's income rose along with the rise in prices the inflation would not be able to achieve its object of reducing consumption, and would become progressively faster. When an inflation utterly fails to achieve its purpose in this direction it collapses into "hyper-inflation."

Redistribution of Income in Inflation

An inflation, however, frequently achieves its object without collapsing into hyperinflation. It does this by bringing about a redistribution of income. We have seen that inflation shifts income away from pensioners, bond and mortgage holders, the receivers of interest, people with fixed or "sticky" salaries or wages, and shifts it toward farmers, businesses and the makers of profit. Wage earners generally occupy an intermediate position. There seems to be some tendency for them to lose ground, relatively, during an inflation, as wages are not so rapidly adjusted as the prices of most consumable goods, but the effect is slight. Paradoxically enough it is organized labor that tends to lose ground most during an inflation. In such a period the wages of unorganized workers generally rise faster than the wages of organized workers.

Generally speaking the people who lose most by an inflation are the "consuming classes," those whose consumption is large in relation to the contribution which they make to the *current* national product: widows, orphans, old people, pensioners, and so on. This is important for Christians to understand, for they are always obligated by their gospel to help those who are made victims of social forces. The people who gain by an inflation are the business classes, the profit makers whose consumption is usually much less than their income. As a result of this redistribution the consumption of those who are hit by the inflation is sharply curtailed, whereas the consumption of those who benefit may not be greatly expanded, and their increased incomes are saved. If this effect is sufficiently large the inflation may be "successful" in the sense that it does not show any tendency to accelerate, and may even slow down.

Taxes and Control of Inflation

We can see now why economists generally regard taxation as the principal key to the solution of the problem of inflation. It may truly be said that taxation is a *substitute* for inflation. Indeed, the principal function of the tax system is not to "raise money for the government to spend." Government, having the power to create money, need never lack for it. The chief purpose of taxation is rather so to adjust the cash holdings of private persons and institutions that there is neither inflation nor deflation. Taxation, in and of itself, operates directly to reduce consumption. It accomplishes directly, therefore, the indirect purpose of inflation.

We can see that this is so if we ask ourselves what would happen if government, continuing its expenditures, neglected to collect any taxes. The goods and services which were purchased by the government would be withdrawn from the private part of the economy, thus diminishing the goods available for household purchases. We see this very clearly during a war, when the absorption of a large part of economic production by government to maintain and equip the armed forces means that less automobiles, washing machines, houses, food and clothing are available for civilians. If government collected no taxes, at the same time that goods were being withdrawn from the civilian population, money would be poured into their pockets by the government expenditures.

These circumstances would issue in a sharp rise in prices, in order to try to "ration" the available goods. This rise in prices, however, as we have seen, may be self-defeating, for it leads to further rise in incomes. It may also lead to an ever more rapid spending as people lose faith in the stability of the value of money. The rise in prices would also lead to ever greater government expenditures and an ever greater quantity of money pumped into the people's accounts. The situation would soon collapse into hyperinflation. If now we suppose the collection of taxes to be restored, two things result. Money is taken out of the private circulation into government by the taxes. And the purchasing power of the public is thereby reduced. If the tax collections are sufficient to reduce the purchasing power of the public to what is available for it to buy at current prices, there will be no inflation.

If there is an expansion in the amount of goods and services absorbed by government (for example, due to a war) at a time when there is full employment, this expansion will be inflationary even if the budget is balanced. The absorption of goods and services by government means that there is a smaller quantity available for private consumers. If the budget is balanced this means that the quantity of money in the hands of private people is not diminished, and we may reasonably expect about the same volume of expenditure as before directed towards a smaller supply of goods, with consequent rise in prices. If an expansion of government absorption of goods and services is *not* to be inflationary there must actually be an excess of taxation over government disbursements, so that there is a removal of money from private hands—that is, there must be a budget surplus. This is such an extremely unlikely event in wartime that it is not difficult to see why wars have almost without exception been inflationary in their effect.

Price and Wage Controls

In concluding discussion of these more technical economic aspects of the problem we should examine now the significance of price and wage control over inflation. We have seen that a rise in the general level of money prices and wages is a symptom of a deep-seated disease rather than a disease itself. Never-

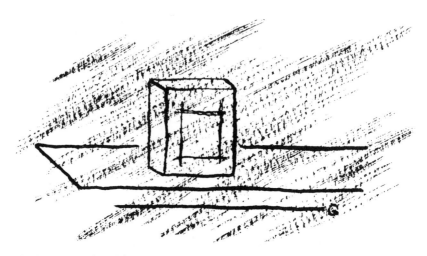

theless we should not rush to the conclusion that any attempt to control the symptoms is undesirable. Yet an attempt to control symptoms merely, without at the same time attacking the deeper sources of trouble, may indeed be doomed to failure.

Price and wage control may be of some assistance in controlling the sources of inflationary pressure as well as in suppressing its expression. In so far as it does lead to rationing, whether formal or informal, it acts as a direct control on consumption. Thus it achieves directly what a rise in prices would only achieve indirectly and by a serious disturbance in income distribution. In so far also as price control leads to confidence in the future stability of prices it leads to a decline in the velocity of circulation and a lessening of the immediate inflationary pressure. If people are afraid that prices are going to rise they will rush to buy almost anything they can lay their hands on, and will want to diminish their holdings of money. This action in itself creates the very rise in prices which was anticipated. If by means of price and wage control we destroy the expectation of rising prices, we destroy also much of the motivation for excessive spending, and hence actually reduce the inflationary pressure.

Price and wage control can only be effective, it must be emphasized, as long as the inflationary pressure is mild. It represents a dam which can help to control a small flood, but is helpless in the face of a great one. If the inflationary pressure is too strong black markets will inevitably develop and the system of control will break down.

Ethical Problems Raised by Inflation

Grave ethical problems are raised by inflation and by deflation to which Christians must become sensitive. At first sight mere changes in the general level of prices might not seem to create any serious ethical problems. It has often been pointed out that the *absolute* level of prices is a matter of very little significance. Thus if we decided tomorrow to call every cent a dollar, wherever it occurred in the economic system, all prices, all wages, all incomes, all debt would rise a hundredfold. But nobody would be any the worse off, or the better off. The change would have no more significance, either economic or moral, than a universal shift in a decimal point.

The economic and moral problems arise in the *process* of inflation (or deflation) and arise because of the fact that all prices, incomes, debts and so on which are measured in money do *not* change in the same proportion. Hence the inflationary process gives rise to these marked shifts in the distribution of wealth and income which we have noticed earlier. In general, the nature of the distribution of income is closely related to the moral problems of achieving a just and free society. In particular, tremendous ethical problems arise because both inflation and deflation create a sharp disparity between the private interest of individuals and the general interest of society as a whole.

Fairly general agreement exists that higher ethical conduct is represented by action in the interest of the "whole" than by action in the interest simply of the individual concerned. For Christians, loyalty to the God revealed by Christ should always widen our interests and concerns. But at once a set of ethical problems confronts us in connection with the *definition* of the "general interest" in a particular situation. To what "whole," for instance, should it refer—family, nation, world, church? And how is the general interest measured?

Real moral problems of this sort are involved where "mild" inflation or deflation is in question. It is by no means certain, for instance, that an absolutely stable price level is most desirable, let us say from the point of view of the majority in our national economy. Possibly a certain amount of instability in the price level is actually desirable. It may, for example, promote a faster rate of economic progress by constantly "disinvesting" the ancient vested interests, and allowing the more energetic members of society to deprive the slothful and foolish of their inherited wealth. Something may even be said, on rather similar lines, for a moderate cycle in employment. Full employment has its "costs" and we should not assume without further question that an absolutely stable level of employment is the most desirable.

Nevertheless, where deflation and depression bring conditions such as those in 1932, or where inflation results in a doubling of the price level in ten years, pretty clearly a real evil is involved. For the kind of inflation and deflation problems with which our society has been wrestling, fine arguments about the exact point at which things are "best" are irrelevant. We are dealing with large and obvious evils, and we need to go after them with meat axes and bulldozers, not with scalpels and salt spoons.

Conflict of Individual and Public Interest

In our situation the most acute ethical problems arise not in theory (what is the right thing to do) but in practice (how does one do it). In both inflation and deflation a sharp conflict arises between behavior which is fairly obviously in the public interest and behavior which is directed toward one's private preservaion or advancement. If a person is sure of a coming inflation, he should in order to protect his own relative position in society sell all bonds and reduce money holdings to an absolute minimum, buying those things which seem most likely to rise in price. This action in itself, however, adds to the inflationary pressure. If indulged in by enough people it may actually create an inflation even in the absence of other inflationary forces.

Similarly if one anticipates a deflation the thing to do, for one's own personal advantage, is to sell as much as one can and hoard money, for in a deflation money is constantly rising in value. The moral problem in this case is particularly acute for a businessman. If he expects a severe deflation with reasonable certainty the only way in which his business can survive may be for him to liquidate as much as possible, fire as many workers as possible and shut down his plant. If he attempts to run his plant in a period of sharply falling prices he will almost inevitably make losses of a magnitude which may bankrupt him. By taking precautions against a depression, however, he helps to bring it on. By selling off his inventories he accentuates the deflationary pressure. By reducing his output and laying off his men he diminishes income everywhere and adds to the deflationary spiral.

Christian Perfection

Now it is clearly part of Christian perfection to follow the general interest even at the complete sacrifice of our own. If we are completely given over to Divine love, if we believe that all children in the world are equally dear to God, then we identify our own welfare with the welfare of the whole family of mankind, or even of all creation. This is what love of our neighbor as ourselves means: to achieve the kind of detachment from interest in self which enables us to see ourselves as we really are, as one among many, and to order our behavior in the light of our apprehension of the whole rather than of the part which we constitute. In the moral sphere this change corresponds somewhat to the new apprehension in metaphysics that we live in a "public" world of space and time, and that we are not actually the center of a real horizon that moves with us as we walk.

The kind of moral maturity which is involved in Christian

perfection, however, is a matter of slow growth, and we do not understand too well the nature of the laws which govern its development. We certainly cannot assume that many people achieve moral maturity, and even those who subscribe to the ideal of Christian perfection are aware of how far they fall short of it in their own conduct. Therefore, the pressing task confronts us of so ordering the institutions of social life that for any individual the private and the social interest do not diverge too far. We may not want to achieve, even if we could, a complete identity of the private and the social interest; otherwise the moral resources of men would never be tested and character would not develop. Perhaps there is an optimum amount of temptation for the development of moral fiber. Nevertheless, in this world our problem nearly always seems to be too much rather than too little temptation. Too great temptation is even more destructive to the moral character than too little. If we are constantly placed in situations where divergence between our self-interest and the general interest is so great that we abandon the general interest in favor of our own, the lapse eventually becomes a habit and the sense of identification with the general interest which is the essence of all morality and the very cement of society itself is weakened.

Law and Public Morals

The whole business of law is to create "artificial"' mechanisms in society which will diminish for each individual the gap between his own and the general interest. The chief mechanism is the creation and enforcement of *penalties* for actions which would otherwise be in the private but not in the public interest. The punishment of theft is a good case in point. Without legal sanctions it would often be in the private interest of an individual to steal. The prosperity of society at large, however, depends upon respect for property rights. Hence, stealing is very rarely in the public interest. The object of legal institutions therefore, is to introduce an element of risk of private loss into actions which otherwise result in a private gain at public expense.

"Theft" by Inflation

Inflation and deflation have almost the same kind of effect on society as theft on an enormous scale. Both inflation and deflation redistribute the wealth of society, as theft redistributes it, without process of law and without consent. Even a small amount of deflation, and large amount of inflation, may have the further effect that much wealth is destroyed in the process. It is evident that the ordinary processes of law are helpless in the face of movements of this kind. This is because the legal concept of property is essentially a *physical* concept. Theft in law is the removal of some physical object from its lawful to some unlawful custodian. The economically significant concept of property however is a *value* concept, which may roughly be identified with a purchasing power concept. Thus a man who steals my purse commits theft; but if by inflation the value or purchasing power of what is in my purse declines, no theft, in the legal sense, has been committed, yet as far as the effect on me is concerned the two are virtually identical. The history of our society indicates that while we have been moderately successful in preserving the rights of physical property, we have been very unsuccessful in preventing that instability of the economy which may be even more disturbing than outright lawlessness.

The Economic Task of Government

The task of maintaining stability in the economic system is inescapably a task of government. Indeed, it may properly be said that the principal economic task of government (that organization within the body of society which is specifically charged with the protection and good order of the whole society) is to "govern" in the sense in which a governor of an engine governs. Government should be a thermostat to keep the economic and social temperature steady. Cycles large enough to bring widespread misery are an evidence of an inadequate governing mechanism.

Thus the house with a hand-fired furnace run by a somewhat inexperienced or absent-minded householder exhibits a marked temperature cycle. Indeed, it may almost be said to have only two temperatures, too hot and too cold. If the house is cold the fireman goes down and opens up drafts and shovels coal on the furnace, with the result that in a little while the house is too hot; whereupon the fireman goes down again and shuts the draft and banks the fire, with the result that in a while the house is too cold again, and the cycle repeats itself almost indefinitely. Even in a house with a thermostatically controlled furnace there is still a temperature cycle; the temperature has to rise a little above the level set in the thermostat before the furnace is turned off, and a little below this level before it is turned on. The lag between turning on the furnace and heating the house will create a small cycle even above and below these points. Nevertheless with a properly adjusted thermostat the temperature cycle can be controlled until it is barely noticeable.

Our economic and political system is beset with many cycles or fluctuations great enough to be seriously disturbing—even to threaten the very existence of the system and man within it. Such fluctuations are clear evidence of the lack of a proper governing mechanism in the system. This inadequacy in the institutions of government creates most of the acute moral conflicts between individual and general interests. We have seen this conflict operating in the economic sphere; it operates equally in the political sphere.

Moral Conflict in Politics

War is a semi-cyclical phenomenon similar in many ways to economic cycles, and indeed related to them. The history of any nation can be divided roughly into "pre-war periods" when things go from bad to worse, as in a depression, and "post-war periods" when things go from bad to better, as in a recovery. The turning point is frequently, although not invariably, war itself, which corresponds somewhat to an economic "crisis." An arms race corresponds in many ways to an economic deflation: every nation tries to improve its relative position by increasing its armaments, a process which renders everybody as a whole all the more insecure. The conflict here between action in the general interest (that is, of humanity at large) and action in the particular interest of the national state becomes unbearably acute. In providing for its own defense each nation is adding to the insecurity of all and even contributing to the downfall of the great society of which it is a part. Yet in the absence of any world "governing" institution every nation feels that it must provide for its own defense, just as during a depression every business feels that it must provide for its own defense by liquidating its assets, even though by so doing it is contributing to the very depression from which it seeks to defend itself.

Principles of Governing Mechanisms

Fortunately the *principles* of governing mechanisms are now fairly well known, especially as they are met with in so many sciences.* If anything is to be stabilized there must be first an *indicator* of the thing to be stabilized which is capable of sending messages showing when there is "too much" or "too little." Secondly, there must be a *controller* capable of receiving these messages and acting upon them in such a way that "more" is created when there is too little and "less" when there is too much. Then every time there is "too much," a force is brought into play to lessen the amount, and every time there is "too little" a force is brought into play to increase the thing to be stabilized. The situation being controlled will fluctuate within limits around its "just right" position to an amount depending on the sensitivity of the apparatus. The thermostat, which sends more heat when there is too little and less when there is too much, is a good example of a simple mechanism of this kind.

Governing Mechanism for Payments

In the economic system a very simple governing mechanism could be set up to stabilize the total volume of *payments*—that is, the total amount of money changing hands in a particular

---

*A detailed discussion of these mechanisms is to be found in Norbert Wiener's *Cybernetics* (Wiley and Sons, 1948), and a more popular exposition in the same author's *The Human Use of Human Beings* (Houghton Mifflin, 1950).

period of time. We already have an "indicator" analogous to the thermometer in the collection of systematic economic statistics. By modern methods of sampling we are now able to get a remarkable amount of information which is accurate enough for our purposes at relatively small expense. Indeed, the improvement in the techniques of obtaining information which has been proceeding at such a rapid pace in the past two or three decades may rank as one of the major technical changes of the twentieth century. These techniques permit the establishment of governing mechanisms and techniques of government which would be unthinkable without them.

What we lack, however, is any clear, objective, or automatic "controller" which can act upon the information in these messages. If we had an agency in society which would automatically act in a deflationary way when the indicator registered inflation, and in an inflationary way when the indicator registered deflation, some sort of stability would be established.

Use of the Tax System

Such a "controller," as far as the total volume of payments is concerned, could easily be set up through the tax system. The collection of taxes as we have seen is a deflationary act. By reducing the stock of money in the hands of the public taxes operate directly to reduce the total volume of private expenditures and receipts (payments).* An increase in tax collections therefore reduces the total volume of payments and a reduction in tax collections increases them. With a pay-as-you-go income tax the total volume of tax collections could be adjusted quickly and easily by adjusting the tax rates. If the tax rates were linked to the *movement* in the index of total private payments, so that every time this index went up, say one per cent, tax rates increased two per cent, and every time the index went down one per cent, tax rates went down two per cent, the total volume of private payments could be stabilized within quite narrow limits.

---

*Every payment is an expenditure to the payer and a receipt to the payee. In a closed society, therefore, the total volume of expenditures is exactly the same thing as the total volume of receipts.

Such a system could be wrecked, of course, like any other, if too great a strain were placed upon it. It would not, for instance, survive the inflationary impact of a major war. For with every rise in government expenditure, tax rates would have to rise in greater proportion and would soon become politically intolerable. I do not believe, however, that there is any way of avoiding inflation in a major, even a quite middle-sized war. The inflation is part and parcel of the social breakdown which war itself represents.

Complexity of Economic Stabilization

Unfortunately the problem of economic unemployment is more difficult than seems to be indicated above, even neglecting the political difficulties of such a scheme. Stabilizing the total volume of payments (which is, I now believe, the only thing which can certainly be stabilized through the tax system) does not necessarily involve stabilizing either output of goods, employment, or prices, though it renders extreme fluctuations in these more important objects of stabilization much less likely. A small output, much unemployment, and niggardly trade at high prices could give us the *same total volume of payments* as a large output with correspondingly little unemployment and much trade at low prices. A payment of $10 may represent a purchase of five shirts at $2 each, or two shirts at $5 each, or 1 shirt at $10 each. With a stable total volume of payments, therefore, it would be quite possible to have widely fluctuating output, employment, trade and prices—the first three moving roughly in one direction and prices in the other direction.

If while we are trying to keep payments stable there is an upward shift in prices two things must happen. Either trade and probably output and employment will diminish, or the stability of payments will break down and in the endeavor to prevent unemployment we will permit the total volume of payments to rise to take care of the higher prices. All too likely, therefore, a society committed to full employment *and* with institutions which permit a rise in the price or money wage level as full employment is reached, may find itself also committed to perpetual inflation. This is particularly likely if a society has extreme difficulty in bringing about a *reduction* in the level of money prices and money wages, a difficulty which may arise in a nation with strong labor and farm organizations.

Possibility of Continual Inflation

These considerations lead to a somewhat discouraging conclusion. Unless we can develop methods for rapid and overall reductions in the general level of money wages and prices from time to time, a policy of stabilizing employment may be achieved at the cost of a perpetually rising price level. If we can never have a fall in money wages and prices, we can never correct a rise. The rise may theoretically be prevented by a permanent system of price and wage control. Price and wage control, however, has never been successful, outside a totalitarian society, except on a strictly temporary basis. Price control can work for a time because it starts off by freezing a system of relative prices and wages which have been developed by the sensitive operations of free markets. The original price and wage system, however, rapidly gets out of date as demands and techniques change. With present knowledge of administration it has never proved possible to catch up with the necessary changes by any system of political administration. The principal technique of bureaucracy is delay rather than rapid and sensitive adjustments.

It is possible, of course, to adjust, as individuals and as a society, to a continually rising price level, but the adjustments may be extremely difficult and painful, especially in a society like ours which has never really had to face the problem. In a society with continual inflation private pension and insurance schemes, private savings in the form of bonds or mortgages may be almost worthless. The problem of provision for the aged becomes one which must be solved either by family or by social "charity" since the individual finds it very difficult to provide for his own security. Unless the nominal rates of interest rise to heights which seem to be institutionally impossible in our present system, "real" rates of interest will be negative. Borrowing and lending will seriously diminish, with a possible adverse effect on the rate of economic progess; that is, productivity gains will decrease due to a decline in investment in capital goods.

We have hardly begun to think about these problems. They may trouble the next generation as much as depression troubled the last. We should remember that inflation at a constant annual rate of five per cent, which seems small enough and has been far exceeded in the past few months, means an increase of thirty-two times in a lifetime. An annual increase of ten per cent means a thousand-fold increase in a lifetime. Changes of this magnitude can disrupt the whole fabric of a society.

Two Aspects of Ethical Conduct

To conclude, the problem of ethical conduct in economic affairs has two aspects. There is first the relatively simple traditional ethics of direct relationship of things to men and persons to persons—the old virtues of honesty, integrity, truthfulness, respect for persons and for property, industriousness, enterprise, and so on. This remains unchanged by anything I have said. These virtues are the cement which holds society together, without which any economic system disintegrates. Even capitalism, which seems at times to be deficient in the warmer virtues of charity, is built firmly on good faith and reasonable hope.

There is, however, a more subtle range of ethical and economic problems which arise because of the closely integrated nature of economic society—because we are in fact, members one of another in the body of social life, knit by the blood streams of monetary circulation and the nerve fibers of information. These problems of social stabilization and control cannot be solved merely by practicing the ethics of direct personal relationship. Our Christian faith requires us to understand the more impersonal forces of social life. It demands the adjustment of our conduct both as an earning and spending person and as a political influence to these more subtle standards of moral health.

present system, "real" rates of interest will be negative. Borrowing and lending will seriously diminish, with a possible adverse effect on the rate of economic progess; that is, productivity gains will decrease due to a decline in investment in capital goods.

We have hardly begun to think about these problems. They may trouble the next generation as much as depression troubled the last. We should remember that inflation at a constant annual rate of five per cent, which seems small enough and has been far exceeded in the past few months, means an increase of thirty-two times in a lifetime. An annual increase of ten per cent means a thousand-fold increase in a lifetime. Changes of this magnitude can disrupt the whole fabric of a society.

Two Aspects of Ethical Conduct

To conclude, the problem of ethical conduct in economic affairs has two aspects. There is first the relatively simple traditional ethics of direct relationship of things to men and persons to persons—the old virtues of honesty, integrity, truthfulness, respect for persons and for property, industriousness, enterprise, and so on. This remains unchanged by anything I have said. These virtues are the cement which holds society together, without which any economic system disintegrates. Even capitalism, which seems at times to be deficient in the warmer virtues of charity, is built firmly on good faith and reasonable hope.

There is, however, a more subtle range of ethical and economic problems which arise because of the closely integrated nature of economic society—because we are in fact, members one of another in the body of social life, knit by the blood streams of monetary circulation and the nerve fibers of information. These problems of social stabilization and control cannot be solved merely by practicing the ethics of direct personal relationship. Our Christian faith requires us to understand the more impersonal forces of social life. It demands the adjustment of our conduct both as an earning and spending person and as a political influence to these more subtle standards of moral health.

ECONOMICS AS A SOCIAL SCIENCE

The Social Sciences at Mid-Century:
Essays in Honor of Guy Stanton Ford
Minneapolis: Univ. of Minnesota Press, 1952, pp. 70-83.

Economics as a Social Science

ECONOMICS in the past has been a very self-contained subject. It may be the antiquity of the science which gives it a certain air of New England self-satisfaction, for it must be remembered that Adam Smith was a contemporary of Boyle, Ricardo of Dalton, and Mill of Darwin, and that therefore economics is older even than chemistry, much older than any of the biological sciences, and of course a positive greybeard compared with such johnny-come-latelys as sociology, psychology, anthropology, and genetics, to say nothing of the innumerable hybrid disciplines. It may also be that past experience with attempts at integrating economics with the other social sciences have discouraged or even frightened the economists. There have been at least two such attempts in the past hundred years — one by Marx and the other by Veblen. The best that can be said of these previous attempts is that insofar as they have been successful, they have been dangerous. The power of the Marxian system over the minds of men rests on the fact that it is a synthesis of economics, sociology, and political science. Its apparent completeness, and its ability therefore to give some sort of answer to almost any question, give it a persuasive power which has enabled it to take in a surprising number of intelligent people, in spite of the crudity of its value theory, the highly special character of its sociology, and its unfailing capacities for false predictions. Men crave closed systems, and want like sophomores to "know the answers." It is little wonder that ingenious integrations, however bad the components, exert a subtle fascination, especially over those who fancy themselves as belonging to the intelligentsia, and that they lead into dead ends of human development.

The task of integration, therefore, is not to be approached lightly. Nevertheless it is not to be set aside. The urge to integrate is there. If we do not have good integrations, we shall have bad ones. Furthermore, in the attempt to defend itself from premature integrations, it is easy for a specialized discipline itself to become a closed system and to lose touch with reality. There is some reason for fearing that economics has not been exempt from this tendency. The ultimate impact of both Marx and Veblen on the main stream of economic thought may have been to make economists draw in upon themselves in the logical and mathematical refinement of their own theories rather than to encourage them to reach out for a broader conceptual base. It is quite possible for an economist — especially a mathematical economist — to become so entranced by the beauty and ingenuity of his analysis that he quite fails to perceive when his conclusions are ridiculous, as occasionally they may be. It is not uncommon, especially for bright young men in the field, to feel that the other social sciences have nothing to offer them as economists, and to write and talk only for the select circle to which they belong.

While, therefore, I am not arguing that we should immediately set about the construction of a Grand Integrated Science of Everything, I *am* arguing for an increase in communication. There is no case for imperialism among the disciplines, and not much case for federation. But there is an overwhelming case for trade. One of the most important propositions of economics is that specialization without trade is useless (the tailor would starve and the farmer would shiver), and conversely that trade without specialization is impossible. In the market of ideas, as in other markets, there is a strange prejudice against the middleman. There is a prestige value about production, whether of theories or of potatoes. The humble trader, who merely disseminates and distributes, is rarely an object of admiration. Nevertheless it is not a breakdown in production which threatens us, but a breakdown in trade and in communication. We are not today perhaps threatened immediately by the kind of breakdown in trade which happened in the 1930's. We are, however, threatened by a far worse breakdown — a breakdown in the communication of ideas, desires, and ideals. It is hardly an exaggeration to say that the violence which is threatening our civilization is a direct result of a breakdown in communication between East and West. It is when we feel that we can no longer argue with people that we want to bash them over the head.

What, then, are the prospects for integration in the social sciences? It has been said that the greatest discovery in agricultural economics was that there is no such subject — there is only economics applied to

agricultural problems. It may be that the greatest discovery in economics will be that there is no such subject — that there is only social
science applied to economic problems. We are not, I think, ripe for
such a discovery at the present stage of the development of the various
social sciences — there is such a thing as marital readiness in science as
there is apparently among young people. Nevertheless there are signs
of courtship, if not of marriage, and we may be in a position at least
to announce some engagements.

The first of these signs is the development of *applied* studies which
clearly cut across all the regular departmentalizations. The field of
labor is a good example, which brings together economics, sociology,
political science, social psychology, law, engineering, psychology, psychiatry, and perhaps even a dash of religion. International relations is
another applied field which should, at least, require the cooperation of
many specialists. We are, I think, on the point of realizing that the
study of any institutional segment of society requires the cooperation
of literally all the disciplines.

Traditionally we have suffered from a sort of cartelization of the
intellectual market, whereby the institutional subject matter of social
science has been divided out among the various departments, giving
economists a monopoly of the study of banks, corporations, etc., giving tribes to the anthropologists, families to the sociologists, states to
the political scientists, and rats to the psychologists. Just as we have
begun to realize that labor institutions cannot be studied with the tools
of the economist alone, so it is beginning to dawn on us that the same
may be true of many hitherto monopolized fields. It would be fun, for
instance; to let the anthropologists loose on the banking system, to
study bankers as if they were a tribe, which in so many respects they
are, governed by custom and taboo as well as by rational calculations.
(One can almost visualize a delightfully racy book on "Coming of
Age in the Federal Reserve.") On the other hand, it is astonishing how
many anthropologists blithely undertake the study of the economic
life of primitive peoples without knowing any economics. It may one
day occur to somebody that the study of the household is a serious
integrated study, not a device for entertaining those young ladies who
insist on coming to college: up to now household economists, family
sociologists, and home economics departments have lived remarkably
isolated lives. One can notice the beginnings of a perception among
economists that the firm is not merely an economic organization, but

that in order to understand it, one must know something about the political process of decision-making in a group and the social psychology of consensus, conformity, and communication.

It is not the purpose of this paper to announce any grand integrated system: its main purpose is to explore some possible contributions of economics to other social sciences, and of other social sciences to economics. Being an economist, I naturally approach the first question from the point of view of the seller who is fairly knowledgeable about what he has to sell, but is a bit uncertain about what his customers want, or even whether he has any customers at all; and I approach the second question from the point of view of the buyer who has some ideas about what he wants, but is somewhat dubious about the capacity of his suppliers to deliver the goods.

The great contribution of economics is the idea of the "model"— i.e., of an abstract system bearing some faint resemblance to reality, but containing far fewer variables, and worked out in complete logical detail. I am not suggesting, of course, that economics has any monopoly on model-building, for all science involves abstraction from reality. Indeed, I suspect that when we say we "understand" anything, what we mean is that we perceive some degree of correspondence between the immeasurably complex operations of the real world and some model which we have created in our imaginations. Economics, however, largely because of certain favorable aspects of its subject matter, has been able to develop two methods of model-building which certainly have applicability in other fields. The first is the definition of a mutually determined, general equilibrium by means of a system of simultaneous equations. By this means the logical completeness of the system can be determined — i.e., whether enough relationships have been postulated to give a determinate position of equilibrium to all the variables. The second is a method which I shall christen the method of *plausible topology*. It is not enough simply to postulate equations and unknowns; we generally want to explore the *properties* of the systems: we want to know, for instance, what will happen to one variable or set of variables when another is changed, or when some of the underlying equations of the system are changed. Generally, however, we do not know the exact mathematical form of the significant relationships, though we know a little more than their mere existence: we postulate, therefore, some plausible topology for these relationships, defining their general shape but not their exact position. This is why geometry has proved so useful in economics, while excessive refinement in algebraic technique is apt to involve inserting illegitimate assumptions into the analysis in order to get a spurious exactness into the assumed relationships.

There are three principal examples in economics of the use of the above methods: first, the maximization models of economic organisms (firms or households); second, the particular equilibrium models of selected economic variables (supply and demand analysis of the Marshallian type); and third, general equilibrium models of the Walrasian-Keynesian type. In constructing a theory of the behavior of the economic organism (say, the firm) the economist assumes that there is some quantity descriptive of the organism (e.g., profits) which the organism maximizes. Thus the firm is supposed to select those outputs, inputs, prices, etc., which make profits as large as possible. For there to be a determinate maximum position, the theory must postulate a function or set of functions relating all the relevant variables to each other and to the maximand. Then, if various other conditions are satisfied, we can set the first differential of the maximand with respect to each variable in turn equal to zero: this is the condition for maximizing the maximand, and it immediately gives us as many equations as there are variables. If these equations have a unique, real solution, this is the "equilibrium" value of all the variables. If now we postulate certain broad properties (i.e., a plausible topology) for these functions — e.g., a law of diminishing returns for the production function, relating inputs to outputs; a law of market imperfection relating outputs or inputs to their prices — it becomes possible to deduce certain principles of behavior for the organism — i.e., certain *responses* to changes in its external environment, such as markets, or its internal environment, such as its production function. Thus we can deduce under what circumstances a rise in the price of the product (or a favorable change in markets) will raise output, and what sort of assumptions about the nature of the fundamental relationships will make this rise large or small.

There are a good many objections to the theory of maximization as a description of real behavior, the most serious being that it is deficient in its informational system: i.e., there is nothing, generally speaking, which tells us when we are *not* at the maximum (except in the important special case where the maximum is zero), and hence it can be argued that it is absurd to suppose that an organism proceeds to a maximum position if it doesn't know where that maximum is and there is nothing in its information-receiving machinery to inform it. In spite of these objections, however, the theory of maximization still holds the field, for want of anything better, and at least is a protection against certain crude errors.

Particular equilibrium models, of which supply-and-demand analysis is the best example, have been very successful in economics. The simplest model supposes that the quantity demanded is a function of price (the demand curve) and that the quantity supplied is another function of price (the supply curve), the equilibrium condition being that quantity demanded and quantity supplied should be equal, the result being three equations and three unknowns. The interpretative and even predictive power of this simple piece of apparatus is remarkable. It predicts that a price fixed above some equilibrium level will create surpluses and one fixed below an equilibrium level will create shortages — a prediction which never fails to surprise some unwary price-fixer. It predicts that monopoly power is more likely to be successful in raising prices where demands and supplies are inelastic — a proposition of great importance in understanding the success of craft unionism. It predicts that under some circumstances a good harvest may bring in less money than a poor harvest. These are substantial achievements for a crude piece of apparatus, and are not to be sniffed at, even by Integrators.

The third type of model which has been successful in economics is the general equilibrium model: it is this concept which perhaps has most to contribute to other disciplines. Formally the model consists of putting each variable of a system as a function of all the others: such a formal equality of unknowns and equations, however, tells us little. These models have become useful insofar as the number of unknowns and equations has been reduced to the point where the "plausible topology" of the model can again be discussed and certain topological conclusions drawn.

This has been the strength of the "Keynesian" type models, in spite of certain grave weaknesses. These models are derived by selecting a group of variables representing the great aggregates of the system, deriving one or more identities among these aggregates by breaking some aggregate down into parts and identifying the aggregate with the sum of its parts and then postulating enough empirical relationships among these variables to determine the system. In the simplest of these systems (which might almost be called the sub-Keynesian system) we first divide the national income (Y) into its two components, consumption (C) and investment (I), thus obtaining the identity $Y = C + I$. (All that this means is that anything which has been produced in a given period and has not been consumed is still around.) Then we assume two empirical functions: a consumption function, $C = F_c(Y)$, postulating the dependence of consumption on income, and a similar investment function, $I = F_i(Y)$. This gives us the requisite three equations for the three unknowns. As a matter of plausible topology certain assumptions can be made about the consumption and perhaps about the investment function — e.g., that consumption even at zero income would be positive, and that a given increase in income produces a smaller increase in consumption.

This slender apparatus throws a great deal of light on the problem of unemployment, for there is nothing in the model which indicates that the *equilibrium* value of income is the full employment value — i.e., under-employment equilibria, at least in the short run, are possible. We now see unemployment therefore as an "attempt" on the part of the system to get income down to the point where it can be absorbed by consumption and by willing investment, under conditions where the consumption and investment functions are too "low" to give a full employment equilibrium. It is hardly too much to say that this simple piece of apparatus makes the difference between "understanding" the phenomenon of unemployment, however imperfectly, and being wholly at sea about it.

The general equilibrium models also enable us to discover certain "macroeconomic paradoxes" — propositions which are true for an individual operating with an external environment, but are not true for closed systems which have no external environment. Thus an individual finds no impossibility in "hoarding" money — i.e., increasing his money stock by the process of not spending as much as he gets — and it is positively easy for an individual to "dishoard," or spend more than he gets. From the point of view of a closed system, however, it is evident that every payment, or transfer of money, is expenditure at one end and a receipt at the other, so that the total of expenditures must be exactly equal to the total of receipts. A closed society, that is, cannot possibly get rid of money by spending it, nor can it acquire money by not spending it. If everyone decides to increase his money stock by cutting down his expenditure, the result is not an increase in the total stock of money, but a decline in the total volume of payments. Strangely enough, the only way to increase the sum of all individual money holdings is by increasing the total stock of money by creating new money. There are other such paradoxes: decisions to save do not necessarily result in saving, but may simply destroy income; decisions to build up business reserves may not result in an increase in net worths, but may simply destroy profits. At a more familiar level, any individual can withdraw his bank deposit in the form of cash or can pay back his debts: any general action either to withdraw deposits or to pay debts would result in a virtual collapse of the system.

There are unquestionably similar paradoxes connected with closed systems in other fields, though they have hardly been explored as yet. A single nation, for instance, can increase its security by building up armaments: all nations taken together decrease their security by building up armaments. In general, any behavior of an individual which implies change in his relative position cannot be summed for a closed system. There must be many such cases, and I leave their discovery to the ingenuity of my colleagues in other fields.

I now turn to some contributions which may be made to economics by other sciences — even by nonsocial sciences. Perhaps the greatest opportunities for economists to learn something from their intellectual siblings arise in connection with the theory of the firm or, more generally, the theory of the single economic organism. Of all the economic models, the model of the theory of the firm based on the maximization principle, from which the marginal analysis is derived, is the least satisfactory. It is so unrealistic, in fact, as to prevent almost all communication between economists and businessmen — a far from desirable state of affairs, as those who study institutions should be able to learn something from those who run them, and those who run them, and who therefore never have time to think about what they are doing, should be able to learn something from those who merely think.

As expounded in the textbooks of economics, the firm is a strange object. It has no balance sheet, no financial statements, no problem of control, and no organization. It maximizes a variable called "net revenue," of which no accountant or businessman ever heard, and having done so, it lives happily ever after. It suffers no crises; it is subject to no neuroses; it shifts without any fuss or feathers in response to the slightest change in its environment, in spite of the fact that it seems to have no organs to inform it as to the nature, and still less the changes, in that environment. In the economics of the firm, moreover, nobody ever *learns* anything: indeed, a student could go through almost the whole of economic literature without finding a suspicion that there is a learning process — everybody is apparently born with the full complement of knowledge about not only his own demand curves and utility curves, but about the obscurest parts of the economic character of everybody else with whom he may come in contact. Even an economist suspects sometimes that this assumption falls short of realism: one can hardly be a teacher for long without discovering, often to one's surprise, that even students are capable of learning, and it is not a wide jump to the conclusion that if they can do it, anybody can.

It would not surprise me, therefore, to find that we are on the edge of a revolutionary change in the theory of the individual economic organism, a change inspired largely by developments outside the present framework of economics. There are a good many signs of the times in this regard. One is the increasing dissatisfaction with the conventional marginal analysis among economists themselves: a considerable controversy on this subject has been blossoming in the journals, and while some of it is due to misunderstanding, many of the objections are legitimate. Reinhold Noyes' monumental work *Economic Man* (Columbia, 1948) has called the attention of economists to some of the insights to be derived from physiology. Norbert Wiener's *Cybernetics* has opened up new vistas in the theory of the organism. Finally, in the field of economics proper, there is the work of a remarkable group of young men at the Carnegie Institute of Technology on the firm as a control mechanism (see especially two articles by W. W. Cooper on the "Theory of the Firm," in the *American Economic Review*, 39:1204 [1949] and in the *Quarterly Journal of Economics*, 45:87 [1951]).

Two closely related concepts seem to be emerging from these discussions. One is the concept of *homeostasis*, the other the concept of a *control mechanism*. The word "homeostasis" is to be attributed, I believe, to the great physiologist Cannon. It is, perhaps, only a fancier way of saying "equilibrium." It means the maintenance of a "state"— i.e., of some variable within a range of tolerable values. There are innumerable instances from physiology. The living organism largely consists of apparatus for maintaining a large number of physicochemical variables approximately constant, variables such as blood temperature, water content, calcium content, and cell count. Thus we can identify in all organisms or organizations, whether cell, mouse, man, family, city, firm, church, or state, certain *critical variables*. Variation in the value of these variables above some upper limit or below some lower limit will call forth *behavior* – i.e., changes in the organism designed to bring the values of these variables within the limits of tolerance.

A very simple theory of the firm, for instance, can be constructed on the assumption of a homeostasis of the balance sheet. We suppose that the firm wishes to maintain a certain set of items on its balance sheet: events which disturb these values call forth action to bring them back to their original values. Thus sales of product increase cash at the expense of inventory: the homeostatic behavior reaction to such an event will be to spend the increase in cash in order to produce more product, thus restoring the old quantities. Depreciation, on this assumption, seems to be the main force compelling activity; the firm must engage in production and exchange in order to be able to maintain its depreciating assets. One visualizes human activity as a desperate attempt to shore up a tottering structure which is being constantly corroded by moth and rust.

The homeostasis of the balance sheet is, of course, only a very first approximation, as it does not allow for income variables or for growth and decay. It is not difficult to include the income variables into a homeostatic scheme. We merely have to assume that there are tolerable levels of profits, for instance, which will not cause change in policy; if profits fall below some critical level, however, or even if they rise above some upper critical level, action will be called for. The theory of maximization can be seen as a highly special case of this more general theory, in which the upper and lower critical levels of profits coincide at the maximum. Growth and decay are more difficult to fit into a homeostatic scheme. We can perhaps suppose that growth is a homeostatic movement towards a size which is regarded as "ideal." The problem of "aging" and death is still, however, largely unsolved, even at the level of physiology. Even if the long run equilibrium for all of us is the grave, it is a little difficult to see why there is so much fuss involved in getting there.

Homeostasis always requires a control mechanism, and the studies of communications experts, evolving into the "new science" of cybernetics have thrown a great deal of light on the functioning of all organisms, economic organisms not excepted. The maintenance even of the simplest variable, such as, for instance, the temperature of a house, requires at least three pieces of apparatus with communication channels attached. There must be a *receptor of information* which can detect divergences of the critical variable from its tolerable values and which can transmit this information to an *interpreter*. The interpreter takes the information received and transforms it into *orders*, which are further communicated to an *effector*. The effector sets operations in motion that result in changes in the actual value of the critical variable. Thus in the simple case of the thermostatic control of temperature, the thermostat is the receptor; if the temperature of the air around it diverges from the level at which it is set, messages are sent to the furnace control (the interpreter), which translates these messages into orders to the furnace (the effector), which in turn by its pipes and radiators affects the temperature of the house. It should be observed that all control mechanisms of this type set up a cycle, and that the amplitude of this cycle depends largely on the sensitivity of the mechanism. Anyone who has run a hand-fired furnace can testify to the fact that being one's own thermostat results in a noticeable, and even an uncomfortable, temperature cycle.

In the theory of social organisms, and more particularly in the theory of the firm, the concept of a control mechanism focuses attention on the *information system* of the organism—i.e., on its receptors. In the firm this consists, first, of the accounting system; next, the whole system of "reports"—e.g., from personnel managers and sales managers; and finally, newspapers, journals, Kiplinger letters, and golf-club gossip as a means of acquiring information about the wider external environment. The executive is the interpreter who receives this mass of information and transforms it into orders or directives, which are in turn transmitted to appropriate persons within the organization (supervisors, foremen, workmen, salesmen) and eventually result in changes (production, sales, financing, etc.), which in turn feed back into the information system. An equilibrium situation presumably is one in which the information that is received by the executive results in orders that result in changes that result in information that is identical with the information previously received. It is a great advantage of this theoretical structure, however, that it is not confined to equilibrium situations, and is particularly well adapted to the interpretation of a dynamic flow.

The theory of control mechanisms may also be well adapted to accommodate certain insights from other social sciences. Sociologists, for instance, have made a good deal of use of the concepts of "crisis and adjustment," especially in their treatment of the family. In economics, except perhaps in the darker reaches of business cycle theory, there are no crises. It may well be, however, that the principal reason why the sociologist's family staggers from crisis to crisis, while the economist's firm floats in a happy-ever-after fairyland of equilibrium, is that practically all sociologists have been in a family, whereas not too many economists have ever had intimate association with a firm. The study of what constitutes a "crisis" in a firm, and what the nature is of the adjustments it makes, is a wide-open field for the promising young empiricist. The "crisis" concept also fits well into the control mechanism picture: there are certain mechanisms which are routine in their operation, and there are others which are not; there are some variables which may have a wide range of tolerance, and some which do not. Where variables have a wide range of tolerance, there may be long, unfavorable movements which produce no action whatever. Eventually, however, the movement brings the variable to the edge of toleration, and dramatic action may result from an apparently very small movement of the variable. We badly need studies of the nature of crises in firms, and the nature of their reactions to them. Why, for instance, do some firms react to an inventory or liquidity crisis by cutting down production, while others react by cutting prices? What are the items in the information system which give rise to changes in price policy? What is it in the information system which gives rise to changes in investment policy? Questions such as these would be most fruitful objects of study.

There is even a possibility that economists might learn something from the psychologists. Every generation or so some economist has had the idea that something might be learned from the psychologists, and almost always has returned from his forays into their strange country empty-handed and discouraged. As a result, economists have simply gone ahead and constructed for themselves whatever psychology they need, which is not much. Now, however, it is possible that a genuine rapprochement may be made in the field of learning theory. The problem here is, How do the behavior patterns, and especially the transformation functions relating information received to orders given, change systematically in response to past experience? Without learning theory of some kind, it is difficult to see how there can be much in the way of economic dynamics, especially in the difficult theory of oligopoly, where the behavior of each firm depends on what it thinks it knows about the possible reactions of others.

This brings me to the last resting place of all discussions on methods — the problem of statics and dynamics. Here I find myself in the curious position of, on the one hand, saying that economics has very important contributions to make to the study of social dynamics, and, on the other hand, finding it almost necessary to deny that there is or can be any such thing as *economic* dynamics. Out of pure economics there have come two important general contributions to the study of processes in time. The first is the method of comparative statics, or comparative equilibrium. In studying change, we first postulate an initial equilibrium position of a "model": then we change certain elements in the model and find the new position of all the variables. Then we have some confidence that a change in one set of variables will "produce" the changes in the others. The second contribution, for which we are mainly indebted to Professor Samuelson, is the application of difference equations to the study of the dynamics of economic models. A difference equation expresses the value of one or more variables as a function of one or more *preceding* values of the same variable. In time series this means that we can express the situation on Tuesday as some function of the situation on Monday, or perhaps on Sunday and Saturday as well. If these relationships are stable, prediction becomes possible; prediction is *only* possible if stable difference equations (or differential equations) can be discovered. This is the basis of the success of celestial mechanics in predicting the movements of the heavenly bodies. Social dynamics is a kind of celestial mechanics applied to the variables (planets!) of society.

The contributions of economics to social dynamics are, therefore, of great importance. Nevertheless it has not been found possible to construct true dynamic systems in economics which have anything like the predictive power of the systems of comparative statics. The reason seems to be that the economic abstraction — i.e., the world of commodities — does not take into account some of the more important variables of actual social dynamics. I can give an example from the study of the introduction of hybrid corn into the Middle West. Here we have a rather simple example of a dramatic technical change, taking place in the space of about ten years. Economics can predict a good deal about the comparative statics of such a change. That is to say, we can consider a rough equilibrium before the change, then another rough equilibrium after the change, and compare the two situations. We have a good deal of confidence that the relative price of corn and of hogs will be somewhat lower, and their outputs somewhat larger, than they would have been had the change not taken place. In studying the actual dynamics of the change, however — i.e., the things which determine whether it will take place in five years, in ten years, or in twenty years — the variables of the economist are not much use. A study of this kind is more in the domain of the sociologist. He, not the economist, is the man to study whether people adopt new processes because of what they hear on the radio, what they read from college bulletins, what they get from farm journals, or what they hear over the backyard fence. (I gather from my sociologist friends that the backyard fence has it over all other means of communication.) The speed with which people react to new ideas also is something which is not particularly in the economist's frame of reference.

I have a strong suspicion, therefore, that the reason why economic dynamics has been such an unsatisfactory subject is that it doesn't exist, which is a serious handicap to the development of any science. I am quite convinced, however, that there is a proper study of social dynamics, and to this study I believe economics has some very important contributions to make. There is real danger that in the general advance which is taking place in sociology and social psychology, the contribution of economics will be forgotten, because of the very self-contained nature of the economist's frame of reference. It would be most unfortunate if in the general movement towards integration in the social sciences economics were left out, both on account of what it has to give and what it has to gain. My final recommendation, therefore, is that a wide bridge be constructed between Ford and Vincent Halls as soon as possible!

RELIGIOUS FOUNDATIONS OF ECONOMIC PROGRESS

Public Affairs, 14, 4 (Summer, 1952): 1-9.

Religious Foundations of
Economic Progress

ONE of the most challenging—and tantalizing—propositions of what may be called the "larger economics" is that the success of economic institutions depends to a large extent on the nature of the whole culture in which they are embedded, and not on the nature of these institutions in themselves. This proposition is of particular importance in two current fields of economic inquiry: (a) the study of the complex forces which underlie economic development and (b) the study of the stability and survival power of the characteristic institutions of capitalism.

Indeed, it is only a slight exaggeration to say that the wealth of a nation is a by-product of certain elements in its culture, cumulated through the years. Over a broad range of human societies within the extremes of the Eskimo and the desert nomad, if one area is rich and another poor, it is not because of anything inherent in the natural resources or in the genetic make-up of the people, but because of the cumulative effect of certain familial, educational, and religious practices. Thus the forbidding soil and climate of New England provided a comfortable—if not opulent—homeland for the Puritan, while under the Turk, in his unspeakable days, the ancient cradles of civilization became barren and starveling deserts.

Of all the elements of culture which shape economic institutions, religious practices particularly play a key role—a doubly important one because many other elements of the pattern of life, such as sex, child rearing, work habits, agricultural and industrial practices, are themselves profoundly affected by the prevailing religious beliefs. That religion plays such an important role is not, however, sufficiently recognized by most people, and it is my purpose here to throw more light on it. More specifically, I shall attempt to survey certain aspects of our own society in the light of the contribution which religious ideas, practices, and institutions have made to its economic development and to its power of survival.

Process of Economic Development

TO appraise the role of religion in economic development, we must understand the process by which economic change takes place. All change may not be for the better, but it is clear that there can be no betterment without some change.

Essential Features of Improvement. There are, then, three essential features of any process of economic development in a society—innovation, imitation, and displacement; and two further features which, though conceivably not indispensable, are almost certain to be present in any kind of economic improvement process of which we have knowledge—accumulation of capital and limitation of population. Let us look more closely at these five features:

(1) There must be an *innovator*, who first makes the change. He can be divided, as was done by Schumpeter, into an inventor and an entrepreneur. But the point here is that whether the function is specialized or not, or whether it is performed by a single individual or by a number, the function itself is necessary. If we are to have progress, somebody, somewhere, must do something in a way that has never been done before.

(2) If, however, there is no freedom to *imitate* a change—still more, if the innovator himself is suppressed by the

conservative institutions of his society—there can be no testing out of the innovation to see whether it in fact constitutes a "betterment" or not. It would be rash to say that all innovations which are widely imitated are in fact "betterments," for even the mass may be wrong. But we can say that unless there is opportunity for imitation, an innovation *cannot* be tested, and nobody can ever find out whether it is in fact a "good" innovation, that is, a "better" way of doing things.

(3) Imitation cannot take place, in turn, unless there is *displacement* of the old methods. It is the resistance to displacement (that is, to "competition") on the part of those whose interests are bound up with the old ways, and who are not flexible enough in their habits or opportunities to change, which is likely to be one of the main obstacles to change.

(4) Next, practically all economic innovation of which we have knowledge involves the *accumulation of capital*, in the broad sense of the increase in "valuable objects." The objects so accumulated are not only material; the acquisition of skills, traits, and abilities constitutes capital accumulation just as much as does the stockpiling of materials and material equipment.

If capital is to be accumulated, production must exceed consumption—production being gross additions to the total stock of capital, and consumption being subtractions from it. Such accumulation is far from automatic. In poor societies it is difficult because the minimum needs of consumption press daily on the meagre and hard-won product; most of the activity of the society is concerned with mere maintenance and litte is left for accumulation. In rich societies the threat may be from more subtle sources—from unwillingness to accumulate (i.e., to invest) leading to unemployment and from levels of production below the society's capital.

(5) Even if there is an increase in the total capital or income of a society, however, economic progress will not necessarily result. Economic well-being must rise on a per-capita basis. Hence the accumulation of capital will not constitute "improvement" unless capital increases, in some sense, faster than population. And hence a permanent high-level economy is not possible unless there is *limitation of population*—that is, unless population is checked by methods other than starvation and poverty (according to the familiar "dismal theorem" of Malthus that if nothing

checks the growth of population but misery and starvation, then the population will grow until it is miserable and starves).

Even if a society starts on the road of economic improvement, then, there are many ·elements in its culture which may prevent the improvement in techniques from resulting in an actual improvement in welfare. The newly won powers may be used merely for the support of larger populations at the old level of poverty, or they may also be squandered in the luxury of a foolish ruling class or in the waste of total war. The pyramids of Egypt and the endless wars of Rome are good examples of the waste of resources liberated by technical improvement.

Influence of the Protestant Ethic

THE past three centuries have witnessed a rate of economic development in the "western world" which, measured by any standard we choose, almost certainly exceeds the achievement of any other period of equal length in human history. We are so much accustomed to this rapid progress, both in techniques and in general levels of income, that we are likely to take it for granted. Nevertheless, looking over the whole range of human history and prehistory, we can clearly see that these last 300 years represent an episode in human development which has no parallel, except perhaps in that dim period when settled agriculture was invented and gave rise to the first civilizations.

The unique nature of the achievement makes it all the more important that we should not take it for granted, but should inquire very carefully into its sources in the culture of the western world. The history of civilizations reveals that it is perfectly possible, indeed easy, to dry up the springs of progress in a society, and that virtually all past civilizations have eventually done so. Therefore, unless we are aware of the nature of those elements in our total pattern of life which are responsible for this rapid rate of development, we may run into grave danger of changing that pattern, without knowing it, in a way that destroys those peculiar elements in the culture from which development springs.

Important among the elements in our complex culture having favorable influence on the rate of economic development are certain religious ideas and practices which comprise the so-called "Protestant ethic."

The thesis of Max Weber and his school that the Protestant ethic has influenced the development of capitalism is now well accepted. Though one's estimate of the quantitative importance of this influence will depend to a great extent on the interpretation of history which one favors, the direction of the influence can hardly be in doubt.

What has not, I think, been pointed out with sufficient force is that the Protestant ethic has contributed to the *success* of capitalist institutions, particularly in regard to their fostering a high rate of economic progress. Economic sociologists like Weber, Sombart, and Tawney, who have emphasized the close connection between religious and economic ideas, have been on the whole unfriendly to capitalist institutions and have consequently tended to lay stress on their failures rather than their successes. This is perhaps because the ethical systems of these writers were conceived in fairly static terms—in terms, for instance, of the problem of justice in the distribution of a given total income, rather than in terms of the encouragement of a growing total income.

It has now become clear, however, that the consequence of even a small rate of economic progress, persistently raising average incomes, is so enormous over even a few decades that from the point of view of long-run human welfare the capacity of a system to generate economic development has come to overshadow all other criteria in judging it "good" or "bad". (Curiously enough, this has also become true of Communism; in·the interest of inducing a rapid rate of economic development the rulers of Russia have thrown overboard practically every other ideal of their ethical system, and have developed degrees of inequality which even the most uncontrolled period of capitalist development could hardly rival.)

In other words, we see now that in practice the abolition of poverty can come only from development—not from redistribution, not from taking from the rich to give to the poor, but by making everybody richer. And it is on this score that the Protestant ethic, which was born with the Reformation, has been so influential.

Innovation in Religion. Innovation, imitation, and displacement in economic life have their counterparts in religious life. Thus the Reformation marked the beginning of a series of innovations in religion. Men like Luther, Calvin, Menno Simons, George Fox, John Wesley, General Booth, and even in our own day Frank Buchman, represent a disturbance of the previously established equilibrium, with a new form of religious enterprise and new arrangements of human time and spiritual energy. They are widely imitated, and the spread of the new technique forces profound adjustments even in those older institutions which do not go over completely to the new ideas.

It generally seems to be true that these innovations in religion have preceded and in some sense paved the way for innovations in economic life. Indeed, the most important innovation in any society is the *idea* of innovation itself, for this represents the Rubicon between the traditional stationary type of society, in which each generation repeats the pattern of its elders, and the "economic," dynamic society, in which innovation becomes an accepted and profitable role. A strong case can be made out for the claim that the principal historical agency bringing about this critical change is a reformation (or revolution) in religion, that this liberates the society from its previous equilibrium and exposes it to all the terrors and delights of dynamics. Once iconoclasm has succeeded in the most traditional and "sacred" area of life, once "free enterprise" has been successful in religion, the spirit of innovation seizes upon all other areas of life.

What in our western society we call *the* Reformation is of course only one among many. The period of rapid innovation which followed the rise of Mohammedanism is another and spectacular example. Within Christianity itself the monastic

reformations—especially of the Benedictines and Cistercians—paved the way for the economic development of medieval Europe. Again—if only to remind us that Protestantism is not the whole story— the Counter-Reformation within the Catholic Church also represents a period of "innovation," though of a less dramatic and less iconoclastic nature.

Individual Responsibility and Perfectionism. The fact remains that the Protestant Reformation has certain specific features of its own which have increased its importance for economic development. I am not referring to the sanctification of economic activity through the extension of the concept of "vocation," as emphasized by earlier writers. The concept of vocation is not peculiar to Protestantism, nor is it so important as what I have in mind.

First of all, there is the "unmediated" character of Protestant religion, that is, the emphasis on the individual's own responsibility for his religious life and salvation without the intermediary of priest or prescribed ritualistic "works." It is this unmediated quality of Protestant religion which underlies the sociological significance of the doctrine of justification by faith. Protestantism, that is to say, represents private enterprise in religion, as opposed to the great organized collectivism of the Catholic Church.

It is not surprising that private enterprise in religion carried over into the economic field. The full effect of this is seen in the eighteenth century, where the immense economic innovations which constituted the beginnings of the technical revolution in banking, trade, and industry were to an astonishing extent the work of the British nonconformists, and especially of the Quakers, who had developed the most unmediated of all Protestant varieties of religion.

Another aspect of Protestantism which relates closely to economic development is its perfectionism. Like the earlier monastic reformations, Protestantism reflects a discontent with compromise with the "world" and a serious attempt to return to the pristine revelation of perfection implied in the Christian vision of perfect love. Unlike the monastic reformation, however, the Protestant Reformation—because one of the things against which it was protesting was the corruption of the monastery and nunnery prevalent in the time of Luther—rejected the monastic solution and became an attempt to lead the life of Christian perfection in the workaday world rather than in cloistered separation.

Such an attempt, however, is almost doomed to fail, and the difficulty of practicing the major virtue of charity will lead to an insensible substitution of the "minor virtues" as attainable ends of the religious group. So the perfectionist subsides into the Puritan, and groups of people arise practicing, with some success, the minor virtues of thrift, hard work, sobriety, punctuality, honesty, fulfillment of promises, devotion to family, and so on. The minor virtues, however, lead almost inevitably to accumulation and increased productivity, and eventually therefore to an escape from poverty.

The Lost Economic Gospel

This all adds up to what I call the "lost economic gospel" of Protestantism. Poverty is the result of "sin," sin being defined in terms of intemperance, loose living, prodigality, laziness, dishonesty, and so on (that is, in terms of violation of the "minor virtues").[1] On yielding to the power of Christ and the discipline of the congregation the individual is converted, gives up his evil ways, and becomes temperate, frugal, thrifty, hard working, honest, and so on; as a result of which he begins to accumulate skill and other capital and raises his standard of life. Thus he becomes respectable, and incidentally, but only incidentally, he may become rich by hitting on a successful innovation.

In the process of the individual's becoming richer, society also becomes richer. Indeed, the improvement of society is nothing more than the sum of the improvements of individuals. In a dynamic and improving society, therefore, the increase in riches of the individual is not thought of as a redistribution of wealth (one individual gaining at the expense of others) but rather as a creation of wealth (the gains of one individual representing net additions to the total and being taken from no man). Economic life is not a "zero sum" poker game in which a fixed volume of wealth is circulated around among the players, but a "positive sum" enterprise in which the accumulation of each person represents something which he brings to the "pot" rather than something which he takes out.

Another doctrine which Protestantism shares with other forms of Christianity has combined with the "lost gospel" to contribute to the success of capitalist institutions: the doctrine of stewardship of charity in the narrower sense of the word. Those whose virtue, energy, or plain good fortune have brought them material success are expected to regard their riches as in some sense a trust, to be used for the benefit of the less fortunate. Over the long pull, this aspect of Christian culture has proved of great importance in modifying the inequalities of capitalism. As in the middle ages the establishment of monasteries was an important agency in the redistribution of wealth and income so in the nineteenth and twentieth centuries the establishment of universities and foundations has provided a means whereby private accumulations have found their way into public uses.

The habit of mind engendered by the doctrine of stewardship has also been important in removing obstacles to legislative methods of correcting inequalities, such as progressive income and inheritance taxation. It is quite possible that this factor may have something to do with the different impact of capitalist institutions in the West and, say, in China, where the acquisitive opportunities have been less likely to be modified by the sense of responsibility for the welfare of those outside the circle of kinship.

It can hardly be doubted, then, that the "lost gospel"—the old gospel of individualism, of self-help—is in many respects a sound one. Indeed, the middle-class nature of Protestantism is a testimony to its long-run success. If Protestants are middle-class, it is largely because their Protestantism has made them so— has developed a culture in which hard work, thrift, family limitation, productivity and frugality have been important values. There is hardly any better over-all recipe for economic development, whether for the individual or for a society.

Decline of the Old Doctrines. Nevertheless to a considerable degree the old doctrines are discredited in the churches today, especially, oddly enough, in the more prosperous ones. The old gospel of self-help flourishes among the little rising sects, the pentecostal people, and the store-front churches, it is actually the poor who seem to be least aware of the new "social gospel" and who cling to the old-time individual virtues. In the large Protestant denominations as represented by the National Council of Churches, it is not perhaps unfair to say that there is more awareness of the weakness of the individualist gospel than of its strength, and that even where the older gospel is preached, it is often the result of the momentum of tradition rather than of any continuing spiritual insight.

There are significant reasons for the decline of the gospel of self-help and the rise of the "social gospel". Part of the cause lies in sheer misunderstanding, stemming from failure to appreciate the ethical significance of economic progress, and a resultant economic ethic based on static assumptions, in which an undue stress is laid on distributing a fixed sum of wealth fairly rather than on increasing the total to be distributed.

More fundamental is a certain inevitable tension between the ethic of the New Testament and the ethic of Samuel Smiles (the old Scottish biographer of industrialists and extoller of thrift and self-reliance). There is an anti-economic strain in the teaching of almost all the prophets and poets. The careful, calculating, economizing way of life is neither prophetic or poetic. It counts the cost; it asks for reward; it has no fine frenzies; it is humdrum, commonplace, even a little sordid. The stimulus to economic progress, therefore, is not in the ethic of

the New Testament itself; rather it is in the "Puritan" substitute-ethic, the product of the impact of the ethic of love on the iron laws of the world.

The substitute-ethic, however, is itself somewhat unsuitable, because it is always subject to criticism by the pure ethic which generates it. Hybrids are vigorous but can generally only be reproduced from pure stock! Thus when the New Testament makes a fresh impact on a sensitive and vigorous mind—as it is likely to do at least once in a generation—the gospel of "be righteous and grow rich" for all its truth and practicality, looks cheap and pharisaical beside the poetic vision of "sell all thou hast and give it to the poor"; and radical forms of Christianity tend to appear. There is something in Toynbee's suggestion that Communism is a Christian heresy!

Technical Weaknesses of Capitalism. Perhaps a still more fundamental reason for the failure of capitalism to sustain the ethic which supports its most characteristic institutions is to be found in certain technical failures of these institutions themselves.

The ethic of capitalism is based firmly on the proposition that wealth is produced by saving and that saving is accomplished by producing much and consuming little. That is why the principal recipe for riches includes hard work and thrift and the other Protestant virtues. Under some circumstances, however, wealth· is not produced by saving. Hard work works the worker out of a job, parsimony produces unemployment, and the fluctuations of the price system redistribute wealth without regard to any of the soberer virtues. The thrifty and hard-working find their net worth disappearing in deflation and their hard-earned interest and pensions evaporating in inflation, while the speculator and the manipulator reap what others have sown.

In conditions of general price and output instability the poker-game aspects of capitalism come to the fore. Instead of wealth being accumulated by carefully contributing to the physical stock more than one takes from it, it is accumulated by taking advantage of the shifting structure of relative values, by buying cheap and selling dear. Every economist will recognize, of course, that there is a legitimate function of speculation, and that some flexibility of the price structure is necessary to reflect changing structures of productivity and tastes. In fact, however, the characteristic institutions of capitalism—especially the organized commodity and security markets and the real estate market—have lent themselves to fluctuations far beyond what the flexibility of the system requires, and have therefore been the instrument of redistributions of wealth which have created a gap between economic virtue (in the sense of contribution to the progress of real wealth) and reward.

The phenomenon of depression has been particularly destructive to the capitalist ethic, because the misery which it has entailed has seemed to be so meaningless: why work and save when the end result is the foreclosure of a mortgage and selling apples in the street! The whole technical weakness of an ungoverned market economy can be summed up in two concepts: (a) speculative instability in price levels due to the dynamics of self-justified expectations and (b) the limited or imperfect market resulting either from monopolistic imperfections in the market structure or from general deflation. Speculative instability leads to essentially meaningless redistributions of wealth. The limited market leads to an undue shift of emphasis away from production, to wasteful advertising and selling costs, to restrictions of output, to featherbedding, and to other familiar devices by which individuals or segments of the economy seek to protect themselves from the impact of general deflations or seek to enhance their own particular power position at the expense of others.

The all-important question is whether these defects are to be regarded as diseases of the free economy, potentially curable within the general framework of market institutions, or whether they are to be regarded as essential genetic characteristics of it, quite incurable without a radical overthrow of the whole market economy itself.

Chances of Survival

IT is in this connection that the contribution of Keynes to the survival of capitalism is so important, for it is the essence of the Keynesian view that the defects of capitalism are curable diseases rather than incurable deformities. While the actual cures may be a matter still in considerable dispute, it is the great virtue of the Keynesian analysis that it gives us a clearer picture than we have ever had before of the nature of the disease, and it has consequently engendered the hope that institutions can be devised within the general framework of a free market economy which will prevent deflation and unemployment, on the one hand, and inflation, on the other.

If such a "governor" can insure the over-all stability of the economy (and it is not the purpose of this article to say how this should be done), most of the ethical objections to a market economy fall to the ground. Given a reasonable degree of stability of the over-all price and output system, the old-fashioned virtues of hard work, thrift, honesty, and so on come into their own.

The Problem of Underdeveloped Areas. Perhaps the crucial test of the capitalist system will turn on its ability to solve what is by far the greatest single economic problem facing the world today; the development of the so-called underdeveloped areas—inhabited by about three-quarters of the world's population —to the point where at least the grim consequences of extreme poverty (malnutrition, early death, constant ill health, superstition, squalor, and misery)are mitigated.

There are, roughly speaking, two kinds of society in the world today. The "high-level" societies have low birth and death rates, an expectation of life at birth rising up toward 60 or 70 years, disease well under control, malnutrition rare, literacy universal, education widespread, a high status and much freedom for women, complex economic and political institutions, and so on. The "low-level" societies, on the other hand, have high birth and death rates, an expectation of life around

30 years, disease and malnutrition rampant, literacy and education confined to a small upper class, a low status for women among the mass of the people, burdensome and exploitative financial institutions, often a colonial status, and so on.

The crux of the problem is how to raise the three-quarters of the world that live on a low level to the high level of the other quarter, for it is precisely this wide disparity that makes our world so unstable. American-Russian relations, for instance, would not constitute the apparently insoluble problem which they now pose if the relationship were simply one of America and Russia; in that event they could perfectly well leave each other alone. The relationship is complicated almost unbeatably by the fact that each power is competing for the support of the vast fringe of underdeveloped countries, which divide them on the globe, from Poland to Korea. These countries are dissatisfied with their present state and are hovering between the two cultures, wondering which offers them the best chance of shifting from their present low-level to a high-level economy.

In this whole difficult situation it is of vital importance to appreciate the relation of economic institutions and economic development to the *whole* culture pattern, and to realize that the success of any set of economic institutions depends of the total culture setting in which they are placed. The success, even of modern technology, therefore, may depend quite as much upon the missionary as upon the engineer. One of the tasks of human inquiry is to discover exactly what the elements are in any culture which perpetuate poverty—whether in family life, in religious life, in education, in politics, or in economic and financial institutions—and then to effect a *minimum* change in the culture which is necessary to eradicate these germs of poverty.

We do not want, of course, the kind of cultural imperialism that insists on giving the Fiji Islanders Coca-Cola and Christmas trees whether these things are meaningful expressions of their present culture or not. Cultural change and cultural impact, however, there must be. Such impact is immensely dangerous and may result in disaster to both cultures; yet with the collapse of isolation such impact is inevitable. If it is to be ultimately fruitful, it must be understood much better than we understand it now; the marriage of economics and cultural anthropology must be accomplished, even at the point of a shotgun!

Inadequacy of Social Sciences. It must not be thought, however, that all that is needed for world salvation is a stiff dose of social science, no matter how well documented empirically and no matter how well integrated analytically. The rise of social science presents man with problems of an ethical and spiritual nature of which he is still for the most part not aware. The spectacular "success "of the physical sciences in expanding the power of man, both for good and for evil, is dramatically symbolized in the atom bomb. The worst that a physicist can do for anybody, however, is to cause pain and death. The social scientist, when he knows a little more, may be able to destroy the soul, that inner core of freedom and integrity which constitutes at once the humanity and the divinity of man.

The nightmare of the "manipulative society"—the brave new world of Aldous Huxley or George Orwell—is not too far from reality. We see it foreshadowed in the crudely manipulative society of Soviet Russia, and it is this aspect of Communism which rightly fills us with disgust and fear. In its very conflict with Communism, however, the West may find itself sliding imperceptibly into a manipulative society more horrible, because more efficient, than the Soviet counterpart.

A world of unseen dictatorship is conceivable, still using the forms of democratic government, in which education has been replaced by training, in which government creates artificially the public opinion which keeps it in power, in which "loyalty" investigations corrupt the whole system of communications, in which only "safe" ideas are expressed, in which love of country is corroded by conscription and integrity is swallowed up in expediency, and in which the springs of technical as well as of moral, progress are eventually dried up. The cleverer we are and the more we know, the more thoroughly we may damn ourselves.

Increased Significance of Religion

WHEN the final history of the human race comes to be written, therefore, the part played by religion and religious experience may be even more significant than I have suggested earlier. I have argued that religion is an important autonomous force in the development of the technical revolution. It may turn out to be even more important in the control of this revolution.

We do not yet realize, I believe, what a portentous watershed in human history we are now treading. Civilization is a product of the increase in human control over environment which resulted from the invention of settled agriculture. All past civilizations, however, have proved to be unstable; the "iron laws" of social dynamics have eventually caught up with them and destroyed them. It is by no means improbable that our own civilization will suffer the same fate.

Yet there is reason for hope. As our knowledge not only of nature but of man and society expands, we may get to the point where man comes not to be ruled by history but to rule it. He may be able to take the iron laws and fashion them into an instrument for his own purposes, to mold the unconscious dynamic which drives him to destroy his civilizations into a conscious dynamic which will empower him to perpetuate them indefinitely.

---

¹Kenneth E. Boulding, "Our Lost Economic Gospel," *The Christian Century*, August 16, 1950, pp. 970-972.

The possibility of permanent and universal civilization therefore rises before us, though the prospect is not necessarily one to be approached without fear. It might be the kindgom of heaven on earth, but it might also be an indestructible and universal tyranny, securely based on the power of both physical and social science. A world of refugees is bad enough, but a world in which there is no place of refuge would be worse.

An increase in human power, therefore, makes all the more urgent the question of the discipline of the human will. Economic development means an increase in our ability to get what we want. Religion, however, raises the question of whether we want the right things. As long as we are impotent, it does not perhaps matter so much in regard to externals whether we want the right things or the wrong things. We cannot get what we want in any case. But if we can get what we want, the question of whether we want the right things becomes acutely important.

There are those who think that as economic development comes to fruition in a humanistic heaven on earth, where war, poverty, and disease are abolished, religion will wither away. In that millennium faith will be swallowed up in knowledge, hope in fullfillment, and love in psychoanalysis and group dynamics. Such a belief seems to be naive. As power and knowledge increase, the question of the *truth* of religion—of what is the "will of God," and how it is discovered and incorporated into the human will—becomes all-important. The feather of religious experience may then tip the great scales toward either heaven or hell on earth.

ECONOMIC PROGRESS AS A GOAL IN ECONOMIC LIFE

Goals of Economic Life, Dudley Ward, ed.,
New York: Harper Bros., 1953, pp. 52-83.

Economic Progress as a Goal of Economic Life

I

The concept of economic progress, difficult and wide as its ramifications may be, is at bottom simple. It may be defined as an increase in efficiency. All the difficulties in the concept center around the definition and measurement of "efficiency," and it is to this problem that we shall first turn.

All concepts of efficiency define it as the ratio:

$$\frac{\text{Quantity of Output}}{\text{Quantity of Input}}$$

Efficiency, that is to say, is a quantity descriptive of some process of production or transformation, by means of which a quantity of something is transformed into a quantity of something else. The difficulties in the various concepts of efficiency all revolve around the definition and measurement of the output and input concerned.

At the simplest level are concepts of "engineering efficiency"— amounts of physical output per unit of physical input. The ratio of available kinetic energy to fuel-energy consumption in an engine is a good example. Engineering efficiency, however, is not necessarily economically significant. One engine may, for instance, have a higher ratio of output to input in terms of energy than another, but it may use a costlier fuel or be more expensive to run.

Accounting as a Measure

Evidently a more "significant" concept is that of accounting efficiency. Here we take into account not merely the energy transformation, but all the other inputs and outputs which are subject to valuation in terms of money. The transformation process here is regarded as a process of transformation of asset values, of "costs" into "revenues." In any process of production, looked at from the point of the balance sheet of the firm, certain assets are diminished. Money is paid out in wages, raw materials are used up, fuels and lubricants are consumed, plant and equipment depreciate, and so on. As a result of all this consumption of assets, however, certain other assets are created—the products of the process. Clearly another interesting measure of efficiency is the ratio:

$$\frac{\text{Assets produced (revenues)}}{\text{Assets destroyed in production (costs)}}$$

Even at this level, however, a second main problem presents itself —that of *valuation.* Both input and output are not now usually homogeneous quantities; they are aggregates of a number of different, incommensurable quantities. If 100 bushels of wheat and 5 tons of straw are produced at a "cost" of 5 acre-years of land, one tenth of a man-year of labor, one hundredth of a tractor and a combine, and one ton of fertilizer, what is the "efficiency" of such a process? This question cannot be answered at all unless we have some way of reducing these heterogeneous quantities to a common denominator; i.e., to a single dimension. This is done by valuation— i.e., by multiplying each quantity by a valuation ratio expressing the number of units of the "measure of value" which are equivalent to one unit of the quantity concerned. Usually, of course, the common denominator is money and the valuation ratio is a money price.

Thus, if in the above example wheat were $2 a bushel, straw were $3 a ton, land use was $10 an acre-year, labor use was $1,000 per man-year, the tractor and combine were worth $2,000, and fertilizer was $20 per ton, the value of both input and output could be calculated and the efficiency ratio derived. The value of the input is $(50+100+20+20)$ or \$190; the value of output is $(200+15)$ or \$215, and the efficiency is $\frac{215}{190}$ or 1.13. With different *relative* values of the different inputs and outputs a different result will be obtained for the efficiency ratio, even with the identical physical quantities of inputs and outputs. Thus, even if all other values remain the same and the valuation ratio of wheat falls to \$1 a bushel, the value of output will now be \$115, and the efficiency is $\frac{115}{190}$, or .61.

Without the valuation ratios we cannot even tell whether the process has an efficiency greater or less than one—i.e., whether it results in an increase or in a decrease in the total stock of assets. Mere physical transformation alone, therefore, can never serve as a measure of efficiency. The necessity for valuation raises acutely the question of *what* valuation ratios should be used. The most obvious ratios to use are, of course, the market prices of the various assets. The concept of a valuation ratio, as well as the process of valuation, is, however, independent of the concept of market price. There are many assets which do not have a market; specialized plant and machinery, for instance, has no regular market and no regular market price. There are other assets for which the market price is an inadequate guide to relative significance—where, for instance, markets are narrow or otherwise imperfect, or where the market price is highly fluctuating. Nevertheless it is to market price, whether actual, average, corrected, or in some sense ideal, that we turn to find an objective system of relative valuation ratios; indeed, there is no other source of an *objective* system.

It is perhaps the greatest contribution of the institution of the market to the conduct of human affairs that over a wide area of life it provides us with some sort of standard of relative values which is objective at least to the degree that it results from a consensus of a multitude of individual valuations. There is an analogy here with political opinion; the market does for commodities what the process of argument does for public opinion—it forms a general judgment out of a multitude of individual opinions.

The most significant concept of accounting efficiency is that of the *rate* of profit; that is, the rate of growth of the value of assets in the course of their transformations. Even this concept, however, is inadequate as a measure of economic progress. The accounting-efficiency concept breaks down for two reasons. One reason is that at the level of the individual account there are a good many costs and revenues which are clearly significant from the point of view of well-being but which slip through the broad net of the accounting system. There are, for instance, social costs which for one reason or another do not get into the accountant's ledger because the assets (or liabilities) concerned cannot be appropriated. A famous example is the nuisance created by smoke, which the owner of the offending chimney (or pipe!) does not have to pay for. Another significant example is the unseen labor costs due to health hazards, etc. There are also social revenues which do not get into the accounts; a man who beautifies his garden thereby enhances the value of his neighbor's property as well as his own. One of the major objects of economic legislation should be to catch these hidden costs and revenues, so that accounting results may bear a closer relation to social costs and benefits. Much rather ill-founded criticism of the private-property economy is based also on the failure to distinguish between this defect in the definition of property and the concept of property itself.

The second reason why the concepts of accounting efficiency are not applicable to social efficiency is more fundamental. Even if the accounting net were made fine enough to catch every cost and every benefit, the accounting concepts would still not yield us a measure of social efficiency, for the costs and benefits cannot be *aggregated*. Accounting, no matter how socially refined, is a device for measuring the *relative* efficiency of different enterprises or of different uses of resources. It is not suited to the measurement of the total efficiency of a society. Suppose, for instance, that we tried to define the efficiency of a whole society by the ratio of its total revenues to its total costs. If we include "profits" in costs, defining costs to include all disbursements out of total revenue, costs and revenues are by definition equal, and their ratio is unity. If we exclude profits from costs the "efficiency ratio" becomes total income divided by total income less profits, and becomes simply a measure of the way in which income is distributed, and is not a measure of efficiency at all.

OTHER MEASURES

In order to get a measure of social efficiency, therefore, we must ask ourselves what are the outputs and inputs which are significant in assessing the total efficiency of a society. Clearly the ultimate input is human time and energy. The ultimate output is human living, human satisfaction, call it what you will. Do we get "more" out of life than our ancestors? This is the crucial problem of progress. And it cannot be answered satisfactorily unless we can ask, more of *what*? What do we get out of life? And what do we put in? Now perhaps we have jumped too far; right outside the realm of the economist, in fact into that of the philosopher and the theologian. Perhaps before asking the ultimate question it would be better to ask some penultimate questions which have more hope of being answered.

Suppose, then, we limit the input concept to human time and the output concept to the value of economic product—i.e., a money value of that product which can be so valued. What we have now is "income per man-hour." We can call this concept without too much strain the "economic efficiency" of a society. There are some points, however, at which we must be careful. If two societies, or two periods in the same society, are to be compared in this respect the same schedule of valuation coefficients must be used in both cases. Otherwise a mere inflation of the monetary unit will result in an apparent rise in economic efficiency. But the use of the same schedule of relative valuation coefficients introduces an inescapable indeterminacy into the measurement, because the set of relative values which is appropriate to the one society or period is not necessarily appropriate to the other, and there are no clear objective criteria for selecting a set of valuation coefficients which are equally significant for both periods. Where the societies or periods compared are not widely different, this indeterminacy does not have a wide enough range to invalidate the use of the concept. Where, however, the societies compared are widely different, the comparison becomes almost meaningless. How, for instance, can we compare the nightingales' tongues and chariots of ancient Rome with the caviar and automobiles of today?

Fortunately the problem of comparison is not quite so hopeless as the above example would suggest, because there are certain products, or categories of products—"necessities"—which are common to all societies. All societies, for instance, produce food and warmth. It is not beyond the bounds of imagination to compare even two very different societies in this respect, in regard to the amount of man-time which is necessary for the provision of the caloric requirements of living. Any actual statistical definition of "necessities," of course, will have to be somewhat arbitrary; the arbitrariness need not be so great, however, as to impair the meaning of the comparisons.

A useful rough index of economic progress is the proportion of the economic resources of a society (say, its labor force) which is not employed in agriculture; for agriculture, by and large, produces the basic necessities.[1] A society in which only 20 per cent of the people are employed in agriculture, leaving 80 per cent to be employed in producing the "conveniences and luxuries of life," is clearly richer than one in which 90 per cent of the people have to be employed in agriculture, leaving only 10 per cent to produce the other things.

As long as the output of necessities is a large part of the total, the measure is likely to be fairly significant. Improvements in techniques in industry, however, may raise general standards of life without affecting the proportion of resources in agriculture, so that especially for more advanced countries the measure is not conclusive. If the demand for necessities is completely inelastic—i.e., if the society will wish to consume only a certain amount of them no matter how rich it is—an improvement in the methods of producing necessities will not result in an increase in the production of necessities (population being held constant) but will result in a

[1] The export industries of a food-importing country should, of course, be included in its "agriculture," and vice versa for a food-exporting country. Thus England grows wheat in her cotton mills, for the final process of the cotton industry can be thought of as the exchange of cotton goods for wheat.

transfer of resources from the "necessities" industries. The end result of the improvement is that the same quantity of necessities as before is produced with fewer resources, and the resources so released are available to produce conveniences and luxuries.

The figure below (related to "Agricultural Power and Machinery" in *Encyclopaedia Britannica*, 1947, Vol. I. p. 381) shows this force operating graphically in the case of American agriculture. The improvements in agriculture in the past hundred years have released something like 30 million workers—about half the present labor force—for employment in producing telephones, automobiles, refrigerators—and, it must be added, guns and bombs.

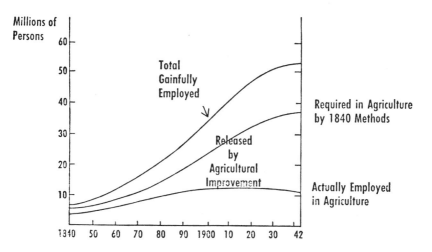

THE FACT, MEASURED OR UNMEASURED

We may well leave the question of the *measure* of economic progress at this point, even though the question must be left partially unanswered. As with all questions involving complex aggregates, there is no single measure or simple answer. We cannot always measure even the direction of economic development. Nevertheless we have a strong feeling that we have made enormous economic progress in the Western world in the past two hundred years, and that no matter how it is measured the figure that measures it must be so large that there can be no doubt of its significance or direction. The crudity of our measures is amply justified by the magnitude of the change.

We are so accustomed to a rapid rate of economic progress in the Western world that we are apt to regard it as a natural law that average real income shall increase at the rate of 3 per cent per annum! In fact, of course, periods of rapid economic progress have been relatively rare even in the history of civilization, and are almost unheard of in precivilized societies. Furthermore, there has never been anything like the last two or three hundred years in human history before. It is no exaggeration to say that all previous civilizations have existed on an economic shoestring, and that the typical abode even of civilized man has been on the edge of starvation. It is doubtful whether any previous civilization was ever able to spare more than 20 per cent of its labor force for all its nonsubsistence occupations. There may have been short-lived exceptions, but two almost universal forces have conspired to make any age of plenty brief. One is the Malthusian principle—that in the absence of deliberate checks on the growth of population, an improvement in the food supply will simply enable the population to grow to the point where numbers are once more checked by malnutrition. The other is the pride of the powerful, which leads to the expenditure of resources on luxury, buildings, and war beyond what the agricultural base can support, with consequent capital consumption and decline.

Over the long pull our own age may be no exception to these dismal "laws." But it differs from all previous ages in the sheer quantity of its economic power. The United States at present produces all the food that it needs, and more, with less than 20 per cent of its population: less than two hundred years ago it required something like 95 per cent of the population to produce its food supply. Nor are we at the end of this process. Even if there is no further improvement in the knowledge of agricultural techniques —even if present techniques were merely applied more extensively —it would be possible to produce our food with 10 per cent of the population or even less. People are not generally aware of the significance of this change. It was shown during World War II that the United States could devote half its national product to war, and still maintain a comfortable level of consumption, without anything (in the mass) that could be called real privation. This hundred billion dollars' worth of extra product could take other forms. In less than ten years, for instance, we could replace all our capital equipment—all our cities, roads, railroads, all our stores and houses and everything which they contain. Economic power on this scale has never existed in history before.

SOCIOLOGICAL FACTORS IN A DYNAMIC ECONOMY

How, then, did this remarkable development come about? Unfortunately we do not really know more than fragmentary answers to this question. The study of economic progress has been strangely neglected by most reputable economists, historians, and philosophers alike, in spite of its being the dominant characteristic of our age. Economic theory has been too much concerned with equilibrium, not enough with change. Economic history has been written largely by literary romanticists, who have not even been aware of what insights economic theory has to offer on this question. Finally, the moral philosophers have argued too much as if we were already in a stationary state, and as if the problem of economic justice were mainly one of distributing a fixed product, rather than encouraging an increasing product.

Any theory of economic progress therefore must be tentative. Nevertheless we can claim to know something. It is evident, for instance, that change, although not synonymous with progress, is at least a prerequisite. Not all change is progress, but without change no progress is possible. A society, therefore, which is resistant to change must also be resistant to progress; one which is open to change has the possibility of progress, though it has also possibilities of retrogression. We need to know much more, therefore, about what determines the willingness to change. This is more in the domain of the social psychologist, where the economist does not feel particularly competent.

One principle may nevertheless be suggested. If change itself, in any connection, is valued highly in itself in any aspect of the culture it is more likely to be valued highly in other aspects, and so will reduce the society's resistance to economic change. In this connection, therefore, the nature of religious attitudes to change is extremely important. One may venture a hypothesis that those societies in which conversion or convincement has been an important part of the religious experience of individuals will be much more open to change than those societies in which the prevailing pattern is to grow up without any conversion experience into a secure and established pattern of life. This may be one of the main reasons for the clear historical connection between "newness" and reforming zeal in religion and progressiveness in economic life. The immense influence of the Protestant Reformation and the Catholic Counter Reformation on economic development is a commonplace among historians. Less well recognized, but perhaps even more important, has been the influence of the perfectionist and evangelical sects, especially the Quakers and Methodists. An astonishing number of the basic developments of the so-called Industrial Revolution were the work of the Quakers and other nonconformists. Looking outside the boundaries of Christendom we find a similar connection between reforming religion and economic development in the early days of Mohammedanism.

The converse side of the medal is, of course, that when a religion gets "old," when it relies for its propagation and maintenance on the coercive power of the family or of the state, when it loses its "prophetic" quality and becomes "priestly," it correspondingly acts as a damper on change of any kind and on economic progress in particular. The greatest enemy of change is the spirit of orthodoxy —the feeling that the fundamental problems of life have been solved and embodied in writing or in organization, and that the main task of each generation is to transmit this solution to the next. Christianity has passed through several such "orthodox" phases; Mohammedanism provides one of the best examples of the ossifying effects of orthodoxy. It now looks as if Russian communism is repeating the same pattern—the vigor of revolutionary days being replaced by the sterile orthodoxy of Marx-Lenin-Stalin worship.

Although the religious element in a culture is of great importance in explaining its attitudes to change, other elements also are at work. We must not underestimate the importance of the high value which the development of science has given to disinterested curiosity. Science can exist only in a world that tolerates change; by its successes it reinforces that tolerance. Nor, in explaining the willingness to change, can we leave out of account the physical factors of climate, nutrition, and disease. Any change involves an expenditure of human energy; the easiest thing to do today is usually what we did yesterday, and the inertia of primitive societies may be closely related to their low human-energy levels. The relation between high productivity and cool, temperate climates is obvious to anyone with even a slight knowledge of human geography. One does not need to go so far as Markham and identify the 70° isotherm as the prime source of civilization;[2] but the northward drift of civilization with the invention of window glass and adequate heating of houses is beyond doubt, and it will be surprising if the invention of air conditioning does not produce a corresponding expansion toward the equator. Malnutrition and diseases such as malaria or hookworm are also important in explaining the failure of the tropics and warm-temperate zones to produce high-productivity cultures. Favorable physical conditions, however, while they may be necessary for the development of high productivity, are by no means sufficient. An almost classic example is the old German-Polish frontier, which divided two economic regions virtually identical in the physical factors of soil and climate, but differing widely in their economic productivity—a difference which could be explained only in terms of the whole culture pattern of the two peoples.

The most difficult question of all is that of the effect of social institutions, organizations, laws, and customs on economic progress. It is clear from human history that there is nothing automatic about economic progress; it is all too easy, in fact, to devise a set of social institutions which will prevent it. We need to know much more about the impact of various institutions and habits in these respects, and in the criticism of institutions their impact on economic progress should receive much more attention.

[2] S. F. Markham, *Climate and the Energy of Nations* (Oxford, Oxford University Press, 1944).

Economic progress cannot take place unless there is some provision in society for processes which are judged in some way "superior" to displace those which are judged by similar criteria to be "inferior." As a dynamic process economic progress means the development of better ways of doing things; this implies as a corollary that worse ways must be abandoned. The opportunity for the better to displace the worse is one of the meanings that may be given to that much-abused word "competition."[3] It is in this sense that competition can be said to be a prerequisite of progress.

Its opposite is "protection"—the setting up of institutions to protect the "vested interests," or the established ways of doing things, and to prevent their abandonment. If enough people and institutions are so "protected" from the necessity of substituting better for worse ways of doing things, progress may be made impossible. There are, of course, ethical problems involved in the "rights" of vested interests. There are also practical problems involved in overcoming the resistances to desirable changes, and modern welfare economics has developed quite an elaborate discussion of the "compensation" of vested interests. All we are concerned to do now, however, is to point out that there must be some arrangements for displacement of the obsolete methods, skills, equipments, and commodities.

There are a number of possible institutional systems under which competition of this sort can take place. One of the main justifications for the free market as an institution is that it permits rapid displacement of one process by another—though there may be real question as to the tests of inferiority or superiority. The free market is not, of course, the only conceivable institutional framework within which competition of this kind is possible; even within a highly organized and planned society it is possible for superior processes to knock out the inferior. The test of superiority, how-

[3] One of the most deplorable failures of modern social ethics has been its inability to develop a proper ethical taxonomy or classification of competition, and hence its tendency to regard all "competition" as bad. The truth is that some kinds of competition are bad and some are very good. The lumping of all kinds of competition together results mainly in a quite false imputation of badness to the good kinds, and imputations of goodness to all kinds of substitutes for competition, both good and bad.

ever, in this case is ability of the successful process to displace the unsuccessful one in the opinions of the planners rather than in the opinions of those who would benefit directly.

Another institutional factor on which economic progress depends is the ability of innovators to acquire control over the resources which are necessary to make the innovations. The capacity for genuine innovation, whether for invention itself or for the practical application of new methods, is rare in society. It would be remarkable indeed if the individuals whose heredity and upbringing had granted them unusual capacities for innovation were at the same time individuals whose position in society automatically gave them control over the resources needed to make innovations. If a society is to progress, therefore, some apparatus is necessary which will enable—or compel—the established controllers of resources to relinquish some of that control to the innovators.

In a capitalist society this is one of the main tasks of the financial system. The ultimate control of resources is invested in the owners of the physical capital and the money stocks of the system. These owners, however, are not necessarily, or even usually, the people best adapted to control these resources, whether as innovators or even as routine operators. Some means need to be devised, therefore, whereby the owners can relinquish the administration of resources to specialists in this task. This "divorce of ownership from control" is the main achievement of finance—i.e., of the system of debt and securities. The banking system is an important part of this process; through its power of creating bank deposits it has enabled borrowers to withdraw resources from unemployment or from the less active members of society by the process of inflation.

In the Western world, therefore, the innovator has obtained the necessary resources by persuading those who have the equity in the capital of society to relinquish to him some of their "purchasing power." Indeed, he does not even have to do the persuasion. The growth of the financial system has bred a class of financial experts whose job it is to persuade capitalists to relinquish their capital to enterprisers, and then discover enterprisers who can be entrusted with capital. It is impossible to assess how much of the rapid growth of the Western economy is due to its specialized system of finance, but there may be a strong connection, and the matter needs careful investigation.

A socialist society, of course, faces the same problem, and has generally found it much more difficult of solution. The virtue of capitalism has been its decentralization. Because ownership has been scattered among many individuals and groups, the man with an idea who is repulsed by one group of potential backers may, and frequently does, find another. Studies of innovations are revealing the importance of *informal* methods of finance in this connection. As society moves toward the formalization of its economic life, the capitalist "angel" willing to take a flyer on a crazy new idea is replaced by the bureaucratic bank and the even more bureaucratic government lending agency, whose operations are conducted in the limelight of politics and which is therefore prejudiced in favor of a cautious respectability. It would be rash to say that a socialist society cannot solve this problem. It is hardly too much to say, however, that the ultimate success of a socialist or of any highly integrated, monolithic society depends largely on its ability to devise administrative substitutes for capitalist casualness and flexibility.

In order to have economic progress there must not only be innovators—there must be imitators. The institutions and customs in a society which encourage the imitation of successful new methods deserve careful study. We have already noticed the significance of the free market in this regard. Innovation often results in a cheapening of the product, which will reduce the rewards of those who are still using the obsolete methods, thus forcing them either to change their occupation altogether or to increase their rewards by adopting the improved methods. There are, however, other factors in society which encourage imitation. To get very far into this problem would involve us in the sociology of fashion—most of which is yet to be written—but it is clear that the greater the positive desire to emulate the successful innovator, the more rapidly will the change take place, and in all probability the less will be the social cost. It is when the practitioners of the old methods are highly resistant to change that the process of competitive displacement results in so much human suffering.

There are also other elements in the fabric of society which may be of great importance in determining the rate of economic progress, and which should at least be mentioned, even if they cannot be treated very adequately.

There is first the whole problem of "incentives." The problem here is how to ensure that the rewards of those who pioneer are adequate to insure a sufficient supply of pioneering, or of productive activity in general. This is a problem which it is extremely difficult for any large collectivized system of distribution to solve. It is interesting to note that the Pilgrim Fathers at New Plymouth started with an "experiment of communal living," but got along much better when this was abandoned and each man was allowed to plant corn for his own household! If in fact productive activity of any kind has a "supply price"—i.e., if there is some level of reward below which the activity will not be undertaken—any system of distribution which results in a return to the productive activity of less than its supply price will simply result in the disappearance of the product. In other words, it is only the surplus of product over and above what is necessary to pay out to producers to keep them producing that is "available" to society, either for pomp, for war, or for redistribution.

There is, however, a difficult problem of fact here. A good deal of economic activity, and even a good deal of innovation, is done for its own sake and has a zero or even negative supply price—i.e., it will be done whether it is rewarded or not, or even if it is penalized. This spontaneous activity, however, has rarely been sufficient for the needs of society. Consequently in virtually all societies it has been necessary to reward the producer somewhat in proportion to his product. By our patent and copyright laws also we seek to reward the innovator. It is a moot question whether the granting of a monopoly, even a temporary one, is the best method of rewarding the innovator. It seems clear, however, that unless the institutions of society permit a reward of some sort there will not be a rapid rate of economic progress. It is desirable, of course, that the "supply prices" should be as low as possible; and insofar as honor, for instance, can substitute for more tangible rewards, that is all to the good. The more unselfish people there are in society, the better it is for the selfish, and, no doubt, for the unselfish as well.

Another factor which is difficult to define but which is unquestionably real is the stimulus of necessity, which is reputed to be the mother of invention, or that challenge, in the language of Toynbee, which is just adequate to provoke the proper response. The importance, in this connection, of a *disequilibrium* in the price system is something which most economists have overlooked. Often it is not the prospect of reward as much as the prospect of disaster which spurs us to effort, and failure is often the goad which has spurred a man on to success. A system in equilibrium in which everybody was doing moderately well might afford much less of a stimulus to progress than a system in disequilibrium in which there was a wide dispersion of profits and losses. There may be a case here for price fluctuations, which perpetually stir up the economic elites and make them circulate; also for interferences with the pricing system, such as the minimum wage, which has sometimes been a spur to innovation. Depressions and even wars have played their part in stimulating innovations. The quantitative importance of this factor, however, is difficult to assess, and I merely warn against overlooking it.

Specific Economic Factors

The factors we have mentioned above might well be called "sociological"; in fact their discussion carries us far beyond the conventional bounds of economics. There are also some more narrowly "economic" factors, most of which have been recognized at least as far back as the classical economists.

There are, for instance, the influence of specialization (i.e., the division of labor) on human productivity and the influence of the "extent of the market" on the development of specialization. Adam Smith's eloquent exposition of these theorems (*Wealth of Nations*, Book 1, Chapters 1-3) has never been bettered. The contribution of specialization to economic progress can be visualized dramatically. Suppose that the present population of the world were placed with each family on its own five acres of land and forbidden to trade with any other, so that each family had to raise its own food, weave its own cloth, build its own houses, paint its own pictures, and write its own books—in short, suppose we had a world of Swiss Family Robinsons. The material and cultural poverty of such a world compared with our own would be beyond measure. It must be emphasized also that specialization and trade are inseparable partners; without trade specialization would be absurd, and without specialization trade would be useless.

There are, however, certain qualifications which must be noticed. Like everything else, specialization can be carried to excess, and in any one state of the arts there is clearly an optimum degree of specialization. Most men employ barbers to cut their hair, but shave themselves. There are also certain human costs of extreme specialization (for instance, loss of significance of daily work) which do not get into the accounting system and which therefore need the attention of social policymakers. There are also certain technical qualifications of the doctrine that an increase in the extent of the market is always desirable, such as the "infant industry" argument for protection or the case for patents and copyright. These qualifications, however, serve but to underline the basic significance of the central doctrine.

Another theorem regarding economic progress which also dates back to Adam Smith is that economic progress almost invariably requires the "accumulation of stock." If we extend the concept of accumulation to include the accumulation of knowledge and skills in the minds and muscles of men, the proposition is incontrovertible. The "better ways of doing things" which economic progress implies nearly always involve the use of more elaborate and costly implements; and so, especially in poor societies, the difficulty of accumulation may be the most significant factor limiting the rate of progress. Accumulation is the excess of production over consumption. If production is small the sheer physical necessities of consumption press so hard upon the heels of the meager productive capacity that it requires the utmost parsimony and "abstinence" to refrain enough from consuming to allow much accumulation. In such circumstances "foreign investment"—i.e., an arrangement which enables the poor region to import without exporting—may be of great help in permitting the poor region to accumulate enough to start it on the path of progress.

In this respect, as in so many others, "to him that hath shall be given." There is some critical point of poverty below which consumption presses so hard on production that no accumulation is possible, and the people tread round and round in an endless squirrel cage—low production meeting only their barest necessities and allowing no surplus for improvement, either of human or of physical capital. Once above this critical point, however, a benevolent spiral is set up, with accumulation leading to higher productivity, and higher productivity leading to easier accumulation, which in turn leads to still higher productivity. One of the great problems facing the world today is how to get the poverty-stricken three quarters of the world over this initial "hump."

In this whole problem of accumulation the vital importance of human capital (i.e., improvement in the abilities of men) must be stressed. Education, training, and health services may easily be by far the most profitable kinds of investment. The rise in the average length of life which is an almost universal characteristic of a progressive society is itself a substantial contribution to economic progress, for it means a reduction in the "consumption" of skills and abilities by death. In a society in which the average age at death is thirty—as it is, for instance, in most of the overcrowded nations of the Far East—a large proportion of the resources of the society must be spent in replacing the population, and little can be devoted to improving it. Where the average age at death rises toward sixty and seventy, as it is doing in the Western world, a much smaller proportion of the resources of the society need be devoted to replacing the population, children and young people will form a much smaller percentage of the society, and much higher standards of education can be attained.

At this point, however, it is necessary to introduce again the "dismal theorem" of Malthus—a theorem which, incidentally, also goes back to Adam Smith. The "dismal theorem" can be stated very simply. It is that if nothing checks the growth of population except misery and starvation, then the population will grow until it is miserable and starves. It is necessary at this point to make a sharp distinction between *technical* and *economic* progress. Technical progress consists in the discovery and application of better ways of doing things. Such technical progress, however, does not necessarily result in economic progress—i.e., in a rise in income per head. This is because income per head depends not merely on the techniques available but also on the proportion of the human to the nonhuman resources.

We have here the famous law of diminishing returns in one of its forms. For our purposes it may be stated as follows: With *given* techniques there is some proportion of human to nonhuman resources at which income per head is a maximum; with given nonhuman resources, therefore, there is some population at which income per head is a maximum. This is usually called the "optimum population." As the population rises beyond this point, with given techniques and nonhuman resources, income per head must fall. And if the only check on the growth of population is poverty and the high death rate which poverty brings in its train, then, no matter how advanced the techniques of the society, the population will grow until poverty checks its growth.

This is a dismal theorem indeed. It implies that the end result of technical progress under strictly Malthusian conditions is an actual *increase* in the sum of human misery—if indeed misery can be summed—for it means that a larger population is enabled to live in precisely the same state of misery as its forefathers.

Fortunately, however, the dismal theorem is a strictly conditional one. Its dismal conclusion rests on an alterable premise, and it can be readily restated in a cheerful form: if there are checks other than misery which prevent the unlimited growth of population, then there can be a stable condition both of population and of plenty. Fortunately, also, rising standards of life themselves seem to bring these preventive checks in their train. Or perhaps the matter should be stated more generally: the same cultural changes which are favorable to technical change also seem to be associated with voluntary limitation of the population.

We are here dealing with a field where more is surmised than is known. The Malthusian specter does seem to have been laid in the Western world—though even there the apparent slowing down of population growth may have been merely a depression phenomenon, and a permanent state of full employment and increasing levels of income may produce results at present unsuspected and may raise the specter once more. Nevertheless the dismal theorem operates in full gloom over the greater part of mankind. If technical change comes too slowly to the underdeveloped parts of the world, its benefits will be swallowed up in population increase before the rising level of living has a chance to operate sufficiently as a check to the birth rate. It may well be that in these areas the change must be rapid and dramatic or it will be worse than useless and will merely set off a disastrous population explosion. Technical change, whether in agriculture, manufactures, transportation, education, or health, must be viewed in the light of the population situation and the whole cultural pattern of the society.

The growth of population is not the only way in which the fruits of technical progress can be dissipated. In some societies these fruits have been dissipated in the pomp and display of the ruling classes —in the building of pyramids, of palaces, even of temples. A much more frequent source of dissipation is war. In a world of warring states there is no true equilibrium of national power, and the normal condition of international relations is that of the arms race. Each nation attempts to establish its security by being stronger than its neighbors. It is only under rare circumstances that this situation can be stable for anything more than brief periods, and the competition for relative strength results in the constant rise in the proportion of the national income which is devoted to defense. In these circumstances the result of technical progress may be simply to enable nations to devote an ever-increasing proportion of their resources to war. This trend is unquestionably apparent in modern history. It is doubtful, for instance, whether any of the wars of the eighteenth century involved more than 5 per cent of national incomes; the Second World War absorbed up to 50 per cent of the national income of the major belligerents. It is a remarkable tribute to the rapidity of technical progress in the Western world that we have been able to witness so enormous a rise in the proportion of national product going to war and still enjoy a rapid increase in standards of living out of the remainder. The race between war and plenty, however (in spite of the spur of military necessity to invention), has usually been won by war, which has been perhaps even a greater destroyer of economic progress, looked at in the long view, than population increase.

The fruits of economic progress can also be dissipated in unemployment. This is a disease which is peculiarly characteristic of rich societies. In poor societies consumption is always pressing on the heels of production, and the problem is never under- but overconsumption. In rich societies, however, productive capacity may be so great that with the existing institutions the capacity and willingness of the society to absorb its output, whether in consumption or in willing accumulation (investment), is insufficient to take care of the great volume of output which results from full employment. When this is the case, full employment will be unstable, for it will result in a volume of accumulation greater than the society is willing to accept. Firms will attempt to reduce their unwanted accumulations by cutting down output, and unemployment will develop until output has been reduced to what the society is willing to absorb. Fortunately this is by no means an insoluble problem. It can be claimed, indeed, that the intellectual and technical problems of unemployment have been largely solved, though the political problems involved are still difficult.

There is no law, however, which says that the attempt of man to improve his worldly lot will always result in the swarming of population, or in the waste of pomp or arms, or in the lethargy of underemployment. Economic progress has taken place in history. It has brought with it improved food, houses, clothes, education, health, not merely for the few, but for the masses. It has resulted in a great increase in leisure, and a lifting of the burden of heavy labor. The hopes of mankind do not have to be confined to another world. A human society is conceivable in which the evils of poverty are completely eradicated, and in which there is sufficient production of this world's goods to enable everyone to live in health and decency. This is the proximate end toward which economic progress moves. It is not a sufficient end, as every religion testifies. But even if the chief end of man is to know God and enjoy Him forever, the enjoyment of goods is surely not inconsistent with the enjoyment of good, and God is better served by a race whose capacities are not stinted by inadequate food, clothing, shelter, education, or health.

II

Economic progress is not in itself an ultimate end of human activity, nor is it a universal criterion for passing judgment on societies. Nevertheless it is a significant partial end, and in making any assessment of the weight which should be given to it other possible ends or criteria of judgment should be considered. Some of these may be in competition with economic progress; others may be complementary to it.

Other Ends of Economic Activity

Economic progress consists in the increase in human power to satisfy human needs. Our evaluation of it therefore depends in considerable degree on our attitude toward power on the one hand, and toward wants on the other. It is by no means a foregone conclusion that an increase in power is desirable. Whether it is desirable or not depends largely on what people want to do with the power. It is probably better for a man who wants to drive down a crowded street at a hundred miles an hour not to have a high-powered car. The problem of the *nouveaux riches* is a familiar one —the people whose debased desires did them little harm as long as they did not have the power to satisfy them, but who rapidly went to the devil when they had the power to do so. There is some case for the suggestion that our whole society is a *nouveau riche* society, and that the result of our economic progress is to enable us to go to hell at a thousand miles an hour instead of at five.

It is perhaps this lack of confidence in the human will that has turned many prophetic figures to "holy poverty" as an ideal in itself. St. Francis immediately comes to mind, as in the delightful story about the novice who wanted a psalter (*The Mirror of Perfection,* Chapter 4). St. Francis reproved him, saying, "After you have a psalter, you will desire and wish to have a breviary. Then you will sit in your chair like a great prelate, and say to your brother, 'Bring me the breviary.'" The saints have usually seen clearly how the power to satisfy desire—of a worldly sort—itself increases the desire, and so power runs a continually losing race with desire, and satisfaction seems ever farther away. There is much wisdom in this prophetic criticism of the quest for riches, whether on the part of an individual or a society.

Nevertheless there is something also to be said on the other side. The idealization of poverty has never proved stable, especially in Christendom, and even the Franciscans were corrupted by the "world." In America the ideal of holy poverty has seemed unsuitable to a rapidly expanding economic universe, and only small groups, such as the Catholic Worker movement, have cherished it. It is hardly represented in Protestantism at all, least of all in the liberal Protestantism of the "social gospel." This is not merely the perversity of human nature and original sin. The power to satisfy existing wants can also be a power to criticize them. The new rich eventually become the old rich. The change of taste which power brings is not always in the wrong direction. And the power to fail is also sometimes the power to learn.

The way of renunciation is the attainment of satisfaction not by expanding our power but by curtailing our wants. It is perhaps more characteristic of the religions prevalent in the East than of Christianity. In a formal sense, if what we mean by economic progress is an increase in the ability to satisfy wants, the way of renunciation would seem to fall under the definition of economic progress just as the way of power. The West gets out its bulldozers and brings the mountain to Mahomet, the East takes things more quietly and Mahomet betakes him to the mountain; but the end result is the same—the mountain and Mahomet are brought together. Indeed, if the satisfaction of desires is really the end in view, the way of renunciation of desires is probably the answer.[4] In Western culture, however, there is little desire for "being" as opposed to "becoming," and the art of static contentment with little is not much regarded.

Another end which frequently rides counter to the objective of economic progress is that of *equality*. Economic progress has gener-

[4] "The Hindus thought this question of happiness through to the end long ago and reached the inevitable conclusion—Nirvana—just enough life to enjoy being dead" (F. H. Knight in *The Ethics of Competition*, New York, Harper & Brothers, 1935, p. 32).

ally arisen not from a concerted effort on the part of all to raise the general level, but by the efforts of individuals to "better their condition." An enforced equality is therefore highly inimical to economic progress—as the Russians, for instance, have discovered in spite of their strong theoretical prejudice in favor of equality. On the other hand, economic progress itself, by raising the general level, makes inequality less necessary. The relations between progress and equality are so important that we must examine them further.

The concept of economic justice—i.e., justice in distribution—has different connotations if we are considering a stationary society or one that is progressing in wealth. In a stationary society in which total capital and income are constant, economic competition reduces itself to what in the theory of games is called a "zero-sum game"—i.e., an affair in which what one gains is gained at the expense of others, the total of gains and losses being zero. In such a society one man's accumulation can be made only at the cost of another's decumulation, or if one man increases his income it can be only by decreasing others'. To an astonishing extent the exponents of the "social gospel" seem to believe that the actual economic system is in fact stationary. Thus Thornton Merriam writes in his famous discussion with Frank Knight: "Modern man wants to do the work of the world in ways that do not require that he put his neighbor out of business at the price of his own success. With all its gilded façade of freedom that is what the free market really means ethically."[5] The assumption here that nobody should ever be put out of business is staggering enough (presumably the railroads should have been taxed to the point where stagecoaches could compete with them), but it is quite evident that the idea that anyone could raise his own level of living without lowering anybody else's is foreign to Mr. Merriam's frame of reference.

In a progressive society, however, economic competition is not generally a zero-sum game but is a positive-sum game, in which the activity of the players results in an increase in the total to be divided, so that my increase is not taken from somebody else but is a

[5] *The Economic Order and Religion* (New York: Harper & Brothers, 1945, p. 271).

net addition to the total pot. The moment this is recognized, both competition and accumulation are seen in a different light, and much of the moral objection to them disappears. Perhaps one of the main contributions which the economist as a technician can make to the moral philosopher in this regard is to render explicit those conditions under which the action of an individual to increase his own net worth results in an addition to the total capital of society equal to, or even greater than, his own accumulation. In contrast are those conditions under which accumulation by the individual results in an increase in the total capital of society less than the increase in his own net worth, and in which therefore the accumulation of one individual is made, at least partly, at the expense of someone else.

One question which must be made explicit by the moral philosophers is the relative weight which they give to the evils of poverty and inequality. They frequently write as if these were the same evil, and as if the way to abolish poverty were to redistribute income more equally. Against this proposition the economist must raise a serious protest. In a poor society even if all incomes were made equal the poverty of the poor would be relieved hardly one whit. There is no avenue to the abolition of poverty save through the increase of productivity. Indeed, even inequality itself is the result to a large extent of the failure of certain groups or societies to raise their productivity as fast as others. America is rich and China poor not because of "exploitation"—not because the Chinese produce a lot and the Americans take it away from them! America is rich because her productivity has been increasing faster than that of the Chinese for the past two hundred years or more.

Even within the United States the great inequality in the distribution of income—the difference between the North and the South—is not due to exploitation; is not due to the North's taking away what the South produces. It is due to the low productivity of the South, which in turn is due to its low rate of economic progress. This is not to deny, of course, that exploitation exists. There is the matter of differential freight rates. There is the matter of immigration restrictions. There is the matter of race prejudice restricting the economic opportunities of Negroes. There is the matter of trade-union restrictions and protective tariffs and Agricultural Adjustment Acts. But all these things placed into the balance together do not add up to one tenth of the causes either of poverty itself or of the unequal distribution of income.

It is arguable, of course, that inequality of income is itself an evil so hideous that considerable sacrifice of other objectives may be justified to attain equality, and that it would be better to have an equalitarian society in which everyone was equally poor than an unequal society in which nobody was poor but some were rich. If such is indeed the objective, it must be stated clearly. Even if this objective is held, however, the difficulties of achieving equality must be taken into consideration. Methods of achieving equality which involve leveling up rather than leveling down, which involve raising the levels of the poorer without lowering the levels of the richer are much more likely to find social acceptance than methods of forcible redistribution. Certain methods of forcible redistribution—e.g., progressive taxation—are entirely feasible and desirable within limits.

Even these methods, however, will meet much less resistance in a society which is rapidly increasing its wealth than in a stationary society. Indeed, it is a defensible proposition that whether we look at the matter from the side of ultimate objective or of ways of achieving those objectives, only a rich society can afford to be equalitarian. If the level of productivity in a society is so low that almost all the resources of the society are needed to maintain its supply of bare necessities, the very existence of any kind of civilization depends on the development of wide inequalities. That is why ancient civilizations all rested on a basis of slavery—which is genuine exploitation—and why only modern civilizations have been able to dispense with it. In a poor society, unless the vast mass of men are ground down to a bare minimum of subsistence, there is no possibility of the development anywhere in the society of the arts of civilization; the very existence of "peaks" necessitates vast and dismal "troughs." The equal distribution of income, even if it were technically possible without lessening the total product of such a society, would result only in an infinitesimal improvement in the lot of the poor and in the complete disappearance of any outstanding human achievement in the physical world.

It is not to be inferred that achievement in the spiritual world would not be possible in such a society of equalitarian poverty. Indeed, much of the preaching of the Hebrew prophets, for instance, is directed at this point—to glorify the "righteousness" of the simple, equalitarian, pastoral society of the hill country as against both the wickedness and the splendor of the cities of the plains. Both the ineffectiveness of their literal recommendations and the effectiveness of their spiritual message, however, point in the same direction—toward the redemption of riches rather than their abolition.

It may well be that in the long view of history inequality must be viewed as a protracted process of transition from the primitive society of equal poverty to the ultimate goal of a society of equal riches. In the long climb from the slough of equal poverty to the plateau of equal riches, certain individuals and groups lead the way, leaving others behind, and inequality develops. But because we are all roped together in the nexus of social and economic relations, the climbers cannot help pulling others after them and the whole level rises. Those who insist that we must all rise together or not at all may be actually condemning us forever to the slough of poverty. And the view that nobody can rise without pushing somebody else down is true only in a stationary state, and is quite foreign to a state of progress. There may therefore be more than mere Scottish optimism in Adam Smith's dictum that "the progressive state is in reality the cheerful and the hearty state to all the different orders of society. The stationary is dull; the declining, melancholy" (*Wealth of Nations*, Book I, Chapter 8).

EQUILIBRIUM VERSUS PROGRESS

The neglect of economic progress on the part of the moral philosophers and social gospelers has implications that are even more fundamental than those raised above. The neglect of progress is part of a quite general neglect of *process*. The very expression "goals," so beloved of the moral philosopher, is a striking indication of the basically static nature of his thinking. The term implies that there is some "right" way of organizing the affairs of men and that anything is "wrong" which does not conform to the ideal system. Such an approach may be useful in arousing moral emotion, and

as such may have a real function, but it is not useful in the attempt
to analyze the real processes of society, nor in the search for the
most powerful levers of social change.

The economist himself, likewise, must be accused of neglecting
process in favor of static equilibrium. There seems to be more
justification for the economist, in that at least his static-equilibrium
theory throws some real light on the processes of society. The very
success of economic statics, however, has led economists into deriving from their theory more implications than it can justify—the
implication, for instance, that distribution according to the equilibrium of perfectly competitive markets represents "commutative
justice" (everybody gets what he produces; see Knight and Merriam, op. cit., p. 111), or the implication frequently made in economic theory that there is something sacred about the system of
prices set up by perfect competition. The introduction of process
analysis (dynamics) into economics creates havoc with many of the
cherished allocational ideals of the economist, as Schumpeter (especially in his Capitalism, Socialism, and Democracy) showed with
great vigor. The case against monopoly, for instance, is much
weaker in a dynamic setting than it is in a static one.

In any attempt to sit in judgment on society, however, which is
presumably the ultimate task of the economist acting as moral philosopher, society must be judged as process; not by how far it falls
short of some "goal," but by how rapidly it is moving in "right directions." It is possible to judge directions without knowing where
movement will ultimately lead. Indeed, we know nothing about the
ultimate fate of the human race. History must be regarded as a
process of ecological succession in the great "ecosystem"[6] of society.
Men, methods, ideas, processes, organizations, institutions, constitute a highly complex system of interacting "populations," some
species rising and some falling, some perhaps stationary for awhile,
closely analogous to the dynamics of a pond, forest, or prairie. Man

[6] Biologists use the term "ecosystem" to describe the totality of living
things, together with the relevant environment, that occupy a single habitat
and form an equilibrium of interacting populations. "Ecological succession"
is the process by which one ecosystem gives place to another, under the
influence of the cumulative and irreversible processes of the ecosystems themselves; e.g., as a pond fills up, or soil accumulates.

is not a passive constituent of these systems, however, any more than he is passive in regard to nature. Once he is past the food-gathering stage, man intervenes actively in nature, producing field crops, raising domestic animals, and so on. Indeed, agriculture may almost be defined as the process of extreme distortion of the natural ecosystem in favor of man, making grain grow where once grew forests, and cattle flourish where there were once only wild animals.

The task of the "policymaker," whether he is the preacher making policy for the individual lives and conduct of his congregation, the teacher making policy for the thoughts and lives of his pupils, the bishop or the trade-union official or the executive making policy for his organization, or the statesman making policy for the state, is essentially the task of "social agriculture." It is to distort the "natural" system of society and the "natural" forces of ecological succession in society, also in favor of man. If there is to be a division of labor between the social scientist and the moral philosopher or the theologian, it is surely here. The business of the social scientist is to throw light on the *effects* of various policies on the significant *kinds and rates of change* in the society. It is the business of the philosopher and the theologian to throw light on what is in favor of man; what changes, therefore, should be speeded up, if possible, and what slowed down or reversed. These changes are not, of course, measured in homogeneous units. Any evaluation of them, therefore, involves "valuation" in almost exactly the same sense that the calculation of a price level or of real income involves valuation; i.e., it involves assigning a "weight" to the various changes —some of which will be complementary and some competitive one with another. In any such weighting I would urge that economic progress deserves to be weighted high, not only for its own sake, but because it is complementary to so many other desirable ends.

The Optimum Rate of Progress

What we are searching for here is some concept of an "optimum" rate of economic or of technical progress. It is impossible to define such a concept exactly. Nevertheless, it is possible to imagine a rate of progress so rapid that it destroys itself and the society in which it takes place. Very rapid growth may produce internal stresses and dislocations which the society cannot survive, just as the 2-4-D weed killer destroys plants by making them grow at a rate faster than they can "take," or the forcing of a child may produce revolt and personality disintegration. On the other hand, there is nothing to be said for stagnation at low levels of living.

The critical question is the evaluation which we place on the "social cost" of economic progress at various rates. If there were no social cost—i.e., if no other good ends had to be sacrificed in increasing the rate of economic progress—there seems to be no reason why indefinitely rapid rates should not be desirable. It is probable, however, that beyond a certain point the social costs of progress rise with increasing rates of progress.

The formal condition for the optimum rate is that at which the benefits of more rapid progress are just balanced by its cost—both capitalized in some way to the present. This is simply an application of the principle of marginal equality familiar to all economists. It is not, of course, sufficient to inform us as to the exact rate of progress we should strive for. Nevertheless some important conclusions can be derived from it—notably the conclusion that the lower the (marginal) cost of each rate of progress, the more rapid the optimum rate will be, assuming that these marginal costs rise with an increasing rate. Any change in society, therefore, which lowers the cost of progress is an almost unmixed blessing.

The human cost of progress depends mainly on the immobility of men. This immobility has two sources: the *unwillingness* to change which is part of the structure of character, and the *inability* to make changes which is imposed by law, custom, or physical circumstances. Both these sources of immobility are susceptible to attack: the one through change in the moral habits of individuals, the other through change in the institutions and equipment of society.

In this connection the economic significance of the Protestant Reformation needs to be thoroughly reassessed. The responsibility of the Reformation for the rise of capitalism has been fairly thoroughly explored, though not enough attention has been paid to eighteenth-century and later developments. Too much emphasis has been laid, however, on the exploitive aspects of capitalism, which are not so significant quantitatively as is its aspect as an extraordinary movement of economic progress.

The progress has taken place not merely in mechanical matters: the progress in techniques of organization, in skills of government and education, and in the art of human relations has almost been as phenomenal as the developments in the techniques of production and transportation. The Factory Acts and social legislation are as much a part of the miscalled Industrial Revolution as the spinning jenny and the railroad. The "technical revolution" through which we are still passing is a revolution in ways of doing almost everything.

A strong case can be made that Protestant and evangelical Christianity, by its stress on conversion, on individual enterprise in religion, and on the minor virtues of industriousness, punctuality, thrift, honesty, truthfulness, and so on, has played a key role in this whole revolution. By its stress on the conversion experience as a radical change in the character of the individual it gives a positive value to change as such which carries over into all spheres of life. By its emphasis on the individual's responsibility to make his own peace with God in an unmediated religious experience it gives a positive value to enterprise as such in all spheres of life. And by its emphasis on personal integrity it has made possible a vast extension of interpersonal relationships in the system of "finance"—a system which, while it may be deficient in charity, at least is based firmly on faith and hope!

Unfortunately Protestantism, and especially liberal Protestantism, has suffered a grave loss of nerve in the past few decades. It has become defensive, ashamed of its own tradition, and even completely unaware of any history or historic mission. Its own scholars and theologians are in considerable measure to blame for this state of affairs. They have accepted much too easily criticisms of capitalism (e.g., the Marxist criticism) which are not for the most part valid, and they have not been able to put their finger either on the significant positive contribution of Protestant capitalism or on its real failings.

More than any other single factor it has been the instability of output and employment in a highly progressive market economy that has undermined its intellectual and moral support. In part, though only in small part, this instability is part of the cost of progress and must be accepted as such. In large part, however, this instability is unnecessary and can be avoided if government is prepared to accept its proper responsibility as a "governor" or stabilizer. Were this difficulty to be cleared out of the way, Protestantism should once more be able to shoulder its prime historic mission as the promoter of enterprise in its best sense, the search for constantly better ways of doing everything. This does not commit it either to "public" or to "private" enterprise—indeed, this distinction is no matter of principle, and the choice among various forms of enterprise should be entirely pragmatic. But it does commit it to economic progress as the most fundamental task of any economic system.

TOWARD A GENERAL THEORY
OF GROWTH

Can. Jour. of Econ. and Pol. Sci.,
19, 3 (Aug. 1953): 326-40.

THE growth phenomenon is found in practically all the sciences and even in most of the arts, because almost all the objects of human study grow—crystals, molecules, cells, plants, animals, children, personalities, knowledge, ideas, cities, cultures, organizations, nations, wealth, and economic systems. It does not follow, of course, from the mere universality of the growth phenomenon that there must be a single unified theory of growth which will cover everything from the growth of a crystal to the growth of an empire. Growth itself is not a simple or a unified phenomenon, and we cannot expect all the many forms of growth to come under the umbrella of a single theory. Nevertheless all growth phenomena have something in common, and what is more important, the classifications of *forms* of growth and hence of theories of growth seem to cut across most of the conventional boundaries of the sciences. In addition there are a great many problems which are common to many apparently diverse growth phenomena.

It is convenient to start with a threefold classification of growth phenomena. We have first what might be called *simple* growth, that is, the growth or decline of a single variable or quantity by accretion or depletion. In all that follows it should be understood that growth may be negative as well as positive, decline being treated merely as negative growth. In the second place we have what might be called *populational* growth, in which the growing quantity is not regarded as a homogeneous aggregate, but is analysed into an age distribution. Growth is regarded as the excess of "births" (additions to the aggregate) over "deaths" (subtractions from the aggregate), and the analysis of the process is conducted in terms of functions which relate births and deaths to the age distribution. Finally we have what might be called *structural* growth, in which the aggregate which "grows" consists of a complex structure of interrelated parts and in which the growth process involves change in the relation of the parts. Thus in the growth of a living organism, or of an organization, as the "whole" grows, the form and the parts change: new organs develop, old organs decline, and there is frequently growth in complexity as well as in some over-all magnitudes. Problems of structural growth seem to merge almost imperceptibly into the problems of structural *change* or development, so that frequently "what grows" is not the over-all size of the structure but the complexity or systematic nature of its parts. Thus the "growth" of a butterfly out of the chrysalis involves an actual decline in over-all magnitudes such as weight or volume, but certainly seems to come under the general heading of phenomena of growth or development.

These three "forms" of growth constitute three different levels of abstraction rather than a classification of actual growth phenomena. Growth phenomena in

*This paper was presented at the annual meeting of the Canadian Political Science Association in London, June 3, 1953.

the real world usually involve all three types. Thus a phenomenon of simple growth such as, for instance, the growth of a capital sum put out to interest, or the growth in the inventory or stocks of a single commodity are in fact part of, and ultimately dependent upon, much more complicated structural processes. Similarly, populational growth as in the case, say, of a human population, never takes place without changes in the organizational structure of the society, that is, in the kinds and the proportions of its "parts"—its organizations, jobs, roles, and so on. Thus all actual growth is structural growth; nevertheless, for some purposes of analysis the structural elements may be neglected and the growing aggregate can be treated as a pure population, and for other purposes even the populational aspects can be neglected and the growth can be treated as simple growth.

II

Turning first then to the analysis of simple growth, the main problem here is that of finding a "law" of growth which will serve to describe the growth curve, that is, which will express the size of the growing variable as a function of time. Perhaps the simplest case of simple growth is growth at a constant rate, for example, the growth of a capital sum at a constant rate of interest. In this case the growth function is the simple exponential $P_t = P_0 (1 + i)^t$, where P_0 is the original sum, P_t the amount into which it has grown in t years at a constant rate of growth i, growth being added at the end of every year. If growth is continuous the function becomes $P_t = P_0 e^{it}$.

Continuous growth at a constant rate, however, is rare in nature and even in society. Indeed it may be stated that within the realm of common human experience all growth must run into *eventually* declining rates of growth. As growth proceeds, the growing object must eventually run into conditions which are less and less favourable to growth. If this were not true there would eventually be only one object in the universe and at that point at least, unless the universe itself can grow indefinitely, its growth would have to come to an end. It is not surprising, therefore, that virtually all empirical growth curves exhibit the familiar "ogive" shape, the absolute growth being small at first, rising to a maximum, and then declining eventually to zero as the maximum value of the variable is reached. Many equations for such a curve have been suggested, though none seem to rest on any very secure theoretical foundation. The most familiar is perhaps that of Raymond Pearl, which graphically is a cumulative normal frequency curve. In any such equation the most important constants are (i) one which measures the total amount of growth, that is, the difference between the initial and the maximum value of the variable, and (ii) one which measures the time taken to grow from the initial position to a value reasonably close to the maximum. All that growth equations can do, however, is to describe growth; they are never capable of interpreting or understanding it.[1]

[1]My recent acquaintance with the work of Dr. S. A. Courtis suggests that this judgment may be much too severe. An empirical "growth law" which fits many cases has at least the virtue that it calls attention to possible unknown sources of disturbance in cases where it does not fit—just as the law of gravity led to the discovery of the outer planets. Courtis's law ($y = ki^r$) may well be of use in this way. See S. A. Courtis, "What Is a Growth Cycle?" *Growth*, I, no. 3, May, 1937.

Turning now to the second level of growth analysis, that of population growth, we find that fairly detailed and complex analyses are possible. A population may be defined as "an aggregation of disparate items, or 'individuals,' each one of which conforms to a given definition, retains its identity with the passage of time, and exists only during a finite interval."[2] "Birth" occurs when an item begins to conform to the definition which encloses the aggregation, and "death" when the item ceases to conform to this definition. A definition may be thought of as a closed fence: everything inside the fence belongs to the defined population; birth consists in crossing the fence into the enclosure; death in crossing the fence out of the enclosure. The population concept as thus defined is a perfectly general one, and applies not only to human or animal populations, but to populations of automobiles, poems, stars, dollars, ideas, or anything that is capable of definition.

Population *analysis* is only useful in the case of aggregates where birth and death rates can be regarded as some function of the *age composition* of the population. The age composition can be expressed most simply as a series of age groups, $a_1, a_2, \ldots, a_n$, where a_1 is the number of individuals between the ages of 0 and 1 "year," a_r is the number between the ages of $r - 1$ and r "years" old. The "age" of any individual is of course the time which has elapsed since birth. The "year" can of course be made as small as we like: in the limit the age composition reduces to a continuous function. If then the number of births and the number of deaths *in each age group* can be expressed as functions of the age composition, $a_1, \ldots, a_n$, the whole course of the population can be traced as far as patience and arithmetic hold out—or the assumed functions do not change. The simplest "birth function" is $B = b_1a_1 + b_2a_2 + \ldots + b_na_n$. This assumes that each age group makes a specific and constant proportional contribution to the total number of births where $(b_1, \ldots, b_n)$ are constants. Similarly the simplest "death function" is $D = d_1a_1 + d_2a_2 + \ldots + d_na_n$, where the number of deaths in each age group is assumed to be a constant proportion of the numbers in the group. Given such a death function, a "survival function" for any given "cohort" of births can be derived, a "cohort" being all those individuals who have a common "year" of birth. Thus of a number of births B in year 0, Bd_0 will die and $Bs_1 = B(1 - d_0)$ will survive into year 1: of these $B(1 - d_0)d_1$ will die and $Bs_2 = B(1 - d_0)(1 - d_1)$ will survive into year 2; similarly $Bs_{r+1} = B(1 - d_0)(1 - d_1) \ldots (1 - d_r)$ will survive into year $r + 1$. If the population is finite (that is, composed of mortals), we must have $d_n = 1$: that is, none of the oldest age group survive into the next year.

Probably the best way to illustrate the process of population analysis is by an arithmetical example, as the algebraic treatment is both easy and clumsy. Suppose a population of three age groups, a birth function $B = 3a_2 + 8a_3$, and a survival function $s_1 = 1$, $s_2 = 0.8$, $s_3 = 0.4$, and suppose we start with a population of 100 in the first age group, 40 in the second, and 10 in the third. The course of the population will be as in Table I.

[2]K. E. Boulding, "The Application of the Pure Theory of Population Change to the Theory of Capital," *Quarterly Journal of Economics*, XLVIII, Aug., 1934, 650.

TABLE I

Year	Births	Age Group 0–1	Age Group 1–2	Age Group 2–3	Total
1	120 + 80 = 200	100	40	10	150
2	240 + 160 = 400	200	80	20	300
3	480 + 320 = 800	400	160	40	600
4	960 + 640 = 1600	800	320	80	1200

Thus in the first year the number of births is $40 \times 3 + 10 \times 8$, or 200; of this cohort of 200 births all 200 survive into year 2, and are then in the first age group: $160 = (200 \times 0.8)$ survive into year 3, and are then in the second age group, and $80 = (200 \times 0.4)$ survive into year 4 and are then in the third age group. Given the number of births and the age composition of year 1 we can get immediately the age composition of year 2; the 200 births of year 1 become the 200 0–1 year olds: the 100 0–1 year olds become the 80 1–2 year olds, and the 40 1–2 year olds become the 20 2–3 year olds. From this age composition we can then derive the birth cohort of year 2 $(80 \times 3 + 20 \times 8)$. Similarly from the birth cohort and the age composition of year 2 we derive the age composition of year 3, and from that the birth cohort of year 3. The process can clearly be repeated for an indefinite number of years.

Table I has been arranged so that the population grows exponentially, doubling every year. It will be observed that the birth cohort likewise doubles every year, as does the number in each age group. Such a population may be said to be in "equilibrium exponential growth." If the rate of growth is 1, of course, the population is stationary and exactly reproduces its composition every year. If the rate of growth is less than 1 the population is declining, but the same principles apply. Now, however, suppose that instead of starting with the age composition of Table I we started with a distorted composition, as in Table II.

TABLE II

Year	Births ($3a_2 + 8a_3$ = Total)	Age Group 0–1	Age Group 1–2	Age Group 2–3	Total
1	30 + 800 = 830	10	10	100	120
2	24 + 40 = 64	830	8	5	843
3	1992 + 32 = 2024	64	664	4	732
4	153 + 2656 = 2809	2024	51	332	2407
5	4857 + 208 = 5065	2809	1619	26	4454
6	6741 + 6480 = 13221	5065	2247	810	8122
7		13221	4046	1124	18391

It will be seen that although the underlying laws of development of the population are exactly the same as in Table I, the immediate course of the population is very different. Instead of growing steadily, the population grows in a series of leaps and checks; indeed, from the second to the third years it actually declines, in spite of the fact that the underlying dynamics of the population imply a doubling every year! It will be observed, however, that in the present case the irregularities of the growth rate diminish as time goes on, and the age distribution becomes less distorted. This is because the birth function has coefficients for more than one age group, so that the contribution of the initial age composition gets "mixed" as time goes on. If the birth function only had coefficients for a single age group the "cycle" in the growth curve would perpetuate itself.

A simple algebraic expression of the above principles follows. Let the age composition in year t be $a_1, a_2, \ldots, a_n$, these being the numbers in the age groups 0–1, 1–2, $\ldots$, $(n-1)$–n. Suppose a birth function

(1) $\qquad\qquad B_t = b_1 a_1 + b_2 a_2 + \ldots + b_n a_n.$

Suppose also a series of survival coefficients, $s_1, s_2, \ldots, s_n$, where s_n is the proportion of the births of any year t that survive into the year $t + n$. Then for the year t we have

(2) $\qquad\qquad a_1 = s_1 B_{1\,t-1}, \ a_2 = s_2 B_{t-2}, \ \ldots, \ a_n = s_n B_{t-n}.$

Combining (1) and (2) we have

(3) $\qquad\qquad B_t = b_1 s_1 B_{t-1} + b_2 s_2 B_{t-2} + \ldots + b_n s_n B_{t-n}.$

Suppose now that we have a population in equilibrium exponential growth (or decline) at a rate g. Then we must have:

(4) $\qquad\qquad B_{t+1} = g B_t, \text{ whence } B_{t+r} = g^r B_t.$

Inserting the appropriate values from (3) and cancelling B_t we have:

(5) $\qquad\qquad \dfrac{b_1 s_1}{g} + \dfrac{b_2 s_2}{g^2} + \ldots + \dfrac{b_n s_n}{g^n} = 1.$

This equation can be solved for g to give the equilibrium rate of growth corresponding to any set of birth and survival coefficients. For a population in stationary equilibrium $g = 1$, and we have

(6) $\qquad\qquad R = \displaystyle\sum_{1}^{n} b_r s_r = 1.$

R may be called the "growth potential" of the population; the population must eventually grow, be stationary, or decline according as R is greater than, equal to, or less than 1. If sex ratios are neglected R is the same as the net reproduction ratio of a human or animal population, that is, it is the average number of births which eventually come from a unit of any given cohort of births in a population in equilibrium exponential growth.

Suppose now that the birth function contains only a single coefficient, b_r. If the initial age composition of the population is $a_1, a_2, \ldots, a_n$, births in year t_0 are $b_r a_r$. In year t_r then the rth age group will have $b_r a_r s_r$ individuals in it, and the number of births will be $b_r^2 a_r s_r$. In the year t_{2r} the rth age group will be $b_r^2 a_r s_r^2$, and the number of births $b_r^3 a_r s_r^2$. In the year t_{kr} the number of births will be $b_r a_r (b_r s_r)^k$. Similarly in the year t_1 the rth age group will be

$$b_r\, a_{r-1} \frac{s_r}{s_{r-1}},$$

and the number of births will be

$$b_r^{\,2}\, a_{r-1} \frac{s_r}{s_{r-1}}.$$

In the year t_{kr+1} the number of births will be

$$b_r\, a_{r-1} \frac{s_r}{s_{r-1}}\, (b_r\, s_r)^k.$$

It is clear that the birth cohorts and also the total population will repeat the pattern set up by the first r years, multiplied by the growth factor in all succeeding periods of r years. If however there is more than one birth function coefficient, the effect will be "damped."

The assumption of constant birth and survival coefficients gives us at least a first approximation to the dynamics of human or animal populations. The fact, however, that such an assumption results in exponential growth (or decline) means that it cannot be more than a first approximation for, as we have seen, exponential growth cannot go on forever. In order to achieve growth patterns of an ogive or logistic form it is necessary to assume that the birth or survival coefficients are themselves functions of the total population or of time, one or both eventually decreasing with increase of population, or lapse of time. A period of growth can then be attributed to a rise of

$$R = \sum_1^n b_r s_r$$

above 1; the ultimate cessation of growth comes about because the growth of the population itself carries R down to 1 again. This is illustrated in Figure 1.

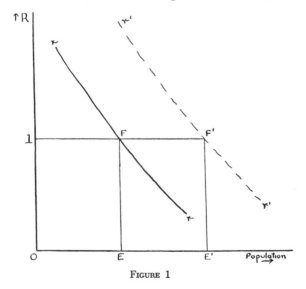

FIGURE 1

We postulate an R-curve rr relating R to the total population. The equilibrium population is OE where $EF = 1$. Suppose now that conditions change—life, say, becomes easier. The R-curve moves to the right to a new position $r'r'$. The equilibrium population is now OE', where again $E'F' = 1$. The exact dynamics of the shift from E to E' of course depend on the nature of the birth and survival functions.

Birth and survival functions need not, of course, be confined to age compositions. In many populations other variables are significant. For instance, for populations of capital goods (e.g., automobiles) we may assume as a first approximation that the object of "births" (production) is to hold the total population either constant, or increasing at a constant rate. In that case the number of births in any year will be equal to the number of deaths, plus the number necessary to maintain the desired increase in the total population. On such an assumption within any given pattern of growth of the total population, considerable fluctuations are possible in birth cohorts, if there are distortions in the age distribution. Thus consider the following population table:

TABLE III

Year	Births	Age Composition			Total
		0–1	1–2	2–3	
0	100	100	100	100	300
1	100	100	100	100	300
2	200	100	100	100	300
3	100	200	100	100	400
4	100	100	200	100	400
5	200	100	100	200	400
6	100	200	100	100	400

Here we suppose a population of "one-hoss shays," with three age groups, and survival coefficients of 1, 1, 1, 0: all deaths occur at the end of the third year. We suppose an initial population of 100 in each age group, 300 in all. This is maintained by 100 births every year, as we see going from year 0 to year 1. Now in year 2 it is decided to increase the population to 400, and in order to do this 200 births are "made." In year 3 we then have an age composition of 200, 100, 100. However, only the 100 in the third age group "die," so that only 100 need to be born in year 4. In year 5, however, the 200 that were born in year 2 die, and have to be replaced by another 200. It is clear that a perpetual cycle is now set up, with 200 births every three years and 100 in the intervening years. This cycle could only be avoided by raising the total population by equal amounts each year for a three-year period. If the survival distribution is more normal, however, so that some of the survival coefficients are less than 1, the effect will again be damped and the intensity of the cycle will diminish.

Very interesting and important problems arise (which are too complex to be examined in detail here) when the growth functions of one population depend upon the size of other populations. This, of course, is the theory of œcological interaction. At the level of comparative statics, that is, the comparison of two positions of equilibrium, the theory is not too difficult, but the dynamics of such systems easily become very complex. Figure 2, however, illustrates the principle on which such systems operate.

We suppose two different populations, P_1 and P_2. Size of population P_1 is measured along the horizontal axis, P_2 on the vertical axis. The solid line R_1 then shows all those combinations of P_1 and P_2 at which the R (growth potential) of population 1 is unity. Similarly the line $R_{1.1}$ shows those combinations for which $R = 1.1$ for population 1, and similarly for the other solid lines. The dotted lines similarly represent those combinations of P_1 and P_2 for which the growth potential of population 2 is 1, 1.1, etc. In the figure as drawn P_2 inhibits the growth of P_1, that is, the larger the population of P_2 the less will be the growth potential of P_1 for each level of P_1 as shown by the family of solid lines.

P_2 is a predator or parasite on P_1. Cases in which both populations are mutually competitive, or in which both are mutually co-operative, can be analysed by the same technique. The point E where the R_1 and r_1 curves intersect is the point of general stationary equilibrium, that is, the point at which the populations in equilibrium will coexist without growth or decline of either. Consider, however, the combination of populations represented by the point P. At this point $R = 0.8$, $r = 0.9$. Both populations will therefore decline, unless their age structures are very distorted. P_1 will decline more than P_2, and the two populations will move following the vector PP'. From P' another movement will take place to, say, P'', and so on until the equilibrium is reached. Lines of movement of the populations such as $PP'P''$ may be called "vector lines,"

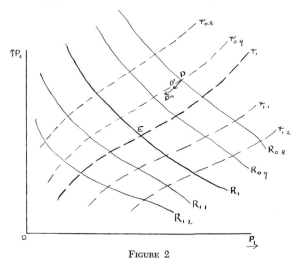

FIGURE 2

and the family of such lines is a good rough description of the dynamics of the system. Examples will be found in my *Reconstruction of Economics*, chapter I.

IV

The analysis of structural growth is much more complicated than the analysis of populational growth, and is much more difficult to reduce to a neat set of propositions. Structural growth includes such complex phenomena as the growth of crystal structures, the growth, division, and differentiation of cells, the growth of organisms, of organizations, of language and other mental structures, of buildings, and of societies. We would hardly expect such diverse phenomena to reduce themselves to a uniform simple scheme. Nevertheless it is striking how many of the problems which rise to special prominence in one field of study also carry over into others, and it is not impossible to formulate some principles of great generality.

The first of these we may call the principle of nucleation, following a term which comes originally from physics. Any structure has a minimum size, which is its "nucleus." Once a nucleus has been formed, it is not too difficult to understand how additions to the structure are made. The formation of the nucleus itself, however, presents many problems which are quite different from those involved in the growth of an already established structure. Thus there is a minimum size of crystal, depending on its complexity: in smaller aggregations of atoms than this minimum there are not enough components to make up the minimum structure. In the case of the cell the problem of nucleation is almost completely unsolved: as far as we now know, all living matter grows from living matter. We know something about how the complex societies of subordinate structures which comprise the living nuclei can grow, divide, and differentiate as "going concerns." We know practically nothing about how such an immensely complex organization ever came to be established in the first place, and up to the present we have not been able to reproduce that mysterious initial act of nucleation. In the social sciences the nucleation problem also exists; here it manifests itself as the problem of innovation, in the Schumpeterian sense. Once a form of organization is established, whether a type of production or a kind of enterprise, a cult, a school, a party, or any distinct type of institution, it is not too difficult to imitate. The initial innovation, however, is something of a mystery, which does not fall easily within the smooth rubrics of historical necessity. We do not understand very well what it is that makes the genuine innovators—those mysterious individuals who establish religions, cultures, nations, techniques, and ideas. In society as in physics, however, we find that very small amounts of "impurities" (say one Edison per hundred million) produce effects fantastically disproportionate to their quantity, because of the nucleation principle. It is also not perhaps too far fetched to speak of "super-cooled societies," where the external conditions call for change to a new state of society, but where the rate of nucleation is so small that the change does not take place.

Another principle which emerges from the study of nucleation is that the nucleus does not have to be homogeneous with the structure that grows around it; thus the speck of dust at the heart of the raindrop! Consequently *impurity* in a universe is a very important factor in explaining change. Examples of this principle are numerous in society. Colleges nucleate around sects, farm organizations around county agents, trade unions around socially minded priests. One cannot be a student of society for long without observing what I have sometimes called the "Pinocchio principle." Some agent or organization sets up a "puppet" in the form of some other kind of organization. Before long however the "puppet" begins to take on a life of its own, and frequently walks right away from its maker. Here we see the principle of "heterogeneous nucleation" actively at work in society. The principle of nucleation applies even to the learning process, which can be thought of as the growth of a " mental structure." Thus in learning a language it is necessary for the language to "nucleate" in the mind of the learner before it can become anything more to him than an unusable bunch of unrelated words. Even in learning economics the student frequently finds that for the first few months the subject makes practically no sense to him, and then quite suddenly he experiences a "conversion"; what had previously been disconnected parts somehow fall into place in his mind, and for the first time he "sees" the subject as an organic whole. The application of this idea to the phenomenon of religious or political conversion would make a most interesting study.

The second general principle of structural development might be called the principle of non-proportional change. As any structure grows, the proportions of its parts and of its significant variables *cannot* remain constant. It is impossible that is to say, to reproduce *all* the characteristics of a structure in a scale model of different size. This is because a uniform increase in the linear dimensions of a structure will increase all its areas as the square, and its volumes as the cube, of the increase in the linear dimension. Thus a twofold increase in all the lengths of a structure increases its areas by four times and its volumes by eight times. As some of the essential functions and variables of structure depend on its linear dimensions, some on its areal dimensions, and some on its volumetric dimensions, it is impossible to keep the same proportions between all the significant variables and functions as the structure grows.

This principle has two important corollaries. The first is that growth of a structure always involves a *compensatory* change in the relative sizes of its various parts to compensate for the fact that those functions and properties which depend on volume tend increasingly to dominate those dependent on area, and those dependent on area tend increasingly to dominate those depending on length. Large structures therefore tend to be "longer" and more convoluted than small structures, in the attempt to increase the proportion of linear and areal dimensions to volumes. It follows therefore that as a structure grows it will also tend to become longer and more convoluted. Architecture and biology— two sciences which are much more closely related than might appear at first sight—provide admirable examples. A one-room schoolhouse, like the bacterium, can afford to be roughly globular and can still maintain effective contact with its environment—getting enough light and nutrition (children) into its interior through its walls. Larger schools, like worms, become long in relation to their volume in order to give every room at least one outside wall. Still larger schools develop wings and courtyards, following the general principle that a structure cannot be more than two rooms thick if it is to have adequate breathing facilities. This is the insect level of architecture (skin-breathing). The invention of artificial ventilation (lungs) and illumination (optic nerves) makes theoretically possible at any rate much larger structures of a "globular" or cubic type, with inside rooms artificially ventilated and lit, just as the development of lungs, bowels, nerves, and brains (all involving extensive convolution to get more area per unit of volume) enabled living matter to transcend the approximately three-inch limit set by the insect (skin-breathing) pattern. In the absence of such devices further growth of the structure involves splitting up into separate buildings (the campus) of which the biological analogy is the termite or bee colony.

The second corollary follows immediately from the first: if the process of compensation for structural disproportion has limits, as in fact seems to be the case, the size of the structure itself is limited by its ultimate inability to compensate for the non-proportional changes. This is the basic principle which underlies the "law of eventually diminishing returns to scale" familiar to economists. Thus as institutions grow they have to maintain larger and larger specialized administrative structures in order to overcome the increasing difficulties of communication between the "edges" or outside surfaces of the organization (the classroom, the parish, the retail outlet) and the central executive. Eventually the cost of these administrative structures begins to outweigh any of the other possible benefits of large scale, such as increasing specialization of the more directly productive parts of the organization, and these structural limitations bring the growth of the organization to an end. One can visualize, for instance, a university of a hundred thousand students in which the entire organization is made up of administrators, leaving no room at all for faculty.

It is interesting to note that the principle of compensation may operate in two very distinct ways—in the direction of attempt to *solve* the problems posed by large scale or in the direction of an attempt to *avoid* these problems. Thus the critical problem of large-scale organization is that of the communications system (nerves and blood!). This being a "linear" function tends to become inadequate relative to the "surface" functions of interaction and production as the organization grows. One method of compensation is to increase the proportion of the organization which is devoted to the communications system as the organization grows larger (the modern army, David Reisman has remarked, marches not on its stomach but on the punched card). Another method however is to diminish the *need* for communication by developing autonomy of the parts or rigid and ritualistic patterns of behaviour. Thus a very large church organization, such as the Roman Catholic Church, not only has to permit a good deal of autonomy to its various parts (in this case, national churches), but can only maintain its structure at the cost of extreme rigidity in its basic operations. The Pope doesn't have to communicate with the priest in the wilds of Bolivia because the mass is removed from the agenda of discussion! In this connection it might be noted also that great size in itself leads to relative invulnerability, and hence very large organizations do not face the same problems of uncertainty and adjustment which face smaller organizations or organisms. The whales and elephants of the universe can afford to have fairly placid dispositions and insensitive exteriors.

A third principle of structural growth follows somewhat from the second, but is sufficiently distinct to warrant a separate status. This might be called the D'Arcy Thomson principle, after its most famous exponent.[3] It is the principle that at any moment the *form* of any object, organism, or organization is a result of its laws of growth up to that moment. Something which grows uniformly in all directions will be a sphere. Something which grows faster in one direction than in others will be "long." Something which grows faster on one side than on the other will twist into some sort of spiral. The shape of an egg is related to its flow down the oviduct. Examples can be multiplied almost indefinitely, and the contemplation of these beautiful and subtle relationships is perhaps one of the most refined delights of the human mind. It is clear that the principle applies in general not only to organisms, but to organizations, though its applications here are more complex and perhaps less secure. An aggressive chairman or department head will cause his department to grow relative to the total structure. Scientific inquiries follow growth patterns which are laid down by previous studies and by the interests of scientists. Economic and technological

[3]D'Arcy W. Thompson, *On Growth and Form* (2nd ed., Cambridge, 1952).

development follows patterns which in turn determine the structure of an economy. Law grows like a great coral reef on the skeletons of dead cases.

Growth creates form, but form limits growth. This mutuality of relationship between growth and form is perhaps the most essential key to the understanding of structural growth. We have seen how growth compels adjustments to changes in relative proportions. It is also true that occasionally growth stops because of "closure"—because the growth itself seals off all the growing edges. We see this frequently in the world of ideas where self-contained ideologies (such as Marxism) exhibit closure in the sense that any development outside the narrow circle of the self-contained system is inhibited. It is often the "loose ends" of systems that are their effective growing points—too tight or too tidy an organization may make for stability, but it does not make for growth. This is perhaps one of the most cogent arguments for toleration in the political sphere; the morbid passion for tidiness is one of the greatest enemies of human development.

There is, I believe, a fourth principle of structural growth, detailed evidence for which it is difficult to find in the biological sciences, but which is clearly apparent in the growth of man-made structures, especially, oddly enough, in building. It may perhaps be called the "carpenter principle." In building any large structure out of small parts one of two things must be true if the structure is not to be hopelessly mis-shapen. Either the dimensions of the parts must be extremely accurate, or there must be something like a carpenter or a bricklayer following a "blueprint" who can adjust the dimensions of the structure as it goes along. If, for instance, we are building a structure out of a thousand identical parts, the tolerable variability of each part would have to be about one thousandth of the tolerable variability of the whole structure, if we were simply adding part to part without making any adjustments on the way. It is only possible, however, to build a brick wall or a wooden house, with bricks and with boards that are in themselves highly variable, if there is exercised during the process of growth a "skill" of adjustment, that is, of adjusting the structure as it grows in conformity with some plan or requirement. It may perhaps be hazarded that the genes perform some such function in the growth of living organisms, though what is the machinery by which these little carpenters of the body operate is still unknown. In social and intellectual structures, however, the principle is of great importance, for the whole development of these structures may be affected profoundly by the existence of a "plan" and of an apparatus by which the growing structure is constantly conformed to the plan. The construction of a building, a machine, or a bridge is an obvious example. The process of academic learning is another example. In the learning of a language, for instance, the existence of a grammar exercises a profound effect on the capacity of the student to develop originality. In any subject, the presence of a textbook exercises somewhat the same influence as a grammar on the process of learning, and the instructor is the intellectual carpenter, trimming the student's mind off at frequent intervals by means of quizzes and examinations. What we have here is essentially a homœostatic process, the divergence which excites action being the divergence at any time between the actual condition of the structure and the "planned" condition.

Even where a detailed "plan" of development is not available the existence of some kind of ideal structure with which present reality may be compared exercises a profound influence on growth, especially in the sciences. One need only cite, for instance, the influence exerted on the progress of chemistry by the existence of the periodic table of elements, an ideal structure which in the beginning had many "holes" (undiscovered elements), but which was gradually filled up as the process of chemical research was directed into filling the obvious gaps in the structure. It may, indeed, be regarded as one of the prime functions of "theory" in any field to set up these ideal structures which are in fact incomplete. In this connection it may be observed that one of the principal advantages which may be derived from interdisciplinary research is the development of a "general theory" which will fulfil this function of the "ideal structure" for knowledge as a whole.

A fifth principle of structural growth emerges fairly clearly from economics, though here also its application to the biological or physical sciences is quite unproved. This may be called the "principle of equal advantage." It governs the distribution of the "substance" of a structure among the various parts of the structure. We assume first that the "atoms" of a structure can be ordered according to a parameter which we label, for want of a better term "advantage," this being defined operationally as a "potential" such that units will tend to flow towards locations of higher, and away from locations of lower, advantage. We then postulate that the advantage of a unit in any location is an inverse function of the relative quantity of units in that location—that is, the fewer the merrier! This implies a concept something like the "demand" for any given location—demand in this case fulfils something of the function of the "plan" under the fourth proposition. We then postulate a principle that "demand" tends to be satisfied, that is, if there are differences in advantage to units ("industries") in different locations, units will tend to move from the low-advantage locations where there are "too many" to the high-advantage locations where there are "too few."

In economic systems the principle of equal advantage, and the fact that the "advantage" parameter can be approximately related to monetary reward, enables us to give reasonably satisfactory explanations of two phenomena which are common in biology, but very little understood. These are the phenomena known as functional substitution and regeneration. If one organ of a living organization is removed, there is an observable tendency for other organs to take over the function of the missing organ. At lower levels of life, also, the organism seems to have a remarkable capacity for the regeneration of lost parts; tadpoles can grow new tails and starfish new limbs. The healing of wounds and of broken bones is an example of the same phenomenon at a somewhat less spectacular level. In the economic system it is possible to observe fairly closely what happens when an "organ" (industry) is cut off, say, by prohibition. In the first place if regeneration of the severed industry is prevented by the cauterizing action of law, other "industries" will begin to take over the functions of the destroyed industry (speakeasies, bathtub gin, etc.). If now the prohibition is removed, the old industry rapidly grows back again into the body economic, under the stimulus of profit (advantage). One may again hazard a guess that biologists will have to look for a variable akin to profit at the level of the cell if they are fully to understand the phenomenon of functional substitution and regeneration.

It is interesting to observe that the "carpenter principle" and the "advantage principle" are to some extent alternative ways of effecting the organization of a society, the first, of course, corresponding to the communist planned economy and the second to the capitalist market economy. In the planned economy, growth is organized by the principle of conformity to the plan: industries which are lagging behind the plan get extra attention to make them catch up, much as a child is taught in an authoritarian educational system. In the market economy, growth is organized by the principle of advantage: it takes place in the directions that "pay off" to the individuals who initiate it or are able to take advantage of its initiation, the "pay off" being derived from "profit," that is, an excess of value of product over cost. There is a certain analogy here perhaps with "progressive" education.

We have not, of course, exhausted a subject so ramified and so universal as growth in five summary propositions, though it may be hoped that there is here presented some indication that general theories of growth are possible. It remains in the compass of a short paper to indicate some of the loose—and therefore growing!—ends of the subject. We have not, for instance, considered the problem of the possibility of equilibrium *rates* of growth in an organism or system such that higher (or lower) growth rates may seriously disturb the functioning of the system even to the point of its collapse and "death." There is evidence in the plant world that too rapid a rate of growth kills the organism; indeed, some very effective weed killers have been developed on this principle, using growth hormones. The growth theories of Harrod and Domar suggest that in the economic system there are "appropriate" rates of growth of a system as a whole which will yield continuous full employment. These theories also suggest, however, that there is nothing inherent in the nature of an unstabilized market economy which will guarantee these appropriate rates of growth. There is a suggestion, indeed, that under some circumstances a continuous equilibrium rate of growth may be impossible, because certain elements, consumption, for example, do not keep pace with the rise in capacity and so force *accelerated* growth on other elements, such as investment, if the system is to maintain full employment. These problems may all turn out to be problems in compensation for structural changes through increasing size, such as we have noted earlier, but particularly where equilibrium seems to require acceleration in certain growth rates some quite peculiar problems may be involved.

The problems of the transition from rapidly growing systems to more or less stationary ones are also very general, and need careful study at many levels. The character of a system frequently has to change not merely because it gets big, but because it stops growing. Thus when a religious movement passes from its initial phase of rapid expansion into the phase of slow or even negative growth it has to make profound adaptations: what is appropriate organization in a "movement" is not necessarily appropriate in a "sect." Any system which passes from a rapidly growing phase to a more stationary one, whether it is a religion, a labour organization, a business firm, a nation, an economic system, or a civilization comes face to face with somewhat the same kind of adjustment.

David Reisman makes the growth phase of a culture the principal determinant even of the typical character of its individuals, attributing "tradition-directed" behaviour to low-level, slowly growing, or stationary populations with high growth potential, "inner-directed" behaviour to rapidly growing populations, and "other-directed" behaviour to high-level, slow-growing, or stationary populations. These connections may seem a little far-fetched, but there can be no doubt that the type of growth which any system exhibits will affect most if not all of its major characteristics.

In conclusion one may hazard a guess as to the growth patterns of the sciences. The remarkable universality of the principles enunciated here in regard to a general theory of growth indicate that perhaps there is emerging from the welter of the sciences something like a "general theory," something which is a little less general and has a little more empirical content than mathematics but which is more general and therefore, of course, has less content than the content of specific sciences. Mathematics is itself, of course, a "general theory" in that it applies wherever quantitative concepts and relationships are encountered. The sort of general theory which I have in mind, however, is a generalization from aspects of experience which include more than mere abstract quantity and which are common to many or even to all of the "universes of discourse" which constitute the various sciences. Growth is one such aspect: organization is another; interaction is another. When, and if, such a general theory comes to be written it will be surprising if the general theory of growth does not comprise an important chapter.

ECONOMICS AND THE BEHAVIORAL SCIENCES: A DESERT FRONTIER?

Diogenes, 15 (1956): 1-14.

ECONOMICS

AND THE BEHAVIORAL SCIENCES:

A DESERT FRONTIER?

One of the important intellectual interests of American scholars and scientists at the present time is the movement toward greater integration of specialized fields and disciplines. The size of the movement must not be exaggerated—it concerns a small minority of scholars, and most specialists are still content to stay comfortably within the cosy walls of their own specialty. Nevertheless there is something which might be called an "interdisciplinary movement" in many areas of knowledge, and if the movement is occasionally more undisciplined than interdisciplinary, this can be charitably ascribed to growing pains.

Three sources of this movement can be distinguished. In the first place there is a certain dynamic process in the development of pure theory which tends toward the integration of different fields. Within each discipline there is a tendency for theory to become more and more general. It is one of the marks of a developing science that old theories can usually be seen as special cases of the newer theories. Thus, in physics, the Newtonian mechanics can be exhibited, I am told, as a special case of the theory of relativity. In economics the "classical" theory of Adam Smith and

Ricardo can be seen as a special case of modern theories of value and employment. It would not be surprising if the increase in generality of theory led to a breakdown of the conventional barriers between disciplines. This has already happened to a considerable extent in the physical sciences, and it is difficult these days to tell where physical theory leaves off and chemical theory begins. Concepts which used to be pure chemistry, like valency, now turn out to have a basis in atomic physics. We still do not have a unified theory of the machinery of life, but we seem to be advancing in this direction with increased knowledge of the physical and chemical accompaniments of life processes. In the social sciences psychoanalytic theory has made a profound impact on sociology and anthropology. Biological theories of the interaction of populations, of growth, of ecological succession, and of homeostasis have an impact on the social sciences, even on economics. Economic theory itself is surely a special case of a much more general theory of society, a general theory which is not quite explicit but which sometimes seems to be just around the corner. Cybernetics seems to offer a clue to the unification of many disciplines; information theory jumps from electrical engineering with a spark of excitement into the social sciences. So widespread is this movement that a new society to enshrine it is in process of formation, known at the moment as the "Society for the Advancement of General Systems Theory."

The second source of the interdisciplinary movement is closely related to the first. It is the development of what might be called "interstitial fields" between two or more old-established disciplines. In the natural sciences the rise of physical chemistry in the second half of the nineteenth century is a good example. Now it almost seems as if the hybrid threatens to displace both its parents. Similarly, the twentieth century has seen marked advances in biophysics and biochemistry. In the social sciences the rise of social psychology as a recognized discipline in the last generation parallels the rise of physical chemistry two generations earlier. Here too there seems to be some tendency for the hybrid offspring to gobble up the parents as the realization grows that society consists of the interaction of individuals, and that individuals cannot be understood apart from the society which grew and which nourishes them. Social anthropology likewise threatens to take over sociology on the one side and anthropology on the other.

The third source of interdisciplinary interest is the growth of specialized empirical and professional fields which utilize theoretical and conceptual material from more than one of the traditional disciplines. Thus, medicine is a professional field which draws on the resources of all the physical sciences, and which is beginning to draw more and more on the social sciences. Many of the advances in biophysics and biochemistry have been stimulated by the demands and opportunities provided by medical and surgical practice. The recent rise to prominence of psychiatry, psychosomatic, and social medicine, with the recognition that the source of many diseases lies in the experiences, perceptions, and social environment of the patient, opens a door to many important developments in the social sciences. Engineering increasingly requires theoretical material drawn not only from the physical sciences but from the social sciences as well. Even in law, the most formal and isolated of the great professions, there is increasing interest in drawing on the resources of the various social sciences, though this movement is still in a very early stage. Other professions are likewise finding that the logic of their own professional activities forces them into a more integrated approach to their theoretical foundations. Social work has perhaps leaned too heavily on psychoanalysis, and needs to reach out to other social sciences. Architecture is awakening to the fact that buildings are made for people and must be built around patterns of behavior as well as engineering necessities. Schools of education, business, nursing, dentistry, and some others have not perhaps yet realized some of the opportunities for integrative research which are open to them. Their problems, however, involve more disciplines than they are often aware of.

Even more than in the "regular" professions, however, interest in interdisciplinary work arises in what might be called the "sub-professions," those specialized branches of empirical study which may perhaps be on the way to becoming recognized professions, but which at present occupy a status somewhere between the full-fledged profession and the "pure" disciplines. Of these sub-professions the most striking example perhaps is industrial relations, an area of study which has had phenomenal growth in the past generation. It draws on economics, for it has to be interested in wage theory and employment theory. It draws even more on sociology for the study of the dynamics of labor organizations and labor-management relations. It draws on social psychology and group dynamics, especially in its study of small-group interactions. It is at least adjacent to the field of industrial psychology. International relations is another specialty which draws on many disciplines—economics, political science, anthropology. The study of economic development and culture change is forcing certain rapprochements between economics and anthropology. In the area of family relations we have a rapidly developing field which draws its theoretical material from psychology, sociology, even from economics. The list is by no means exhaustive.

To these three sources of the interdisciplinary movement one should perhaps add a fourth—the stimulus given to the "behavioral sciences" by the Ford Foundation. It is not wholly clear even now what defines a behavioral science. The operational definition—a science which can get support from the Ford Foundation—perhaps illustrates the difficulties of operational definitions better than it defines a behavioral science. But if the edges of behavioral science are not altogether clear, this is probably as it should be—concepts should spread out from a center rather than be enclosed by a fence. And the center of the behavioral sciences, it is fairly clear, is social psychology. Social psychology and its two parent fields, sociology and psychology, are clearly within the fold. Social anthropology is hard to tell from sociology these days, and gets a first-class ticket. Physical anthropology (if there are any people left who go around measuring skulls) probably gets no ticket at all. Political science is divided: the students of political behavior, who are really social psychologists in disguise, come in as approximately full members. Political theorists and institutionalists are admitted only on promise of improvement. History of the traditional sort is barely allowed to peek in the back door. There is a certain tendency for those outside the behavioral sciences to be suspicious, and perhaps a little envious, of the support they have received. The impartial observer must admit, however, that the behavioral sciences are not merely a whim of the Ford Foundation, but that they do represent a certain core of disciplines and methods which have growing unity, and a certain common culture. The Ford Foundation's support rests on an already existing movement, and while it no doubt encourages this movement, it has in no sense created it.

Up to this point I have not mentioned economics. The main task of this article, however, is to examine the relation of economics both to the general movement for the integration of knowledge and to the particular movement for unity in the behavioral sciences. It must be confessed that at least at first sight economics stands somewhat aloof from this general movement. Economics is an old, rather self-contained discipline. It has some claims, after all, to being the second oldest of the sciences, emerging in systematic form with Adam Smith in 1776, a century later than Newton but earlier than Dalton, Darwin, or Freud. Economists live in something of a world of their own, and do not, for the most part, feel any strong urges to communicate with or to learn from sociologists, psychologists, and so on. Some attempts have been made to bring economics and psychology together,[1] but it cannot be claimed that there is any discipline of "economic psychology," or of "economic sociology" corresponding in status to social psychology. There was a time when "political economy" was a respected name. In a sense, however, it was prematurely born and died in infancy. Economics had to escape from this entanglement with political science and develop an abstract discipline of its own in the middle of the last century—an escape which is symbolized by the very substitution of the older name "political economy" by the term "economics." Only within the past few years has there been some revival of interest in what perhaps had better be called "economic politics"—an attempt to develop a unified view of the economic and political processes in society.[2] There have been some attempts to develop the study of economic anthropology.[3] On the whole, however, anthropologists and economists have gone their separate ways with the minimum of contact, and even the current interest in the relation between culture change and economic development has not, as yet, produced any major theoretical integration.

The reasons for this relative isolation of economics lie partly in its history as an "old" discipline, inclined to be self-contained and indifferent or even hostile to the "upstarts," and partly in the nature of the economist's abstraction. The economist's universe consists not of men but of commodities and the quantities associated with them—prices, outputs, stocks, consumptions, rates of interest, and so on. His data consists for the most part of time series of these variables. Economics is therefore a kind of astronomy of commodities, studying the movements and interrelations of these various time series, and if these movements are regular enough the incidental fact that commodities are moved by men can be neglected. Astronomers can, in similar fashion, neglect the question whether the planets are moved by angels, because whether they are so moved or not, angels are so delightfully regular in their behavior that they can be neglected, or at least replaced by differential equations. Unfortunately for the economist, however, men are not as regular in their motions as angels, and it is more difficult to replace them by equations. It may be worth while, therefore, to explore some possibilities of advance in this "desert

1. See especially George Katona, *Psychological Analysis of Economic Behavior* (New York, McGraw-Hill, 1951), and Albert Lauterbach, *Man, Motives and Money* (Ithaca, N.Y., Cornell University Press, 1954).

2. *Politics, Economics, and Welfare*, by R. A. Dahl and C. E. Lindblom (New York, Harper, 1953), represents a major attempt in this direction.

3. See M. J. Herskovitz, *Economic Anthropology* (New York, Knopf, 1952).

frontier" that lies between economics and the other social or behavioral sciences.

Part of the difficulties of this frontier, and one reason for the self-sufficiency of economics, lies in the fact that whereas economics organizes itself around a *level of abstraction*—the "commodity universe"—the other behavioral and social sciences tend more to organize themselves around various forms of *method of procedure*. It is not altogether easy to identify the various levels of abstraction at which the other behavioral sciences operate. We may say, for instance, that psychology centers around systems of stimulus and response, sociology around systems of interaction of persons, and anthropology around the study of simple static states of culture. Each of these propositions, however, would be disputed vigorously by many competent experts in the various fields and important counter-examples could easily be given. It is much easier to set up a classification of methods on which there would be fairly general agreement and which would cut across the traditional division into departments or disciplines. In examining the possible contribution of the behavioral sciences to economics, then, we will find it more fruitful to examine the contribution of the various methods, rather than the contribution of various disciplines. The four methods which I propose to consider are: (1) the experimental, (2) the observational, (3) the metrical, and (4) the clinical. These methods are not, of course, peculiar to the behavioral sciences. It can be claimed, however, that the behavioral sciences have been more self-critical and more self-conscious about their methods than any other group of sciences in recent years, and that all the sciences might do well to subject themselves to at least something of this process of self-examination.

The experimental method is a familiar one in science. It consists essentially in setting up and observing an artificial situation in which the variables are fewer and more subject to control than in "nature." In the behavioral sciences it has been most employed by psychologists, especially animal psychologists. The rat threading his maze, the pigeon pecking for food, the monkey solving his problems, are the trade marks of this craft. Human subjects have not been lacking. Studies of perception and cognition owe much to experiment with humans, especially college sophomores. The processes of learning, the formation of mental images, and the whole complex interaction of stimulus and response have been subject to inquiry through experiment. The method has also been employed, with more difficulty but still with some success, by the social psychologist in the study of small groups. The tradition of Kurt Levine and "group dynamics," the fascinating studies of communication and interaction in small groups by Alex Bavelas, and the elaborate studies of group organization and behavior at the RAND Corporation are all examples of this method. Even in anthropology the experimental method is not entirely lacking. Cornell University, for instance, under the leadership of Allan Holmberg, is conducting what might be called a quasi-experiment in culture change in a whole community in the mountains of Peru, by keeping close watch on the effects of a planned series of innovations.

Up to the present, economics has been little influenced by the experimental method: it is difficult to get the banker or the corporation executive or even the housewife into a laboratory and subject them to simplified artificial economic situations to see what they would do. Nevertheless, there are some recent developments, for instance, in the theory of games, in decision theory, and in utility theory, which point toward certain possibilities of experimental verification. The phenomenon which is most subject to investigation here is that of choice under conditions of uncertainty. We can, for example, give subjects the choice between various outcomes, rewards, or punishments of varying degrees of probability and see whether their responses are consistent with various assumptions about utility functions. It may be doubted whether the results of these experiments will throw any startlingly new light on the processes of choice in the real world. Nevertheless, choice, or the decision-making process, especially under conditions of uncertainty, is so fundamental to the economic process, and is so little understood, that any light shed on it is welcome.

The observational method is again common to many sciences—astronomy, geology, the various branches of natural history, as well as the social sciences. It may be divided roughly into observations in space and observations through time, though all observational studies should ideally consist both of observations of variables, structures, and relationships existing at a *moment* of time and of records (time series) of these observations at regular intervals through time. In the behavioral sciences much sociology and most anthropology follows this method. Sociologists of the type of Max Weber draw upon historical record for their data, and derive their generalizations from careful study of this material. Sociologists of the questionnaire-interview school and anthropologists in their field work also rely almost exclusively on the observational method. Economics relies heavily on this method. If a distinction were to be drawn between its use in economics and in the other behavioral sciences, one might say that economics is more interested in observation of variables through time (that is, in time series), whereas sociology and anthropology are more interested in·observations in "space" of some kind. The space need not be geographical space—it may be one of many "social spaces" or "sample spaces," but the main interest is in the structure and relationships of variables as they exist at a moment, or through a fairly brief interval of time. One might say also that economics is more interested in variables which are capable of fairly exact quantitative measurement, whereas sociology and anthropology are more interested in qualitative descriptions and relationships. A third possible distinction is that economics is apt to be content with data obtained as a by-product of social processes which have other main objectives. Thus, much economic information comes as a by-product of tax systems—income data, for example, from the income tax, and trade data from customs. The behavioral sciences on the other hand are less apt to be satisfied with "by-product" data and have developed many ingenious methods for the deliberate and careful collection of information.

It must be emphasized that these distinctions are very rough, and important exceptions could be found to all of them—they define foci of interest rather than clear boundaries. Furthermore, in part under the stimulus of the "interdisciplinary movement" these distinctions are breaking down. One of the most important developments in economics in the past ten or fifteen years has been a great development of specialized data-collection, especially through the survey method. The Survey Research Center at the University of Michigan, for instance, conducts at regular intervals an elaborate survey of consumer finances. Thus, the economist no longer has to rely on data drawn from the haphazard, but unfortunately not random, processes of the tax and customs system, but has an independent source of information carefully designed to yield the maximum of information per unit cost. Sociologists and anthropologists are getting more aware of the importance of time series, and there has been some growth of "longitudinal" studies which follow a certain situation through many years. Much remains to be done in this connection, however, and it is perhaps the greatest weakness of these sciences that they have too many "one-shot" studies relating to a particular time and place, and that the information gathered does not feed into a continuing time series in the way that most economic information does. It is hard to overestimate, for instance, the importance for economics of the *continuous* collection of national income data which has been going on now for twenty-five years or more. There is nothing like this, as yet, in the other social sciences. In economics we have a reasonably clear and accurate picture of the over-all magnitudes of the economy and a picture of how these magnitudes proceed through time. Current data is always seen as the last element of a long time series, and this gives it a richness and significance which it would not otherwise possess. In the other social sciences each piece of information tends to stand alone, without reference to any over-all picture either in time or in space.

The third method which may be distinguished is the metrical method. This is in a sense a subdivision of the observational method, but it has so many characteristics of its own that it is perhaps worth a separate heading. In the past generation or so there has grown up in many different disciplines an interest in quantification, in indices, in exact measurement of variables, and in the attempt to discover stable functional relationships among these variables by methods involving fairly advanced mathematical and statistical technique. So widespread is this movement that it might almost be identified as a "metrics" movement. Thus, in economics we have seen the rise of econometrics; in psychology, psychometrics; in biology, biometrics; and even in sociology, sociometrics. The curious thing about this movement, however, is that it is in the main one of isolated and unrelated disciplines. In spite of the fact that it uses the one basic language of mathematics, the metrics movements in the various disciplines have been surprisingly isolated, largely unaware of each other's work, and have remained for the most part within the framework of their respective disciplines. Thus, psychometrics has developed mainly around the problem of psychological testing. Its main tools have been correlation and factor analysis; its main interest has been the identification of stable traits or elements in test performance. Sociometrics is perhaps the least successful, or perhaps one should say respectable, of the various metrics. Its focus of interest has been in the quantification of distributions and of spatial relationships. Econometrics has undergone a phenomenal growth in the past twenty-five years, and has had a significant impact on theory and practice in economics. Its main focus of interest is the identification of stable functional relationships among economic variables, such as demand and supply functions, consumption functions, and so on. It is also interested in discovering stable difference equations among economic variables with a view to the possibilities of predicting their time course. The next few years may bring considerable convergence among these various metrics. They share many basic mathematical and statistical tools, and many of the basic models may turn out to be more closely related than is now apparent. Thus, models of learning in psychology attempt to relate time series of stimuli and responses: this is not wholly unrelated to the problem of economic dynamics, which also seeks to relate "earlier" to "later" variables in stable difference equations.

The fourth method of the behavioral sciences is the clinical method. Psychoanalysis is the chief monument of this method. It is used, however, in clinical psychology, in social work, in criminology, in town planning. The emphasis here is on the "cure" of a pressing practical problem. In one sense we may say that this also is an example of the observational method. The observations in this case, however, are of "cases"—that is, of situations which have some degree of morbidity, and they are directed mainly toward prescription of remedies. Verification comes, if at all, from the further observation of the effects of the remedies prescribed. In spite of the biased sample and the unsystematic nature of the verification processes, much has been learned from clinical observation, and a good deal of the theoretical structure of the behavioral sciences stems from data derived by this method. The impact of psychoanalytic theory on all the behavioral sciences has been great, even where it has not been accepted as quite scientifically respectable. The theory of personality and of motivation has been largely drawn from psychoanalytic sources. Cultural anthropology has also been deeply influenced by psychoanalytic theory in its theories of the mutual interaction of culture and personality, of the importance of child rearing customs on the dynamics of cultural preservation or change, and so on.

Economics has been affected very little by the clinical method, and practically not at all by psychoanalytic theory. Economic man had no parents and never was a child. The interest of economics focuses on rational, conscious, and reflective behavior rather than on irrational and subconsciously motivated behavior. Nevertheless, there are areas in economics, such as the field of labor relations, where not only is a clinical approach possible, but where psychoanalytic theory also has considerable relevance. One does not need to go all the way and confine labor relations to the discussion of the employer as the father image or to attribute labor disputes to the unsatisfactory love of foremen, but one can still admit that the industrial relationship is not a purely economic relationship and that there are usually more things in dispute than wages and hours. It may be also, as Lauterbach has suggested, that childhood experiences in depression affect the outlook of the decision-makers of the next generation, and that this may account for something of a long cycle in economic affairs. There is so little direct evidence for this proposition, however, that it cannot be awarded higher status than that of an interesting but unproved notion.

It is clear that the frontier between economics and the behavioral sciences is by no means wholly desert. It is true that beyond the safe departmental boundaries the ear is unusually sensitive to the voice of the Windy Platitude, and what is glimpsed around the corner of the sagebrush is frequently only the Obvious. It is true also that professional hazards are unusually high for the traveler, and academic rewards are more likely to go to those who stay at home and cultivate their departmental gardens rather than to those who venture forth on interdisciplinary territory. The economic psychologist is apt to find himself regarded as a psychologist by the economists and as an economist by the psychologists, and is pushed out from both departmental cases, and the same is apt to be true of any hybrid specialist, unless, like the social psychologist, he can get together with his kind and establish an intermediary oasis of his own. Nevertheless, the desert is irrigable, especially by the welcome springs which flow from the foundations, and under, these circumstances it may turn out to have astonishing reserves of intellectual fertility.

Irrigation, however, always raises the awkward question of which desert should be irrigated—assuming what is usually the case, that water is scarce. One may raise therefore a final awkward question—whether there are not other interdepartmental deserts which would be even more fruitful under irrigation than the one which stretches between economics and the other behavioral sciences. There is some evidence that it is not always interaction between closely related sciences which produces the most fruitful results, but that frequently hybrid vigor results from the crossing of two highly unrelated parent stocks. One should certainly not assume that it is only from the social sciences that economics will learn new tricks, and there are signs of fruitful interactions outside the traditional framework of the social sciences. One of the most exciting theoretical developments of the past ten years, for instance, has been the rise of information theory, which originated—and one cannot help expressing a little surprise —in electrical and communications engineering. Up to the present the impact of information theory on economics has been small. It is clear, however, that we are never going to solve the problem of economic dynamics unless we know something of how economic information—or more generally, information relative to economic decisions—is transmitted around the system. The particular abstract concept which the communication engineers have called "information"—which is simply a convenient measure of the improbability of the symbols in a message—may not be a suitable abstraction for this problem, but at least economists are being stimulated by these developments to re-think the problem of information in their own discipline. We have gone too long in economics on the assumption that economic man never has to learn anything—that he is somehow mysteriously equipped from birth with all the knowledge necessary to rational behavior. Under assumption of perfect competition, where all economic man has to know is a set of prices which he can see plainly with the naked eye, it may well be that information or learning concepts are unnecessary. The introduction of imperfect competition into economics, however, means that poor old economic man now has to know all sorts of complicated relationships like demand and cost functions (and much worse things in game theory!) if he is to behave "rationally," and how he gets to know these mysterious facts of his environment nobody ever asks. Once we abandon the assumption of perfect competition, then, the problem of the place of information and learning processes in economic behavior cannot be avoided.

Of more immediate importance to economics than information theory are certain developments in a rather ill-defined field which might be called the "theory of organization." Some of this comes out of the biological sciences, in the notion of homeostasis and homeostatic mechanisms—those beautiful and subtle devices which regulate the constancies of the body—its temperature, blood pressure, and chemical and biological composition. The union of biology and electrical engineering produced cybernetics, the science of steersmanship, or of control mechanisms, so ably developed by Norbert Wiener.[4] From this and various other sources, some from outside of traditional economics, some from inside, comes the lusty new discipline—which its enemies would describe as a cult—of "operations research" and "management science." Mathematicians and even philosophers have been taking an increasing interest in problems which economists used to think were their private property. The theory of games comes out of a liaison between pure mathematics as embodied in Von Neumann and economics as embodied in Morgenstern.[5] It is basically an attempt to define the nature of rational behavior under conditions of uncertainty of various kinds and degrees, in an environment which includes other "rational" beings with whom various agreements

4. Norbert Wiener, *Cybernetics* (New York, Wiley, 1948).

5. J. Von Neumann and O. Morgenstern, *The Theory of Games and Economic Behavior* 3rd ed. (Princeton, N.J., Princeton University Press, 1953).

may or may not be made, and where all the participants abide by some minimum set of rules. The theory of games has stimulated renewed interest in utility theory because of the necessity of finding some measure of the "pay-offs" involved in various strategies. Philosophers and logicians vie with each other in devising axiomatic systems which will permit the construction of a utility function, while the poor economist looks on in some amazement, not quite knowing whether to be flattered or insulted. Just what will come out of all this ferment is hard to predict, but there is at least a good deal of intellectual excitement even if as yet the fruits seem to be largely a matter of promise.

Finally, it is my personal conviction, not perhaps shared by many other economists, that there is an important field of interdisciplinary advance between economics and the biological sciences. There are two grounds for believing this. The first is that there is a certain similarity in the theoretical problems of the two sciences. The problem of the "ecosystem"—the community of living organisms—in biology has many similarities with that of the price system in economics, and the idea of history as an ecological succession of temporary equilibria is fruitful and attractive. The biological organism and the social organization also show marked similarities. The great processes of metabolism (exchange), growth, internal transformations, homeostasis, information, and entropy exchange operate in both social and biological bodies, and it is not unreasonable to hope that a general theory of organization is possible which would serve as a first-approximation model for cells, animals, firms, states, and societies. This is not to say that a single theory can cover all these diverse organisms and organizations—the introduction of consciousness into the model, for instance, makes a profound modification. Nevertheless, it helps in the systemization of thought if these organizations can be placed in something like a continuum of increasing complexity.

The second possibility of interaction between economics and biology is at a more practical level. Economists are apt to forget that man is part of a complex biological system and that this imposes certain limitations on him. Biologists, on the other hand, especially those interested in conservation, are apt to forget that man is more than a biological species, in that he is capable of communication, learning, and problem solving on a scale far beyond the capacity of any other form of life. Somewhere between the economic naïveté of the conservationists and the biological naïveté of the economists it should be possible to establish a solid "interdiscipline" of economic biology which would take account of both characteristics of man—his biological base as a member of an ecosystem and his rational aspirations as an intelligent being.

If the reader is confused by the picture I have given, he is merely reflecting the realities of the situation. Nevertheless, even though the situation is confusing, it is also exciting. We live in a time of many intellectual frontiers. Some of these may turn out to be deserts. But many are capable of permanent academic settlements, and the crazy men and adventurers of today may be the classicists and the founding fathers of a respectable tomorrow.

PARITY, CHARITY, AND CLARITY

Michigan Daily, Sept. 16, 1956.

Parity, Charity & Clarity

Ten Theses on Agricultural Policy

1. **FARMERS HAVE** been grumbling for at least 6000 years, not wholly without justification. It is the food-and-fiber surplus from agriculture—what the farmer produces over and above what he eats and wears—that feeds the non-agricultural population. In an oppressive society the forces of law and the state combine to take this surplus away from the farmer without giving him much in return.

Even in a **progressive** society like ours however the farmer gets short-changed for a more subtle reason. In a progressive society, especially one in which agricultural techniques are improving, the proportion of people in agriculture steadily declines. (In the United States, for instance, it has declined from over 90 per cent at the time of the Revolution to about 16 per cent today.

There must therefore be some force operating to chase people out of agriculture into industry. If this is not done with the stick it must be done with the carrot—that is, industry must be more attractive than agriculture. The relatively depressed incomes in agriculture therefore are paradoxically enough the necessary consequences of agricultural progress.

2. **THE MAGNITUDE** of the differential between agricultural and industrial incomes depends on the mobility between the two groups—that is, one the ease with which the relative transfer of resources from agriculture to indus-

try can take place. If farmers are wedded to the land it takes a big differential to divorce them. If they can move easily, a slight differential will suffice to effect the necessary adjustments.

3. **IN AMERICAN** commercial agriculture of the North and West the mobility problem is not serious except in so far as government price supports have made it so. In America we are witnessing a phenomenon unique in history—the disappearance of the rustic. All previous civilizations have rested on a sharp differential between urban (and urbane) culture and rural, or rustic culture. The differentiation has usually proved to be their undoing.

Only in the present century is a society emerging in which the basic culture of town and country is the same. Never has there been less justification for agricultural discontent than in present-day American commercial agriculture.

4. **THE ONLY** serious economic problem in American agriculture is that of non-commercial agriculture—the two million small subsistence farms, mostly in the South and in the mountains. Here is really rural poverty: here is our great domestic underdeveloped area.

5. **NEVERTHELESS**, it is the rich farmers who squawk the loudest, and the fundamental principle of Democracy is Government by Squawk. On the whole, American agricultural policy is designed to make rich farmers a bit richer,

not to solve the problem of the poor farmer.

It has been put over on the people partly because the agricultural population is outrageously over-represented in Congress, especially in the Senate, but also because of an essentially mistaken concept of Justice. You cannot do justice to a commodity: you cannot do justice to an industry: you can only do justice to people. Failure to realize this humble truth is at the bottom of most of the muddled thinking on agricultural policy.

6. AMERICAN Agricultural Policy revolves around the notion of **parity price.** This is the price, whether of a single commodity or of agricultural products in general, at which a given quantity of the agricultural commodity would purchase approximately the same amount of the goods that farmers buy that it commanded in some "base period"—historically, 1909-1914. The idea arose in a mere statistical calculation by the economists of the Department of Agriculture. During the depression however it became the rallying symbol for agriculture discontent, and it retains a powerful emotional appeal to farmers.

7. THE ATTACHMENT to the parity symbol is not wholly unreasonable, because a depression hits farmers mainly through a fall in the relative price—that is in the purchasing power—of their products, not through loss of jobs. Hence the labor movement is "job conscious" and the farm movement is "price conscious."

In 1932 farmers were working as hard and producing as much as in 1929: a bushel of their produce however purchased less than half as much as in the former year. It is because agricultural production stays up in a depression that agricultural prices fall so low. Because of this also, however, we eat just about as well, on the average, in a depression as in prosperity. The price of parity in a depression would be hunger.

8. ALTHOUGH the attachment to the parity symbol is understandable, it is nevertheless a grave obstacle to the framing of a more rational agricultural policy. Because agricultural policy is price-centered and backward-looking, it fails to come to grips with the income problem and with the real problems of agricultural poverty.

High prices are only good for those who sell something, and are best for those who sell a lot. Hence price supports benefit rich farmers more than poor, commercial farmers more than subsistence farmers.

Even worse, high price supports tend to "freeze" an obsolete commodity structure and prevent necessary adjustments of output. They therefore tend to create "surpluses" which are an embarrassment to all. These surpluses create pressures which are seriously inconsistent with our trade and foreign policies.

9. IF WE must "help farmers" then a policy based on income supports rather than price supports is intrinsically much more sensible. The defunct and not much lamented Brannan Plan had this to its credit. Income supports, however, smack of "charity," and have the reputation, at least, of being politically unacceptable. They also raise the awkward question of Justice. If we are to have income supports for farmers, why not for everybody? Why should poor farmers be helped and not poor shopkeepers or professors?

10. THERE IS a lot to be said for the proposition that the best agricultural policy is a general full employment policy. As long as there is generally full employment it is easy for people to transfer out of agriculture to keep pace with advancing technology and we do not face the "depression price" problem. The present decline in agricultural incomes, for example, is little more than a necessary readjustment after a period of unusual agricultural prosperity. Agriculture did very well out of the war, and it is no more than justice that their incomes should decline a little relative to those who did not so benefit. This is not to deny the existence of a few problem commodities and problem areas. Special cases however demand special treatment.

The political importance of the present small decline in agricultural incomes is probably due more to the fear that, as in the 1920's, it preages a general collapse like that of 1929-32. There are good reasons for supposing that this will not happen.

THE PUBLIC IMAGE OF AMERICAN
ECONOMIC INSTITUTIONS

American Perspectives, Robert E. Spiller
and Eric Larrabee, eds., Cambridge:
Harvard Univ. Press, 1961, pp. 117-133.

THE PUBLIC IMAGE OF AMERICAN ECONOMIC INSTITUTIONS

In ECONOMIC and political life it is not the images of the philosopher or the specialist that decide the course of history — important as these may be in the long run. It is, rather, the images of businessmen, factory workers, union men, farmers, housewives, and so on that make up the workaday world and guide its immediate destinies.

Although often widely divergent, these images have something in common. It would be surprising if they did not, since all presumably originate in the general experience of the society and in the same external reality. They are also very complex, and their complexity is not diminished by their frequent lack of definition. We are dealing here not with the clearly expressed ideas of scholars, but with the half-formed, vaguely delimited, and often unexpressed perceptions, attitudes, prejudices, and views of the world of people in the ordinary business of life. This chapter deals mainly with a single predominant aspect of these images — the perceptions and evaluations, by various groups in the society, of business and the businessman. This aspect will be dealt with first as it expresses itself in a polarity of attitude, "pro-business" or "anti-business," a great over-simplification of a complex and many-dimensioned image. Yet, as a first approximation it is useful to look at the history of the general image of business in the first half of this century as a process of gradual resolution and synthesis of these two opposing states of mind.

Discussion of "pro" or "anti" views implies either that there are opposing ethical systems — differences in valuations of the same set of perceived "facts" — or that there are differences in the perceptions of the facts themselves. These are not unrelated, since differences in valuations usually lead to differences in perception of fact. If, for instance, by reason of something in our basic valuation system we look unfavorably on the institution of business, we will be more likely to perceive the bad consequences of the institution than the good. It is important, therefore, to look into our value systems — especially polarities of value — in order to trace the sources of different images even of the facts of the business institution, and still more of its evaluation. A polarity of value is a quality (or quantity) that can be ranged on a linear scale, such as "honesty–dishonesty." Frequently opposite descriptive terms apply to each end of the scale, so that the polarity can be described as a movement from more to less of the one, or less to more of the other. Thus, a movement from more to less honesty is the same as a movement from less to more dishonesty.

Behind both the "anti" and the "pro" business image there are a number of these polarities of value, and the over-all position of the image on the "anti–pro" scale will depend largely on the weight given to these various polarities or qualities. There is the quality of *publicness* versus *privateness*. Both Christian and Nationalist ethical systems preach the virtues of the public interest as over and against the private interest; the public interest is noble and self-sacrificing, the private interest is mean and self-seeking. Insofar as the business institution gets identified with the private as over and against the public interest, this polarity leads to a distrust of the business institution and a corresponding prejudice in favor of governmental institutions which seem to symbolize the public interest.

Closely related to this polarity is the further quality of "profit" as opposed to "service." Here again the Christian and Nationalist ethic lays much stress on the ideal of "service," again, it relegates profit-seeking to the less praiseworthy level of human motivation.

Insofar as business becomes identified with profit as opposed to service, again we are apt to move toward the "anti-business" end of the scale. Another related polarity is the "competitive–coopera-- tive." Here the church and the school stress the cooperative aspects of life; "uncooperative" has become a strong term of abuse in American childhood. Business, therefore, gets another black eye for being "competitive" — which comes to have the sense of "uncooperative."

These three polarities are all perhaps derived from a more fundamental scale which might be called "familistic–mechanistic." In religious teaching and in formal education much stress is laid on the virtue of familistic behavior and institutions. The family is held up as the ideal type of human relationship, where informality, love, service, and cooperation reign. By contrast, the market institutions are formal, cold, selfish, and competitive. A further polarity emerges which likewise grows out of the high value given to small groups and informal relationships. This is the "big guy–little guy" quality. I think it was Christopher Morley who coined the delightful jawbreaker "infracaninophilism" to describe the love of the underdog! This is a powerful value symbol; it leads us to value "small business" at the expense of "big business"; it moves us toward sympathy with the worker rather than with the boss. This is the identification with Oliver Twist, with Peter Pan, with Cinderella. It reinforces the unfavorable image of business.

These value systems based on identification of business with private, selfish, nonfamilistic modes of behavior have been much more important in creating an unfavorable image of business in the United States than has Marxist ideology. Marxism has never attracted more than a splinter group of convinced adherents, plus a few hangers-on among the intellectuals. Among those whom it has influenced, of course, Marxism contributes to an attitude hostile to the whole concept of a business civilization. This hostility may have some emotional roots in familistic attitudes, but its intellectual foundations lie in the Marxist concept of history as a succession of dominant classes. The United States has failed so dismally to conform to the Marxist predictions that it has required unusually self-contained minds to maintain the Marxist interpretations in the face of so much obvious evidence to the contrary. The Great Depression seemed at the time to be evidence for some of the Marxist claims, but, as it has become clear that this was an episode rather than a fundamental collapse, it has become harder and harder to maintain the Marxist interpretation in all its purity.

Balancing the anti-business image, there have been strong value systems making for a pro-business image. The polarity "businesslike–unbusinesslike" has an important value connotation in American society. We admire the businesslike: the efficient, the well-planned, the uncluttered desk and the uncluttered mind. We do not like the unbusinesslike: the inefficient, the careless, the cluttered. Government has a certain reputation for being unbusinesslike: wasteful, bureaucratic, lackadaisical. Hence the success of Coolidge's slogan: "More business in Government, and less Government in business." To be businesslike is to be progressive, to welcome new methods, to be willing to scrap the old. In this polarity the world of business is a world of shiny machines, of constantly growing output, of ever improved technology. A sourpuss like Veblen may try to persuade people that it is the engineers who are responsible for all this lovely technology, and that the businessmen are sinister figures trying to sabotage the noble efficiency of the engineers in the interest of monopoly profits and stock market jiggery-pokery.[1] But the word for efficiency is still "businesslike" and not "engineerlike." The engineer is perhaps too much linked in the public imagination with the oily rag, and only the businessman has the clean, efficient desk and the clean, efficient mind that goes with it.

Another polarity making for a favorable image of business is that of independence and democracy on the one hand, compared with subservience to government and arbitrary power on the other. This is the great "Jeffersonian" image of America as a land where "they shall sit every man under his vine and under his fig tree; and none shall make them afraid." [2] The business-man is the independent man, because he is not dependent on the favors of a few, nor on the whims of a superior, but on his own ability to satisfy the desires of many customers, none of whom has individually any authority over him. In its modern form this is the theory of what may be called the "polylithic" society, as opposed to the monolithic society of the totalitarian, communist, one-form state. A business society is a society of "many stones" — many different organizations, many niches, many bosses — and hence may hope to avoid the tyranny that comes from the concentration of power. The rise of the great bureaucratic corporations and of the "organization man" has somewhat blurred this image, for the Jeffersonian image is that of a nation of small businessmen and proprietors, not of great corporations. It tends therefore to unite with the familistic dislike of "bigness" in favoring small rather than large business.

The competitive–cooperative polarity, which lent itself to unfavorable appraisal of business as "cutthroat competition," appears now in a different form as the competitive–monopolistic polarity, in which it is favorable to business. Competition is here associated with rivalry for the consumer's dollar — that is, rivalry in service, at least according to the standard of consumer preferences. Competitive business is here seen as serviceable, as opposed to monopolistic business, and even more to monopolistic government which is under no obligation to be serviceable in order to survive. Just as the rise of big business somewhat dims the Jeffersonian image, so the rise of advertising and public relations somewhat dims the competitive ideal, as business is now visualized as wheedling or bamboozling the customer out of his dollar rather than as being rivals in service. Still the ideal of competition in service remains strong and does much to counteract the contrary image of business as the selfish profit-seeker which we noticed earlier. If profits are the measure of service performed, much of the sting of the "profit motive" is removed.

It is from this image of business as purified by competition that the ideology of the antitrust acts is derived. The image of government is now that of a watchdog, seeing that business behaves itself in such a way that profits are made by service and not by deception, chicanery, or conspiring against the public.

Finally there may be an increasing sense of business as the noncoercive element in society as over against the coercive power of the state. Two of the best unintentional advocates of business in the twentieth century were Hitler and Stalin. Compared with these heads of states, the president even of the most selfish, sinister, and powerful corporation seems like an angel of light, or at worst only a feeble little devil. The assumption — which was perhaps not so implausible in 1900 — that public institutions had a certain moral superiority over private institutions is more open to doubt today. The peccadilloes of business even at its worst in the days of goon squads and Joe Hill, seem insignificant when compared with Dachau, the liquidation of the Kulaks, and Hiroshima. In the long run a business can survive only by being serviceable, by being of more use to more people than alternative organizational coagulations. In the very long run this may be true of states as well, but in at least a fairly long run, states can survive merely by being cruel, simply because of their virtual monopoly of the means of cruelty. The view that all problems can be solved by turning them over to the state therefore received a considerable setback as the ambiguous moral nature of the state became clearer.

Business is by no means the only institution of economic life, and a word should be said about the image of other economic institutions. The image of the labor union exhibits many of the same complex polarities that are involved in the image of business. Anti-union images are derived from the perception of unions as monopolistic, as greedy, as seeking gains for their members at the expense of the rest of society, and sometimes as corrupt, exploiting their own members or conniving with corrupt employers.

More sophisticated anti-union images perceive unions as agents of inflation, pushing up money wages and thereby forcing a monetary expansion, or as the creators of unemployment in deflation by holding money wages up. Pro-union images are derived from the perception of unions as the defenders of the rights and status of the worker against the arbitrary power of the boss or the straw boss and so, as the instruments of democratic industrial government, or as the defenders of the poor, the "little guy" against the rich (infracaninophilism again?). Once more, there is a sophisticated pro-union image of the union as an agent of integration of the working class into the general fabric of society, and therefore a conservative rather than a disruptive force, helping to prevent the alienation of the masses and rectifying what would otherwise be serious sociological defects of capitalism.

The image of government as an economic agent is an important element in the total image of economic life. This is a peculiarly complex image, as it is an image of functions rather than of the institution as such. That is to say, the question is not what government *is* but what it *does,* not whether it should exist, but whether it should do certain things. Thus there is a libertarian-socialist polarity of attitude. Toward the libertarian end the economic functions of government are conceived in very meager terms as little more than the protection of the rights of person and property, with the market and the right of contract being left to take care of all economic problems. Toward the socialist end government is seen as an appropriate agency for the organization of major industries and areas of economic life and for the control of the system of prices and the distribution of income. There are no sharp breaks however along this continuum. Few libertarians would advocate turning the post office or the state universities over to private enterprise, and few socialists want to socialize everything or to abolish the market entirely.

The image of government as a referee in the conflict of special interests is a curious and complex one, especially when it reveals government as an ally of the weaker interest. Much of the justifi-

cation of government support of labor unions, government assistance to agriculture, and government programs of social security
is in terms of this doctrine. There is also a somewhat less reputable image of government as a pork barrel, as a booty to be
divided among the constituents by the process of logrolling. The
government role in the process of economic competition is also
a peculiarly complex image. On the one hand we have the image
of government as the promoter and defender of competition; on
the other, we have an image of government as the protector of
special interests against *foreign* competition. An industry threatened by competition of imports feels free to call on government
to protect its inefficiency in a way that it does not when threatened by technological improvements in the domestic economy.
Then the image of government as the defender of competition
falls foul of the image of government as the ally of the weaker
interest. We find ourselves torn between the defense of the weak
and the encouragement of the efficient.

Images are kaleidoscopic patterns, made up of many polarities
and pieces of values and perceptions. The course of events constantly changes them, both by the introduction of new pieces and
by rearranging the old ones. Insofar as value images especially
contain many inconsistent polarities, these may change rapidly
as the perception of events brings one or another of these polarities to the fore. Since 1900, events have been large, loud, and
insistent. It would be surprising indeed if images were not affected by them. We can trace this effect through what may be
called the "great cycles" of war and peace, depression and prosperity, and also through the "great trends" of rising income, rising population, rising organization, rising and increasingly progressive taxation, and the rise in education, religion, and militarism, and what might be called the decline of the proletariat.

Consider first the impact on the economic image of the "great
cycles." The century to date divides conveniently into three
periods. From 1900 to 1919 we have an inflationary period,

broken by a brief depression in 1907 and culminating in World War I and the wartime and postwar inflation. From 1919 to 1932, we have a period of deflation — a sharp deflation and depression in 1920, a plateau of moderate stability from 1921 to 1928, then the Great Depression of 1929–1932. From 1932 to at least 1958, we have a long inflationary period — a slow recovery from 1932 to 1940, broken by a sharp depression in 1937–38, then wartime and postwar inflations to 1951, with moderate stability to 1957, and a moderate depression in 1958. On these long swings of inflation and deflation a great deal of economic, social, and political history is hung; it is a most useful clothesline on which to hang out the rags of particular events.

These long cycles likewise produce great changes in the image. Thus, the image of business tends to become less favorable in periods of deflation and depression, more favorable in periods of full employment, and perhaps less favorable again in periods of sharp price inflation when the image of the "profiteer" comes to the forefront. By contrast, a period of depression produces a more favorable image of labor unions and a more favorable image of active government intervention in economic affairs. A period of recovery and rising employment is favorable to the growth of labor unions and of reform movements in government, as the discontent that gathered in the previous depression is now expressed in the easier climate of a rising market. The depression creates the steam; the recovery provides the engine. A long period of prosperity, on the other hand, especially following the stresses and strains of a war or reforming period, produces a conservative reaction, or what might better be called a period of consolidation — for example, the eras of Coolidge and Eisenhower.

The rise and fall in the warmth or coolness of public attitudes toward various economic institutions follow the great cycles fairly closely. In the period 1900–1919 there is a rather sharp division of opinion between radical and conservative views. The pro-business view, however, is clearly dominant, in spite of certain anti-business overtones of Wilsonian reform. Public attitude toward labor is at best neutral or mildly hostile. Government economic programs hardly exist. These attitudes carry over somewhat into the next period, though some change is perceptible even in the twenties. The Great Depression, however, produces a major shakeup. The depression is visualized as a serious breakdown of the business system and of the market mechanism. Public attitude toward business becomes increasingly hostile, even though business is on the whole the worst sufferer from the depression, and profits is the share of income that takes the worst beating. Conversely, attitudes toward labor become warmer, as reflected in the Wagner Act of 1935. The New Deal represents a major shift in attitude toward the economic functions of government, even though most of the New Deal activities were ill-planned and very small in scope. (The share of national product going to government actually *fell* from 1932 to 1938!) The attitudes, however, were more important than the policies, and such experiments as the N.R.A. and A.A.A., the T.V.A., and other alphabetical agencies, would have been inconceivable a decade earlier. Since World War II, we have again seen a shift in the image, which grew more favorable to business, less favorable to labor (as reflected in the Taft-Hartley Act and in the state right-to-work laws) and slightly less favorable to government enterprise and intervention in the market.

In the long view, however, the trends may affect the image more than the cycles; 1958 is *not* 1928, and still less is it 1908. The effects of the cycles are obvious and often spectacular. The trends are like the movements of the ice cap, imperceptible over short periods but enormously powerful. There is, for instance, the trend in growth of population, checked by the immigration laws after 1920 and by the low birth rates of the depression years, but now resumed in full and somewhat alarming flood. There is the trend in increased wealth and in real per-capita income, again interrupted by the depression, but, if anything, stimulated by the two world wars. There is the continuing "organizational revolution," the rise in the scale of organizations of all kinds: businesses, labor unions, professional associations, farmers' associations, trade associations. There is a continuing rise in the educational enterprise, and in the proportion of people who enjoy higher levels of education. There has been a fairly continuous rise in the size, and perhaps also in the power, of the churches. The proportion of the population included in church membership has risen fairly steadily through the century till it is now about 60 per cent. Especially since the outbreak of World War II, there has been a great rise in the size, power, and influence of the armed forces. Expenditures on national security were about 1.5 per cent of the Gross National Product even in 1939; in 1960 they were about 10 per cent.

The structural changes within the over-all totals of these trends have been just as striking since 1900 as have the changes in the totals themselves. The proportion of the population in agriculture has declined sharply as a result of a great revolution in agricultural techniques — the mechanization and "biologizing" of agriculture — which enables one man to grow much more food than he could in 1900. People living on farms formed almost 50 per cent of the population in 1900, 25 per cent in 1929, and 13 per cent in 1957! In 1900 one might still say that the "average" American lived on a farm; in 1929 his parents had lived on a farm, and in 1958 his grandparents! Manufactures have about maintained their proportion of the population; the great increase has been in the professions and the service trades. With the coming of automation this trend should continue.

Another trend of great importance is the rise of consumer capital and the shift in the center of gravity of the stock of wealth away from the factory and the business toward the home. This is the age of the home-owning, the car-owning, and the washer-and-dryer, household-equipment-owning family. Even entertainment has moved into the home with the coming of TV. The "average American" is increasingly a surburban family man with a working wife and three or four children. This improvement in the efficiency of the home as an economic unit is releasing increasing numbers of women to the labor force. Even from 1942 to 1956 the percentage of women (20–64 years old) in the total labor force rose from 22 per cent to 27 per cent.

What all these trends add up to is a great movement of economic success, punctuated with one serious interruption in the Great Depression of the 1930's. It is not surprising under these circumstances that economic radicalism has declined, that socialism is no longer even the very mild threat that it may have seemed in 1900, at least as far as internal affairs are concerned. On the whole we seem to have entered an era of economic good feeling where something of a synthesis of the conflicting images has been achieved. This "mid-century synthesis" can be seen at three levels — the level of the academic and the intellectual, the level of the "informed" businessman, and the level of political action.

At the academic level, economic dissent in this country took the form of "institutionalism" rather than of Marxism. The Institutionalists were a group of professional economists, most of them professors, among whom the names of John R. Commons, Thorstein Veblen, and Wesley Mitchell stand out. Their most productive period was about 1900 to 1920. Their protest against the "orthodox" economics of the universities took three main forms. They objected to the static nature of the prevailing Marshallian and Austrian price theory, and its neglect of dynamic and evolutionary processes. They objected to the narrowness of the economist's abstraction, and wanted to bring sociological and psychological considerations into the treatment of economic problems. Then they objected to the divorcement of economics from the facts of life — and, Commons and Mitchell, at any rate, pioneered in empirical economic research. All the protests of the Institutionalists had an important degree of justice in them. Their positive contributions were less fruitful, and with the exception of a handful of faithful disciples, the Institutionalists left no direct descendants and made little direct impact on the course of American academic life. Their indirect influence, however, has been very great. As with many reformers, their reforms were carried out by other (more conservative) men, and in ways which they would never have envisaged. Within the last twenty-five years or so, the revolution in economic thought, justly called the Keynesian Revolution, has had as profound an effect on American thinking as it has on other parts of the non-Communist world. The revolution walks on two legs. One is the theoretical reformulations of Keynes which gave economists a new box of tools, crude but effective, to deal with the problems of mass unemployment, depression, and inflation — that is, with the "great cycle." The other leg is the development of national income statistics, pioneered by the National Bureau of Economic Research in the 1920's, and beginning on an official scale with the Department of Commerce in 1929. The situation is not unlike that of the Copernican revolution in astronomy which was a new theoretical viewpoint combined with a new source of information, the telescope. Before the development of national income statistics, economists moved in a world of occasional lights and flashes; afterward, however shadowy, the outlines of the *whole* economic landscape became visible.

The Keynesian Revolution undermined the most serious and far-reaching criticism of capitalism — that it was inherently incapable of solving within the broad framework of its own institutions the problem of recurrent depressions, and was therefore necessarily doomed to be succeeded by a centralized planned economy. The Keynesian conclusion is that the vices of an uncontrolled capitalism are not inseparable from its virtues, and that its major defects can be remedied within the framework of its basic institutions of private property, free enterprise, and the market mechanism. The remedy, however, involves the acceptance of a certain basic responsibility by government for "steersmanship." We might describe this system, using the term of Norbert Wiener, as "Cybernetic Capitalism." Its image is, appropriately enough, not the socialist streetcar, following the rigid rails of a predetermined, bureaucratic plan, but the automobile, family-owned and privately driven and free to go where fancy calls, but provided with a steering wheel and brakes and guided by stop lights. The remedy for the high-powered but steerless car of uncontrolled capitalism is not to jam everybody into the socialist trolley but the much simpler solution of fitting the car with a steering wheel. In less fanciful language this means that government must be prepared to act in the *opposite* sense to the way in which the private economy is going — to be deflationary when the private economy is inflationary and inflationary when it is deflationary — and to see that aggregate demand is maintained at a level which yields high employment and reasonably full-capacity operation of the system. The ideas involved in this "revolution" are very simple yet they imply a shift of viewpoint from which many objects of the economic landscape are regarded. Thus, we now look upon the tax system not merely as a device to raise money for government to spend, but as primarily an instrument to control aggregate demand. The national debt likewise is looked on as an instrument for providing the economy with an adequate amount of government securities and for satisfying the demand for savings in the absence of investment, rather than as the shameful offspring of financial incontinence. We may sum up the conclusion of the Keynesian Revolution by saying that the main economic task of government is to be a governor, not an engine.

It is a little too early to say that this revolution has been accomplished in practice as it has in thought; one will be a little happier about the permanence of this "new era" if we get through, say, another five years without anything more than minor depressions, and with continued steady growth in percapita income. The memories of the "New Era" of the 1920's, when the Federal Reserve System was supposed to have done away with depressions for good and all, still rankles a little. The wise economist knows that there are "ifs" and "buts" even in the new theoretical and informational system, and that the problem of steersmanship — with a slack steering wheel, or maybe with two steering wheels — is not as easy as it sounds in the textbooks. There are still more "ifs" and "buts" in the political system; it remains an open question whether the government would be able to act fast enough, or even in the right places, if we were faced with another situation like those of 1930 or 1931. There is a further gnawing long-run uncertainty as to whether the price of a full-employment policy is not continued creeping inflation, and if so, whether we can adjust to this situation. There is even an unpleasant doubt as to whether economic progress is not to some extent stimulated by depressions, so that steady progress might be a little slower than the kind of unsteady progress which we have experienced.

In spite of these hesitations, however, there is room for cautious optimism. On the side of government there is the commitment involved in the Employment Act of 1946. The commitment is not spelled out in any detail, but the act had at least the virtue of setting up a fire alarm in the shape of the Council of Economic Advisers and a small fire department in Congress in the form of the Joint Committee on the Economic Report. The Joint Committee has acted through the years as a seminar in economics inside Congress, and has developed as a result a small group of congressmen in both houses who have an above-average level of understanding of economic problems. It is to be hoped that in the event of a serious economic emergency, this core of more expert congressmen might give leadership which their less experienced colleagues would accept. The Council of Economic Advisers performs a rather similar function within the executive branch.

On the side of business, an influential group of business leaders in the Committee for Economic Development accepted the new ideas, and have been influential in getting them broadly accepted within the business community. The C.E.D. did much to break down the wall between the business and the academic communities, at least in its earlier years. We must not overdo the idyllic picture; there are still large numbers of the unreconstructed on both sides. Still, a certain change in atmosphere is perceptible; even the National Association of Manufacturers and the United States Chamber of Commerce have come around to a rather grudging acceptance of some of the new ideas, and the essential continuity in economic policy between the Truman and Eisenhower administrations is evidence of the permanence of the change.

In industrial relations also we see a certain "mid-century synthesis," as symbolized perhaps in the five-year contract of General Motors and United Automobile Workers. The change here is again not unrelated to the intrusion of academic ideas into what used to be a preserve of practical men. A new academic discipline of industrial relations, drawing on all the social sciences for its theory and methods, and embodied in institutes of industrial relations in many of the major universities, emerged in the 1920's and 1930's. The impact of this development on the practice of labor relations has been important, though credit must also be given to the practical wisdom learned from the often bitter experience of industrial warfare. Thus, in many industries there has been a transition from industrial warfare, with the employer and the union fighting each other tooth and nail, through a period of "cold war" in which the union is accorded a grudging coexistence, to a genuine industrial peace in which the union is fully accepted as a necessary part of the industrial picture and in which the worker achieves a dignity and status within the enterprise which is something more than that of a mere hired hand. Here again one must not paint too idyllic a picture. The 1958 depression shook the Great Detroit Truce. The great steel strike of 1960 evoked dim reminiscences of 1919. Much of the South is still in the stage of industrial warfare, and there are great underlying tensions there. The very growth of the labor movement has brought with it serious problems of corruption, of internal democracy and control of irresponsible leadership. On the whole, however, a mood of cautious optimism is still in order; looking back on 1900, one is conscious of a real change in attitude. There has been an integration of the working class into the over-all structure of the society in a way that perhaps has never before been achieved in history, and which certainly has not been achieved in the communist countries for which this is theoretically a major objective! There has been a similar movement in agriculture — the farmer is much more like his city cousin than he was in 1900. The integration of the Negro has been slower, but it has been steady. If the twentieth century does not go down in nuclear disaster, then, it may stand out in history as the great age of integration, in which for the first time a classless society was created by everybody becoming middle class.

SOME QUESTIONS ON THE MEASUREMENT AND EVALUATION OF ORGANIZATION

Ethics and Bigness: *Scientific, Academic,*
Religious, Political, and Military,
Harlan Cleveland and Harold D. Lasswell, eds.,
New York: Harper and Bros., 1962, pp. 385-95.

Some Questions on the Measurement and Evaluation of Organization

THE CONCEPT of organization is perhaps the most central, and also the most puzzling notion in the scientific view of the universe. The great quest of the scientist is for *ordered structure* in space and time, whether this is in the nucleus, the atom, the molecule, the virus, the gene, the organ, the animal, the human person, or the social organization. An ordered structure capable of behavior and perhaps capable of growth is however precisely what we mean by an organization. All these ordered structures are essentially role structures—open systems with a throughput of components consisting of lower level organizations, in which however the components are forced by the related roles around them to play a certain role in the organizational structure. Thus individual electrons come and go in an atom, but once one is captured it must behave in a certain way until it is lost. Similarly atoms come and go in a molecule, but the molecule remains, molecules come and go in a cell, but the cell remains, cells come and go in a body, but the body remains; persons come and go in an organization, but the organization remains. What "remains" in the midst of all this flux of components is the "role," the "place," and the relations of roles one to another. A role is a hole, an organization is a related and orderly set of holes, and one sometimes catches a fleeting and slightly nightmarish vision of the scientific universe as a set of holes bounded and defined by other holes! The significance of almost anything, like that of a word, is derived largely from its context; everything, however, is the context for other things; context creates itself, *ad infinitum*.

In the processes of the universe we seem to see two apparently opposite, though not essentially contradictory processes at work. One is the constant increase in entropy, that is in "chaos" or "disorder" as work is done and processes are carried out, according to the Second

Law of Thermodynamics. Everything that happens destroys potential, and so makes "happening," which is made possible by potential differences of some kind, less possible. According to this image of the universe all processes in time lead eventually to a universe which is a kind of thin soup of undifferentiated matter and energy, all equally distributed, all at the same temperature, and in which nothing whatever can happen. This gloomy view of the ultimate future may be in process of modification by current controversies among the astronomers, but whatever the outcome of these, whether the universe is a stationary state with continuous creation of hydrogen, as Hoyle supposes, or whether the more conventional views are correct, there is no doubt about the general validity of the increase of entropy with process.

We observe, however, another process at work in the universe which we call "evolution." This is a process by which the population of organizations comes to have more and more complex members in it. The elements evolve in the primordial explosion, at a certain point in time life appears, living forms grow in complexity and culminate in man; man himself forms social organizations which also evolve rapidly toward greater and greater complexity. Here is a process which seems to go in the opposite direction to that of "time's arrow" as measured by entropy. What is happening here is not that entropy is failing to increase, but that entropy itself is getting increasingly *segregated*. There are redistributions of entropy going on, leading to greater organization at some points no doubt at the expense of other points. "Life," as Schroedinger says, "feeds on entropy." In the course of the evolutionary process even though chaos continually increases and "unchaos" diminishes, out of these diminished reserves of order evolution builds increasingly complex castles. The universe on this view is like a rich man continually losing his capital, but in the process transforming his diminishing stock into ever more intricate and differentiated forms.

The first question therefore which I want to raise is whether it would be possible to find a *measure* of the extent of evolution in the *distribution* of entropy. This would be in itself a measure of the degree of organization of the universe or of any part of it, though it would not in itself be an adequate description of organization. No single measure, of course, can describe a complex structure such as an organization. Nevertheless these "indices" which single out certain quantitative aspects are helpful in reducing the complexity of reality to a form which our inadequate minds can grasp. Thus a price index reduces a long list of prices to a single number, and expresses something "important" about the list. Similarly a measure of the degree or quantity of organization, if we had one, would be a useful way of symbolizing something essential and significant in these very complex structures.

It would provide, for instance, a rough measure of the rate of evolution. We have a certain intuitive sense that in the course of evolutionary change "something" is evolving; that there is, in other words, an evolutionary vector, and that it makes sense to say that evolution moves "faster" at some times than at others, or even that it occasionally reverses itself. From the hydrogen atom to the amoeba, and from the amoeba to man we seem to detect "progress," that is, increase in some quantity which measures progress. It may be that this "upwardness" is an anthropomorphic illusion, and that in some scale of values the retrogression from the ascetic simplicity of the hydrogen atom to the monstrous corruption of mankind may be deplored. It is not the value sign which matters here, however, but the vector, that is, the sense of both direction and magnitude. Few could deny that the process which leads from the hydrogen atom to the amoeba to man has both direction and magnitude, and that it would be very useful to have even a rough measure of the magnitude.

Several important problems might be closer to solution if we had a measure of evolutionary change. It is difficult, for instance, to test any theories of the machinery of evolutionary change, whether in biology or in the social sciences, without some measure of the extent of this change. Furthermore a simple measure of the quantity of organization would almost certainly force us to examine higher levels of organizational systems, simply because it would prove unsatisfactory in dealing with the complexities of the higher organizational forms. Consider, for instance, the view that the key to the understanding of the process of evolution is an analysis of the *teaching* process. Here is the one clearly observable process in the universe where the strict laws of conservation do not hold. Energy and matter can only be exchanged: knowledge can be *produced*. When a teacher teaches a class, if the hour has been successful, not only do the students know more as a result of the process, but the teacher frequently knows more, too! Teaching is in no sense an exchange, in which what the student gets the teacher loses. We can break down the teaching process perhaps into two others: the first might be called the *printing* process. It is the process by which a certain structure or organization is imposed on some carrier around it by simple transfer of pattern. The pattern of a page of type imprints itself on many pieces of paper in exactly the same shape. The gene evidently has this property of printing in three dimensions: its self-reproducing quality arises because it can attract to each atom of itself a like atom, which forms a mirror image of the structure, which then exercises the same power of imprinting itself and so reproduces exactly the original pattern of the gene. Similarly a teacher may simply "teach" verbatim something that he knows, like the multiplication table: this is "rote teaching," which results in rote learning.

There is also however a more fundamental process at work: I shall call it, for short, *"inspiring."* This is the process by which the teacher supports and cooperates with a process of internal growth in the mind of the student. This is also the process by which the gene organizes the growth of a phenotype or body quite unlike itself. It is the process also by which ideas and ideologies inspire the growth of cultures and societies. This is clearly a complex and puzzling process, which we understand very imperfectly at present. It has some similarities to the process by which a building is built to follow a blueprint—the blueprint, indeed, might be described as a special case of the "inspiring" process, for the building which it "inspires" is very different from the mere two dimensional plan which maps it. The building of the body, however, or of a society, is inspired by more complex processes than that of the blueprint. The gene seems to be able to change its blueprint in the course of executing it, and society likewise does not develop toward a predetermined end, but according to certain broad principles of change and continuity in a process which is constantly liable to a shift in direction both from conscious images and from unconscious causes.

It is clear that in the "teaching" process we are dealing with something akin to the growth of organization. Knowledge, indeed, can be regarded as a form of organization. In its verbal expression it consists of a structure of related contexts, in each of which any "word" or symbol can play the appropriate role, provided that the code is understood. Thus "house," "domus," "maison," etc., are different words or symbols each of which however plays the same *role* in a language. One despairs, indeed, of ever getting any simple measure of the quantity of knowledge. Nevertheless a measure of the quantity of organization would be of some help here, and might be valuable in testing the "success" of a learning process.

These considerations may seem very abstract and remote from the pressing problems of today. Nevertheless I hope to show that the questions I have raised lie at the heart of most of our major, practical problems. Consider, for instance, the problem of economic development. What we have here is a process of social evolution from an economy at a lower level of organization to one at a higher level. The difference between a rich and a poor society lies mainly in the level of organization which it has attained; rich societies are rich not usually because they are amply endowed with natural resources but because they have learned how to organize themselves into complex processes of production extended through time. Extreme poverty of resource base, of course, like that of the Bushmen or the Eskimos, may condemn any society which lives on it to a low level of organization and a low standard of living. Once these extremes are excluded, however, the level of living, or per capita real income of a society is overwhelmingly a function of its degree of organization. Iceland, which is a fairly well organized society, makes a moderately good living in a most unprepossessing natural environment; there are countries by contrast with fair climates and rich soil "where every prospect pleases" but man ekes out a miserable existence in dire and disorganized poverty.

In the case of economic development we actually possess a rough measure of the degree of attainment of a society and of its rate of progress in the per capita real income. At first sight this seems to be wholly unrelated to the "distribution of entropy" measure which I suggested as a possible index of degree of organization. The relation is a subtle one, but I believe it exists. Consumption is clearly a process which increases entropy: we eat more highly ordered substances than we excrete, automobiles are more highly ordered than scrap iron, clothing is more highly ordered than rags or dust, and so on. Consumption means therefore reducing order to disorder: it is a typically "entropic" process. By contrast production is "anti-entropic." It takes soil and air and water and makes wheat and bread; it takes ore and rock and makes steel and machines; it takes fiber and makes cloth, or cloth and makes clothes. In each case the act of production is that of imposing a greater degree of order in one place, at the cost, however, of greater disorder elsewhere (mine tailings, waste materials, etc.). Production therefore is typical of the evolutionary process in that it segregates entropy and builds up highly ordered, low entropy "products" (commodities) at the cost, no doubt, of producing high entropy "wastes" elsewhere.

Per capita real income is a measure of the rate of production, in some index of units of commodities per unit of time. It is clearly therefore related to the rate at which entropy is being segregated in economic processes. We may ask, however, what about consumption? If all production is consumed, does not the entropy increasing character of consumption just offset the entropy decreasing character of production so that there is no net segregation of entropy or increase in organization? This raises the question whether increase in organization does not come from *accumulation,* that is, from the excess of production over consumption, rather than from production or consumption itself? On this view the rate of progress of a society would be measured by its rate of accumulation rather than by its real income: two societies might have the same real income, but if one consumed less and accumulated more than the other it would be advancing faster.

There is a good deal of truth in this view, especially if we take a broad enough concept of accumulation. There is some confusion of thought here even among economists because of a failure to distinguish between income in the sense of production or consumption, that is, additions to or subtractions from the capital stock, and income in the sense of "use" or enjoyment *of* a capital stock. Thus my enjoyment or use of furniture, houses, clothing, etc. is almost independent of their consumption—that is, the rate at which they wear out. I have argued in an earlier paper[1] that it is this enjoyment or use of a capital stock which is the true measure of human wellbeing, not the rate at which this stock is consumed or produced. Nevertheless there is likely to be a fairly monotonic relation between the amount of use or enjoyment, the total stock which is used or enjoyed, and the rate at which this stock is consumed or produced, especially under fairly constant techniques. We must bear in mind here that the capital stock consists not only of physical objects like furniture, but also of the furniture of our minds and the states of our bodies. Thus the acquisition of memories, the learning of information or skills, and the inculcation of pleasant states of mind is as much capital formation as the building of a dam. When we go to a movie we build a state of mind called "just having

[1]"Income or Welfare," *Review of Economic Studies,* volume 17, 1949–1950, p. 77.

been to a movie." This state depreciates or is consumed just as a chair or a breakfast depreciates, and needs to be restored at suitable intervals. I do not propose to resolve the question here whether economic organization or welfare can be discussed equally well in its "stock" aspect as capital or in its "flow" aspect as income. I am prepared to argue that both these aspects may be of importance, and that neither can quite be reduced to the other. This dilemma also faces us, we may note, in general evolutionary theory. Is it the "stock" of organisms or species which is significant in measuring the rate of evolution, or is it some rate of "throughput" or metabolism which is most significant? We should not be much interested in a "stock" of things, however complex, which never "did" anything—that is, which had no throughput—evolution is more than the elaboration of skeletal forms. On the other hand, *mere* busyness, mere throughput, mere metabolism is not the sole object of interest either; evolution is not merely the development of vast outputs of slop and enormous appetites and excretions. It is this curious combination of the development of intricate structures which *do* things that are significant to them, or to something, which constitutes the peculiar charm of evolution, and I am not prepared to argue at this point whether this apparent two-dimensionality can be reduced to one dimension or not.

The transformation of a society from a lower level to a higher level of organization is not a process of simple homogeneous growth (indeed, the fashionable term "economic growth" may be quite a misnomer) but is an evolutionary, developmental, and almost embryological process not unlike that of the development of a chicken within (and out of) the egg. The "egg" is the relatively undifferentiated, unorganized subsistence economy of small farmers and craftsmen, without large organizations, without much in the way of complex equipment or formal education. The "chicken" is the developed society, with large and complex organizations, complex accumulations of capital in the form of material, skill and educated and informed intelligence, and an extensive division of labor and differentiation of function. As the chicken grows, it gradually absorbs the "yolk"; subsistence farmers and unskilled laborers get jobs in larger organizations, they get education and skill and they end up as highly differentiated members of complex organizations. One of the problems which a developing society faces which is not usually faced by an embryo is that the "yolk" may revolt and refuse to be absorbed in the chicken: it may even carry the revolt to the point where the chicken is killed and the developmental process stops. Because of this possible resistance the developmental process in society requires a certain identification of the "yolk" with the whole developing society: the undeveloped people must either enjoy vicariously the pleasures of the developing middle class which they themselves are not enjoying, or they must identify themselves with the *hope* that they or their descendants will enjoy the fruits of progress, or they must be coerced into cooperation by the superior power and will of the developing part of society in control of the means of coercion. The first is the British pattern, the second the American, and the third (one fears) the Chinese.

The problem of the measure of the level of organization is quite crucial in the argument of the "cold war" between Communism and capitalist democracy. The Communists claim, in effect, that their system is at a higher level of social evolution, and a higher level of organization, than capitalism, and that it must therefore ultimately triumph, as all higher levels of organization have supposedly triumphed in the evolutionary process. We must beware, incidentally, of a tautology here: if we *define* "higher" by "survival," then of course the higher organism always survives! The "survival of the fittest" slogan is quite empty if fitness is defined as fitness to survive. This underlines the necessity of an independent measure of organization or "fitness" so that the proposition that the fit survive may be *testable* in experience. The Communist claim to be a higher level of organization rests mainly on the assumption that hierarchy is the only organizing instrument. The Communist society is a "one-firm state"—that is, a society organized hierarchically into a single economic organization. It is simply General Motors (or perhaps more realistically, the Pentagon, which is in terms of national income the world's third largest Communist society) expanded to include the whole economy, with the possible exception of a few Nepmen and some surreptitious private trade. A capitalist society by contrast is "ecological" where the Communist society is "organic." A Communist society is a true Leviathan, a vast social whale; a capitalist society is more like a pond with a great multitude of interacting organisms bound together in a system of mutual exchange, or markets.

The biological parallel gives us a certain reason for not accepting the

Communist claim without very careful scrutiny. The key to the problem here is what the economist calls "diminishing returns to scale." In society, as in biology, it by no means always follows that "the bigger the better." Beyond a certain point in the development of a particular type of organism a further increase in size leads to a decline in efficiency, a decline therefore in the "quantity of organization," and a lessened chance, we presume, of survival. Where this point comes at which diminishing returns to scale set in depends on the *type* of organization. Chemical elements seem to show diminishing returns in terms of stability as the atomic number increases, and beyond Bismuth (atomic number eighty-three) no stable (nonradioactive) forms are known. Inorganic molecules form larger structures than the elements, but these rarely exhibit molecular weights above 100. Organic molecules with carbon chains go much farther; cells are much larger organizations again, but again have a limit—no one celled animal reaches more than microscopic dimensions. Differentiation of cells permits the growth of larger organisms: plants get to be quite large, though not very complex: insects achieve great complexity, but cannot break through the size barrier of about three inches in length, and their optimum size seems to be between the ant and the bee. The endoskeleton and the convolution of the lung, the bowels, and the brain permitted the construction of still larger complex forms in the vertebrates, culminating in the mammal, just as the steel frame (an endoskeleton) and air conditioning permits the development of larger buildings than solid walls (exoskeletons) and mere windows permit.

Now, however, the biological parallel, no doubt to our alarm, gives some possible comfort to the Communists. Admitting (which in general Communists do not) the existence of diminishing returns to scale beyond a certain point for *any one form* of organization, do we not see in the evolutionary process the constant transcending of an old size barrier by a new form of organization—the molecule transcending the element, the cell the molecule, the animal the cell, the vertebrate the invertebrate, the mammal the reptile? Can we not argue then that new and more perfect forms of social organization now have enabled us— or shortly will enable us—to transcend the old size barrier and establish, literally, a whale of a society in the Communist state? The question here is crucial to the world's future: it is however an empirical question which cannot be answered *a priori*, but only by studying the organizations themselves. Here again we see how useful would be an acceptable measure of the degree of organization against which we could test the hypothesis that diminishing returns to scale set in at a point far smaller than that of the whole society. It is on this hypothesis, if "returns" are interpreted broadly enough to include all things which are valued by men, not merely commodities, that a market (capitalist) society stands or falls by comparison with an organic (Communist) society.

Somewhere lurking in the wings of this whole argument is, of course, the whole problem of value. The bigger is not necessarily better, the more is not necessarily better, so what *is* better? This unfortunately is a question too important to be left to the philosophers, and too unanswerable to be left to anyone else. The value coordinate is clearly a vector, like organization. We compare two constellations of perceived reality, and we say that one is "better" than the other, that is, is further "out" from some origin of goodness. Insofar as we believe that the evolutionary process carries us not only to more organized systems but also to "better" systems we imply a generally monotonic relationship— which does not, of course, have to be linear—between degree of organization and "goodness." Such a relationship may of course be questioned —indeed even to state it so baldly looks like a reversion to the uncritical Spencerian optimism of the nineteenth century, and one can hardly question that for short, or even for fairly extended periods, evil may clothe itself in organization superior to good. Nevertheless it is surely an implication of the basic long-run optimism of most religious or even secular faiths that the course of evolution toward higher organization is also a movement toward the "good." If this seems homocentric it is at least not surprising in *homines!*

If large and complex constellations of organizations are to be reduced to a one dimensional vector of "goodness" we must have something like a "price system" of valuation coefficients by which the diverse and many dimensional elements of the constellation can be reduced to a single dimension of value. Thus suppose we ask whether a man who is loyal but stupid is "better" or "worse" than a man who is unfaithful but intelligent. The answer we give will clearly depend on the *value weights* which we give to the various qualities. If we give loyalty a low value weight and intelligence a high one, we are likely to rate the intelligent man "better" than the stupid one even if he is unfaithful: if we give loyalty a high value weight by comparison with intelligence the reverse result may obtain. Many of the difficulties of ethical valuation arise because of the absence of a "salient" and clearly agreed upon system of value weights. In economic valuation of course—as in, for instance, the valuation of a heterogeneous constellation of assets in a balance sheet—we have the advantage of a system of value weights given us initially by the structure of relative prices, even though we may modify this considerably in the evaluation process. In ethical valuations we do not have the same advantage, and the difficulties of ethical agreement are a direct result of the absence of an agreed system of value weights.

I would not wish to imply that a measure of organization would automatically yield a system of ethical value weights which would enable us to do perfect "ethical accounting." Nevertheless, because I have some confidence in the generally monotonic character of the relationship between organization and "goodness"—that is, that both generally increase together—I would argue that the development of a workable measure of organization would at least be a first step toward the construction of an ethical calculus. The want of this measure however may impede progress toward the solution of many problems, not only in biology and in the social sciences, but also in ethics.

AGRICULTURAL ORGANIZATIONS AND POLICIES: A PERSONAL EVALUATION

Farm Goals in Conflict, Ames, Iowa:
Iowa State Univ. Press, 1963, pp. 156-66.

Agricultural Organizations and Policies:
A Personal Evaluation

THE DILEMMA of the price system is that it has at least three roles to play in society and these roles may easily be contradictory. The first of these three roles is the allocation of resources in response to changes in technology and demand. That is, one of the functions of the price system is to move society in directions such that there isn't too much in the way of resources in any one occupation. We see this in agriculture. For example, in this country we have moved from 90 percent of the population in agriculture to 8 percent in 200 years. We've done this in large measure through the operation of the price system. Nobody said to the farmer, "You have to get out of farming." He just followed Mr. Staley's good advice and got out of it. In this sense the price system has been a very powerful organizer of our society.

The price system also has a great deal to do with the distribution of income. I am personally very much interested in the price of economics being high and the price of everything else being low. The real income of any individual or group depends on the relative price structure. The higher the price of the commodity you sell and the lower the price of what you buy the better off you are.

The third responsibility of the price system is not, I think, as generally recognized among economists as the other two, but I wish to put it in the trinity on an equal basis. This is the role of organizing the process of economic growth and change and particularly the process of economic development. One of the things the price system does is to decide which are the things we are going to work on in the way of improvements. That is, if something is scarce and its price is high, we are more likely to work on it to make it more plentiful and cheaper than if it is plentiful and its price is low.

One of the major dilemmas arises between the first two roles. Frequently the role of the price system in organizing the allocation of resources runs up against our sense of what is right and just in the way of distribution of income. We see this of course very clearly in agriculture. In a progressive society, and particularly in a society which has institutions like Iowa State University, agriculture continually declines as a proportion of the total economy. One of the major causes of this is Iowa State University itself! That is, the greater the productivity of labor in agriculture, the fewer farmers there are going to be.

The dilemma is, however, that if you are to get resources out of any occupation, you have to squeeze it. The only way I know to get toothpaste out of a tube is to squeeze the tube, and the only way to get people out of agriculture is likewise to squeeze agriculture. It just has to be made less profitable than other occupations. When the price system is doing this, it's doing fine; this is just what it's supposed to do. If we had a progressive society in which agriculture was profitable, this would be a sure sign of social decay. A high profitability of agriculture would be a sure indication that something was definitely wrong with the society. We have succeeded in progressing for over 200 years pretty well. So agriculture has been unprofitable for 200 years; people have been squeezed out of it for 200 years; it has been technically progressive for 200 years, and all this is just fine.

However, from the point of view of social justice we get uneasy. We look at the 8 percent of people in agriculture and we see that they get only 4 percent of the income. Maybe we can find some other 8 percent of the labor force that nobody bothers about at all who also only get 4 percent of the income. It's just because agriculture is visible that we notice it. But then we still feel, quite rightly, that this is unjust. But the economist says that the only recipe for this problem is increased mobility: if the toothpaste is thin you don't have to squeeze the tube very hard; on the other hand, if the toothpaste is thick you have to put real pressure on it. If you can't get people out of agriculture easily, you are going to have to squeeze agriculture very hard to get them out. You are going to have to do farmers severe injustice in order to solve the problem of allocation.

Suppose the economist says that mobility is the solution both to the problem of allocation and to the problem of justice — that is, of course, if we are looking only at the price system. Now of course the difficulty is that the price system is not the only organizer of social life and it is not the only organizer of the economy. Besides the exchange system we have what I call the grants system, the system of unilateral transfers. This is composed of taxes, subsidies, grants, budgets, philanthropy. In short it is that part of the economy where you shovel money out and it gets taken away. This is very different from the price system. As a matter of fact, economics does not have any very good theory about it. I've been struggling with the theory of philanthropy. This is quite difficult, really, because foundations are quite incomprehensible organizations. There is no way of telling whether they are doing any good, and I suspect that many are not. That is, after studying philanthropy I decided that we may eventually have to do what Henry VIII did with the monasteries — liquidate them. Foundations can be dangerous centers of irresponsible private power, and the least we can do is to have an anti-trust law for them. The mere fact that you said you were doing good did not mean you could not be a menace to society. The people who set out to do good often did a great deal more damage than the people who didn't — but that is a nasty-minded economist's point of view.

We have to recognize that there is a "grants" sector of the economy and that it can alter the distribution of income, it can alter the allocation of resources and it can alter economic development quite substantially. I would agree with Mr. Thompson that it is quite legitimate to use it. In spite of the fact that I am an economist I don't really think the price system can do everything, although I think we underestimate what it can do. I think also that the hostility towards the price system, especially among the theologians, is really quite unfortunate. The market is really a very useful form of organization and we shouldn't really have any prejudice against it.

The way in which society effects allocation and distribution of wealth outside the price system is through coercion, taxation and subsidy, and also prohibitions and law. For instance, as Mr. Hamilton pointed out, we put quotas on tobacco and this gives a present to all the people who were growing tobacco in 1942. What this has to do with justice I don't know, but as an economist I have a very strong prejudice against it. I have an extraordinarily strong prejudice against coercion as such. This is why I think government is fundamentally demonic. It is an intrinsically evil thing which can occasionally be subverted to good ends. I don't know how this is theologically, but I have a feeling that the

Lord uses the devil for His own purposes and that as a matter of fact if it were not for the devil we might not have such an interesting world. Where would redemption be if it were not for the devil? Not that I think we can wholly avoid being coercive. Even though I have always wanted to be an anarchist, I have never quite been able to make the grade; I have to admit the need for a little government in society. But I have a certain sympathy with the feeling that whenever you decide to employ coercion you want to look at it three times. Coercion is a dangerous shortcut to social justice. It often goes along with the use of quotas, quantitative restrictions and the limitation of supply, and these can easily result in a freezing of an obsolete system.

FARM POLICY PROBLEMS

It is now time to turn to the problems of agricultural policy. Now this isn't economics, and I am not speaking authoritatively as an economist. In the first place, I think it is unjust to discriminate either in favor of agriculture or against it. I am against agricultural fundamentalism and I do not agree with the view that virtue peculiarily resides on the farm. In fact, a case can be made the other way: that farmers are dull, cloddish and selfish and that almost anything decent that has ever gone on in the world has happened in the city. Civilization, after all, is a product of the cities; the very word tells us that. As a matter of fact, even most agricultural improvement is a product of cities. The improvement of agriculture is not due to farmers, who have usually resisted it. It is due to all these city folks who come out and shake it up. So in a way I am almost an agricultural nonfundamentalist, though on the whole I would like to think that virtue is fairly evenly distributed. Christianity, incidentally, is unfailingly marked with the stamp of Jerusalem and Tarsus. There's nothing rural about it; it is an extremely urban product.

But all joking aside, I think the principle of no discrimination is a vital one, whether this is about Negroes or farmers, and it is just as wrong to discriminate in favor of people as it is to discriminate against them. Now this is not to say that we exclude counterdiscrimination. You can sneak in a case for the state discriminating in favor of the farmer on the grounds that everybody else discriminates against him. I will admit this in theory. But on the whole I won't <u>really</u> admit it in practice, because I think we have put far too much into agriculture. We have over-redressed the balance absurdly. We now know too much and do too much about agriculture and not enough about other things.

Counterdiscrimination may justify helping the poor but it does not justify helping the farmers. Agricultural policy has been sold under the name of justice on the basis of a wholly fallacious syllogism. The major premise is, "We ought to help the poor." We all agree to this, especially professors. The minor premise is that farmers are poor, and the conclusion is that we ought to help farmers. The difficulty here is in the minor premise. Some farmers are poor and some farmers are filthy rich. When you help farmers you tend to help the rich more than the poor; this has been pointed out previously.

My next point is that we do want to continue Iowa State University. We do need to continue the process of technological development and the increase in knowledge even if this does away with agriculture altogether, as I suspect it will do. Agriculture is really a terribly primitive way of raising food. I expect that this process of the diminution of the agricultural population will go on until what we have always thought of as agriculture becomes perhaps almost a negligible part of the economy. Whether we approve of this or not there is not much of anything to do about it. Anyone who advocates plowing under Iowa State University is under a delusion. We are not going to stop this process and we have to learn how to ride it. Once we have been chased out of Eden there is no way back; the angel with the flaming sword stands there. Once we have eaten of the fruit of the tree of knowledge there is no place to go but onward to Zion. We cannot go back to innocence and ignorance. The basic principle of my goals and values for agriculture is that if we are going to have policies they ought to be people-centered and not commodity-centered. We cannot do justice to a commodity; we can only do justice to people.

This is why I advocate abolishing the Department of Agriculture and also the Department of Labor and the Department of Commerce, for it is absurd to have commodity pressure groups in the executive branch. We have got quite enough of them in the legislature. I would very much like to reorganize the executive branch and have a Department of Science and Research, a Department of Poverty and Economics. That is about all we would need. That policy should be directed towards poverty, towards knowledge. There is practically no excluse for directing it towards agriculture as such, for agriculture is not an important enough sector of the economy.

We may soon get to the point where drycleaning is a more important industry then agriculture, and I want to worry about the family drycleaner just as much as I want to worry about the family farm. These laments about the family farm seem to me mainly hokum. In the first place, I think the family farm is here to stay — we aren't going to get rid of it. It is an efficient unit, especially in livestock enterprises. Cows almost have to be part of a family, as they need tender loving care. When we go over to algae, perhaps this will be the end of it. But this is still a long way ahead.

PROFESSOR'S GRADES ON FARM POLICY

How bad is American agricultural policy? The only physical product of a professor is grade sheets, outside of books, which don't really count. So I suppose what I am expected to do in evaluation is to give out A's, B's and C's, and I am quite prepared to do this. It may be a gross example of the original sin of human pride and presumption, but it is still what professors are paid to do.

What I have tried to do is to assess, first of all, American agricultural policy in general, and then the policies which are advocated and promoted in the preceding papers to see how they stack up against the three tasks of the economy: allocation, distribution and growth.

For American agricultural policy as a whole, in point of allocation it gets a B, because we <u>have</u> succeeded in getting a lot of people out of agriculture. We could have done it better and more humanely. We could have done it faster. We ought to do it faster. But we aren't doing so badly. So this gets a B. In point of distribution (social justice) I think it gets a D. Social policy is clearly unjust if it subsidizes the rich. We have an agricultural policy which is based on price supports. If you don't sell anything, however, it doesn't matter what price you don't sell it at. Agricultural poverty arises out of the fact that the poor have so little to sell. From the point of view of distributional justice, therefore, we make quite a low grade.

From the point of view of growth and development we make an A plus. We might even make it an A plus plus. We have done extraordinarily well on this — and all for the wrong reasons. The genius of our whole society is that we always do the right thing for the wrong reasons. This is much better than doing the wrong things for the right reasons, which is what I think the Communist side often tends to do. We have been extraordinarily lucky. For instance, we set up Iowa State University, which is very much against the interests of agriculture and particularly against the interests of agricultural fundamentalists. We did this on the grounds that the way to make agriculture prosperous is to make it efficient. Of course this isn't so. If you make agriculture efficient you make agriculture unprosperous and all the rest of us prosperous. So you see the non-farmers really ought to have to set up Iowa State. But it was the farmers who did it. This is one of the cases where ignorance was bliss.

I would argue that even our price support policies, foolish as they are, have been good from the point of view of economic development. They have introduced a certain stability into agriculture which has, I suspect, increased the rate of technological change in it, and we would not have had this degree of technological change if it hadn't been for the price supports. So everything we have done for justice has created injustice and growth, and on the whole growth is much more important than justice. If we don't have growth we can't afford to have justice. This is the best of all possible worlds, obviously.

If you compare our agricultural policy with policy in almost any other sphere of life, it stands up extremely well. Compare it with national security policy: here we have spent 500 billion dollars on national security since 1950 and the answer is, "Dig your own holes, boys." If we had achieved a corresponding degree of success in agricultural policy, we would be saying, "Look, we're terribly sorry. We don't have any food, but how about digging you own garden?" By these standards agriculture has done very well indeed. Compared with almost all other policies, agriculture stands at the top, in spite of the fact that we have done most of the right things for the wrong reasons.

In conclusion, let me go down the list of the various organizations that seem to be represented in these papers and see if I can hand out a few grades. The Farm Bureau first: I would give it a B on allocation, because it is almost the only farm organization which is not fundamentalist and which recognizes that if agriculture is going to prosper, it has got to be small and people must get out of it. This point of view is very sensible. On distribution I give it a D. The Farm Bureau consists mostly of people who have licked, personally, the problem of poverty in agriculture, and they have no interest in people who have not. The Farm Bureau has persistently fought any attempt to solve the problem of poverty in agriculture, apart from the solution of letting things take their course. This, of course, is a solution of a kind — but a very expensive one. In regard to growth I would give the Farm Bureau an A, especially in regard to commercial agriculture. But on second thought I might reduce this to a B for failing to care about economic development in the poorer sectors.

The National Farmers' Union gets no more than a C on allocation. The Brannan plan, while not perhaps an official doctrine of the NFU, is nevertheless close to its heart. This would have pauperized American agriculture permanently and subsidized people to stay in it instead of subsidizing them to get out of it. It would indeed have eliminated the surplus of commodities but not the surplus of farmers. On distribution of income I am tempted to sneak the NFU a B on account of its warm heart and its real sensitivity to the problem of poverty. On the other hand, its remedies are either worthless or discriminatory. The danger of all policies of price or income support is that they might be generalized, on the grounds that anything which is good for farmers is good for everybody. I have been advocating around Michigan, for example, that we declare automobiles an agricultural commodity. It would solve our problems nicely if we could put a parity support price on them. If we could not sell them at that price, the government could stockpile them. We could ship them abroad under P.L. 480, and they could be used as chicken coops in Siam. This would be (for Michigan) the best of all possible worlds. From a growth position, here again NFU gets a B. It is not hostile towards technical development but it is not what I would describe as enthusiastic about it.

I've given the Grange a C on all three counts. The Grange ought to go back to whatever classical gods or goddesses it worships and think again. Really, it ought to get past the 1920's. I think that on almost any score its policies have been unrealistic. It is still wedded to McNary-Haugenism. It hasn't learned that dumping is a thing that makes you lose friends and alienate people. From the point of view of the growth objective this is absurd. The way to get income parity is to get people out of agriculture, and the way to get people out of agriculture, as I suggest, is to increase mobility. But the Grange doesn't want to do anything about this, as Mr. Thompson suggests; it just doesn't have any policy, really, as far as I can see, except what it had at the time of Calvin Coolidge's veto. Where has it been since 1920? I don't know. It's my business to be frank.

I think the National Farmers' Organization also ought to get a C on all counts. This seems to me a most extraordinary pipedream if ever I saw one. It should read some of the studies of whether labor unions have succeeded in diverting the national income to labor, which on the whole economists agree they haven't. Collective bargaining is extraordinarily inefficient as a means of redistributing income, absolutely the least efficient and the most costly method there is of doing it. If anybody can organize enough farmers to do collective bargaining on any scale which would make any difference I would be extraordinarily surprised. Here again, from the point of view of realism it doesn't make any sense.

The NFO doesn't organize mobility out of agriculture; it tries to keep people in agriculture. It is not even really proposing to control production. If you want a monopoly you have got to control production. If you want to exploit the rest of society you have got to control production. Just holding a few supplies off the market occasionally has little effect. In fact, the more successful you are at it the less successful you are going to be. People will stay in agriculture. They will produce more. You will just have an increasing problem and a fundamentally unstable social system. The NFO is very good for morale. As a matter of fact this is also the main function of the trade union: the NFO keeps people busy (I'm all in favor of this) and gives them an interest in life. Thus, sociologically I think it's wonderful. But economically it makes no sense.

Now we come to the churches, and I propose to jump the gun and amalgamate the Catholics and Protestants — while amalgamation is perhaps a hundred years off. From the point of view of social policy the Catholics and Protestants are almost indistinguishable. This is one of the things that I find gratifying. The ecumenical movement has gone a long way here and the differences seem to be small. I seem to have given them a B on all counts, not quite an A. On allocation I would say they are almost going up from C to A. They used to be agricultural fundamentalists but they are beginning to realize that this is unrealistic. On the other hand, they are beginning to think about how to organize mobility, which is a very important ethical problem. Too few people are concerned with this and I think this is enough to raise them to an A.

On distribution I'm not going to raise them to an A — especially the Protestants on account of the Mexicans. I am very annoyed with the National Council of Churches and I have been fighting it for several years now because it wants to discriminate against Mexicans. That is, it's a national council of churches; it preaches an American Christ; it wants to keep Mexicans out so that we can all be nice little rich Americans together. Very often the only hope for really poor people is migrant labor. At this point the church is not facing up to the realities of the world at all. It thinks America is secure in its little Tokugawa Empire; it is willing to dole out little bits to the rest of the world, but it is not going to let them in. I have been fighting this battle of ethnocentrism and nationalism in the National Council for quite a while and I have finally decided that from the ethical point of view this is the weakest link in the council's whole structure, just as the weakest link on the part of our Catholic friends is their unrealism about population.

Population is another question and a large one. But obviously if we are going to have death control we have got to have birth control too, just as, if we are going to have Iowa State, we can't have a lot of farmers. If we are going to have modern medicine we have to control population. There is no way out of this. We have got to control it morally, of course, and I expect that is the only way to control it. The worst thing, however, is not to face the problem and to refuse to talk about it. The Catholic Church has a very grave responsibility at this point which, incidentally, it shares with the Communists. But this is beside the present point and does not have much to do with agriculture or even with farmers. I doubt if the birth rate is any higher among commercial farmers than it is among professors. I am always embarrassed about this because I have five children myself, which makes my Malthusian speeches sound a little hollow.

On growth I think the churches get a B in the sense that they are not quite aware of the implications of it but that they are coming along in this way, and perhaps I can almost say that they get an A.

Now we turn to the United States Department of Agriculture. I give it a D on allocation, and I am in favor of abolishing it. There is no excuse for that big building in Washington. It deals with much too small a part of the economy. There has been a tremendous misallocation of very scarce resources into what I call the intellectual side of agriculture, which has resulted in a severe absence of these resources elsewhere. I can give it a C on distribution, actually, because it has not really emphasized the major problem; but perhaps that really is unfair because it gets bullied by the Farm Bureau. The Department did try to tackle poverty in the Farm Security Administration and things of that kind, but the great agricultural middle class didn't want to have anything to do with poor white trash, and that was the end of that. On the whole, therefore, I would say that we have done very little and that our conscious policies have done practically nothing towards abolishing poverty in agriculture. On growth I think the Department gets an A. I think it is very good on this.

I have got now to the universities and the extension services, which will be the last. I give them a C rising to A on allocation; that is, I think 25 years ago they were not realistic about it. Now, thanks to Iowa State University, I give the universities a pretty good score. On distribution I am not sure how good a grade I can give them because the universities and the extension services are still very fundamentally middle class. I am terribly worried about the thing I mentioned earlier, which is the separating out of our economy the 75 percent who make it to affluence and the 25 percent who don't. The universities are not doing anything for that 25 percent; they just can't be bothered with it. From that point of view they don't get a very good grade on distribution. On growth they get an A plus; this is where most of it comes from.

For those who like tables, my grades are summed up below. And for those who do not like my grades, I can only suggest what I once told a student who made a similar complaint — that this was an unjust world and that education was intended to prepare us for it. Perhaps even conferences have the same objective.

EVALUATION OF AGRICULTURAL POLICIES

Organization	Allocation	Distribution (Justice)	Growth
The United States	B	D	A+
The Farm Bureau	B	D	A
National Farmers' Union	C	B	B
The National Grange	C	C	C
National Farmers' Organization	C	C	C
The Churches	B	B	B
The U.S. Department of Agriculture	D	C	A
The Universities and Extension Services	C to A	C	A+

THE FUTURE CORPORATION
AND PUBLIC ATTITUDES

The Corporation and its Policies, John W. Riley, ed.,
New York: John Wiley and Sons, 1963, pp. 159-75.

THE FUTURE CORPORATION AND PUBLIC ATTITUDES

The title of this chapter is a clear invitation to brainstorming and social science fiction. The corporation is an institution of great complexity. Its structure and perhaps even its objectives have been undergoing rapid change. It is rash, therefore, to predict what is going to happen to it very far in the future. In so far as this chapter indulges in prediction, then, it must be regarded as highly speculative. These speculations, however, are not necessarily worthless for they may in themselves play some part in directing the future course of events. We do not necessarily move toward that which we anticipate, but what we anticipate is an important factor determining whither we shall move.

If we are thinking of the corporate institution as a dynamic social system, what are the variables that we should include? A dynamic social system consists of a succession of states, S_0, S_1 . . . S_n. Each of the states consists of a set of values of significant variables. The transition from one state to the next is determined by the rates of change of the variables involved. If the state at any one time, say S_0, is defined so as to include these rates of change, it automatically gives us the next state, S_1.

Thus, if we are on a train traveling at sixty miles an hour, we know that in one minute's time we will be one mile from where we are now. Similarly, if a corporation is growing at the rate of 5 per cent per annum, in one year's time its net worth, total assets, or whatever measure we take of its size, will be 5 per cent larger than it is now. A dynamic theory attempts to relate these rates of change, either to the existing structure at the point of origin, to some past rates of change, or to some past structures. If stable relationships of this kind can be obtained, then prediction is possible.

For the purposes of this chapter, I have classified the significant variables of the corporate institution into six heads. The first of these is its *size* and rate of growth. The second is its *complexity* as measured, for instance, by the number of different products, related or unrelated, by the number of different departments, by the extent and number of ranks in its hierarchical structure, or by the number of different roles in its job structure. The third relates to the *locus of power* within the organization and its constitution, formal or informal. The fourth relates to its *objectives,* overt or covert. The fifth relates to its *emotional affect,* and the extent to which it can command affection or loyalty, etc., or the extent to which it is disliked. The sixth is the general nature and quality of the *environment* in which the organization operates. Other classifications may occur to the reader, but these six boxes seem to be able to hold most of the things I want to put into them.

The first of these variables and perhaps the one that is most tractable to analysis is size. The important question here is whether the rate of growth of an organization is a function of its size, that is its absolute size. If the rate of growth is uniquely related to the size of the organization a curious paradox emerges. The organization will grow, of course, until its rate of growth is zero. This is its maximum and, in a certain sense, its equilibrium size. If the rate of growth, however, is related to the efficiency of the organization, it may well be that the most efficient size is smaller than the maximum. For, at the most efficient size, there is still a positive rate of growth. The most efficient size, therefore, is not an equilibrium size. Efficiency inevitably

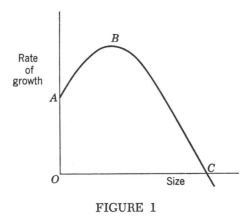

FIGURE 1

destroys itself through growth, simply because an organization cannot grow without becoming larger.

This system is illustrated in Figure 1. Here we measure size on the horizontal axis and rate of growth on the vertical axis. The curve *ABC* relates these two variables. There must be a positive rate of growth *OA* at 0; otherwise the organization will never come into being. A fascinating problem here, incidentally, is how something which does not exist can have a positive rate of growth. This is the problem that the physicists call *nucleation*, but we will have to pass this by for the moment. We suppose, therefore, that the rate of growth is a maximum at *B* and is zero at *C*. If the rate of growth itself measures the efficiency of the organization, which is not necessarily true, this would be at the maximum at *A*. The organization must continue to grow, however, until it gets to *C*, at which point it reaches an equilibrium. In a strictly ecological sense, *OC* is its optimum size and is a true equilibrium. If it grows beyond this size, it will decline back to it. At a smaller size growth will continue until equilibrium size is reached.

The rate of growth of a corporation may fall to zero for a number of different reasons. In the first place, there may be what economists have called *decreasing returns to scale*. This means that the organization runs into certain internal difficulties as its size increases. Communications become harder, mistakes become easier and costlier, and the replacement of individuals in their roles becomes more difficult. All this is reflected in a decline of output per unit of input at larger sizes. In some cases, as in agriculture, this phenomenon becomes apparent at quite small scales. In other cases, such as in the automobile industry, it is doubtful whether it comes into operation at all at the kind of scales with which we are familiar. This principle has an important analogy in the biological world. Each form of organization there has a size boundary which it cannot transcend without incurring severe penalties. The one-celled animal, for instance, must be microscopic. The insect with its exoskeleton and primitive breathing apparatus cannot transcend the size of the praying mantis, and it seems to be most efficient somewhere between the ant and the bee. The land animal cannot be much larger than the elephant, and the blue whale seems to be the absolute limit of size of living organizations on the earth as we know it at present.

The second set of limitations relates to what might be called the metabolic or market environment of the organization. All organizations exchange with their environment. The corporation exchanges its product for money and it likewise exchanges money for labor, raw material, and the services of borrowed funds. The ability of an organization to grow depends upon these rates of exchange. In particular the ability of a corporation to grow depends upon its ability to sell its services above cost, that is, to make profits. As an organization becomes larger, however, it often finds that the rates of exchange with its environment become less favorable. The more product a corporation has to sell, the less price it can get for it or the more it will have to spend on selling; the more it has to buy, the higher the price or the more buying costs will have to be incurred in making the purchase. These market limitations operate even where the diseconomies of scale are not yet felt. Indeed, if there are no diseconomies of scale the size of the organization must be limited by the market limitations. A market limitation on one commodity may, of course, be transcended as far as the whole organization is concerned by adding another commodity to the line of products. This, as we shall see, involves what might be called *costs of complexity*.

A third source of expansion of the corporation, which we may also think of as a source of limitation upon size, is the ability or inability to merge. This is a phenomenon which is virtually unknown in the biological field but which is quite common in social organizations. The size of a social organization such as a corporation, therefore, depends not merely on its ability to grow out of its own peculiar operation, that is, by simple accretion. It may grow also by the absorption of other organizations by merging. A political analogy is the federation of states. The ability to merge is not necessarily the same as the ability to grow out of profits or even the ability to borrow, although these various abilities may not be unrelated. It is frequently, indeed, the lack of profits which makes a firm attractive as a partner in a merger for tax purposes!

A fourth factor in the growth of organizations, even of corporations, which is not wholly taken care of in the preceding list is the propensity and ability to receive grants out of the budget of another organization. This proclivity might be called *budget-sucking*. It is somewhat different from sales in the market in so far as it represents, on the whole, unilateral transfers from the account of the donor to the account of the recipient. Subordinate departments within a larger organization are, of course, budget-suckers. Their growth depends entirely on their ability to persuade the larger organization to devote more resources to them. Many ostensibly independent organizations, however, are finding themselves more and more in a budget-sucking rather than a market environment. This includes the universities, the research and development corporations, and armaments firms.

The complexity of an organization and especially of a corporation may be determined in part by the dynamics of its drive toward growth. As we have seen, a one-product firm runs rapidly into sharp market limitations. If it wishes to continue expanding as an organization it must add more products to its line. We find this holds true for religious and educational organizations also. A sect can afford to have a single spiritual product, but a church must be many things to many different people. Similarly a large university provides many more kinds of educational product than a small denominational college. The problems here are sociological rather than economic. There does seem to be a certain drive for growth in itself in organizations quite apart from the profitability or advantages of growth. This may in part be due to ambition and the search for status on the part of executive officers. It is also, however, a result of the dynamics of adjustment within an organization. It is always easier to adjust something up than down. Consequently, if one part of an organization is too big, it is frequently easier to rectify this by making the other part larger than by making the over-expanded part smaller. Thus the search for *relative* adjustment results in a drive for *absolute* growth.

Complexity, however, has a cost. The more products a firm adds to its line, the harder it is to keep track of them all and to maintain a homogeneous and integrated organization. Notably firms tend to develop what might be called *industrial style*. An automobile firm may go into things like refrigerators, but it would not generally go into textiles, furniture, and powder puffs. Chemical firms keep to chemicals, drug firms to drugs, etc. We find, that is to say, product specialization of firms. We never find one firm producing all the commodities of an economy. The problem again is one of sociology more than economics. We are not discussing the advantages of specialization in the classical economic sense either as between individuals or as between plants. A large firm like General Motors or a one-firm state like Soviet Russia can enjoy most of the advantages of the division of labor. The real question here is whether there are advantages in the homogeneity of the *style* of the individual firm or enterprise. The diseconomies of complexity seem to arise because at the core of every organization there is a small subculture of strongly interacting individuals, and there seem to be limits on the complexity of this subculture. It seems to be beneath the dignity of steel producers to make powder puffs and beyond the imagination of garment makers to make steel.

The third box of variables relates to the locus of power and the political constitution of the corporation. Traditionally and formally the center of power in the corporation is supposed to be the capitalist. The owners of the net worth of the corporation are the *sovereign people* of its political entity. Much has been written in the past generation to prove that the sovereignty of the capitalist is mythical—perhaps even more mythical than the sovereignty of the people in a democracy. We have, at least, ceased to be surprised that ownership is usually separated from control. Indeed, I have emphasized strongly in previous writings that the whole purpose of the financial system is precisely to separate ownership from control. A system of freely disposable and inheritable private property is bound to move toward a condition in which most of the actual owners of the capital of a society are in no position to administer or control it. There is a strong tendency, indeed, for the ownership of capital to fall into the hands of elderly widows and maiden aunts. It would be most unfortunate if these poor ladies could not relinquish the control and administration of this capital to abler hands. They do this, of course, through the agency of financial instruments, stocks, bonds, mortgages, etc. On the other side of the coin, these same financial instruments enable people who are skilled at the management and administration of capital to manage and administer much more than they themselves own.

Nevertheless, this necessary and on the whole benevolent aspect of the financial system raises some curious political questions for the corporation. Legally, almost without exception, the management is supposed to be responsible to the owners of the net worth. He is supposed to be hired by these owners and to be their servant. In reality, as we know, management is often a self-perpetuating oligarchy which can be removed by the stockholders only with the greatest difficulty. Furthermore, management, as we shall see in a moment, frequently is responsive to many other pressures outside the stockholder group. Indeed, the pressures brought upon him by the stockholders often seem to be the least of his worries. Government with its anti-trust division, its Food and Drug Administration, its Taft-Hartley Act, and its Fair Employment Laws often seems to be pulling at him from one side. Organized labor pulls at him from the other. Most important of all, his peers in the management profession breathe down his neck. The professionalization of management represents a profound change in the sociological power structure of the corporation, and there seems to be no retreat from this.

The relations among the power structure of a corporation, its formal constitution, and its formal and informal lines of communication is a very interesting problem. We suspect sometimes that the higher an employee goes in a hierarchy the more the decision-making power is circumscribed by regulation, by custom, and by ignorance. The larger the organization the less the man at the top really knows about it. Consequently, we suspect that the real decisions are frequently made at middle levels in the hierarchical structure, particularly at what might be called the *information turnstiles,* where the information that goes to the executives is sifted. Executive decisions can be made only on the basis of information received and he who controls the information frequently controls the decision. This does not necessarily mean, of course, that there are machiavellian manipulators in the lower ranks who deliberately distort the information streams flowing upward. It is much more likely that no real decisions are ever taken by anybody. The larger the organization the more likely this is to be true. Everybody reacts and nobody acts. The organization lumbers along under the impetus of its own implacable dynamism somewhat in the manner of Tolstoy's *War and Peace.* Nobody, very much, is responsible either for its success or its failure.

The fourth box contains the objectives by which the decisions, when they are made, are justified and by which the success of the decision-maker is measured. In the old days, of course, profit was supposed to be the sole objective of the firm. There is, at least, a beautiful simplicity about this objective. Forgetting for the moment that no wise man should believe his accountants, 6 per cent is always better than 5. The economist, moreover, delights in profit maximization because it gives him a beautiful theory. The truth, alas, is more complex. All firms will sacrifice profits for something. The banker sacrifices them for liquidity, the insurance company sacrifices them for respectability, and nearly everybody sacrifices them for public relations.

The decay of profit maximization may go hand in hand with the decline in the sovereignty of the capitalist, which we noted earlier. It becomes harder and harder to tell nasty, money-grubbing corporations from virtuous, non-profit institutions. Indeed, I suspect sometimes that a type of organization called the *not-very-profit organization* is going to gobble us all up. The university, the research corporation, the hospital, the mutual insurance company, and the cooperative all seem to be moving toward profit making while the plain old money-making corporation moves in the direction of good works, contributions to the

Community Chest, support of universities, allotments to pensions, welfare funds, and Christmas turkeys. Pretty soon it is going to be hard to tell General Motors from the Salvation Army. There is both gain and loss in this. The large corporation, especially, cannot help being *affected with the public interest*. The nationalization of the Bank of England hardly created a tremor in Threadneedle Street because it affected so few of the public criteria by which the decision-makers of the bank had acted. It may not take us very long to get to the point where the nationalization of the Ford Motor Company or General Motors would make as little difference.

This is probably why nationalization seems to be increasingly unattractive in most of the western world. It makes so little difference that it hardly seems to be worth the trouble. This does mean, however, that there has been a subtle change in the standards by which the behavior of the corporate executive is judged not so much by outsiders as by himself and his peers. In this, as in any other subculture, it is the judgment of the peers that is all important. We are justified by the grace of the approving phrase and nod at the country club or the cocktail party.

This change in objectives is related to the variables in the fifth box—those that relate to the emotional affect with which the corporation is regarded. This set of variables has been examined very little. Adam Smith took a dim view of those joint-stock companies which were the forerunners of the modern corporation. At their best he thought they were useful work horses and well-adapted to digging ditches and canals, while at their worst they were cruel exploiters and monopolists. On the other hand, somebody must have loved the East India Company, otherwise it is hard to see how it could have conquered a subcontinent. There must have been something about it which commanded devotion and self-sacrifice. Some of Adam Smith's attitude persists to the present day. The nation and the church are supposed to command greater loyalties than the corporation. Welfare capitalism is rightly suspect as a device to destroy the labor market and to tie the worker to his job. On the other hand, it is the job that gives status; it is the identification with the employing organization which is often the most important identification in the person's life.

There is a real dilemma here. On the one hand, there is something to be said for the work-horse theory that the corporation should demand and receive an honest day's work for an honest day's pay, and that should be the end of it. The employer should not be allowed to poke his golden fingers into the dark recesses of private life provided that what a man does outside the firm does not affect what he does inside it. On the other hand, there is also a great need to recognize that the work group is a vital subculture within which the individual spends much time, from which he needs to receive emotional support, and toward which he needs to give emotional identification. Perhaps the resolution of this conflict is the maintenance of lively and important subcultures outside the work group such as in the family, the church, the club, and the interest group. Only thus can we be defended against the grotesque identification of the work group with the whole life environment which we find in the Soviet Union and which is perhaps the most repulsive aspect of Communism.

The last box perhaps does not contain much that has escaped the others. It is useful, however, to have a box labeled *environment* in which we can put the many variables outside the corporation itself which its decision-makers have to take in mind. In the ideal model of the economist, of course, the only environment which the firm has to worry about is the market for its output and for its inputs. In the real world we find that other environments continually are pressing upon the attention of the economic decision-maker. The rise of public relations as a form of corporate expenditure testifies to the extent to which the nonmarket environment has become important. The business of public relations is, of course, to sell the organization not the product. For the budget-suckers, who now especially cluster around the Pentagon, the ordinary market environment has almost completely disappeared, and it is replaced by a budget-manipulating operation. In the communist state, of course, this type of environment dominates. The Soviet trust is certainly not unresponsive to its customers, but it is probably much more responsive to its opposite numbers in the *Gosplan*.[1]

[1] The State Planning Commission's unified plan for Soviet industry.

This chapter has outlined what seem to be the major variables of the corporate institution as a social system with some indication as to their present position and possible movement. Now, of course, comes the more speculative part of the chapter. Where do we go from here? Are there any indications that present trends will continue, accelerate, or reverse themselves? Perhaps the dominant factor here is the changes which are going on in the information system of the organization. *The Organizational Revolution* [2] argued that the communications revolution from about 1870 on involving the telegraph, the telephone, the mimeograph, the trained secretary, and the vice-president was the main cause of the increase in the scale of organizations which began about that time and to which I gave the name of the *organizational revolution*. General Motors, the Pentagon, and the Soviet Union are all part of this process.

As far as the corporation in the United States was concerned, this movement seemed to have spent itself by about the First World War. From that time on, even though the big corporations got bigger, they did not grow much faster than the total economy and so remained about the same proportion of it. An important question for the future is whether this situation will continue, or whether the development of IBM machines and data processing has not sown the seeds of a new organizational revolution which makes possible, if it does not make necessary, a very large increase in the size of the organization beyond the existing limits. The continued existence of the Soviet Union illustrates that a very large organization is possible though it does not demonstrate that it is either efficient or desirable.

The Pentagon is a "communist state" with roughly the national income of Communist China. The gross income of a large American corporation like General Motors is of the same order of magnitude as that of a small communist country like Yugoslavia. It is one of the paradoxes of our time that the more successful General Motors is in solving its own internal problems, the better the case for Communism, at least on a small scale! This is not, of course, the whole story. The fact that General Motors exists within the framework of a larger society means that its

[2] K. E. Boulding, *The Organizational Revolution*, Harper and Bros., New York, 1953.

dissatisfied citizens have power to *emigrate* far beyond that of the citizens of Yugoslavia. This, in itself, is a very important check on the power of General Motors which is not possessed by the communist state except perhaps in a world of smaller communist states and of much freer migration than we have today.

IBM may have removed the internal barriers to almost indefinite growth of the corporation, but, of course, the market and environmental barriers remain. It is probably fear of the nonmarket environment which prevents General Motors from expanding to cover the whole automobile industry. Up to now, the family farm has shown remarkable strength in the face of new technology in agriculture. It is possible, however, that a revolution in agricultural administration may render a very large expansion of the scale of the enterprise in agriculture feasible. Here again, the nonmarket environment may prevent what the internal and the market environment would permit. It is possible, however, that we may find ourselves in the future with a dilemma which in the past has been more apparent than real. It concerns whether we should preserve the family farm at the cost of some sacrifice in agricultural efficiency. Even at the staid level of the university rumbles are being heard. We visualize a university of 200,000 students in the future in which the teaching machines have taken over, and the student can be graduated practically untouched by human mind.

The future of the financial corporation against the manufacturing enterprise is an interesting object of speculation. A strong case can be made that the financial corporation, especially the commercial bank, is closer to what Talcott Parsons calls the *polity* than it is to the economy. In economic and financial theory it is always temptingly easy to nationalize the banking system in the model and to regard the banking system essentially as an outpost of government. With the growth of social security, insurance, likewise, becomes more a part of the polity than it is of the economy. A strong case can be made for private solutions to the social problems of personal finance. However, we have never accepted this in education and we are increasingly uneasy about the private solution in health. It is at this point that the limits of public and private organization are hardest to define.

More, perhaps, than any other single factor the future of the private corporation depends upon the extent to which it can be legitimated in the mind of the general public. In a country like the United States this presents little problem. On the whole we accept the private corporation as a legitimate aspect of the social scene, and as long as the economy continues to perform efficiently, there seems to be no reason why this state of affairs should not continue. Discontent in the United States takes mostly personal and private channels. If a man is not happy in General Motors he gets out of it and he finds a job elsewhere. He does not usually devote his life to its destruction or nationalization.

The many opportunities for personal advancement within the existing system in the United States make it remarkably stable politically and enabled it to survive even the great trauma of the Great Depression. In many other parts of the world, however, things are very different. The corporation is often an alien institution. The individual feels trapped by his environment and has no sense of personal freedom to escape it. Under these circumstances discontent is channeled along political lines, and the future of the private corporation is correspondingly more uncertain. Under these circumstances its role is difficult. If it tries to be a "good employer" it will be accused of being paternalistic. If it tries to accept political responsibility, it will be accused of interfering in the internal affairs of the country in which it operates. The threat of possible expropriation will hang continuously over its head. In the face of these dilemmas, it would hardly be surprising if American capital decided to stay home and mind its own business. This, however, is no answer either. This delays the development of the poor countries and exposes them all the more to left-wing influences. The future may well depend on whether new forms of organization appropriate to these peculiar circumstances can be devised which somehow reconcile the claims of foreign capital with the claims of domestic politics.

One thing we can look forward to with some confidence is an increase in the richness and variety of corporate forms of organization. It may be, indeed, that we shall see a certain blurring of the distinction between the private and the public corporation as well as between the profit and the nonprofit organization. Prediction in social systems is extremely hazardous. This is particularly true where the rise of new and unprecedented forms of organization is concerned. Social invention is just as hard to predict as any other kind, for, if we could predict it, we would already have it, at least the idea of it. I cannot help being impressed with the fact, however, that, much more than its constitution or legal form, the *size* of the structure of an organization determines its behavior, its attributes, and its impact on the individuals who compose it and who are affected by it.

All large organizations tend to be very much alike whether they are Soviet trusts or American corporations. This is true at least in their productive activities, internal communications, and structure. They differ most, perhaps, in the activities directed toward the environment, especially those activities directed toward the control of the environment. These are very different in the Soviet trust and in the American corporation. In both cases, however, these activities may be seen as a "problem." In one case, this is because they distort or undermine the sacred sovereignty of the consumer. In both cases, also, these activities are likely to be with us for a long time, and we will no doubt continue to put up with them. We turn back here to the classical simplicities of competitive economics and wonder perhaps whether by some counterorganization or countervailing power, the grand simplicities of perfect competition can be simulated— in the budget-sucker as well as in the market oriented corporation.

It may well be that the ultimate future of the corporation, whether in its capitalist or its socialist form, depends more on the nature of the matrix in which this organization exists than on the nature of the organization itself. In the classical economic model this matrix is, of course, the market environment of the different firms and consists only in the ability to buy and sell. In the model of perfect competition this ability to buy and sell is at some price or set of prices which is independent of the activity of the firm itself. The market, however, itself coordinates in an orderly, although unplanned, way the innumerable decisions and activities of the different economic organizations in the society. This is a theory of the general equilibrium of demand and supply. The price-profit mechanism is supposed to insure that the activities of the producer are coordinated with the demand of consumers. For if this is not so, it will pay somebody to make changes in the direction of this coordination. An industry that is too small will be unusually profitable and will grow. An industry that is too large will be unusually unprofitable and will decline. This is the "hidden hand" which organizes what might be called the unprogrammed economy.

At the other extreme, we have the totalitarian, socialist economy in which the whole system is organized as a single firm. Here the coordinating agent is not the impersonal market but the (still almost impersonal) budget or plan. The guiding hand here is only moderately hidden, but it is still by no means obvious. The coordination of decisions is made by an hierarchial information system in the central planning agency. Industries expand, not necessarily because they are profitable, but because they can get a large allotment of the planned budget. Similarly, they contract if they are unsuccessful in getting these allotments.

Both in the unprogrammed market society and in the programmed socialist society, the coordinating network is influenced by those whom it is supposed to coordinate. In the market society markets are never perfect or hardly ever perfect. Monopoly pays off and is eagerly sought, and monopoly power means that the monopolist manipulates the signals that are supposed to coordinate him. In the socialist society, likewise, it is surprising if industrial groups do not act as pressure groups on the political decisions of the plan, and he who gets the ear of the dictator prospers. In both societies, therefore, there is a profound tendency for the coordinators to be controlled by the coordinated. This is a principle, incidentally, which is noticeable in the regulatory bodies of advanced capitalist societies, such as the Interstate Commerce Commission and the Federal Trade Commission. What starts off as control often ends as protection. The distinction between the corporation and its matrix is thereby blurred.

There are problems here which are extremely difficult, although they are important. Is there, for instance, some kind of equilibrium distribution of organizations by size and by type in the society? As an organization grows, for instance, its depart-

ments become more and more independent and more and more
like organizations of their own. The most monolithic organization of society is never as monolithic as it looks. There are
organizations between organizations. There are always cracks,
holes, and interstices. In the biological world organisms are
always subdivided into organs. Even the cell has its mito-
chondria. Society likewise always breaks up into separate organizations, and there may be some equilibrium principle at
work here of which we are not now aware.

On the other hand, in social theory it is always dangerous to
yield too easily to mechanical interpretations. Neither persons
nor organizations are machines. If they are machines they are
of much higher order of complexity than the most complicated
machines which we can make. Consequently the element of
consciousness must be taken into account. The social organization, whether it is a sect, a party, or a corporation, is always a
result of some kind of conscious image or vision, and its history
is in no small measure determined by the nature of this vision.
The entrepreneurial function in society is strangely similar to
that of the prophet and the dreamer. Organizations must be
dreamed up before they can be embodied. They are, indeed,
of such stuff as dreams are made of. In the last analysis, therefore, we must perhaps relate the future of the corporation as
much if not more to these intangibles of the conscious mind
than to the processes of mechanical dynamics. Without a continuing vision the organization perishes.

These reflections lead to one concluding thought. It may be
that, in the long run, the most critical problem of the corporation, as of every organization, is how to maintain and nourish,
especially at the top levels of the hierarchy, the vision which
gives it life. The greatest dilemma of the corporation, especially
the large corporation, is that it is all too likely to have expelled
for insubordination at the age of thirty, the man who ought to
be its president at the age of fifty-five. The qualities which lead
to a man's rising in a complicated hierarchy are by no means
necessarily those which are desirable at the top. A man rises,
on the whole, by pleasing his superiors. At the top this ability
is useless. A man who rises to the top, therefore, by pleasing his

superiors is apt to find himself ill-adapted to the role that he finds there.

Indeed, the longest-lived organizations like the church, are precisely those in which the top roles have been stylized by tradition and ritual to the point where the role almost completely imposes its own image on the occupant. No matter who is pope, he has to behave like a pope. In the corporation there is much less chance of ritualizing the top role. For this very reason there is a certain long-run insecurity about the future of the corporate institution. The corporation as a major social form is not very old. It barely goes back one-hundred years and in this brief experience there are many instances of a painfully short length of life, even in large corporations. It would be absurd to suppose that these problems of long-run survival are insoluble. It would be optimistic to pretend that they have been solved.

THE MISALLOCATION OF
INTELLECTUAL RESOURCES

Proceedings, Amer. Phil. Soc.,
107, 2 (April, 1963): 117-20.

THE MISALLOCATION OF INTELLECTUAL RESOURCES

ECONOMISTS have always been interested in the problem of allocation of resources. It is, indeed, a central problem of their science. In equilibrium price theory, for instance, an equilibrium set of prices of all commodities, on the one hand, and of outputs of all commodities on the other, results in an equilibrium set of returns to factors such that there is no incentive for factors or resources on balance to switch from one occupation or from the production of one commodity to another. If there were no obstacle to the movement of resources, the returns to their use would be equal in all uses. Where there are obstacles to movement, returns to factors in the equilibirum situation may be unequal, provided that the differences are not large enough to overcome the obstacles to movement.

The weakness of this elegant schema, particularly when it comes to examining economic development and the dynamic course of an economy through time, is that it takes no explicit account of the intellectual resource and the learning process. In the classical economics, the three factors of production are identified as labor, land, and capital; labor is little more than manpower, analogous to horsepower—indeed, Adam Smith at one point speaks in the same breath of the laboring poor and the laboring cattle. Capital is conceived as a stockpile of commodities, and investment is simply the addition to these stocks by the process of producing more than is consumed. Land is little more than simple area. Alfred Marshall tried, somewhat unsuccessfully, to add a fourth factor of production which he called organization, which looks a little more like an intellectual resource. In all this scheme, however, there is very little explicit recognition of the fact that economic development is essentially a learning process, and that the nature and allocation of the intellectual resource is the key to it.

The above statements should be qualified by the observation that Adam Smith, with his usual insight but also with his usual lack of an explicit analytical framework, comes very close to ex-pounding what might be called an epistemological theory of development in his account of the effects of the division of labor. In the very first chapter of *The Wealth of Nations* he says,

This great increase of the quantity of work which, in consequence of the division of labour, the same number of people are capable of performing, is owing to three different circumstances; first, to the increase of dexterity in every particular workman; secondly, to the saving of the time which is commonly lost in passing from one species of work to another; and lastly, to the invention of a great number of machines which facilitate and abridge labour, and enable one man to do the work of many.[1]

Each of these "three different circumstances" represents a learning process and an allocation of an intellectual resource. The increase in dexterity is a learning process in the lower nervous system. The diminution in what Adam Smith in another place calls "sauntering" as we go from one occupation to another also reflects the fact that there has to be a brief period of relearning when we take up a new pursuit, even if it is one we have pursued in the past; and the invention of machines is, of course, the most important learning process of all, and the only one which seems to have an almost unlimited horizon. Later in the chapter Adam Smith observes that improvements in machinery may in part come from the workmen who operate them (the suggestion box!), but then he goes on,

Many improvements have been made by the ingenuity of the makers of the machines, when to make them became the business of a peculiar trade; and some by that of those who are called philosophers or men of speculation, whose trade it is not to do anything, but to observe everything; and who, upon that account, are often capable of combining together the powers of the most distant and dissimilar objects.[2]

In his tribute to the philosophers Adam Smith foreshadows the increasing importance of research

---

[1] Adam Smith, *The wealth of nations,* 7, New York, Modern Library edition, 1937.

[2] *Ibid.,* 10.

and development as a source of economic progress. These important hints which were dropped by Adam Smith, however, were not much taken up by subsequent economists, and it is only very recently that the problem of the intellectual resource as opposed, say, to the mere accumulation of capital has risen to prominence as a key to economic development. I should add that it is a key likewise to the even more important, though less easily identifiable and measurable, processes of political and social development.

An allocation problem implies that a resource is scarce, in the sense that the more we apply to one use the less we can apply to others. If we define the intellectual resource in terms of the learning process, it is clear that it is scarce in the above sense and that an allocation problem arises. An individual cannot know everything and cannot learn everything in the course of his lifetime. In any particular year, if he learns one thing there are things that he cannot learn as a result. A society as a whole has to cope with the consumption of knowledge as a result of old age, incapacity, and death. A large part of the educational activity of a society consists in the replacement of knowledge which is lost in this way. The ability of a society to expand its stock of knowledge—what Adam Smith himself calls the "quantity of science"—depends on its having an intellectual resource which is greater than that needed for the mere maintenance of the knowledge which is lost by death and other means. One reason why primitive societies are apt to be stable is that it takes their whole intellectual resource merely to replace the loss of knowledge by death, and hence there is nothing to spare for an increase in the stock of knowledge. The fewer intellectual resources are necessary, therefore, to maintain the existing knowledge structure, the more can be spared for increase and improvement. This is why, for instance, an increase in the expectation of life introduces a dynamic process into almost any society. If the expectation of life at birth is only thirty years, a much larger proportion of resources will have to be devoted to simple maintenance of the knowledge stock than if the expectation of life is sixty years. There is even something, though not much, in Bernard Shaw's suggestion that we shall have to go back to Methuselah before we can spare enough intellectual resource for improvement.

Perhaps the most important question that any society can ask itself, therefore, is: what are the signs of misallocation of the intellectual resource, and, if these signals are flying, what can be done to correct the situation? We have no simple measure here in the shape of a rate of return, as we have in the case of allocation of financial capital. The same general principle applies, however, that, if the rates of return on the investment of intellectual resources are much larger in one employment than in another, this is a sign that the resources are being misallocated and there should be a transfer out of the low-return employment into the high-return employment. We would have to define the returns to intellectual investment in terms of the relevance of knowledge to the "problems" of the society. The definition of "problems" presents real difficulty, as a definition in terms of *perceived* problems is not always satisfactory. A society may have unperceived problems which are of great importance to its survival and ultimate success. The best we can do, perhaps, is to start off with the perceived problems and then inquire into the reality testing to see whether there are unperceived problems which are important and whether the perceived problems are not real ones.

For any particular society, therefore, we could visualize a process of self-examination which might go something as follows. We first of all would examine the whole learning process in the society, including not only the institutions of formal education and research but also the less formal learning which goes on in the field, the shop, the factory, the family, the church, and so on. We then look at how much of this total process can properly be ascribed to mere replacement and how much is *net* in the sense of a net addition to the total stock of knowledge. We then look at whether there are unused intellectual resources. There is a problem in the use of intellectual resources somewhat akin to the problem of underemployment as a result of deficient social organization. In most societies the underemployment of intellectual resources is likely to be massive, for the biological capacity of the human organism for learning is usually much larger than the actual performance. We need to look therefore at the blocks to learning and particularly for the points at which social organization can improve the learning performance. We must also look at the distinction between useful knowledge and useless knowledge, difficult as this may be. A society in which knowledge of an elaborate ceremonial structure unrelated to real problems has to be maintained, generation after generation, is clearly wasting its intellectual resources. Finally, we must look at the extent of redundancy in the information system, and the absence of significant communication channels.

We then ask whether that proportion of the intellectual resource which is devoted to development and the increase in knowledge is in fact being directed along the right lines. This is a delicate question, because it is part of the mythology of science that this should not be a problem—knowledge is supposed to grow by a spontaneous process by which there is a gradual division of labor into specialized disciplines and by which the problems on which people work are determined by the growing-points of the structure of knowledge itself. That is, the questions which science asks of nature are supposed to be determined by what we already know. Unfortunately this myth becomes more and more divorced from reality, especially in an age in which research and development has become such big business. Knowledge always grows towards payoffs, like any other growth structure, and the payoffs in this case consist not merely of the rewards of distinterested curiosity; they consist of very tangible economic rewards which are determined by the structure of the society. We need to look at these economic rewards, therefore, to see whether they are introducing any malfunctioning into the growth of knowledge, and particularly whether they are directing intellectual resources towards the solution of unreal, unimportant, or insoluble problems.

Even the most cursory inspection of the allocation of intellectual resources in the United States according to the above criterion suggests that we are, in fact, suffering from a massive misallocation of current intellectual resources. There are two aspects of this problem. In the first place, we are not increasing the stock of already known, useful knowledge in the population as a whole to an adequate extent. The image of the world held by the mass of the people is now unrealistic to the point where this constitutes a grave danger. This is because the folk knowledge on which we mostly rely for our image of society is not adequate in a period of rapid change in the social system, and especially in the basic parameters of that system. An even more basic problem concerns the allocation of resources to research, that is, to the development of knowledge that nobody knew before. The problem may be summed up by saying that, whereas our major problems lie in the field of social systems, our major intellectual resource is still being devoted towards physical and biological systems. As a result of this, the growth of knowledge has become so one-sided that it actively threatens us. The change in the parameters of the social system which results from increased knowledge of physical and biological systems is so great that we are threatened all along the line with a collapse in social systems as a result of our inability to understand them and to operate them successfully. In a brief paper of this kind one can do no more than outline a few cases where this principle is at work.

(1) After spending four billion dollars on flood control in this country, we are more in danger of major disasters than before, because we have treated floods as a problem of the river, not as a problem of people, and we have attempted to deal with the problem in engineering terms instead of in terms of social institutions such as zoning and architectural design. Transportation policy is not much better, because of the strong prejudice in favor of cement.

(2) The health revolution in the tropics, made possible as a result of our increasing knowledge of biological systems, is threatening the world with a major social disaster in terms of unmanageable rates of population increase, a shift in the age composition of these societies out of the labor force groups into both the young and the old, and the consequent imposition on these societies of a problem in education and knowledge formation which may be beyond their powers to solve.

(3) In agricultural policy we have created an almost insoluble problem in the misallocation of agricultural resources, because again our capacity to solve biological problems has run so far in advance of our capacity to solve social problems.

(4) Lest we should think that these problems are confined to Western society, we should note that China is facing a major disaster in terms both of agriculture and of industrial development, because of the application of a premature and inadequate knowledge of social systems, as enshrined in an unrealistic quasi-Marxist ideology.

(5) In regard to war and peace, we are all traveling on the edge of almost irretrievable disaster because of our attempt to achieve national security by concentrating almost exclusively in physical systems, in terms of weaponry. Because of this we have changed the parameters of the international system so radically that the concept

of national defense as an international system has collapsed. Specifically, we put billions of dollars' worth of intellectual resources into attempting to operate an unworkable system, and we put practically nothing into the study and operation of conflict resolution in the international social system, which is where the problem really lies.

(6) Above all, we are putting quite inadequate resources into the study of the learning process itself, which seems to be the key to all the other problems. An improvement in the efficiency of the learning process would have a tremendous leverage; it would not only enable us to replace depreciating knowledge with a smaller expenditure of intellectual resources, because of increased efficiency in the educational process, but it would also increase the efficiency of intellectual resources expended in the production of new knowledge. For the processes by which old knowledge is disseminated and new knowledge is acquired are not essentially different.

The basic difficulty seems to be that whereas in the area of physical and biological systems we have accepted long ago the inadequacy of folk knowledge and the necessity of scientific knowledge, in the field of social systems we have not yet reached this point. Consequently in the operation of the political, social, economic, and educational systems we are still operating to a large extent with "wisdom"—that is, folk knowledge rising out of the ordinary experience of life. No one will deny that wisdom is better than folly, that is, good folk knowledge is better than bad folk knowledge. We have now reached a point in the development of man, however, where wisdom is inadequate to operate the increased complexity of his social systems. We must improve both our theoretical structures and our information-processing apparatus. We live in the day when even the best wisdom is not far from folly, and a major intellectual effort in the field of social systems is going to be necessary if our trust in wisdom in the face of a lack of knowledge is not to betray us.

THE DIMENSIONS OF ECONOMIC
FREEDOM

The Nation's Economic Objectives, Edgar Edwards, ed.,
Univ. of Chicago Press, 1964, pp. 107-22.

The Dimensions of Economic Freedom

Freedom is a troublesome concept and all the more important for being troublesome. It is not something which can be measured easily on a linear scale so that we can say, without equivocation, that one person or one society is more or less free than another. It is a concept which frequently has more emotional than intellectual content. We all use it to mean what is fine, noble, and worthwhile about "our side." It is significant, for instance, that "*Freiheit*" was one of Hitler's slogans; that the Four Freedoms, which now, alas, seem almost to have passed from public memory, were the watchwords of the Atlantic Charter; that Engels' great phrase, "The leap from necessity into freedom," is a powerful weapon of Communist ideology; and that Portugal, Spain, Haiti, and even Mississippi belong to the "free world." Amid such a confusion of tongues it is almost, but not quite, pardonable to be cynical. Cynicism, however, is never good enough. A confusion of tongues is a challenge to an intellectual enterprise to clarify the sources of the confusion and evaluate its consequences.

The confusion arises because freedom is a concept with more than one dimension, and all its dimensions are important. A great deal of unnecessary political controversy and many false images of the world arise out of the failure to recognize the existence of these various dimensions. A person or society may be moving toward more freedom on one dimension and less freedom on another. Under these circumstances it is not surprising if we concentrate on the dimension which is favorable to us and neglect the dimension which is not. Hence we get into seemingly irreconcilable arguments about the meaning of these movements, with each party perceiving himself as becoming more free and the other party as becoming less. In this paper I shall distinguish three major dimensions of freedom which I shall symbolize by the names power, law, and understanding. These three dimensions almost certainly do not exhaust the concept; they do, however, seem to represent the three *major* dimensions, and the failure to distinguish among them seems to be the principal source of controversy.

The first and most obvious dimension of freedom is power, that is, the generalized ability to do what we want. Power in turn has a number of dimensions, depending on the social system in which it is embedded. I have elsewhere distinguished three major organizers of society, corresponding to three major subsystems within the larger social system, which I have called exchange, threats, and love. To each of these there corresponds a dimension of power. In terms of the exchange system, power is purchasing power and is equivalent to wealth or riches. The richer a person or a society is, the more commodities can be commanded, the more can be bought of that which is offered for sale, and the more can be produced that has exchangeable value.

The second dimension of power relates to the threat system. Power here signifies the capability of doing harm and the capability of preventing another from doing harm to one's self. This is a complex and unstable system with some very peculiar properties, very little explored by social scientists. Violence is an important, though not the only, aspect of this system, and the institutions of national defense are of course its main organizational embodiment. Whereas in the exchange system we increase our power by increasing our ability to do things which others regard as good for them, that is, by being productive, in the threat system we increase our power by producing things which enable us to do to others what they regard as evil. For this very reason, exchange systems have a much better chance of being positive-sum games in which the total of everybody's welfare constantly increases, and threat systems tend to pass over into negative-sum games.

The third dimension of power relates it to what might be called the "integrative system." This is the kind of power which is given by status, respect, love, affection, and all those things which bind us to each other. The power of the teacher over his students, who acknowledge his superior knowledge and ability to teach; the charismatic power of a political or religious leader over his followers; the power of a beloved parent or a respected friend—these are examples of this dimension. Power in this sense is also an important organizer of society, the study of which has again been much neglected. Integrative systems, like exchange systems, are likely to develop into positive-sum games in which everybody is better off. In general we may venture the hypothesis that threat systems, as embodied, for instance, in slavery, oppression, and conquest, have a low horizon of development; exchange systems, a much higher one; and the integrative systems, the highest of all.

In all these three systems, freedom or power must be measured by the distance from the party concerned of the boundary which separates what is possible to him from what is impossible. This I have called the "possibility boundary." Each individual, organization, or society stands, as it were, at any moment of time at a point representing the existing state of the world. There are a large number of other conceivable points representing other states of the world, and we can divide the set of conceivable states into two subsets, the possible and the impossible. The impossibility of the impossible may be for a number of different reasons. There are states of the world, for instance, which are technologically impossible to reach at the present time. I can be in Detroit tomorrow, but I cannot be on the moon. The exchange system imposes limitations on me depending on what I can afford. It would be technologically possible for me to be sunning myself in Hawaii tomorrow, but I cannot afford either the time or the money for this agreeable excursion. There are limitations likewise which are imposed by the threat system. It is technologically possible for me to refuse to pay my income tax next month, but I am constrained from advancing toward this delightful state of the world in part, at least, because of the threat system which is involved in the law and its sanctions. I would very much like to go to China, and I would be willing to afford both the money and the time to do this, but the law prevents me. The integrative system likewise imposes a boundary depending on my status and on my position in the whole web of personal and organizational relationships. For some reason which is a little mysterious to me, I seem to have the power, once suitable preliminaries have been arranged, to get up and make a speech in a perfectly strange city, and a few people, at any rate, will come and listen to me. This is a power not possessed by everybody, and it depends clearly on the position of the individual in the integrative system.

As the main subject of this paper is economic freedom rather than freedom in general, we should perhaps give particular attention to that aspect of power which is most concerned with economics, that is, wealth, or its converse, poverty. In the absence of any good measurements of power or of freedom, any propositions regarding which are the *most* severe limitations on freedom are debatable, but it can at least be argued with some cogency that the most severe limitation on freedom for the mass of mankind is sheer poverty. In spite of two centuries of rapid economic development in some parts of the world, most human beings still do not have the freedom to travel much beyond the confines of their native village. They do not have the freedom to have full stomachs and healthy bodies; they do not have the freedom to provide their children with education; and the most severe limitations which are imposed on them are imposed by the sheer scarcity of commodities. For the very poor, the economic limitation is so severe and constricts them in so small a living space that other possible restrictions on freedom, such as those arising out of political dictatorship, are like distant mountain ranges beyond the close, high wall of poverty which shuts them in. It is only as economic power is increased from this extremely low level at which so much of the world still lives that other aspects of power become important. The relations here are complex. It may be, for instance, that a change in a political relationship and an increase in political freedom may be necessary before a process can be set in motion which will eventually lift the burden of poverty. The poor themselves, however, have very little say in whether this happens or not.

The second dimension of freedom concerns itself not so much with power, that is, with the distance of the boundary which divides the possible from the impossible, as with the nature or quality of the boundary itself. A slave and a free laborer may be equally poor and equally impotent, and the boundary of possibility may be drawn tightly around them by their sheer poverty. They may both be unable to enjoy full stomachs, physical ease, wide sources of information, and travel. In one case, however, the boundary is perceived as the will of another, that is, the master, whereas in the other case the boundary is an impersonal one, imposed by the market.

I have identified this aspect of freedom with "law" with some hesitation, because the concept of law itself is certainly wider than the notion of the kind of boundary which forms the limits of power. The problem of law also includes more than the problem of freedom. It includes, for instance, justice, which is an independent and equally important object of social organization. Thus in the sense in which I am using the word it is perfectly possible to have an unjust law, but it still remains a law. The extreme opposite of law in this sense, perhaps, is "whim," which is irrational and unpredictable behavior, especially toward another.

The difficulties of measurement and even of conceptual clarity in this dimension are great, and it is hard to tell whether a man or a society has more or less freedom in this regard. We are faced here with a multidimensional network of interlacing relationships, and in a brief essay we cannot do more than point to some of the major problems. There is, for instance, the dimension of certainty or uncertainty about the position of the boundary which limits our power. Sometimes we do things which we think we have the power to do, and we turn out to be disappointed. One of the difficulties here is implied in the very notion of a boundary: as long as we stay well within the boundary it is very hard to find out where it is. The effort to find out where a boundary lies involves probing operations which may be costly and which may even result in an actual constriction of the boundary. Our image of the nature and quality of the boundary therefore is almost inevitably derived from hearsay, that is, from written or verbal information rather than from actual experience. Most of us stop, if not within the boundary of the law, at least within the boundary where we think the law will catch up with us. We all, almost without exception, break traffic regulations up to the point where we think it may get us into trouble. Frequently, a few detections and penalties may be necessary before we learn where that boundary lies.

Another quality of the boundary of freedom which is of great importance is the quality of legitimacy. This is a very puzzling concept which nevertheless is obviously of great importance in establishing social organizations and the course of social dynamics. A boundary is legitimate when it is accepted as just and proper by a person who is limited by it. We can regard it, perhaps, as a threat-submission system in which the submission is not merely made out of fear of the consequences of not submitting but is made because the system as a whole is acceptable and is considered in the interests of the person submitting. A good example of a system of this kind is taxation. Most of us submit to be taxed, not merely because certain penalties will be imposed if we refuse, but also because we recognize that taxation in some degree is necessary for our own welfare. If taxation were completely voluntary, a lot of people would escape it. I do not mind, therefore, being forced to pay taxes myself as long as everybody else is forced to pay them likewise. Here freedom—and a specifically economic freedom in the sense of the freedom to enjoy a larger income—is limited by the tax system, presumably, however, in the interests of a larger freedom, that is, most of us feel that we might have less income, if there were no tax system at all, than the net income we enjoy under a tax system. At this point the problem of freedom seems to be inseparable from that of justice, for only limitations of individual freedom which are seen as just are likely to enhance this freedom in the long run.

Many of these problems fall into a category which might be called problems of conflict resolution. These are problems which arise when the power of one person or organization limits the power of another. Conflicts of this type all arise out of scarcity in some sense, where, if A succeeds in pushing his boundary of freedom away from him, this at the same time pushes B's boundary closer to B. A great deal of the political and organizational apparatus of society is concerned with situations of this kind. The institution of property, for instance, is a socially legitimated boundary system which divides a field of scarce goods into areas of freedom around each particular owner. Within limits, I can do what I like with my own. Property rights, of course, are never absolute and they are always created by society. The process of creating and limiting them, however, must also be legitimated, and this is one of the main functions of law. A good example of this kind of conflict resolution is a stop light at an intersection. The use of the intersection is scarce in the sense that two parties cannot occupy it at the same time. If there are no means of regulation, the exercise of the freedom of all is likely to result in the freedom of none —the parties will be dead. The traffic light creates property; it gives the right of way part of the time to travelers on one thoroughfare and part of the time to travelers on the other. It is inalienable property and not usually subject to exchange in the market, but it is property nevertheless, and when the fire truck comes by it may even be alienated. It is property, furthermore, which is established by some kind of legitimate process which is recognized as legitimate by all parties. Legitimate process is *due* process, which suggests, incidentally, why this concept is so important to civil liberties and to political freedom.

The constitution of a society is a set of rules for deciding conflicts. These rules may be either written or unwritten, and there are indeed always a good many unwritten rules which constitute, as it were, the tacit part of the social contract. Majority rule, for instance, is one such constitutional compact; in practice, however, it is always modified by unwritten restraints on the arbitrary power of the majority, for otherwise the social contract tends to break down. In the international sphere we still have no adequate social contract, and the development of a world social contract, whether written or tacit, is the highest-priority task of our time. Without this there is likely to be no freedom for anybody.

The "law" aspect of freedom, as applied to the particular arena of economic freedom, presents some problems of peculiar interest. In classical economic theory, the concept of perfect competition itself can claim to optimize the nature of the boundary which is imposed on individuals by economic constraints. In the first place, under perfect competition the boundary is not subject to the arbitrary whim of any person. Under perfect competition the seller faces many buyers; the buyer, many sellers; and if he cannot make a bargain with one he can make a bargain with another. Perfect competition is thus the state of affairs the furthest removed from slavery, in which the slave has no choice of master. The very existence of a labor market is an important guarantee of personal economic freedom and is a powerful check on the arbitrary power of organizations. In perfect competition, the eco-

nomic power of the individual is limited by what seem to be impersonal forces, namely, the systems of relative prices which face him. It
is true, of course, that these impersonal forces are the result of the
aggregation of a large number of personal ones, but in the aggregation, at least, the arbitrary quality of personal forces is lost, and the
individual is faced with a boundary which may perhaps be affected
by the whims of fashion but is *not* affected by the whim of any one
person. Under perfect competition, furthermore, economic conflict
scarcely arises, simply because the range of bargaining is so small.
Economic conflict arises between two parties over the terms of a
bargain: where, for instance, a commodity is bought and sold for
money, the seller would like to have a high price; the buyer, a low
price. Under perfect competition, however, there is practically no
occasion for conflict of this kind. If a seller tries to raise his price
above the market, nobody will buy from him; if a buyer tries to lower
his price below the market, nobody will sell to him. If, in addition,
people are highly mobile between different occupations, there is practically no change in the state of the society which is capable of making one group of people permanently better off at the expense of
another group. If a commodity suffers a loss of demand, or if it is
taxed and becomes unprofitable to produce, those who produce it will
simply quit their occupation and go and find another one, up to the
point at which those who are left receive normal returns.

As we move away from perfect competition toward monopoly
and—alas!—reality, the situation, of course, changes. Under monopoly, the quality of the boundary of freedom changes severely for the
worse. The monopolist is felt to exercise a personal or organizational
power over those who have to buy from him, for if there are no other
sellers there is no way to escape the relationship. As we move toward
bilateral monopoly, the situation gets even worse. Here economic
conflict becomes intense and obvious; bargaining is difficult and costly and often breaks down; and each party has a sense of being limited
by the will of the other, which is seldom regarded as legitimate. The
problem of how to develop institutions by which the bargaining
process can be legitimated in the case of monopoly power may be
regarded as one of the major unsolved economic problems of our society. In the case of the unilateral increase in steel prices, for instance,
there seemed to be no recourse but the presidential anger. In the case of
a failure of collective bargaining in the labor market, as in the newspaper strike in New York City, there does not even seem to be this
recourse. Once we get away from perfect competition, the whole
process of legitimation of the relative-price structure is in total con-

fusion. The arbitrary and confused nature, for instance, of the whole antitrust enterprise is a case in point.

The problem of legitimation becomes even more acute as we move from the exchange economy into what I have called the "grants" economy. A slowly increasing part of our economic life is governed by essentially unilateral transfers rather than by exchanges, which are bilateral transfers. In an exchange, something goes from A to B and something else from B to A. It is not always easy to tell a grant from an exchange; interest payments, for instance, have a good deal of the character of a grant in the short run but may be exchange in the long run. Tax payments have a good deal more of the character of a grant, although we can conceive ourselves as getting something rather tenuous for them. Subsidies, whether to industries or to individuals, and philanthropic donations clearly have the character of grants, though even here we have tricky cases. The support of the aged and also of the young can be regarded as part of a long-run exchange between those in middle life and those at the extremities. In youth and in old age we are recipients of grants, that is, we get more than we give; in middle life we tend to be makers of grants—we give more than we get. Part of this may be thought of as paying back what we received when we were young; part of it is paying out in the expectation of receiving grants when we are old. Even when we have eliminated all elements of long-run exchange, however, the grants system still looks pretty large. Here, unfortunately, we have practically no institutions of legitimation—indeed, practically no theory of what is legitimate, apart from some vague notions of merit. Philanthropy, whether public or private, seems to be a part of the economy where the rules are even less clear than they are in the case of antitrust legislation and prosecutions. The problem is hidden by the fact that the receipt of a grant always looks like an extension of the freedom of the recipient, whereas those who do not receive them are not conscious of any diminution of their freedom. In fact, however, insofar as resources are scarce, the giving of grants diverts resources from the non-receivers to the receivers and hence represents a real economic conflict of which (and perhaps this is fortunate) we are not fully aware.

The third great dimension of freedom is freedom from error, both intellectual and moral. A man may have a lot of power, and the boundary which limits his freedom may enclose a wide field. This boundary, furthermore, may be subject to the full blessings of law and legitimacy and free from dependence on the will of another or from uncertainty and arbitrariness. This man, however, can still be the slave of his passions and his stupidities. The more power he has and the wider the boundary of his freedom, the more quickly he may be able to damn himself. The mere quality of the boundary itself and all the majesty of law assembled will not save him. This is a dimension of freedom which is not, I think, encompassed in the other two, and yet which can be neglected at our great peril, for freedom misused will soon be destroyed.

Here again we face a problem of formidable size and complexity. We cannot discuss freedom from error without knowing something about the nature of truth. Pilate may not have been jesting, and he might not even have got the answer had he stayed, but his question, "What is truth?" has lost little of its difficulty. Nevertheless there is something both appealing and meaningful in the idea that "Ye shall know the truth, and the truth shall make you free." Freedom in this sense means the ability to fulfil an image of the future. If my image of the world contains my being at a certain place on a certain date in the future, and if when that date arrives, I find myself where I expected to be, this is a fairly convincing demonstration that the relevant part of my image of the world was true. A difficulty arises, of course, in that all images of the future have a degree of probability attached to them, and the mere fact that a particular expectation is fulfilled says nothing about the correctness of that probability. My being at a particular place at a particular time may, in fact, have been very improbable, but if I am there, in fact, there is no way of finding out how improbable it was. The test, therefore, of both truth and freedom in this sense is the amount of disappointment in the long run. If I am constantly disappointed, it is clear that there is something wrong with my image of the world; what I think is truth must in fact be error, and in consequence my actual forecasts are constantly falsified by this ignorance.

Freedom in the first sense of power is, of course, highly dependent upon knowledge of the truth. That knowledge is power is no mere copybook platitude, but perhaps the first law of social dynamics. The technology which so enormously increases our freedom in the physical sense is a direct and obvious result of increased knowledge of the nature of matter, energy, and space. One may hope also that in human relations and social systems an increase in knowledge will lead to a social, political, and economic technology which will preserve us from some of the disasters of the past.

In regard to economic freedom, the major problem here is the relation of the prevailing image of the economic system, especially among important decision-makers, to its actual development. It is perfectly possible, of course, to do the right thing for the wrong reasons, and in economics this is not treason at all but just sheer good luck. Our own agricultural policy, for instance, which was based on what seems to me to have been a wholly mistaken view of the nature of economic justice and of the effects of altering the price system, in fact has turned out to be a powerful stimulus to technological development, not only in agriculture, but in the whole economy. It is quite likely that if we had known better we would have done worse. Ignorance is bliss, however, only in the short run and in stochastic processes. In the long run, ignorance can hurt us and only knowledge can save us. What Engels meant, I think, by the "leap from necessity into freedom" was that when man achieves an understanding of the dynamics of his own society, he can then develop an image of the future for that society as a whole into which it has the power to progress. Man is no longer then the object of blind social or natural forces which he cannot control, and he can move forward into a future of his own making. This is a noble idea and should not be rejected out of hand. In our day, indeed, it is accepted by all—except, perhaps, by the most unreconstructed obscurantists. It is one thing, however, to say that we *can* know the truth and quite another thing to know it. The difficulty here is that it is the convincing image which is powerful, and the convincing is not always true. A good many people have come along, among them even Marx and Hitler, and have claimed that *their* service was perfect freedom. Man has never lacked for false prophets. Furthermore, in the absence of a process of cumulative social learning it is very hard to learn to tell the false prophets from the true. Merely because it is difficult, however, the problem cannot be pushed aside. In a great many of these matters we cannot simply suspend judgment; we must act upon *some* view of the universe. The hope here, as I have suggested, lies in a careful, cumulative process of long-run information collection, processing, and dissemination which can do for social learning what the scientific method has done for our knowledge of the physical universe. This goal may seem a long way off, but there are signs that we are moving toward it.

The economic aspect of this third dimension of freedom relates, of course, to the growth of economic knowledge itself. This is seen, for instance, in relation to two of the major economic problems of our day, economic development and economic fluctuations. That extraordinary process of economic development which began to accelerate with such force in the eighteenth century, in the full tide of which we find ourselves today, was certainly not initiated by any conscious plan or any clear knowledge of the dynamics of economic systems. Its origins lie deep in latent and unconscious processes which can, perhaps, be understood in retrospect but which certainly were not and could not be understood at the time. Who would have guessed, for instance, that the turnip and the potato would have engendered so great a revolution? The failure of economic development in many parts of the world, however, indicates that it is not a necessary process and that the West may simply have been lucky. We are now, therefore, desperately trying to understand the nature of this process in order that we may prescribe what needs to be done in those parts of the world that, to judge by results, have not yet done it. The full understanding of the process may not therefore be necessary to "lucky" economic development but may be necessary to make it certain and independent of luck.

Economic fluctuations represent an area where, in the Western world at least, an increase in economic knowledge has had a profound effect on the dynamics of the system. It would have been almost inconceivable, for instance, for Herbert Hoover to have proposed a substantial tax cut as a remedy for his depression. To do so requires not only a sophisticated economic theory—it requires an information-processing apparatus in the shape of econometric models and national income statistics which we simply did not possess thirty years ago. One of the critical problems at the moment, indeed, is that the image of the economy which is possessed by virtually all professional economists extends only a little way beyond their ranks; many of the people and perhaps even a majority of congressmen are operating with an image of the economic system which is so far removed from reality that we are in grave danger of being enslaved to our own ignorance and of failing to make our system operate successfully because those who have to make the important decisions do not possess the truth about it. On the other hand, we have to recognize that it is easy for economists to be wrong; that the truth about an economic system is very hard to obtain, especially in a system as complex as ours; and that there must be room for knowing when we don't know as well as when we do.

Beyond these matters of what might be called economic technology, there are more fundamental questions of the critique of values or objectives themselves, which not even the economists can escape, even though they frequently like to disclaim responsibility in this area. We do not have to go all the way toward believing in objective values and natural law to see that a critique of ends may be necessary even for quite positivistic social dynamics. Nazi Germany was fairly successful in solving the problem of depression and might even have done fairly well with economic development, but it used its freedom for such outrageous ends that it was destroyed. We cannot escape the fact, therefore, that there are ends which can destroy us, and it is important to identify them. If we use wealth for futile idleness, for meaningless luxury, for corrupt gratifications, and for the expression of hatred and prejudice, then the richer we are the sooner we will be damned. Besides the knowledge of means, therefore, there must be a very real knowledge of ends, and if we do not have true ends we will be enslaved by false ones. In this sense, too, the truth makes us free; but in this sense also it is hard to come by.

By way almost of an epilogue, it may be of interest to test the theory of the dimensions of freedom which I have outlined above in terms of the current ideological struggle between the Communists and the "free world," to see if we can throw any light on where the argument really lies and on what the conflict is about. This exercise is all the more important because both ideologies claim to be champions of human freedom, and the differences between them, important as they are, are at times surprisingly subtle. The image which the Communist has of himself is that of a liberator of mankind from age-old error and poverty, even if in that process man must be temporarily subordinated to a dictatorship. In the mind of the West, these promises are false and have been disproved by painful experience, and ideologically, therefore, the West envisages itself as the defender of political freedom, individual rights to privacy and non-conformity, and economic development which is mainly private and based on these virtues. The struggle is deeply felt and represents, in many cases, honest differences on both sides. Evangelical fervor, however, can easily turn into xenophobic fury when it is frustrated, and in a world of nuclear weapons this presents a constant and present danger. Where great and noble words like "freedom" and "democracy" are used in different senses by both sides, there is danger of misunderstanding and, worse, mounting mutual frustration which can end only in violence. It may be something more than a mere intellectual exercise, therefore, to apply the concept of freedom as I have analyzed it to this outstanding problem of our day.

I have equated the first dimension of freedom with power, and economic freedom in this sense is wealth. It is now becoming apparent that economic development from poverty to wealth is not a property either of socialism or of capitalism as such, but of a process of cumulative social learning of the kind which increases the productivity of labor. This cumulative process of social learning depends more than anything else on the proportion of resources which are devoted to it and on the efficiency of their use. It has become clear in recent years that it is not the mere accumulation of physical capital which brings about economic development, but a restructuring of the form of that capital in ways which represent greater and greater quantities of information. The learning process in society as a whole in all its institutions, not only those of formal education, is therefore crucial to the whole movement. In this regard the argument between socialism and capitalism is largely irrelevant. If we think of capitalist societies as guided mainly by the market and the price system, and socialist societies as guided mainly by the budget and the economic plan, we see that while both the market and the budget are, under certain circumstances, agents of the social learning process, neither of them by itself is sufficient. Market-oriented societies are old enough so that we have a number of examples of unsuccessful market development as well as of successful market development, and the difference here, one suspects, lies largely in the nature of the non-market institutions. Totalitarian socialism is so young that we have not yet had time to experience any clear examples of socialist failure, mainly because existing socialist countries have encouraged the educational process on which economic development rests. I suspect, however, that we shall find cases of unsuccessful socialist development, perhaps even in China, and we shall see that from this point of view the argument between socialism and capitalism is in large part irrelevant. The United States certainly would never have been a success if it had not been for the large non-market element in its social system. On the other hand it seems pretty clear that the prejudice against the market in socialist countries is a real handicap to them, and that those socialist countries which can most successfully overcome it, such as Poland and Yugoslavia, are the most likely to make rapid development.

Freedom in its second dimension is measured by the rule of law, the development of legitimacy, and the successful resolution of conflicts. In this sense democratic capitalism gets very good marks and totalitarian socialism very bad marks, though totalitarian market societies, too many of which are included in the so-called free world, fare pretty badly too. Political liberty and the absence of spiritual monopoly are very precious aspects of freedom, and ones in which the socialist countries do poorly. It is a bad sign when one of the principal exports of a society is refugees. This is a sign of gross domestic failure to provide personal liberty, the rule of law, and successful conflict resolution. The socialist societies of East Germany and Cuba are particularly to be indicted on these counts. It is the great virtue of a market-oriented society that it lends itself to the rule of law, that it operates more successfully under conditions of political liberty and impartial justice, and that discrimination and the denial of civil rights are a severe economic handicap—as the southern states have found to their cost. In market-oriented societies, furthermore, there is likely to be a wide diffusion of economic power. Up to now at any rate, we have discovered no administrative devices which can solve this problem in a socialist state, where all the economic activity in the society is concentrated in a single firm, which is the state; where the concentration of economic power in the matter of decision-making reaches its height; and where mistakes on the part of a few powerful individuals can cause universal suffering. In the absence of a true labor market, the almost inevitable limitations on the right of the individual to change jobs can easily be a more fundamental limitation on individual freedom than the deprivation of political liberty. When we add to this the denial of the right of the individual to start enterprises of his own, or to hire labor, or to create organizations outside the monopoly of the one-firm state, simply because of a theology of surplus value, we can see the socialist state as imposing limitations on individual freedom in which the boundary is of very low quality, often arbitrary and essentially meaningless.

On the other hand, we must not underestimate the ability of the socialist state to acquire legitimacy in the minds of its citizens. With the exception of East Germany and Czechoslovakia, there is no widespread alienation or denial of legitimacy in the socialist camp, even among those, like the Christians, who are discriminated against. It seems to take an enormous amount of discrimination to create alienation, as the experience of the Negro in the United States, the Christian in the socialist states, the outcastes of India, and the eta of Japan seems to indicate. Legitimation, however, is a variable that is very hard to evaluate. The Tsar of Russia seemed unshakably legitimate in 1914, in spite of widespread dissent. The Emperor's legitimacy in Japan survived an even more shattering defeat and occupation.

In the third dimension of freedom, in which freedom is equated with "truth" or a correct view of the world, there is obviously plenty of room for controversy. One can concede this much to Marxism: that the idea of social self-consciousness, that is, the idea that society as well as an individual can have a realistic image of its own future into which it can progress, is an idea of far-reaching importance for the whole future of mankind. In a sense, like a great many things in Marxism, it goes back to Adam Smith, whose *Wealth of Nations* is largely a study of the "progress of society" and how to get it. To say that a society *can* have such an image, however, is not necessarily to give it a true one. The Marxist image, in particular, is a case so special that for most societies it is grotesquely untrue. It involves an absurdly oversimplified notion of class structure, a fallacious view of the dynamics of the distribution of income, and a quite insufficient appreciation of the ability of capitalist society to develop itself along evolutionary lines while still retaining its essentially market-oriented character. The fact that Marx's own predictions have been largely falsified is well known. Communism has come, not in the countries of advanced capitalism, but in countries of very early capitalism which have a strong feudal and "folk" residue. Its success, insofar as it has been successful, has not been the result of appeal to class conflict, which has been almost universally disastrous, but in its ability to keep real wages low or even declining; to exploit the present generation ruthlessly, presumably for the benefit of the future; and its determination to devote large resources to education and investment in people. Communist development, however, has been achieved at a high social cost not only in terms of class war, refugees, the extermination of whole groups in society, and social disorganization but also in terms of the atrophy of much artistic and intellectual life, in the development of a harsh, barren, provincial puritanism, full of false values and heavy sentimentality, without even the grace notes of religion. The Communist's image of the world is quite reminiscent of that of the Prohibitionist, with its oversimplified and unduly moralistic approach to complex social problems. It is, of course, changing, and mostly for the better. One hopes for the rise of a liberal generation, as a result of so much investment in higher education, who will revolt against sterile austerities and moralistic platitudes. In the present generation, however, the oversimplified and distorted view of the social system which the decision-makers in these societies possess has involved them in severe social costs and grave errors.

By contrast, capitalist society frequently has no general public image of the future at all. The strength of a market economy lies often in the fact that there is, indeed, a "hidden hand," and that, as Adam Smith remarked, the market itself exhibits a tendency toward health which even the greatest absurdities of governmental doctoring cannot quite overthrow. On the other hand, capitalist society is also subject to certain diseases which the mere operation of the market mechanism itself cannot cure. It does not necessarily distribute income or even the fruits of progress in such a way as to prevent the alienation of large numbers of its people, as we saw in Cuba. Without any governmental stabilization, the market mechanism is subject to essentially meaningless fluctuations which can cause unnecessary loss and distress. It is not clear also that the market-oriented society will necessarily devote enough of its resources to social overhead and the investment in human capital to guarantee a sufficiently rapid rate of development. For all these reasons, knowledge of society itself is needed. Right-wing capitalists frequently have an image of society which is as grotesquely unrealistic as that of the Marxists and which can have equally disastrous consequences. There are, indeed, striking similarities between the right and the left. They are both impatient and moralistic, eager for short cuts, and unwilling to take the long, hard road that leads to truth. The conservative whose image of his own society is untrue, no matter how much he loves it, will not be able to conserve it, just as the revolutionary whose image is untrue will not be able to reform it. In both socialist and capitalist societies, therefore, deeper understanding is the key to freedom in the third sense. Freedom, if I may be pardoned for parodying Holy Writ, is power, law, and understanding; and the greatest of these is understanding.

In all these various dimensions then, is there any way in which it makes sense to say that there can be a "policy" about freedom? For some people the very idea of a policy for freedom may seem contradictory, for to them freedom means the absence of policy. It will be clear from the above that I do not hold this view and that though some freedom grows wild in the great jungle of social species, it flourishes best when it is intelligently tended. In each of the three dimensions which I have outlined above, therefore, I would argue that a policy for freedom is possible. It is possible to have an image of the future in the furtherance of which present decisions are made, and in that future, freedom in any or all of its senses may grow. Policy in this sense is not a monopoly of government, for decisions of private persons also may be taken in the light of an image of a future of increasing freedom. Government also, however, may be a servant of freedom as well as its enemy, and one of the great objects of political development is precisely to learn how political institutions may be devised and used in the service of freedom. But if political power and, still more, military power are often illusory and self-defeating, and if the law which is imposed from above often seems to destroy more freedom than it creates, the reasons must surely lie in our deficiencies of understanding. It is only as we come to understand the social system and the long-run dynamics of power that we can learn to use even coercion in the service of freedom, once that coercion is legitimatized and constrained. This once again points to the dimension of understanding as the greatest of the three, and the one without which the others will be in vain.

THE ECONOMIST AND THE ENGINEER:
ECONOMIC DYNAMICS OF
WATER RESOURCE DEVELOPMENT

Economics and Public Policy in Water Resource Development,
Stephen C. Smith and Emery N. Castle, eds., Ames, Iowa:
Iowa State Univ. Press, 1964, pp. 82-92.

The Economist
And the Engineer:
Economic Dynamics of
Water Resource Development

I T CAN BE STATED almost as a political axiom that water resources are developed by engineers. Economists usually have very
little to do or to say about it and perhaps in all decency they should
keep silent. However, the engineer in general is not apt to be aware of
the contributions the economist can make to this problem. It is perhaps
these contributions which are the main justification of this chapter.

I may say I have no wish to be derogatory to engineers — indeed,
some of my best friends are engineers. If I am going to live below a
dam I would much rather have it built by an engineer than by an economist. Nevertheless, the economist comes into the picture perhaps by
asking the awkward question as to whether the dam should have been
built in the first place.

DIFFERING ATTITUDES

We can sum up the distinction between the economist's point of view
and the engineer's by saying that, on the whole, the engineer is project
oriented whereas the economist is system-oriented. In other words,
the business of the engineer is concrete while the business of the

economist is abstract. The engineer is concerned with particular projects in particular places; the economist is concerned with the impact not only of actual projects but of potential projects upon all of society. It is this difference perhaps which makes criticism by the economist so distasteful to the engineer. The economist is always concerned with "might-have-been", the engineer is always concerned with "what will be"; the engineer is concerned with plans, the economist with unrealized alternatives. Hence, on the whole, the engineer is talking about "what is" or "what shortly will be" — the economist is always talking about "what is not" — giving the economist a certain disadvantage in the argument. A big dam is a very solid argument compared with all the things that might have been done if the dam had not been built, yet it is precisely with these invisible alternatives that the economist is primarily concerned.

Project Versus Value

One is tempted to say also that the engineer thinks mainly in physical terms whereas the economist is interested primarily in values. This is an overstatement, for many engineers and certainly all good engineers are deeply concerned about the valuation of their projects and do, in fact, evaluate these projects in highly economic language. Nevertheless, the heart and soul of the engineer is in the project rather than in the impalpable value which may attach to it. It is all the more difficult for the engineer to think in terms of values, because the value is something which is not inherent in the construction itself, but consists of alternative uses of resources. Value again is in the shadowy realm of the might-have-beens.

There is a third and still more subtle distinction between the mode of thinking of the economist and the engineer: the engineer tends to regard his activity as a kind of "war against nature"; the economist, on the other hand, thinks of nature as a factor of production to be treated gently in a cooperative manner. It may, of course, be a mere accident that the care of our rivers and particularly of our floods has been given to the army engineers. Again perhaps this is no accident. Perhaps there is something very deep in our culture which regards the conquest of nature somewhat in the same sense as the conquest of an enemy. I shall suggest later that this seems to me a profoundly mistaken attitude and one that can only lead to ultimate failure and frustration.

Price System: A Variable or a Constant?

Perhaps the greatest difference between the economist and the engineer lies in their respective attitudes towards the price system, interpreting this in a broad sense. The engineer on the whole takes the price system for granted and tends to regard prices as cost. The economist, by contrast, regards the price system as essentially a variable and is always interested in the question as to what would happen if prices were different from what they are now. The engineer tends to regard the price system as a mere obstacle to the attainment of his engineering ideals — he would like to build wonderful dams, beautiful aqueducts and magnificent roads. But the nasty economist and accountant and financier stand behind him reprovingly, always preventing him for reasons which seem to have nothing to do with engineering.

Perhaps the classic expression of his attitude comes not from engineering at all but from a misguided economist, Thorstein Veblen, in his book *The Engineers and the Price System* (publisher B. W. Huebsch, New York, 1921). Veblen clearly regards the price system as simply a nuisance in the way of ever-expanding miracles of engineering. If only we could dispose of it, giving the engineers complete leeway, the world would soon be transformed into something like an engineer's paradise.

A special case of this difference in attitude toward the price system may be seen in the difference in attitude toward the rate of interest. For the engineer the rate of interest often is seen as an arbitrary obstacle to the attainment of his cherished projects. He tries to justify the building of a dam, shall we say, where the benefits are a long way in the future, and he finds that if they are discounted at a high rate of interest the project is clearly not financially feasible, whereas if they are discounted at a low rate of interest, the project is clearly justified. If I may quote one of my own verses:

> Around the mysteries of finance
> We must perform a ritual dance
> Because the long-term interest rate
> Determines any project's fate:
> At two percent the case is clear,
> At three, some sneaking doubts appear,
> At four, it draws its final breath
> While five percent is certain death.

It is hard to blame the engineer if he feels often that the rate of interest is merely an arbitrary obstacle to the attainment of his plans. For most economists (although I must confess there are exceptions to this) the rate of interest is a reflection of some basic conditions in the economy. If the high rate of interest is not merely the result of the country's political instability or mismanagement by the monetary authorities, this is an indication that in the society there is a certain unwillingness to sacrifice present enjoyments for future benefits. This means that projects from which the benefits are to be found a long way into the future will have to fight harder for their lives or will have to promise larger net benefits than those which will be realized in the near future. It must be confessed that the problem of the socially optimal rate of interest is one which economists have not solved, and until they have solved it they can hardly blame the engineer for a certain restiveness under the restriction imposed by high interest rates which seem to be arbitrary.

THE ECONOMIST AND THE ENGINEER

Engineer a "Politician"

Another distinction between the economist and the engineer — which perhaps does more credit to the engineer than to the economist — is that the engineer is by nature more of a politician. This is particularly true of the water engineer and the highway engineer. Funds for projects frequently come from public treasuries, and if he is to see his projects carried through, he must be sensitive to sources of political power and the strange forces which bring about political decisions. The economist, on the other hand, is inclined to stand aloof from society and to make judgments in terms of the abstract standpoint of social welfare, in which each man counts as one and one only. The engineer in a sense is more realistic. He knows that a small benefit which is ' clearly obvious and which goes to a politically powerful group is of much more weight politically than a larger benefit which is not visible and which is diffused over a large and politically inactive and impotent section of society. Consequently, it is hard to blame the engineer for keeping his ear to the political ground, and for designing his projects to appeal to those decision makers in whose hands the fate of the project ultimately lies.

Nevertheless, there is a certain virtue in the economist's point of view because he seeks a standard by which the actual performance of a society may roughly be judged and from which significant deviations may be properly denounced. It has always been a cherished function of the economist to point out that benefits to the few are obtained at the cost of much larger injuries to the many. This is what sometimes we call the "welfare criterion" of judgment upon political decisions. Even though it may be unrealistic in a narrow sense, the very fact that these judgments are made affects somehow the grounds upon which political decisions are taken. It is the business of the economist to see that special interests have a bad conscience.

I am inclined to think that engineers and economists unite somewhat against the accountant and the financier when it comes to assessing nonreimbursable benefits of various projects. In defense of this project the engineer is likely to bring together as many nonreimbursable benefits as he can. The economist, however, is quick to point out that financial returns alone are not sufficient justification for any human endeavor and that financial returns must be modified by many imponderable factors — not only those described as "human factors" but also what the economist calls "external economies and diseconomies." By this we mean the impact which expansion of a particular operation or industry in society will have upon other sectors of society which cannot, however, be financially chargeable to the operation which induces them. Engineers have not been slow to pick up this conception, particularly where it seemed to favor the expansion of their projects. They have naturally been slower to seize on those external diseconomies which likewise may follow from the expansion of particular industries or occupations.

WATER RESOURCE DEVELOPMENT

PUBLIC VERSUS PRIVATE DEVELOPMENT

Let me now descend from the high altitude of generality and come down to the problem of water resources. One of the first things that strikes the economist as he looks at the water industry is the extraordinary extent to which water is not treated as a commodity. Again perhaps I may be forgiven if I quote my own verse:

> Water is far from a simple commodity,
> Water's a sociological oddity,
> Water's a pasture for science to forage in.
> Water's a mark of our dubious origin,
> Water's a link with a distant futurity,
> Water's a symbol of ritual purity,
> Water is politics, water's religion,
> Water is just about anyone's pigeon.
> Water is frightening, water's endearing,
> Water's a lot more than mere engineering.
> Water is tragical, water is comical,
> Water is far from the Pure Economical.
> So studies of water, though free from aridity,
> Are apt to produce a good deal of turbidity.

Of all the easily recognizable physical commodities, water seems the one we are least willing to leave in private hands, and even in the least socialized countries there is a strong tendency to socialize the "water industry." It is a useful exercise in nonpolitical economy to ask ourselves what would happen if in fact the state did nothing about water and if the provision of this estimable commodity were left entirely in private hands. It is clear that water would in general be supplied to people who wanted it and who are prepared to pay for it. There would be problems requiring political solution in the field of eminent domain, the transmission of pipelines and so on; but these presumably would be no more difficult than we face in the transmission of private gas or oil lines or electric power lines.

But when we ask this question it is by no means clear why water is so sharply differentiated politically from oil, gas and electricity and why the private water supply has become the exception. I suspect we may have to find the answer to this somewhere outside economics, perhaps even in the deeply symbolic nature of water in our society and in our almost neurotic fear of being without it. One even gets a feeling abroad that if the state or municipality did not supply water, nobody would! This clearly is absurd. Indeed, I think it can be argued quite seriously — although I do not have enough evidence to be sure that the argument is correct — that we would have been better off if the state had never intervened in the supply of water, or even if the municipality in general did not feel itself obliged to take on this enterprise but instead had provided legal framework for the use of private enterprise.

THE ECONOMIST AND THE ENGINEER

Irrigation

In the case of irrigation, the case is much clearer. In the early days of irrigation, private enterprise did most of the work. It is only as irrigation has moved, as it were, into the public and political domain, that it has become an enterprise so firmly concerned with government and the struggle for appropriations. It can be argued cogently that the first 10 million acres of irrigation in the West made so much sense that private enterprise would have done it and, for the most part, did do it. The second 10 million acres perhaps can be justified as a public enterprise in terms of external economies and the advantages derived from the building up of denser population. The third 10 million acres is of much more dubious value, and the fourth 10 million acres, on which we now seem to be embarking, is of very dubious value indeed and can only be explained in terms of the momentum of a large political organization designed to do a certain thing.

I am not, however, fanatical on the subject of private enterprise, and I have no prejudice against public enterprise, particularly in this kind of industry where there are substantial advantages in monopoly. I have no particular desire to turn municipal waterworks back to private companies, although I confess to having a certain itch to ask embarrassing questions about the Bureau of Reclamation.

It may well be that a lot of the difficulties in this field arise from the failure of people to recognize that under most circumstances water is a commodity and not a free good. We are so accustomed to thinking of rain as a free good that we confuse rain with water. Rain is no more water than grass is milk, and water supplied to a particular person in a particular place is just as much a commodity as oil. There seems no reason to suppose why, in the first place, it should not be supplied in the cheapest possible way and, in the second place, once it has been supplied it should not pay its full cost. Furthermore, the situation is often confused because of the failure to realize that water is not one but many commodities. Water supplied to the urban bathtub is not the same commodity as water supplied to the field, the factory or the recreational area.

ECONOMIC ISSUES IN WATER DEVELOPMENT

Let me now approach still closer to earth and ask what the main economic issues in water development are. I would argue that the first issue is the apparently simple one of *how much*. If we think of the water industry as an industry, we question if it is overexpanded or underexpanded. Are we putting too much into this particular occupation of resources or too little? My guess would be (and this may not be a very well-informed guess) that in urban water supplies on the whole we are doing about right; that in regard to irrigation we are doing far too much in the dry areas, and probably not enough in the moist ones; and in regard to flood control we are creating disasters for ourselves in the future and are living in a fool's paradise.

In the case of urban water supplies we have a commodity with a fairly elastic supply in most cases. Where adequate local government exists, not much of a problem tends to arise. There are some places, perhaps in the arid areas, where too little investment is going on. There are almost certainly other places, such as Los Angeles, where too much has gone on and is still going on. Los Angeles is going to run out of air long before it is going to run out of water. This is almost a classic example of economic presbyopia — farsightedness in the optical sense of the term. In Los Angeles water is not a commodity but a religion. There is a strong tendency for religions to expand their use of resources beyond the strict needs of their practitioners.

Flood Control

I have already suggested the possibility that the development of irrigation has gone far beyond the point of proper social returns and that social return to investment in a great deal of irrigation is now negative, especially in view of bounding agricultural surpluses. The real scandal, however, is flood control. Professor Gilbert White of the University of Chicago has suggested that after spending four billion dollars on flood control we are more in danger of flood damage, and indeed disaster, than we were before. This is largely because we have regarded flood control as a problem in engineering rather than in sociology. I suggested earlier that we invite trouble if we regard nature merely as an enemy to be conquered rather than as a friendly home. It may be perhaps accidental that army engineers have been responsible for flood control. The truth is that what we call "flood control" means the eradication of little disasters every 10 years or so at the cost of a really big disaster every 50 or 100 years in any given floodplain. No flood-control program is able to protect a floodplain against the 100-year flood. After all, that is why the floodplain is there!

When, however, we build dams and levees, we give people the illusion that the problem has been conquered whereas, in fact, it has merely changed from a benign to a very dangerous form. The danger of flood damage increases despite flood control because people have confidence in the works themselves, which leads them to build out over the floodplain. It is because flood control is *not* linked in any sense with social policy nor especially with the growth of urban areas that the more flood control we have the more damage we are likely to have from floods.

It is particularly striking to visit a city such as Sacramento in California, where the old houses have long stone stairs leading up to the first floors, where the ground floor is devoted merely to storage and life begins at 15 feet. In the old days when there was a flood the family went upstairs and waited till the flood went down. Now with dams and levees constructed, everybody builds low ranch-type houses on the floodplain. It may be next year or it may not be for 100 years or for 200 years, but one of these days the really big flood is going to come, the levees are going to break and the dead will be counted in tens of thousands, and the water will be several feet over the rooftops of most of the new housing developments. The same story could be repeated in floodplain cities all over the country.

It seems to me that we need an entirely new philosophy for flood control which may involve treating the river not as an enemy to be conquered but as a rather dangerous friend with whom one has to learn to live. It is perfectly possible to design cities on the floodplain to *accommodate* floods instead of taking on the impossible task of trying to prevent them. There is no reason, for instance, why we should not build our floodplain cities on stilts; there is much to be said for this architecturally and from the whole point of view of city design. It would provide parking spaces under the buildings and would enable a separation of levels of traffic.

Development and the Distribution of National Wealth

The other question an economist asks besides "how much," is "to whom." What is the impact of our resource development on the distribution of wealth and income? This is a difficult question to which we do not know the answer. Nevertheless, there are some fairly clear pitfalls which we may avoid. There has been a tendency, for instance, to justify a subsidy to irrigation on the grounds that this redistributes income away from the rich taxpayer towards the poor farmer. The fallacy of this proposition is the general fallacy of trying to do justice to a commodity or an industry rather than to individuals. It is true that some farmers are poor but some are rich; so when we subsidize *water* as such, we aid the rich more than we aid the poor because the rich use more. It is true that the Bureau of Reclamation has tried to avoid this dilemma by imposing a 160-acre limitation on subsidized water. In California, however, and I am sure in many other parts of the country, there are a good many ways of getting around this. I would be surprised if a careful study did not reveal that the impact of the subsidy is more favorable to the larger farmer than it is to the smaller. Even if we want to redistribute income from the rich to the poor, this is one of the worst ways in which to do it, for it encourages people to stay in an occupation that they should leave. It contributes to agricultural surpluses and to the general maldistribution of resources.

Price Structure of Water Industry

This brings us to the large and difficult question of the water industry's price structure and of the positive or negative subsidies which may be implied in it. It is surprisingly difficult to define what we really mean by a subsidy, particularly where we have a commodity which is only one of many joint products. This is usually the case with water.

There is always an arbitrary element in the allocation of fixed costs among a number of joint products, and under these circumstances it is often hard to say when a given price for a given use involves a subsidy or a tax. We must evaluate this whole question from the viewpoint of a sound philosophy of the whole price structure and particularly from a clear view of the functions of the price structure.

One of the great difficulties in price policy is that there are at least three functions of the price structure which may not be compatible one with another, and a good deal of the pulling and hauling in economic policy arises because we are trying to make the one institution of the price system perform three incompatible tasks.

Allocate resources. The first of these three tasks is the allocation of resources to different industries so that the structure, i.e., the relative proportions, of different commodity outputs is such that each output can be distributed without difficulty. The function of the price structure here is to prevent shortages and surpluses in the sense of unwanted accumulations or decumulations of storable commodities or in the sense of unsatisfied buyers or sellers of nonstorable commodities.

Distributor of income. The second function of the relative price system is that of the distributor of income. Given the distribution of property, the distribution of income is largely a function of the relative price system. If we raise the price of wheat, the income of wheat farmers will be raised at the expense of wheat consumers. If we make the price of water very low, as a result those who use a lot of water will be better off and those who use a little will be worse off than they otherwise would be. It is one of the great dilemmas of economic policy that the attempt to rectify what are regarded as socially undesirable distributions of income through use of the price system almost inevitably involves the misallocation of resources or the development of shortages and surpluses. Water is no exception to this. If we "subsidize" water — that is if we lower its price in some sense below the Marshallian normal — this means that from the standpoint of ideal resource allocation too much has been devoted to water and not enough to other things. Water will be produced in quantities too large and will be used wastefully.

Direct technical change. The third function of the price system is seldom mentioned in the textbooks, but in the long run it may be perhaps the most important. This is the function of directing the course of technical change and of the larger dynamics of the economy. Inexpensive products are not economized, and attention is not drawn towards their economization. On the other hand, the course of technical change always tends to work toward eliminating the costly and dear. This is a principle of great importance in the development of water resources. If we have a commodity which is fairly plentiful today, but which is likely to be much scarcer in the future with expanding population and perhaps increasingly costly sources of supply, the slogan of the water resource man should be "water should be dear and plentiful." It should be dear because only if it is dear will people bother to economize; only if it is dear will technical change move in the direction of water-saving improvements.

I came across a striking example of this in California. In the Los Angeles area where even agricultural water is quite expensive, there is a regular profession of water savers, men who teach farmers how to use as little water as possible in order to irrigate their fields. In the Central Valley where water costs little, thanks to the taxpayer and the public enterprise of the Bureau of Reclamation, no such occupation exists. The farmers use water as wastefully as they like and it is hard to blame them, for there is no incentive to economize and particularly no incentive to develop water-saving improvements.

The same principle applies to industrial water. In the steel mills in Fontana in the desert the water is used again and again. In the Great Lakes area it is used wastefully and quite rightly so. But if any substantial water-saving technology is to emerge from the steel industry, we would expect it from Fontana and not from Cleveland. There is therefore a strong social case for making water expensive in the hope that this will persuade technical change to go in the direction of water-saving improvements.

The easiest way to make water dear is to tax it. Water is an excellent commodity for tax. It has a fairly inelastic demand, so the yields of taxation should be high. The rich use a lot more than the poor, so the tax should not be unduly regressive. Moreover, when the overhead of the economy at the state level is nowhere being met on an adequate scale and where the balance between the public and the private sector, as Galbraith has suggested, is deficient on the public side, an almost unobjectionable object of taxation such as water should not be overlooked, especially as a source of state and local revenue.

It is not impossible that we are on the edge of large changes in water-saving technology. One of the crucial questions in the economic dynamics of the water industry is how such changes may both be foreseen and encouraged. It is possible, for instance, that one by-product of the enormous amount of resources in space research may be the development of the totally self-sufficient household in which water, along with other necessities of life, is continually processed through a closed circuit of human intake and output and purification. The results of sea water purification research have been disappointing to date, and it may be that the energy requirements are too great to make it cheap enough to get fresh water from the sea, even though the freshening of brackish water seems to have great possibilities. Nevertheless, we have scarcely begun to ask the right questions about the *use* of sea water. It does, after all, support a great deal of life and metabolism, and the payoff here may come through the biological approach and through developing better ways to take salt water directly into the human bio-economy. As far as the immense resource of the sea is concerned, we are still in the food collection stage and have not even domesticated any plants or animals, if we except the humble oyster. A marine equivalent of agriculture might make a lot of land irrigation unnecessary!

Another line of technical development which may have a great impact on water resource development is the cheapening of sea transport of liquids (or even granular solids) through the use of floating plastic bags. Rather than getting its water from the Feather River through immense and costly aqueducts, Los Angeles might well import it from Alaska by sea. Engineers, like the rest of us, like to do what they have been trained to do. In economic dynamics, however, it is frequently through doing what nobody has been trained to do that brings about the critical "entrepreneurial" breakthrough into a new technology.

It may well be that in the future it will be the skills of the biologist, the meteorologist (in weather control) and the mariner which will dominate the development of water resources rather than those of the hydraulic engineer. What is pretty certain, however, is that the skills of the economist will not have much impact and that the economist will continue to be a voice crying in the wilderness. If he cries loudly and long enough, however, somebody may listen to him out of sheer irritation. To that irritation this chapter is intended to be a small contribution.

RESEARCH AND DEVELOPMENT
FOR THE EMERGENT NATIONS

Ohio State University Conference on Economics of Research and Development, Richard Tybout, ed., Columbus, Ohio: Ohio State Univ. Press, 1965, pp. 422-37.

RESEARCH AND DEVELOPMENT
FOR THE EMERGENT NATIONS

TO AVOID ANY POSSIBLE MISUNDERSTANDING, it should be made clear that the following paper does not purport to describe what is going on in research and development in the emergent nations, for the very good reason that the author does not know. It is rather an attempt to state the nature of the problem which is involved in the development of these countries and to try to identify the role which should be played in the process by research and development.

Economic development is a polite name for a revolutionary change in the state of mankind. This has been said many times before, but it can hardly be reiterated enough. In particular it must be stressed that we do *not* mean by economic development mere "growth" in the sense of an increase in population of the same kind of people producing more of the same kind of things. Economic development means different kinds of people producing different kinds of things from their ancestors and ancestral goods. I elsewhere call this the "second great transition" in the state of man, the first transition being, of course, the change from precivilized to civilized societies which followed upon the domestication of crops and animals and the concentration, by fair means or foul, of the resulting food surplus to feed the emerging cities. The transition through which we are now passing is at least as large and spectacular as that first transition which began some eight or ten thousand years ago—so much so that I have described the new state of man toward which we are moving as "post-civilization."

This great transition from civilized society of the classical type to post-civilized society has many facets: economic, political, social, psychological, philosophical, educational, and religious. It is indeed a change which affects every area of human life and reaches far down into the human personality. Nevertheless its base is an economic change, and it is not surprising that most of the discussion of the transition take place under the heading of economic development. The essence of both of the great transitions consists in a rise of the productivity of human labor and particularly an increase in the product per man-hour. The transition from precivilized to civilized societies depended essentially on the development of agriculture, which increased the productivity of human labor in food production to the point at which the food producer could produce a surplus of food beyond his family needs for subsistence. It was this surplus that fed the artisans, the craftsmen, the builders, the priests, the philosophers, and the soldiers who built the classical civilizations. The second great transition represents an increase in the productivity of labor even more spectacular than the first. In classical civilization that is represented, say, by ancient Rome in the time of Augustus, or by Indonesia today, it takes 75 to 80 per cent of the population to produce the food that feeds the total. In the United States today, we can produce all the food we need with 10 per cent of the population, and pretty soon it will be 5 per cent, and we still have burdensome agricultural surpluses. Not only in agriculture, but in all fields of manufacturing, the increase in the output per man-hour has likewise been spectacular. With the advent of automation, we may find that we can produce all the manufactured goods we need with 10 or 15 per cent of the population as opposed to the 30 per cent which we require today. A day is within sight in the United States when we will be able to spare some 80 per cent of the population for the tertiary industries, and we will have indeed a leisure society. Europe is following rapidly behind the United States in this development and may, indeed, at the present rate of progress, overtake the United States in another generation or two. Japan is enjoying a similar development, and so is the Soviet Union, for the great transition pays no attention to the cold war. It can be argued that socialist development, while it may be more rapid at first, has a lower ultimate ceiling than development in what might be called cybernetic capitalism. What is more important, however, is that the socialist countries, at least in the temperate zone, are participating successfully in this movement toward post-civilization; and, as a result, in spite of the great ideological gulf, the difference in technology and general modes of life between, say, the United States and the Soviet Union is much less than between either of these two countries and their neighbors to the south, which are still in the age of civilization.

I

The quantitative aspect of economic development can be expressed in a very simple formula. Let us suppose first that for any particular country we can divide the labor force into two parts: L_d, which is the number of people employed in domestic industry, and L_e, which is the number of people employed in export industries. If then P_d is the productivity of labor in domestic industries and P_e is the productivity of labor in export industries, and T is the terms of trade, that is, the quantity of imports received per unit of exports, the total real product of the society, Y, is given by the equation

$$Y = L_d P_d + L_e P_e T .$$

If y is the per capita income, this is given by the second equation:

$$y = \frac{L_d P_d + L_e P_e T}{L_d + L_e + L_n}$$

where L_n is the number of people not employed, that is, not in the labor force, so that the denominator of the second equation represents the total population.

What we mean by economic development is a long, persistent increase in per capita income, y, which carries it to ten or even twenty times its "civilized" level, and which may even carry it beyond this. Per capita income in the United

States today, at about $2,000, is about twenty times the per capita income of $100 which is characteristic of "classical" civilized societies; and a per capita income of $5,000 is by no means inconceivable. We now look at the second equation to see what element in the equation can result in such a steady increase in y. The answer is obvious from a mere inspection of the equation: it will have to be an increase in P_d or in P_e or in both. This does not rule out the possibility of short-run movements within the society which can increase per capita income without changes in the over-all productivity of labor. Thus, if $P_eT > P_d$, that is, if the productivity in terms of domestic products or imports is greater in the export industries than it is in the domestic industries, we can increase per capita income for a time, at any rate, by shifting the labor force from domestic industry into export industry. This is a process, however, which eventually comes to an end simply because, as it goes on, P_d is likely to rise and P_eT is likely to fall, either because of declining productivity or worsening terms of trade. Similarly, for a period a country may enjoy an increase in per capita income because its terms of trade are improving, that is, T is increasing. This also, however, is a process which cannot go on forever and which is quite likely to be reversed after a time, and it cannot be relied on to produce that long and persistent increase in per capita income, y, which is the essence of economic development.

There is no escape from the conclusion, therefore, that it is only by a large and persistent increase in the productivity of labor in both the domestic and the export industries that economic development in the sense in which we have been using the term can be achieved.

The next question is obvious: what are the factors in the structure of the society which lead to a long, persistent increase in the productivity of labor? I have said hardly anything so far which is not either in or just below the surface of Adam Smith's *Wealth of Nations*, and Adam Smith has some sage words to say on the causes of increasing productivity likewise:

This great increase in the quantity of work which, in consequence of the division of labour, the same number of people are capable of performing, is owing to three different circumstances; first, to the increase of dexterity in every particular workman; secondly, to the saving of the time which is commonly lost in passing from one species of work to another; and lastly, to the invention of a great number of machines which facilitate and abridge labour, and enable one man to do the work of many.[1]

It is important to observe that all three of the causes which Adam Smith mentioned are aspects of the learning process in man. By dexterity, we mean essentially the diminution in the time of performing any particular act which results from constant repetition. This involves a learning process mainly in the lower nervous system, and it has, of course, a fairly well-defined upper limit which is generally reached fairly early in the life of the specialized laborer. A man with a machete acquires, for instance, a skill in the cutting of sugar cane which is far beyond the capability of the amateur, but he usually acquires his maximum skill in his teens. His productivity does not rise thereafter, and indeed declines in later life.

Adam Smith's second cause, the time lost in going from one task to another, is seldom mentioned nowadays. Nevertheless, it also represents an interesting application of the learning problem. When we take up a task newly, even though we may have done it many times before, a certain process of relearning has to go on before we hit our stride. This process is economized if we can devote a substantial period of time to the same task. The professor who must go from teaching to research to conferences and back to teaching again, and who longs for a solid slab of time in which he can do any one thing, may testify to the acuity of Adam Smith's observation. Nevertheless, this also is a learning process the horizon of which is reached very quickly. If we try to concentrate the task too much, we fall into monotony, which may even impair dexterity; and in a good many assembly-line processes it has been found advantageous to

---

[1] Adam Smith, *Wealth of Nations* (London, 1926), p. 7.

vary the task when it has become too monotonous and too concentrated.

Adam Smith mentions only incidentally in connection with his second cause the problem of intensity of application to a task. He observes that when the task is changed frequently, "a man commonly saunters a little in turning his hand from one sort of employment to another." Sauntering is certainly a major problem in a good many emergent nations, and it is a habit of life which the tropical sun, especially, makes extremely agreeable. The psychological origins of the orientation of the person toward achievement rather than toward sauntering through life is a problem of great subtlety and complexity. As David McClelland has pointed out, the division of labor is merely part of this problem, for even though the division of labor itself, by making tasks simple and well-defined, may help to encourage the achievement motive, the division of labor is by no means a sufficient explanation of the differences we find in different societies. This problem extends to cover the Weberian thesis regarding the relation of the Protestant ethic to the origin of capitalism and indirectly to the achievement motive, and also raises very interesting questions regarding the various substitutes for the Protestant ethic which have been found in other cultures. Even the elimination of sauntering, however, and the development of a society of eager beavers is a learning process that likewise has a limited horizon from the point of view of economic development. Hard work might increase the product two or three times in a society dedicated to the delicate social arts of laziness, but it is inconceivable that hard work alone should increase the product by twenty times.

It is when we come to Adam Smith's third cause, therefore, that we find the key to continued development with high horizons. Adam Smith observes that even the division of labor itself is likely to promote invention, and he quotes the delightful and possibly apocryphal story of the boy who tied the string on the handle of the valve to another part of the machine. He goes on, however—and the temptation to quote from him is irresistible—

All the improvements of machinery, however, have by no means been inventions of those who had occasion to use the machines. Many improvements have been made by the ingenuity of the makers of the machines, when to make them became the business of a peculiar trade; and some by that of those who are called philosophers or men of speculation, whose trade it is not to do anything, but to observe everything; and who, upon that account, are often capable of combining together the powers of the most distant and dissimilar objects. In the progress of society, philosophy or speculation becomes, like every other employment, the principal or sole trade and occupation of a particular class of citizens.[2]

Now we feel that old Adam has put his finger on the heart of the matter. It is as we develop a specialized class of people engaged in research and development and, one would like to add, education, that we find at last a learning process whose horizon seems to be almost unlimited, and the rate of economic development toward these broad horizons would seem to be determined mainly by the proportion of specialized resources which the society is prepared to devote to this end, modified, of course, by the efficiency with which these resources are used. Adam Smith goes on to observe, incidentally, that the division of labor even within the sciences themselves enhances the productivity of this activity. "Each individual becomes more expert in his own peculiar branch, more work is done upon the whole, and the quantity of science is considerably increased by it."[3]

It is interesting that in these early chapters Adam Smith hardly mentions the accumulation of capital as a force in increasing the wealth of nations. He does so later on, in Book II: "As the accumulation of stock must, in the nature of things, be previous to the division of labour, so labour can be more and more subdivided in proportion only as stock is previously more and more accumulated."[4] It is clear, however, that he does not regard capital accumulation as the most essential element in economic development, but rather as a

2 *Ibid.*, pp. 9–10.
3 *Ibid.*, p. 10.
4 *Ibid.*, pp. 241–42.

prerequisite and a co-operator with that process of division of labor and human learning by which productivity is mainly increased. In this he shows a sound instinct. The statistical studies by Moses Abramovitch of the growth of the United States economy, for instance, show convincingly that the mere increase of capital makes a relatively small contribution to economic development, and that the increase in productivity on which economic development rests is mainly the result of changes in the structure and form of capital and in the structure of human skills and knowledge rather than mere accumulation as such. Economic development is not the mere piling up of old things; it is the making of new things which were not made before in ways that were not done before. The learning process is therefore absolutely crucial to it. It is a process which has its parallel in nature in the structuring of living bodies by the genetic material, and the teaching-learning relationship is central to it. We can indeed think of material capital as frozen knowledge, for it would never come into existence were there not images of it in the minds of men; and the more complex these images, the more complex and productive are the material capital structures which these images produce. The mere piling up of stocks of wheat, for instance, is not in itself economic development. It is only as these stocks are used to feed people who think, plan, design, and construct new material forms of capital that these stocks become part of the living, ongoing, developing fabric of society.

This structural process, then, which is the foundation of continued economic development, has three aspects: research, education, and development. Research is the acquisition of knowledge which nobody knew before. Education is the dissemination of this knowledge among the population. It is hard to measure the amount of knowledge in any particular head, but the notion of the per capita amount of knowledge in a society is at least qualitatively admissible. Without education, of course, research does very little to increase the per capita knowledge of a society, as it remains in the head of the original discoverer. Education includes not only formal education in schools; it also includes the innumerable agencies and activity by which the knowledge of any person may be increased. It includes, for instance, the press and the mass media; it includes gossip and personal conversation; it includes personal observation; it includes much of what goes on in the family and in face-to-face groups; and we must regard formal education essentially as a part of this larger process. It is a part, however, which has a peculiar responsibility, which is that of supplementing and frequently correcting the informal learning processes. We can roughly distinguish two types of cultures: the one, folk culture in which the learning process in the society, the transmission of the culture from one generation to another, is accomplished largely through face-to-face groups—the family, grandmothers, and other informal institutions. At the other extreme, we have scientific culture which is transmitted mainly through formal means and through formal educational institutions. Interesting problems arise where there are contradictions and tensions between these two educational processes, and a good deal of the social and political upheaval in emerging societies can be attributed to the tension between these two competing cultures.

Development, in the narrow sense in which it is contrasted with research and education, is not, perhaps, very different from education. There are, however, processes which are distinct enough to deserve a particular name. These are the processes by which new knowledge is translated into patterns of human behavior and into human artifacts of new kinds, such as new machinery and equipment. This might be thought of as the engineering function as distinct from the function of pure science, and it is in a sense a mixture of research and education. For new knowledge to be effective, it must be implanted in a good many more heads than those of its originators, but pure theoretical knowledge must also give rise to knowledge of a practical kind. There must be know-how as well as know-what. Know-how is as much a matter of the development of organization and of teaching patterns as it is the development of new material structures.

II

I have contended that if we have enough of research, education, and development (R, E, and D), we do not need to be either Red or dead. The evidence that we have, such as, for instance, the studies of Zvi Grilches on the rate of return on investment in research in hybrid corn, and the various studies which have been made of the rate of return of investments in education, suggest that the general rate of return on R, E, and D is substantially above the rate of return of investment in material capital. When this is so in any country, we can state with a great deal of confidence that a mere quantitative increase in the absolute amount of resources devoted to R, E, and D will increase the rate of economic development, even if diverted from low-return material investment. There is a certain tendency for countries which have been influenced by European culture to regard research, education, and development as if they were frills or social services—that is, things which are nice to do for people if you can afford it. There is hardly any point of view which is so potentially disastrous. R, E, and D must be thought of as investment with a high rate of return, and it must be given top priority in any society that is ambitious for development.

The mere quantity of resources devoted to R, E, and D, however, is not necessarily an indication of the effectiveness of those resources. One of the most urgent needs of our time is research into R, E, and D itself, that is, into the social rates of return that attend different kinds of research, education, and development. If we look upon the whole developmental process as a learning process, it is obvious that some processes and some institutions teach people faster and better than others. It is obvious also that there are some things which it is more important to learn than others. A research effort which is devoted mainly to increasing man's destructive power or his capacity to get to the moon will probably have less impact on the rate of growth of human welfare than research which is more directly pointed at that end. Similarly, education which is devoted to memorizing the classics and holy books is not likely to be so useful in economic development as education in science and engineering. Likewise, in many areas development can be sadly misapplied, and there is no country in the world in which the boondoggle is unknown.

I have been arguing that when we look at the world effort in R, E, and D, we find a very profound misapplication of intellectual resources. The most acute problems of the world lie in the area of social systems. This is even true of problems of water supply and health, which we often think of as belonging exclusively to physical or to biological systems. The problem of war and peace is very clearly a problem in social systems. Yet we persist in devoting the major part of our intellectual resources, by far, to research, education, and development in physical and biological systems, with the result that the very existence of man is threatened by his incapacity at handling the social system. Peace research, for instance, which easily could have rates of return in terms of sheer disaster insurance reckoned at thousands or tens of thousands of a per cent, is almost totally neglected; and we see much the same pattern of neglect of social systems in the treatment of water resources, flood control, irrigation, agriculture, urban development, transportation, recreation, and social security.

Next to the neglect of peace research, the neglect of an adequate R, E, and D program in economic development is the most striking. Perhaps one of the most spectacular benefits from disarmament would be the release of the intellectual resources which are now tied up in plotting man's destruction or in furthering his vanity and idle curiosity in space exploration for use in solving the intractable problems of the emergent nations. With the amount of intellectual resources we presently devote to this problem, I think it is extremely likely that economic development in most of the tropical belt will be unsuccessful. We have in the making, indeed, a major human tragedy on a scale unknown to all previous history. We all know that the impact of civilization on precivilized societies has been almost without exception disastrous. In one or two cases borrowings from the more advanced societies gave the precivilized societies new resources and new vitality, such as, for instance, the introduction of the horse among the Plains Indians. In the long run, however, the impact of civilized on precivilized societies has been like that of an iron pot on a clay pot. The precivilized societies have been shattered, and they exist either in a decadent state or their members are absorbed, often unhappily, in the form of minority groups and second-class citizens, into the civilized societies which have overcome them. What we may be facing in the world of today is an even more frightful tragedy: that impact of post-civilized societies on the civilized societies. It is easy to spread some of the techniques of post-civilization to the civilized societies, for instance, movies and DDT. These innovations, however, may easily create a dynamic to which the society cannot adapt. Movies, radio, and other modern forms of communication destroy the traditional image of the world and create the "revolution of rising expectations." DDT, by controlling the mosquito, produces a dramatic diminution of mortality and creates a 3 per cent annum population increase which in itself can easily frustrate the expectations which communications have aroused. The combination of aroused expectations and the inability to fulfil these expectations may be totally disastrous, and the civilized societies of the tropical belt may easily lapse into violence, anomie, anarchy, or even apathy. This is a gloomy view which one hopes history will falsify. Whether it comes true or not, however, depends in no small measure on the amount of intellectual resources which we devote to solving the problem on a world scale. The terrible fact today is that we are devoting so little to this problem that the chance of failure is very high. It needs, I suspect, a degree of intensity and an absolute amount of R, E, and D at least equivalent to what the space programs of the two great powers now involve. Yet nothing like this seems to be forthcoming from any direction.

We need, for instance, a massive research program on the methods of population control which are appropriate to particular cultures. The fact that two countries as culturally diverse as Ireland and Japan have both had a reasonable success in population control indicates that this is something which can be adapted to widely differing cultural milieux. In some parts of the world, such as the West Indies or Ceylon, India, and China, this problem is of desperate urgency. Unchecked growth of population at present rates even for a few years may create a situation so difficult that these countries will start to go downhill. Haiti is a terrible object lesson of what can happen to a small country where independence has meant quarantine by the world, internal anarchy and anomie, unrestricted population expansion, soil erosion, and cultural erosion to the point where per capita incomes are now not much above $50 per annum.

Another large program which needs to be pushed beyond the present pioneer stage is that of the development of machinery and equipment which is appropriate to the early stages of technological advance. It is not easy to jump immediately from digging sticks to tractors. Western technology frequently cannot be imported as it stands into the emerging nations simply because the existing material and human structure of society is not ready to receive it. In the development of society, as in the development of the phenotype from the egg, there are certain stages which may have to be gone through, and there is some sense in which phylogeny recapitulates ontogeny. This is not to say that the poor countries must go through a stage of Satanic mills and cumbersome steam engines before they can emerge into the sunlight of the electronic age. It does mean, however, that for any given society there is a next step, and it is frequently quite difficult to perceive what this next step should be. It may be a long-handled hoe; it may be an atomic reactor. At this point we often have to reckon with national pride, which sometimes puts the symbols of development, such as steel mills and reactors, in front of the realities, which may be primary schools and a better breed of mule. India has experimented, apparently without too great success, with small solar furnaces, but it may be that the development of many of these countries waits on the development of a small but cheap source of small amounts of power. The problem is not completely neglected, but compared with what needs to be done the gap is a shocking one.

Another problem which cries out for attention is the study of the locus of political power in emergent nations and the problem of how to get power into the hands of those who will use it best. Development of any kind grinds to a halt when those who have the power do not have the will and those who have the will do not have the power. In the West the system of banking and finance provided an important answer to this question, for this enabled the enterprising and ambitious to attract resources away from the rentier, the aristocrat, and the defender of the status quo. In other countries bloody revolution and social disorder have tried to achieve the same end, sometimes with success, sometimes not. This is a problem which we must face and which we are not facing—which, indeed, we are not even studying adequately.

Let me conclude, therefore, by pleading for a massive intellectual effort, of at least the magnitude which we are devoting to space exploration, devoted to solving the intellectual and organizational problems which surround this great transition to the developed world society. An effort of this kind would involve the co-operation of all disciplines and all countries. On the physical and technological side, the problems of permanent high-level technology are still unsolved. Man's existing high-level technology cannot last for more than a few hundred years because it depends on the use of fossil fuels and ores which he is rapidly using up. A permanent high-level technology, however, is conceivable, based on the sea and the atmosphere as ultimate resources, and either on the sun or on nuclear fusion as the source of energy. The Haber process for the extraction of nitrogen from the air and the Dow process for extracting magnesium from the sea are signs of things to come, but we must not deceive ourselves: we are still a long way from the kinds of scientific knowledge and engineering applications which will enable us to operate a truly self-sustaining earth spaceship without using up our long accumulated geological capital. It is probable that the biological sciences will make an important or perhaps the crucial contribution to the solution of this problem, for life itself is the major antientropic process and is the one which operates with the greatest efficiency. The solution of the problem of the utilization of solar energy for high-level societies may well lie in the development of artificial low forms of life which utilize this energy more efficiently than existing forms.

Another section of the program should be devoted to the study of population and population control. This clearly calls for a giant effort on the part of biological, medical, and social scientist, for we still know very little about the human biology of fertility and sterility, and we know still less about the all-important motivational problems which are at the heart of population control. Furthermore, we do not know even to an order of magnitude what is the population which a stable high-level technology would support on earth. It might be as small as a hundred million or as large as a hundred billion. This is an area of ignorance which it should be possible to clear up in a very few years if a concentrated effort were made, and a great deal of subsequent human history is going to depend on the answer to this question. If stable high-level technology can support only a hundred million people, then the earth is in for a grotesque agony before its utopian state can be achieved. If earth can support ten billion at high levels, we have a little time to make this transition reasonably painlessly.

The third major area of research and development should be that in the dynamics of social systems. The problem of peace research and the control of organized violence falls in this section; likewise the problem of disarmament and the release of the $120 billion now wasted on the world war industry for use in the great transition. Also in this section lies the question of political power and organization and the political development of societies toward institutions which permit the orderly transfer of power from those who use it less well to those who use it better. Political development is a concept less clear than that of economic development, but it is equally important and the two clearly go hand in hand. In the economic development of a country which is politically immature, there can be disasters both for the country and for the world, as the history of Germany so dramatically shows.

Finally, I would like to see a fourth department of this great enterprise devoted to man's cultural, spiritual, and religious development. This is the most delicate and difficult of all the problems involved; it is entangled in man's deepest emotions, and the very notion of an intellectual effort devoted to this problem is repugnant to many sensitive persons. Nevertheless, there is no point in making man rich if he does not know what to do with his riches. The great transition represents an enormous increase in the power of man, but power in itself is neutral; it can be used either for good or for evil. There is in the human personality an enormous potential both for good and for evil, and the increased power which the new technology will bring man may release either the potential for good in him or the potential for evil. It can lead him toward divinity or drive him to destruction. Even though power itself, therefore, may be morally neutral, an increase in power is not, because it causes us to raise the question of the will, that is, of the ends toward which power is to be used. As long as man is impotent, it does not matter so much what his ultimate ends are as he cannot get them anyway. If these ends are evil, however, the increase of power is undesirable. It enables man to damn himself all the faster. Any intellectual effort devoted to the great transition, therefore, must raise the question of the nature of man himself and of how his nature may be changed and how the good will in him may be encouraged and the evil will discouraged. These are the great questions with which philosophy and religion have struggled for many thousands of years They do not become obsolete merely because we can put men into space.

It is an awesome thing to have been born in the twentieth century. This is perhaps the most critical century in the whole history of the planet. Never before has man's future and indeed the future of the whole planet rested in man's own hands. This is a terrible responsibility from which we may well shrink; it is a responsibility, however, from which we cannot escape. I believe that man has the capacity to rise to this challenge, and in that fact lies our hope.

THE CHANGING FRAMEWORK
OF AMERICAN CAPITALISM

Challenge, 14, 2 (Nov., 1965): 39-42.

The Changing Framework of
American Capitalism

AMERICAN CAPITALISM stands at an unprecedented peak, both of power and of wealth. It is often precisely at the moment of greatest success, however, that societies have made fatal mistakes and have collapsed. One can indeed reverse the familiar aphorism and say that nothing fails like success, simply because success inhibits learning. If we are successful, we don't have to learn anything; we have it made already. Success, however, may be due to accidental causes, or it may be due to circumstances which change; and under these circumstances what we learn from success may quite unfit us for the task of perpetuating it.

I do not necessarily want to sound a note of doom. Indeed, I happen to think that American capitalism is in pretty good shape, and is showing remarkable vigor. It is disturbing, however, that as a people we seem to be so unaware of the importance of the *legitimacy* of our system. If we fall into the trap of relying on the wealth and the threat capability which we have achieved, without paying attention to the framework of legitimacy in which it is used, we may be in for a very rude awakening. The most obvious threat to the legitimacy of American economic institutions is the challenge of Marxism and international communism, and all those questions which revolve around the Cold War. The Cold War itself is a struggle of competing

► This is the first in a series of articles examining the changing character and institutions of the unique form of capitalism that has evolved in the United States. In the January issue Neil Chamberlain, Professor of Economics at Yale University, will discuss the changing nature of the American corporation.

legitimacies. Marx challenged the legitimacy of the whole institution of private profit and private enterprise by appeal to a macroeconomic form of the labor theory of value, which asserted that as labor produced all the product, any nonlabor income was fundamentally illegitimate.

Around this beautifully simple principle has grown a tortuous maze of ideological argument on both sides. It is a doctrine which has a strong appeal in more primitive societies, where the landlord obviously reaps what he does not sow and where the rich do seem to be living off the backs of the poor. It is a doctrine which has little appeal in successful and developed capitalist societies, where it looks as if the only alternative to private enterprise and private profit is government enterprise, and experiences with government enterprise are not such as to inspire confidence in it.

I HAVE a doctrine, indeed, which I would like to sell to the Marxists and which I call the Doctrine of the Missed Bus. This is the doctrine that the bus for socialism comes along at a certain point in the evolution of a society, when it has had some development, has a small bourgeoisie, a large working class, a self-conscious Socialist or Commu-

nist party, and some sort of revolutionary upheaval. If at this moment the society gets on the Socialist bus, it is hard to get off it again; if, however, the bus goes by and the society continues a successful process of capitalist development, the bus never comes by again, and socialism becomes increasingly irrelevant. This, one would certainly argue, is the case with the developed capitalist societies today.

Nevertheless, there is an implied threat to the legitimacy of these societies in the very existence of the Socialist countries which not only seem to have had a modest success in economic development, but seem to be able to produce governments which have at least fairly widespread popular support and which even seem to be moving in the direction of greater political and civil liberties. One could almost identify the right wing in the United States as those people who suspect in their hearts that the Communists are right and who think, therefore, they can only be opposed by suppression, coercion and violence.

Those of us who really think the Communists are wrong, and that centrally planned economies are fundamentally a pretty poor way of organizing economic life, are actually likely to be much more tolerant of communism in practice, simply because we do not believe that it will survive indefinitely in competition with free societies and free ideas.

Fortunately, the more confused the Cold War becomes, the less dangerous it is, and the less anybody's legitimacy is really threatened. If, for instance, we were to measure the success of different systems in terms, say, of the rate of economic development and the extent to which the benefits of development are widely diffused, it is not difficult to end up with four major categories.

At the top we have the successful market economies, with Japan in the lead, Western Europe not far behind, and with Britain, Canada, the United States, Australia and New Zealand just managing to stay in the league, at least on the basis of the last 20 years. Then a few notches below this level we have what we might call the successful Socialist countries, with Yugoslavia at the top and many of the Eastern European countries not too far behind, the Soviet Union somewhat in the lower middle range and China probably at the bottom, especially on the basis of the last five or six years.

Then in the third category we have what might be called the unsuccessful market economies, which comprise many of the successor states of the old European empires. Latin America is perhaps the best, or the worst, example of the failure of development under predominantly market institutions, perhaps because of the lack of an adequate political framework and the absence of the right kind of educational system.

At the bottom of the list we have what might be called the unsuccessful Socialist countries, Indonesia, Burma, Ceylon (with India doubt-

to draw a legitimacy from their successful confreres which their standards of living do not warrant.

One of the problems that faces us in assessing results in complex social systems is what might be called the "package principle" in social evolution. A lot of things survive and are apparently successful, not because they contribute much to the success of the whole system, but because they come in a package with the things that do so contribute. Hence, everything in the package gets credit for what should be credited only to a few items in it. The economic success of the more successful Socialist countries is a good case in point. It is almost certainly due to the fact that these societies have put a great deal into education and the development of human resources, and that this part of the package is mainly responsible for what success in development they have had.

The rate of development depends on two things: (1) how much a society puts into development, and (2) the efficiency with which this resource is applied. On the whole, in Socialist societies there is a good deal of evidence that the resource is not applied very efficiently, but the fact that these societies put such a large proportion of their resources into development is enough to account for their relative success. Sim-

achieve a successful mix of public and private, and also a successful mix of economic institutions with other institutions. It is perhaps no accident that market economies have been most successful in those societies which lay a great deal of stress on such nonmarket virtues as private generosity and the fulfillment by private persons of obligations to the public. Thus both Japan and the Western countries have been deeply influenced by philosophical, religious and ethical systems which have laid great stress on the social obligation of private persons.

In the united states we can distinguish two broad processes by which we have sought to legitimate private profit and enterprise. One is through the doctrine of the invisible hand—that is, that under conditions of perfect or at least of workable competition, the quest for private profit produces public good. This doctrine had led to the antitrust laws, to various kinds of antimonopoly legislation, and also to regulation of monopolies.

The other line of legitimation is through what might be called public oversight of private enterprises, first by the incorporation laws, through which the privilege of incorporation is clearly granted by government and implies certain responsibilities of oversight on the part of government. Stemming in a way from this is a whole network of legislation which sets up instruments of government oversight, such as the Securities and Exchange Commission, the Federal Trade Commission, the Interstate Commerce Commission, and so on. At the far end of this spectrum we have actual government operation and ownership, as in the case of some public utilities, and especially the lone case of the Tennessee Valley Authority. Actually, even these government enterprises are supposed to assist in the legitimation of the private enterprises which surround them, and which perhaps compete with them, through the provision of a "yardstick."

In addition to these more formal methods of legitimation, a number of institutions which started out as challenges to the legitimacy of the existing order have actually turned

ful, but probably rising out of this class), which somehow manage to deny themselves both the virtues of the "invisible hand" and the virtues of a well-constructed and implemented central plan.

The Cold War has tended to lump together the first and the third of these categories, and the second and the fourth, while it ascribes legitimacy to whatever side one happens to be on. Because of this symbolic and ideological link, both the unsuccessful market economies and the unsuccessful Socialist economies tend

ilarly, in the unsuccessful market societies the lack of success may not be due so much to reliance on the market rather than on central planning, but on the fact that these societies do not allocate sufficient resources in, for instance, public education, in the general public underpinning of the private economy and in general investment.

One may even venture on a still more dangerous thought, that the success of the successful market societies may also have been due in considerable part to their ability to out to be agents of legitimizing it. The labor movement is perhaps the best example of this. In its early days, certainly the labor movement, or at least substantial segments of it, visualized itself as a challenge to the existing order. In the extreme form of the Industrial Workers of the World, it rejected the existing order altogether.

The failure of radical unionism, however, and the success of business unionism, which by now is virtually universal in the labor movement, clearly indicate that the main impact of unionism on American society, and to perhaps a smaller extent on Western European society, has been to remedy certain institutional, emotional and integrative defects of capitalism, and has therefore established its legitimacy all the more securely.

This has gone so far in the United States, indeed, that the labor movement is a major internal supporter of the Cold War and of the hard line, partly, perhaps, because of its bitter internal experiences with communism in the Thirties, but also because it has identified itself so completely with capitalism as an institution. The spectacle of the destruction of a free labor movement in the Communist countries and its replacement with a rather nauseating type of company unionism has undoubtedly reinforced the role of the labor movement as a legitimator of private enterprise and even private property.

The cooperative movement likewise, which in its origin certainly was conceived as a challenge to the legitimacy of the stockholder-owned corporation, or even the private entrepreneur, has likewise become a powerful agency for the legitimation of capitalism. Partly this has happened because the cooperative form of organization of business does not get away from the fact that business is business—that is, merely because an enterprise is organized under the cooperative form does not exempt it from the laws of survival in the market economy. Hence the difference between the cooperative form and the stockholder form of organization gets almost swallowed up in the similarity which all businesses have to each other.

There may be a rather curious by-product here, also, in the case of the consumers' cooperative movement of the United States, which, especially in the 1930s, introduced considerable numbers of intellectuals to the difficulties and dangers of business and made them, perhaps in the long run, more supportive and understanding

of the problems and difficulties of all kinds of businesses. Thus the cooperative, which started off as a challenge to the conventional form of business, may actually have increased the legitimacy even of its competitors, the chain stores and the supermarkets. The cooperative movement at least introduced a lot of intellectuals to the fact that a profit system is also a loss system and that one cannot indulge in business enterprise without risk-bearing.

The rise of other forms of nonprofit organization, which is certainly noticeable even if not spectacular (it has risen from about 3.7 per cent of the gross national product in 1929 to 5.1 per cent in 1963), is perhaps more an indication of the shift in the structure of the economy into things like medical services, which are traditionally in the nonprofit sector, rather than a sign of any fundamental change in our attitudes toward the legitimacy of profit.

It may be, indeed, that the labor movement and the cooperative movement between them have done more to establish the legitimacy of private enterprise than the whole body of antimonopoly legislation. Neither the labor movement nor the cooperative movement, as a matter of fact, has ever subscribed very wholeheartedly to the principle of legitimation through perfect competition. The labor movement is not at all averse to monopoly if it can get its hands on some of the spoils; and the cooperative form of organization, especial-

ly in agriculture, has likewise been used to achieve a monopoly power and even monopoly profits.

One is almost tempted, indeed, to regard the whole antitrust movement in the United States as an essentially ritualistic enterprise inspired by the official ideology of the society, much as in the Socialist countries there has to be a good deal of ritualistic invocation of Marxism and Leninism before anything very sensible can be done or said. This, however, is probably being unfair. In spite of the fact that antitrust legislation has never achieved any coherence and that it often gives one the impression of a knight in shining armor mounting his white horse and riding off in all directions at once, nevertheless I am inclined to believe it has had a salutary effect, even by the very uncertainties which it has produced. The famous remark (whose author unfortunately I have forgotten) that the ghost of Senator Sherman sits at the table of every American board of directors has a sharp edge of truth to it, and at least the antitrust acts provide a challenge to American business, to which it frequently makes at least a startled and sometimes a creative response.

Nevertheless, I must confess that I am left with a deep uneasiness. Part of this arises out of the sheer size of the larger corporations. There are only about 11 or 12 countries with a GNP larger than that of General Motors. This represents an aggregate of private economic power and of rather unified control, which is, to put it mildly, large. Unquestionably one of the best defenses of the legitimacy of a free market society is that it permits a great diffusion of economic power and prevents this power from being concentrated in a few hands. If, however, what is good for General Motors is good for the country, what is good for General Motors also seems to be good for socialism; for General Motors is a larger economic organization than many Socialist states.

Carrying the question of size even further, the United States Department of Defense is the second largest Socialist institution in the world, lying between the Soviet Union on the one hand and the People's Republic of China on the other, again in terms of GNP. The comparison is certainly not wholly fair, but it still has a barb. It may be, indeed, that the whole business of the legitimacy of size is something with which we shall have to wrestle in the next period of man's history. I confess to having strong prejudices in favor of small scale myself, but I might be proved wrong in this. However, we have to face the fact that the case for General Motors is distressingly similar to the case for communism.

It MAY BE instructive at this point to take a brief glance at the American economy from the point of view of the changes in its structure, which may or may not be due to changes in our concepts of legitimacy. Some of these central changes, of course, are the result of almost purely technological forces. The decline in the proportion of the labor force in agriculture, for instance, is primarily a result of the relative technological success of that segment of the economy. The rise in the proportion of the economy devoted to government, however, whether measured by the proportion of the labor force or the proportion of GNP, is perhaps the most striking structural change in the last 25 or 30 years, and this has a great deal to do with our conceptions of what is legitimate, more, perhaps, in the political than in the economic realm.

The military segment of the economy, for instance, has risen from a little over one per cent in 1929 to almost 10 per cent today. This is a result partly of our changed perception of the threat postulated by the rest of the world, but also in considerable measure to a change in the national image itself, as we have come to visualize ourselves as the dominant power in the world, inheriting the role of the British in the international system. Consequently, a military budget which would have been regarded as wholly illegitimate in the 1920s and 1930s is accepted almost without question today, in spite of the fact that it seriously cripples our future economic growth.

The problem of the legitimation of the profit institution and profit-making organizations underlies a good deal of American history. The marble columns of banks, the dome of the Capitol, the splendor of churches and the glossy house organ of the corporation are all indications of resources devoted to the production of legitimacy. Sometimes, however, the very resources devoted to the production of legitimacy in fact produce negative results. The ostentatious vulgarity of the nouveau riche, the preposterously ineffective propaganda of business, or for that matter even of the Communists, provide examples of expenditure of resources on the production of legitimacy which had quite the opposite result.

The case of resources devoted to increase the legitimacy of the business institution or the corporation is a peculiarly delicate one. By its very nature the corporation is a

donkey or workhorse rather than a charger or racehorse. Any attempt to make it sublime, therefore, only succeeds in making it ridiculous, and the lofty immediately becomes the top-lofty. I am inclined to think that the public relations propaganda of General Motors may have a negative effect for this very reason. It may be, therefore, that we should look to the organizational symbol rather than to the verbal symbol, or at least the verbal symbol alone, for the solution of this problem.

The great organizational symbol, of course, is representation, and this is a very powerful source of legitimation. The state has been forced to employ this as it has moved from absolute monarchy toward representative government, and as *L'État, c'est moi* is replaced by *L'État, c'est nous*. Similarly, business may find it advantageous to legitimize itself through representation, even though this representation may, in fact, be largely symbolic and may not much affect the real sources of power. Certainly the representation of trade unions on boards of directors, as we have seen especially in Germany, has had much more effect upon legitimacy than upon power. If representatives of government were to sit on the boards of the large corporations, still more if representatives of the United Nations were to sit on the boards of the international corporations, their legitimacy would be substantially enhanced and their operations would probably not be much interfered with.

Often the greatest obstacle to the preservation of legitimacy is the attempt to cling to it in a monopolistic sort of way. Legitimacy shared is often legitimacy enhanced. There have been many occasions in history when the preservation of legitimacy has depended on the abandonment of coercive power or even of unregulated wealth. The movement from absolute to constitutional monarchy, from empire into commonwealth or community, and even from the priestly and sovereign to the monastic and serviceable aspects of religious or even other institutions, are all examples of this kind of process. Whether the great corporation will likewise have to follow this pattern is perhaps one of the big questions of the next 100 years. ∎

WAR AS AN INVESTMENT: THE STRANGE CASE OF JAPAN

(with Alan Gleason)
Peace Research Society (*International*), *Papers,* Walter Isard
and J. Walpert, eds., Philadelphia, 1965, pp. 1-17.

WAR AS AN INVESTMENT: THE STRANGE CASE OF JAPAN

The history of Japan in the last hundred years is perhaps one of the best case studies in the impact of war and military institutions on the whole life of the nation. The main object of this paper is to pursue certain aspects of this history from the standpoint of economics. This means that we look on the war industry as a segment of the economy, just as agriculture might be a segment. The war industry is defined here as that segment of the economy which produces what is purchased with the total military expenditure of the government. We inquire about the effects of the war industry on other segments of the economy as it rises and falls, and we ask ourselves why it is as big as it is at any one time. The answers to these questions, of course, go far beyond economics. Nevertheless, there may be economic elements in the answers.

What might be called the crude statistical story is shown in Table 1 and in Figures 1 and 2. We have expressed the data in real per capita terms, eliminating the gross effects of the growth of population and inflation and deflation. The story can be summarized very simply. From the 1880's to the 1930's, real per capita product in Japan grew at a rate of about 2.4% per annum, and with minor fluctuations, grew rather steadily. Consumption kept pace throughout most of the period. Military purchases in real terms were rather low, averaging about 5% of GNP. In the 1930's we see a change. Real per capita consumption declines, even though per capita gross product continues to increase. From 1937 on, military purchases increase remarkably. This process culminates in what the Japanese call dramatically "the valley," which reached bottom in the great disaster of 1945. All the gains of the previous decades were wiped out. The cities were in ruins, the Empire taken away, the merchant marine destroyed, all foreign investments confiscated, three million Japanese had been sent home from overseas; and from this point on the rate of growth is about 8% per annum, which constitutes a world record! We have here what seems like an unusual episode in political mental ill health and recovery. The full study of this, of course, would require all the resources of the social sciences, and here we are concerned as economists with what is actually a fairly minor aspect. It is an aspect, however, which throws a great deal of light on the whole process, partly because economic development and change is a great trend around which many other aspects of social life revolve, and also because in this case there seems to have been a great difference between the *image* of the economic situation as it determined the behavior of the major

* The authors are associated, respectively, with the Economics Department, University of Michigan and the International Christian University, Tokyo. The paper is an interim report arising out of a research project sponsored by Research on the International Economics of Disarmament and Arms Control, directed by Professor Emile Benoit, Columbia University.

TABLE 1*   Real Gross National Product and Components Per
Capita for Japan, 1887–1960
(1934–36 Prices in Yen)

	(1) GNP	(2) PCE	(3) PDI	(4) GP				(5) NFI
				GPnmi	GPnmc	GPmp	Total	
1887	71.7	57.6	6.5	1.4	4.9	2.4	8.6	−1.1
88	73.5	60.9	5.0	1.3	4.9	2.3	8.6	−1.1
89	69.2	55.9	6.2	1.6	4.3	2.3	8.2	−1.0
1890	83.8	68.5	10.4	1.7	4.9	1.8	8.4	−3.5
91	76.7	55.8	12.5	2.4	4.2	2.2	8.8	−0.4
92	78.8	60.0	11.1	1.7	4.9	2.1	8.7	−1.0
93	81.1	62.1	12.5	2.6	3.9	2.1	8.6	−2.1
94	97.7	76.8	6.4	1.9	4.2	10.1	16.1	−1.5
95	92.4	74.2	5.8	1.5	4.3	8.4	14.2	−1.8
96	87.3	74.0	6.9	2.5	4.4	4.5	11.4	−5.0
97	88.0	70.5	9.1	3.0	4.1	6.1	13.2	−4.8
98	113.2	98.7	9.8	2.7	4.7	5.9	13.3	−8.5
99	102.0	84.1	5.3	3.2	6.1	6.4	15.7	−3.1
1900	105.2	82.0	11.5	3.5	6.0	6.6	16.1	−4.3
01	109.1	86.4	7.7	3.8	7.0	5.3	16.1	−1.1
02	93.8	76.1	6.4	3.7	6.9	4.1	14.7	−3.5
03	104.7	86.0	7.4	3.7	6.7	6.4	16.8	−5.5
04	105.6	70.9	10.0	2.4	5.1	25.4	32.8	−8.1
05	95.3	70.6	8.1	2.9	4.4	24.5	31.8	−15.2
06	104.1	79.4	10.2	2.9	5.8	13.7	22.3	−7.9
07	110.6	91.9	8.4	4.4	6.2	7.4	18.0	−7.8
08	117.9	95.8	9.7	5.7	6.7	7.8	20.1	−7.7
09	114.6	88.5	12.8	5.2	7.7	6.5	19.5	−6.2
1910	113.4	87.6	9.4	6.1	8.2	6.7	21.0	−4.6
11	127.3	94.5	14.4	7.4	10.3	6.9	24.6	−6.2
12	135.9	111.2	12.4	6.2	7.1	6.2	19.5	−7.2
13	131.6	100.4	20.5	6.3	6.7	5.7	18.7	−8.0
14	132.1	105.0	11.4	6.0	7.3	7.1	20.4	−4.7
15	132.2	102.8	9.1	4.9	6.7	7.8	19.4	1.0
16	141.2	109.6	9.2	3.9	5.1	7.9	16.9	5.5
17	148.6	114.0	8.1	3.8	5.4	8.8	18.0	8.5
18	173.3	134.3	11.9	4.1	4.3	11.1	19.7	7.4
19	195.8	152.6	24.9	6.3	4.0	13.5	23.8	−5.6
1920	153.9	110.5	24.1	7.5	7.6	11.5	26.7	−7.5
21	157.1	118.8	17.5	8.7	9.8	11.1	29.7	−8.8
22	144.5	117.7	17.1	9.6	11.7	9.0	30.3	−20.7
23	164.0	145.3	13.7	9.3	11.8	7.1	28.3	−23.3
24	180.4	153.0	21.5	10.0	12.6	6.5	29.1	−23.2
25	194.1	161.4	18.9	11.9	11.5	5.0	29.5	−15.6
26	190.2	154.6	22.1	13.6	12.7	6.0	32.4	−18.8

TABLE 1* (Continued)

(1) GNP	(2) PCE	(3) PDI	(4) GP				(5) NFI
			GPnmi	GPnmc	GPmp	Total	
27	183.1	143.6	23.8	14.1	16.4	6.8	37.3	−21.7
28	194.5	150.1	19.0	14.1	20.7	7.2	42.0	−16.6
29	194.1	148.0	22.4	13.9	17.7	7.0	38.6	−15.0
1930	179.1	141.1	19.1	7.5	18.3	6.9	32.7	−13.7
1930	209.8	169.8	15.5	7.9	18.9	7.1	34.0	−9.4
31	213.1	166.2	17.7	6.5	27.0	8.4	41.9	−12.7
32	212.6	163.2	15.8	8.1	26.0	12.1	46.2	−12.6
33	218.1	161.3	20.9	6.2	25.0	13.9	45.1	−9.2
34	238.7	162.3	35.3	8.4	22.5	14.6	45.5	−4.4
35	241.0	155.4	38.0	7.5	22.9	15.0	45.3	2.2
1936	245.1	157.4	41.1	7.4	22.5	14.8	44.7	1.9
37	299.5	163.7	56.3	8.4	22.9	36.0	67.4	12.2
38	307.7	160.5	57.4	9.5	27.6	48.2	85.3	4.5
39	310.4	152.0	73.1	11.0	17.3	48.8	77.1	8.2
1940	289.1	135.4	70.2	11.4	20.9	48.2	80.6	2.9
41	294.4	131.2	72.3	11.5	23.2	64.1	98.8	−7.8
42	291.1	124.0	72.2	12.0	13.8	76.8	102.6	−7.9
43	292.2	116.4	64.6	12.8	6.5	97.7	117.0	−5.8
44	276.3	95.9	67.8	14.4	—	—	114.4	−1.8
45	—	—	—	—	—	—	—	—
46	148.6	90.1	34.4	13.5	8.7	7.6	29.8	−5.7
47	159.4	94.9	34.5	25.3	3.9	7.5	36.6	−6.5
48	178.9	104.9	41.5	21.6	10.5	6.9	39.1	−6.6
49	178.7	113.7	32.2	18.1	14.6	5.4	38.1	−5.3
1950	194.7	121.1	38.9	9.0	17.1	4.9	31.0	3.7
51	215.1	130.7	42.0	13.8	19.9	3.8	37.5	5.1
52	235.6	150.7	40.3	15.9	24.0	3.7	43.6	1.1
53	249.2	161.6	42.8	20.6	24.7	3.7	49.0	−4.2
54	257.3	166.0	38.9	20.0	24.2	5.4	49.5	2.8
55	279.6	177.4	45.2	23.5	26.1	4.6	54.3	2.7
56	298.8	186.4	66.6	20.4	27.2	4.4	51.9	−6.1
57	320.8	196.7	70.8	23.8	28.3	4.9	57.0	−3.8
58	329.5	205.7	60.3	29.4	30.2	4.9	64.5	−1.0
59	382.5	219.3	100.9	34.2	32.5	5.0	71.7	−9.4
1960	428.0	236.2	128.3	40.3	36.2	5.0	81.5	−18.0

* Notes and sources for Table 1 may be found in the Appendix. All results are tentative and currently under revision.

decision-makers and the realities, at least as revealed by statistics. It is a common picture even outside Japan that the aggressiveness and militarism of the period from about 1880 to 1945 were the result of economic pressures and economic forces. The evidence seems to point quite the other way. Economic difficulties did not cause the military expansion. Indeed, it was economic success that permitted it. A good deal was heard in this period, for instance, of Japan's overpopulation, lack of natural resources, and small area, only a sixth of which is arable. In terms of the economic reality of rising consumption, however, the overpopulation argument for military expansion appears to have been little more than a convenient myth which served to stimulate the laggards at home and to lull the gullible abroad.

Another image which the statistical realities do not confirm is that Japan's military expansion was the result of her difficulties in international trade, in finding, for instance, markets for her exports or sources of supply for her imports. Whatever problems there may have been in this area, however, her attempt to acquire political control of her trading areas contributed very little to their solution. Her principal acquisitions during the pre-1930 period were Korea and Formosa. These and other lesser possessions accounted for about 25 per cent of the external trade of Japan proper in 1928–30.[1] It is difficult to say, however, what the trade with these possessions would have been in the absence of political control. Structurally, at least, it might have been more beneficial to Japan. Lockwood, for example, points out that much of Japan's sugar came from Formosa through tariff preferences, which, if removed, might have permitted cheaper purchases elsewhere.[2]

The period around 1930 is particularly crucial in the rise of the military in Japan, and its economic environment requires particular attention. Japan's trade problem in 1931 was due primarily to the collapse of the United States silk market during the depression and to Finance Minister Inouye's determination to reinstate the gold standard in January 1930, thereby preventing for two years a fall in the value of the yen which would have offset in part the decline in world demand. After the gold standard was abandoned in December 1931, exports increased rapidly and Japan's deficit in her current account was not only reduced, but became a surplus in 1935. This situation continued, with the exception of 1938, until 1941. Her exports, excluding those to Korea and Formosa, showed a steady increase in both monetary and physical terms from 1931 to 1937 when full-scale war began with China.

Much is sometimes made of the restrictions on Japanese exports during the early 1930's.[3] It was, of course, not the first time Japan had been subjected to an increase in tariff rates. The United States, Japan's major trading partner, had already passed the Fordney-McCumber Act in 1922 establishing the highest rates in American history. But Japan's exports to the United States flourished during the 1920's with the bulk of them consisting of raw silk. The Hawley-Smoot Act in 1930, passed over the futile protests of 1028 economists, provided further increases, but left raw silk, the critical item, on the free list. On the

---

[1] From data in Bank of Japan, *Historical Statistics of Japanese Economy*: 1962: Tokyo, 1962, p. 90.

[2] William W. Lockwood, *The Economic Development of Japan*, Princeton, 1954, p. 51.

[3] See, for example, Edwin O. Reischauer, *Japan Past and Present* (Second Edition), New York, 1953, pp. 164–65.

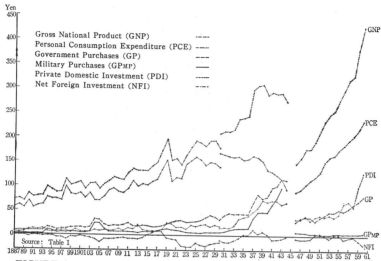

FIGURE 1:   Real Gross National Product and Components Per Capita
            for Japan 1887–1960 (1934–1936 Prices)

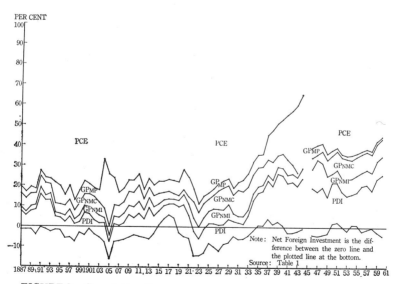

FIGURE 2:   Cumulative Percentage Distribution of Components of Real
            Gross National Product for Japan 1887–1960

whole, it is likely that the Hawley-Smoot Act had more of a psychological than economic effect on Japan. It came at a bad time and added a valuable propaganda weapon to the arsenal of the militant ultra-nationalists. In spite of the act's restrictions and the loud cries of protest from American protectionist groups, Japan's exports to the United States improved after 1931, although they never, during the 1930's, regained the value levels attained during the silk boom of the 1920's. The United States remained Japan's largest single buyer until 1934 when it became a close second to China (including Manchuria and Kwantung province). Until the events of 1937, its purchases remained fairly close to those of China, in spite of the growing hostility toward Japan in the United States. While military conquest and political control may have expanded trade with Manchuria after 1931, these gains may have been more than offset by a retardation in the expansion of trade with other countries as a result of adverse reactions to Japan's military expansionism. If so, the Japanese militarists were responsible for creating one of the very conditions they cited as justification for their activities.

While there was little basis in fact for the overpopulation argument as used by the ultra-nationalists, it could still have provided a primary motivation for aggression as a belief held sincerely even if mistakenly. Evaluation of this possibility requires scrutiny of the many other elements entering into the complex background of the Manchurian Incident and ensuing all-out war. The impact of these elements on the motivations of the decision-makers is frankly a matter largely of inference and conjecture. Even apparently sincere pronouncements of the leaders must be treated with caution, for, as a French philosopher observed, *le coeur a ses raisons que la raison ne connait pas*. In addition to the problem of the aims of the militarist leaders, we are confronted with the necessity of explaining the widespread popular support they apparently received. The simple answer is always the risky one. All one can do is list plausible contributing causes and give the supporting evidence.

It should be emphasized first that Japan's expansion into Asia was a continuation of a movement dating back many decades, perhaps even centuries.[4] Certainly the desire for military expansion showed itself long before population growth and industrialization created a substantial need for foreign markets and sources of supply.[5] Even before 1600, Japanese ships roamed the Asian seas, colonies were established in areas of Southeast Asia, and in 1592 Korea was invaded in an extraordinary, but abortive, attempt to conquer China. This phase of imperialist expansion, paralleling that of Europe during the same period, was interrupted for two and a half centuries by the Pax Tokugawa when Japanese leaders chose isolation rather than conquest as the best defense against expanding European colonialism. But the Meiji government, once isolationism had been abandoned, resumed the imperialistic practices of the earlier era. The policy of expansion was supported by a powerful traditional nationalistic sentiment or pride which rested on the belief that the Japanese were a nation divinely established and favored, a kind of chosen people of the

---

[4] The following historical sketch is based largely on materials in Hugh Borton, *Japan's Modern Century*, New York, 1955; William L. Neumann, *America Encounters Japan*, Baltimore, 1963; and Reischauer, *op. cit.*

[5] See Lockwood, *op. cit.*, p. 534, for a similar comment.

Orient, destined to rule the less favored. Encouragement came from the example of Western nations who had just entered an unusually active period of imperialism of their own. During the 1870's, while the new government was still in the process of consolidating its power at home, it sent punitive expeditions to both Formosa and Korea, affirmed its claim to the Bonin Islands, obtained possession of the Kurile Islands by treaty with Russia, and formally announced control over the Ryukyu Islands which were claimed by China as tributary vassals.

Efforts to dominate Korea culminated in the successful war with China in 1894–95. Formosa was annexed and influence in Korea extended. In 1897, a clash with the United States over control of the Hawaiian Islands was narrowly averted. The seizure of territory in China and the Pacific by various other countries added further incentive to Japan's expansionist tendencies.

Russia's interference in Korea was met by the Russo-Japanese War in 1904–05.[6] Russia was forced to cede the southern half of Sakhalin, turn over concessions, including her railroads in Southern Manchuria, and recognize Japan's control in Korea. A few years later, Korea was formally annexed by Japan. Japan entered World War I on the side of Great Britain and France and promptly seized Germany's Kiaochow leasehold on the Shantung Peninsula plus certain island possessions in the Pacific area.

In 1915, Japan presented her "Twenty-one Demands" to China. Of these, China accepted the demand for formal approval of Japan's various economic activities in China and the demand for a pledge to refrain from making future coastal area concessions to any third power. China did not agree, however, to certain requests which were designed to extend Japan's political control over China. The demands aroused furious protests in the United States as a violation of the so-called "Open Door" policy. Japan's position as an ally in the struggle against the Central Powers, however, prevented the United States from acceding to the clamor for strong action. An accord was reached in 1917 in which the United States publicly recognized that Japan's proximity to China created "special interests" and both powers, in a secret protocol, agreed to refrain from seeking concessions in China which would abridge the rights of other friendly powers. In all this, Japan was only playing a game engaged in by the United States and various European countries over a considerable period of history. In the process, however, her interest in ultimate control over China and certain neighboring areas of Asia became increasingly evident.

During the 1920's, a brief reaction against imperialism set in. A civilian government, which had little sympathy for the military, restored to China the Kiaochow area and certain other concessions in northern China formerly held by Germany. A pact signed at the Washington Conference in 1922 limited Japan's naval strength. In 1925, the government reduced the standing army from twenty-one to seventeen divisions. The demilitarization process, however, should not be exaggerated. The ministers of the Army and Navy Departments continued to be military officers selected by the armed forces. While military expenditures were reduced, compulsory military training was introduced into

---

[6] Japan began the hostilities with a successful surprise attack on the Russian naval forces before formally declaring war. This strategem, while loudly hailed at the time in America for its brilliance, received a quite different reception when used again in 1941.

the middle schools, higher schools and universities on a nation-wide basis, staffed in part by the officers who were released by the reduction in the standing army. Here was an extraordinarily economical method of building a powerful war machine using the existing facilities of the nation's educational institutions. And here also was a matchless opportunity simultaneously to indoctrinate the youth on a mass basis in the military tenets of ultra-nationalism. Certainly while many Japanese during the 1920's may have forgotten or rejected Japan's ancient ambitions, certain members of the military and ultra-nationalistic groups had not. They made their preparations and they waited for an occasion and adequate popular support. An opportunity first came during the economic crisis of 1927 when Baron Tanaka, army general and leader of the political party called the Seiyukai, formed a cabinet which lasted for two years. He achieved some expansion of military expenditures and used Japanese troops to check the northward advance of the Chinese Nationalist government. Even Baron Tanaka was a moderate compared with extremists in the Kwantung Army, who, on their own initiative, assassinated Chang Tso-lin, an uncooperative Manchurian war lord. Tanaka wished to punish the culprits, but was blocked by the Army Chief of Staff and others on the grounds it would weaken army discipline. Public reaction to the incident was unfavorable. Tanaka's government fell in 1929 and the Minseito, an anti-military, business-dominated party, came into power under Prime Minister Hamaguchi. It was not long, however, before a series of political and economic events, combined with other tensions building up during the 1920's, provided the climate for an effective militarist take-over. All that was lacking was an occasion and this had to be created.

We have seen so far that viewed in historical perspective, Japan's militaristic expansion during the 1930's was not something unexpected arising suddenly out of an overpopulation crisis. Rather it was a consistent continuation of a movement which could be traced back for many decades and possibly even centuries. It was supported by a powerful, traditional nationalistic sentiment; it had the sanction of the actual behavior, if not the pronouncements, of other major nations of the world up to that time; and it had enjoyed complete success from the beginning of the Meiji Era to the end of World War I.

Some of the quantitative aspects of this history are reflected in the tables and figures. We see, for instance, that even up to 1936, the proportion of the gross national product taken up by the war industry was relatively small. The Russian war of 1904–1905 was the only one of anything like major proportions. Military purchases rose sharply from about six percent of GNP in 1903 to about twenty-five percent in 1904–05. This was accompanied by a moderate decline in consumption and a large import surplus, without much change in private domestic investment. There is some evidence that the war gave a temporary check to Japanese economic development, but in the long run, of course, the effect was small.

The economic history of the first world war in Japan is particularly illuminating. Japan's participation in the war was negligible in terms of actual military involvement, and economically the war was enormously profitable. Japan exported large amounts of supplies to the Allies at inflated prices, and built up a very large foreign balance, mainly in European currencies. In the '20's, Japan proceeded to spend these funds at much lower prices, and even though it has not been possible to calculate the terms of trade on this particular transaction, it must have been very favorable indeed. The first world war is an interesting example of what might be called the deceptiveness of rational appearances. To all appearances Japan behaved with almost complete rationality, following her national interest with extreme skill. Economic behavior seems to be clearly in command; there is very little in the way of military heroics; and in spite of the fact that this must have seemed like a golden opportunity to the more aggressive militarists to expand, say, into the Russian Maritime Provinces or Manchuria, at a time when Russia was disorganized and the European powers and the United States were busy. Troops were sent to Siberia to join those of other nations, but were eventually withdrawn as a more civilian-minded government came into power during the 1920's. It looked as if Japan was deterred by highly rational considerations, in part perhaps by fear of the rising power of the United States. The line between rational and irrational behavior, however, is a thin one, especially in large and complex social organizations, as the contrast between the first and second world wars shows. Rational considerations of national interest would seem to suggest that Japan should have played exactly the same role in the second world war that she did in the first, and would have done even better out of it. The military take-over of the 1930's, however, threw the decision-making process of Japan into the hands of "heroic" hotheads, displacing the careful economic decision-makers of the previous generation with disastrous results.

Among the psychological factors which have been suggested as leading up to the take-over of the 1930's we find two major blows to a sensitive national pride. They came at a time when Japan was riding on the crest of a wave of national self-esteem, the culmination of a thirty-year period in which she had defeated in war a major Asian power and two major European powers. The first blow was the limiting of Japanese naval power at the Washington Conference in 1921–22 which, in effect, made it clear that Japan was considered a second-rate power and was to be kept that way. The second, and probably more critical event, was the exclusion of Japanese immigrants in the United States Immigration Act of 1924. The exclusion provisions were the culmination of a growing hostility in the United States toward the Japanese, especially in the West where the steady influx of Japanese laborers and farmers into California had led to economic and racial strife. As far back as 1906, San Francisco had attempted to confine Japanese and Chinese to segregated schools, but the uproar in Japan was such that President Theodore Roosevelt personally intervened and the attempt was abandoned in exchange for a "gentlemen's agreement" on the part of Japan to stop voluntarily the flow of migrant labor. This arrangement was no more palatable to the Japanese than her prewar and postwar "voluntary" agreements to limit certain exports to the United States under threat of formal restrictions. Japan had faithfully kept her "gentlemen's agreement" and the exclusion provisions could only be interpreted as a gratuitous slap in the face. Hugh Borton asserts that up to the time of the attack on Pearl Harbor, "This American Law was thrown in the faces of Japanese recruits and subjects alike as proof of the American attitude of disdain and superiority toward Japan."[7]

---

[7] Borton, *op. cit.* p. 307.

Japan's expansion in the 1930's was probably in part an attempt to restore her international prestige through means of proven historical reliability, and the war with the United States had elements of revenge.

While the population pressure argument was probably little more than a rationalization, though powerful in its psychological effects, economic factors were undeniably involved in the events leading up to the 1930's. We believe that central among those factors was a severe agricultural depression which began as early as 1925 and not in 1929 as some may have assumed. In 1925, the two major sources of farm income were rice and silk cocoons, providing together about two-thirds of the total value of agricultural output. Raw silk prices, after reaching a peak in 1925, began to fall and dropped thirty-two per cent by 1929. The collapse of American demand during the depression brought raw silk prices down to a level in 1931 only one-third of their 1925 peak. They remained low throughout the 1930's, further affected by the growing competition of rayon. In 1926, the price of rice began a steep decline, reaching a trough in 1931 which was fifty-six per cent below its 1925 level.[8] Contributing factors were: growing imports of rice from Korea and Formosa, four large crops in succession beginning in 1927, and a slackening in urban demand during the industrial depression following 1929. The result was an economic disaster for farm cultivators and for those rural workers who depended upon the silk market for employment in reeling and weaving establishments. These people constituted about half of the labor force in 1930 and the decline in their living levels probably accounts for the decline in the national level of consumption after 1925 (see Table 1 and Figure 1).

Strong economic dissatisfaction undoubtedly contributed to rural support of the ultra-nationalists who promised economic prosperity among other things. The rural situation, in addition, may have contributed to the personal motivation of many members of the military groups. From the early Meiji period, most of the soldiers and sailors were recruited from the rural areas. Many of the officers, especially those trained during the 1920's and 1930's, were sons of rural land-owners and occasionally of peasants. It is quite likely that Allen is right in arguing that the intense rural discontent "was communicated to the Army . . . and undoubtedly contributed to the overthrow of the 'liberal' Government and the transference of power to those who favored military aggression."[9] Reischauer also stresses the close relationship between the army and the peasantry and claims that the "Younger army officers . . . gradually came to champion the economic interests of the peasantry against the big city groups . . ." while "In return, the peasantry gave the army and its officer corps blind but inarticulate support."[10] It was the younger, rural-oriented officers, rather than the more conservative, urban-oriented, older top-ranking officers, who initiated the militarist period in 1931 and who maintained control when necessary through terrorism. Indeed, one of the major battle grounds for the struggle for power between moderates and extremists was within the armed forces themselves. Mr. Mamoru Shigemitsu, one of the leading participants in

---

[8] The statistical data are from G. C. Allen, *A Short Economic History of Modern Japan* (Second Revised Edition), London, 1962, pp. 114–15, 117, 139, and 202; Lockwood, *op. cit.*, pp. 56–7; and R. P. Dore, *Land Reform in Japan*, London, 1959, p. 21.

[9] Allen, *op. cit.* p. 117.

[10] Reischauer, *op. cit.* p. 160.

the events of the period, claims that three rather than two groups in the army were actually involved: 1) the so-called "young officers"—2nd lieutenants, lieutenants, and captains who were hotheads with assassination their favorite weapon; 2) *chuken* officers—lieutenant colonels and colonels who "connived at the excesses of the young officers because they hoped that the resulting disorders would further their own ends"; and 3) generals, presumably a more moderate group. Majors were split largely between the first and second groups. Naval officers were divided in a similar fashion.[11] It seems plausible to assume that the impact of rural economic distress on the motivations of the officers diminished as their rank became higher. Borton reported that, in 1932, "After agrarian support of the military was assured, General Araki (the War Minister) opposed money grants to the farmers and in the fall suggested that 'mutual aid among the peasants and small traders and owners of small enterprises' would be the best solution."[12] Increased military domination of the government, mainly by the *chuken*, generals, and admirals, brought little help to the farmers outside of a few measures of a purely "palliative nature."[13] There is no evidence that the Japanese military was noted for its sophistication in economics. Their solution to the farm problem, where they were interested in solving it at all, was apparently a military one based on the mystical concept that victory solves all problems.

The role of the great business groups, the Zaibatsu, in the events of the 1930's is highly controversial. It is natural to assume that most capitalistic organizations of that era would and did welcome the profit-making opportunities of war and territorial acquisition. It was still an age when the techniques of war did not visit mass destruction upon industrial areas. The Sino-Japanese War, the Russo-Japanese War, and World War I had proved immensely profitable to large business organizations. Yet there is strong evidence that the Zaibatsu were considerably less than enthusiastic about the plans of the military expansionists in the 1930's. Business was very good for the Zaibatsu and many other concerns in the 1920's. Industrial production doubled between 1920 and 1929,[14] stimulated partly by the reconstruction necessary after the disaster of the earthquake of 1923. Exports, in yen terms, increased about seventy per cent from the recession low in 1921 to the peak in 1929.[15] The financial crisis in 1927 afflicted mainly smaller enterprises, and the Zaibatsu seized the opportunity to acquire bankrupt concerns and fatten their empires, especially in the financial fields. Mitsui used its financial power to extend its control over small producers even in the rural areas.[16] Simultaneously with the growth of economic power, the major Zaibatsu took advantage of the power vacuum left by the gradual passing away of the ruling aristocrats who had dominated the Meiji government, and extended their political influence through the major parties of the period.

---

[11] From notes by Oswald White, translator of Mamoru Shigemitsu, *Japan and Her Destiny*: *My Struggle for Peace*, London, 1958, pp. 20-1.

[12] See Hugh Borton, *Japan Since 1931: Its Political and Social Development*, New York, 1940, p. 92.

[13] *Ibid.*, p. 93.

[14] Nagoya College index cited in Bank of Japan, *Historical Statistics of Japanese Economy*, Tokyo, 1962, p. 12.

[15] *Ibid.*, p. 93.

[16] For details, see Allen, *op. cit.*, Chapter VIII, "Economic Policy and the Zaibatsu, 1914-1932."

Their interest apparently lay in avoiding any military adventurism which would raise taxes and hamper Japan's economic relations with other countries.[17] The industrial depression which followed 1929 was a relatively mild one in Japan and provided little incentive for Zaibatsu cooperation with the military. The index of industrial production declined only sixteen per cent between 1929 and its low point in 1931, compared with a thirty-three per cent drop in the United States during the same period. The real gross national product per capita dipped only about six per cent in 1930 and rose slightly in 1931 (see Table 1). The real crisis, as we argued previously, was in the rural areas.

While some of the older, more conservative army officers may have had sympathy for the viewpoint of big business, there was apparently no love lost between the Zaibatsu leaders and the younger military officers. In May 1932, after violent attacks on the Zaibatsu for allegedly having exploited the peasants and small business concerns, a young officer group assassinated Baron Dan, the head of Mitsui. Allen repeatedly refers to the mutual hostility between the Zaibatsu and the military generally.[18] Much of this arose from the desire of the military to establish a quasi-wartime economy (Junsenji Keizai) completely under their control and designed solely to serve their own strategic purposes. The leaders of the Zaibatsu, now at the height of their economic and political power, were scarcely eager to relinquish their hard-won position of eminence whatever doubtful economic advantages might accrue. Certain non-Zaibatsu firms, however, with less concern for control and relatively more for profits, participated eagerly. They formed the nucleus of the "new Zaibatsu" (Shinko-Zaibatsu) upon whom the military relied heavily in developing the resources of Manchuria and China. Such cooperation as the Zaibatsu rendered in the military industrial build-up appeared, at least at the start, the result more of fear of terrorist tactics than of mutual interest.[19] Later, after the Manchurian die had been cast, there may have been less reluctance as the opportunities grew for profiting from expanding military expenditures.[20]

On the whole, as far as the period under discussion is concerned, the case for collaboration between the Zaibatsu and the military extremists in the initiation of the expansionist program is extremely weak. The weight of the evidence supports the view that the Zaibatsu actively opposed the extremists in a struggle for both economic and political power and then reluctantly cooperated when it

[17] Reischauer says that "The Japanese businessmen of the 1920's influenced by the philosophies of the victorious Western democracies, tended to look with disfavor on the high taxes required for large naval and military establishments. They were also inclined to believe that economic expansion—building up a great export trade and acquiring economic concessions abroad through diplomacy—was less costly and more profitable than colonial expansion by war and conquest. This seemed particularly true in China, the chief field for Japanese expansion. The Chinese, with a newly awakened sense of nationalism, were beginning to boycott foreign merchants whose governments were considered to be pursuing an aggressive policy against China. Consequently, military intervention in China cost the double price of lost markets and increased military expenditures." *Op. cit,*, p. 149.

[18] Allen, *op. cit.*, pp. 155–56.

[19] See G. C. Allen, *Japanese Industry: Its Recent Development and Present Condition,* New York, 1939, pp. 15–17.

[20] Reischauer implies this, *op. cit.*, pp. 179–80, but it is difficult to know whether he is referring to the "old" Zaibatsu or the Shinko-Zaibatsu.

was obvious popular opinion was against them and there was little more than a shotgun choice.

The industrial depression from 1929 to 1931 is sometimes mentioned as contributing to urban unrest and providing support for those who sought to overthrow the government. As we noted above, the industrial depression was not severe. Real wages of workers actually improved in 1930 and continued high in 1931 primarily because the sharp drop in the price of rice lowered the cost of living faster than money wages fell. Thus the curse of the farmer was the blessing of the urban worker. The number of unemployed in 1930 was only 1.1 per cent of the total gainfully employed population.[21] The export slump affected primarily the silk reeling and cotton textile industries whose labor force consisted largely of farmers' daughters. This added more to the woes of the rural families than to those of the urban proletariat. It is likely that whatever contribution unrest among urban workers made to the revival of militarism, it was small in comparison with the impact of the rural disaster.

The recital of contributing causes leading to the Manchurian Incident in 1931 should include certain inept government economic policies, especially those which related to rural distress. Among these were, first, continued encouragement of rice imports from Korea and Formosa in the face of declining domestic rice prices after 1925. Secondly, there was the re-establishment of the gold standard at just the wrong time, and its continuation even after it was obvious that this was detrimental to exports, especially those of raw silk on which the rural areas depended so heavily. The unpardonable sin, however, as far as the military was concerned, was the effort to reduce military expenditures. In 1930, the government approved the London Naval Treaty which further limited Japan's naval strength. A few months later, Prime Minister Hamaguchi was wounded by an ultra-nationalist. In reducing military expenditures, the government was only trying to achieve a balanced budget in accordance with the accepted, pre-Keynesian economic philosophy of the day. Perhaps it was inept only in the context of the situation where popular support required more spending to relieve the agricultural and industrial distress and also where the extremist militarist clique was looking for an excuse to take matters into its own hands. In September 1931, apparently without the approval or knowledge of the government, Japanese army units stationed in Manchuria to protect· the South Manchurian Railway began the conquest of all Manchuria on the grounds that the Chinese had tried to blow up the railway. The Minseito government fell, the new Seiyukai government accepted the *fait accompli*, the gold standard was abandoned, Finance Minister Inouye was assassinated, Japan withdrew from an unsympathetic League of Nations and the long march began down the road which led to a nightmare of destruction.

Again, the quantitative aspects of this period are shown in the table and figures. The conquest of Manchuria was almost fantastically cheap, and it involved practically no expansion of the war industry. This in itself is highly significant, because it suggests a process of false learning, and created an

---

[21] Lockwood, *op. cit.*, p. 156. Actually unemployment figures are a poor indicator of economic distress in Japan. This is due in large part to the very high proportion of family workers, in urban as well as rural occupations, who are not apt to be observedly unemployed.

impression of high returns to military investment which subsequent events were to prove completely unjustified. The real point of no return seems to have been the advance into China proper in 1937. This led to an expansion of military enterprise and the war industry up to the point where by 1945 it had gobbled up most of the economy, and consumption had been reduced to almost thirty per cent of a greatly diminished national product.

All human activity is in some sense investment, for all activity is undertaken in the light of some image of future costs and benefits. These costs and benefits, of course, may not be measurable in terms of money or even of easily-recongnizable goods and services. Nevertheless, they must exist in the mind of the decision-maker. The image of the world on which activity is based is created by a learning process. There is no other way to create it, for it is certainly not given to us genetically. As we stand at any moment of time, the decisions of the decision-makers are based pretty largely on the experiences of their own lifetime, both what they have experienced directly and what they have learned from others or from books. It is tragically easy to learn things which are not so, and to build up an image, especially of the social system, which is unrealistic to the point where decisions become disastrous. The present study clearly points to the need of a much deeper study of this whole period in Japan with a view to finding out exactly how these false images of the world were created, and how there came to be such a fantastic divergence between the image and the reality.

Out of this study also emerges another question of enormous importance. This is the question of how would we estimate in statistical terms the costs and benefits of the war industry to the society which sustains it. War industries are presumably maintained because the societies who decide to do so believe that the benefits exceed the costs. A cost-benefit analysis of the war industry is difficult, not only because of the extreme difficulties of measurement involved, but also because the very concept is repugnant to the "heroic" ideology from which the institution of war draws much of its strength. The most casual inspection of the table and the figures in this paper suggests that while the war industry in Japan may have had a positive rate of return in the early years of the period, taken over the period as a whole the cost has been enormous and the returns very small. The conceptual problem is complicated by what we might call the indirect effects, especially of defeat. The astonishing rate of growth of the Japanese economy since 1945 is unquestionably due in part to the "shock treatment" imposed on Japanese society by the war. We might almost say that the main product of the war industry in Japan was a mentally sick nation, and the defeat not only cured the mental illness but released a flow of creativity and energy which had not been released before. The crucial question here is, what is the contribution of the war industry to the rate of growth of the economy? Unfortunately, this is a question which cannot be answered easily. In the case of Japan, there is a good deal to suggest that in the early days of the period the war industry was an important spearhead of modernization, simply because it was at this point that the motivation was strongest. Even here, however, it is clear that the Russian war created a temporary slowing-down of growth and not enough of a shock to change the rate perceptibly. A rough estimate of the loss due to the industry is the size of the "valley." Suppose, for instance, that Japan had continued her economic development, from say 1930 on, at the rate which she had previously achieved, without military adventure and a major war industry; she would have achieved her actual income as of about 1960, following the line, say, from A to B in Figure 3. The shaded area is then the economic loss due to the war industry. It exceeds by many times the direct damage done to Japan by the American war industry.

It is little wonder that under these experiences Japan has become one of the least aggressive and least militaristic nations of the world, apparently quite content to withdraw from a position as a world power and to live as an American protectorate, quietly getting rich at a fantastic rate. We should beware of

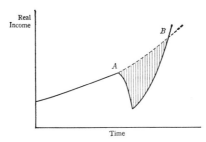

FIGURE 3.

projecting this situation with too much confidence too far into the future. Nevertheless, there is evidence to suggest that Japan has made a radical adjustment in her national image in the way, for instance, that the Swedes must have done in the early 19th century, and that if she continues to have economic success, this situation may be quite stable.

APPENDIX

Notes and Sources for Table 1

Notes: Component do not always add to totals because of rounding.
 Symbols: GNP=Gross National Product
 PDI=Private Domestic Investment
 PCE=Personal Consumption Expenditures
 GP=Government Purchases
 GP_{nmi}=Government Non-Military Investment
 GP_{nmc}=Government Non-Military Consumption
 GP_{mp}=Government Military Purchases
 NFI=Net Foreign Investment
 1946–1960 are fiscal years beginning April 1. All other years are calendar years.

Sources and Methods:
a. Column (1) was obtained by adding together the components, each of which was separately deflated.

b. Column (2): for 1887–1930 the series was computed from personal consumption expenditures in current prices in Kazushi Ohkawa and Keiko Akasaka, *Kobetsu Suikei no Sōgōka* (Integration of Estimated Components), Working Paper D 21, Hitotsubashi Institute of Economic Research, September 28, 1962 (Addendum of November 15, 1962), pp. 1–3. The deflator is a weighted average of a rural consumer price index (excluding rent) and an urban consumer price index (including rent) given in Ohkawa and Akasaka, *Kobetsu Suikei no Sōgōka*, Working Paper D 11, December 18, 1961, pp. 16–17. For 1930–60, the series was computed from personal consumption expenditures given in Economic Planning Agency, *Shōwa 36 Nendo Kokumin Shotoku Hakusho* (National Income White Paper: 1961), Tokyo, 1963, p. 84. The deflator is a weighted average of the urban and rural price indices obtained from *ibid.*, p. 100 and Economic Planning Agency, *Keizai Yōran* (Economic Abstract), Tokyo, 1963, p. 46.

c. Column (3): For 1887–1930, the series was computed by:
    1) subtracting government non-military investment in current prices (given in Koichi Emi, *Government Fiscal Activity and Economic Growth in Japan, 1868–1960*, Tokyo, 1963, pp. 168–70) from gross investment (including government non-military investment) given in Ohkawa and Akasaka *op. cit.*, Working Paper D 21 (Addendum of November 15, 1962), pp. 1–3; and
    2) deflating with a producers' goods price index given in Ohkawa and Akasaka, *op. cit.*, Working Paper D 21, pp. 18–20. For 1930–1960, the series was computed from Economic Planning Agency data for gross private domestic capital formation in current prices given in its *Shōwa 36 Nendo Kokumin Shotoku Hakusho*, p. 84, using as a deflator an index of producers' goods prices from the same sources cited in (b) above.

d. Column (4): Government Military Purchases (GP_{mp}) in current prices for 1887–1936 were obtained from Emi, *op. cit.*, Table A-2(1), col. (6), pp. 145–47; and, for 1937–1960, from *ibid.*, Tables A-2(2) and A-2(3), pp. 148–51, excluding expenses in occupation areas most of which were financed by foreign currencies or army occupation currency (see *ibid.*, p. 150). Payments for pensions, annuities and military "allowances in aid" are excluded as not representing current purchases of goods and services. Other "tranfers" may still be present in the data. They are apt to be especially large during war periods. We adjusted for some of them for 1894–98 and 1903–08 by subtracting from Emi's figures such items as gratuities, loans, interest, and subsidies which were listed as war expenditures but which should probably be excluded in estimating purchases of goods and services according to national income concepts. Data for the adjustment were taken from Giichi Ono, *War and Armament Expenditures of Japan*, New York; Oxford University Press, 1922, pp. 273–74; 286–87; and 291–94. The deflator for 1887–1930 is a weighted average of a consumers' goods price index and producers' goods price index given in Ohkawa and Akasaka, *op. cit.*, Working Paper D 21, pp. 18–20, and designed for deflation of the Gross National Product. The combined index was used because military purchases contain both consumption and investment components, though the relative proportions are difficult to determine. The deflator for 1930–1960 is a weighted average of a consumers' goods price index (75% weight) and a producers' goods price index (25% weight) given in Economic Planning Agency, *Keizai Yōran* (Economic Handbook) for 1963, p. 46, and for 1958, p. 48.

Government Non-Military Consumption (GP_{nmc}) for 1887–1960 was obtained by subtracting the above series of Government Military Purchases (in current prices) from Emi's series of government "current purchases of goods and services" (excluding investment) in current prices, *op. cit.*, Table A–6, col. (1), pp. 168–71. The result was then deflated with the same index used in obtaining real personal consumption expenditures in (b) above.

Government Non-Military Investment (GP_{nmi}) for 1887–1930 was obtained in current prices from *ibid.*, Table A–6, col. (5), pp. 168–70, and for 1930–1960, from Economic Planning Agency, *Shōwa 36 Nendo Kokumin Shotoku Hakusho*, p. 85. (The EPA data are also given in Emi, *op. cit.*, p. 170.) The deflator was the same used in deflating Private Domestic Investment (PDI) in (c) above.

The data for 1944 did not permit a proper breakdown into government non-military consumption and government military purchases.

e. Column (5): Net Foreign Investment (NFI) in real terms was estimated by subtracting a deflated series of debits (mainly visible and invisible imports) in the current account of the balance of payments from a separately deflated series of credits (mainly visible and invisible exports) in the current account. Figures in current prices, for 1887–1930, were taken from Ohkawa and Akasaka, *op. cit.*, Working Paper D 21, pp. 6–8, and, for 1930–60, came from Economic Planning Agency, *Shōwa 36 Nendo Kokumin Shotoku Hakusho*, p. 57. The deflator for credits was computed by linking together three indices of export prices and the deflator for debits was computed by linking together three indices of import prices. The indices used came, for 1887–1900, from Kiyoshi Kojima, "Japanese Foreign Trade and Economic Growth: With Special Reference to the Terms of Trade," *Annals of the Hitotsubashi Academy*, Vol. VIII, No. 2, April 1958, pp. 166–7; for 1900–1930 from a preliminary series by K. Yamada, Institute of Economic Research, Hitotsubashi University, cited in Bank of Japan, *Historical Statistics of the Japanese Economy*, Tokyo, 1962, p. 99; and for 1930–1960 from Economic Planning Agency, *Shōwa 36 Nendo Kokumin Shotoku Hakusho*, p. 100. The EPA series (for import prices and for export prices) were broken at 1953 when the base was changed. We linked them to their post-1953 sections by using Bank of Japan postwar import price and export price indices given in *Economic Statistics of Japan: 1955*, Tokyo, 1956, pp. 289–90.

f. Sources of population data used in computing per capita figures are: for 1887–1920 and 1946 to 1960, Office of the Prime Minister, *Japan Statistcal Yearbook: 1961*, Tokyo, 1962, pp. 10–11; for 1920–1945, Ministry of Welfare, *Vital Statistcs: 1960*, Vol. I, Tokyo, 1961, p. 241. Okinawa is included up to 1945 and excluded after 1945 to provide consistency with the gross national product estimates. Figures from 1887 to 1944 are for July 1 in order to correspond to calendar year data. They were obtained by linear interpolation. Figures for 1946 to 1960 are for October 1, as given in the sources, and correspond with fiscal year data.

THE CONCEPT OF NEED
FOR HEALTH SERVICES

Milbank Memorial Fund Quarterly,
44, 4 (Oct., 1966): 202-225.

THE CONCEPT OF NEED FOR HEALTH SERVICES

The concept of need is often looked upon rather unfavorably by economists, in contrast with the concept of demand. Both, however, have their own strengths and weaknesses. The need concept is criticized as being too mechanical, as denying the autonomy and individuality of the human person, and as implying that the human being is a machine which "needs" fuel in the shape of food, engine dope in the shape of medicine, and spare parts provided by the surgeon. Even if the need concept is expanded to include psychological and emotional needs, the end result would seem to be a wire run into the pleasure center of the brain which could provide a life of unlimited and meaningless ecstasy. Demand, by contrast, implies autonomy of the individual, choice, and a tailoring of inputs of all kinds to individual preferences. Only the slave has needs; the free man has demands.

In spite of the economist's uneasiness about it, a considerable demand exists for the concept of need. As even the most liberal of economists cannot deny the right of a demand to call forth a supply, the development and elaboration of concepts of need can hardly be denied. The demand, however, may be for a number of different concepts, and a single concept will not serve the purpose. The demands for this concept are quite varied, and the supply must be correspondingly differentiated. No single concept of need exists, and especially no single concept of need for health services.

One demand for a concept of need arises because the concept of demand itself has serious weaknesses and limitations. It assumes away, for instance, a serious epistemological problem. The very idea of autonomous choice implies first that the chooser knows the real alternatives which are open to him, and second that he makes the choice according to value criteria or a utility function which he will not later regret. Both the image of the field of choice and the utility function have a learning problem which, by and large, economists have neglected. This problem is particularly acute in the case of medical care, where the demander is usually a layman faced with professional suppliers who know very much more than he does. The demand for medical care, indeed, is primarily a demand for knowledge or at least the results of knowledge. In the case of ordinary commodities the knowledge that is required is fairly easily available and the market itself is a learning process. If one buys something he does not like he will not buy it again. In the case of medical care, however, as in the case of certain other commodities such as automobiles, the learning process can easily be fatal, in which case it is not a learning process at all. In any case the experience of the market cannot teach people what they have to know in regard to the choices they have to make, or even what preference functions they should use in evaluating these choices.

The concept of need which emerges from the criticism of demand is that of professional choice. It is implied to some extent in the very idea of the patient or the client, and it is expressed in the aphorism that doctor (or father, or lawyer, or preacher, or president) knows best. One's demand for medical care is what he wants; his need for medical care is what the doctor thinks he ought to have. The demand for medical care leads to the proliferation of drug stores, patent medicines, osteopaths, chiropractors and faith healers.

That is the market for medical care and it is a large one. It spills over into the medical profession itself, in private practice and the reputation of particular doctors and surgeons, in the prestige of Harley Street and its equivalents in many cities, and it includes both the medicine cabinet in the bathroom and the psychiatrist's couch. It can be thought of as an "industry" or segment of the economy; it is subject to the general principles of the price system, in the sense that wherever a demand is sufficient to make a supply profitable it will arise, even though this principle has to be limited also by the power of the ingenious supplier to create his own demand.

In contrast with the market in medical care, an increasingly professionalized, socialized, organized structure satisfies what the professional conceives of as needs. The periodic medical examinations in corporations and universities, the veterans' hospitals, the school doctor, public health, the professional public provision of clean water and sewage disposal—all this represents a professionalized sector of the economy, characterized by professions which set their own standards of what they ought to do and which are financed by taxation or near-taxation. Among these are Blue Cross and other health insurance plans, Medicare, or even private clinics supported by monthly assessments. Here the activity originates from the profession rather than from the client, from the supplier rather than from the demander. In its extreme form it takes on the flavor of, "What you need is what I as your professional advisor have to give you; what you want is quite irrelevant."

The idea of professional need always rests on some definition of homeostasis or state maintenance of the client, his property or his environment. The professional defines a certain state of his client and his related systems as a state of "health" which he has a professional interest in maintaining. The course of operations of any system, however, involves consumption. That is, the state of the client and his environment changes in some way and become "worse," or diverge in a downward direction from the ideal. The ideal in this case is the professional's ideal, that is, his impression of what state should be maintained. The maintenance of a state, however, requires certain inputs to replace what has been lost by consumption. It may also require the professional handling of certain outputs, such as excreta, which must be removed and disposed of if the organism or organization is to continue to maintain its state of activity. A very fundamental principle in nature implies that any state of activity can only be maintained by a throughput involving both inputs and outputs. In part that may be because inputs come in packages in practice, only part of which can be utilized, and what is not utilized must therefore be excreted as output. Even more fundamental reasons, however, dictate the presence of output in the form of excreta, whether gases from automobile exhaust, carbon dioxide given off in breathing or waste products of the digestive process. The transformation of chemical into mechanical energy, on which all organization seems to depend almost universally, seems to require an input of oxygen and an output of an oxide.

This suggests that certain minimum mechanical, chemical, biological, physiological, even economic and sociological requirements exist for the functioning of any organism or organization. That in turn suggests that the concept of professional need can be broken down into two further problems; one the problem of what might be called homeostatic need. That is, what is actually required to maintain a given system in operation. The other is the problem of perception or knowledge of homeostatic need. That is, can the system itself be trusted to maintain the inputs and outputs necessary to satisfy homeostatic need, or is a professional required with a wider body of knowledge who can perceive and prescribe the homeostatic needs? Homeostatic needs can be divided into two categories, those which can be taken care of by the organism itself and those which require a professional decision.

These categories can be illustrated by pointing to certain undignified analogies between the human being as an organization and an item of material capital such as an automobile. Both require inputs of air if they are to function, and the air must be reasonably pure, though usually only automobiles are provided with air filters. Each of them pollute the air they breathe with the byproducts of combustion, and unless fresh air can be constantly supplied continued operation will become impossible. Both the man and the automobile require food; carbohydrates, proteins and fats in the case of the human, gasoline and oil in the case of the automobile. A certain parallel can even be drawn between the vitamins of the human and the various additives of gasoline. The parallel is particularly striking in Scandinavian countries where automobiles are "buttered," not greased. Food input is usually administered on a fairly nonprofessional basis. The automobile owner buys gas for his car in very much the same way as he buys food for himself, with a certain amount of professional advice but not much professional interference. In the course of operation of the system, internal stocks of food are used up fairly continuously and they have to be replaced at intervals. The automobile takes its dinner at the gas station, which is a kind of automobile restaurant.

The input of food and of fuel and the output of its waste products are not, however, sufficient. In the course of operation, both of the automobile and of the human, wear and tear occur. Consequently, not only are gas stations, restaurants and food stores needed, but also garages and hospitals. At this level need becomes professionalized. The greasing every thousand miles or the annual physical examination may be fairly routine, though at this point one begins to think of medical care for either automobile or man rather than simple fueling and feeding. The professional need is most apparent in breakdown, that is, when the subject simply refuses to function even when fueled and fed. Then the car goes to the garage, where mechanics perform operations on it, and the human goes to the hospital where surgeons perform operations on him. The atmosphere of the garage, indeed, is curiously like that of the hospital. The garage is permeated by the same air of professional importance, the same feeling that the customer is rather in the way, the same rather offhand bedside manner, the same assumption that the customer or the patient is, professionally speaking, an ignoramus, if not a fool. In fact, the principal difference between the garage and the hospital seems to be that the hospital is cleaner and more expensive. The concept of professional need appears in the helplessness of the customer. All he knows is that he hears a funny noise in the gear box or has a pain in his stomach. Once he puts himself into the hands of the professional, demand disappears and no substitute exists for trust in the professional's concept of need.

The difficulty with homeostasis as the basis for a concept of need is that homeostasis is never really successful. No matter what occurs in the way of inputs, virtually all known organisms and organizations exhibit the phenomenon of aging, which is closely related to the phenomenon of growth. Aging is common both to machines and to biological organisms, and it might almost be defined as that adverse change in state of the organism which no known input can remedy. In biological organisms, growth is actually rather similar. It can be thought of, indeed, as a kind of negative aging. The inputs of the growing child have to be sufficient not only to provide for replacement, but also to provide for growth. Growth, however, is almost as unpreventable as aging. Mechanical organizations such as the automobile are not generally subject to growth. They are more like the moth or the butterfly in that they emerge fully grown from the chrysalis of the factory, and henceforth are subject only to aging. Up to now very little is known about aging, at least in the case of the biological organism. It can perhaps be hastened by certain inputs or outputs or by certain deficiencies in input, which is also true of the automobile. In both cases, a life of hard work and poor nutrition results in premature aging. Up to now, at any rate, any inputs which would postpone the aging process beyond the allotted span have not been discovered. If they are, as seems not impossible, at least in the next 100 years, the human race will probably be faced with the greatest crisis of its history, for no existing human institution would survive in its present form the extension of active human life even to 200 years.[1]

Aging introduces a very tricky problem into the concept of need for maintenance, which is difficult enough even in the case of the machine, more difficult in the case of the horse, and a problem of excruciating delicacy in the case of the human being. The problem with the machine is at what point in its history it should be scrapped. The formal answer to this is fairly easy: a machine should be scrapped when its present value as a functioning apparatus, derived by discounting the future costs and benefits to be allocated to it, has fallen just below the net value of a possible replacement. The net value is defined as the present discounted value of future benefits less that of all future and installment costs of the replacement plus the scrap value of the machine which is replaced. With no technical progress and if the machine is replaced by one exactly like it when new, the main factor determining the age at which it will be replaced is the increase in the maintenance cost and perhaps a decrease in its output as it gets older. Where technical change occurs a machine may be scrapped because of obsolescence, that is, because of a rise in the net value of what might replace it.

A machine is generally regarded as having no value in itself, that is, its value is purely instrumental; hence the owner feels no qualms about scrapping it if he feels such action is necessary. Even horses, however, when they can no longer fulfill their economic function, are sometimes put out to pasture in honorable retirement at some cost to their owners. In the case of the human being, the problem of the person himself becomes very acute, because persons cannot be regarded as purely instrumental. That is, they are not merely good for something else, they are good in themselves. They are, in other words, something *for which* other things are good. Whereas the death of a machine is determined mainly by economic forces, this principle as quite inapplicable to persons, where, in theory at any rate, the person supposedly possesses a positive value even up to the moment of death, and death, therefore, is always regarded as a loss. When death occurred mainly in childhood or middle life, this principle could evoke no criticism. As medical science, however, has successively eliminated the causes of early death, the fiction that death is always an "act of God" is increasingly difficult to maintain.

At this point the concept of professional need for medical care becomes most difficult. Should the medical profession devote a relatively large proportion of its resources, as it does now, in keeping miserable and senile elderly people alive, when their capital value even to themselves has become negative? Men, even physicians, have a reasonable aversion to playing God and to introducing a nonrandom element in what has hitherto been sanctified as random. The only solution may be to substitute an artificially random process for the natural randomness by which death came in the past. If death could be arranged by drawing a random number, perhaps by hiding one euthanasia pill in the nursing home diet each week, the Godlike power of the medical man might be laid on the shoulders of Chance, and death might be restored to its former dignity.

A proposal such as the above will seem deeply shocking to many people, and indeed, is put forward only in the form of a most tentative question, intended merely to illustrate a problem which is likely to be more and more prevalent. One principle in the spirit of the Hippocratic Oath to be argued for very strongly is that the person himself must decide at what point death or the chance of death is preferred to life, and no one else should have the right to make this decision for him. At this point, surely, demand must take precedence of need, and the autonomy of the patient be reasserted. Even at the moment of making this assertion, however, and nailing it to the masthead, realistic doubts arise. At what point, for instance, do people become incapable of making decisions for themselves? That is a question of immediate practical importance for the medical profession, for even if they do not have the power at the moment of consigning people to eternity, they do have the power of consigning them to what is often the living death of the mental hospital, and the moral problems of the latter are surely of the same order of magnitude as those of the former. Nevertheless, people do become incompetent and incapable of managing their own affairs. Society has decided that mental hospitals must exist, and along with them the machinery for committing people to them. Who is better able to estimate that professional need than the medical profession, especially when its decisions are mediated through the apparatus of the law? One sobering thought, however, is that a person virtually ceases to be a legal person when he ceases to have demands and has only needs.

Some of the above problems may well reflect a lag in society in the development of a professional sense of what the needs of the incompetent and the aged in fact ought to be. A marked shift has taken place in the care of the aged, from the family into hospitals and nursing homes. Even two generations ago most people died in their own beds in the bosom of their families, amid the consolations of religion and the ministrations of a beloved family physician. Such, at least, is the idyllic picture; the reality was probably more disagreeable. Nevertheless, of the people who die of old age today, most die in nursing homes, old people's homes, and hospitals, away from the comforts of the familiar and the ministrations of kin. No great deal of thought has been devoted to the needs of the departing, and none at all to the need for death. Death, however, is a medical matter. It is certainly part of the need for medical care, if such exists, and it deserves to receive a great deal more care and attention than it has in the past. That is not to suggest that the medical profession should abandon its concern for the needs of the incompetent, the aged and the dying; rather that more attention be given to this problem, both in medical research, so that vigor and physical well-being can be prolonged until the end, and in social and moral research that can devise economic, financial, architectural and social institutions which will give dignity and serenity to the last years of life and will not deprive its end of the majesty which is due it.

At the other end of human life, the increasing control, which the biological sciences seem to be opening up in genetics, presents even more difficult problems in regard to the need for medical activity. If the rights of the living and the dying are hard to determine, the rights of the unborn are an even more difficult problem. The whole problem of population control, in fact, in regard to both quantity and quality, is moving more and more onto the shoulders of the health sciences, and it is a problem for which they cannot escape responsibility. In the last 15 years, the spectacular decline in infant mortality which followed the introduction of malaria control in the tropics has created social problems which seem to be virtually insoluble in the next 15 to 20 years.

One must think here in terms of the homeostasis, not merely of the individual, but of a whole society. When, as a result of the introduction of certain public health measures, a society which previously was in approximate demographic equilibrium, with high birth rates and high death rates, suddenly finds the death rates drastically reduced while the birth rates continue high, an enormous long-run social disequilibrium is created which may have quite unforeseen consequences, both for good and for ill. Many societies in the tropics are now increasing in population at unprecedented rates—between three and four per cent per annum—and this in itself places an enormous burden on the poor society which is anxious for development. When the population doubles every 20 years a whole new country must be built, and the whole physical apparatus of a society doubled in a relatively short space of time, even if per capita capital is not to decline. If the country is already fairly thickly populated, with no unused land areas of any magnitude, the sheer problem of doubling the food supply in 20 years is almost insoluble, and a slow and deadly reduction in nutritive levels can easily follow.

Add to this gloomy picture the fact that in these countries most of the working force was born before the great decline in infant mortality and hence is small. That small working force has to support an enormous number of children and young people—in many of these countries more than half the population is now under the age of 18. Furthermore, very large teenage generations now exist which cannot be absorbed in the traditional structure, especially of the village society, and are forced to migrate to the towns. The towns, because of the phenomenon of what has been called the "rural push," are growing much faster than the population itself, some of them as much as 15 per cent annually which means doubling every five years. Under these circumstances providing housing and municipal services is impossible, and enormous slums and shack towns spread over the landscape like a blight. These circumstances dictate an extremely pessimistic forecast for the next 25 years for many of these countries. On the other hand, if a massive campaign for birth reduction takes place now, so that birth rates could be halved in five or ten years, then the next generation will be a large labor force able to cope with the smaller numbers of children and that will be the moment when these countries may be able to make the leap into the modern world. In the absence of substantial reduction in birth rates, however, the outlook is bleak indeed. Enormous famines, disastrous internal strife and even total civil breakdown may be expected. All this may well be the result of the World Health Organization's malaria eradiction campaign in the years around 1950.

On the other side of the picture, without a substantial increase in the expectation of life, and particularly without the elimination of mortality in the productive years, economic development is also very difficult. An essential step toward the modern world is the introduction of modern medicine and the elimination of the appalling waste of human knowledge and human capital which occurs in countries where human life expectancy is little more than 30 years. The ideal situation would be a sharp reduction in the death rate and an equally sharp reduction in the birth rate, so that the demographic equilibrium was not unduly disturbed. Even if this happy result were unobtainable, a certain disturbance of the demographic equilibrium is entirely desirable in the interest of development, and a public health campaign is at least a start in disturbing the low-level equilibrium of a traditional society.

These problems present great difficulties, even for social scientists, and up to now at any rate the medical sciences have been extraordinarily lax in attending to them. Medicine has considered health mainly in terms of inputs to an individual, not to a society. The possibility of an acute conflict between the health of the individual and that of his society is a problem that has received scandalously little attention. Now the tables have been turning, and birth control has become fashionable and respectable, almost to the point of being advocated as a panacea for all developmental difficulties. Quantitative population control, however, is only a part of the general problem of what might be called societal health, which is not the same thing, incidentally, as public health. Public health concerns itself primarily with the environmental factors affecting the health of the individual. Societal health deals with the factors that determine the health of the whole society, and societies can be sick even when the individuals in them are medically well.

The problem of qualitative population control is beginning to rise seriously onto the human agenda. The eugenics movements of the nineteenth century were premature, and based on wholly inadequate genetic concepts. With the enormous advance in genetics in this century, however, the problems of the genetic composition of future populations are no longer as random as they used to be. Indeed, a recurrent nightmare is that all the medical advances will eventually prove ineffective simply because the improved techniques of individual survival will enable more and more adverse genetic strains to penetrate the population. In his argument against that position, Medawar says that if a genetic adaptation to medical knowledge produces more people who have to be kept alive by "artificial" means, nothing is particularly wrong with that, because genetics always adapts itself to the environment and medical knowledge is part of the environment of man.[2] The argument, however, is not wholly satisfactory, simply because of the cost of medical care for those whose genetic constitution requires it. If the existence of medical care produces a population of the genetic composition which requires it, the whole system seems to be self-defeating. Whatever level of medical care is established, no matter how high and how elaborate, one can argue that in the long run the genetic composition of the population will deteriorate to the point where the established level of medical care becomes necessary. In this case the level of medical care creates its own need. No objective need exists which determines the level of medical care.

Looking to the rather long run, therefore, one would expect to find large payoffs in research devoted to altering the genetic composition of the population in directions which would minimize the cost of medical care. Conceivably, genetic control might eliminate medical care almost entirely, except for accidents; for some genetic constitutions are extraordinarily resistant to disease, and if these could be propagated in the population, the need for medical care would correspondingly decline.

In the next few decades, the possibility of changing genetic constitutions even after birth is not wholly off the agenda, although it certainly seems to be difficult. Even without that, however, the possibility of genetic control at the moment of conception opens up an enormous and rather frightening horizon to the human race, even though this would also open up enormous possibilities for good. Certainly the elimination of the more obvious genetic-related diseases or conditions would be a great gain. The ethical problems involved at this end of the scale, however, are just as severe as those at the other end relating to death. At what point, for instance, in the life history of a person does he have any rights? Opinion seems to have shifted in this regard toward the moment of birth as the point at which human rights are acquired. The increasingly favorable public opinion in regard to abortion would seem to imply that the embryo has no rights, whereas the infant does, as infanticide is still severely censored. If, however, the process of conception can be controlled and, for instance, selective gene structures implanted in the egg, the question of the human rights even of the fertilized egg becomes acute. That again is a problem because the ethical standards and ideas of the human race have been adapted to processes of birth and death which in the past have been essentially random, and substituting nonrandom for random processes always produces an acute moral crisis. Perhaps some consensus might be salvaged with elimination of certain obviously maladaptive genetic traits, for instance mongoloidism and obvious feeblemindedness. Even considering the elimination of haemophilia, enough distinguished people have had this disability to suggest that something might be lost by eliminating it. The ethical problems become even more acute with the proposal to alter genetic structures positively. The production of a race of supermen who would supersede the present generation might not be regarded favorably by ordinary mortals.

Underlying all this discussion is a seldom-discussed specter regarding the idea of health itself. Even assuming the very simple position that need involves merely the maintenance of homeostasis, the question as to what state of the organism is to be maintained still has to be answered. That is like the problem of at what temperature the thermostat should be set. Every homeostatic mechanism implies an ideal, and the question of the critique of the ideal itself, therefore, cannot be brushed aside. In particular, the conclusion cannot be avoided that within limits which may be quite broad, health is a matter of social definition. Societies and cultures do exist in which what is now defined here as ill health is somewhat admired. One recalls W. S. Gilbert's pale young curate, whose tubercular charms in the eyes of the village maidens even outweighed those of gilded dukes and belted earls. In some societies, epilepsy is regarded as a sign of divine favor. The limits of what is socially defined as physical health are so narrow that not much of a problem arises.

With mental health and human behavior in society, however, the limits seem to be broader, and the matter of social definition more important. For instance, should the problem of homosexuality be considered a problem in mental health, to be "cured," even if no cure seems to be currently available, or should it be regarded as a legitimate variation of human behavior, to be accepted and regulated by custom and law? A rather similar problem involving the acceptance of deviant subcultures has descended upon society with the development of the psychedelic drugs such as mescaline and LSD. Some claim that these are legitimate avenues to the expansion of human consciousness and others claim that these are dangerous drugs the use of which should be prohibited by law, except under medical supervision, and that unauthorized users should be punished as criminals. A similar conflict of voices is raised on behalf of marijuana, some people claiming that it affords a legitimate expansion of human consciousness and is no more dangerous than alcohol. The prevailing sentiment, however, is to lash out at the use of these drugs with all the ferocity of criminal law.

The failure to deal with alcohol, which has been with the human race for a long time and is certainly the earliest of the psychedelic drugs, is not an optimistic indication that society will be able to deal with a succession of new chemical and perhaps electrical devices, such as the "pleasure wire," which produce various types of euphoria. One remembers with a slight shudder the use of soma as a social tranquilizer in BRAVE NEW WORLD. Even in the medical field, not very much is known about the impact on society of the enormous use of the tranquilizing drugs both in medical practice and in private life in the past few years. The frightening possibility of a society steeped in agreeable chemical illusions to the point where it becomes quite incapable either of recognizing or solving its real problems is by no means a matter only for science fiction.

Different societies have given very different answers to these questions, and they constitute merely one aspect of a much larger question as to the boundary between health, morality and law. In many fields the problem is defining the point at which behavior which is in some sense disapproved or regarded as below normal is defined as sickness or is defined as turpitude. In this society a long-term movement has attempted to push this boundary to define fewer things as turpitude and more things as sickness. Nevertheless, no golden rule dictates where this line should be drawn. In Samuel Butler's EREWHON, crime was treated by doctors and illness by policemen, and one has an uneasy suspicion that this might work too. The problem of the overall effects upon society of its system of punishment is very little understood, and the line between the need for medical care and the need for criminal prosecution is really quite hard to draw.

A question which is even more fundamental and still more difficult to answer, but which should not remain unasked, is whether the concept of ill health can be applied to moral and political ideas themselves. For instance, do diseases of the moral judgment exist, and if so, are they subject to epidemics? How are these epidemics spread? The rise of National Socialism in Germany and McCarthyism in the United States, of witch-hunting, war moods and irrational hatreds in innumerable societies, indicates that the concept of disease in the moral and political judgment is worth taking seriously, even though it is very hard to define. One may be able to define something like mass infections of unrealistic images of the world, if only one could be sure what is realistic. Whether these phenomena fall under the purview of the medical profession is, of course, a debatable point. The medical profession has long been required in forensic medicine to advise on the medical status of a possible criminal act. Perhaps, one day it may be called in to determine the medical status of a political act or even of a moral exhortation. The difficulty here, and it is a real one, is that, up to now at any rate, a clear physical correlate of mental, moral and political ill health does not exist. The idea is not wholly far-fetched, however, to suppose such physical correlates do exist and that the discovery will be made one day of a drug against malevolence or another that increases good will. Even if the physical correlates are hard to find, the status of psychoanalysis as a medical speciality suggests possible extensions into therapeutic communication in moral, political and social systems.

Society is so accustomed to thinking of the problem of the inter-relations of government, science and medicine in terms of the impact of government on science and medicine that people are at a loss when asked to consider the impact of science and medicine on government. Nevertheless, that may well become one of the major questions in advanced societies in the next generation or two. Political decisions are still made largely in the light of what might be called folk knowledge or at best literary knowledge. The scientist is supposedly to serve the values and interests of the folk but he is not to insert any values and interests of his own. He is supposedly an instrument of the state or at least of the people and not an autonomous creator of values and needs. That is the point of view of the famous aphorism that the scientist in government should be on tap but not on top, and that he should be a humble servant of folk and national values. That, however, is a most unrealistic estimate of the present situation. Science is not a passive servant of existing values. It has its own culture, it creates its own values, and because of its enormous impact on the world, it compels a re-examination of values everywhere.

The role of the social sciences in this respect is even more striking than that of the physical and biological sciences. The physical or bio-logical scientist operates in a different field from that of the politician. The special skills of the scientist in, say, physics or physiology give him very little comparative advantage in attempting to answer a question in social systems. In respect to the economic system or the international system, the physicist or biologist has as much right to be heard as any intelligent citizen, but no more. The social scientist, however, occupies the same field as the politician and is in direct competition with him. The possibility of severe conflict between the folk culture and the scientific culture is thus present at this level. Up to now the conflict has been muted only because it has hardly begun; because the social sciences are only barely at the point where they can begin to challenge the folk wisdom of the politician. Economics already has a kind of establishment of "Lords Spiritual" in the Council of Economic Advisors and in the Joint Economic Committee in Congress. The impact of this establishment is already noticeable in economic policy, and the United States is by no means the most advanced country in this regard. The other social sciences, and least of all what might be called the sociomedical sciences of clinical psychology and psychiatry, still seem to be a long way from any such status. The possibility, however, that one of the needs for medical care may be defined in the future as political mental health, though it may sound absurd at the moment, should not be taken lightly. Society is already beginning to see that the automobile is a problem in public health; to regard the Department of Defense as a similar problem is a simple logical extension of this position, for the present international system is almost certainly more dangerous to health than the automobile and far more dangerous than most communicable diseases.

Even at this point, the ambiguity can be maintained between demand as defined by the consumer and need as defined by the professional. All fields of life seem to feel the necessity for working out an uneasy compromise between these two concepts. Undiluted consumer sovereignty, whether in economics or politics, where it takes the form of the absolute sovereignty of the voter and the sovereignty of the nation, is ultimately intolerable and leads to corruption and disaster. On the other hand, total professionalization, in the case of the doctor, the economist, the sociologist or the political scientist, is likewise intolerable, if only for the reason that having that much father-image is intolerable; and the revolt against paternalism, no matter how benign, is an essential aspect of the human identity. Somewhere between the proposition that the customer is always right and the proposition that the public be damned must be an uneasy Aristotelian mean, and toward this the concept of professional need for medical care or for anything else uneasily steers itself.

The word need has a number of meanings, and the idea of homeostatic need or professional need which we have been discussing does not exhaust it. Another very important connotation of the word is that implied in the word "needy." One's need in this sense is not merely what some wise professional person thinks one ought to have, but what one cannot afford because he is poor. In this sense also, need is thought of as something which stands in contrast with demand, and the need for a concept of need arises because of certain deficiencies in demand as a principle of allocation. The concept of need as a criticism of demand here refers to the fact that effective demand is closely related to income and to the distribution of income. Need is an equalitarian concept. It recalls the famous communist slogan, "From each according to his ability, to each according to his need."

Demand, perhaps because of its very stress on autonomy and freedom, is libertarian rather than equalitarian, and liberty is seldom equally divided. If medical care is distributed according to demand, the rich will get most of it and the poor very little. One of the main concerns of society for the need for medical care, therefore, is the fact that a sizeable proportion of the population is "medically indigent" in the sense that its income is not large enough to provide a demand for the minimum medical care which a society, or a profession, identifies as need. That may be a part of the general problem of the social minimum. At present nearly all societies have a deliberate policy to establish a minimum standard life below which citizens are not supposed to fall. Whether the policy is in fact successful is another matter, for in almost all cases some people do fall below the minimum, and all the machinery of society is not powerful enough to elevate them. Nevertheless, the principle of a social minimum has been established for a long time and today is almost universally accepted.

Even the acceptance of a social minimum, however, does not necessarily resolve the conflict between need and demand. Some argue that insofar as the problem is one of poverty, the only solution to this is to make the poor richer, either by giving them money, by improving their skills or by integrating them more fully into the culture around them. Once the poor have been made richer, the problem of the need for medical care resolves itself essentially into the problem discussed earlier of a consumer's demand versus professional need, between which poles some uneasy compromise must be reached.

In the case of medical indigency, however, the temptation is to deny consumers sovereignty as the price of the relief of indigency, and to say that the poor must have what the professionals think is good for them whether they want it or not. This is part of a very old and still unresolved question as to whether the grants economy should content itself with grants of money, leaving the recipient to spend it as he will, or should consist essentially of grants in kind supplying needs as defined by the professionals. Those who are somewhat liberal are inclined to emphasize demand even in the case of the indigent, and to give them at least some freedom to reject medical care if they prefer a short life and a merry one, though the liberty to preach against such behavior should also be preserved.

One of the great problems of the grants economy—which appears in the relief of medical indigency just as it does elsewhere—is that it can easily result in quite unintended administrative distortions of the price structure which in turn can cause social loss and quite unnecessary individual misery. If, for instance, a grant system bases a grant on a cost of service which is wrongly estimated, it can severely discourage the services which are undervalued and unnecessary and encourage the services which are overvalued. For example, certain casual administrative regulations in the social security system have stimulated a profitable practice of keeping indigent patients in nursing homes in bed, simply because the nursing homes are paid an extra amount for keeping people in bed. Hence nursing homes make more money on bed patients than on ambulatory ones. As a result of the strong financial pressure patients are kept in bed, in spite of the fact that this may be quite unwarranted medically and may contribute to the already bad enough miseries of old age and incompetence.

Generally any system which sets out to administer a price structure will get it wrong so that some things will be underpriced and some overpriced. The same problem may be seen in the universities, where teaching is underpriced relative to research, or where good administration is underpriced and bad administration overpriced. Under these circumstances a kind of universal Gresham's Law operates: the overpriced bad always drives out the underpriced good. No proposition as far as is known says that this problem is insoluble. Unless it is solved, however, socialized and administrative medicine will operate under some handicaps. The uneasy compromise between need and demand takes the form that if needs are to be well satisfied, demand, if it is not to be free, must at least be simulated. If administrative terms of trade are established in the system, it must also have an apparatus that can get feedback from their consequences and review them and adjust them rapidly in the way that the market does.

The last question of this discussion relates to the problem of the effectiveness of medical activity and research. Probably only in the last 100 years has the medical profession done more good than harm in promoting health. Now, although the direction of the effect is not in doubt, a certain amount of doubt remains about its magnitude. Certainly the most spectacular productivity of human activity in the production of health is only indirectly related to the medical profession as such. That is the kind of activity involved, for instance, in antimalaria campaigns, in cleaning up water supplies, in improving nutrition and even in teaching more desirable habits of child-rearing. This fact should not be surprising, nor does it redound to any discredit to the medical profession. Nothing is wrong with the assumption that the business of the doctor is sickness rather than health, just as the business of the garage mechanic is the repair of automobiles, not their production, or the provision of roads on which they may safely be driven. The medical profession is only a single input in the enormous network of social inputs which together determine the general level of health of the population. No one wishes the medical profession to lose its interest in sickness, for that is when a doctor is most needed. On the other hand, one also likes to see a strong interest in preventive medicine and in public health and in what might be called the larger environment of the health sciences. The need is also strong for the development of a social science of health, not only in economics but also in sociology and psychology. Considerable strides have been made toward this, but not in many centers in the world—to bring even one to mind is difficult—is the social science of health studied and taught as a whole.

One would like to see a research operation of at least the magnitude of the Rand Corporation, the object of which would be to study health in all its aspects, social, biological and physical, in a manner permitting a good deal of interchange among specialists. Such a study would clearly reveal that the need for medical services will depend on a very large number of other variables, economic, sociological, biological, and on the whole system of this planet. That answer may not satisfy those who are seeking quick results to solve administrative dilemmas, and the importance of administrative shortcuts cannot be denied. Nevertheless, in the long run, a very substantial intellectual endeavor still awaits mankind in the study of this problem, and at the moment its solution is not near.[3]

The Rand Corporation is used merely as a symbol of the magnitude of the research effort in the social science of health which would probably be profitable. Whether the effort should be concentrated in a single institution or scattered around the academic community is a matter of research strategy on which may rest very valid differences of opinion. Something is to be said for the theory of the "critical mass," especially in interdisciplinary research; and the extraordinary fruitfulness of the Center for Advanced Study in the Behavioral Sciences at Stanford, indicates that a critical mass of this kind may actually be quite small under some circumstances. On the other hand, a research strategy should certainly not be confined to any particular institution, and should envisage the whole intellectual community as its field. Research strategies which are too specific can easily do more harm than good, and even the concept of the need for research needs to be looked at with a slightly quizzical eye. The growth of knowledge is much more like an evolutionary than it is like a mechanical process, and this means that it is fundamentally unpredictable. This can be seen very clearly by asking the question, can anyone predict what will be known 25 years from now? The answer is obviously no, or it would be known now. If the results of a research program are known in advance, the point in doing it has been lost. Hence the growth of knowledge must always contain what is called fundamental surprise, and any research strategy must be built around the capacity to expect and react creatively to surprise.

If any research strategy emerges out of these considerations, it is that one should be extremely suspicious of research devoted specifically to finding out the need for medical care. Too much of such research has already been done, all of which has outlined "needs" which are absurdly inflated, and which, if allowed to be fulfilled, would justify themselves with the greatest of ease. A research program which concentrated solely on quantitative estimates of need would inevitably neglect the problem of demand and the problem of the price structure. A great deal in research depends on how questions are framed. If the question is asked, how does one use a combination of the grants economy and the price structure in producing a system of medical care that compromises between needs and demands, a much richer and more satisfactory answer will likely result than if one simply asks, what is the need for medical care? Almost everyone who has raised children has heard the anguished cry, "But I need—" and soon learns to interpret this as meaning, "I want something badly but I am not prepared to pay the price for it." This cautionary note seems a suitable place to end what is mainly an appeal to move gingerly into an inevitably uncertain future, without forgetting that the movement must be made.

REFERENCES

[1] Boulding, K. E., The Menace of Methuselah, *Journal of the Washington Academy of Sciences,* 55, 171–179, October, 1965.

[2] Medawar, P. B., THE FUTURE OF MAN, New York, Basic Books, Inc., Publishers, 1960.

[3] *See* Ginzberg, Eli, The Political Economy of Health, *Bulletin of the New York Academy of Medicine,* 41, 1015–1036, October, 1965.

ECONOMICS AND ECOLOGY

Future Environments in North America, F. Fraser Darling
and John P. Milton, eds., Garden City, New York:
Natural History Press, 1966, pp. 225-34.

ECONOMICS AND ECOLOGY

The two sciences whose names are derived from the same Greek root, economics and ecology, have had surprisingly little contact, no doubt because of our deplorably compartmentalized systems of education. For some reason the sociologists and the ecologists seem to have had much more in common, for human ecology, at least, has long been a recognized branch of sociology. This is perhaps because sociology and ecology, as recognized departments of science, are about the same age, whereas economics is much older, dating back as a systematic body of theory at least to Adam Smith's *Wealth of Nations* in 1776. Even though, as we shall see, there are striking parallels between the concepts of ecology and economics—and I believe the two sciences can learn a good deal from each other—up to this point, there has been little interaction between them. From the Greek root one would suspect that each science is devoted to the study of households, one to the household of nature, the other to the household of man, and in a broad, though very broad, sense this is true. One of the central concerns of ecology is the way in which all natural species earn their living—that is, attain the input which is necessary for their survival. Economics likewise is concerned very largely with how man earns his living. Nevertheless, both ecology and economics go far beyond this initial concept and devote themselves essentially to the study of how the interaction of individuals and species constitutes a total system.

I have detected at least five basic similarities between ecology and economics, and there are probably more. In the first place, they both study not only individuals as such, but individuals as members of species. The concept of a population of like individuals constituting a species is indeed fundamental to ecology. The corresponding concept in economics is that of the commodity, and it is easy to see the population of commodities as a simple extension of natural species. The automobile, the pair of shoes, and the loaf of bread are just as much members of species as the whooping crane and the horse, or indeed man himself. A somewhat casual observer from outer space indeed might well deduce that the course of evolution in this planet had produced a species of large four-wheeled bugs with detachable brains; peculiar animals which rested when they sent their brains away from them but performed in rather predictable manners when their brains were recalled.

Commodities, of course, are not the only social species. We also have organizations, such as farms, steel firms, PTAs, schools, churches, and so on. It is just as reasonable to talk about the distribution and habitat of the Kingdom Halls of Jehovah's Witnesses or the supermarkets of the A&P as it is to discuss the distribution and habitats of field mice. Each of these species is equally part of an ecological system. In this sense we see economics as a subspecies of ecology, studying that restricted group of species and individuals which enter into exchange—that is, commodities, and studying particularly those kinds of organizations, such as firms or even households, whose activities center around exchange.

Like all populations, populations of commodities consist of individuals which are born, which age, and which even die. The analysis of a population of automobiles differs in no respect from the analysis of a population of horses, as long as we stick to the birth, aging, and death phenomena alone. I have indeed (1955) analyzed the population of automobiles from the point of view of finding out the results of some distortions in the age distribution,[1] exactly as one might analyze a similar population of natural species. The principal difference between populations of commodities and natural populations lies in the genetic apparatus by which births are made. The death or survival functions are highly similar in both cases, though there may be more infant mortality in the case of natural populations. When it comes down to the birth functions, however, striking differences occur. It only takes the cooperation of a horse and a mare to produce a colt, whereas the cooperation of two automobiles has never produced another. Sex and sexual reproduction are vir-

[1] Boulding, K. E., "An Application of Population Analysis to the Automobile Population of the United States," *Kyklos* 2(1955): pp. 109–24.

tually unknown in the world of man-made commodities, although, of course, insofar as natural species become commodities, such as domestic animals, the natural processes of sexual reproduction are significant. Even here, however, the effective birth rate depends much more on the decisions of man than on chances of nature, and there is really more similarity in principle between the reproductive processes of the domestic animal and the domestic automobile than there is between the domestic and the wild animal.

A second similarity between economics and ecology is that both have an important concept of general equilibrium. In the case of ecology this is a concept of general equilibrium of population, depending on a proposition that the birth and death rate of each species is a function of the numbers of all species, and that an equilibrium system can be postulated in which the birth rate and the death rate are equated for all species in the long run. The struggle for existence, indeed, can be regarded as a rather elaborate computer for solving these equations. If there is no solution to a particular set of equations, one or more of the species must disappear, and this will go on until a solution is found. Frequently when a solution is found, it is surprisingly stable in what might be called the medium run. The equilibrium of species in a lake or a pond, for instance, seems to be stable for quite large disturbances. If we take 25 or even 50 per cent of the individuals of a particular species out of the system, in a year or two the old numbers are restored. Any ecological system, of course, is likely to exhibit what are sometimes called watershed points, beyond which the old system will not be restored but a new process will be set up leading to a new equilibrium. In economics we do not usually postulate a simple system of ecological equilibrium of populations of different commodities, even though there is no fundamental reason why this could not be done. The general equilibrium of the price system, however, as developed, for instance, by Walras or by Hicks, or even as implied by Adam Smith and Alfred Marshall, has many basic similarities to a system of ecological equilibrium. It implies, for instance, that the birth rate, which is the rate of production, and the death rate, which is the rate of consumption, of all commodities should be equal, so that the stocks of commodities should remain unchanged. In the case of economic equilibrium, we generally postulate that production and consumption are functions of the set of prices rather than of the set of stocks of commodities. Nevertheless, as the set of prices is itself functionally related to the set of stocks, it is clear that the price set is in a sense an intermediary or an additional set of variables in the system, and its introduction does not alter the basically ecological framework of economic equilibrium. Indeed, it is quite easy to extend the concepts which are analogous to the price system.

This, indeed, is the third basic similarity. Both ecological and economic systems involve a system of exchange among their various individuals and species as an essential element in determining their final equilibrium. In the case of economics, this system of exchange is symbolized in the price system, which is the set of rates of exchange of different commodities with each other. In the case of ecological systems, the exchange consists of the metabolic system—that is, the ratios of inputs to outputs of different individuals, organisms, or species. In both cases there has to be a system of balances of payments. That is, for any segment of the system and for any particular input or output, input must equal output in the long run, otherwise there will be accumulations or decumulations of something in different parts of the system which will destroy the equilibrium. Thus in ecological systems we have a subtle balance of payments in, for instance, the nitrogen cycle and all the various nutritive cycles, by which the various elements which comprise the organisms are circulated through the system. The one important difference between ecological and economic systems is that there seems to be no parallel in ecological systems for the economic concept of money, perhaps because in ecological systems there is no overriding species in the interests of which the value of the system is gauged. Man needs a medium of exchange and a measure of value in the form of money, because he needs to refer the whole system of commodities to his own welfare. In ecology no single species has the temerity to arrogate to itself the character of judge of everything that goes on, and hence no general and uniform measure of value is needed.

A fourth similarity between economics and ecology is that both imply some concept of development. Neither of them is content with the concept of equilibrium as such. In the case of ecology, this involves the concept of ecological succession—that is, the process by which the underlying determinants of the system of ecological equilibrium change in the course of the operations of the system. A famous example, of course, is the gradual filling up of the lake bed by the operations of the ecological system which comprises the lake. The plants and animals gradually absorb carbon from the air, more is washed into the lake than is washed out, and in the course of time the lake shrinks and eventually becomes a swamp, a prairie, or perhaps a forest. In the search for sources of development we have to look for irreversible processes. In the case of ecological systems, we find these not only in certain cumulative processes which violate the principle of equilibrium of balance of payments—that is, balance of inputs and outputs—but we find it also in the phenomenon of genetic mutation. Genetic mutation, by creating individuals of a new species or a potential new species, introduces new parameters into the equations of ecological equilibrium. In the great majority of cases, the old equilibrium is stable enough so that the new species are rejected and perish. In a few cases, however, the mutation is favorable enough so that it survives and then a new equilibrium has to be found for the ecological equations. The whole process of evolution can then be written in terms of successive solutions of the ecological equations under the impact of genetic mutation.

Social evolution exhibits many parallels to the process of natural evolution, and we have ecological succession in society just as we do in the pond or the forest. Here again there seem to be two major processes at work which correspond to the processes of simple accumulation on the one hand and processes of genuine mutation on the other. It is harder to tell these apart in social systems because of the extreme complexity of the genetic process of social species, but the distinction seems to be an interesting one. The cumulative growth of population and the accumulation of capital in the form of larger numbers of the same kind of good represents the sort of thing which seems to go on in the filling up of a pond, and as both population and capital accumulate, certain changes take place in the social system simply as a result of the greater densities of people and things. This, however, is quite inadequate to explain the great processes of social evolution, and again we have to introduce something that looks like mutation in the form of new ideas, new ideology, and new inventions, both mechanical, biological, and social. As in systems of natural evolution, a great many mutations do not survive, but enough survive to introduce what seems to be a constant irreversible succession of social and economic equilibria.

A critical problem in social evolution which also has important implications for natural evolution is that of the growth of knowledge. This is the principal source of the irreversibility of the process of social evolution, and once mankind got past the paleolithic and entered the age of agriculture and metals, this process seems to have been virtually irreversible and constantly cumulative. In the paleolithic period, there seem to have been many times when the slow growth of knowledge was interrupted by an epidemic or a natural disaster which simply carried off the few people in whose heads the accumulated knowledge resided. With mankind living in small clusters and without the aids of writing or records, the "wisdom of the tribe" must have been in constant danger of loss by death, simply because it was contained in so few heads. With the advent of agriculture and especially of writing, the chance of loss of knowledge was much less, and it seems to have entered into its irreversible cumulative phase. There were, of course, periods of retrogression, especially in particular localities, but if we look at the whole world as a single system it seems pretty clear that in the last 8000 years there has been practically no period in which the "quantity of science," as Adam Smith calls it, has diminished. Furthermore, the growth of knowledge seems to be not only cumulative but it seems also to accumulate at an increasing rate. The more knowledge there is, the easier it seems to be to find still more, for one of the items of knowledge which grows is the knowledge of how to find more knowledge.

If we think of knowledge as a species, we see that this also grows, in part, by simple accumulation—that is, the addition of more items than are subtracted in a given period, as, for instance, the simple growth of vocabulary in a language. There is also, however, a phenomenon that looks very much like mutation. This is the reorganization of knowledge into a new system, a new theory, a new way of looking at things, or even a new ideology. This happens usually in a single mind, from which, however, it can be propagated rapidly through a whole society if it happens to fit the particular ecological system of ideas which is prevailing at the moment. The spread of the growth of knowledge therefore seems to follow many of the principles of ecology, and the various kinds of knowledge flourish or decline according to the competition of other kinds of knowledge and according to the general habitat in which they are found.

We may note parenthetically that while there are some elements in this process of socioecological succession which might be called dialectical; in fact, the dialectical scheme adds very little to our understanding of this process, and most of the great processes of ecological succession are in fact nondialectical, in the sense that they do not operate through a process of thesis, antithesis, and synthesis, but rather through the introduction of small parametric changes into the equations of equilibrium. There is competition and conflict, of course, in the processes of ecological succession, but the conflict is among a particular species, not among systems as a whole. Even the phenomenon of ecological revolution, in which a small change in some parameter of the system leads to a total transformation in the habitat of the numbers and kinds of species in equilibrium, there is nothing that really looks like a dialectical process. When, for instance, a slight change in rainfall or perhaps in temperature destroys the equilibrium of the forest and eventually produces the prairie, this is not because the prairie as antithesis challenges and conquers the forest as a thesis, but simply because of the fact that under some circumstances a relatively small change in the parameters of the habitat controls large changes in

final position of equilibrium. For this reason it seems to me the ecological point of view is profoundly unfriendly to the Hegelian-Marxist view of the nature of the world, and leads into what I have elsewhere called a developmental rather than a dialectical philosophy of history, in which emphasis is placed not on the Hegelian-Marxist type of revolution in which one system is overthrown by another but on the long, slow, quiet nondialectical processes by which equilibrium positions change.

A fifth important parallel between economics and ecological systems falls under the general head of policy. That is the distortion of the equilibrium of the system by man in his own favor. In the case of ecological systems, we see this most clearly exemplified in agriculture. Here man deliberately interferes with the "natural" ecosystem of a piece of land, producing corn and hogs instead of prairie grass and gophers, or trees and squirrels. This distortion of the natural ecosystem requires constant intervention in the shape of plowing, harrowing, sowing, harvesting, and so on, and indeed many domesticated species of both plants and animals have now got to the point where they would be quite incapable of surviving without a symbiotic relationship with man. Corn, for instance, in its present form could not possibly survive in a wild state, and the same is probably true of many domestic animals, although there is some possibility that these might retreat toward a state in which they were capable of surviving in the absence of man, were his hand to be removed. Corresponding to agriculture in the natural ecosystem we have policy at all levels in the social system. The law, for instance, is supposed to discourage criminals in much the same manner that harrowing or weed killer discourages weeds. Similarly, the institutions of education and religion are supposed to promote intelligent citizens and happy families. I recall once walking in the jungles of Brazil with a distinguished British economist and remarking as we contemplated the tangled growth that this at least showed that anarchy was possible. He came back immediately with, "Yes, but it also shows that it is not desirable." Without some form of policy as expressed primarily through political organization, the social ecosystem tends to degenerate into a jungle, and the well-ordered society seems to require a "farmer" in the shape of government to distort the natural social ecosystem in favor of some ideals or values.

Both in the case of agriculture and in the case of social policy, however, the fact that we distort the ecosystem in favor of man does not mean that we destroy the principles of general equilibrium of populations. Unless, indeed, we know something about the laws which govern this general equilibrium, we shall not be very successful in distorting it toward our heart's desire. If man is to achieve a distribution of populations of all kinds which conforms to his own values, he must at least learn to cooperate with the great ecological forces which determine the equilibrium of coexisting populations, otherwise he is likely to be grievously disappointed. His crops will fail, his irrigated acres will turn saline, his animals will fail to produce or will die, and his social policies will turn out to have unintended and undesirable consequences. It is hardly too much to say that the failure to appreciate the ecological point of view and to see society as an enormous interacting network of coexisting populations is behind the failure of most social policies.

Up to now we have looked at the similarities between economics and ecology, and indeed these are striking. For the rest of the paper I intend to look more closely at the differences, for these also are important and without proper appreciation of these differences, false

analogies may be drawn and the two disciplines will fail to learn the appropriate lessons from each other. The differences arise, I think, not out of any fundamental principle except insofar, as already noted, that the genetic apparatus of social species and populations is very different from that of biological species. The differences arise out of different sets of values, particularly as applied to the whole system. Economists are irretrievably and irredeemably man-centered. Economics is the theory of the household of man, not the household of nature. Ecologists, by contrast, tend to have a value system which encompasses all species. In their underlying value systems, ecologists often tend more toward Hindu or Buddhist values, in which man is seen as only part and perhaps not even a very important part of a vast natural order. Economics, however, emerged out of a civilization, part of Western Europe, that was created largely by Christianity and which regarded man as the measure of all things and the universe as existing mainly for his pleasure and salvation. Ecologists, therefore, have a strong tendency to look with affection on the whooping crane, to regard the disappearance of any species as a major tragedy, and to regard man on the whole as a nuisance, upsetting the balance of nature, destroying the ancient equilibria of the world, and generally behaving like an outrageous and irresponsible caretaker of his delightful planet. The economist, by contrast, is much more apt to look at things from a strictly human view and while he would no doubt regret the passing of the whooping crane, when the chips are really down, the question he asks himself is, what would it cost to preserve it?—cost in terms of strictly human values.

The contrast is seen very clearly when we reflect that ecology has really no concept corresponding to the enonomists' gross national product. It never occurs to the ecologist to try to evaluate the ecological system in terms of a single measure. One sees occasional references to the total mass of living matter which a given habitat will support, but I have never seen ecologists pay much attention to this, and they certainly would not judge the desirability or interest of a habitat by this measure. I have never heard any mention of the gross carbohydrate product or the gross protein product of a habitat, and indeed concepts of this kind are quite foreign to the multidimensional, structural, interactionist point of view of the ecologist. The economist, on the other hand, has seized upon the concept of the national product with the avidity of the dog seizing a bone. The sophisticated economist, of course, knows that the concept involves a great many dubious assumptions and that it has to be interpreted pretty carefully. Nevertheless, he is not at all displeased to find this concept becoming important in political discourse and used in measuring the over-all progress of the society or the comparative position of different economies. The absence of any gross-product concept in ecology and its presence in economics stem directly from the human orientation of economics and the tendency of economists to reduce large complex systems to some single-value parameter descriptive of their value to man, whereas ecologists have no such interest.

There is, indeed, a deep ethical problem involved in this difference, and one which is by no means easy to resolve. It is a problem which becomes more acute all the time as the power of man over nature increases. The problem has become particularly acute because of the pressure on the resources of the earth which comes from man's exploding population. In a world of a few hundred million human beings, most other species can survive fairly easily. The growth of the human population may, perhaps, threaten a few highly localized species, but does not threaten to upset the general constitution and distribution of living populations. When the human population grows to three billion, even more when it grows to ten billion, as it soon will, the pressure on all other populations becomes acute. In the next hundred years, indeed, if things go on the way they are going, we face the extinction of very large numbers of species of both animals and plants, as man in his insatiable pressure for food supplies gobbles up all the wilderness and turns it into agriculture or something like it for his own use. The lion, the elephant, the tiger, the hippopotamus, the rhinoceros, the ostrich may soon go the way of the passenger pigeon or the dodo, and very little can be done about it. If the price of not extinguishing the lion population, for instance, is the survival of a few thousand humans, who would pay the price? It is one thing when a little care and conservation will preserve a nonhuman population, such as the whooping crane. It is quite another thing when the survival of another species must be paid for in human life. The question, therefore, becomes one almost of theological import. Is man going to conceive of himself as a steward of the planet, conserving a priceless heritage of germ plasm and genetic code material which, once lost, can never be replaced, so that like a good steward he is willing to sacrifice himself in order to preserve his charge; or is man in himself literally the only thing that matters, in which case we face the brutal fact of the future (and the not really very distant future, at that), that in the absence of very stringent control of the human population, any species which cannot in some sense be domesticated is doomed.

The ultimate resolution of this question is clearly far beyond the scope of this paper. All one can hope to do is to put up a few warning signs, such as

Dead End Road for the ecologist or Thin Ice for the economist. The Dead End Road is a blind conservatism which simply takes the existing distribution of populations, particularly of natural populations, as given, sacred, and sacrosanct. It digs in its heels and regards any departure from the existing world ecosystem as undesirable. The economist, I think, can run rings around this position, and the cause of conservation has been substantially weakened because it has been associated in some cases with this blind and obstinate conservatism which regards all dynamic movements as bad. The logical outcome of this position would be the conclusion that the invention of man himself was deplorable and the only decent thing the human race could do would be to feed itself collectively to the lions and hope the evolutionary process would not make the mistake of creating intelligence of this kind again.

Whatever kind of sense we try to make out of the evolutionary process, it is clear that nature abhors a stationary equilibrium. Nature, in other words, is not a conservative. The evolutionary process destroyed more species than it created long before man appeared on the scene, and it is absurd to suppose that the existing distribution of genetic material in the shape of phenotypes represents the *summum bonum* of this part of the universe. Whether we like it or not and even whether man is here or not, the evolutionary process will continue, and to its blank and random stare nothing is sacred, not even the whooping crane. We have to face the fact, therefore, that since the advent of man the evolutionary process has been enormously speeded up, and that man, for good or ill, now has some kind of control over it, a control which is likely to increase even more dramatically in the future as the practical consequences of the recent revolution in biology are

worked out. Suppose, for instance, that in the next hundred years, as is by no means impossible, man is able to modify directly the gene pool of the earth and produce new species quite unheard of before, cranes with louder whoops, more ferocious lions, more absurd hippopotamuses, and even perhaps to re-create the dodo. One feels somehow that the ecologist will look with a kindlier eye on the creation of new species than on the destruction of old ones, but the ethical problem is much the same. The right, or the absence of right, to be born is just as much a moral problem as the right or the absence of right to survive. If the moral impact of the ecological point of view is to be felt, as it should be, it will have to develop a dynamic ethic which will accept the role of man as an evolutionary agent and seek to develop standards and criteria for evaluating this role, rather than taking refuge in a hopeless and obscurantist conservatism.

If, therefore, one wants to put up a few Dead End signs for the ecologist, one also wants to put up some Thin Ice signs for the economist. In his pursuit of purely human values, the economist may easily be running mankind itself into grave dangers. The Greeks were perhaps all too aware of the dangers of *hubris*, that pride and overweening self-confidence in the power or good fortunes of man which so easily leads to his downfall. The extraordinary achievements of the last 200 years have given us certain delusions of grandeur and a certain feeling that man can accomplish anything if he only puts his mind to it. We see this in its extreme form among the Communists, where a belief in the infallibility, omnipotence, and immortality of man and his societies reaches absurdities beyond the most extreme religious dogmas. Even Western economists, however, are by no means exempt from the belief that there are really no limits on man's capacity to manipulate the world to his own advantage. It is highly necessary, therefore, for the ecologist to take these flights of omnipotent fancy and bring them down solidly to earth, and to a highly limited earth at that. Man is beginning to inhabit a pretty small and overcrowded space ship, destination unknown, and the possibility that he may ruin it and himself in the process is by no means negligible. Here the conservatism of the ecologist is badly needed. The technical achievements of the last 200 years have been achieved largely with the aid of the spending of a long accumulation of geological capital in the shape of fossil fuels and ores. A very few hundred years, a mere tick of the clock even on a human time scale, will see these exhausted. One of the most critical questions before us is whether man can achieve a stable high-level economy with high energy and information input and high product output which is not dependent on fossil fuels and ores and exhaustible resources. There are certain indications that such an anti-entropic economy, as I have called it, is possible, and indeed may be just around the corner, but that particular corner has not yet been turned.

Economists, and indeed mankind generally, have tended to treat the economic system as if it could enter into continuous exchange with an infinite reservoir of nature. Thus we have regarded the atmosphere and the oceans as if they were infinite reservoirs which we could pollute indefinitely and from which we could draw indefinite supplies of what they had to offer. Similarly in regard to mines and fossil fuels, we have tended to treat the earth as if it were an infinite reservoir of these substances. This attitude has been less noticeable in the case of land, where, perhaps because of the relative smallness of the habitat, man in many of his societies has developed soil conserving practices which make him and the land together virtually a closed system, in which land is regarded not as an infinite reservoir but as a scarce resource which constantly has to be replenished. Even in the case of land, there has been a good deal of soil mining, often with disastrous results.

It is the peculiar virtue of the ecologist that he does look upon his system as essentially a closed system, in the sense that there are no imports from or exports to the outside apart from those which bring about the processes of ecological succession. In economics, this is what might be called the "space ship" point of view. If man is ever to make long voyages in space, he will have to develop a self-sustaining economy on a small scale, in which the very small capital stock which he is able to take with him will have to be circulated constantly through the system in such a way as to maintain his life and, in some degree, his comfort. We are now beginning to see the earth as a space ship, not only politically but also in economic terms. Even today it is clear that the oceans and the atmosphere are by no means inexhaustible reservoirs. It may be fatally easy, for instance, for man to change the composition of either of them in such a way that the earth will pass some watershed point—for instance, through something like the greenhouse effect of the accumulating carbon dioxide in the atmosphere—which will destroy the existing equilibrium and move us to a new equilibrium which may be much less desirable for man. As the human population increases, the chance of man's activities seriously interfering with the whole balance of the planet becomes greater and greater. One of the greatest contributions of the ecologist, therefore, is to point out that the earth is in fact a total ecosystem of which man's activities are only a part, and that he can no longer regard himself as operating with infinite reservoirs.

This does not mean, I think, that the

problem of operating the earth as a high-level space ship without any inexhaustible reservoirs is insoluble. In what might be called traditional agriculture, indeed, man has already largely solved the problem of a self-sustaining economy on a permanent basis. Even though our existing economy is essentially suicidal, depending as it is on past accumulations of natural capital in the shape of ores and fuels but also in the shape of the atmosphere and the oceans, it is not unreasonable to look upon the present era as a chance which man has (and probably a unique chance at that, which will never be repeated) of translating his natural capital into enough knowledge that will enable him to do without it. We can certainly imagine a world economy at a high level in which man's life and comfort depend on a self-sustaining process in which the input of energy and knowledge is enough to counteract the otherwise inevitable increase of entropy. Either the energy input will have to come from the sun, which from the point of view of mankind has to be regarded as inexhaustible, or of course it may be supplemented with energy from nuclear fusion, which is, in a sense, the same thing. We do not know how large the knowledge input has to be. I think this is a problem which is theoretically capable of some kind of answer. At the moment, however, we do not really know whether the knowledge input is just a little more than what we have today or whether it requires knowledge of another order of magnitude than what we now have, in which case man's long-run situation is probably hopeless. There is no point, however, in acting upon hopeless assumptions. We might as well assume that there is hope, and get on with the business of trying to realize it.

A critical question on which, as far as I know, very little work has been done is: What is the optimum total population of the world under this space-ship type of self-sustaining economy? It may very well be that out of the space research of the next generation an answer to the question will emerge, and I know of no question of greater import for the long-run future of mankind. If it turns out, say, that only something like a hundred million people can live in real comfort on this particular space ship, a terrible agony is in front of man, for he has never succeeded in reducing his population without enormous disaster. If the earth can support three billion, we still have time to catch the population increase, though not much. If it can support ten billion, we have a fair amount of time, at least a couple of generations. The problem, however, is urgent, and it would be quite easy for the current population expansion to carry the load of this planet beyond a point and the world would, in an almost literal sense, sink. Ecologists have sometimes compared the present growth of population rather gruesomely to the explosive expansion of the first occupants of new or changed habitats, like the fireweed after a forest fire. These first occupants, however, are rarely the last occupants, and the climactic ecosystem is usually very different from the initial one. This is a grim note to sound, but it is, I think, the peculiar business of ecologists to be pessimistic. In these days ecology may well take the mantle of doom and the name of "the dismal science" from economics.

BIBLIOGRAPHY

Boulding, K. E. 1955. An Application of Population Analysis to the Automobile Population of the United States. Kylos 2:109–24.

IS SCARCITY DEAD?

The Public Interest, 5 (Fall, 1966): 36-44.

Is
scarcity
dead?

Economics is first and foremost
the science of scarcity. Its problems only arise if there is not enough
to go around. This is why it is a dismal science. Now, there is a fundamental conflict, which has gone on through almost all of recorded
history, between the heroic and the economic, between greatness and
prudence, between extravagance and sobriety, between glory and
common sense. Economics is the good, gray, rational science. After
the charge of the Light Brigade, economics asks the reason why.
Byronic frenzy may inspire us to say, "Let joy be unconfined"; the
economist says, "you'll have to pay for this tomorrow." Even when
St. Francis urges us to give and not to count the cost, the economist
says that *somebody* has to count the cost; and when someone wants
a Great Society, the economist asks, "Who is going to pay for it?" It
is no wonder that the economist is not very popular.

At this point someone is sure to come up and say, "Oh, but we
have changed all that. Science and technology have produced the
Age of Affluence. Scarcity has been abolished. Let us eat, drink, and
be merry; there is plenty for all. Between science, automation, and
systems engineering, we can produce all we need with a fraction of
the labor force; and today not even the sky is the limit."

This view seems to me to involve delusions of grandeur and a
totally unwarranted euphoria derived from the careless observation
of a few special cases. It is true, of course, that where there is eco-

nomic development, where the total to be distributed is increasing, then it is possible that the more there is of yours, the more there is of mine, too. We can all indulge in the delightful "positive-sum game" of getting richer together. It is true, too, that the process of economic development in a very real sense diminishes not only scarcity, but also the urgency of rational choice. This is the essential point that Galbraith is making in *The Affluent Society,* and it is perfectly valid. One of the principal delights of being rich is that we do not have to economize so much — that is, we do not have to devote so much time and attention to the careful balancing of gain against loss at the margin, to what Wordsworth decried as "the lore of nicely calculated less or more." There is a familiar proposition in economics that the richer we are, the less is the marginal utility of money — i.e., the less significance for our welfare does the expenditure of an extra dollar have. We can expand this proposition to say that the richer we are, the less is the marginal utility of a unit of general resources, and the less it matters, in effect, whether we make mistakes in allocation. A rich society can afford to be careless and magnificent: another billion dollars is only two thousandths of the GNP, so why not spend it? Furthermore, even though unemployment is now down below 4 percent, we should be able to get it down to 3 percent; there is thus still a good deal of slack in the economy and, by absorbing this, we could easily raise the GNP by five or ten billion; under these circumstances, practically anything we want to do is virtually costless, since it simply comes out of unemployed resources. Come on in, everybody, the water's fine!

Skeletons at the feast

By this time, any economist who defends scarcity looks like a Prohibitionist at a country club. Truth, however, requires me to inaugurate an anti-euphoria campaign. In the face of the "Scarcity is Dead" theology, which is now celebrated with such enthusiasm, the economist needs to remind the celebrants of a few skeletons at their feast.

In the first place, there is no evidence that we are undergoing anything very unusual in the way of technological change and economic development. If we take, for instance, the indices of output per man-hour calculated by the Department of Labor, we find that in the last eighteen years the average rate of increase of output per man-hour has been 3.4 percent per annum for the total private sector; 5.9 percent in agriculture and 2.8 percent in the non-agricultural industries. The only thing here which approaches the spectacular is the remarkable increase in agriculture, though even this is only a speeding up of what has been going on for more than a hundred years. In spite of automation, the rate of increase in output per man-hour in non-agricultural industries is not spectacular; and as agriculture is a constantly declining proportion of the total economy, its impact on the total gets smaller all the time. It is, indeed, one of the paradoxes of economic development that the more successful any segment of the economy is in achieving rapid technological progress, the more it is likely to decline in importance. Hence there is a constant tendency for the more stagnant sectors of the economy — such as government, education, the service trades, and so on — to increase in the proportion (of resources used, etc.) which they bear to the total. In this way, a rapid technological change in one sector of the economy has, as it were, the seeds of declining influence in it.

Furthermore, the American economy is by no means the most rapidly developing in the world. It is indeed quite a long way down the list. Direct productivity measures are not easy to come by for comparative purposes, but in cases where the proportion of total resources employed is approximately constant, the rise in the gross national product per head is at least a good first approximation of the rate of technical change. On this score, the record of the United States in the last twenty years is by no means impressive. In the 1950's, there were 45 countries who had a higher rate of economic development than the United States. This figure is a little unfair, because the 1950's were, to some extent, a period of relative stagnation for the United States and of unusually rapid development in other countries; the record of the 1960's will unquestionably look rather different. Nevertheless, in the last twenty years, some countries, notably Japan, West Germany, and some other European countries on both sides of the Iron Curtain, have achieved rates of development which are unprecedented in human history. A sustained rate of development of 8 percent per annum per capita, as in the case of Japan, for instance, represents almost a quantum jump from anything which has happened before. In the period before the Second World War, no country sustained a rate of increase in per capita GNP of more than about 2.3 percent. The difference between 2.3 percent and 8 percent may be dramatically illustrated by pointing out that, under conditions of what might be called successful prewar development, the children are twice as rich as the parents — i.e., per capita income approximately doubles every generation — while at 8 percent per annum, the children are six times as rich as the parents. Whether this can be kept up for more than a generation is, of course, a question.

The two scientific revolutions

Even when we have made all these downward adjustments, however, the fact remains that we seem to be in the presence of a new phenomenon which is associated with what might be called the second phase of the impact of the scientific revolution on economic life. The first phase was the period from, shall we say, 1860 to the Second World War, in which we began to get the science-based industries such as electrical engineering, chemical engineering, the nuclear industry, and so on. (Before 1860, the impact of science on the economy was very small. The so-called Industrial Revolution of the 18th century was in fact the tag-end of the long process of developing folk-technology of the Middle Ages.) The impact of science on economic life, in the second phase, since 1945, is reflected in very widespread scientific technologies in a great many sectors, in agriculture, in virtually all forms of industry, in organization and in information processing, and so on. It is this second phase of the impact of science on economic life that produces those 8 percent per annum rates of growth, whereas 2 to 3 percent per annum was characteristic of the first phase. On this criterion, the United States is still in the first phase, and is in a very real sense a backward country; or, we might say more politely, a developing country of the second rank, in spite of the fact that we are, by reason of our past growth and history, still by far the richest country in the world. If present trends continue, however, we will not remain in this relatively privileged position for very long. I have calculated what I call the "overtake dates." That is, at what dates would various countries overtake the United States in per capita real GNP if the growth of all countries continued at the rate of the 1950's (see Table below). In the 1960's, of course, the picture looks rather different. The rate of economic growth in the

OVERTAKE DATES FROM THE 1950's

	Per Capita GNP, 1957 $ U.S.	Rate of Growth 1950-1960 %	Year in which Country overtakes U.S. in Per Capita GNP
United States	2577	1.6	
West Germany	927	6.5	1979
Switzerland	1428	3.7	1986
Japan	306	8.0	1992
Italy	516	5.2	1999
France	943	3.5	2011
Netherlands	836	3.6	2014
Sweden	1380	2.6	2020
Norway	1130	2.6	2040
Denmark	1057	2.6	2047
Belgium	1196	2.3	2069
United Kingdom	1189	2.2	2086
Canada	1947	1.2	Never

Sources: Bruce M. Russett, *World Handbook of Political and Social Indicators,* p. 155

Angus Maddison, *Economic Growth in the West,* p. 30

United States has increased — mainly, however, because we have been absorbing unemployed resources, not because our rate of technological progress has increased. Rates of growth in many other countries, especially in the "socialist camp," have declined, perhaps because of certain horizons which socialist organizations tend to impose, especially in agriculture. The table of overtake dates, therefore, was obsolete as soon as it was calculated. Nevertheless, it represents a certain possibility which cannot be ignored, and certainly any blithe and unthinking optimism about the future of economic development in the United States would be quite unjustified.

The best that can be said about economic policy in the last twenty years is that we could have done worse. The level of unemployment which we have tolerated has probably prevented a more rapid spread of technological improvement, and the fact that it has been concentrated so heavily in two segments of the population, the Negroes on the one hand and young people on the other, is enough to offset much that has been done in these twenty years towards the integration both of youth and of the Negro into the larger society. One should not, of course, overlook the genuine accomplishments of the American economy in this period. In the last generation we have approximately doubled per capita real income, and this increase has been quite widely distributed. The real wages of the employed have almost doubled; the proportion of national income going to labor has actually shown some increase; and the record of the twenty years after the Second World War is unquestionably much superior to the record of the twenty years after the First World War, which was a tragic failure.

The costs of power

At least of equal importance with fiscal conservatism in explaining the sluggish performance of the American economy is the absorption of the whole American society in international political and military competition, its neurotic determination to be the only great power, and the consequent absorption of a large proportion of our total effort in the war industry, or what might be called the space-military complex. The rise of the war industry has been far and away the greatest internal change in American society in the last generation. In the 1930's it was barely 1 percent, of the gross national product; today it is between 9 and 10 percent, and, if the Vietnam war continues to escalate, will almost certainly go higher. This change exceeds by whole orders of magnitude any other change in the system. The only other proportional change in the last generation which anywhere approaches it is the decline in agriculture. Furthermore, from the point of view of growth and development, the 10 percent of the gross national product which is absorbed by the war industry greatly understates its impact. Seymour Melman has estimated that some 60 percent of the total research and development effort is channeled into the space-military operation. Melman's claim that the technological development of the civilian sector of the economy has been severely and adversely affected by this absorption of what might be called "the growth resource" in the space-military complex is to be taken very seriously. It is one of the astonishing facts of our times that there has been no comprehensive economic study of the distribution and impact of technological change in detail over the economy as a whole. The many instances which Melman cites, for example, of depletion and at least relative technological stagnation in our society, in, for instance, railroad, shipbuilding, and machine tools, in civilian electronics, in education and health, in construction — the list is frighteningly large — are of course instances, and they can be offset to some extent by reports of spectacular technical change due to automation, for example, in selected cases. Nevertheless, the evidence for widespread technological malaise in the American economy is not to be dismissed, and the most obvious explanation is the absorption of such an enormous proportion of our intellectual, research, engineering, and growth resources in the relatively sterile activities of the space-military complex.

It may be argued, of course, that these activities are not as sterile as I have accused them of being, and that there are, in fact, considerable spillovers from the space-military industry into the civilian economy. In the early days this may have had some truth to it. Certainly, for instance, we would not have had the civilian jets as early as we did if it had not been for the enormous research resource devoted to military aviation. It is becoming increasingly apparent, however, that these spillovers are declining, mainly because the space-military complex is now at least a whole technological generation ahead of the civilian economy as a result of the enormous resources which have been put into it. There are very great difficulties involved in the transfer of technology between two societies, or even between two parts of the same society, where one is more than a technological generation ahead of the other. (We see this problem in its extreme form in the difficulty of translating Western agricultural techniques into forms which have any use whatever for the poor countries of Asia and Africa.) The two technologies speak such totally different languages that they cannot communicate at all. So while there may be long-run technological payoffs on earth for all this investment in space and rocketry, miniaturization, and so on, the payoffs do not seem to be for this generation.

The "space ship earth"

The evolutionary process, throughout its whole vast span of time, has been characterized by short periods of very rapid change followed by rather long periods of slow change, and one sees this also in human history. We have already gone through two transition periods of very rapid change, one from the paleolithic to the neolithic, the other from neolithic to civilization, and the present period is entirely comparable to these, and of even greater magnitude. If we are interested in development, therefore, it is quite legitimate to ask: what does the developed society look like? — even though we are not going to be able to spell it out in detail, and even though the developed society itself will undergo a continuous change and transformation, though one suspects at a somewhat slower rate than we are having now.

The present transition is characterized by, and indeed largely caused by, a mutation in the process of growth of human knowledge which we call science. We are still very much in the middle of this process; indeed it is doubtful whether we have yet reached the middle, and it seems probable that the next fifty years will see a rate of change at least equal to what we have seen in the last century, perhaps even greater. Certainly the impact of the biological sciences on the condition of man and the nature of his social system is going to be as spectacular as the impact of physics and chemistry, and we have hardly seen the beginning of this. Some people tend to view the transition as opening a prospect of absolutely unlimited expansion. This tends to be the Communist view, with the deification of man and what seems to me a naive faith in his absolutely unlimited powers. I take a somewhat more restricted and pessimistic view myself. To me, the real significance of this transition is that it represents a change from an "open society" — with an "input" of material from mines and ores and fossil fuels, and with pollutable reservoirs as recipients of "outputs" — to a closed society in the material sense, in which there are no longer any mines or pollutable reservoirs, and in which, therefore, all materials have to be recycled. This is what I have called the "space ship earth." In a space ship, clearly there are no mines and no sewers. Everything has to be recycled; and man has to find a place in the middle of this cycle. The "space ship earth" simply repeats this on a larger scale — though when we look at the earth from space, we realize very clearly what a small, closed, crowded space ship it is.

In economics, this represents a transition from what I have called the "cowboy economy" of exploitation and pollution to the "space man economy," which is characterized by extreme conservation. Whether the desperate necessity of conservation will produce conservatism is an interesting problem. It is certainly not beyond the bounds of possibility that one of the things we will need to conserve is change itself, and the ability to change. In the space ship economy, consumption is no longer a virtue but a vice; and a mounting GNP is to be regarded with horror. Human welfare will clearly be seen to depend, not on the through-put of the society — that is, not on the amount it can produce and consume — but on the richness and variety of its capital stock, including, of course, the human capital. Consequently, anything which will conserve consumption and enable us to maintain a larger and more elaborate capital stock with smaller production would be regarded as desirable. Great stress would have to be placed on durability, both of things and of people. We may find indeed that the space ship economy is not feasible without a substantial extension of human life, as George Bernard Shaw suggested in *Back to Methuselah*. I have discussed elsewhere[1] the appalling short-run consequences of cracking the aging barrier and extending human life beyond the Biblical allotted span. Nevertheless, if the space ship earth is to be tolerable at all, it may well be that the consumption of human knowledge which takes place by the frightful toll of aging and death at the average age of 70 will be more than the resources of a depleted planet can cope with.

A space ship society does not preclude, I think, a certain affluence, in the sense that man will be able to maintain a physical state and environment which will involve good health, creative activity, beautiful surroundings, love and joy, art, the pursuit of the life of the spirit, and so on. This affluence, however, will have to be combined with a curious parsimony. Far from scarcity disappearing, it will be the most dominant aspect of the society. Every grain of sand will have to be treasured, and the waste and profligacy of our own day will seem so horrible that our descendants will hardly be able to bear to think about us, for we will appear as monsters in their eyes.

Toward the modest society

How far does the Great Society assist in making this transition? It is hard to avoid giving it some rather bad marks. Greatness is a totally inappropriate moral attitude for a space ship society, which has to be above all things modest. Greatness is all right on the great plains; it is wholly inappropriate to a tiny, fragile sphere. A space ship cannot afford cowboys; it probably cannot even afford horses, and it certainly cannot afford men on horseback. It looks like a tea ceremony, not a parade ground. The slightest touch of grandiosity could ruin it. It involves conservation, coexistence, extreme care in conflict resolution, and above all, no rocking of the boat.

It seems to me that what we need today is less rhetoric about the great society and more thought about the dynamics of the transition to the "modest" society. Revolution is out, as this just creates and

---

1. K. E. Boulding, "The Menace of Methuselah: Possible Consequences of Increased Life Expectancy," *Journal of Washington Academy of Sciences*, 55:7 (Oct. 1965), 171-179.

reinforces greatness, pomposity, corruption of taste, and is likely to establish tyrannies. If revolution is out, however, we need to have an image of a dynamic by which legitimacy is gradually withdrawn from the old system and is acquired by the new, to the point where eventually the old system becomes merely a shadow and cannot cause any trouble. I am convinced that the dynamics of legitimacy is the key to this whole problem; the trouble is I don't know anything about the dynamics of legitimacy. I take heart, however, in the fact that the collapse of empire in our time, and the doubling of the number of nations in the last twenty years, is a symptom of something very important — the realization that national greatness is too expensive and that the people of a modest nation have a much better time, or at least a better chance in the long run of a better time.

VERIFIABILITY OF
ECONOMIC IMAGES

The Structure of Economic Science, Sherman Krupp, ed., Englewood Cliffs, New Jersey: Prentice Hall, 1966, pp. 129-141.

THE FIRST TASK OF THIS PAPER IS CLEARLY to take a brief look at the concept of "verifiability" itself. It is a concept which may appear fairly obvious on the surface; nevertheless, there is hardly any other concept around which so many philosophical banshees howl. It has been the subject of a still unresolved argument among philosophers almost as long as there have been philosophers. The problem, stated very simply, is this: Every human being has an image of a world of time and space, causality, value, and so on in his mind. This we might call the "subjective world." Part of this image consists of a conviction that corresponding to the subjective world inside him there is an objective world outside him to which his subjective image corresponds. If he is a normal person, he can distinguish quite readily between those parts of his image which he regards as "real," that is, corresponding to something outside, and those parts of his image which he regards as unreal or fantasy. The image which he has of his home, his street, his

The

Verifiability

of

Economic

Images

town, his place of work, he regards as real. The image which he has of Santa Claus or fairies, or little green people from outer space, he usually regards as fantasies.

It now seems pretty clear, especially from what we now know about the development of sense perception, that this distinction within the image between the real and the unreal is developed by a process of testing. Testing is a complicated process, and there are many things about it which are still very puzzling. There can be no doubt, however, that such a process in fact goes on. It involves a number of elements. The first is an expectation or prediction, that is, an image of what we expect the "real" part of our image to be like at a certain date in the future. Because of the sheer passage of time, the date in the future eventually arrives, and then we are faced either with confirmation or with disappointment. Confirmation means that the image of reality as we experience it in the present corresponds with our expectation, that is, with the image as we conceived it in the past. For instance, I may have an image of going out to the mail box to pick up the mail. This is an image of the future, even though a very near future. Then when the future "arrives," I in fact go out to the mailbox to pick up the mail, and if there is mail in the mailbox, my image is confirmed. If there is no mail in the box, then my image is disappointed. On a more elaborate scale, the scientist may set up an experiment in which he expects a certain result. The result may be confirmed, or it may be disappointed.

The learning process is the process by which images are changed, presumably in the direction of reality. Crucial in this process is the nature of our reaction to disappointment. If our expectations are confirmed, there is practically no pressure to change the image, even though confirmation is no proof of the correctness of the image on which the expectation was based. Confirmation might be an accident, but if it is, there is no way of discovering this. It is only as we are disappointed that we are placed under any pressure whatsoever to readjust our images of the world or to change our distribution between reality and fantasy. There may, however, be three reactions to disappointment. The first is the rejection of the message which informed us regarding the reality of our present image. Thus, if I open the mailbox and find no mail, my first reaction may be to open it wider and look further inside, thinking that the message which first informed me that there was no mail was inaccurate and was to be rejected. The illustration points out that this is by no means always a stupid reaction. It is just as rational to do this, however, when messages are confirmed as when they are not, for there is nothing in the nature of things which says that confirming messages are more reliable than disappointing messages. The fact is, however, that we are much less likely to take a second look if the message confirms our expectation than if it disappoints it. This is why disappointment is a much more powerful source of change than is fulfillment.

Suppose, however, that in spite of the second look the message remains that there is no mail. I may then reject the inference which gave rise to the expectation in the first place. An inference is a derivation of an expectation from an image of the world. My image of the world says that there is a mail service and that mail is delivered regularly in my mail box at a certain time each day. The inference is that on this particular day there will be mail in the mail box at a certain time. If I go out and find there is no mail, I may simply reject the inference. I may say, for instance, that even though there is a mail service on this particular day, nobody has sent me any mail. The inference here is a probabilistic one— that there is a certain probability of there being mail in the mail box at a certain time, and that if there is no mail, this merely means that the slightly improbable has occurred (which, of course, it always may). If our expectation is probabilistic, that is, if we expect something with a certain probability, then disappointment is probabilistic too. In other words, we do not really know whether we have been disappointed or not. Even if I have a 99 per cent chance of finding mail in the mail box, it is certainly not unreasonable to suppose that if there is no mail in the box the 1 per cent chance has come off. At some point, indeed, it is likely that a very low probability is equated psychologically with zero probability; that is, there is some just-noticeable-difference of probabilities, as psychologists say, and if a probability is below this, this will be equated with zero. Under these circumstances, failure of expectations will inevitably produce sharper impact than if the failure is within the recognizable range of probability.

Rejecting the inference is also sometimes a perfectly rational thing to do, especially where the expectation is probabilistic. It may even be rational where the probability of the expectation is 1, that is, the expectation is certain, because, like messages, inferences on re-examination may prove to have been false. It is one of the virtues of mathematical inference that if it is false, there are strong rewards for somebody finding this out, and hence, false inferences are likely to be discovered. In the case of more vague verbal inferences, however, the rewards may go the other way. That is, the person who points out that the inference is wrong may be received with something considerably less than joy, especially by people who have taken a firm stand on their inferences.

The third possible reaction to disappointment is a reorganization of the basic image of the world itself. If, for example, I find there is no mail in the box, I may suddenly remember that it is a public holiday and that there is no mail delivery. If I had recalled this earlier, I would not have made the inference that there would be mail in the box. It is a peculiar virtue of the method of science that it protects itself very carefully against rejection either of the message or of the inference; hence, when scientific experiments result in the disappointment of expectations, there is hardly anything to do but to reorganize the basic image of the world. This, indeed, is what we mean by scientific testing.

Images of the world may be classified roughly in the order of the ease or of the difficulty with which they may be tested. In general, it may be asserted that narrow and relatively unimportant images are fairly easy to test but that the wider, the more extensive, and the more fundamental the image under consideration, the harder it is to test. It is fairly easy to test whether there is any mail in the box. It is harder to test whether the absence of mail is due to the fact that nobody has written or whether it is due to a breakdown in the mail truck. It is still harder to test whether the postal system in general is efficient, and it is extremely hard to test whether, for instance, a postal service run by a privately owned but regulated utility would be more or less efficient than the present state-owned and state-run operation. It is fairly easy to test the existence of chemical elements; it is very hard to test the existence of God.

In economics, it is not difficult to make a rough classification, finally, of economic images in the order of the difficulty of testing them—that is, in the order of verifiability. A good starting point might be to discuss first what we mean by economic images and how we distinguish these from other parts of our image of the world. This, however, should emerge in the course of the discussion, and for the moment I will simply suggest that economic images are those which revolve around the concept of exchange as a central focus. It is not easy, and indeed probably is fruitless, to try to define the boundaries of economics, for it merges indistinguishably into its related disciplines. Economic theory, however, abstracts from the social system those aspects of it which are closely related to the phenomenon of exchange. Economic institutions, such as banks, insurance companies, and corporations, are those in which exchange is a dominant aspect of the institution's history and behavior; and economic behavior, if it is indeed to be distinguished from rational behavior in general, is that behavior which is particularly associated with exchange and with objects of exchange, that is, commodities. An economic image then is some image of the world related to exchange, or to the whole system of exchanges, or to the production and consumption of those things which are or which may be exchanged. The problem here, therefore, is that of the testing of images of this kind. I shall use four very rough categories which will be described as: (1) easy to test, (2) hard to test, (3) very hard to test, and (4) impossible to test.

Among the images which are easy to test are images of prices and of commodities offered for sale or for purchase. Suppose, for instance, I read an advertisement in the paper that a certain store is advertising shirts for sale at five dollars. I have an image that if I go to the store and place five dollars on the counter, I will get a shirt in return. It is very easy to test this image by simply trying it out. If the store is in fact selling shirts for ten dollars, I would not only be disappointed, I would be indignant, for the disappointment of easily tested images usually creates emotional stress.

Every time we make a purchase or sale we are in fact testing out an image of the price system. This is done frequently in the case of ordinary commodities. For those commodities which are frequently bought and sold, then, our image of the price system is likely to be highly realistic, simply because if it is not, we will be rapidly disappointed.

What this means is that for any seller or buyer who is operating under conditions approximating perfect competition, it is very easy to test the nature of his market environment. If he can buy or sell an indefinite amount of a commodity at a given price, all he has to do is to look at the price tag and he has a great deal of confidence that his image of the market is correct. Similarly, if production functions are fairly simple, it is quite easy to find out what they are, especially when they are linear. The cookbook is a good example of a set of rather simple production functions. If we follow its instructions correctly, we would certainly be quite surprised if things did not turn out as expected. This, however, is only because we are operating within a fairly narrow range of quantities. The cook who is cooking for a thousand people certainly has to use a different kind of a cookbook than one who is cooking for a family. The more complex the process, the more difficult it is to test. Nevertheless, the image which most firms have of their production functions—that is, of how much of what inputs produce how much of what outputs—is likely to be fairly accurate, here again, because the process is going on all the time. Where there is much repetition, testing is easy.

Testing becomes harder as the systems get more complex. A buyer or seller with imperfect markets has a much more difficult time finding out what is the nature of his market environment. If, for example, the quantity which the buyer can buy or the seller can sell is a function of the price itself, it is by no means easy to find out the parameters of this function. In the case of perfect competition all we need to know is the price; in the case of imperfect markets we need to know a function relating the price and the quantity. Here we encounter the difficulty that often recurs, which is that testing becomes difficult because the act of testing alters the thing that is tested. We can test whether a pie is good by eating it, but then we do not have a pie. A firm often is unwilling to test the nature of the demand curve which faces it because if, for instance, it lowers its price and is disappointed, it fears it may not be able to raise the price again to its previous level without suffering a loss of sales. The act of lowering the price itself alters the nature of the market.

At this point the problem of the cost of testing, that is, the cost of search (as it is sometimes called), may have to be taken into consideration. The problem may be summed up in the dilemma that there is sometimes, indeed frequently, a better way of doing something, but it costs so much to discover the better way that the reward is not worth the trouble. This problem frequently bedevils large and complex organizations of any kind. In the case of a large business organization, it is very common. There is a good deal of evidence that the search process is not very well organized and that the search for better alternatives either tends to be done in a rather random fashion or else is unduly influenced by spectacular or noticeable phenomena. Thus, as Richard M. Cyert and James G. March have indicated,[1] a particularly spectacular industrial accident may set in motion a very substantial process of search that may have quite unintended consequences for an organization far beyond the search for greater safety that gave rise to it. This again points up the proposition noted earlier—that disappointments are more likely than confirmations to result in revision of images. We can perhaps extend this to the proposition that when things are going well, little search is likely to be made for methods or decisions which would make things go even better. It is only when things go badly that the process of search is brought into play. Perhaps the greatest danger to the advance of knowledge or even to the survival of organizations is when things are going well for reasons which are not properly understood. Under these circumstances the search for better ways of doing things will probably not be made, and if circumstances change and things do not go well, the organization will be quite unprepared because it did not understand why things went well in the first place. Nothing fails like success, especially a misunderstood success.

From the point of view of the system as a whole, the process of competition, especially insofar as it results in bankruptcies and reorganizations, can be thought of as a rather rough but effective method of testing the validity of images according to which economic decisions are made. The testing is quite expensive, insofar as it represesents loss of capital invested, both in physical resources and in human time and commitment. However, perhaps one of the most fundamental principles of economics is that knowledge cannot be acquired for free, and that any testing process involves some sort of expense. Indeed, the expense of testing can be taken as a rough measure of the ease or difficulty of testing.

What is very hard to test is the method of testing itself. In fact, a good deal of present-day history can be interpreted in terms of a search for cheaper methods of testing. Much of the emotional drive behind socialism, for instance, is a result of dissatisfaction with the perceived costs of the kind of testing of economic decisions which characterizes a system of private enterprise and free capitalism. It can be argued, of

---

[1] *A Behavorial Theory of the Firm* (Englewood Cliffs, N.J.: Prentice-Hall, 1963), pp. 48 ff.

course, and very convincingly, that the socialists have not proved their case that the testing of economic decisions in a centrally planned economy is any cheaper than in the competitive market economy. Indeed, one of the major criticisms of socialism is that centrally planned economies are singularly deficient in any kind of process by which the decisions of the central planners can be tested. The mistakes of capitalists are very easily discovered. For example, the Ford Motor Company produces an Edsel. The fact that a mistaken decision has been made is very rapidly found out, simply because not enough people buy Edsels. Consequently, there is very rapid feedback into the organization. An attempt is made to correct the mistake, and the Edsel is discontinued. If a centrally planned economy makes a similar mistake, there is very little feedback. There is, indeed, a powerful tendency for the information system itself to be corrupted by the exercise of political power. We saw this, for instance, under Stalin, when some disastrous mistakes in agricultural policy were made, for instance in the first collectivization and even subsequently, and yet no one really dared to tell Stalin of this. Those who did try to tell him were sent to Siberia or worse. In an atmosphere of universal fear and purges, extraordinarily little information could get through. In a market society the cost of testing economic decisions consists of the losses of bankruptcy and of bad investments, which after all are not very severe, whereas in a totalitarian socialist society the losses due to bad decisions could add up to millions of deaths and disastrous losses of capital.

Nevertheless, the experiences of the past do not dispose of the future, which is why I would place the problem of the comparative economic systems in the "very difficult" category of testing. The Great Depression certainly taught Western capitalism that it could not rely on the unregulated processes of the market, in the kind of society it had, to insure full employment. Here again was a process of very costly testing; on the other hand, it does seem to have resulted in some expansion of knowledge which makes the probability of severe depressions in the future much less than it has been in the past. It may equally be argued that Stalinism also taught the socialist countries a good deal, even though the Chinese do not seem to have learned this lesson yet. We cannot categorically assert that a centrally planned economy is impossible in which there are extensive feedbacks of information from the society into the planners and in which therefore, mistakes can be tested fairly easily and corrected. I would not venture to predict, therefore, what the argument between centrally planned and market economies will look like in a hundred years, after we have had a continued modification of both systems.

Democratic election in a two-party system can likewise be regarded as a testing process. We may assume that there is a certain difference in the image of the economic system in the two parties, even though there may be a great deal of overlap. If the election of one party is followed by a period of prosperity and successful government, the ideas of the unsuccessful party are likely to converge toward those of the successful one. If, on the other hand, the election of one party is followed by a depression, or a disastrous war, or some sort of social failure, the ideas and image of the world of the party in power will be discredited, the other party will move even further away from it and is likely to be elected in the next election. This process of testing can be very costly, especially if the process by which one party or the other gets elected has strong random elements in it. The election of a party which has an unrealistic view of the world, hence, may be quite disastrous and involve a very high cost.

However, a workable two-party democracy can be defended by contrast with any totalitarian system on the grounds that the cost of testing social images and ideas in a democratic system is much less than it is in a totalitarian system. Certainly the mistakes of democracy seem to have been much less disastrous than the mistakes of a totalitarian dictatorship, whether Hitler, Stalin, or even Sukarno. Once again, we have to be on the lookout for the dangers of partial success. The very success of democracy in the Western countries perhaps inhibits them from conducting further search for political and constitutional change. It is conceivable, therefore, that the totalitarian countries of today, simply because of the glaringly high cost of totalitarian government, have a pressure for search for better solutions to the political problem, and it is not impossible that this search might result in something which is superior to the solution of two-party democracy—superior in the sense that it is able to test competing images of the social system at less cost.

Finally, the discussion turns to things which are impossible to test by their very nature. Many such images are held with great tenacity and have enough importance for the people who hold them so that they cannot be dismissed out of hand, despite all the protests of the logical positivists. The Roman Catholic doctrine of the transubstantiation of the elements in the Mass is one such image, for transubstantiation takes place by definition in aspects of the elements which are not testable. The Marxist doctrine of surplus value is not very different. The amount of socially necessary labor embodied in a commodity is not to be detected by anything so crass as its price. The man who says "My country, right or wrong" or the ardent Communist who thinks that whatever the Soviet Union does is for peace is likewise inhibited by definition from testing his belief. It may be that there is a deep need in mankind for a belief in something that is untestable and that therefore cannot be shaken. Perhaps we should recognize such a need rather than attack it and seek to provide for it in ways that are least harmful.

Another situation where testing is impossible is where the universe itself is random and subject to no law. The movements of stock prices, for instance, have so strong a random element in them, especially in regard to relative stock prices, that anyone who detects a law in their behavior is probably as much under illusion as he who detects a law in the fall of the dice. Under these circumstances neither experience nor disappointment can be a teacher simply because there is nothing to learn. The human mind, however, seems to have an extraordinary distaste for randomness, and experiments have shown that even when subjects are presented with totally random data, individuals will always seek to interpret it in terms of a law, that is, "superstition." The psychologist B. F. Skinner has demonstrated how superstition may be produced even in pigeons. This problem becomes particularly difficult when the system is mixed, in the sense that it contains both random and nonrandom elements. Predictions can then only be made with a certain degree of probability, and if they are not fulfilled, we are never quite certain whether this is because of a random event or whether it is because the image or inference upon which the prediction is based is faulty. It is only through many repeated experiments and predictions that we can ascertain what are the random and what are the nonrandom elements of such a system. Unfortunately, social systems are nearly all of this type, which is one reason why it is so hard to be sure what the essential nonrandom elements of such systems are.

The previous section was concerned primarily with the testing of common, or folk images, of economic life. This section is concerned with the problem of testing the sophisticated images of economic theory. These images are the result of many generations of reflection and debate among economists.

Economic models fall roughly into two categories—static or equilibrium models, which comprise by far the largest body of economic theory, and genuinely dynamic models, which are expressed in terms of difference or differential equations. In the former category are supply and demand analysis, a large portion of the theory of the firm, much of the theory of imperfect competition, and the Keynesian analysis of underemployment equilibrium. These models almost without exception consist of a set of equations, one or more of which is an identity and the others of which express certain propositions about human behavior. The identities, of course, do not have to be tested, as they are true by definition; thus it is not necessary to test the proposition that in an exchange the quantity bought is equal to the quantity sold, these being exactly the same thing, or the proposition that saving, defined as income minus consumption, is equal to investment, which is also defined as income minus consumption.

The testing of the behavior equations is more difficult since they are supposed to represent properties of the empirical world and hence may or may not be true. The testing of equilibrium theory is particularly difficult because equilibrium is never actually observed in nature. All that can ever be observed is an approximation to it or perhaps a tendency toward it, but it would be extremely unlikely to find that at any one moment there would be an actual state of equilibrium. It is particularly hard to test equilibrium theory if there are no major divergences from the equilibrium position, for then any tendencies observed are almost by definition small and barely noticeable.

The best tests of the equilibrium theory occur when there are wide divergences from the equilibrium position—for example, during price control or in a time of severe inflation or depression. Thus we predict that if we interfere with the price system in order to raise certain prices, as for instance in agricultural price supports, surpluses are likely to result; whereas if we interfere, as in wartime price control, in order to lower prices, shortages are likely to result. The impact of rent control on housing is a classic case in point. In depressions, when investment is low and there are no offsets in the way of increased consumption, there is unemployment. When investment or government expenditure is high, as in a war, there is full employment. These might be described as qualitative tests of the theoretical system. The predictions are in terms only of direction, not in terms of the magnitude of change. It is both easier to predict and to detect changes in direction than it is to predict and detect changes in magnitude.

In order to predict changes in the magnitude of the various variables of the economy, we would have to know the exact parameters of our system of equations. Econometrics attempts to discover these, but its success can only be regarded as modest. The classic example of failure in this respect was the prediction of large-scale unemployment after the end of World War II, which almost all economists made for very good reasons, but which fortunately, were totally disappointed. These predictions were made on the assumption that certain parameters, such as those defining the consumption function which had been characteristic of the economy in the 1930's would persist into the 1940's. In fact they did not; the consumption function was much higher. Hence, the postwar disarmament in 1945-1946 was accomplished with astonishingly little difficulty and completely failed to fulfill the gloomy predictions of the economists. The failure of prediction here can be regarded either as a difficulty which is inherent in the system where the magnitude of the parameters is subject to certain random shifts, or it can be regarded as a failure to develop an adequate model with a sufficient number of equations and unknowns. It may not be enough, for instance, simply to postulate consumption as a function of income; it may be necessary to postulate it as a function of a number of other variables as well. The difficulty here is that it is virtually impossible to find out what the parameters of these systems are unless in the first place the parameters are reasonably constant and in the second place the system itself exhibits variation. Without change, knowledge is impossible. The consumption function is a good case in point. We might have made much better predictions of the postwar level of output and employment if we had used a consumption function which included not only income but also stocks of liquid assets. In the 1930's, however, though there was enough variation in income to permit the development of an empirical consumption function relating consumption to income, the variation in liquid assets was not large enough to permit the development of any secure relationship to consumption. Consequently, economists were quite unprepared for the effects of the enormous accumulation of liquid assets that took place during the war.

The predictability of dynamic models fares little better than that of the equilibrium models. The only dynamic model with which we have achieved any success at all in prediction is in the projection of movements of population, and even this has been subject to massive failures in prediction, again in the 1940's. Population projections rest on a simple set of difference equations, the principal one being that any group of members of the population who are x years old in a particular year will either be $x + 1$ years old next year or dead. Our ability to predict, as opposed to project, populations depends upon the assumption either of stable specific birth and death rates or birth and death rates which are subject to a dynamic law expressed as a function of time. The failure of population predictions, especially again in the 1940's, was a result of a sudden and unexpected change in these parameters. In the advanced countries there was a sudden unpredicted increase in the birth rate; in the countries of the tropics in the late 1940's there was a dramatic decline in the death rate as a result of the introduction of chemical insecticides. These changes made all the predictions of the 1940's completely worthless. Perhaps one should say that they were false rather than worthless, for at least one understands why they were falsified.

All predictions, even in the physical sciences, are really conditional predictions. They say that if the system remains unchanged and the parameters of the system remain unchanged, then such and such will be the state of the system at certain times in the future. If the system does change, of course the prediction will be falsified, and this is what happens in social systems all the time. In astronomy, however, we have now reached the situation where predictions are highly successful, except in the case of the incidence of artificial satellites. Prediction is successful in astronomy because we have discovered a system which has extremely stable parameters. In social systems, up to this point at any rate, no such stable systems have been uncovered. It may be, indeed, that in social systems there are no stable systems to be discovered because stable systems do not exist in reality. That is, social systems may contain essentially random elements, which impose as it were a generalized Heisenberg Principle on the social scientist in his search for knowledge.

What this means is that the failure of prediction in social systems does not lead to the improvement of our knowledge of these systems, simply because there is nothing there to know. This may seem like an unduly pessimistic conclusion, and I do not doubt that we are capable of developing models of society with parameters much more stable than those we now use. The development of social science is by no means at an end; indeed, perhaps it is only just at its beginning. Nevertheless, the possibility that our knowledge of society is sharply limited by the unknowable is something that must be taken into consideration. The boundary of the unknowable may still be some distance off, but the fact that it exists is indisputable.

A factor in the testing of economic images, especially economic models of the system as a whole, which has become of great importance in recent years is the development of improved data collection and processing. The development of national income statistics since 1929, for instance, has made an enormous difference in our ability to test certain images of the economy. I remember Professor Schumpeter once saying to me as a student, "How nice economics was before anybody knew anything," meaning of course that in the old days before the development of data collection, anybody could spin any theories he liked, whereas now the development of improved information made it possible at least to check the wilder absurdities. Karl Marx's theory of "immiserization" finds rough going in the face of national income statistics which reveal that the proportion of a constantly increasing national income which goes to labor also almost constantly tends to increase.

The development of scientific sampling as a means of getting information of a degree of accuracy from a large universe has enormously increased the capacity for getting information out of the social system. A good example of the kind of testing process which modern methods of data collection and processing permit is to be found in the effects of the 1964 tax cut. It is now possible to follow the effects of such a cut quite closely through the economic system. Even though the prediction of the effect of such a move is always subject to a certain degree of ignorance about the possible parameters of the system, within what are now fairly narrow limits there can be a good degree of confidence in a prediction for at least short-run movements. It is much harder, of course, to predict the impact of policies which have long-run effects, simply because the long run has such a long waiting period for it to take effect. It is a general problem of science, indeed, that systems which exhibit lags between causes and effects which are longer than the life of a single investigator are extremely hard to investigate. Social systems may have a good many relationships of this kind, and the testing of propositions involving long-run effect needs a research organization which extends beyond the lifetime of a single investigator. In a way this holds true, for example, for national income statistics, the annual survey of consumer finances, and so on, which build up cumulative data. In astronomy the building up of records beyond the lifetime of a single individual was of great importance in permitting the development of highly predictable systems; a similar pattern can be anticipated in the social sciences. In economics the fact that we have had national income series since 1929 is beginning to make a real impact on our image of the economy.

One may conclude, therefore, on a note of cautious optimism. Economists do know something. They do have a certain amount of testable knowledge, and indeed they know a great deal more than they did fifty years ago. This in itself has a marked impact on the operation of the economy. One need only contrast the operations of the economy of the Western world in the twenty years following the end of World War I with the twenty years following the end of World War II. The contrast is striking indeed. The first period saw laggard growth and the Great Depression and an almost total failure to deal with major economic problems. The second period has seen relatively rapid growth, indeed spectacular growth in some countries, and there has been no great depression. This relative success can be attributed in part to the increase of economic knowledge, and how it affected the policies of governments.

The record is much less encouraging for the poor countries, and it may look even worse in many parts of the world in the next twenty years. In a way the transition from a stagnant traditional society to a developing one is a social system of greater complexity even than that of the operation of the advanced economies. We cannot pretend to understand it very well, and we certainly cannot claim any great successes for predictions concerning its behavior patterns. On the other hand, the same kind of process of ferment of thought in regard to this problem seems to be occurring that took place in the 1920's and 1930's regarding unemployment and depression. It may well be that as a result of this ferment a new body of testable knowledge will arise, the fruits of which may not be seen for the next fifty years, but which will eventually produce enormous benefits for mankind. The stakes here are obviously very high, and the payoffs for genuine knowledge are enormous.

I have suggested that it is impossible to know everything about social systems or even about economic systems because of some very fundamental obstacles which these systems themselves place in the way of advancing knowledge. To state that we cannot know everything, however, is not to state that we cannot know anything. We can know a great deal, and virtually everything that we know can be of use. The difficulties of the task should inspire us not to despair, but to renewed effort.

HUMAN RESOURCE DEVELOPMENT
AS A LEARNING PROCESS

Farm Policy Forum,
19, 2, (1966-67), pp. 27-35.

Human Resource Development As A Learning Process

THERE IS A GENERAL problem of development in society. Thus, we are concerned not only with economic development but development in all its forms, political, cultural, artistic and moral. The development of society is essentially a continuation of the evolutionary process that began with the first big bang of creation or whatever it was that started developing the elements, then went on to life, on to man and then on to society.

I regard biological and social evolution as essentially a single process, though social evolution is more complicated, simply because of the complexity of man himself. All development and evolution involves the learning process because the only thing that can evolve is knowledge or information.

I think of knowledge as the capital stock of information and information as an improbable arrangement of something. You and I are among the more improbable things in the universe; the more we know, the less probable we get.

Matter in the form of the chemical elements did not seem to evolve much after the first twenty minutes of the universe until man got into the game and started making new elements. Apart from nuclear transformations, matter is conserved and so is energy. Even in nuclear transformations, matter and energy together are conserved.

Available energy is not even conserved in the sense that the deplorable second law of thermodynamics, which nobody seems to have been able to repeal, states. That is, energy gets less and less available. Obviously, then, if we are going to have evolution the only thing that can evolve is complexity of structure which is almost the same thing as knowledge. In this sense, helium "knows more" than hydrogen, and all the other steps follow from this.

Evolutionary Process . . .

Looking at society from this evolutionary point of view, we can see human learning as an evolutionary process. It is a process essentially of mutation and selection. Mutation creates new images through the imagination, and then the critical faculties, including the senses, select those which are most valuable. Before the advent of the human nervous system, mutation as far as we know was random. Since the development of the human nervous system, evolution has been going on inside the human head probably faster than outside it. Soon, indeed the evolution inside the head begins to affect the world outside it.

The advent of man therefore signalled an acceleration in the evolutionary process in this part of the universe. This has not been the only acceleration; as we look at the history of evolution it seems clear it goes into higher gear every so often and the intervals between these gear changes get less and less. This may, of course, be an illusion because of something that is happening to the nature of time, but that is speculative.

Economic development is also a mutation-selection process. Commodities are species, just like animals. They are indeed animals which have a genetic apparatus consisting of human society. The automobile is obviously a large four-wheeled bug with a detachable brain that entered the ecological system about 70 years ago.

It has displaced the horse, and if we are not careful, it may displace people.

The main biological difference between an automobile and a horse is that the genetics of an automobile are more complicated. Commodities are born through production, they die in consumption and they form a population. They form an ecological system along with all other species. Like biological species they can be eliminated in competition for food, in this case the money of the consumer. They then become extinct, like the bustle.

Economic development, then, is not just having an excess of production over consumption, and it is certainly not piling up agricultural surpluses. It involves a mutation of commodities into more and more complex forms, that is, into objects which have more knowledge embodied in them. Thus, the microphone which I use to amplify my voice is an extremely improbable arrangement of matter. Its much less probable than, say, the speaking trumpet which might have been used a hundred years ago. The microphone came into existence because of mutations and selections which went on in the human mind. All capital, indeed, is frozen knowledge, that is, human knowledge imposed on a material world.

Human Capital . . .

Knowledge in the mind is not only prior to capital formation, that is, knowledge in matter, but it is very much superior to it. We can see this very clearly if we look, say, at the development of Japan in the last twenty years by contrast with the development of, let us say, Indonesia.

In Japan the material capital was largely destroyed in 1945. Nevertheless it only took a few years to get all the material capital back, even in improved form. This occurred because the human capital, that is, the image in the mind which created it, was still there. In fact, the human capital of Japan was probably improved by defeat. It seems to be a fundamental principle of development that nothing fails like success, because the more successful you are the less you learn from it.

In the case of Japan, the military defeat acted as a kind of shock treatment curing its political mental ill health and as a result it has made a world's record for economic development in the last twenty years, growing at the rate of about 8% per annum per capita.

This fantastic record is almost wholly the result of the extraordinary capacity of the Japanese for learning. They seem to have very few psychological obstacles to learning of the kind that bedevil us.

Our rate of development in the U.S. has not averaged more than 3%, and in recent years, in some areas of the economy, we even seem to have some technological decline, as anyone who has ridden on a railroad lately or even mailed a letter lately can testify. It looks almost as if in some fields our *rate of forgetting* has exceeded our *rate of learning.*

There are some interesting conclusions that can be drawn from this view of development as learning and of learning as a mutation-selection process. Thus, there are some things which have a survival value in the long run which do not have survival value in the short run. Economists are familiar with this interesting problem under the heading of the infant industry argument.

Biologists are familiar with the same problem in what might be called the Sewell Wright principle of the optimum degree of cellulation. If too many species are in contact and if competition is too intense, the rate of evolution will slow down because all mutations will be adverse. There is a strong probability anyway that most mutations will be adverse, because obviously if you are where you are you must have gotten there because you survived. You must be all right, Jack, and anywhere you go from where you are is bad.

This is biological conservatism, or what might be called the republican view of evolution, that all mutations are for the worse. The trouble is that probably 99.4% of mutations *are* for the worse. Only a small fraction of mutations are for the better, and in a way the more the system has survived, the less likely is it to suffer change.

One of the problems we face in economic development is the appalling stability of low-level societies, like the Indian village, which has an astonishingly stable equilibrium. Outside agencies try to disturb it, but when they go away it all sags back the way it was before.

Predominance of Knowledge . . .

The moral of all this is that in any kind of social development process, it is human knowledge that is dominant. The reason is simply that human beings are brighter than other animals, and even the brightest commodities that they produce are still terribly dumb. If you leave an automobile to itself it will run off the road. Even the brightest computers probably do not reach the native intelligence of the one-year-old human. It is the human organism, therefore, this very peculiar non-linear computer produced by largely un-skilled labor, which is the real clue to social evolution.

One of the most astonishing facts about the growth of human knowledge is the fact that all human knowledge is lost every generation and has to be transmitted to a new set of minds. It sounds rather shocking to say this so bluntly, but the only place that human knowledge exists is in human heads. There is no knowledge in a library. If all the humans died off, the library couldn't do a thing. The books would just sit there and rot. There is a curious illusion I find among scientists that knowledge exists in the bindings of scientific periodicals, but this isn't true.

If it doesn't exist in the mind, it exists nowhere. The rate of consumption of knowledge is appalling, because of the short length of human life. This is why the great acceleration in the rate of social evolution took place with the development of agriculture.

This is the first time, I think, I have ever said anything nice about agriculture, and perhaps it is about time. Agriculture, however, is the key to all subsequent development, because it probably increased the span of human life by five or ten years, as we moved from the paleolithic to the neolithic. This, of course, is speculation, as records do not exist.

It is hard to believe, however,

that improved food supplies and greater security, stable settlements and moderately comfortable houses did not increase the expectation of life by at least five or ten years. This would be enough to set off an irreversible process of the accumulation of knowledge. Now the human race could learn more in every generation than it lost by death.

Thus the key to all accelerations in the rate of social evolution is to be found in new methods of transmission of knowledge between the generations. In traditional society the main transmission belt is the family, especially the grandmother. One of the problems of economic development is that this transmission belt has to be broken and new methods of transmission through the school, the library, the mass media, radio and so on have to be introduced.

It is not surprising that this introduces certain traumatic experiences in the early stages of development. You have to teach people that what they learned at their mother's knee is largely nonsense. It is not surprising that economic development is tough and that economists who go around giving good advice about it are not always as delighted by the reception they get as they might be.

The Stationary State . . .

Another interesting proposition that is derived from the evolutionary point of view is in regard to the probability of the stationary state. The interesting thing about the stationary state is that it is always on the way and never comes. This has been happening now for four billion years and we can justifiably get a little tired waiting for it.

Any given method of knowledge transmission would eventually produce a stationary state, simply because the greater the stock of knowledge the greater its consumption in every generation by people getting old, stupid, and dead. The larger the body of knowledge, therefore, the larger is the proportion of resources that have to be put into the knowledge industry just to maintain it. The stationary state arrives at the point where the maintenance of existing knowledge takes all the available resources of the society.

There have been many societies which have exhibited something which looks like a temporary stationary state. China may have been an example for a considerable period, and certainly many of the so-called primitive societies have looked like this. Primitive societies, of course, are never as primitive as they look at first sight. They frequently have a very large stock of rather useless knowledge, like baseball scores. They do not develop because they have to put an enormous amount into reproducing useless or even pernicious magical knowledge.

We put a lot into this sort of thing also, but we seem to have something to spare. Even though the increase in the stock of knowledge enables us to produce it faster, there may be some sort of diminishing returns here. Hence the rising rate of consumption of knowledge eventually overtakes the falling rate of production of knowledge, and we have a stationary state in which production equals the consumption and there cannot be any increase.

Everything then goes into education, nothing into research and development. According to one estimate, the knowledge industry in this country absorbs now about 30% of the gross national product. The rate of increase of knowledge is still so great that it certainly doubles every generation and in some fields seems to double about every fifteen years.

If there are no further improvements in the methods of transmitting or creating knowledge, the business of simply replacing existing knowledge every generation could grow until, say, by the middle of the next century it would absorb the whole knowledge industry. The increase of knowledge would then grind to a halt. Enor-

mous universities would cover the landscape wholly devoted to preserving what is already known. Research will disappear because there will be nobody to do it.

Nonetheless, this seems to be what has always tended to happen in the evolutionary process, and is puzzling why the universe has not come to a stationary state long ago. If it has not been reached, perhaps it is because of mutations in the methods of transmitting and acquiring knowledge. We may be on the edge of great changes in the teaching process at the moment, involving, say teaching machines, even learning drugs, or even perhaps surgical operation for the differential calculus. If this happens the stationary state is postponed still further.

Economic Development . . .

I would like to apply this evolutionary theory to two problems of economic development. One of the depressing things about the economics of development is how little there is, in spite of the fact that we seem to put considerable resources into it. It is very depressing to go back to Adam Smith on this subject, as we don't seem to have improved on him very much in almost 200 years.

The first problem that may be illustrated is the question of whether you ought to have balanced or unbalanced growth. The evolutionary approach suggests that there are some activities in which knowledge has a kind of multiplier, and it is these activities we want to stress. We clearly do not want to increase knowledge equally in all parts of society, and in all industries.

In the early stages of development it is clear that there are very large payoffs to the increase of knowledge in agriculture. These payoffs are to the society at large rather than to agriculture itself, because the increase of knowledge in agriculture tends to make agriculture unprofitable and chases people out of it. I have often pointed out that the principle reason for the unprofitability of agriculture in this country are the land grant universities. The more technically progressive such an industry becomes the more people have to be chased out of it, and the only way to chase people out of something in a free society is to make it relatively unprofitable.

We have now got to the point where agriculture is only 5% of the gross national product. It may be, therefore, that research and development in agriculture is not very important any more, simply because it cannot release much in the way of resources to go into other things. It is now these *other things* which have the larger poten-

tial for multiplying knowledge.

One of the interesting things about development is that those industries which are successful technologically will often tend to decline and the industries which are technologically stagnant, like haircutting and education, grow and grow. We may get to the point, therefore, where the technologically progressive industries are all very small and the stagnant ones are enormous. This is presumably when the process comes to an end.

We may be at a point where we need radical readjustments in the distribution of intellectual resources in this country, and the misallocation of these resources is becoming a serious problem. There is, therefore, a certain validity in the unbalanced growth thesis. As anything grows, its structure, that is, the proportions of its part, has to change. We can never preserve the structure of a thing that is growing and we always have to be on the lookout for what structural changes are necessary.

Terms of Trade . . .

The second problem of economic development might be called the "Prebisch problem" after its most distinguished exponent. This is the argument that the poor countries, especially the Latin-American ones, are in a very sad way because they produce primary products and in the course of development the terms of trade turn against them. Thus, they have a parity problem, just like agriculture. The argument is certainly not absurd. On the other hand, when one asks what one does about it, apart from wringing hands and arguing that the rich countries must simply make large grants to the poor ones, we do not seem to get very far.

What we must do here is to look at the dynamics of knowledge and ask the question, "Can a poor country that wants to get rich quick, pick a winner in technological development and specialize in that?" This is, of course, hard to do, and I have come to the depressing conclusion that the only really good recipe for getting rich quick is to be lucky.

This is an unfriendly and an unpleasant thing to say to people because we have always believed before that the way to get rich is to be virtuous. No matter how virtuous you are, if you back the wrong horse in your specializations, you won't get rich. A lot of the poor countries have been in this unfortunate position and only a few of them have really picked the winners.

Obviously if your terms of trade are bad, you should not be producing what you are producing. The answer to bad terms of trade is to get out of your present occupation and produce something else. On the other hand, how do we know that what we are going to get into is going to be all right? The answer is, we do not know. In the development of Japan, for instance, the terms of trade were quite important in the early days, say the 1880's and 1890's, mainly because of an unexpected piece of luck. Japan was specializing in silk and the European silk industry was severely affected by disease, hence the Japanese had extraordinarily good terms of trade in silk for a whole generation. Though this was not a crucial factor in their development, it certainly helped.

A similar example is Malaya, which has surprised everybody in the last twenty years. Twenty years ago, Malaya looked like a hopeless case, but it has forged ahead, whereas Indonesia has been going backwards, Burma has retreated into traditionalism and Ceylon has torn itself apart with racial conflict.

Part of the reason for this was that the Malayans were simply lucky. I'm not sure how self-conscious they were about it, because they were producing rubber, which everybody thought was going to be a drug on the market, especially with the development of synthetics.

Actually, they made a bet that technologically, biology was going to beat chemistry and they turned out to be right. The decline in costs of natural rubber due to a rapidly advancing technology, has more than outweighed the worsening of terms of trade.

Even though they did not have very good terms of trade in the old sense, they were able to beat this through technological development. It doesn't really matter what your terms of trade are as long as you can reduce your costs fast enough. Whether the Malayans will be able to do this in the next 20 years is another matter.

These cases illustrate why the problems of economic development are so difficult, much more difficult, in fact, than most economists are willing to admit. The difficulties arise because all development involves decision-making under uncertainty and indeed under very large uncertainty. If you have to make a decision under uncertainty, it is easy to make the wrong one. There is no rule which tells you how to make the right decision. For the purpose of development, a dangerous and unwise right decision may be the only thing which can really get a society off its launching pad. The decent, conservative wrong decision may be disastrous.

I am fairly well convinced that the development of the United States and the West has in some measure been due to a succession of lucky accidents. I have been tempted to write a little American history on the principle that we always did the right things and always for the wrong reasons.

When one looks at history in these terms one gets an uneasy feeling about how long luck can continue.

Even if virtue cannot guarantee development, one has more confidence in the proposition that certain kinds of vice can prevent it. There are a good many countries, for instance Argentina, which have stopped an active developmental process because of their foolish governmental policies. It is certainly not entirely out of the question that we might do the same thing in this country, especially if we continue to have delusions of grandeur about being the world's policeman.

THE SCIENTIFIC-MILITARY- INDUSTRIAL COMPLEX

The Virginia Quarterly Review,
43, 4 (Autumn, 1967): 672-679.

THE SCIENTIFIC-MILITARY-INDUSTRIAL COMPLEX

A NUMBER of recent books have concerned themselves with the problem of the changes in the structure of the American economy and indeed the whole American society as a result of the rise of the war industry and large-scale industrial organization, especially in the last twenty years. The two which are particularly noted in this review are "The New Industrial State" by John Kenneth Galbraith and "In the Name of Science" by H. L. Nieburg.

Both of these books are well written, Galbraith's with the touch of the phrase-maker which Nieburg does not quite possess. Both of them stem from much the same political philosophy, which might almost be described as that of American institutionalism. One is almost tempted to call this the "Wisconsin philosophy," especially as Professor Nieburg teaches at the University of Wisconsin in Milwaukee, were it not for the fact that Professor Galbraith's Canadian origin and Harvard location make him a dubious candidate for Wisconsin citizenship. Both these men, however, and a considerable legion of others could well claim John R. Commons, the sage of Madison in the early years of this century, as their spiritual ancestor. They are both deeply committed to certain fundamental values of American society. On the other hand, they are also deeply alienated from certain aspects of the organization of that society. If this tension between commitment and alienation produced a certain querulousness, this may perhaps be excused as an almost inevitable consequence of this otherwise quite creative tension. Both of them, one feels, mourn an Eden lost, a simpler, sweeter, and healthier state of society, of good-natured, simple people, small firms, innocuous government, and a very modest rôle on the world scene. Each of them is eloquent in denouncing the unpleasant world that lies outside the gates of the lost paradise. Neither of them is very convincing about how paradise may be regained.

In both cases we might say that Eden is lost by eating too heavily of the tree of knowledge. Galbraith, with his usual capacity for the memorable phrase, identifies Eden with what he calls the "accepted sequence" and the cold world outside in which we live by what he calls "the revised sequence." The accepted sequence is that of classical economics and classical democracy; demands are supposed to originate with individuals operating either as consuming households or as voters. These demands are transmitted in sequence to firms and producers on the one hand, or to politicians on the other, who then proceed to jump smartly to attention and to satisfy the demands within the limits of scarcity. The producer or the politician is here supposed to be passively receptive to the demands of the consumer or the voter. The consumer, shall we say, develops an increased passion for pizzas, and pizza manufacturers and pizza parlors spring up as if by magic almost overnight to supply this new demand. Similarly, a great grass-roots movement among the voters demands, shall we say, prohibition, and the Congressmen snap to attention and pass the law.

Both producers and politicians now eat the tree of knowledge and Eden is lost. Producers learn how to manipulate consumers' tastes through advertising, politicians learn how to obtain voter consent by propaganda, so we get "the revised sequence." The automobile industry decides that for purposes of its own convenience and because of its own high commitments in development, if not in research, the American public is going to have big, fat, overpowerful, and dangerous automobiles, whether they want them or not. If they did not want them, they could easily be persuaded to take them by the psychological tricks of Madison Avenue. Similarly, if for reasons of its own, the United States Government decides to have a war in Vietnam, this is then sold to the public by appeals to patriotism, to not letting our boys down, and the creation of a national image which is large, sleek, overpowered, very dangerous, and satisfying to frustrated masculinity.

This loss of Eden, according to Galbraith, has happened because of the rise of what he calls "the technostructure." This consists of the people and the rôles they occupy who, largely in committee, make the decisions in large-scale organizations, whether this is the Pentagon, General Motors, the University of California, or, I am tempted to add, the National Council of Churches or the AFL-CIO. As Galbraith pictures them, they seem like anonymous, faceless, although not entirely brainless, entities, conforming to a strong sub-culture around them, not taking many risks themselves, but adept at passing risks on to somebody else, and retiring eventually to a rather dismal and unnoticed old age. They manipulate each other as well as the general public and their main concern is the continuity, survival, and growth of the organization with which they are associated.

Nieburg is looking at much the same phenomenon as Galbraith, from a slightly different point of view. Most of his book is an historical, factual account of the rise of what he calls "the contract state" in the last twenty years, thanks largely to the enormous increase of the war industry, which has risen from some one per cent of the gross national product in the 1930's to about ten per cent today. He is critical of the scientific community for allowing itself to be prostituted. He sometimes, indeed, seems almost hostile to science as an institution and in regard to the nature of science and its content he strikes one as being even more "lay" than the average political scientist and historian. Nevertheless, he tells a good story and it is in some of its aspects, as the dust jacket suggests, "chilling." What is supposed to produce the chill, however, is the contemplation of undeserved private profit at the expense of the public purse as a result of the contract system. There is not much questioning of the basic objectives of national policy in becoming a super-power. There is no mention of napalm or of cruel and un-usual weapons. There is no great indignation about the use, past or potential, of nuclear warheads on civilian popula-tions. These things, apparently, are all part of the national game. What horrifies Professor Nieburg is the spectacle of the explosive growth of private firms in what is essentially a public sector, the abdication of public responsibility, espe-cially on the part of the Air Force in its procurement pro-gram, the dismantling of the "yardsticks" such as the Red-stone Arsenal of the Army and the research institutions of the Department of Defense, and the general myth that pri-vate contracts to single suppliers somehow salvage the great socialist enterprise of the Pentagon for free private enter-prise and all that.

There is a good deal to be indignant about in Professor Nieburg's indignation, and I may perhaps be prejudiced by the fact that my own line of indignation goes somewhat higher and deeper. This is a book, in other words, somewhat in the tradition of the great muckrakers, but the muck that is raked is a relatively clean pile of a few billion dollars of undeserved dough, rather than a putrid puddle of roasted civilians. In the Nieburg scheme of things, even Wernher Von Braun, the hero of the V-2 rockets and their subse-quent offspring, emerges as a kind of hero, in sharp contrast to the world view of Tom Lehrer, whose pithy little song, "And I'm learning Chinese, says Wernher Von Braun," re-flects a rather different set of values. Another of Professor Nieburg's heroes is Secretary of Defense, Robert McNa-mara, and it may be indeed that McNamara, besides saving the taxpayer a few million bucks in procurement, may also be acting as a force moderating the madness of those who are driving us towards a nuclear holocaust or even those who are inflated by the paranoia of being a great power.

Still, it is a little discouraging to reflect that the McNamara savings are now wholly gobbled up in the expansion of the total defense budget and that we seem to be engaged on a course from which there may be no return.

Galbraith's heroes are somewhat different from Nieburg's. Robert McNamara, indeed, only appears in his earlier incarnation as a Ford executive, and one suspects that to Galbraith he is as much part of the technostructure as the faceless executives of General Motors or the contract negotiators of the Air Force in spite of his agreeable personal qualities. Galbraith rather pins his hope on what he rather grandly calls "the educational and scientific estate," especially those located in those presumed colonies of Eden, the universities. Nieburg, on the other hand, perceives perhaps more realistically that Galbraith's idol has feet of clay. The scientific estate, alas, swills as enthusiastically at the trough of a contract state as their more worldly brethren in the profit-making, and, alas, even in the non-profit-making, institutions. Neither Galbraith nor Nieburg, indeed, devotes much attention to the problem of how the contract state is undermining the universities as communities, yet in the long run this may easily be its most horrendous aspect.

Neither Galbraith nor Nieburg gives any very satisfactory analysis of the system which has produced the evils that they deplore. Nieburg, indeed, is hardly to be blamed for this, for his book is essentially a work of what might be called historical journalism, telling the story rather than analyzing the system. Galbraith has somewhat more pretensions to be analytical and he has, indeed, an analytical gift for the perception of what is happening and the translation of that perception into a few mordant phrases. Neither of these two authors, however, has a social theory which is in any sense adequate to explain or really to prescribe for the pathological dynamic processes which they describe. They might reply with some justification that nobody has such a theory and that they are not to be blamed for lacking what does not exist. Nevertheless, works of this kind, perhaps even because of their liveliness and the social passion which underlies them, serve all the more to emphasize the defective state of social theory. One can legitimately complain, indeed, that neither of these two authors utilizes adequately even those insights which are presently available. Nieburg, for instance, is highly insensitive to the function of the structure of relative prices as a social organizer. This is an insensitivity which seems to be bred right into the whole institutionalist school, perhaps as a result of their overreacting to the exaggerated claims for the price system made by classical and neo-liberal economics. Nevertheless, to an economist Nieburg seems to underestimate the extent to which the contract state which he deplores, so often rightly, has arisen as a result of desperate need to break down the inflexibilities of governmental pricing and especially government wage rates. If the contract state is seen as a device to bypass the control of Congress and the civil-service regulations, it can be claimed that this bypass in fact bypassed an intolerably congested street and that without it the rapid expansion of the space-military sector of the economy would have been impossible. With my values, of course, such inefficiency would have been most desirable, just as I think that the inefficiency of the Eisenhower régime had a most desirable effect on the international system, my own view being that a stupid system requires rather slow people to run it successfully. Nieburg, however, does not share these values. On the whole he approves of the expansion of the space-military complex, and is only critical of the way in which it was brought about. One is reminded a little of the oscillation between a corrupt and a reformist government in urban administration. It seems to be an almost inevitable consequence of the inflexibility of civically administrated prices and wages.

Galbraith as an economist should be more sensitive to the social dynamics of the relative price structure and indeed he is well aware of the way in which the large private corporation corrupts the market and thereby produces an almost irresistible pressure for long-run inflation. There is something in his liberal half-socialist intellectual ancestry, however, which makes him relatively blind to the same problem as it applies to government. The great liberal illusion is that the private is automatically bad and the public is automatically good, whereas it seems closer to the truth to say that good and evil are pretty well randomly scattered over virtually all varieties of social organization.

The principal theoretical deficiency of both these writers is an inadequate appreciation of the dynamics of what I have elsewhere called "the integrative system," that enormous structure of communications, behavior patterns, habits, associations, rôles, and cognitive and valuation structures which produces such social constructs as communities, identities, allegiances, legitimacies, and loves. These two authors, however, should not be blamed for not knowing what nobody else knows either. The plain fact is that the theory of this aspect of the dynamics of society is hardly out of its swaddling clothes. It is precisely this deficiency, however, which leads to the most doubtful conclusions, to Galbraith's reliance, for instance, on the educational and scientific élite, which is to a very large extent part of the technostructure, and his failure to see that it is the church rather than the universities which is the principal countervailing power, feeble as it may be, to the appalling potency of the merciless state and its corporate and labor allies. Similarly, Nieburg does not see that it is precisely the prevalence of identities and values which he himself holds which has created the system which he deplores, and that his heroes are too much part of the whole community of dragons to be really successful in the long run as dragon-slayers.

It is only those who withhold legitimacy from the national state itself when it goes beyond the bounds of human decency and sensitive morality who can really challenge the total system. Goliaths will always hang together; it is only David with a sling-shot who can bring them down. Both Galbraith and Nieburg are relying on Goliaths to tame each other and this may be unrealistic.

AMERICA'S ECONOMY: THE QUALIFIED UPROARIOUS SUCCESS

America Now, John G. Kirk, ed., New York:
Atheneum, 1968, pp. 143-161.

America's Economy: The Qualified Uproarious Success

"The mere fact that capitalism has been economically successful . . . is not a necessary guarantee that it will continue to be legitimate."

The American economy, says the eminent economist Kenneth Boulding, can only be described as an uproarious success. But that is not quite the same thing as saying that the ways in which we habitually characterize it are accurate or that it is as nearly perfect as it might be or that its form cannot change for the worse. Indeed, the very success of our economy may be one of the most dangerous things about it. And in order to understand how this may be true, says Professor Boulding, the first thing we must do is clear our minds of cant.

T HE ASSUMPTIONS listed at the beginning of this section reflect a vague sentiment that many people still feel about the American economy. But as useful descriptions of the reality, these assumptions are nearly worthless. They are worth little, too, as guide lines for the future, for in addition to being unspecific, they contain implications which we could accept uncritically only at our peril. There are, at present, ambiguities about the national economy that may be of the most fundamental importance, yet about which the old assumptions tell us next to nothing. It is vital, therefore, that we try to understand the real nature of our economic system without reference to slogans and that we try to anticipate as objectively as possible which current tendencies might develop into major problems.

The American economy is a segment of the total condition and activity of about 200,000,000 people residing within the geographic limits of the United States, plus a rather ill-defined set of activities of Americans residing abroad and of American organizations operating abroad. The first task in describing the American economy is to define the boundary that separates the economy from the other aspects of the total society. There is no absolutely clear line of division between what is inside the economy and what is outside of it. A rough division can be made, however, between those conditions and activities which are governed primarily by exchange and those which are governed by other relationships such as threat, fear, love, hate, identification and so on. Just as economics is the study of how society is organized through exchange, the economy is that segment of the total social system in which exchange predominates. It consists, therefore, in those activities that are directed either toward the production or use of exchangeables or toward the act of exchange itself. Because of the fact that by far the greater part of exchanges either have money as one of the exchangeables, or have exchangeables that can be measured in terms of money, it is only a slight poetic exaggeration to say that the American economy is everything which is stamped with a dollar sign either actually or potentially.

We begin describing the American economy, therefore, with the concept of the stock of objects which can be valued in terms of dollars. This is sometimes called real capital. It consists of the houses, automobiles, clothing, food stocks, inventories, factories, machines and so on which dot the landscape so plentifully. The total value of this stock is not regularly calculated but it may be estimated as between two and three trillion dollars. When we contemplate the capital stock we immediately run into a curious paradox. In the accounting system the capital stock does not ordinarily include people, especially in a non-slave society. Occasionally a human life is valued, as when a jury sets a sum of dollars as compensation for the loss of a breadwinner. Ordinarily, however, we do not put the dollar stamp on the capital value of a person, although we do on his income. Logically, however, the bodies and the minds of the human population are just as much part of the capital stock as the cows, sheep and machines; and the economy certainly cannot be understood without them. Indeed, some of the difficulties of the American economy arise because of the fact that whereas we have an elaborate and rather accurate accounting system for nonhuman capital, the accounting system for human capital is very imperfect. In understanding the American economy, we must realize that the capital value which a man has inalienably in his own body and mind usually exceeds by far the material capital that he works with, even though no dollar figure is usually put on it. Nobody has ever dared to put a figure on the total value of human capital, but under very modest assumptions it could very easily turn out to be from five to ten times the physical capital; yet it usually does not appear anywhere in our accounting systems.

As we turn from the stock of capital to the flow of income we pass from an area of surprising ignorance to an area of knowledge which at least in the past generation has become reasonably broad. The capital stock of both material and human capital has a "throughput." At one end it is consumed—that is, destroyed—by eating it; by wearing it out; by the sheer passage of time with moth, rust and decay; and through forgetting, aging and death. In order to maintain, and still more in order to increase, the capital stock, there must be *production*—that is, additions to the stock through building, weaving, tailoring, farming and through people being born and educated. The first, and almost the last, principle of economics is what I have elsewhere irreverently called the bathtub theorem: that the difference between production (what is added to the stock) minus consumption (what is subtracted from the stock) must be equal to the addition to the stock if these concepts are properly defined. One can divide production into *maintenance* and *investment*. Maintenance is the process by which consumption is simply replaced. These are the processes of homeostasis by which the erosion of the soil is replaced by adding fertilizer, by which the decay of buildings is replaced by repairs, and in which the cooling and tissue loss of the human body is replaced by eating and drinking. Production over and above maintenance is investment, which adds to the stock, whether of human population or of material capital. In the course of maintenance the stock can also be transformed. As housing decays, for instance, we do not merely replace it as it was before; we rebuild it in a new form. Similarly, horses are replaced by automobiles and clerks by computers.

National income accounts give us a great deal of information about the nature and dimensions of the processes of production and consumption, although they are often tantalizingly incomplete. Thus in 1966 the gross national product was about $743,-000,000,000 and for 1967 the preliminary figure is $785,000,-000. To understand the meaning of a figure like this, we first divide it by the population—now almost exactly 200,000,000. This arithmetic reveals immediately that the gross national product per capita is now about $3,900 a year at current prices. Not all of this is available as personal income. From the $785,000,-000,000 gross national product in 1967 we deduct capital consumption (67 billion dollars) and some indirect and direct taxes and transfers to get national income (650); more additions and subtractions give us personal income (626); subtracting personal taxes (82) gives us disposable personal income (545), of which we spend for consumption, expenditures, interest paid back by consumers, plus a few minor items, about $506,000,000,000. This still means that the average American has about $2,700 a year to dispose of, or nearly $11,000 for a family of four.

As an average this looks like a pretty good performance, whether we compare it with the past or with other economies around the world. In terms of the past, if we use per capita dis-

posable income as the most significant measure of economic welfare, this has about doubled since 1929. We might say roughly
that it has doubled in forty years. If we take out the Great Depression, it has doubled in less than thirty years, that is, in about
a generation. A society in which the children are twice as rich as
the parents is obviously not doing too badly. By comparison with
other countries, the United States is, of course, the richest country in the world by almost any standards. Per capita disposable
income even in Northern Europe, Canada and Australia—which
are its closest competitors—tends to be about half what it is in
the United States. In the socialist countries, per capita disposable income is probably about a third; and in the poor countries
of the tropical belt, per capita disposable income is about one-
twentieth of the United States level. Economically the United
States can only be described as an uproarious success. If what
follows sounds mainly critical, it has to be interpreted against this
background of overall success.

Averages, of course, can be very misleading. We must look beyond a figure like that of per capita real income to the structure
of the economy both in time and in space before it can be properly evaluated. In time, the critical problem is growth. There is a
very fundamental principle of nature which states that everything
is what it is because it got that way; in other words, we must look
at the history of a structure before we can really understand it. If
some countries have per capita real income of $100 a year and
others of $2,500, this must be a result of a difference in their
history. Rich countries are rich simply because they have been
getting richer at a sufficiently rapid rate for a sufficiently long
time. If we think of the process of "getting rich" as a process
whereby per capita real income doubles in a certain period of
years, it takes about five or six doublings to give us the difference
between the poorest countries with about $50 per capita per
annum and the richer countries with over $1,600. The doublings
go $50, $100, $200, $400, $800, $1,600. With the kind of development which has characterized the successful countries in the

last hundred and fifty years, this has amounted roughly to a doubling of the per capita income every generation. A country that can keep this up for six or seven generations will end up being as rich as the United States is now, even if it starts from the barest subsistence. One of the most important questions about the United States economy, therefore, is why it has been subject to *sustained* growth over such a long period of time, for it is only this sustained growth which has made it as rich as it is now.

It is much easier to state this question than to answer it. Sustained growth at the doubling-every-generation rate has not on the whole been characteristic of human society. It is something, indeed, which has only come into existence in the last hundred and fifty or two hundred years. It is not just a matter of geographical expansion or increase in population; these will account for increase in the total product but not necessarily increase in the product per head. If we ask ourselves what element in society is capable of sustained growth of this kind, only one answer can be given: human knowledge. The growth of the United States economy, therefore, as with other successful economies, is primarily a result of the fact that the total social system encouraged the growth of human knowledge and the application of new knowledge to the techniques of production. Historically, we can distinguish at least two stages in this process. The first is the period before about 1860 when most of the new knowledge which was applied to economic life was what might be called "folk knowledge," the sort of thing one thinks of as "Yankee ingenuity." After 1860, we begin to see the science-based industries—chemical, electrical and, of course, in the twentieth century, the nuclear industry—which are based on the wide expansion of knowledge as a result of science. It may be that we are at the beginning of a third stage now with the development of computers and systems analysis, which represents, as it were, the application of the scientific method to the increase of science itself. It is too early, however, to know whether this really constitutes a major long-run acceleration in rate of development.

Another aspect of the position of the American economy in time is its position relative to other nations. At the moment the world can be divided pretty sharply into economically successful countries and economically unsuccessful countries, with the economically successful ones lying mostly in the temperate zone (plus one or two in the Caribbean), and most of the unsuccessful ones lying in the great tropical belt. Among the successful countries the rate of growth depends quite sharply on the existing per capita real income or per capita gross national product, with the poorer countries (like Japan) growing at a more rapid rate than the richer countries. This is not surprising, of course, for any growth process in nature tends to follow a pattern of declining rate of growth with increasing size. A boy that is growing several inches a year in his early teens is not necessarily going to be a giant when he is thirty. In so far as the economically successful countries are all growing in a similar pattern of development, we should expect the poor ones to grow faster than the rich ones.

The long-run effect of this, however, is that the successful countries will all become more similar. If present trends continue, by even the early part of the twenty-first century we should find that almost all the countries in the temperate zone have approximately equal per capita incomes. The world will then have separated out into a rather uniform rich belt around the temperate zone and a poor belt around the tropics. In the tropical countries there seems to be no relationship between the rate of growth and existing income. These countries may be expected to become more diverse, though as average rates of growth are low, they will remain poor.

One of the most striking facts about growth is that latitude seems to be a much more significant variable than the type of economic system. Both the socialist and capitalist countries of the temperate zone are all in the "successful" bracket, so that from this narrow point of view socialism seems to be almost irrelevant.

We should now take a closer look at the internal structure of the American economy, not only because this is important in it-self, but also because it may throw some light on the reasons for the success of the economy. The first thing to look at is the distribution of income. A high per capita income, as, for instance, in Kuwait, where statistically the per capita income is almost as great as in the United States, may hide very large inequalities. If income is very unequally distributed, no matter how high the per capita income of the economy, it cannot be given very good marks.

On this score the American economy has an oddly mixed record. On the one hand, it is clear that the American economy has not in the slightest degree followed the Marxist prediction that economic development would simply increase the income of property owners while the working class remained at, or even below, the subsistence level. In terms of the distribution between labor income and property income, the record of the American economy is impressive. The national income statistics themselves do not allow for an exact description of this distribution here, but a rough approximation can be made. At the present time the American economy distributes well over 80 percent of its total income to labor income in some form. By labor income I mean that which is derived from the sale of the activity of human capital. Probably not much more than 15 or 20 percent goes to the owners of material property as such. Thus, even judged by the socialist criterion of how much of an economy's income goes to labor, the American economy compares very favorably with any socialist state—especially when we recall that at any given level of technology, our economy is almost certainly substantially more efficient in producing income than a centrally planned economy. It is not surprising that under these circumstances Marxism has been so unsuccessful in the United States. In so far as it has any validity, it represents a special case which is irrelevant to most of the American pattern. Not only does the American economy return a surprisingly large amount of its income to labor, but historically this proportion has been increasing. It was probably something like 50 percent in the nineteenth century and 70 percent in the mid-twentieth century.

In spite of the success of the American economy in returning income to labor, there is a strange paradox: it has a persistent and intractable problem of poverty at the bottom end of the income distribution. The Bureau of the Census defines a poor family as one with a money income of less than $3,000 in 1966 prices. The proportion of total families that qualify as poor has fallen slowly from about 30 percent in 1947 to 14.3 percent in 1965. The absolute number of poor families, however, has not declined very much. The situation seems to be that while nearly 80 percent of the population—what might be regarded as "middle class" and above—have been increasing their incomes rather sharply, about 20 percent of the population have not been participating in this general increase. Here we have a pattern that is almost a parody of the Marxist model, in which 80 percent are getting richer and 20 percent are staying about where they are. This means that the relative position of the poor has been worsening—relative, that is, to the middle classes. A critical question, therefore, is the extent to which the poor represent a distinct "kith" in society, to use a technical anthropological term. That is, are the children of the poor themselves poor, or are there a fair number who rise out of the poverty and others who correspondingly fall into it? One suspects that in the United States, to a very considerable extent the poor are a "kith" in this sense, and that they do reproduce themselves genetically, if only because of the fact that Negroes and Spanish-Americans are so disproportionately represented in them, as are also poor Southern and Appalachian whites.

We do not really know the *extent* to which a "culture of poverty" exists, in which poverty perpetuates itself from parents to children for generation after generation. In so far as it exists, it is being eroded slowly as the numbers of the poor decline; but we certainly cannot contemplate this situation with any great satisfaction, especially as the poor are concentrated to such an extent in the central cities, the South and Appalachia. What is more, the poor are moving out of the South into the central cities. The social disorganization which results, as reflected in recent riots and burnings, can be attributed in part to a certain failure of the American economy—a failure at least to provide for a uniform rise in per capita incomes among all sections of the people.

The reasons for this partial failure are buried deep in the social structure of American society. One of the reasons, indeed, may lie in the nature of the developmental process itself. Economic development, whether of a whole country or of a segment of a country, is a process which involves profound cultural change. It means especially that the way of life of the children will be profoundly different from that of their parents. On the whole, the family is an institution for perpetuating the way of life and the values of the parents. The parents usually try to instill their way of life in the children, and often succeed in doing so even if they do not try. Cultural change from one generation to the next involves changes in values as well as in knowledge, and changes in values are often perceived as threatening our identity. Development therefore usually requires some agency beyond the family to break into the pattern of transmission of culture from parents to children. This always involves certain psychological costs.

In the United States our main agency of culture change has been the public school. At the level of the bottom 20 percent of the income scale, however, the public school system has not functioned effectively because of the local nature of its finance. Rural schools, Southern schools, Appalachian schools and central-city schools are notoriously below the level of our suburban schools. Thus finance is perhaps the most fundamental reason for this defect in the American economy. We must also recognize that the American problem in regard to public education is more difficult than it is in more homogeneous societies. Culturally the United States is a heterogeneous country with large numbers of cultural, religious and racial minorities. This makes the problem of the "culture of poverty" more intractable than in homogeneous societies such as the Scandinavian countries. Nevertheless, the resources which are needed to solve the problem are quite readily available; what is lacking is the political will and the institutional framework.

This brings us to the next question—that of the organizational structure of the economy. The main characteristic here is one of astonishing diversity if we include, as we must, the economic operations of government. The organizations of the American economy range in size all the way from the United States Department of Defense—which is essentially a planned economy with a gross product larger than that of the People's Republic of China—through a bewildering variety of semipublic and private organizations of all sizes. The gamut runs from General Motors, which has a gross product approximately equal to that of Brazil, down to the independent artisan, the family farm, the corner grocery and the boy with a newspaper route. Oddly enough there is no easily available breakdown of the product of the American economy by size of organization, but it is certainly safe to say that the American economy is dominated by large-scale organizations, both public and private. The largest of these is, of course, the federal government, which accounts for about 11.4 percent of the national product. Of this, about 9 percent is accounted for by the Department of Defense, which stands, therefore, as the largest single economic organization. The largest private corporation, General Motors, has total sales of about a quarter of the budget of the Department of Defense, and accounts for a still smaller proportion of the gross national product. If state and local governments are taken together they are almost as large a proportion of the gross national product (11 percent) as the federal government. This sector however represents a very large number of organizations—fifty states, over 3,000 counties, and about 35,000 townships and municipalities, not to count school districts and special districts of many kinds. The largest of these organizations, the state of California, has a budget of over $6,000,000,000 (only 8 percent of the gross national product).

However we look at it, the business of America is still business. Private business still accounts for about three-fourths of the gross national product (74.3 percent). Of the 22 percent or so contributed by government, about one half constitutes "government business," that is, activities of government which are really in the exchange sector of the economy. The contribution of households and farms to the economy is astonishingly small: about 6 percent of the gross national product.

TABLE I

PERCENTAGE OF U.S. GNP CONTRIBUTED BY VARIOUS SECTORS

	1929 (GNP = 103.1 billion)	1967 (GNP = 785.1 billion)
Government Total	8.2	22.5
Federal, Defense	} 1.3	9.3
Federal, Civilian		2.2
State and Local	7.0	11.0
Government (Non-Business)	4.2	10.9
Government (Business)	4.0	11.6
Business, Private	88.2	74.3
Business, Total	92.2	85.9
Business, Non-Farm	82.8	82.8
Business, Farm	9.4	3.1
Households	2.6	2.7
Rest of World	.6	.6

Table I shows these relationships and also shows changes from 1929 to 1967. If we were to characterize what has been going on in the structure of the American economy in this generation, we could summarize it in a single sentence by saying that the resources which have been released by the decline in the farm sector —a result of the extraordinary technological development in agriculture—have been almost entirely absorbed by national defense. In thirty-eight years the proportion of the GNP contributed by farms has fallen from 9.4 percent to 3.1 percent, whereas the proportion absorbed by national defense has risen by an almost equal amount, from something under 1 percent to over 9 percent. If we include government business in the total, non-farm business has hardly changed at all as a proportion of the gross national product, although government business has increased substantially. These figures throw considerable light on whether the United States is suffering from (or enjoying) "creeping socialism." It is pretty clear that the only place that socialism has crept very far in the United States is in the Department of Defense, which is, of course, the socialist organization next to the Soviet Union in size. Nevertheless, the private sector still dominates the American economy quantitatively.

Quantity, to be sure, is not everything. Qualitatively these figures unquestionably hide an increased role of government in the American economy. The Great Depression of the 1930's was a deeply traumatic experience for American business—indeed for the whole American society. It represented a massive failure for the existing system, a failure represented in quantitative terms, for instance, by a decline in the real national product by 30 percent in four years (1929–1933). This seemed like utterly meaningless poverty in the midst of plenty. The decline, furthermore, was very unequally distributed; and it was the productive members of the population who were particularly hard hit, both profit makers and the labor force. In the face of this massive failure of the Great Depression, the surprising thing is that so little structural change has taken place in the American economy. That little, however, has had a great effect, especially in the acceptance by government, in the Full Employment Act of 1946, of the responsibility for maintaining a reasonable stability in the economy. The success of this policy in the last twenty years unquestionably restored confidence in the existing system. If we want to devise a phrase to describe the American economy as it exists today, we could very well describe it as "Cybernetic Capitalism": a predominantly market type of private-property, private-enterprise economy, in which government plays an essential stabilizing role.

It now seems clear that the Great Depression, traumatic as it was, acted as a kind of shock treatment for American society. It broke it out of a box of complacency and put it onto a new track of development. In retrospect, indeed, the American economy in the generation before 1932 seems flabby and unprogressive. Per capita disposable income was not rising very fast, if at all. Our agricultural technology was relatively stagnant. The business cycle, even before the Great Depression, was a very serious problem. Social technology was primitive, there was little social insurance and old age and unemployment created unnecessarily severe hazards for large masses of the population. By contrast, from 1932 on, productivity in agriculture has increased spectacularly at nearly 6 percent per annum, social technology has undoubtedly improved and the business cycle has become a relatively minor element.

While a mood of mild self-congratulation seems to be in order, therefore, this mood should not divert us into neglecting the still unsolved problems of the American economy and the difficulties which it may run into in the future. Some of these have already been noted. For example, there has been the failure of the economy and its developmental process to reach the bottom 10 or 20 percent of the income distribution. This may well be the most serious of the unsolved problems. Nevertheless it is not the only one.

Another, the cumulative effect of which may be quite frightening, is the apparent inability of the American economy to achieve a satisfactory level of employment without running into a certain amount of wage and price inflation. In the fifties the fear of inflation dominated the policy makers, and we paid for this fear by a level of employment and operation of the economy which was too low to be satisfactory, though in no sense as disastrous as the Great Depression. On the whole, the level of unemployment in the fifties ranged about 6 percent of the labor force. If we take 3 percent as at least something to shoot at, representing what might be called reasonable capacity operation, this is a loss of about 3 percent of the product each year. Over a generation this amounts to a whole year's national product. In so far as the deflationary bias of the decision makers—the federal government and the Federal Reserve banks—discriminated against investment, the cost may be even greater in terms of growth. It comes as a shock to many Americans to learn that in the 1950's over forty-five countries had a higher rate of growth in per capita gross national product than the United States! It is a little unkind to call this the "Eisenhower stagnation," for the stagnation was only relative; but the implied criticism is not wholly unjust. Furthermore, the basic problem is still unsolved. It seems clear that even when unemployment gets down to 4 percent, there is a pretty sharp upward pressure on the wage-price structure. Surprisingly little effort has gone into thinking about this problem, even on the part of the economics profession. The most constructive suggestion, indeed, has come from Gardiner Means, who has proposed a discriminatory tax on rising money incomes, when the rise is a result of price or wage increases rather than a result of increased production or productivity.

The problem in a nutshell is that while it is fairly easy, especially through fiscal measures, to manipulate the money value of the gross national product, if the increase in the money value is a result of price increases, there may be no—or insufficient—change in the real product in which we are really interested. The problem then is how to create an adequate level of effective demand and at the same time prevent money, wages and prices from rising. The difficulty here is that there seems to be no way of controlling the general level of prices and wages without controlling individual prices and wages. Individual price and wage control, however, is anathema—and rightly so—in the American economy. It can be suffered only in times of extreme national emergency, for the administrative inefficiencies of any price and wage control system are so great that they could not be tolerated in reasonably normal times.

Another aspect of the American economy which gives cause for reasonable concern is the rise in the national defense sector which we have previously noted. This has implications for all aspects of American life. It has risen *not* primarily in response to economic needs or motivations, but mainly in response to threats from the rest of the world, especially, of course, from the socialist countries. There has also been a change in the national image itself—toward militarism and "national greatness," and away from isolationism and a modest appraisal of the national role in the international system. Whatever the reasons, the impact on the economy has been profound. There is indeed a military-industrial complex, against which President Eisenhower warned the country in his farewell address. The rise of the war industry is undoubtedly the most striking single change in the structure of the American economy in the past generation. It has consequences for the labor movement, for the educational system, for family life and especially for the young who are its principle victims. These consequences go far beyond the more than 9 percent of the economy which it absorbs. If we are not careful, it can become a cancer within American society. It represents an ethic, a state of mind and even a form of organization which is sharply at variance with the business tradition and the civilian culture of the society. It is ironic that we may be in danger of the same type of business-military alliance which essentially overthrew the business system in Nazi Germany. In fact, militarism in the United States is a greater threat to the business system than socialism. Businessmen seem singularly unaware of the essential inconsistency in their support of militarism.

There is a widespread myth in American society that it is only military expenditure which preserves prosperity and prevents us from having a great depression. This myth is widespread in both the business community and the labor movement. Like all myths, it has some foundations in the empirical world; the belief that it was Hitler that got us out of the Great Depression has some elements of truth in it. As our understanding of the economy increases, however, we should have growing confidence in our ability to insure full employment even when the level of the war industry is much less. If we compare the structure of the American economy in the 1920's with the structure today, we see that one of the major differences is the rise in the war industry and the fall in consumption as a proportion of the gross national product. The war industry, as we have seen, has risen from less than one percent to over 9 percent. Consumption expenditures by contrast have fallen from about 75 percent of the gross national product in 1929 to 63 percent today. The "bite" of the war industry comes almost wholly out of personal consumption. If the reconstruction of the international system permitted us to reduce the war industry to the 1929 level, with the application of our existing skills in fiscal and monetary policy to preserve full employment, American consumers would be about 15 percent better off. The view that the war industry creates prosperity can therefore only be described as an illusion.

From the point of view of long-run development, the situation may be even more serious, because the war industry absorbs a much larger proportion of what might be called the "growth resource" in the economy than the 9 to 10 percent which is absorbed out of the gross national product. There is indeed a "brain drain" internally into the war industry which is severely affecting the technical development of the civilian segment of the economy.

In taking a final long look at the American economy we must ask ourselves, "What are the underlying conditions in the total social system which are likely to affect its future?" We will confine ourselves here to two problems, both of them, however, of overwhelming importance when it comes to the future. The first concerns the kind of people which the society produces. At least three or four times in a century a new generation takes over the conduct of affairs. The people who are operating the American economy today will nearly all be dead or retired fifty years from now, and a completely new set of people will have taken over. This transference of culture from one generation to the next dominates the history of mankind. We noticed it earlier in the problem of the "culture of poverty." It may be a problem in a different sense for the "culture of wealth," for the culture of those who are economically most active and who comprise what is rather inaccurately called the "middle class." These are people characterized in a greater or lesser degree by a certain type of personality. They tend to be energetic, achievement-oriented, hard-working, with a strong image of the future and much activity directed toward the future. They are interested in economic calculation. They make decisions by some kind of cost-benefit analysis, however informal, and consequently they count cost; they ask for rewards, they save and invest. These are people dominated by what Max Weber called, rather unfortunately, the "Protestant ethic" (it has, in fact, been characteristic of American Jews and Catholics, and doubtless of many Japanese, for that matter), and which I prefer to call the "economic ethic."

The dynamic and developmental quality of the American economy has, for a number of generations, been the result primarily of the fact that the society produced the economic type of personality in large numbers, not only among those who went into business, but also in the labor force. Societies which do not produce this type of personality find economic development very difficult.

Among American young people today another type of personality seems to be on the increase. There is no very good name for this. We might simply call it the "non-economic" personality. This type is represented in its most extreme forms by the hippies, but one perceives it also among more conventional types. It is reflected in an increasing tendency, especially among able young people, to go into the professions rather than into business in general and the large corporations in particular. Whether this is a passing fad or whether it is the beginning of change in the character of American society, is too early to say. Nevertheless, it is clear that something is happening, and the future of the American economy depends a great deal on what it is. The personalities of adults are produced on the whole from childhood experiences. If, for example, there is any radical change in methods of child-rearing, we may expect to find this reflected in the adult character of the population of the next generation. But of course early childhood experiences are not the sole source of adult character. There are also profound changes going on in school and adolescent experiences. How important this is quantitatively nobody knows, but it is about time somebody found out. We might be making a great mistake in projecting the habits and the character of the past generation into the future.

Somewhat related to this is a wide range of questions involved in what might be called the dynamics of legitimacy. Unless an institution can retain legitimacy both in the minds of those who operate it and in the minds of those who constitute its environment, it cannot survive. Legitimacy is intimately related to success, both in relation to power (threat capability) and wealth (exchange capability). Nevertheless, power and wealth do not create their own legitimacy, and the relationships are often unexpected. Thus the threat of socialism to capitalism is a threat to its legitimacy and to very little else. The mere fact that capitalism has been economically successful, as it has been in the United States, is not a necessary guarantee that it will continue to be legitimate. Within limits, failure and trauma often do more for legitimacy than success. The Great Depression, for instance, far from its shaking the belief of the American in his own system, reinforced that belief simply because the whole society had gone through a disastrous experience together. The very sacrifices involved may have reinforced belief in the system. Success might, therefore, possibly be more dangerous to capitalism than a certain amount of failure.

These are very tricky questions, and at the moment we certainly do not have any satisfactory answers. They must be asked, however, if only to prepare us for possible surprises. At times, though not always, it has been at the height of its success that an institution has suddenly lost its legitimacy and disintegrated. The very success of the American economy may be a reason for increased caution about the future. It is never safe to take the future for granted, least of all when one is successful.

GRANTS VERSUS EXCHANGE
IN THE SUPPORT OF EDUCATION

Joint Economic Committee, Congress of the United States,
U.S. Gov. Printing Office (1968), pp. 232-238.

GRANTS VERSUS EXCHANGE IN THE SUPPORT OF EDUCATION

If we take any segment of the economy such as education it is clear that there is some sense in which its accounts must balance, at least in the long run. Every segment of the economy must draw inputs from the rest of the system in the shape of labor and materials, having a certain dollar value. Corresponding to these inputs there must be an equivalent value of outputs of some sort. If for the moment we think of this process in terms of money flows, then corresponding to the inputs there will be outflow of money, and unless there is an equal inflow of money from various sources, the money stocks of the segment will soon be exhausted and it will no longer be able to continue the purchase of inputs. The input of money into a segment, however, can come from three major sources. 1. It can come from the sale of currently available goods or services. 2. It can come from borrowing, which is roughly equivalent to the present sale of future goods and services. If we borrow a million dollars now we will have to sell something over a million dolars of goods and services at some future date in order to repay the loan with interest. 3. Money can be received from grants, a grant being a one-way transfer for which nothing tangible or measurable is given in exchange.

The distinction between exchange and grants is very fundamental in economic life although it has been surprisingly neglected by economists. Exchange is a two-way transfer. A gives something to B and B gives something to A. A grant is a one-way transfer. A gives something to B and B makes no tangible transfer in return. The distinction between exchange and grants is not always clear. Many things, for instance, which look like grants in the short run such as the support of children by their parents are in effect are deferred exchange or investments, for in some societies at least the parents expect their children to support them in their old age. In a great many grants also there are intangible and unmeasurable benefits which are returned from the grantee to the grantor. Thus a gift of charity to a beggar returns to the giver a certain intangible return in the shape of status or self-satisfaction or a warm feeling of having done the right thing. These intangible things do not constitute reallocations of assets so that even though there may be difficult marginal cases, by and large the distinction between grants and exchange is fairly easy to make.

The "grants economy," that is, that part of the economic system which consists of grants, has been steadily rising in importance, especially in the 20th century. Depending somewhat on the definitions which we use (according to one estimate in 1966 it was about $100 billion), the grants economy accounts for a little less than a sixth of the gross national product. In billions of dollars this represents individual grants 10.6, corporation grants 0.8, foundation grants 1.2, and government grants 87.6. We must be careful not to interpret these figures too literally as this represents very heterogeneous collections of activity, some of which certainly ought to be placed in the exchange sector. By contrast in 1929, the total of grants in the United States was barely 5 billion, which was about one-twentieth of the gross national product. We obviously have here a phenomenon of great importance and yet one which has received surprisingly little attention in its total impact.

Unfortunately, my studies of the grants economy have not yet proceeded to the point where I can give a figure for the education sector, though in view of the enormous predominance of public schools at the primary and secondary level and even the extensive subsidization of higher education, it will be surprising if the figure for the proportion of the total receipts of the education sector which comes from grants will be less than 90 percent. Outside of national defense, which is, of course, almost wholly a grants economy, education is probably the largest segment of the economy which is almost completely dominated by grants. It is all the more important, therefore, that we take a look at some of the conceptual and theoretical problems which are involved in the grants economy, particularly as these affect education.

We can begin by asking: "Why should there be a grants economy in the first place? Why should anybody make a one-way transfer for which he does not get anything tangible in return?" The most obvious and perhaps the most satisfactory answer to this question is that a grant is an expression of community or human solidarity. It is an expression of the fact that individuals are not self-sufficient in their identity but in order to obtain a satisfactory personal identity they have to identify in some degree with other people. This widening of the personal identity to include others may also quite legitimately by described as "benevolence," a phenomenon which can be defined objectively, not as a Pickwickian emotion, but as a property of a utility function. When welfare or utility is increased, when I perceive that the welfare of another person is increased, then I am technically benevolent toward that person. The parent who takes satisfaction in the welfare and achievement of his children, the citizen who gives to relieve the poor, the person who gives to an organization with which he identifies are all expressing the benevolent aspect of human behavior by which the personal interest is expanded to some kind of community. Without this kind of identification it is indeed doubtful whether community could exist at all. Benevolence, of course, has a negative aspect—malevolence—which exists when one person regards his own welfare as increased in the contemplation of the diminution of the welfare of another. This also, unfortunately, is an important aspect of human behavior, especially in the international system and is a sign of what we might call negative community.

Exchange tends to be neutral on the benevolence-malevolence scale. As Adam Smith says in *The Wealth of Nations*:

> It is not from the benevolence of the butcher, the brewer, or the baker, that we expect our dinner, but from their regard to their own interest.

Malevolence, of course, may destroy exchange, as we see in the current hostility of many people toward trade with the Socialist countries even though this would be mutually beneficial. Those people who feel malevolent toward the Socialist countries would rather have us injure ourselves so that we may injure them more. Exchange is best developed when there is a mild degree of benevolence in a society, enough at least to make us polite to the store clerk and trusting of the banker. On the whole, though, exchange does not require much benevolence, simply because there is no sacrifice involved. In exchange, indeed, each party benefits so that there is very little in the way of redistribution even though some problems arise in regard to the distribution of the benefits from exchange. Thus in collective bargaining, for instance, in the labor market, some malevolence frequently develops between the employer and the employed and if this goes too far the whole industrial relationship may break down into destructive strikes and sabotage. The very fact that uncoerced exchange is beneficial to both parties, however, exercises a constant pressure toward the diminution of the malevolence that so clearly is costly to all sides. This probably accounts for the development of the kind of live-and-let-live neutrality which is characteristic of most of the American labor scene today.

Benevolence, of course, is not sufficient to explain grants to education. Here we must pause for a moment to consider the role of the tax system in the grants economy, for education is largely financed, not out of voluntary grants, but out of taxes, which might be described as involuntary grants. The tax system occupies a somewhat uneasy midpoint between what might be called the threats economy and the grants economy. At one end of the scale we might have a situation in which taxes were collected by pure threat, in which the taxpayers did not identify in any sense with the objectives of the taxing authority and in which the taxes were paid simply because of the fear of consequences of not paying them and for no other reason whatsoever. A country occupied by a foreign power, the policies and principles of which were repugnant to most of the inhabitants, would be such a case. Here there would be no sense of community with the authorities and taxes would only be paid out of response to threatened consequences. At the other extreme we have something like the United Fund where there is a slight element of threat in the sense that the person who does not contribute often receives sneers or hard looks or a low opinion of his character, but where on the whole the grant is given because of a certain sense of identification with the purposes for which the grant will be used.

The tax systems of democratic countries fall somewhere between these two extremes. Certainly if they were to rely on United Fund techniques of raising money for government, the collections would be much less than they are now. On the other hand the threat system which enforces the collection of taxes is not a naked threat, but it is legitimated in some sense, especially insofar as the taxes are voted by the representatives of the people. The people then have a kind of a counterthreat against the Government, as a good many Congressmen are feeling at the moment. Here we run into a rather odd principle which we might call that of voluntary coercion. There may be sufficient identification with the purposes of the tax-collecting authority so that most people will be willing to pay taxes if everybody else paid them. If taxes were placed on a purely voluntary basis, however, a good many people would avoid paying them, even though they might believe in the purposes for which they were being collected, because the purpose might still be fulfilled even if a single person did not pay his taxes. Under these circumstances a system of legitimated coercion may be quite rational and, indeed, to a considerable extent this is what we have.

In a well-integrated democratic society, therefore, it is by no means unreasonable to regard taxes as a segment of the grants economy, a little different no doubt from voluntary contributions, but nevertheless also representing a sense of identity of the individual with the community and with the purposes of the community. On the other hand, there are limits to this sense of identity at which point the community begins to run into tax resistance, taxes become not merely personally unpopular, as they always are, but generate a strong sense of malevolence toward the existing officers of government. A political party which neglects this tax resistance may easily find itself voted out of office. In extreme cases, tax resistance may take the form of greatly increased and privately legitimated evasion, or it may even take the form of deliberate defiance of government in tax refusal or "voting with the feet"; that is, emigration. There are a good many signs at the moment that we are reaching some boundary of tax resistance in the United States, both at the Federal and at the local level. The Vietnam war has not unified the country behind the Government. It has, indeed, divided it and there is widespread resistance to the present objectives and purposes of the administration. At the local level we find increasingly that bond issues and millage increases are being voted down, which again are symptoms of the fact that there is a growing lack of identity of large members of people with purposes of the taxing community.

In this situation the education "industry," if we may use so undignified a term, is in a curiously ambiguous position. On the one hand, there is a long tradition in the United States of identification of individuals with the purpose of public education, and a striking willingness to submit to taxation for this purpose. Hardly anyone will question, not even the extreme rightwing, that in this country education is a proper subject of subsidy; that is, for grants. On the other hand, in real terms it is clear that education participates in the exchange economy simply because education is an investment. Many studies have shown that almost every year formal education, at least up to the level of the M.A., increases the life income of the educated person. In this sense, education is an industry which produces a product which can be valued in dollar terms, that is, in terms of the increased income of the educated person, as well as producing intangible products in the shape of the good life, a greater capacity for enjoyment, and a greater ability to make good decisions. It is a good general principle that the best cases for applying grants are those in which an activity produces intangible and inappropriate benefits We regard contributions to churches, for instance, as being largely in the grants economy (though there may be some argument about this), mainly on the grounds that the benefits which are received from religion cannot be evaluated in dollar terms and hence will not be elicited in response to pure market or exchange institutions. National defense, likewise, cannot be evaluated in market terms. Education, however, is mixed from this point of view. Some of its benefits cannot easily be evaluated, and some of them can be measured in dollars without difficulty. A legitimate question can be raised, therefore, as to whether we have achieved the appropriate mix of grants and exchange in the educational industry, or whether what we have today is simply not a leftover from an earlier period, and requires serious reexamination.

The case for this reexamination is reinforced because of the rise in both the size and the cost of the educational industry, a rise which is likely to continue and perhaps even to accelerate. The expansion of the total resources devoted to education arises from two sources. One is the fact that in the modern world human knowledge is the major source of productivity. Hence investment in human resources has become recognized as not merely a legitimate, but an essential form of investment, the limits of which have by no means been reached. Furthermore, the growth of knowledge itself means that a larger proportion of the resources of society have to be devoted to maintaining it and replacing it. Every year a substantial proportion of the knowledge stock of society is removed by death, aging, retirement, and human obsolescence. Even if the knowledge stock were to be simply maintained and prevented from decay, therefore, an increasing proportion of the activities of society would have to be devoted to education as the knowledge stock itself rises. The rate of growth of the stock of knowledge, however, has itself been increasing dramatically. In the first millenium of our era, it probably took about a thousand years to double the stock of human knowledge. Today in many fields knowledge doubles in less than a generation. Under these circumstances the proportion of resources which have to be devoted to the simple maintenance of the stock increases all the time and seems to increase at an accelerating rate. We certainly cannot see any end to this process at the moment. We may expect, then, in the next hundred years that the proportion of resources devoted to education will continue to increase dramatically simply to prevent the loss of what we already know. For every physicist who dies, for instance, we must train up a new physicist to take his place at the cost, perhaps, of 25 years of formal education.

The second reason for what almost might be called the education explosion is the fact that, technologically, education is not a rapidly advancing industry. Its techniques, indeed, have changed very little even since the time of Plato. There are some signs of technological change now in the shape of teaching machines and programed instruction, but these increases in productivity are relatively small and may not even do much to diminish the cost of education. Because of this backwardness in technology, which may incidentally be something quite inherent in the nature of the process, not merely the result of the fact that we have not devoted much in the way of resources to it, the unit cost of education relative to agricultural and manufacturing commodities, especially, continues to increase. Hence what might be called the real burden of education rises even faster than the quantitative increase of the industry itself. The financial crises which education is encountering and which seem likely to deepen in a spectacular way in the next 25 years if nothing is done about it, is mainly a reflection of the increased size and the increased burden of the industry. A system of finance which is quite appropriate for a small establishment may be quite inappropriate for a large one.

It is this increase in the relative size and the burden of the educational industry, therefore, which is forcing a reexamination of the extent to which it should be financed by grants and the extent to which it should be financed through the exchange mechanism. If, as I suspect is the case, a grants economy reaches a limit at a certain point and the supply of grants as it were becomes inelastic in response to the demand for them, we may have to face much more seriously than we have done hitherto the possibility of shifting part of the educational industry onto an exchange basis rather than supporting it through a grants economy. Fortunately, it would seem that this could be done fairly easily, simply because of the fact that education for the individual who undertakes it is an investment, in terms of increasing his income with a fairly high rate of return. Investments, however, which have a high enough rate of return can be financed through financial mechanisms; that is, through some form of borrowing, and there seems to be nothing inherently inequitable about this. On the other hand the conventional financial instruments and the conventional forms of borrowing are clearly inappropriate to investment in human resources, simply because of the long time periods involved and the peculiar nature of the risks. It is for this reason that the private financial sector has not produced financial instruments or institutions such as educational banks in the way in which it has produced mortgage banks and a large financial apparatus for investment in housing.

Thus, education would seem to be an example of a segment of the economy where private financial institutions, for very good reasons, are not able to adapt themselves to meet financial need. There is a case here, then, for the development of what might be called a public exchange economy. All Government operations do not consist of grants. Many of them, indeed, such as social security have only a relatively small grant element and consist essentially of what might be called a public deferred exchange system. Education would seem eminently suitable for such an arrangement and proposals such as that of Professor Killingsworth should receive very serious consideration. Most of these proposals involve the setting up of a public educational bank which would be prepared to extend loans to any qualified student in sufficient amount to enable him to continue his education for as long as it seems profitable for him to do so. These loans would then represent not a chattel mortgage, which is quite inappropriate to the human person, but a general claim on future income which could easily be satisfied by a 1- or 2-percent addition to the person's income tax over a fairly long period of years which would then, of course, be repaid to the educational authority. This avoids the unpleasant implications of the chattel mortgage and it represents a distribution of the burden of repayment which is in proportion to the economic success of the education. This is more like ordinary share financing than it is of bond financing, but there seems to be nothing inappropriate in this.

There are many practical problems involved in schemes of this kind and a great many details which need to be worked out, especially regarding the conditions and the rules for granting the educational loans.

The success or failure of the system, indeed, may well depend on success in working out these details, and we should certainly not assume that this is necessarily going to be any easy problem. Nevertheless, the payoffs of this system would seem to be so great that it deserves a most serious consideration.

Proposals for an educational bank do not in any way imply that the whole finance of the educational system should be removed from the grants economy and put over into the exchange system. The critical problem of the political decisionmaker here is that of the appropriate mix of grants and exchange. There is certainly no reason why a national educational bank should not be combined with extensive subsidies either to educational institutions themselves or to students. There are, however, problems here which need a great deal of thought, especially in regard to the impact of a system of student-centered finance on the structure and the policies of the educational institutions themselves. There is a good deal to be said for the argument that the deficiencies of the educational system are, in part, a result of the fact that it has been too monopolistic and made too much use of the police power and has not relied on the competition of educational institutions for students. I am not suggesting, of course, that the educational system can be governed by wholly perfect competition, which would be absurd. Nevertheless, if students were able to pay for their own education because of reform in the system of educational finance, this would unquestionably have a very marked effect on the nature and the performance of the educational institutions themselves. They might need to be protected under these circumstances from too much student domination: if the student is a paying customer, would he be always right? One has an uneasy suspicion, however, that a little competition from students might be good for both schools and universities.

The purpose of this paper has been to raise questions rather than to answer them and unfortunately a good deal of the information which is required to give answers to these questions does not yet exist. We now need a period of serious questioning and research in regard to the whole educational industry and there are many encouraging signs that this is beginning.

THE LEGITIMATION
OF THE MARKET

Nebraska Journal of Economics and Business,
7, 1 (Spring, 1968): 3-14.

THE LEGITIMATION OF THE MARKET*

The central concept of economics is exchange. In its most primitive form this is a small social system which involves two parties, call them A and B, and two exchangeables, say, X and Y. The exchange consists of a transfer of a certain quantity of X from A to B and a corresponding transfer of a certain quantity of Y from B to A. Out of this relatively simple element, constantly repeated, has grown the whole vast structure of markets, division of labor, specialization of production, and an enormous variety of social institutions: firms, corporations, banks, insurance companies, and so on, all in fact that we call the "economy."

The question of the legitimacy of exchange has rarely if ever been raised by economists. On the whole, we have simply taken the elementary phenomenon for granted. This is perhaps because we have always regarded exchange as essentially a positive-sum game with payoffs for both the parties. Like mercy, it is twice blessed; it blesses both the seller and the buyer, otherwise it will not take place at all, provided that it is uncoerced. Consequently, we have regarded the institution as self-legitimating and have thought very little about the environmental conditions which in fact have legitimated it. The insensitivity of economists, however, to the problem of legitimacy has sometimes led them into serious error, for legitimacy should never be taken for granted. It is an aspect of the social system which has a dynamic of its own, and a very subtle dynamic at that, which is by no means easy to comprehend or to forecast. Furthermore, the dynamics of legitimacy frequently dominate other aspects of the social system. It is perhaps the most important single aspect of any institution in regard to survival power. If an institution loses its legitimacy, it loses everything, for it can no longer continue to function as a constant organizer. The bandit for instance may organize a brief social system by unlegitimized threat. He says, "Your money or your life." You give him your money and he gives you your life. If, however, he wants to do this every week, he must become either a tax collector or a landlord, that is, the threat system must be legitimated. Similarly, even though exchange can occur in conditions where it is not regarded as legitimate, and an occasional bargain may be struck, there can be no continuing organization which is based on it.

Illegitimacy in exchange can be derived either from the parties,

---

* This paper was presented as the C. Woody Thompson Memorial Lecture at the annual meeting of the Midwest Economics Association, April, 1967, Chicago.

or from the exchangeables, or from general attitudes towards the whole process. Exchange is sometimes defined as illegitimate because it involves at least a neutral relationship between the two parties, and if their relationship is defined by the society as one of hostility, exchange between them may be regarded as illegitimate. A good example of this is the Trading with the Enemy Act, which prohibits even works of mercy and charity in the interests of the malevolence of the national state, and regards trading for merely private gain with persons defined as enemies as both illegitimate and illegal, and subject to heavy penalties.

Even where trading with the enemy is regarded as illegitimate, it often becomes apparent that it is also profitable, that is, there are mutual payoffs. If the malevolence is not too great, therefore, there may be some institutionalization of exchange even with enemies. A very interesting example of this is what the anthropologists call "silent trade" in which two tribes, each of which regards the other as an enemy, each of which has malevolence towards the other and each of which, therefore, cannot afford even to meet the other without the expression of hostility, may institutionalize trade by the device of laying commodities out in some neutral spot with the expectation that the enemy will come up after the first party has withdrawn and replace the proffered commodities by other goods given in exchange. A good deal of this goes on even during modern war through the intervention of neutrals.

Another source of illegitimacy in exchange relates to the *status* of potential parties to exchange in a society where status depends on an ability to exploit a favorable position in the threat system; the high status person may consider it beneath his dignity to indulge in exchange with low status persons. Thus in aristocratic societies, the aristocrats are frequently not supposed to indulge in trade. One of the most interesting characteristics of exchange is that in the formal model there is an implication of equality of status between the parties simply because of the formal symmetry of the process. A gives something to B, B gives something to A, and there is nothing in this process which identifies either A or B as having higher status. Exchange, therefore, is a very real threat to hierarchy, and where an exchange takes place between persons of different status it always has a certain flavor of illegitimacy. We see this for instance in the obsequiousness of the shopkeeper, which is an attempt to preserve an illusion of inequality of status in the transaction, in order to reassure the customer of his actually higher status; whereas, in fact, in the exchange process, it is the shopkeeper who is really at an advantage, who really knows the commodities, and is perhaps able to obtain the superior position in bargaining.

The difficulties which have always surrounded the labor market are another example of the difficulties of exchange under conditions of hierarchy between the exchangers. Within the organization of the firm, the employer is in a superior status position to the worker. Insofar as employing a man is an act of exchange, however, the very fact that it is an exchange brings an aura of equality to an otherwise hierarchical situation—"an honest day's pay for an honest day's work." The constant insistence of the labor movement that "labor is not a commodity" in spite of the fact that it is clearly something which is bought and sold is a reflection of the sociological tensions which underlie the phenomenon of exchange in the labor market. The organization of labor unions can be interpreted in large measure as an attempt to create a greater equality of status between the parties of the labor market. Unions hence become an important agency for legitimating the very labor market which they seem at first sight to challenge.

Sexual exchange is another interesting example of the difficulties of legitimation of exchange in a situation where the status relationships are extremely complex. There can be no doubt that the pure model of exchange applies in considerable degree to the sexual relationships. Each of the parties certainly gives something to the other. On the other hand, the very complexity of this relationship has in almost all societies made what might be called the pure market solution, which is prostitution, both illegitimate and rather stable. Here we have what might almost be called the legitimation of illegitimacy. It is because prostitution is illegitimate that it persists. If it were to be completely legitimated and if a brothel were to be regarded as legitimate as a supermarket, the very complexities and peculiarities of this kind of exchange would be likely to create psychological strains which would recreate its sanctioned illegitimacy again. In marriage the exchange is fully legitimated by the device, oddly enough, of destroying the free market and establishing bilateral monopoly.

These cases of illegitimacy arising from the nature of the parties to exchange shade off almost imperceptibly into cases which involve the illegitimacy of the exchangeable or the definition of the commodity. Exchange cannot be legitimate unless the thing which is exchanged, that is, the exchangeable, is regarded as a legitimate subject of transfer and of trade. Perhaps the most striking example of illegitimacy of the commodity is the prohibition of slavery. In societies of classical civilization there was no such prohibition. The human body was considered just as legitimate a commodity as a horse or a cow. Even Adam Smith in the heyday of the Enlightenment speaks in one breath of "the laboring poor and the laboring cattle." It is only with the development of the sense of community of all men and the rise of what I call the "integrative system" that slavery has become illegitimate and hence has virtually disappeared from the exchange system, except in the special case of military conscription, where the legitimacy of the national state is used to overcome the illegitimacy of involuntary servitude. General Hershey is Simon Legree dressed up as Uncle Sam.

The illegitimacy of prostitution in a sense combines both the illegitimacy of the exchanger and the illegitimacy of the exchangeable and it may be that in all cases where the exchanger and the exchangeable are combined there tends to be a threat to the legitimacy of the exchange.

Another interesting example of the illegitimacy of the commodity is alcohol and drugs. The status of alcohol is peculiarly interesting because the controversy about its legitimacy tends to run rather sharply upon class lines. It was Adam Smith again who pointed out that there are two systems of morality, one for the rich, and one for the poor, so that we may even see prohibition as an example of class warfare. The poor, or rather the upwardly mobile lower middle class, tend to regard as illegitimate those commodities the use of which may impair their upward mobility. Consequently we get what might be called a puritan definition of the legitimacy of commodities in which those which impair productivity are regarded as illegitimate. The class aspects of legitimacy of what might be called "sumptuary" goods produces even a kind of counter legitimacy in the ruling class which develops what might be called an alcohol subculture in which the consumption of alcohol is a symbol of legitimacy rather than of illegitimacy. The shrill joviality of the cocktail hour and the beery geniality of the saloon are interesting examples of a class response to a challenge—one from below and the other from above. The sumptuary legislation of the Middle Ages is another interesting example of an attempt to destroy the equalizing tendencies of exchange by reserving certain commodities to certain classes and status groups in society.

Besides the legitimacy of the exchanger and the exchangeable there is a third source of legitimacy or illegitimacy in the exchange phenomenon which is hard to classify, but which does not seem to fall in the other categories, that might be described as the legitimacy of the exchange process and the kind of human relationships which it involves. Historically, exchange has often been regarded as something rather grubby, disreputable, and low class. The merchant, for instance, has always had an aura of illegitimacy about him, and even in American society, where the business man probably has a higher status than he has ever enjoyed in any other, he still feels conscious of a certain inferiority in his intrinsic status position as compared, shall we say, with the supreme court justice, the military leader, or even the clergyman or the professor. Part of the reason for this "bad press" of the exchange phenomenon is the very equalitarian nature of exchange itself and the threat which it presents to hierarchy. Another part of the picture is the tension between the "threat system" as an organizer of society and exchange as an organizer of society. In the development of civilized society the threat precedes exchange as a social organizer and if it is to be successful it has to be highly legitimated either by appeal to divine sanction or by appeal to the heroic ethic. The hero is the great legitimator of the threat system. By incurring danger and by making sacrifices he legitimates the ugly fact that his support is largely by unilateral transfers, that is, that he gets a great deal from the rest of society and gives it precious little. Exchange is a threat to the heroic. It is grubby, commonplace, it denies the histrionic splendors of malevolence, and it has the unpardonable quality of making everybody better off. It is not surprising, therefore, that the heroes and the saints and the poets have despised it, for it runs counter to the heroic ethic of not counting the cost, not too visibly asking for reward, asking not the reason why, asking not what your country can do for you, and so on. As Gerard Manley Hopkins says, "All is seared with trade."

Another source of the illegitimacy of exchange is what might be called the "material fallacy" that only production is virtuous whereas exchange simply consists of the pushing around among various owners of things which have previously been produced. There is a good deal of this feeling in agrarian fundamentalism, the feeling that the farmer is the real producer and that the merchant and still more the financier is exploitative in the sense that he simply pushes around what the producer has produced. Every economist recognizes this as a fallacy, but it is a very popular fallacy nevertheless. This is related also to the Marxist concept of alienation which may be related to Freudian concepts of toilet training, that we resent the loss of our product, even when we get something else in return. I confess I feel something of this as an amateur artist. Quite apart from the fact that nobody has ever wanted to buy one of my productions, I would feel psychologically embarrassed if anybody came along and offered to do so, simply because one's own productions are in a very real sense extensions of one's own personality, and giving them up almost has the psychological impact of cutting off a finger. Thus all exchange takes on a little bit of the air of prostitution.

The point where exchange is most vulnerable in regard to the loss of legitimacy is in financial markets. Here its legitimacy may be attacked on all three counts: there is the populist and socialist feeling that bankers and financiers are illegitimate people, cleverly exploiting for their private gain a system which ordinary people do not understand. There is a corresponding feeling that the exchangeables with which the financial system deals are also in some sense illegitimate. We see this in a book like Bazelon's *The Paper Economy*, in which there is a strong feeling that whereas dealings in real things, in wheat, copper, and land, may be all right, the economic system is governed far too much by dealings in paper, in stocks and bonds, debts and loans, even such gossamer exchangeables as bank deposits which are not even visible as paper in the hand. The populist feeling against Wall Street is a symbol of the denial of legitimacy to exchange; it reflects in large part the feeling of the producer against the exchanger and especially against the specialized exchanger.

Another source of illegitimacy of exchange which is related to the above pertains to the relative legitimacies of the public versus the private as a mode of institutional form. There is something private about exchange. It organizes society through the operation of the invisible hand of private benefit, rather than through the visible grandeur of the public will. Simply because exchange is of mutual benefit, and it does have large payoffs for the individual parties, the institutions of exchange do not generate the loyalty, affection, and respect which institutions of the threat system or the integrative system generate. As somebody has said, the main thing that is wrong with capitalism is that nobody loves it, and this could also be said of the stock exchange and the banking system. An institution which demands little in the way of sacrifice also gains little in the way of loyalty and affection. We love our country quite literally because our terms of trade with it are so bad, because we give it a lot and it gives us very little. We don't love General Motors because on the whole our terms of trade with it are quite good. These are curious subtle phenomena of which the economist is largely unaware, yet when the things which he takes for granted are suddenly not granted he may find himself in queer street.

Another aspect of the legitimacy of exchange which relates most closely to the legitimacy of exchangeables but which also is involved in the legitimacy of the whole matrix of the exchange relationship is the legitimacy of the concept of property itself. Exchange is impossible without some concept of property, for unless I *have* something I cannot give it to you. Exchange is essentially the redistribution of properties among owners, and if there is no concept of property there can be no exchange. Property itself, however, is not automatically legitimated. In its origins it rests uneasily on the threat system. My property is what I have because I am able to threaten you who want it. There is here therefore a certain tension between the exchange system and the threat system which arises because the origin and even the maintenance of the institution of property is dependent to some extent on the existence of a threat system, and yet without the institution of property the exchange system itself cannot come into being. The problem of the legitimation of property would take us much too far afield for this paper. The notion of Locke that property originates in that with which man has mixed his labor is certainly part of the legitimation process. On the other hand, property is in no sense an absolute right. It is a creation of the total social process and it may lose legitimacy almost as readily as it gains it. The problem of maintaining the legitimacy of different forms of property is probably at the heart of the problem of maintaining the legitimacy of exchange.

We cannot proceed with this question further without taking a little time to look at the whole problem of the dynamics and the sources of legitimacy, to see how far this can be applied to the exchange institution. At least six sources of legitimacy can easily be distinguished: positive payoffs, negative payoffs, age, mystery, ritual, and alliances with other legitimacies.

The relation between positive payoffs and legitimacy is a straightforward one, though it is a long-run relationship which may not be observed in the short run at all because of the familiar phenomenon of social lag. Institutions which acquire positive payoffs tend to acquire legitimacy, institutions which lose their payoffs and become unprofitable tend to lose legitimacy. Economics has always stressed the positive payoffs to exchange and rightly so. Nevertheless, there may be some negative payoffs to the system as a whole; that is, there may be diseases of the exchange system which can discredit it. One possible negative payoff is the discomfort associated with the bargaining process itself in bilateral exchange, where there is a range of possible bargains. It is not wholly clear whether this aspect of exchange is a positive or a negative payoff; some people undoubtedly enjoy bargaining, and others do not. On the whole, however, there seems to be a tendency for bargaining to diminish and for conventions like the fixed price to replace it. This suggests that the overall payoffs of bargaining are negative in terms of wasted time and the exacerbation of conflict. Consequently, institutions like the custom of the fixed price and the development of organized markets, which largely eliminate bargaining, may help to legitimate exchange. The 'worst disease of the exchange system is deflation, which is very destructive. The opposite disease of inflation is much milder in its impact, though still a disease. A severe deflation, like that of 1929–1932, discredits the exchange system simply because there is an apparently sharp reduction in payoffs to it. Hyperinflation likewise discredits it and diminishes the legitimacy of the whole institution. Nevertheless, the payoffs to exchange in general, by contrast for instance with the threat system, are so enormous that they operate as a constant long-run pressure towards establishing its legitimacy.

It may seem paradoxical to suppose that negative payoffs also establish legitimacy but this paradox represents a profound truth. Sacrifices, that is, one-way transfers not only act as one measure of legitimacy, the legitimacy of an institution being in part measured by the willingness of people to sacrifice for it, but sacrifices also in part *create* legitimacy because of a phenomenon which I have called "sacrifice trap." If we ever get involved in making sacrifices for anything it is very hard for us to admit that the sacrifices have been in vain, for this would be a threat to our own identity. Consequently, we persuade ourselves that the sacrifices have been worth while simply because we grant legitimacy to the institution for which they were made. Thus, families persist even though one of the partners may be getting a raw deal and have very poor terms of trade with the other simply because to admit this would be too great a threat to the identity. In a similar way, the blood of the martyrs is the seed of the church, and the blood of the soldiers the seed of the state. We even find this in fiscal relationships, where there is a certain tendency to throw good money after bad because again we cannot admit to ourselves that we have been deceived. Thus, both sacredness and legitimacy are a result of sacrifice as well as its cause. This leads in the long run perhaps to a somewhat unstable dynamic in which sacrifice demands further sacrifice until finally the breaking point comes and the whole institution collapses. This happens sometimes with a religion, as with the Aztecs, or political institutions, as in the case of the monarchy. It could even happen in the university, when students decide they have put up with enough foolishness, and revolt. It could even happen to the national state which today is the most legitimate of all institutions and the one that demands the most sacrifices and probably provides the worst terms of trade.

On the score of legitimation through sacrifice, the exchange institution fares badly. On the whole those institutions which exist mainly in an exchange environment, such as banks, insurance companies, and business firms, do not expect much sacrifice and do not get involved in the sacrifice trap, except perhaps in the case of their executives, their principal investors, or those who are most deeply involved with them in their personal identities. Consequently these exchange institutions do not attract to themselves much in the way of loyalty or emotional affects. Nobody is going to die for the dear old Federal Reserve or even make any financial sacrifices for it. This introduces a certain vulnerability into the exchange institution. It does not have, as it were, a reserve fund of legitimacy but it has to rely on what legitimacy it can derive from its positive payoffs and this may under some circumstances be precarious, if only because the payoffs are largely invisible.

The conferment of legitimacy by age is a familiar phenomenon and arises perhaps from the importance of habit. A thing which has been around for a long time, which is familiar, tends to attract legitimacy simply because it *is* familiar. By contrast the *nouveau riche*, the new state, the new university, even the new science, like the young person, has to worry about legitimacy, and has to work at creating it. The Pope has enormous legitimacy simply because the Church has been around for such a long time. Similarly, an old country like the United States which has maintained a constitution for nearly 200 years acquires a stability in its political system which is very hard to shake. The legitimacy which is conferred by age, however, like that which is conferred by sacrifice, may be subject to a sudden collapse as age passes into senility, or as styles, fashions, or institutions become old-fashioned and obsolete. Again, paradoxically, novelty may create legitimacy just as age may, and the new look, the young idea are also capable of creating a legitimacy of their own. There may, indeed, be a certain quadratic relationship between age and legitimacy. An artifact or an institution may start off by being the latest thing. Then it becomes old-fashioned. If it survives long enough, however, it becomes an antique, a revered institution or an elder statesman.

It is clear that age has something to do with the stability or instability of the institutions of exchange, especially those of capitalism. Where the exchange institutions have been around for a long time, as they have been in Western Europe and the United States, they become familiar and acquire a patina of legitimacy due to just having been around. It is significant that socialist revolutions have all taken place in those countries in which the institutions of capitalism were relatively young and did not have time to get themselves firmly established, such as Russia, Eastern Europe, and China.

Mystery, as a source of legitimacy, may seem less important today than it was in the classical civilizations, but it should not be underestimated. Many of the attributes of the priesthood have been taken over both by scientists and by the military and even by the lodge. The ordinary man often gives respect to that which he does not understand. The secrecy and mystique of the military is a particularly important aspect of the establishment of its acceptance. From this point of view the institutions of exchange fare rather badly. The banking system, and especially central banks, create a certain aura of mystery about their operations, but on the whole exchange is matter of fact, it belongs to the commonplace rather than to the mysterious aspects of life, and from this point of view, therefore, it does not have the sources of legitimacy which political, military, and religious institutions possess. Like most of the other sources of legitimacy also, the impact of mystery may be nonlinear; up to a point mystery creates legitimacy; beyond a certain point, however, it becomes threatening, a source of anxiety rather than of confidence, and can destroy legitimacy. Where the national state, for instance, has relied on secret police, as in Czarist Russia or in the CIA, it has tended to undermine its own legitimacy, because the mystery has in some sense become ominous, an apparition rather than a holy ghost. There may be something of this in the populist fear of Wall Street and financial markets, and of the mysterious financiers who pull the strings which manipulate the economic system. The difference here between the capacity to inspire respect to the point of awe, or anxiety to the point of total repudiation, may be a hair's breadth.

The fifth source of legitimacy, ritual, is related to mystery but not quite the same thing. This is a loose term which covers what Adam Smith called "state," the paraphernalia of achitecture and dress, the crown of the monarch, the robes of the academic or the cleric, even the white coat of the doctor and the scientist, and the frock coat of the banker are all part of the rituals of the communication of legitimacy. The ritualistic churches, such as the Greek Orthodox and the Roman Catholic, or the Shingon Buddhists, are adepts at the creation of legitimacy by ritualistic communication. Exchange and the institutions of exchange, just as they are weak in mystery, also tend to be weak in ritual. The marble halls of the bank, the pomp of the medieval guilds, or the Lord Mayor's show in London, seem rather small beer when compared with St. Peter's or the dome of the Capitol. The only economic institution in this country which seems to have gone for this sort of thing is the railroad, as expressed in its terminals, and the sad fate of the Pennsylvania Station in New York suggests how little good it did them.

Finally, the whole problem of the dynamics of legitimacy is enormously complicated by the fact that institutions exist in symbiosis with others and that hence we get what might be called legitimacy syndromes in which one institution derives legitimacy from another with which it associates itself. Thus the young and somewhat illegitimate Republic of the United States builds a capital city which looks like ancient Rome and so allies itself with the ancient legitimacy of the Caesars. A parvenu university builds itself a Gothic campus to associate itself with the ancient legitimacies of Oxford and Cambridge. A church with a new revelation, like the Mormons, takes the old Bible as part of its sacred books and simply adds to it. Here again, of course, we also find non-linearity at work. The newly-rich soap manufacturer who builds himself a palatial mansion may be rewarded only with quiet sneers behind the hand. A new country which builds itself an elegant capital at the cost of its more fundamental development may earn only the suppressed sniggers of diplomats.

The legitimacy of the institutions of exchange are tied in, in a highly complicated manner, with other legitimacies and other institutions. Only Italy has dared to have a Bank of the Holy Spirit.

The institutions of exchange, however, are frequently legitimated by tie-ins with the legitimacy of the state. We see this particularly in central banking. We see it also, oddly enough, in government regulation of business, in things like the Securities and Exchange Commission, the antitrust law and the Federal Trade Commission, even the National Labor Relations Board, which grant legitimacy to economic institutions, even at the same time that they may seem to be threatening them. An institution can derive legitimacy, indeed, even from its ostensible enemies. Thus in American society the labor union has unquestionably contributed to the legitimacy of the business institution, even though it may seem to be in conflict with it. Even the cooperative society movement has helped to legitimate the business institution as a whole.

The greatest challenge to the legitimacy of exchange and exchange institutions in the last hundred years or so has come from socialism and the rise of socialist states. The principal key to the understanding of the socialist movement, indeed, lies in an appreciation of the fact that it is basically an attack on the legitimacy of exchange at many different levels. It attacks the legitimacy of certain exchangeables, such as stocks and bonds and other financial instruments, especially when issued by private corporations. It attacks the legitimacy of the private organization as an exchanger, especially the private firm. More fundamentally, it attacks the legitimacy of the market as the principal organizer of society. It denies the legitimacy of the invisible hand and insists that only the visible hand of a centrally planned economy is legitimate. In those countries where the socialist attack has been successful, market-based organizations—that is, those organizations which derive their survival value from the opportunity to buy and sell and exist in a market environment—have virtually disappeared except at the margins of society, and have been replaced by essentially political organizations, the guiding principle of which is the budget rather than the market, and which survive because of their ability to find a place in the overall budget of the society rather than because they can obtain revenue by selling things to customers.

This shattering attack on the legitimacy of exchange has come from many sources and would take much more than a brief paper to analyze. Insofar as the attack has come from intellectuals, and without intellectuals it is fair to say that socialist revolutions would never have been accomplished, it comes partly perhaps from intellectuals' feeling that their product has an aura of sacredness about it, being the Word, and that it should not be subject to the grubby manipulations of the market. As a class, intellectuals have frequently been alienated from the merchant and from those elements in the society which have specialized in buying and selling. They have tended to be aristocratic in origin and attitudes, laying great

stress on those integrative relationships which are one of the products of the intellectual and hence divorced even from the positive
contributions of exchange. At the other end of the social scale, as
we have seen, the labor market produces severe psychological and
sociological strains because of the peculiarity of labor as a commodity which sometimes leads the worker to reject the whole concept of the labor market as inconsistent with his human dignity
and his aspirations to status, even though, as I have suggested, this
may represent a fundamental misunderstanding of the essentially
equalizing function of exchange. Finally, the labor theory of value
represented an intellectual focus for a great many of these vague
dissatisfactions and delegitimizing tendencies. It gave an excuse
for the denial of legitimacy to all types of exchange relationships
which give rise to the appropriation of surplus value by anyone
other than the laborer.

Now that the first shock of attack has passed we see a certain
process of the relegitimation of exchange taking place, even in the
socialist countries, mainly, one suspects, because of the payoffs
involved. Whether it is regarded as legitimate or not, a system of
exchange has high payoffs to all parties participating. Furthermore,
no society can exist without something like a price system, or at
least a system of real terms of trade. Every person, every organization, and every segment of society has inputs and outputs, and the
ratio of these inputs to the corresponding outputs is a very important quantity in determining welfare and the distribution of welfare. Furthermore, there are good reasons to suppose that over a
large field of human activity freedom of exchange increases the
welfare of all parties. It is not surprising therefore to see the socialist countries move towards what has been described as market socialism, at least in commodity and labor markets, even though they
are very unwilling to extend this into the capital market. Whether
the process of convergence of East and West will proceed so far
as to make the two types of society virtually indistinguishable is a
matter which only the future will show, but the fact of convergence
is very obvious, and a great many of the problems involved can be
stated in terms of the legitimizing of exchange of different kinds.
Neither perfect competition nor competition stimulated (or perhaps
one should say simulated) by antitrust legislation, nor government
regulation, nor absorption of the whole economic process into the
overriding but dubious legitimacy of the national state is wholly
satisfactory, as a recipe for the legitimation of the total exchange
process. It is clear that we need to give much further thought to
this problem; and it is clear also that the theory of the dynamics
of legitimacy is an instrument through which many problems of
great difficulty in the past may be solved and even some quite
intractable controversies resolved.

THE ROLE OF ECONOMICS IN THE
ESTABLISHMENT OF STABLE PEACE

Economisch-Statistische Berichten (Rotterdam, Netherlands),
53, 2639 (April 10, 1968): 332-334.

The role of economics in the establishment of stable peace

Stable peace is a recognizable phase of the international system which is characterized by the diminution of mutual threat, the abandonment of deterrence, that is, a threat-counterthreat system as the basis for international relations, and by the removal of the location of frontiers from the agenda of the international system except through mutual consent. This is a phase of the system which has already been established in North America and Scandinavia and there is a distinct possibility that this may be established throughout the whole Temperate Zone in the course of the next generation. If this happens there will be a major transformation of the nature of the international system, transforming it from the system we have lived under for the last two hundred years, of unstable peace with islands of stable peace developing within it, to a system in which the major part of the international system will be in stable peace but which may still exhibit islands of unstable peace, especially in the Tropics.

It should be noted that while international organizations such as the United Nations and its related agencies may assist the establishment of stable peace they are not strictly necessary to it, for stable peace depends primarily on re-adjustments in national images and in the conception of national interest. Nevertheless, the most likely dynamic which would lead to stable peace is a combination of the development of world organizations on the one hand and a maturing process on the part of the national state itself which will lead towards a mature conflict behavior and national images which are consistent with stable peace.

THE IMPACT OF MOVEMENTS
IN THE WORLD ECONOMY

Even though the development of stable peace is primarily a dynamic process within the international system, movements both in the world economy and in the science of economics may have profound effects on the international dynamic process. The critical problem here is what is the effect of changes in the economy on political and national attitudes and particularly on what might be described as „political mental health". In this respect, the development of the economy may have different effects at different times and places. Where the national image and the national identity are immature, so that hatred of the foreigner or desire to impose national culture on others are characteristic attitudes, economic development may easily lead to imperialism and to a worsening of the international system and may lead also to a decrease in the stability of peace with an increase in war. This phenomenon has been noticed in a number of nations; as they have begun to enjoy the fruits of economic development they have used these fruits to a considerable extent for imperialism and national aggrandizement. This happened, for instance, with Britain and France in the eighteenth and nineteenth centuries, with

Germany in the late nineteenth and early twentieth century, with the United States and Japan in the early twentieth century and so on. It is quite probable that if the Asian and African countries today have a successful economic development, especially if this is disproportionately distributed among the various countries, greater economic power may easily permit an aggressiveness which is now latent to become actual. Fortunately, there does seem to be some tendency for this process to reverse itself as development proceeds. The richer countries today, with the possible exception of the United States, seem to be increasingly pacific and isolationist in their attitudes.

Another aspect of economic life which can easily lead to a worsening of the international system is the failure of expectations about the economy, which may be occasioned either by a depression, especially a great depression, or by a failure of expected development to materialize. The Great Depression in the 1930's unquestionably produced a severe worsening of the whole international climate. Had it not been for the Great Depression indeed it is likely that Hitler would have never have come to power in Germany, and it is quite likely there would have been no Second World War, at least not at that time. The hypothesis that it is the failure of expectations rather than any absolute change in the economy itself that is significant is perhaps borne out by the Russian experience where the first collectivization (1928-'32) was an economic disaster, at least as large as the Great Depression in the West, but where a repressive regime placed all expectations very far in the future and conditioned large masses of people to expect sacrifices in the present. The present military posture in the United States can even be attributed in part to a delayed reaction to the Great Depression, for a great deal of the international support for American aggressiveness in the international scene stems from the „myth", which unfortunately has some basis in reality, that it was only the Second World War that really aroused the United States from the traumatic experience of the Great Depression. Hence war and appropriations for the war industry are associated, especially in the imaginations of the American working class and its representatives in the labor movement, with prosperity and full employment.

The above hypothesis suggests a very depressing conclusion that the „revolution of rising expectations" which has dominated the tropical world in the last decade or so may easily lead to grave disappointments, as population increase, the shift in the age distribution towards children, and the massive inertia of traditional societies frustrates the desire for development. This then may easily lead to increased aggressiveness in the international system especially towards somewhat weaker neighbors. One fears especially for the future of Africa in this regard as the nations which have resulted from the liquidation of colonialism have been set up with highly arbitrary boundaries

and with very little cultural homogeneity, so that the opportunities for future boundary disputes seem almost unlimited. It is incidentally one of the elements in the present situation which leads to modest optimism in regard to the Temperate Zone, that as a result of the two world wars most European nations are now culturally homogeneous by comparison with what they were fifty years ago, hence the possibility of stabilizing national boundaries is much greater than it was.

THE ROLE OF ECONOMICS AS A SCIENCE

The science of economics by contrast with the economy itself may also make important contributions towards the establishment of stable peace, both through changing the images which people may have of both the economic and the international system, and also by the subsequent development of economic policies which are consistent with stable peace. One can perhaps distinguish three major lines of development along which the study of economics impinges on the international system.

The first of these is not easy to assess, though in the long-run it may be the most important. This is the role which the study of economics plays in developing a „rational" or „economic" attitude even toward institutions which are not ordinarily regarded as economic like the national state. Historically, economics has developed an attitude of mind which looks towards a „cost-benefit analysis" of all sorts of institutions. It is unfriendly towards the romantic and heroic attitude towards life and it develops a system of measurement which is at least supposed to be based on economic welfare. Traditionally at least since the day of the classical economists, economic welfare has been identified with the human welfare of all the individual persons in the society. Economic thought, therefore, by its very nature develops an ethic which is unfriendly to notions of national grandeur or racial pride or even heroic idealism, all of which are likely to produce pathological states in the international system. Under the impact of ideas which are largely derived from economic thought we are now beginning to apply cost-benefit analysis and rational models of decision-making even to such irrational and heroic enterprises as war and national defense establishments. Like the „acids of modernity", the acid of the economic attitude eats deeply into the whole ideology of war as an institution, simply because in the modern world war, especially major war, is clearly uneconomical and results in severe loss to all parties. Thus when the economist gives a cost-benefit analysis of the present international system it shows that the cost has to be reckoned in terms of about 180 billion dollars a year, which is the approximate cost of the world war industry. Then the question of what benefits could possibly be worth such an enormous cost becomes acute, and the international system which has been the darling of historians and an object of human pride becomes exposed as the most deeply pathological of all elements of the world social system.

Another aspect of the development of the science of economics closely related to the above is the development of measures of economic success or failure which make visible as it were the economic approach and attitude towards the world. Of these measures the most spectacular has been the development of measures of the gross national product or national income in the past thirty or fourty years. This has made visible economic success or failure on a large scale and has also made the evaluation of the economic success of political or international policies more open to public view. It has improved feedback even to the decisionmaker himself. Even though, as all economists know, these measures are greatly defective, they have had an enormous impact in changing the image of the world especially on the part of people who are politically conscious.

In the last generation especially the economic impact both of empire and the loss of empire and of victory and defeat have become clarified through economic measurement in a way that has sharply revised the image of „payoffs" in the minds of large numbers of people, especially of important people. Thus, national income statistics have revealed very clearly that empire was mostly a burden to the imperial powers and actually lowered their economic growth and that the liquidation of empires has been a greater gain to the imperial powers than to the former colonies. Neither Britain nor France nor the Netherlands nor Belgium have suffered appreciably economically from the loss of their former empires. After some possible short periods of adjustment indeed the losses have rapidly swallowed up in economic gains. Even in the nineteenth century it is now clear that countries like Sweden which did not try to be part of the great power system had a more rapid rate of economic growth than the imperial powers such as Britain and France.

In the last generation what might be called the paradox of the „poverty of power" has been revealed even more sharply in the contrasting experiences of the victorious and the defeated parties of the Second World War. The defeated powers, West Germany and Japan, had unprecedented rates of economic growth, Japan for instance having registered 8 % per annum per capita for over twenty years, which is a world's record. Even what might be called the partially defeated powers like France and Italy have done very well, whereas the victors such as Britain and the United States have had rather slow rates of growth. Japan is the classic example of a case in which total military defeat, the loss of empire, and the destruction of the military establishment released quite extraordinary forces for domestic growth and evidently operated as it were as a „kind of shock treatment" for restoring political mental health after a period of political paranoia, which initiated an enormous surge of economic development.

Thus the very cumulation of economic information destroys the image of war as a good investment and makes it clear that a nation's own armed forces do much more damage to it economically than do the armed forces of the supposed enemy. A study of the impact of the war industry on the Japanese economy, for instance, suggests that even in the Second World War the withdrawal of economic resources from Japanese civilians into the Japanese war industry was so enormous that it may well have exceeded all the damage done by the American war

industry to Japan. It seems equally certain that the economic and social costs of the war in Vietnam to the United States far exceed any damage which is being done to North Vietnam. Under these circumstances, the sheer accumulation of quantative economic information continually undermines the case for the present international war system.

A third impact of economics on the international system lies in the changes in the economic policy of nations, particularly toward their domestic economies, which has resulted from the development of the „new economics" and especially the development of policies for domestic full employment through fiscal and monetary means. Before the Second World War it may have been true that national economic policies which were designed to „export unemployment" through tariffs and restrictions on imports may have served to increase international conflict and led to a deterioration of the international system. There may in those days have been some slight basis of fact for the theories of Hobson and Lenin regarding the economic sources of imperialism. With the triumph of the „Keynesian revolution", however, it has become clear that economic policy can create satisfactory levels of employment domestically without any adverse consequence to the international system. In the last twenty years indeed the advanced nations have been exporting employment to each other rather than unemployment. These increased skills in the management of each separate national economy have unquestionably lessened the tensions of the international system and have been a strong force making for the slow movement toward stable peace. The role of economics indeed can be judged if we contrast the twenty years which followed the First World War, from 1919 to 1939, with the years that followed the Second World War. The first period was a disastrous failure. It developed a dynamic which led to the Great Depression, to the rise of Hitler, and inevitably to the Second World War. Twenty-three years have now elapsed since 1945. We have had no great depression, there have been unprecedented rates of economic development, especially in the advanced countries, even though development has lagged in the tropical belt, and in spite of the disaster of Vietnam we are certainly further from the third world war today than we were from the Second World War in 1944!

The great unsolved problem of economics as Tinbergen suggests is the development of the tropical belt. Conventional economics as Myrdal has pointed out so convincingly in his great new work on Asia, has made very little contribution to this problem. This is the great challenge which faces the next generation and if economics, which in this case must be allied to the larger body of social science, cannot solve the problem the outlook for the international system may be very bleak, for as we have seen, the frustration of expectation can easily produce the political poisons which lead to the breakdown of peace. The East-West conflict, due in part at any rate to improved knowledge of economics, is dying down and has a fair chance of solution. The North-South conflict between the „successful" Temperate Zone and the „unsuccessful" Tropics may be much more difficult and of longer duration and here it seems we must look to the development of a general social science to give us the intellectual foundation which will enable us to solve this most difficult of all human problems.

THE UNIVERSITY AS AN ECONOMIC AND SOCIAL UNIT

Colleges and Universities as Agents of Social Change,
W. John Minter and Ian M. Thompson, eds., Boulder, Colorado:
Western Interstate Commission for Higher Education, 1968, pp. 75-87.

THE UNIVERSITY AS AN ECONOMIC
AND SOCIAL UNIT

$\mathcal{E}$conomists have been surprisingly tardy in recognizing that education is an "industry" which is a significant sector of the economy. It is now a little larger than agriculture as a proportion of the gross national product and the prospects are for its continued growth, partly because the sheer growth of the total stock of knowledge means that a larger proportion of real resources must be devoted to transmitting knowledge from one generation to the next and partly because, being an unprogressive industry technologically, its relative price keeps rising, like haircuts. In spite of this, if one contrasts the number of agricultural economists with the number of educational economists, the disproportion of the effort is a beautiful testimony to social lag.

There is no generic name for a unit of economic organization. The word "firm" is usually restricted to profit-making organizations. There is no general word for nonprofit or what might be called "not very profit-making" organizations such as universities, schools, hospitals, municipalities, and so on. Surprisingly little attention has been paid to this sector of the economy even though it is growing very rapidly. Still less is there any general term for a unit of organization considered as an organizational behavior unit in the total network of social relationships.

In economics there is a quite elaborate theory of the firm based on the assumption of profit maximization. There is no corresponding theory of the nonprofit organization, even though this occupies very much the same kind of position as the firm in the total social system. The only nonprofit organization which has received much attention from economists is the household or the family spending unit, but the problems involved in large-scale nonprofit organizations (NPO) are quite different and cry for attention. The university may be taken as typical of this important class of organizations.

A look at balance sheets

A good many elements in the theory of the firm can be applied directly to the NPO. In the first place, any organization has something like a balance sheet in the form of a position statement or state description of it at a moment of time. A physical balance sheet or general position statement consists of a simple list of physical assets and liabilities. These include, on the asset side, cash, debts due, accounts receivable, inventories, buildings, land, and certain intangible but extremely important items which might be called reputation, good will, or morale, representing the capacity of the organization for continuing to function as an organization. On the liability side we would have such things as accounts and other debts payable, and perhaps some items of negative good will representing disadvantageous personal relationships, personnel, traditions, or reputations.

In making a state description, the role of the existing personnel is of great importance. We need to distinguish between the role *structure* on the one hand, which consists of all the clearly recognizable positions in the organization, and the role *occupants* on the other. The role occupants may either under fulfill or over fulfill the role and hence may contribute positively or negatively to the good will items in the balance sheet.

In some cases, such as professors with tenure, the role occupants have a considerable degree of contractual permanency. In other cases, there may be a high turnover. In either case, an accurate state description would have to involve some kind of estimate of the value of the various role occupants to the institution on the asset side, and some account of the obligations of the institution to the role occupants on the liability side.

An essential element in the state description is the inputs into and outputs out of the institution for some accounting period. An income account also has to include items of depreciation of the existing assets or conditions, such as the running down of buildings or equipment or (strictly) the decline in skills and reputation of the faculty members.

The dynamics of an organization are closely related to its inputs, outputs, and depreciations. Its processes may be divided fairly sharply into those which are subject to what I have called the "bathtub theorem" in which the relation of inputs, outputs, and stock is that of simple addition and subtraction. An input adds to the stock and an output subtracts from it, so that the net increase in the stock in any period is equal to the input minus the output, just like water running into and out of the bathtub. An excess of input over output raises the stock by exactly that amount. An excess of output over input lowers the stock similarly.

This principle applies in exact form, for instance, to cash balances. The increase in a cash balance in a period is exactly equal to the difference between what has been paid into it and what has been paid out of it. In the case of other physical assets, again, the bathtub theorem applies if the increase in the stock of any particular asset is equal to the input minus the output. The output in this case, however, may include depreciation as a form of consumption. Input may be either production or purchase; output may be either consumption or sale.

When we come to the more subtle assets and liabilities involving reputation and good will, the relations between inputs, outputs, and stock may be much more complex than the simple additive relationship. These might be called the informational variables. Here, even though there are clearly functional relationships between inputs, outputs, and stock, these relationships may be very complicated and not follow simple principles of addition or subtraction. Thus, in the case of an individual, an increase in his knowledge is not simply the result of an excess of input of information over its output. Information is not conserved as money stocks, and, as to a considerable degree, the physical capital are conserved.

The university is particularly subject to this principle because one of its major activities is teaching, which is a prize example of nonconservation. When the teacher teaches a successful class, the class knows more and so does he. There is no sense in which teaching results in a loss of information in the mind of the teacher and a corresponding gain in the mind of the student. Everybody gains together. Good will or benevolence and the closely related concepts of morale and reputation are also nonconserving quantities. A "good" administrator creates good will among the faculty which in turn makes it easier for him to be a good administrator. An abrasive person by contrast can easily create cumulative ill will and declining morale and reputation.

One of the problems of all organizations, profit-making as well as nonprofit, is that accounting systems are designed primarily for those inputs and outputs which are subject to the law of conservation and are not adapted at all to deal with those elements in the organization which involve information and which do not obey the law of conservation. As a result, all organizations tend to operate with a perverted information system, with good information about certain aspects of the organization and very poor information about other aspects which may be equally important from the point of view of the organization's success or survival.

This means that, while there is a clearly defined ritual in financial accounting, the all-important informational accounts are never made explicit and one has to rely on the good sense and almost on a kind of unconscious skill on the part of administrators and others in keeping the nonfinancial accounts in good shape.

A "good administrator" is precisely the man who is sensitive to the total state or condition of the institution. Therefore, he does not sacrifice the nonfinancial aspects to pettifogging detail or accounting formalisms. Nor does he neglect the necessity for making financial accounts balance and for keeping the institution continually capable of meeting its financial obligations.

The fuzziness of nonfinancial accounts introduces a bias into the decision-making process. This is a problem even in profit-making organizations where, even though the financial accounts contain a large part of the measure of the success of the organization, the nonfinancial aspects of the institution frequently determine its financial success or failure. Under these circumstances, a decision-maker in almost any organization is like a man with a telescope attached to one eye and a frosted glass over the other. He might be able to see something very well, but he would certainly not have binocular vision.

Any theory of the organization, whether profit or nonprofit, must have some sort of abstract view of the process of decision-making. In the elementary theory of the firm, information is supposed to be virtually perfect and costless and the decision-making process is simply based on profit maximization, that is, the firm is supposed to select those inputs and outputs at which the profit is at a maximum. In the case of the nonprofit organization, this view is clearly inadequate from the start. Nevertheless, it is not easy to find a substitute for the maximization principle. We can, of course, restore the maximization principle formally for all organizations by supposing that what is maximized is utility. All this really means, however, is that everybody does what he thinks is best at the time, which can hardly be denied but is a principle that does not necessarily have a great deal of content.

Maximization theory, however, does have one virtue. It implies that all decision-making processes involve some kind of evaluation of the changes which are believed to result from a decision. The weakness of maximization theory is that it has prevented the development of a taxonomy of decisions simply because it assumes implicitly that all decisions are alike. This may not be so. In a university, for instance, decisions about appointments and promotions may be made on very different principles from decisions about curriculum, about fees, about recognition of student organizations, or about the building of dormitories. The list could be extended almost indefinitely.

Furthermore, the decision-making process always has to be studied in the light of its organizational setting. The authoritative legitimator of a decision in an organization may not correspond at all, for instance, to the "real" slot or level from which decisions actually emerge.

The structure of authority

Every organization has a certain written or unwritten constitution which represents the generally accepted structure of authority. The points of authority may be a single role such as department chairman or dean; they may consist of a committee which has to make a collective decision; or they may consist of certain veto powers. No matter what the written constitution, every organization tends to have an informal constitution consisting of the people who control channels of communication or who are influential with the authoritative decision-makers.

The larger the organization, the more important this informal constitution is likely to be, simply because the formal lines of communication lead to a progressive impoverishment of the information flows to the higher executives. A hierarchy is a set of wastebaskets designed to sift out what each member of the hierarchy regards as the essential information which will go up to the next level. It may well be that the information which is really wanted at the top is sitting in the wastebasket somewhere in the seventh level of the hierarchy.

If large organizations are to operate successfully, they must develop a good deal of redundancy and informal communication. These informal redundancies are often very hard to identify. Nevertheless, "knowing" the organization becomes one of the principal avenues of advancement in the hierarchy, and this consists essentially of a sensitivity to who it is that really makes the decisions. These informal organizations are apt to be particularly important where the occupants of roles which are high in the hierarchy are incapable of handling the information overload which is always the penalty for authority. Under these circumstances, the supposedly powerful members of the organization tend to rely on cronies and informal communications which may not be part of the formal organization network at all.

One sees this principle operating most clearly in political organizations where the upper members of the hierarchy do not "rise" through the hierarchy but are imposed on it from without, as for instance, the President of the United States. In universities and also in corporations, where promotion at least in the middle levels of the hierarchy is often made from within, there tends to develop an "official family" within the administration who have a strong subculture among themselves and lively communications among themselves but not very good communication with the rest of the organization, either informally or formally.

This situation can often cause a great deal of trouble as decisions are made in the light of increasingly imaginary images of what the situation is like. There is an iron law of hierarchy, that hierarchy in itself tends to corrupt communication because there is always inadequate feedback between superiors and subordinates, but also a man gets promoted to the hierarchy by pleasing his superiors. This is a skill which may make for euphoria but not necessarily for survival. It also leads to a progressive elimination, as people rise in the hierarchy, of the kind of capacity which is needed at the top where there are no superiors to please. This is perhaps why, in universities and in many other organizations, presidents and even deans are frequently brought in from outside.

Maintenance decisions and growth decisions

A real taxonomy of decision is beyond the scope of this paper, but it may perhaps start with the fundamental distinction between what might be called maintenance decisions and creative or growth decisions.

Maintenance decisions, as the name implies, are designed to maintain the institution as an open system. The Office of Admissions, the search for replacement of faculty and administrators, and the bulk of financial decisions fall into this category. The larger, the older, the more respectable the organization, the more likely it is to confine itself largely to maintenance decisions. The danger here is that maintenance may not be adapted to a changing environment, and an institution which neglects the creative decision may find itself at a sharp competitive disadvantage in rapidly changing environments.

Even in universities, it is very hard to get recognition for the really creative decision-maker. He is often somebody who stands outside the regular respectable channels of academic and institutional life. This is the sort of man who opens up a new field, who creates a new department, or a new institute, or a new kind of activity such as extension, new fields of teaching, and so on. The long-run success of an institution, and this is especially true of universities, depends in no small measure on the ability to tolerate and even to encourage people of this kind. Here again, the capacity of an institution to recognize the intangible accounts is often the key to its success.

The problem of location

A very interesting problem in the theory of the university which has not been very much studied is the problem of location. A university which is too isolated will find it hard to maintain a constant input of stimulating visitors and also the circulation of its faculty among other institutions and assignments. On the other hand, an institution which is too close to the center of things may find it hard to maintain its inner integrity because it is too distracted by easy access. This is perhaps why Washington has not produced a major university in this country and why one is almost tempted to describe the ideal situation for a major university as 30 miles from a major airport. These, however, are speculations without much evidence.

Especially at the level of second and third rank institutions, the random element is often very important. There are large numbers of people, for instance, who are capable of what might be called "maintenance operations" in the role of the president of a university. There are very few people who are capable of a creative operation in this role, and for any particular institution it is largely a matter of luck whether they get a maintenance man or a creative man. Two creative presidents in a row and the university is either ruined or advanced into a higher rank. Like the selection of presidents of the United States, however, the process of selection of university presidents has a very strong random element in it.

The problem of financial survival

The problem of financial survival of the university is closely related to its function as an economic unit in society. The financial survival of any institution depends on its capacity to maintain an input of cash adequate to cover its cash outflow. In growing institutions the input of cash should be slightly larger than its outflow to allow for growth in the total stock of liquid assets. An input of cash, however, corresponds to an output of something else and an outflow of cash to an input of something else.

It is usually fairly clear what the outflow of cash creates in the way of inputs of something else, for the outflow of cash is, for the most part, paid out in exchange for something. It purchases inputs in the way of supplies, equipment, buildings, and the services of faculty and employees. The input of cash, however, is derived only in part from the exchange system, for instance, from student fees, medical fees, hospital charges, royalties, and payments for contract research. A large part of the cash input of any university is in what is called the "grants economy" and is derived either from appropriations from legislatures, either state or federal, which are in turn derived from the tax power, or they are derived from endowments, alumni contributions, private gifts, or foundation grants, all of which represent one-way transfers.

The economic position of a university is very deeply involved in the total grants economy, and up to now we have not had very much study about this or theory about it. We can perhaps stretch the economist's concept of exchange and suppose that grants are made in response to some "product." The product in this case, however, is not a physical or exchangeable product, but it is a state of mind of those who have the power to make grants. Just what it is, however, that produces a willingness to make grants on the part of those who make them is often quite mysterious. I suspect that the best theory of the foundation is that it is a 90 percent random process. I am not sure that government is much better. One of the problems here is that the willingness to make grants is often quite unrelated to the performance of the grant-recipient. By contrast, one of the nice things about the exchange economy is that the institution which produces a saleable commodity has at least some control over what it produces, and hence its own decisions may affect its cash input. In the case of a grant-recipient, the grant often strikes, or does not strike, as the case may be, like lightning—the risk, however, being much less insurable.

A factor in the university situation which is receiving increasing attention today is a very remarkable change in the nature of the market for university services. This has two aspects—the increase in the proportion of income derived from research as opposed to teaching and the increase in the proportion of income which is derived from the federal government by contrast with either state or local government, private endowments or fees. There has been a shift also in the relative support which is given to different sections of the university. In the last 25 years, for instance, there has been a great increase in support of the natural sciences and of the medically related sciences. We are now seeing a similar rise in support of the social sciences, while the support of the humanities lags.

These changes in the market environment inevitably have profound impacts on the condition and on the decision-making processes of the whole institution. There is quite a strong case for a certain amount of viewing with alarm. How much alarm is appropriate is not easy to say. It is particularly hard to evaluate this change in the financial environment from the point of view of its impact on the intangibles, such things as loyalty to particular institutions, the willingness to perform roles which are not directly rewarded, and the relative role of the university itself, and outside sources of funds.

Anxiety is at least being expressed that this change in the market environment is corrupting the integrity of the university as an institution. It is feared that the tradition, which goes back to the Middle Ages, of the university as an academic community with widely shared responsibility among the faculty for its decision-making and a corresponding identification of the faculty with the institution itself and with its welfare, is giving way to the notion of the university as a convenient source of status, a kind of launching pad from which appeals can be made for outside funds.

It can be argued that we should simply accept this phenomenon and adapt ourselves to it. What is significant is the total republic of the intellect, not any particular embodiment of this in a local university. In American universities, especially, the very political structure of the university as a corporation, usually governed by a self-perpetuating oligarchy or occasionally by an elected body of regents or trustees, has tended to undermine the notion of faculty responsibility for the particular university and its governance. The American university has been described as a benevolent tyranny checked and balanced by an active labor market, and while this is a caricature the face is recognizable. The active labor market, however, has one unfortunate consequence. It creates a pretty sharp distinction within the university itself between the visible "cosmos" who participate in the active labor market and who are, therefore, largely independent of the particular institution which they condescend to grace with their presences and the "locals" who are less visible and who do all the work around the house. It is not surprising that, under these circumstances, severe internal strains may appear.

The status of students

In these days one cannot allow one of the strands in the composition of the university to go unnoticed, that is, the students. Although there are times these days when one gets almost a little nostalgic for apathy, certainly this is a very remarkable student generation raised as it has been from babyhood on Dr. Spock and TV. The great problem here is that students occupy an uneasy status within the university. They are not merely customers, although they do have somewhat the relationship to the organization that customers have to Sears Roebuck. Neither are they quite *members* of the community, though they are perhaps closer to this these days than to being mere customers. It is this intermediate status between the customer and the member which makes the problem of student unrest and dissatisfaction so hard to handle.

Universities are reluctant to admit students to full membership in the community with decision-making rights simply because it is felt that they are not around long enough. They do not have sufficient responsibility for the long-run future. A university which would be parallel to a consumer's cooperative in which the students are not only members but the owners and the ultimate governing authority would be conceivable. This could almost be called the "Legend of Bologna." Up to now at any rate this form of organization has not even gotten off the ground. Nobody really knows whether it could survive.

One does not have to go to this extreme, however, to recognize that there is increasing pressure these days for the recognition of students as members rather than as customers, and the universities have to respond to this in some way. One possibility is elected student representatives on the Board of Governors. Certainly what has passed for student government in the past is proving increasingly incapable of carrying the weight of the new demands.

It has become apparent this year also that, as legal and judicial organizations, universities leave very much to be desired. This aspect of the university has functioned in the past partly because it has not been seriously challenged. When it is challenged, the universities find they have no repertoire to fall back on. In matters of student discipline there is no "graduated deterrence"—nothing between the slap on the wrist of admonition or probation and the blockbuster of suspension or expulsion. Perhaps universities are going to have to set up small jails under the heading perhaps of meditation chambers to provide suitably graduated deterrence for suitably graduated assaults. The disturbances of the last few years raise very acutely the question of the judicial status of the university within the framework of the larger society. Is the campus part of the city it is in, or is it not? The medieval tradition of the university as a sanctuary still remains but is perhaps becoming increasingly impractical.

A look at the future

As one looks into the future one sees the university as an institution of increasing importance in society, with great resilience and staying power, but also as an institution in some degree of continual crisis. Part of this is a matter of sheer growth. The kind of decision-making processes which are appropriate in small institutions are not appropriate in large, and the sheer lag of organization in universities tends to give them growth trauma. Part of this is conservation of tradition and the fact that most faculties, especially, see little reason for doing anything today that they did not do yesterday, which after all is the simplest decision-making rule even if it is not always successful.

A very interesting question is whether universities increasingly are going to run into competition with other types of teaching and learning institutions. Corporations, for instance, are increasingly taking on functions of teaching, learning, and research which previously were regarded as somewhat the preserve of the university. Certainly if the universities do not adapt themselves to the modern world they will very rapidly run into new institutions which will provide them with stiff competition, which is good at least from the point of view of society. This is perhaps the most optimistic note on which to end.

BUSINESS AND ECONOMIC SYSTEMS

Positive Feedback, John H. Milsum, ed., Toronto: Pergamon Press, 1968, pp. 101-117.

BUSINESS AND ECONOMIC SYSTEMS

Introduction: Equilibrating and Disequilibrating Feedback

As discussed elsewhere, a system has feedback if its input–output components are linked in such a way that there is at least one circular (closed) loop in the system, that is in which the output of one component is related back to its own input through the chain of subsequent components in the input–output sequence. The simplest case is illustrated in Fig. 6.1, which has an element with two inputs, I_1 and I_2, and two outputs, O_1 and O_2, which are functionally related and in which the output O_2 becomes the input I_2. This is really too simple to be a true cybernetic system. It is rather a system of eddies or vortices. For a true cybernetic system we must postulate at least two input–output processes, as in Fig. 6.2, in which the process F_2 translates the output O_2 into the input I_2 of the process F_1. The properties of this system then depend on the nature of the functions involved. Let us

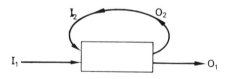

FIG. 6.1.

suppose, to simplify the system, that we have linear functions of the form:

$$O_1 = aI_1 + bI_2, \qquad (1)$$

$$O_2 = a'I_1 + b'I_2, \qquad (2)$$

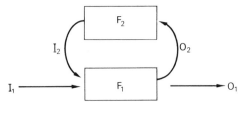

FIG. 6.2.

and that we have a feedback function,

$$I_2 = cO_2. \tag{3}$$

These functions all assume that if there is no input there will be no output. Solving these three equations, for the output, O_1, as a function of the input, I_1, we obtain,

$$O_1 = \frac{a + c(a'b - ab')}{1 - b'c} I_1. \tag{4}$$

It is clear from equation (4) that if $b'c$ is less than 1, there is an equilibrium of the system in the sense of a static relationship between the output O_1 and the input I_1. If there is negative feedback, c is negative, hence no matter what the coefficient b', which relates the output O_2 to the input I_1 in the process F_1, there will be a position of equilibrium. Negative feedback, therefore, always gives some kind of static equilibrium or homeostasis.[1] If there is positive feedback, that is, if the coefficient c is positive, there may or may not be equilibrium, depending on the size of the coefficient. The important distinction, therefore, perhaps is not between positive and negative feedback as such, simply in terms of algebraic sign, but whether the feedback coefficient c is greater than, equal to, or less than the critical value $1/b'$. Perhaps it would therefore be better to talk about equilibrating feedback and disequilibrating feedback. In those systems with disequilibrating feedback, the process literally feeds on itself to the point where there is a continual increase or decrease of some variable, and there is no true point of equilibrium.

A system with disequilibrating feedback may exhibit what

[1] However, this equilibrium is not necessarily stable if the input–output F functions are dynamic rather than static.

might be called a quasi-equilibrium, if it reaches some kind of system boundary, or even if it oscillates between two boundaries. Thus a body falling freely *in vacuo* under the influence of gravity with a constant force exercised on it and therefore a constant acceleration may be regarded, perhaps, as a limiting case of disequilibrating feedback, in which the output of the system is the velocity at one moment, which is a multiple greater than one of the input which is the velocity of the moment before. When such a body hits the ground and finally comes to rest, there is a system change, action and reaction become equal and opposite, the net force and therefore the net acceleration fall to zero, and the velocity likewise is zero as the object rests on the ground. We might imagine a cyclical equilibrium in such a case if the body had perfect elasticity and were bouncing between a floor and a ceiling. In practice, especially in very complex systems, it may not always be easy to tell whether we are faced with a true equilibrating feedback, as we are, for instance, in the uniform motion of an engine or an automobile under the influence of a governor, or whether we have a system with disequilibrating feedback which is operating within limits that are so constrained that they give the appearance of equilibrium. One does not want to use the invidious words "true" and "false" here, so perhaps we might reserve the famous word homeostasis, which has the prestige of being derived from the Greek, for those cases of dynamic equilibrium in which there is an equilibrating feedback, as there is in the case of the governor of an engine, the thermostat of a furnace, or the innumerable homeostatic mechanisms of the body, to distinguish this from the kind of static equilibrium of the book resting on the table, which is, strictly speaking, destabilizing feedback operating under severe constraints.

Accelerators and Multipliers

In economic processes, we find examples both of true homeostasis, or equilibrating feedback, of disequilibrating feedback which may actually continue for quite long periods, and of disequilibrating feedback operating under more or less broad constraints of "floors" and "ceilings". In general, as we shall see, *accelerators* are symptoms of positive feedback, which may or may not be disequilibrating, depending on their magnitude;

whereas *multipliers* are symptoms of negative feedback, and tend to produce homeostasis, even though they may also give rise to fluctuations around the homeostatic equilibrium. Accelerators are found wherever a rate of change induces an increase in the input or the process which produced the change itself, in the direction of the existing change. Processes of this kind must underlie all phenomena of growth.

Material, Energy and Information

Before going into the question of the positive or negative, disequilibrating or equilibrating character of economic feedbacks, we should take a look at the "loops", that is, the places where the output of one process becomes the input of the same or earlier processes in a sequence. We see this to some extent in *materials*. Scrap iron, for instance, which can be thought of as an output arising from the consumption of commodities made of iron and steel, is fed back into the iron and steel producing process and is a not inconsiderable part of its raw material. Similarly, the universities produce Ph.D.s which go back into universities to produce more Ph.D.s. In ecological systems in nature we find many such circular flows, such as, for instance, the nitrogen cycle, without which the system could not be sustained. In the very long run, indeed, all systems must be circular, but up to now we have not had to face this problem in the economic system, because we have had sources of economic input in the shape of mines, ores, fossil fuels, and so on, and we have had pollutable reservoirs into which the ultimate output in the form of refuse of the system could be dumped. As population increases, however, as mines get exhausted, and as reservoirs get polluted, we come closer all the time to what I have called the "space-ship economy" in which man must face the fact that earth is a closed circuit of materials. Because of the second law of thermodynamics, of course, there must always be energy inputs, but the input of energy can be used to prevent what might be called material entropy. Our existing economy is profoundly entropic, in the sense that it diffuses the concentrated. It takes metal ores and diffuses them eventually in innumerable dumps, it burns fossil fuels into the air and flushes sewage into the sea. An anti-entropic economy, or at least one which is entropically neutral, which concentrates as much as it diffuses, is theoretically possible, even though we are a long way from this technology.

The *energy loops* are perhaps less obvious than the material loops; nevertheless they are of great importance in the process of economic growth. When energy is applied to the creation or the liberation of new sources of energy, a disequilibrating positive feedback is created which leads to a continuous increase in the amount of energy available for human use. The whole process of economic development is highly dependent on this kind of feedback.

An even more subtle but yet more fundamental form of loop is the *information loop*, in which information is fed into the system and creates further sources of information, which multiplies itself and in turn becomes input to the system. Without the information loop, indeed, the others would soon run themselves to a standstill. Information, I suspect, is the major source of positive and disequilibrating feedback in the economy, simply because this is the one place where the cybernetic coefficient of Fig. 6.2, c, can be really large. Information is able to multiply itself simply because many people can listen to one speaker, even larger numbers can read one book or can hear one broadcaster or telecaster, and the printing process can impose information on an enormous number of copies. The mass production of commodities is merely three-dimensional printing. In information processes, therefore, the input–output process F_2 of Fig. 6.2 is an enormous multiplier, and I_2 the output of this process, may be much larger than the input O_2. Under these circumstances, the total process is almost certain to be a disequilibrating feedback, and indeed almost all economic and human development proceeds from this. Especially it would seem that once man domesticated crops and livestock and developed a settled agriculture, his life span increased to the point where the gross accumulation of knowledge by information intake exceeded the loss of knowledge through death, and a process of net accumulation of knowledge was set in motion which seems to have been accelerating ever since. The acceleration which is so striking in the last 300 years is also a result of a positive feedback in the information process, arising out of the fact that the more knowledge we have, the easier it is to acquire new knowledge and disseminate old knowledge, so that again in terms of Fig. 6.2, the more knowledge there is, the greater the ratio of I_2 to O_2 and the greater the rate of growth of knowledge. The process that we call rather tamely economic development is in fact an enormously long-drawn-out process of disequilibrating positive feedback in the information system. This applies strictly even to physical capital, which we can regard as frozen knowledge or some kind of structure imposed out of the epistemological content of man's mind upon the material world around him. The automobile in man's head almost literally imprints itself on steel and rubber and other materials in the process of production, and so creates the material structure which is the counterpart of the knowledge structure in which it originated.

Inventory, Production and Money

At somewhat less exalted levels, we find positive disequilibrating feedback processes in ordinary investment, for instance in the accumulation of inventories. Suppose, for instance, that inventory policy follows what used to be a rather common rule of thumb before the advent of linear programming, operations research, and sophisticated inventory control, that inventory should be a given proportion of sales. If this rule is applied strictly, then when sales rise, inventory will rise also, hence a rise in sales will produce a larger rise in production, or at least in orders for production. Similarly, when sales are falling, inventories are reduced, and production tends to fall faster than sales. For a single firm, these processes soon come to an end. If, for instance, there is an increase in the rate of sales which is then maintained, production will first rise faster than sales in order to build up inventory, but then will fall to the new level of sales once the inventory has been built up to the desired proportion of sales. Here an equilibrating feedback in the information process soon brings to an end the acceleration in production. In the economy as a whole, however, the process may go on much longer, because of of the circular nature of the system of exchange and the circular flow of money and payments. The circulation of money is a true feedback loop, and it is quite easy for it to exhibit positive and disequilibrating feedback. Thus the increase in production of one segment of the economy may increase the sales of another segment, which will increase the sales of another segment, and so on until there is a further increase in the sales of the initiating segment; and if there are unemployed resources to start with, there may be a general increase in employment, incomes, production, inventory, and so on, which can go on for a considerable time, at least until some constraints appear on the system, either in the shape of approaching full employment or in the shape of financial constraints rising out of the unwillingness or inability of the banking system to finance increased inventories, or even through fiscal constraints in the shape of increased taxation.

Inflation and Economic Stabilization

The general processes of inflation and deflation are good examples of positive disequilibrating feedback on an economy-wide scale. Inflation can happen even under a banking system, as Wicksell pointed out,[3] as long as the banks are free to expand their loans and deposits. The process may originate with some new investment opportunity, as a result perhaps of an invention, which is financed by additional bank loans. The loans create deposits, which increase the total volume of payments in the society. If there are unemployed resources, these may be absorbed; if there are not, there will be a general rise in prices and wages. As prices and wages rise, however, the value of collateral also rises, more bank loans are made, more deposits created, which leads to a fresh rise in prices and money wages. This process can go on until something limits the capacity of the banks to expand loans further, for instance a fall in their reserve ratio to the point where they fear for their liquidity. A similar process may then set in on the deflationary side, with banks calling in loans, destroying deposits, diminishing payments, which will result in a decline in money wages and prices, which in turn will call forth further withdrawals of loans, a decline in deposits, and so on.

A similar process can take place through government finance. This is indeed the commonest form of inflation, and is indeed the only cause of hyper-inflation, the situation in which the system loses all equilibrium and the price level moves toward infinity. This type of inflation, which might be called fiscal inflation, arises when, either because of some breakdown in the tax system

[3]Knut Wicksell, *Interest and Prices*, trans. by R.F. Kahn, London, Macmillan, 1930.

or because of unusual expenditures, almost invariably for internal or external war, a large budget deficit is met by the creation of new money, either through the sale of government bonds to the banks, which creates bank deposits, or through the direct printing of government money. This increases payments, increases prices and wages, and increases government expenditures thus creating a further deficit and a wider gap between government receipts and expenditures which leads to still further increase of prices and wages, and so on.

The process just described is particularly likely to happen where the taxes of one period are based on the income of the last, which used to be the case almost universally before the development of pay-as-you-go income-taxes. In this former case the expenditure of government was related to the current price level, its receipts to the price level of the period before. If therefore there was a rise in prices in the interval, this automatically led to substantial budget deficits and an increase in the quantity of money, with a further continuation of the rise in the price level. With a given tax structure and expenditure commitments, this process might go on almost indefinitely, or at least up to the collapse of the system. There have been a good many such cases, for instance in Germany in 1923, in Hungary and in China after the Second World War, and so on.

It is interesting to note, however, that a relatively slight change in the tax system may easily turn this disequilibrating feedback into an equilibrating feedback, especially if taxes are paid concurrently with income and if the taxation system is progressive,[4] so that people with large incomes pay a larger proportion of their incomes in taxes. Thus in the United States the tax system has undoubtedly operated in the last twenty years to stabilize the economy, even though it can be argued that it stabilized it, at least in the 1950's, at an undesirably low level of income and employment. The stabilizing feature arises because of the fact that if there is a rise in prices or wages and a corresponding rise in incomes, this gets more people into the upper brackets, and if the tax system is progressive, this means that the proportion of income which they pay in taxes rises. Hence any inflationary movement tends to raise the receipts of government more than its

---

[4]Non-linear increasing function,

expenditures, which means that the government absorbs cash, that is, liquid assets from the public, the total quantity of money declines in the hands of the public, and this introduces a deflationary force. If money prices and money wages are rigid, the deflationary force may operate mainly on employments and outputs, which is most undesirable; but if there is some flexibility in prices and wages, the deflation will be felt in the price-wage level rather than in output. In this case there is a strong equilibrium force operating to stabilize the total volume of payments.

The same equilibrating force operates at the other end. If, for instance, there is a deflationary move in the economy which reduces the total volume of payments, this will reduce government receipts, as people get into lower tax brackets, more than it reduces expenditures, the government will begin to run a deficit, which will increase the money supply and increase the volume of payments. In general there will be some critical set of values of the essential parameters of the tax system, on one side of which the system is equilibrating, on the other side of which it is disequilibrating.

It should be pointed out that even when there is a stable volume of total payments, R, it is still possible to have fluctuations in opposite directions in the price-wage level (P) on the one hand and the output and employment level (Q) on the other. As any payment for something is equal to the product of its price times its quantity, that is, $R = PQ$, the total payment may be constant if one of these components rises while the other falls proportionately. As it is Q that we really want to control, controlling R is not enough unless we can also control P.

Economic Development – Disequilibration and Equilibration

The whole long-run process of economic development is a process of expansion of per capita real income, with no boundary yet in sight. Not all growth processes imply disequilibrating feedback, except in a limiting sense. Thus it is stretching the concept quite a bit to suppose that the growth of a crystal in a saturated solution as more atoms are added to it from the solution than are lost from it to the solution, is a process of disequilibrating feedback, though even in this case there may be subtle structural interactions which affect the rate of growth. In growth processes in more complex systems, however, we are almost always justified in looking for disequilibrating feedback, and this is especially true in social processes. Economic development is based largely on the growth of human knowledge in one form or another. This may take the form of a simple increase in skill, which is knowledge at the level of the lower nervous system, that comes with the division of labor, and the specialization of particular productive acts. It may come even as Adam Smith supposed, from the saving of time which is lost in going from one occupation to another, when occupations become specialized. The principal source of development—that is, increase in the "productive powers of labor", as Adam Smith also saw—is the specialization in the production of human knowledge. Fig. 6.2 illustrates the process quite well. Here we suppose that I_1 represents the input of human labor in terms of hours of productive activity, O_1 represents the output of consumable, enjoyable goods, O_2 represents the output of capital goods, which may include knowledge in the human head and also may include machines, equipment, and so on, which represent knowledge imposed on the material world. O_2 in the process F_2 then produces another input, I_2, of aids to labor, and the larger I_2 is, the larger will be both O_1 and O_2 for any given input of I_1. The real secret of this process is that I_2 is a function of the total capital stock rather than that of the additions to it, that is, we can think of O_2 as implying a gross investment. As long as this is greater than the consumption or depreciation of the capital stock, whether of things or of knowledge, the capital stock in F_2 will increase and I_2 will increase accordingly. As I_2 increases, however, so does O_1 and O_2, and we have a characteristic process of disequilibrating feedback. The accumulation of physical capital makes it easier to produce more and to accumulate more, and similarly the accumulation of knowledge also enables us to accumulate it and to teach it more easily and more rapidly.

These processes may eventually reach an equilibrium in what economists have called a stationary state, simply because as total capital and knowledge accumulate, its rate of consumption likewise increases, and when this is increased to the point where it is equal to the gross additions to it in O_2, further accumulation will stop, further increase in I_2 will stop, and for a given I_1, further increase in O_2 will stop, and the system will reach an equilibrium.

This seems to be an equilibrium of a rather different character from that which is produced by an equilibrating feedback of the ordinary kind, as in a system in homeostasis. It is more like the equilibrium of the book on the table than it is the dynamic equilibrium of the cybernetic or thermostatic system. It comes about, that is, at the end of a dynamic process of growth when this process has, as it were, exhausted itself because of the fact that the forces of action in gross investment and reaction in consumption are now equal. Nevertheless, this can be a true equilibrium in the sense that if the capital stock goes beyond the equilibrium level, the consumption of it will exceed the additions to it, and it will decline towards equilibrium level. Similarly, if it is below the equilibrium level, additions to it will exceed the subtractions from it and it will grow towards the equilibrium level.

Once a developmental process of this kind has been set under way, it does seem to follow a kind of "creode" as the biologists call it, or equilibrium path through time, simply because of a certain stability in the functions of the system. Even great disturbances, like the Great Depression in the United States, or the Second World War in Japan, do not throw the society very far off its long-run path, particularly in the early stages of a developmental process, where the long-run equilibrium seems to be a long way ahead. There seem to be other cases, however, in which the developmental potential of a society seems to be exhausted at a fairly early stage, and it stagnates even after a considerable process of development. China, for long periods of its history, seems to have been in this condition; so do Spain and Portugal in the last two centuries; so do many Latin-American countries and Islamic countries. What seems to account for this is a weakness in the O_2 function, so that not enough of the total output of the society is devoted to the increase of knowledge, the improvement of skills, and the development of new methods. In many such societies there does seem to be something like a negative feedback in the developmental process, in the sense that any change which seems to threaten the existing power structure or the prevailing ethos of the society is severely repressed. This may well be a true cybernetic system of equilibrating feedback, in the sense that undesirable change, from the point of view of the people who have the power in society, is perceived as such and forces are immediately set into action to counteract it. Innovators are penalized or exiled, conformists are honored, and the whole socialization process in society tends to produce a simple reproduction of each generation by the next. One sees this even in such subcultures as the Amish, within the enormously dynamic society of the United States. The Amish have preserved their culture largely unchanged, even in its material components of clothing and furniture, for almost 200 years. They do this by developing severe sanctions against any innovation, also by having a very high birth rate and expelling the innovators. There have evidently been enough conformists left within the group in each generation to perpetuate its pattern of life.

Population

The Malthusian equilibrium of population is another example of a dynamic disequilibrating process which ends in a kind of static equilibrium. As long as the number of births exceeds the number of deaths, population will increase. As it increases, however, on a given resource and knowledge base, it eventually gets to the point where further increase produces either an increase in deaths or a decrease in births or both.   In the "dismal" Malthusian system, we suppose that the whole effect operates on deaths, and that as the population rises, the pressure on the available resources means that the people in it become more hungry and miserable until finally the death rate rises to the relatively fixed birth rate and we reach an equilibrium with birth and death rates equal and everybody very miserable. The theorem can be cast in a more cheerful form if we suppose that there can be an impact on birth rate as well as death rate and if we suppose that as population increases, awareness of the need for birth restriction developes, and births decline until they equal the death rate. This system is another example of the stationary state system mentioned above. It should be observed, however, that the nature and quality of the stationary state, whether it is one of utter misery or cheerful affluence, depends on the nature of the dynamic process by which it is achieved.

Another social process which possesses the potential, at least, of disequilibrating feedback, is that of the arms race and the international system. This is more closely related to the political rather than the economic system; nevertheless, it is a phenomenon of enormous economic importance. The instability of the system rises from the fact that the size of the military budget of any one country is a function of the military budgets of others. Hence we get a situation in which an increase in the military budget of A produces a similar increase in B, which produces another increase in A, which produces another increase in B, and so on. This process may or may not produce an equilibrium, depending on the size of the parameters of the system. In the simplest case, let us suppose that the functions are linear, so that if x, y are the military budgets of two countries, the equations of the system are as follows:

$$x = m_x + r_x y,$$
$$y = m_y + r_y x,$$
(5)

with the solution

$$x = \frac{m_x + r_x m_y}{1 - r_x r_y},$$
$$y = \frac{m_y + r_y m_x}{1 - r_x r_y}.$$
(6)

These coefficients have simple interpretations. The coefficients m_x and m_y might be called the coefficients of militarism, and show how much a military budget will be even in the absence of a foreign threat. The coefficients r_x and r_y are the coefficients of reactivity, and show how much each country will increase its military budget for each unit increase of the other. The reactivity coefficients represent the feedback system, each part of the system in this case feeding back into the other part. A necessary (but not sufficient) condition for the system to have an equilibrium at all, is that either r_x and r_y or the product $r_x r_y$ must be less than 1. If we think of the reactivity coefficients as "normal" when they are equal to 1 (a dollar increase in the Russian budget produces a dollar increase in ours), the system must be abnormally unreactive to have any stability in it at all. It is easy to show that with more than two countries the situation is even worse, and that the more countries there are, the more unreactive they have to be in order to produce any equilibrium.

Subsystem Competition within System

A problem which arises in the long-run dynamics of the international system and in the social system as a whole is that of the division of the social universe, or as it is sometimes called, the "sociosphere" (that is, the total sphere of human activity) into subsystems, each with a particular disequilibrating feedback process of its own. We see this problem even in the case of individual firms. Some grow rapidly, some slowly, some do not grow at all, and some decline into eventual bankruptcy and extinction. The difference here is largely a matter of the nature of the disequilibrating feedback. At one stage of its development, a firm finds itself in an unusually profitable situation so that high profits lead to internal growth through self-financing; that is, the profits are not all distributed as dividends but are used to expand the total net worth of the firm. The high profits also lead to easy financing from outside, so that we get a disequilibrating feedback sequence in which profits lead to growth and growth leads to profits. This may turn into an equilibrating feedback if growth proceeds beyond the optimum scale and hence growth leads to a decline in profits which cuts off growth. The overall dynamics of the distribution of wealth and power in a society depends very much on the extent to which the society is cellulated into more or less independent feedback systems with different properties. The subsystems with high positive feedbacks will grow at the expense of the others, and may eventually even absorb the whole society. We find a similar problem in the international system, where the relative power position of nations depends to a very large extent on what their rates of economic growth have been in the past. Here again, there may be a long-run process at work in which a positive feedback eventually results in a negative feedback, a process which can be expressed in the simple aphorism that wealth creates power and power destroys wealth. A nation which plays a small role in the international system but concentrates its resources on economic development eventually becomes richer than the others, its wealth tempts it into becoming a great power, but being a great power is so costly, both economically and psychologically, that the nation eventually overreaches itself and falls in relative position again, relative to other nations which have concentrated on wealth rather than power; and the cycle begins again.

System Self-consciousness

A final question of great interest relates to the question of feedback at the level of the conscious image, in which the image of the system itself determines the behavior of the actors in it, especially as the system approaches crisis or critical change. An important vector of the evolutionary process is the development of increasing degrees of insulation of subsystems against changes in their environment. A stone falling out of a cliff or a salt crystal dissolving in water is absolutely helpless in the face of environmental change. A living organism maintains a degree of homeostasis, and has cybernetic machinery with feedbacks to protect it against environmental change. The more complex the organism, the more environmental changes it is protected against by its internal constitution. We can think of consciousness as the last link in this long chain of development, which enables the conscious system to project an image into the future and hence protect itself against change which has not yet happened. It is this image of time stretching back into the past and forward into the future with a degree of system regularity, which perhaps distinguishes consciousness from mere awareness, such as an animal has when it chases its prey. In social systems this appears as social self-consciousness, that is, consciousness of the time patterns of the social system in which one is placed and for which one has to make decisions, whether this is a family, a business, a nation, or a world. The development of social self-consciousness is perhaps the greatest achievement of man in the last 200 years, and it is an achievement of incalculable consequences for the future. Instead of being a helpless pawn of uncontrollable historical forces, he now visualizes himself as a planner, and this no matter whether he lives in a socialist or a capitalist country, capable to some extent of controlling his future and the future of his own system by anticipating change, preparing for crisis, and developing social cybernetic machinery with an information system adequate to detect impending undesirable change and an apparatus of effectors sufficient to counteract it.

The System's Challenge

This self-consciousness of social systems is perhaps the greatest contribution of the social sciences, and we see it making an impact in all fields of life. In economic policy, for instance, we no longer are content to suffer the swings of the business cycle; we are not even interested in predicting it; we want to control it, and we have done so in the last 20 years with at least a modest success, in regard to major fluctuations. Just as a thermostat reduces fluctuations of indoor temperature to a small and tolerable cycle, so social cybernetics, as reflected, say, in monetary and fixcal policy, can control fluctuations of the economy to tolerable dimensions and amplitude. We now face the same problem of introducing cybernetic machinery into the international system, where up to now it has been sadly deficient, and where the system has been characterized by violent swings from war to peace and from peace to war, and by continual crises. In this case what we are looking for is equilibrating feedback. In other cases we may be looking for disequilibrating feedback, as in the case of economic development, where one of the major problems is to destroy the equilibrating feedbacks of the traditional society, traditional culture, and traditional village life, and to introduce disequilibrating feedbacks into the society which will break it out of the low-level trap in which it finds itself and set in motion an irreversible process of development and change.

At the other end of the scale, it is sometimes necessary to reintroduce equilibrating feedbacks into a system once it has developed to the point where something like a new equilibrium must be sought. We see this, for instance, in a business where the approaching end of a period of growth often produces a crisis, which may even destroy the organization. Growth itself has positive feedback; it produces euphoria, improves morale, encourages innovation, develops "slack" in the organization which can be devoted to further growth, and so on. When a period of growth comes to an end, as inevitably it must do, for nothing can grow, at least exponentially, for ever, and all growth curves eventually flatten off, there is often a crisis which can only be averted by a highly self-conscious appreciation of the nature of the system, the course of its future, and what has to be done in order to introduce stability into it. On the national and world scale, the development of social self-consciousness may be even more important for survival, especially in times of profound system change like our own, where the parameters of the social system are altering so rapidly that the whole quality and character of the system is continually threatening to change. Under these circumstances, an adequate social theory from which feedback into all kinds of behavior and policy can be made is of the utmost importance. Without this, the disequilibrating feedbacks of the system can easily drive it to destruction.

ECONOMIC EDUCATION: THE STEPCHILD TOO IS FATHER OF THE MAN

Journal of Economic Education,
1, 1 (Fall, 1969): 7-11.

Economic Education:
The Stepchild Too
Is Father Of The Man

It may seem a little unkind or even discourteous to call economic education a stepchild in the first issue of a journal which is to be devoted to it. These are days, however, in which we are urged to "tell it as it is" as the only sound basis for legitimation. Let us admit openly that the progeny of economics and education are not the children of a passionate first love. Economics was born as political economy and the love affair of economics with politics has been indeed long, stormy, and passionate. The urge to give Advice to the Sovereign has always inflamed us with intellectual passion. The urge to give advice to the teacher, we must admit, comes to us late in life when the reforming fires are perhaps a little banked. Furthermore, education—and I see this metaphor is carrying me into deeper and deeper water—has to be shared with many other disciplines. Is economic education, for instance, any different as far as education goes from political education or historical education or even sex education? One still finds in the remnants of the burgeoning teachers' colleges the doctrine that teaching is teaching no matter what the subject, and if this is true, economic education would be even less than a stepchild and merely the dubious offspring of an extremely polyandrous relationship.

Let me hasten to add that this is too gloomy and superficial a view. The relationship between economics and education is more intimate, more profound, and of more consequence to both parties than is the relationship between education and many other disciplines. In the first place, in the last generation economists have come to realize, in a way they perhaps have not done before, that what might be called the educational industry is not only an integral part of the economic system but plays a key role in the developmental and dynamic process. With all this rather belated recognition of its importance, the educational industry is still neglected as a field of study by economists. It is now, for instance, a larger proportion of the gross national product than agriculture in the United States. Nevertheless, there must be a hundred or more agricultural economists for every one educational economist. We are just beginning to award advanced degrees in economic education, such as the ones at Ohio University in Athens, New York University, and Purdue, but as far as I know, there are still very few professors of economic education.

A number of good reasons can be cited for this neglect on the part of the economics profession, but none of these reasons are very good excuses, that is, they do not excuse us. One reason perhaps is that education is largely in what I call the "grants economy" and mainly in the public sector of that. Economists, therefore, who are more familiar with the phenomenon of exchange and the market find this problem unfamiliar and intractable, though this excuse does not seem very cogent, as public finance is an ancient specialization within economics. Another argument perhaps is that education does not have the tangible and measurable commodities and price structure of, say, agriculture, and that hence the methods and the concepts of economics do not apply to it so easily. There is some merit in this excuse. The production of Ph.D.'s is not so susceptible to input-output analysis as the production of potato chips. Still, in the last analysis, this also is only an excuse; for the fact that we cannot easily measure something which is important is no excuse for neglecting it. One certainly cannot deny that the concept of a production function and even that of optimization under various constraints is as important in education as it is in any other segment of the economy.

It is true, of course, that the educational industry operates in an environment which is much more political than it is economic or market. In particular, the revenue of public educational "firms" is derived not from the sale of a product to its user, that is, to the child or student or even to the parent that wants his child educated, but it is derived from an allocation out of public funds ultimately paid for by the taxpayer. Nevertheless, the incursion of economic thinking into the study of political structures is now so far advanced that we can hardly excuse ourselves by turning the whole matter over to the political scientists.

Some of my readers will already be uneasy because I seem to be confusing the economics of education with economic education, and it is quite true that these are fairly different subject matters. A question, for instance, of what determines the size of the educational industry, the nature of its inputs and outputs and finance, may not seem closely related to the question of how we teach seniors in high school the concepts of national income analysis. I can see some people arguing indeed that this *Journal* could either be a journal of the economics of education or it could be a journal for the teaching of economics, but that it could not possibly be both. I shall argue, however, precisely the opposite, that the relationship between economics and education goes far beyond that of the relationship between education and many other subject matters simply because the process of human learning itself has a great many of the characteristics of an "economy." Human learning is a process whereby inputs of information, reinforced by internally generated information and by feedbacks from outputs of information, are processed into a growing structure of knowledge. Thus, knowledge is in some sense a capital stock of information, although the relations between information input and output and this capital stock are much more complex than they are in the case of ordinary commodities. Commodities, for instance, follow what I have elsewhere called the "bathtub theorem," that production (which is inputs into the capital stock) minus consumption (which is output from the capital stock) is equal to the increase in the capital stock in a given time period. Information and learning do not obey the bathtub theorum; the stock of "bits" of information in the human nervous system for instance is not equal to its past inputs minus its past outputs. Indeed the "bit" itself is a wholly inadequate measure of the knowledge structure, useful as it is for the purpose of Bell Telephone. Nevertheless, the economic way of thinking is not irrelevant here. We find, for instance, scarcities and limitations which force us to consider the problems of economy. The information channels are not infinite. Hence if we learn or teach one thing we cannot learn or teach another. We see this in its most obvious form in the struggle for a place in the curriculum, a struggle which is also "economic" in a quite literal sense of the word. The specialized skills of the economist would be particularly useful in problems of this kind.

As I see it then, this *Journal* will have two distinct, but closely related, functions. In the first place, it will serve as a journal of "natural history" of the teaching of economics. Natural history is the description of a universe of study, usually involving a fairly standardized terminology which will facilitate the rapid assimilation of a large body of empirical observation. The social sciences have always been rather weak on natural history, that is, on the simple description by observation of social systems and social patterns. One of the great problems of the study of teaching has been precisely the absence of an adequate natural history of the teaching operation. Each teacher over his lifetime works out certain techniques and patterns that he finds are successful. There is no active mechanism, however, for describing and passing on these patterns to others or to a succeeding generation. Hence they all too often represent a kind of "craft" wisdom which dies with the craftsman, like the glass flowers of Harvard. The problem of the standardization of description and terminology is something which should engage us here, and I confess I do not see the answer to it at the moment. We are still a long way from having a taxonomy of teaching methods and experiences and we are still further from a Linnean language. One thing we have lacked is a specialist who will observe many kinds of teaching and learning experiences and hence, when the need for comparison arises, will almost be forced into a standardized language. Up to now, most descriptions have been made by the teachers themselves and these may be a little unreliable and also not lead to standardization of descriptive language.

As a second function of the *Journal,* one would like to see the encouragement of both theoretical and empirical work directed at the economy of the teaching and learning process as such, in both its institutional aspects and also in its more informal aspects. Learning is the fundamental concept, not education. We have to think of formal education indeed as only one among many instruments and inputs which affect the total learning process in the society. The mass media, especially newspapers, radio and television, informal discussion and folk lore, conversations with the faculty and among friends, probably contribute as much to the development of knowledge, or error, about the economy as do formal classes and textbooks. The more formal education can visualize itself as an integral part of the total learning process, the more effective it is likely to be. If it is isolated, it is in grave danger of becoming a self-perpetuating process for transmitting "trained incapacity," as Veblen called it.

A problem which is of peculiar importance for economic education and which also should not be shirked by this *Journal* is the problem of the learning of values and attitudes. One thing a social scientist cannot assume is that the values of the society are given independently of the social process itself. One would hope to see a place, therefore, for studies of the development of values and attitudes towards economic institutions and problems, not only in our own society, but also in societies where the values and attitudes differ from our own. It would be desirable, indeed, to make the scope of this *Journal* as worldwide as possible. Comparative studies of economic education in different societies would be particularly valuable.

The great poets have a way of saying much more than they know, and Wordsworth's famous remark that "the child is father of the man" has a literal truth far beyond what he perhaps himself had in mind. If there were no other reasons for economists being interested in the teaching of economics, the fact that, if there were no such teaching, economics as a discipline would die out in a single generation is surely enough to justify profound interest. Human knowledge is a very perishable commodity. It is totally consumed in every generation and must be reproduced in new minds. If this process of reproduction goes astray, as it frequently has done in human history, the progress of knowledge, and with this the progress of man himself, is interrupted. We can now see a grave crisis in the knowledge process looming ahead which arises out of the enormous accumulation of knowledge which the scientific revolution has engendered. Even if the stock of knowledge were to double only every generation (today this is probably a substantial underestimate), it would not take long, as human history goes, for us to reach the point where the stock of knowledge is so large that it requires the whole energy of the society, and especially of its "knowledge industry," to transmit it from one generation to the next. Then no resources would be left over for growth. Under these circumstances, and we may be closer to this than we think, an increasing economy in the transmission of knowledge is a prerequisite for continued growth. In the days when we did not know very much, the efficiency of the transmission of knowledge did not matter. Today when we know so much, unless we devote the cream of our intellectual resources to the problem of economies in the transmission of knowledge, that is, to education, we may find the whole growth process grinding to a halt. This is a sufficient reason why the specialists in knowledge of all kinds should be actively interested in its transmission from one mind to another.

In economics again, however, the case is particularly urgent and of peculiar importance. There are some areas of knowledge which it is agreeable to have, but which are not of great significance for human survival. An accurate and workable image of the social system in general, and the economic system in particular is, however, increasingly essential to human survival. If the prevailing images of the social system are unrealistic and inaccurate, decisions which are based on them are likely to lead to disaster. The more complex society becomes the more important it is to have a widespread realistic and complex image of it. If we suppose, as is not wholly unrealistic, that the occupants of powerful roles are selected by a process with strong random elements in it, it is all the more important that sophisticated and realistic images of the society should be widespread. Then whoever is thrown by our political Monte Carlo processes into powerful roles may reasonably be expected to have realistic images, and will be able to make good decisions. Economic education, therefore, along with education in other aspects of the social system may well be one of the most important keys for man's survival in the coming centuries or even decades. In a complex world, unfortunately, ignorance is not likely to be bliss, and a society in which important decisions are based on fantasy and folk tales may well be doomed to extinction. Especially in a democracy, knowledge, no matter how good, which is confined to a small elite stands in danger of lying idle in the decision-making process. To be effective, it must be widely disseminated. The study of dissemination, therefore, and its impact on the total social process should have a very high priority. Hence the interest which has given rise to this *Journal* is not marginal, but lies at the very center of social science and the social process.

THE FORMATION OF VALUES
AS A PROCESS IN HUMAN LEARNING

Transportation and Community Values, Washington, D.C.:
Highway Research Board, Special Report 105 (1969), pp. 31-38.

The Formation of Values as a Process in Human Learning

One of the unfortunate consequences of speaking an Indo-Aryan language is that we tend to turn things into nouns that really should be verbs, according to the famous Whorfian hypothesis. Thus, the "it" in the expression "It is raining" is a beautiful example of a nonexistent noun or pronoun forced upon us by the structure of the English sentence. The word for "values" used as a plural noun may be another example of a group of virtually nonexistent objects that stands as a grammatical substitute for what is essentially a process. Consider, for instance, the two sentences, "I value you highly," and "You have a high value to me." In terms of meaning, these are almost exactly equivalent, yet the first is much more accurate as a description of what is going on. When value is used as a verb, as in the first sentence, it is clear that it represents something that somebody is doing. When it is used as a noun, as in the second sentence, it seems to suggest a quality that is intrinsic in the object. A search for nonexistent intrinsic values inherent in the commodity object plagued the classical economists for a hundred years, until the ghost was finally laid to rest by Jevons and the marginal utility school.

Valuation can express itself either in verbal statements or in actual choices and behavior. I may make the verbal statement, "I value you highly," but if I will not inconvenience myself to the slightest degree in order to add to your welfare the statement may rightly be suspect. Economists have laid a good deal of stress on what they call "revealed preference," which is what one may deduce about people's preferences, that is, values, from their behavior. We may, however, be justified in speaking of "values" as a noun in terms of the description of a state or condition of preference on the part of an individual or even an organization or other unit of choice. Economists since Pareto have defined preferences in terms of indifference curves or, more generally, in terms of a utility or welfare function, which relates the state of the individual in his environment to some measure of his well-being or welfare. Thus, suppose we have a field that consists of combinations of two elements of choice, A and B, measuring A vertically and B horizontally. Then on Cartesian coordinates we can draw the contours of a welfare or utility function, as in Figure 1. This may be visualized as a mountain rising above the plane of the paper. It may have a summit at S, which represents a point of satiation of both the elements A and B beyond which they become "bads" rather than "goods". Each of the contours of the welfare surface is an indifference curve that is the set of all points in the field representing the same level of welfare or well-being. A whole welfare function represents a "value system" and may quite properly be thought of as a property of the person, group, or organization that it describes.

Within a given value system, such as is shown in Figure 1, the value, whether absolute or relative, placed on either of the elements A and B depends entirely on where we are in the field. From any point in the field the absolute value of an element may be defined as the increase in welfare or utility that would result from a unit increase in the element itself. Thus, suppose we start at the point L with an amount OL of B and zero of A and increase the amount of A. Between L and M, welfare increases, that is, A has a positive value. At M, a small increase in A produces no change in welfare and beyond M, as we move from, say, M to N an increase in A results in a decline in welfare; A then has a negative value or is perceived as a "bad". Similarly, as we increase the amount of B along PQR, between P and Q welfare increases with an increase in B, beyound Q it diminishes.

The relative value of, say, A in terms of B is measured by the slope of the indifference curve at any point, or between any two points. Thus, between the points E and F, which are on the same indifference curve, A is highly valued relative to B. This is

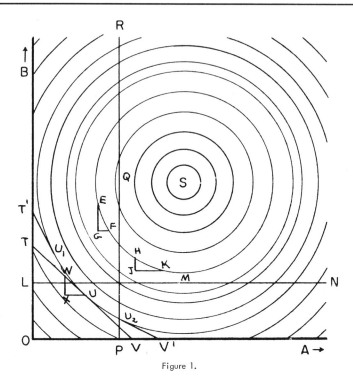

Figure 1.

reflected in the fact that we would be willing to give up a large amount of B (EG) in order to get a small amount of A (GF) and still be just as well off as we were before. By contrast, between H and K, B is valued highly and A not so highly, as reflected in the fact that we will want a lot of A, equal to JK, in order to compensate us for the loss of a little B (HJ). Thus, we do not have a single "value" for either A or B; what we always have is a value system that consists of different values for A and B depending on how much we have of either of them.

Economists have always insisted that actual choice depended not only on the value system but also on the opportunities that were open. A choice is necessitated when the elements in the set of choices are scarce, in the sense that there is a limitation on the quantities that can be obtained, which prevents the chooser reaching the point of satiety. In the field like Figure 1 this is represented by an opportunity boundary, such as the line TUV. What this means is that all combinations of the elements A and B inside the area OTUV are possible for the chooser, that is, constitute a feasible set, assuming at the moment that A and B cannot take negative values and that all combinations beyond this feasible area are impossible of attainment. Economists generally assume that the chooser maximizes his welfare, that is, the point he actually selects is that represented by the point U, where the possibility boundary touches an indifference curve. The point U has the highest welfare that can be attained in the feasibility area.

The concept of a possibility boundary produces another value concept—that of alternative cost. Alternative cost is the slope of the possibility boundary; thus, between, say, W and U we would have to give up WX of B in order to get XU of A. This is value in the sense of how much we have to sacrifice of one thing in order to get a unit of another. We might perhaps call it objective value by contrast with the subjective value, which is the slope of the indifference curve. At the point of choice these two are the same, given certain assumptions about the nature of the functions, which may, however, by no means always be true.

One proposition of considerable importance that is frequently overlooked follows immediately from this analysis. It is that under some circumstances, which are by no means implausible, a small change in either the opportunity structure or in the preference structure can produce large changes in the optimum point that is chosen. Choice, in other words, can easily be a highly sensitive system responding to small changes in the parameters by large changes in the equilibrium position. This is particularly likely to be the case if the indifference curves and the opportunity boundaries have approximately the same slope. If, indeed, the opportunity boundary and the indifference curve coincide over a range, the position of choice is indeterminant, that is, we have a "dilemma". We quite literally do not know what to choose and a very slight change may take us to one extreme or another. Thus, suppose in Figure 1 the opportunity boundary was $T'U_1U_2V'$. Choice would be indeterminant between U_1 and U_2 where the opportunity boundary and indifference curve were identical. A feather in the balance might move it from U_1, with a little A and a lot of B, to U_2, with a little B and a lot of A. This principle has great potential for explaining why value systems tend to cluster around what are often widely diverse points. Thus, as between socialist and capitalist countries the actual preferences and opportunities may not differ very much, but a small difference in the underlying conditions produces large differences in the actual choices made.

This economic approach to valuation, although it clarifies certain concepts and develops the possibility of some important propositions, such as the ones just mentioned, nevertheless has serious defects, most of which relate to the absence of any adequate dynamic considerations in the model. The most serious defect is that economists in general simply assume the preference or welfare functions on the one hand and the opportunity functions on the other without further inquiry and particularly without inquiring as to how these functions come into existence. This is what I have called elsewhere the "doctrine of the immaculate conception of the indifference curve." The opportunity functions and the production functions on which they are based are almost equally immaculately conceived without inquiry into their origins. If we are to receive any understanding of the dynamic processes of society this obviously is not good enough, because both value systems—i.e., preference functions and the opportuntity functions that rest on production functions—are learned in a long process of individual and social learning.

Only a very small part of the human value system is genetic in origin, unlike that of the birds and the lower animals whose value system is imparted mainly by their genetic structure. The human comes into the world with certain preferences that are presumably genetically controlled. The baby likes milk, warmth, and mother or some reasonable substitute, and he dislikes hunger, pain, cold, and being wet. On this primitive foundation, the whole elegant structure of human values is learned by a process of information input, output, and feedback. Even sexual preferences seem to be very largely learned, although there are certain potential preferences implicit in the structure of the nervous system. If, however, some people like caviar and red flags, and others like rice and little red books, while still others like hamburgers, French fries, and red, white, and blue, the answer has to be found in the life experience of these people, rather than in their genetic structure. What we know very little about, however, is exactly what elements in the input, output, and feedback history of the individual or society produce what structures in either values or production functions. Production functions perhaps are easier. The Balinese learns how to make batik and how to conduct elaborate and complex interpersonal relations. The American learns how to make automobiles and how to enjoy baseball.

One thing we do know: As people communicate with each other, individual preferences and value systems tend to converge into something that might almost be called a "common value system". A common value system is what defines a culture or a subculture, which consists essentially of a group of people all of whom have rather similar value systems and welfare functions. A common value system almost inevitably determines an ethical system, which is a common value system in which the value system itself is highly valued, so that people who do not hold it are regarded with suspicion and distaste. Tastes are values about which we can agree to differ. If I like coffee and you like tea, there is no great reason why we should not agree, provided both are available. If two sets of tastes are complementary the case is even better, as with Jack Spratt and his wife. You may recall that Jack Spratt could eat no fat, his wife could eat no lean, and so betwixt the two of them, they licked the platter clean. Tastes that are too similar indeed may lead to conflict, such as the two rival princes who were in complete agreement—they both wanted Milan. On the other hand, with any group of people who are in close communication, these very communications produce conformity in all those things that symbolize membership in the group, whether speech, dress, taste in food, even taste in symbols and ethical principles. We must recognize indeed that in one sense there are no purely individual tastes, just as there are no pure individuals. We are all artifacts of our society. Only those tastes are allowed to the individual that society permits. Any man in our society who has a taste for communism or bigamy, young people who have a taste for pot or LSD, a chemist who has a taste for the phlogiston theory, or an astronomer who has a taste for Ptolemaic theory will soon find that, even in the scientific community, and still more in utopian communities, there are not many tastes that are really private.

The proposition that choice is a highly sensitive system may throw a certain amount of light on how the total structure of preferences developed into cultures and subcultures, i. e., into what might be called "preference clusters". If we could map the value systems or preference structures of all the individuals in the world onto some kind of field, we would find that they would not scatter uniformly around the field but would cluster into value constellations much as the matter in the universe is clustered into stars and the stars into galaxies with large empty spaces between.

The evolutionary model of mutation and selection is perhaps the best one that we have at the moment to interpret the total human learning process, which includes both the learning of value systems and preference functions and also the learning of techniques and production functions. These functions can be thought of as "species" that inhabit the human nervous systems of the world. They propagate by means of communications, i. e., through outputs, inputs, and feedbacks of information, feedback being an input that is perceived as being related to a previous output. As an individual person grows from birth his image of the world or what might be called his "internal universe" continually changes under the impact of information input and output. This is a growth process in the image that is very imperfectly understood. In part it grows by its own internal systematic processes, largely through the generation of internal information inputs in the imagination. In part it grows because of inputs and feedbacks from outside. In this process, dissonances or disappointments are of particular importance. At any one moment we have certain images of the future and as time goes on these are either realized or not realized. If they are realized our general image tends to be confirmed; if they are not realized—if we are disappointed—some revision of the image usually has to be made.

We start off with a genetically constructed value system, with some things having high value (rewards) and others low value (punishments). Our images tend to grow toward the rewards and away from the punishments. However, the value system itself does not remain stationary, but changes as the image develops; that is, we have to learn most of what we regard as rewards and punishments beyond the most obvious physiological level. In particular, we find the approval of those around us rewarding and their disapproval punishing, unless we also learn to put a low value on approval and a high value on disapproval, as may be done at a late stage of development, if the individual rejects the society around him, as some do. Most people, however, do not get to this stage and are socialized into the society in which they grow up, accepting its preference structures and learning its technology. We thus see the process of socialization as something like the reproduction of the gene in biological evolution, by which images, value systems, preference functions, and so on are transmitted from one person to another by a process of simple reproduction, so that the children grow up with much the same value systems as the parents. This is not wholly dissimilar from the process by which genes reproduce by a kind of three-dimensional printing. In social evolution, however, printing is much less accurate and much more subject to change in transmission. The value systems of children may be very much like that of their parents, but they will rarely be identical and sometimes they may be drastically different.

If we are to understand the processes by which value systems change, we have to look at the phenomenon of social mutation. This consists of the development of images in the mind of a single individual that are different from those around him. This happens presumably because of the internal processes of growth in the image within the individual, and represents in a sense an alternative method of reducing dissonance. If there is dissonance between the incoming messages and the existing image, this may be reduced in at least two ways. We may deny the validity of the messages or we may deny the validity of the existing image and reorganize it. Consider, for instance, the case of a young person who has grown up in a small sect, hearing nothing but the doctrines and the value systems of the sect, who then goes out into the world—to college, for example—and finds himself exposed to a whole set of communications that are dissonant with his values. He may reject these communications as invalid and remain with the sect, or he may decide that the previous communications and images are invalid and may undergo a radical restructuring of his image of the world and his whole value system. Another possible reaction to dissonance is compartmentalization, that is, having one value system for one part of life and another for another. The more complex the society, the more compartmentalization is likely to take place, simply because of the differentiation of roles. The value system that man professes and even practices on Sunday may not be the same as that which he obeys on Monday. The value system that man employs in his professional life may not be that which he employs in his political life. Scientists, for instance, have been known to be quite unscientific when they go into politics.

The situation is further complicated by the fact that in social systems communications do not merely flow from one individual to another, but are dispersed over large numbers of people through mass media. The communications system is not even confined to the present time. We have a very large volume of communications with the dead through their artifacts and especially through their books, their paintings, and other semi-permanent means of communications. A great deal of what happens to a student in college is communication from times past, that is, from the dead. One sees, for instance, the enormous impact of books like the Bible, the last author of which died almost 2,000 years ago. We also have an increasing amount of communication through the mass media, the newspapers, radio, television, and so on by which messages from one person will reach millions of others. In spite of this mass communication, however, face-to-face dialogue, or what might be called "double feedback," is of enormous importance in the formation of value systems. Feedback is one of the most important sources of credibility and, in the case of the mass media, feedback is very remote. Indeed, a conversation that begins "What did you think of the TV show last night?" may have much more impact in changing value systems than the show itself.

Social evolution exhibits much more instability than biological evolution and hence is much more difficult to predict. This is particularly so in the case of evolution of value systems, less so perhaps in the case of the evolution of technology. It is extraordinarily hard to identify evolutionary potential in social systems at the time when it appears. This is why history is always surprising to us as it develops. The great mutations and value systems associated, for instance, with the names of the founders of religions, the prophets, and the poets, are virtually impossible to predict in advance, though perhaps we can say something about what it is that gives them survival value. We look, however, at the impact of individuals like Jesus, Mohammed, and Marx; we see the enormous importance of individuals who become exemplars and who may set a process of reproduction of value systems in the minds of men that profoundly changes the whole social structure. It is hard to see, for instance, how anything in the information system of the Roman Empire could have alerted Tiberius to the fact that in an obscure prophet of humble origins in a small corner of his empire was going to set in motion such an extraordinary chain of events. Similarly, who would have thought that a wild old scholar with a beard in the British museum in the mid-nineteenth century would have had such an impact on the twentieth. Those who will be the prophets of the twenty-first and twenty-second centuries are likely to be hard to identify now.

In the evolution of value systems, the development of organizations, and the skills of organizations, and especially organizations that are specialized in propagation of value systems, clearly play an important role. One thinks particularly of such organizations as churches, political organizations—especially the national states and political parties, and economic organizations, such as firms and corporations. For any organization to survive in the great ecological system of the social world it must be able to get inputs from its environment and it must be able to send outputs into its environment, and its capacity to do this depends in considerable measure on the structure of value systems and perferences of that environment. The firm, for instance, that is producing something that nobody wants will soon find itself out of business. Political parties, likewise, whose product falls into disfavor are likely to be voted out of office. A church whose doctrines do not appeal to the people around it will soon disintegrate. It is not surprising, therefore, that all organizations become modifiers of the value environment around them. In the case of the firm this is advertising and selling activity; in the case of the church and the political party and the national state, there is preaching and propaganda, often under the name of education, which is designed to change the value environment around it in favor of the survival of the institution. From the point of view of survival of an organization, the value environment may have several aspects, i.e., what in the first place might be called "simple demand" for the product of the organization. If the product is highly valued in the environment the organization will be able to survive in a market environment provided that the market itself is highly valued and legitimated.

At another level there are value systems in the environment regarding the nature of the organization quite apart from its product. Some organizations are valued for their own sake. We might express the same proposition by saying that organizations have outputs that are not commodity outputs; outputs such as, for instance, identity, security, and those subtle outputs that produce inputs of approbation and identification. This relates to the part of the social system I have called the integrative system, which deals with such matters as status, identity, security, approbation, community, identification, legitimation, love, and so on. The survival of organizations, however, is a very complex business. The corporation that nobody loves may survive by producing goodies; the country or church that nobody loves will probably not survive for very long.

The functional relations involved in the integrative system are very tricky and obscure and exhibit all sorts of nonlinearities and discontinuities. Nevertheless, I am convinced that the dynamics of the integrative system dominate all the other elements in the social system, in the sense, for instance, that if an institution loses legitimacy for whatever reason it has a very poor chance of survival. We get, however, extremely complex systems of both negative and positive feedback, sometimes leading to growth and expansion of particular institutions and syndromes, sometimes leading to decay.

Another very interesting problem in the dynamics of value systems is the interrelationship between technology and values, that is, between the growth of knowledge as embodied in production functions and input-output relationships in the commodity world and the development and change of preference and value systems. The problem can almost be summed up by saying "Do we get what we like or do we like what we get?" A value system, or a preference function, is never independent of the field of choice over which it is exercised, and in particular, widening the field of choice through changes in technology may profoundly affect value systems even in those areas where the technology has not changed. The invention of the automobile is an almost classic case in point. There is hardly any area of the value structure that has been left unchanged by this invention. It has changed our religious life, our sexual life, family life, the structure of our cities, and even in some degree the form of government. Television may have an even greater impact in the long run, for by introducing a new and rich channel of information into the home environment, it changes not only the family structure, but the whole learning process of the child and is resulting in a generation far more different from its parents than any generation in human history before. This impact of change in opportunities on the preference structure itself has been almost completely neglected by economists, though businessmen and politicians have known about it for a long time, and it raises enormously difficult questions for the evaluation of social processes.

We may conclude by applying some of these principles briefly to the transportation industry. This industry exists because the total value system puts a sufficiently high value on moving things and people from one place to another. The proposition that mobility has survival value emerges very early in the game of evolution. This is, indeed, the great difference between animal and vegetable life. Vegetables do not get around, animals do. On the other hand, vegetables are still here in very large numbers, so that obviously mobility has not been essential to evolutionary survival. It may be, indeed, that there are certain disadvantages in mobility and it was this that forced the animal kingdom into those frantic attempts to improve itself that essentially ended in man, whereas the vegetable kingdom was able to realize the survival advantages of immobility and was not forced to develop so much complexity. Perhaps we should conclude therefore that mobility leads to complexity, but not necessarily to survival. We see this principle operating in the social system too. Transportation is a cost rather than a benefit and the less of it we can get away with in a sense the better off we are. The benefit aspects of transportation are nearly always associated with variety. This is especially true of the transportation of humans because, although this has some importance for dissemination, that is, moving people to where they are most useful, the main function of human transportation is the provision of variety of experience, which is something that we do tend to value highly and certainly has to be included as one of the elements in the field of choice.

The transportation system also provides something that has very little to do with transportation as such, namely, identity. A man on horseback not only can travel farther faster than the man on foot, but he is also bigger and more impressive, and he has a larger threat capability, at least in some circumstances. It is not surprising, therefore, that aristocrats were chevaliers, which is simply the French for men on horseback. The domestication of the horse probably did more to destroy equalitarianism and to establish hierarchical social systems than any previous technological development. The fact that if you fed a horse you could not feed a man in an era when the surplus from the food producer was quite small was a very effective guarantee that horses would be scarce and not very many people could have one. This again established hierarchy. The horse, indeed, in a crowded, agricultural society, produces feudalism and the whole feudal set of values, with a distressing degree of probability.

By contrast, the automobile has been a great democratizer. In a technologically advanced society it is feasible for everybody to have one as long as oil supplies hold out, for it does not require a food surplus because it lives on gasoline. The automobile is an extension of the human body just as the horse is, but where the man on the horse is a centaur, proud and domineering, the man in an automobile is just a fast turtle, protected by a shell from the world around him and on a fundamental level of equality with his fellow man in fellow automobiles. The difference between a man in a Volkswagen and a man in a Rolls Royce is much less than the difference between a man on a horse and a man on foot. This is why I suspect that, in spite of the architects and city planners who hate automobiles because they destroy the human scale of the urban environment, the automobile is here to stay as long as we have anything to power it. This large four-wheel bug with detachable brains may in a sense be the evolutionary successor to the pedestrian. The pedestrian, of course, will survive in protected places like college campuses, but we are going to have to face the fact that the pedestrian, like a vegetable, survives as an example of an earlier stage of evolutionary development. The universality of the demand for the automobile and the difficulty that even the communist countries have in suppressing it suggests that we have something here very fundamental and universal in the development of value systems. The automobile indeed is the temple of a new religion, more universal than any of the great religions of the past. It is religion of personal power and human sacrifice and this fact alone makes it extremely difficult to control. We should not be unaware, however, of the possibility of value mutations that will change the automobile culture. We see signs of this in the hippies for whom a "trip" does not connote transportation, and also in quite respectable elements of the society such as the conservationists, environmental scientists, pollution experts, preachers, and planners.

A problem of particular importance to the transportation industry is the extraordinarily subtle and complex relationships that exist between political decisions on the one hand and the value systems of the electorate on the other. The relation between the value systems of political decision-makers and those of the electorate is loose in the sense that a great many political decisions are made arising out of the structure of political organization that probably do not correspond to the value systems of the electorate. In matters of highway development, for instance, a tax system that gives highway departments large funds only loosely controlled by legislatures has probably had more impact on the development of transportation in this country than any overt electoral process. Political decisions, like technology, also have a back-effect on the value systems of the electorate. There are bandwagon effects, for instance, that suggest that political decisions are, up to a point, self-justified, no matter what they are. Nevertheless, there is a residue of electoral power and of independent dynamic processes of formation of value systems among the electorate that cannot be neglected, and it is this perhaps more than anything else that produces long-run changes. About this sort of thing, however, we do not have a very good information system.

One concluding observation is that even though every institution, organization, and sector of the social system depends heavily for its survival and success on what might be called its value environment—that is, on the value systems of those persons who constitute its environment—the information system regarding this value environment is almost universally defective and this is perhaps one of the prime causes of decisions that lead to disaster. The most glaring case of this is the international system, which has an information system that is almost deliberately designed to produce misinformation and ignorance, but we find much the same thing in decision-makers in regard to domestic policy and particularly in regard to organizations and segments of the economy. A more explicit recognition of the importance of the value environment, therefore, and the development of an information system that can create more accurate images of it could hardly fail to improve the quality of decision-making in all fields.

FUN AND GAMES WITH THE GROSS NATIONAL PRODUCT: THE ROLE OF MISLEADING INDICATORS IN SOCIAL POLICY

The Environmental Crisis, Harold W. Helfrich, Jr., ed.,
New Haven: Yale Univ. Press, 1970, pp. 157-170.

Fun and Games with the Gross National Product—
The Role of Misleading Indicators in Social Policy

The Gross National Product is one of the great inventions of the twentieth century, probably almost as significant as the automobile and not quite so significant as TV. The effect of *physical* inventions is obvious, but social inventions like the GNP change the world almost as much.

The idea of the total product of society is fairly old, certainly dating back to Adam Smith, but the product's measurement is very much a matter of the second half of the 1900s, which I suppose we can call the fortieth half-century. Before 1929 we did not really have any adequate measure of the Gross National Product, although its measurement was pioneered by Simon Kuznets and others at the National Bureau of Economic Research from 1919 on. We began to get theories which used it in the '30s, and the cumulative effect has been substantial.

Every science must develop its own Tycho Brahe, the sixteenth century Danish gentleman who painstakingly plotted the planets' positions and thus paved the way for Johannes Kepler and Isaac Newton. In a way, Wesley Mitchell was the Tycho Brahe of economics. He painstakingly collected time series of economic quantities, although (like Tycho Brahe) he was operating with a largely erroneous theory. However, the studies at Mitchell's National Bureau of Economic Research led to the invention of the Gross National Product as a measure, and this has had an enormous effect on economic policy.

It is hard to underestimate the impact of economic measures on the world. A good example of a rather deplorable measure was the parity index, which had a tremendous impact on our agricultural policy—especially in the 1930s and '40s. The Bureau of Agricultural Economics in the Department of Agriculture developed indexes for the prices paid by farmers and for the prices received by farmers; then some enthusiast divided one by the other and came up with the parity index, which is a measure of the terms of trade of agriculture. This then became an ideal.

The danger of measures is precisely that they become ideals. You see it even in the thermostat. If we had no Fahrenheit, we would not be stabilizing our room temperature too high. There is a magic about the number 70, and we tend to stabilize the temperature at it, when for the sake of health it might be better at 64 degrees. Certainly, one should never underestimate the power of magic numbers. We are really all Pythagoreans. Once we get a number, we sit down and worship it.

The parity ideal was a mistake, but it proved to be astonishingly successful. I do not want to get into this because it is another subject, but one of these days after I retire I want to write a history of the United States on the principle that we always have done the right thing for the wrong reasons. Our agricultural policy for the last 30 years is a prize example of this. Parity was sold to the people and to Congress under the name of social justice. The measure of social justice was the parity index, which was an index of terms of trade of agriculture with 1909-14 as a base.

Well, how stupid can we get? There is nothing sacred about terms of trade if the differential rates of productivity change, and they have changed. You do not establish social justice at all by stabilizing terms of trade. Terms of trade of progressive industries often worsen, as in agriculture; the terms of trade of stagnant industries like education ought to get better, as they have done. Educators today are richer, not because *they* are more productive (which they are not) but because *other people* are more productive. As education's terms of trade have improved substantially, the unit cost of education has correspondingly risen.

Incidentally, when we tried to establish social justice with "parity," which meant, of course, that we raised agricultural prices, we subsidized the rich farmers and penalized the poor. If you try to establish social justice through the price system, you always benefit the rich because the rich have more to start with. Agricultural poverty is always the result of people having not very much to buy and sell. If you do not have anything to buy and sell, it does not matter what prices you do not buy and sell it at. So manipulation of prices—whether of agricultural policy or of cheap education—always succeeds in subsidizing the rich in the same way that state universities subsidize the rich.

All of this may seem to be a long way from the GNP. Actually, I am trying to illustrate this: when you measure something, you inevitably affect people's behavior; and as a measure of the total gross output of the economy, the GNP has had an enormous impact on behavior.

A fascinating book, *The Fiscal Revolution in America* (University of Chicago Press, 1969), has been written by Herbert Stein. He is a member of the Council of Economic Advisers who are the Three Wise Men in our society, the bishops of the modern world, Congress having established an economic episcopate. Stein has done an extremely interesting study, an intellectual history explaining the great change in economic policy from the administration of Herbert Hoover to that of John F. Kennedy.

In the depths of the depression, Hoover engineered a tax increase which exacerbated the depression. That dark hour in the global economy contributed to the rise of Adolf Hitler who precipitated World War II. Had it not been for all those developments we might not have had today's Russian problem; we might not even have had Vietnam. Hoover never knew what hit him because he did not have a Council of Economic Advisers. We did not know much economics in those days. We did not know about the GNP.

Kennedy, in a much milder situation, fostered a tax cut which was an enormous success. As a result, we have had the bloated '60s, the decade without a depression. That should go down in the history books as something spectacular. It is the longest boom ever enjoyed in the United States. Economics has had something to do with it. So has the GNP.

These days, if the GNP starts to go down, an economic adviser will go to the President and say, "Oh, look, Mr. Nixon. The GNP dropped half a point. We have to do something about this." This is the beauty of having social cybernetics, an information system that we can use to our advantage.

I suspect that without economics we might have had a Great Depression in the 1950s and '60s. The rate of return on investment in economics may be at least 10,000 percent per annum, because we have not put much into it and we have gotten a lot out of it. On the other hand, this very success worries me. I have revised some folk wisdom lately; one of my edited proverbs is "Nothing fails like success," because you do not learn anything from it. The only thing we ever learn from is failure. Success only confirms our superstitions.

For some strange reason which I do not understand at all a small subculture arose in western Europe which legitimated failure. Science is the only subculture in which failure is legitimate. When astronomers Albert A. Michelson and Edward W. Morley did an experiment which proved to be a dud (in some eyes), they did not just bury it the way the State Department does. Instead, they shouted the results from the housetops, and revised the whole image of the universe. In political life—and to a certain extent in family life—when we make an Edsel, we bury it. We do not learn from our mistakes. Only in the scientific community is failure legitimated. The very success of the GNP and the success of economics should therefore constitute a solemn warning.

I am something of an ecologist at heart, mainly because I am really a preacher, and we know that all ecologists are really preachers under the skin. They are great viewers with alarm. Is there any more single-minded, simple pleasure than viewing with alarm? At times it is even better than sex.

I propose, then, to view the GNP with alarm.

The Gross National Product is supposed to be a measure of economic success, or economic welfare, or something like that. Of course, it is not. So we have to modify it.

In the first place, the Gross National Product is too gross. It includes a number of things which should be netted out. If we are going to get the net benefit of our economic activity, we have to net the national product, and the real question is how net can we make it? We get first what we call the Net National Product, which technically is the Gross National Product minus depreciation.

The GNP is like the Red Queen in *Alice Through the Looking Glass:* it runs as fast as it can to stay where it is. It includes all the depreciation of capital, so we net that out.

We really ought to net out all sorts of other things such as the military, which is also in the GNP and does not produce much. The world war industry is really a self-contained exercise in mutual masochism. The war industry of each country depends on the other's war industry, and it is a largely self-contained system. It has little to do with defense. It is extremely expensive and very dangerous, and we certainly ought to net it out of the product. That takes out about 10 percent.

Things like commuting and pollution also should be netted out. When somebody pollutes something and somebody else cleans it up, the cleanup is added to the national product and the pollution is not subtracted; that, of course, is ridiculous. In fact, I have been conducting a mild campaign to call the GNP the Gross National Cost rather than the product. It really represents what we have to produce, first to stay where we are and second to get a little farther along.

I have been arguing for years (and nobody has paid the slightest attention) that the real measure of economic welfare is not income at all. It is the state or condition of the person, or of the society. Income is just the unfortunate price that we have to pay because the state is corruptible. We have breakfast, and breakfast depreciates; so we must have lunch. The sole reason for lunch is metabolism, and metabolism is decay. Most change is truly decay. Consumption is decay—your automobile wearing out, your clothes becoming threadbare. It is burning up the gasoline. It is eating up the food. Consumption is a bad, not a good thing; production is what we must undergo because of consumption.

Things will not stay as they are because of a reality which I sometimes call the Law of Moth and Rust. What causes our illusion that welfare is measured by the Gross National Product or anything else related to income (that is, any flow variable)? The more there is, the more is consumed; therefore, the more we must produce to replace what has been consumed. The bigger the capital stock, the more it will be consumed; hence, the more you have to produce to replace it and, of course, add to it if you want to increase it. In this sense the GNP has a kind of rough relationship with the stock or state, but I think it should always be regarded as a cost rather than a product.

Another minor item, perhaps just a technical point: as we measure it, the GNP neglects household production and only includes items in the market. If a man marries his housekeeper, the GNP falls; I argue that if he was a moral man the GNP ought to rise because he is enjoying all he had before and then some. Obviously, there is a small technical defect. However, household production probably is not much more than 5 percent, certainly not more than 10 percent, of the GNP, and thus it is a minor issue.

Much more fundamental is that all of economics, the whole GNP mentality, assumes that economic activity is a throughput, a linear process from the mine to the garbage dump.

The ultimate physical product of economic life is garbage. The system takes ores and fossil fuels (and in a boom the unemployed) out of the earth, chews them up in the process of production, and eventually spews them out into sewers and garbage dumps. We manage to have state or condition in the middle of the throughput in which we are well fed and well clothed, in which we can travel, in which we have buildings in which we are protected from the atrocious climate and enabled to live in the temperate zone. Just imagine how the GNP would fall and welfare would rise if man abandoned the temperate zone and moved into the tropics. An enormous amount of the GNP is heating this building because the plain truth is that nature is very disagreeable. It is cold, damp, and miserable, and the main effort of human activity is to get away from it. As a matter of fact, we do not even like pure air. Otherwise we would not smoke. All of this indicates that a great deal of man's activity is directed toward what we might call desired pollution.

The throughput is going to come to an end. We are approaching the end of an era. People have been saying it for a long time, but nobody has ever believed them. Very often they were wrong in their forecasts, but this time I suspect they are right. We really are approaching the end of the era of expanding man.

Up to now, man has psychologically lived on a flat earth—a great plain, in fact a "darkling plain" where "ignorant armies clash by night," as Matthew Arnold says. Man has always had somewhere to go. There has always been a Kansas somewhere to beckon him as a virgin land of promise. There is no longer any Kansas. The photographs of the earth by astronauts in lunar orbit symbolize the end of this era. Clearly the earth is a beautiful little spaceship, all blue and green and white, with baroque cloud patterns on it, and its destination unknown. It is getting pretty crowded and its resources rather limited.

The problem of the present age is that of the transition from the Great Plains into the spaceship or into what Barbara Ward and I have been calling spaceship earth. We do not have any mines and we do not have any sewers in a spaceship. The water has to go through the algae to the kidneys to the algae to the kidneys, and so on, and around and around and around. If the earth is to become a spaceship, we must develop a cyclical economy within which man can maintain an agreeable state.

Under such circumstances the idea of the GNP simply falls apart. We need a completely different set of concepts for that eventuality, and we are still a long way from it technologically because we never had to worry about it. We always have had an unlimited Schmoo, Al Capp's delightful cartoon creature that everlastingly gets its kicks from being the main course for gluttonous man. We could just rip the earth apart and sock it away. We used to think Lake Erie was a great lake; now it smells like the Great Society. We used to think the oceans were pretty big, but events like the oil leakage in California have spotlighted that fallacy. Suddenly, it is becoming obvious that the Great Plain has come to an end and that we are in a very crowded spaceship. This is a fundamental change in human consciousness, and it will require an adjustment of our ethical, religious, and national systems which may be quite traumatic.

On the whole, human society has evolved in response to a fairly unlimited environment. That is not true of all societies, of course. It is not so true of the Indian village, but the societies that are mainly cyclical are almost uniformly disagreeable. Even the societies which are cyclical (where you return the night soil to the farms) are not really circular. They rely on water and solar energy coming down from somewhere and going out to somewhere. There is some sort of an input-output.

Up to now we have not even begun to solve the problem of a high-level circular economy. In fact, we have not even been interested in it. We did not have to be, because it was so far off in the future. Now it is still a fair way off. Resources for the Future says, "We're all right, Jack. We've got a hundred years." Its report points to our fossil fuels and our ores, and reassures us that they will be adequate for a century. After that, the deluge. I would not be a bit surprised if we run out of pollutable reservoirs before our mines and ores are exhausted. There are some signs of this happening in the atmosphere, in the rivers, and in the oceans.

The nitrogen cycle, the extraction of nitrogen from the air, exemplifies the development of what looks like the beginning of a spaceship technology. Surely, when man looks back on the twentieth century, he will regard the development of the Haber process in 1913 as its most important event, even though it did permit World War I. If it had not been for Fritz Haber, the Germans would not have been able to fight that war because they were cut off from Chilean nitrates. Historically, there was a famous viewer-with-alarm about 1899, the English chemist Sir William Crookes, who predicted the exhaustion of Chile's nitrates and consequent global starvation by 1930. His prophecy did not pan out, thanks to the Haber process.

That process was the beginning of an anti-entropic process of production, entropic in the sense of material entropy. We need a word for this, and it does not exist. Ordinary economic processes diffuse the concentrated. We start off with concentrations of ores and fuels, and we spread them over the earth into dumps or into oceans. This is entropic in the sense of returning to chaos. The Haber process concentrated the diffuse; it showed that if you put energy into the system, you could reverse the material entropy.

That is an old trick. It is called life, and it was invented a long time ago. However, Haber's process marked the first time that any living organism had invented a new formula for it. Without Haber we would certainly be in much worse shape than we are today. We would have had mass famine in this century, without question. Barry Commoner, Professor of Plant Physiology at Washington University, says that in the Middle West, for instance, we are now dumping into the cycle about twice the amount of nitrogen we used in the days before artificial fertilizers were developed. This means that nearly all the rivers in Illinois are now eutrophic, and where will it all lead?

Can we overload the nitrogen cycle without creating extremely alarming ecological consequences? That is something we shall have to answer. My IBM spies tell me that a fundamental doctrine applied to computers is called the Gigo Principle, standing for "garbage in, garbage out." It is a basic law that what you put in you have to take out. This is throughput. Otherwise, we have to recycle everything, and we have not begun to consider the problems of a high-level, recycled economy. I am pretty sure there is no nonexistence theorem about it. I am certain that a recycling technology is possible which, of course, must have an input of energy. Nobody is going to repeal the second law of thermodynamics, not even the Democrats. This means that if we are to avoid the increase of material entropy, we must have an input of energy into the system. The present system has an enormous input of energy in fossil fuels which cannot last very long unless we go to nuclear fusion. In that case there is an awful lot of water around, and it would last a long time.

Fission is not any good; it is just messy. I understand that if we began using uranium to produce all our power requirements in this country, we would run out of it in ten years. So actually nuclear energy is not a great source of energy; this planet's coal probably has more. Nuclear energy is not a great new field opened up. I suspect it could turn out to be rather dangerous nonsense.

What does this leave us with? The good old sun. At the most pessimistic, you might say we have to devise a basic economy which relies on the input of solar energy for all its energy requirements. As we know, there is a lot of solar energy.

On the other hand, what we do not know is how many people this spaceship earth will support at a high level. We do not know this even to order of magnitude. I suggest that this is one of the major research projects for the next generation, because the whole future of man depends on it. If the optimum population figure is 100 million, we are in for a rough time. It could be as low as that if we are to have a really high-level economy in which everything is recycled. Or it could be up to 10 billion. If it is up to 10 billion, we are okay, Jack—at least for the time being. A figure somewhere between 100 million and 10 billion is a pretty large area of ignorance. I have a very uneasy feeling that it may be towards the lower level, but we do not really know that.

We do not really know the limiting factor. I think we can demonstrate, for instance, that in all probability the presently underdeveloped countries are not going to develop. There is not enough of anything. There is not enough copper. There is not enough of an enormous number of elements which are essential to the developed economy. If the whole world developed to American standards overnight, we would run out of everything in less than 100 years.

Economic development is the process by which the evil day is brought closer when everything will be gone. It will result in final catastrophe unless we treat this interval in the history of man as an opportunity to make the transition to the spaceship earth.

Now that I have been rude to the Gross National Product, let me show how it *can* be used and the things it suggests. In an interesting little empirical trick (it is not much more than that) I have plotted the *GNP per capita,* which is a very rough measure of how rich a country is already, against the logarithm of the *rate of growth* of GNP per capita for all the countries where information was available. Despite the measure's defects, I think that the data are meaningful.

The GNP per capita varies from about $50 for Haiti to more than $3000 for the United States; when the range is that much it must mean something—even if you do not know what. The yearly rate of growth per capita ranges from about 10 percent in Japan to minus 2 percent for Uruguay in the first half of the 1960s.

The countries of the world then divide clearly into two groups. One, which I call the A countries, includes Japan, the USSR, Yugoslavia, Hungary, Belgium, Italy, Denmark, and, indeed, most of the countries of the temperate zone; they lie along a downward-sloping straight line, with Japan at the top and the United States at the bottom. In this group the richer you are, the slower you grow. This is a fundamental law of growth and, so far as I know, all natural growth systems obey such a rule. Certainly, exponential growth of anything never goes on for very long. If it ever did, it would be the only thing in the universe. Obviously, there is a nonexistence theorem about exponential growth. The A countries exhibit logistic growth, or at least the appearance of it.

The other group, the B countries, are all in the tropics with some exceptions, mainly in Latin America. They occupy a circular area in the bottom left-hand corner of the figure. They do not seem to be going anywhere, but they have sort of a Brownian movement. Their rates of growth are far below countries of equal poverty in the A group. This suggests that the developmental process has a "main line." If you are on this line, you will go on getting richer; but as you get richer, you get rich more slowly— which is not surprising. If this goes on for a century, all the A countries will begin to slide down the line to the bottom, and will be equally rich and equally slow. In the meantime, unless some of the B countries get on the main line they are not going anywhere.

This is the most significant example I have found to illustrate the use of the GNP as a measure of some kind of process. Consequently, I am not prepared to ditch the GNP altogether. It is a measure of some process in the United States that took us from about $100 per capita at the time of the Revolution to $3000 today. It is a real process, and the difference between Haiti and the United States is very real. We are rich and they are poor; no question about it. This is mainly a result of the development process, not of exploitation. The one thing it suggests is that exploitation is a minor element in explaining the differences of wealth in the world. If some countries are rich and some are poor, it is because the rich countries are on the main line of development, or have been on it longer, and the poor countries are not. The reason for the United States' wealth today is that we have had fairly consistent economic growth for well over 150 years.

The American Revolution cost a generation of growth, as all revolutions do, whether they are one-generation revolutions like ours or two-generation revolutions like that of the Soviet Union. Revolutions always set nations back, although they may start off the process of growth. We recovered from the Boston Tea Party by about 1815, and then we took off. From that point on, we approximately doubled the per capita income every generation. If you do that, you go 100, 200, 400, 800, 1600, 3200. It takes six generations that way. On the whole, this has been the rate of development before World War II.

Now the Japanese GNP is growing at 8 to 10 percent per capita per annum, which is absurd. This means that in Japan the children are six times as rich as their parents, which I think is greedy. I am quite happy with a 4 percent rise, which makes the children twice as rich as the parents, as in the United States. In the same 150 years India (or Haiti even worse) has gone 100, 100, 100, 100, 100. Or perhaps 100, 110, 120, 90, or something like that. It is the difference in the rate of development which explains the difference in per capita GNP.

On the other hand, this kind of process does not at all answer the question that I raised in the first half of this discussion. When we get to $10,000 per capita, what does it really mean? Does it simply mean that we are exhausting the resources of the earth at a much more rapid rate? Of course, we have a process here of increased efficiency in exploitation of the earth, not exploitation of man. We go on, we become terribly rich, and suddenly it is all gone. We may have a process of this sort.

What may happen is that we are going to have to face something of this sort in the next 500 years. Unquestionably, we will have to aim for much lower levels of growth, because the cyclical process costs more than the throughput does. However, if we devote our knowledge industries to solution of the problem of the cyclical economy, maybe it will turn out all right.

The idea that we are moving into a world of absolutely secure and effortless abundance is nonsense. This is an illusion of the young who are supported by their parents. Once they have children of their own, they realize that abundance is an illusion. It is a plausible illusion, because we have had an extraordinary two centuries. We have had an extraordinary period of economic growth and of the discovery of new resources.

But this is not a process that can go on forever, and we do not know how abundant this spaceship is going to be. Nobody here now is going to live to see the spaceship, because it is certainly 100 years—perhaps 500 years—off. I am sure it will be no longer than 500 years off, and that is not a tremendously long period of historic time.

An extraordinary conference was held last December [1968] on the Ecological Consequences of International Development. It was an antidevelopment gathering of ecologists, who presented 60 developmental horror stories, among them predictions that the Aswan Dam is going to ruin Egypt, the Kariba Dam will ruin central Africa, DDT will ruin us all, insecticides will ruin the cotton crops, thallium will ruin Israel, and so on all down the line. Some of these forecasts I take with a little grain of ecological salt. The cumulative effect, however, is significant, and suggests that no engineer should be allowed into the world without an ecologist in attendance as a priest. The most dangerous thing in the world is the completely untrammeled engineer. A friend of mine was at the Aswan Dam talking to the Russian engineer in charge. He asked him about all the awful ecological consequences: snails, erosion, evaporation, and such. The engineer replied, "Well, that is not my business. My job is just to build the dam."

We are all like that, really. I have recently discovered the real name of the devil, which is something terribly important to know. The real name of the devil is *suboptimization,* finding out the best way to do something which should not be done at all. The engineers, the military, the governments, and the corporations are all quite busy at this. Even professors try to find the best way of giving a Ph.D. degree, which to my mind should not be done at all. We are all suboptimizers.

The problem of how to prevent suboptimization is, I think, the great problem of social organization. The only people who have thought about it are the economists, and they have the wrong answer, which was perfect competition. Nobody else has any answer at all. Obviously, the deep, crucial problem of social organization is how to prevent people from doing their best when the best in the particular, in the small, is not the best in the large.

The answer to this problem lies mainly in the ecological point of view, which is perhaps the most fundamental thing we can teach anybody. I am quite sure that it has to become the basis of our educational system.

I have added a verse to a long poem I wrote at that ecological conference. There are some who may still shrug off its somber tone, but the wise man—and nation—will take heed.

With development extended to the whole of planet earth
What started with abundance may conclude in dismal
    dearth.
And it really will not matter then who started it or ran it
If development results in an entirely plundered planet.

WAR INDUSTRY AND
THE AMERICAN ECONOMY

De Kalb, Illinois: Department of Economics,
Northern Illinois University, 1970.

The War Industry and the American Economy

I define the war industry as that part of the economy which produces the product which is purchased by the military budget. Some people dislike this name, but I think it is accurate. The world war industry is the sum of all the war industries of the world. Last year it was about 182 billion dollars, which is quite a lot. This is roughly equal to the total income of the poorest half of the human race. So, as you can see, it represents a considerable burden on the planet.

Today, however, I want to talk about the war industry in the United States and its impact on the American economy, especially in the last forty years. It has, as you all realize, been the most highly fluctuating element in the total economy. It has fluctuated from about 0.6 per cent of the economy under Herbert Hoover, to 42 per cent in the Second World War, to about 9 per cent today. Fluctuations of this magnitude naturally have had a considerable impact.

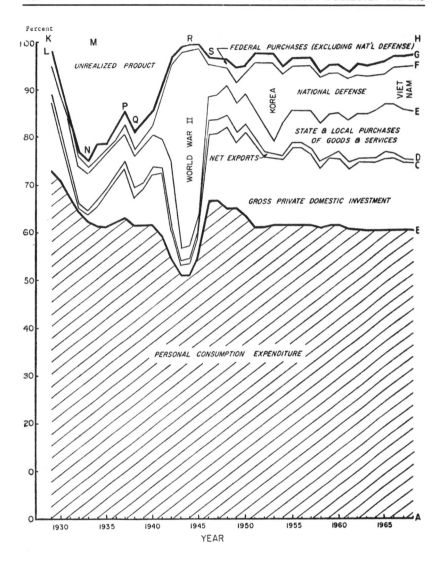

Figure 1.
Unrealized Product and Major Components of GNP
as a Per Cent of Gross Capacity Product

Figure 1 shows the proportional structure of the American economy for the last thirty-nine years. We measure the total size of the American economy, not by the Gross National Product, but by a concept which I call the Gross Capacity Product (GCP), which is the Gross National Product adjusted for unemployment. Thus, for the year 1968, AH, representing 100 per cent, is the Gross Capacity Product. GH is Unrealized Product, that is, the measure of the per cent of the Gross Capacity Product which is lost because of unemployment. We calculate this simply by increasing the Gross National Product by the proportion of the labor force unemployed, so that GF is actually the percentage of the labor force unemployed. This is not completely satisfactory or an accurate measure of the Gross Capacity Product, but it has the virtue of identifying Unrealized Product with the proportion of unemployment. AG is then the proportion of Gross Capacity Product as represented by the Gross National Product. Components of this are then AB, which is the proportion of the Gross Capacity Product accounted for by Personal Consumption Expenditure (a little over 60 per cent), BC, the proportion of Gross Private Domestic Investment, CD, the proportion of Net Exports, DE, the proportion of State and Local Government Purchases, EF, the proportion devoted to National Defense, and FG, the proportion devoted to Federal Purchases for Civilian Uses.

The story told by this diagram is dramatic. We see first of all the Great Depression in the huge bulge of the Unrealized Product between 1929 and 1942. The fantastic slide from L to N, with unemployment rising from 3.2 per cent in 1929 to 24.9 per cent in 1933 (MN), illustrates the almost unbelievable severity of the Great Depression. The slide from L to N symbolizes an amount of human suffering and defeat which is hard for this generation to appreciate.

The diagram shows dramatically the relative failure of the New Deal, from N to P, and the second traumatic depression of 1938, from P to Q. The New Deal produced important long-run spillovers in the shape of labor legislation and Social Security, but in dealing with the major problem of the day it was a dismal and dramatic failure. The reason for the depression and the failure of the recovery is also suggested by this diagram. It was the disappearance of Gross Private Domestic Investment, which fell from 15.3 per cent of the Gross Capacity Product in 1929 to 1.3 per cent in 1932, without there being any offsets either in consumption or in government, which was the prime force leading to the rise in unemployment and un-used capacity. If, for instance, we had kept up Personal Consumption Expenditure, which also fell sharply because of unemployment, by means of remission or even abolition of taxation and if we had increased the government sector, the decline in Gross Private Domestic Investment would also probably have been less severe and the De-pression would have been avoided. The war industry, we should note, in these years was negligible—a mere 0.7 per cent of the Gross Capacity Product in 1929.

Looking now at the years from 1940-1945, we see how Hitler got us out of the Great Depression. The figure shows clearly the source of what I have called the "great American myth," that only a large war industry can save us from depression and unemployment. Like a great many myths, it rises out of the misinterpretation of some pro-foundly true experience. From Q to R we see the virtual disappearance of unemployment and the expansion of the war industry to a maximum of 41.9 per cent of the Gross Capacity Product in 1943. We should notice, incidentally, that only about half of the Second World War was financed out of unemployment; the other half had to come out of all the other sectors of the economy. As we see, Personal Consumption Expenditure was squeezed the least; indeed, because of the rate in the GCP it fell very little in absolute amount. Gross Private Domestic Invest-ment and Civilian Government were squeezed very se-verely.

From 1944 to 1946, from R to S in the figure, we see the Great Disarmament. National Defense falls from 41.3 per cent of the economy in 1944, to 34.3 per cent in 1945, and 6.8 per cent in 1946. In a little over a year, we transferred about a third of the economy from Na-tional Defense into civilian industry, without unemploy-ment rising even to 4 per cent. It is odd that the Great Disarmament did not become another "great American myth." For some reason or other, it has simply escaped out of the national consciousness, yet is one of the most remarkable achievements of economic adjustment in human history and very much needs to be studied. One myth about it is that we achieved it by hungry consumers buying domestic appliances. The figure at least dispels this myth. It is true that Personal Consumption Expenditure rose fairly sharply from 51.2 per cent in 1944 to 66.3 per cent in 1946. Nevertheless, as we see in Table 1, the major burden of the adjustment was borne by the increase in Gross Private Domestic Investment, Exports, and Civilian Government.

Table 1. The Great Disarmament

	Per Cent of Gross Capacity Product		
	1944	1946	Change
Unrealized Product	1.2	3.9	+2.7
Federal Government, National Defense	41.3	6.8	−34.5
Federal Government, Civilian	0.8	1.2	+0.4
State and Local Government	3.5	4.5	+1.0
Net Exports	−0.9	3.5	+4.4
Gross Private Domestic Investment	3.4	14.1	+10.7
Personal Consumption Expenditure	51.3	66.3	+15.0

After 1950, we see the expansion of National Defense, first due to the Korean War, which brought National Defense to 13 per cent of the Capacity Product by 1953. The Post-Korean disarmament was rather poorly handled and unemployment rose to 5.5 per cent in 1954. However, from 1954 to 1955 we have the interesting phenomenon of a fairly noticeable decline in National Defense, from 10.7 per cent to 9.3 per cent of the GCP, going hand in hand with the decline in unemployment from 5.5 per cent to 4.4 per cent, the main reason being the more than countervailing expansion of Gross Private Domestic Investment and State and Local Government. We have a similar phenomenon in what might be called the "Mc-Namara Disarmament," from 1963 to '65, when National Defense fell from 8.2 per cent of the GCP to 7.0 per cent and unemployment likewise fell from 5.7 per cent to 4.5 per cent. It is clear that it is quite easy for other segments of the economy to compensate for a fall in National Defense if conditions are right. We may note finally the Vietnam expansion from 1965 to '68 which is surprisingly small in relative terms—from 7.0 per cent to 8.9 per cent of the Gross Capacity Product. We see that proportionally Vietnam is a much smaller war than Korea, yet because of the absence of legitimacy it has created an enormous qualitative upheaval. This should warn us that quantity is not everything and that the quantities which are revealed in Figure 1 have to be interpreted with care.

A very interesting phenomenon which emerges from Figure 1 is the proportional stability of the American economy in the last eighteen years. We notice the three small depressions—1954, 1958, and 1961—which mainly originate in Gross Private Domestic Investment and within that quite largely in inventory changes. Apart from that there is a slight tendency for State and Local Government to expand at the expense of National Defense. The proportional stability is quite astonishing, especially the remarkable stability of Personal Consumption Expenditure as a proportion of the Capacity Product. This possibly reflects the cybernetic effects of the deductible-at-source currently collectible progressive income tax. A very interesting phenomenon is the impact of the federal tax cut of 1964, which is not perceptible in household consumption at all, but which is immediately apparent in a rise in State and Local Government. I get the feeling that State and Local Government stands like a great big crocodile just waiting to gobble up every dollar which the federal government releases. We don't even have to have revenue sharing! All we have to do is give up federal taxes and snap, off it goes into state and local taxes. I think there is a case for revenue sharing for distributional reasons, but I think it clearly is not necessary from the point of view of producing any expansion out of state and local government. When we reflect that within this period the Gross National Product, in current dollars, rose from 345.5 billion in 1952 to 862.7 billion in 1968, and even in real terms about doubled, the proportional stability is all the more remarkable.

Figure 2 now points up another aspect of the problem and perhaps dispels another myth, that the war industry produces large profits. Here we show the division of the National Income, which is now taken as 100 per cent, as between its various components—Net Interest, Corporate Profits (which includes an inventory valuation adjustment), Rental Income of Persons (which is a rather miscellaneous and not very significant category), Income of Farm Pro-

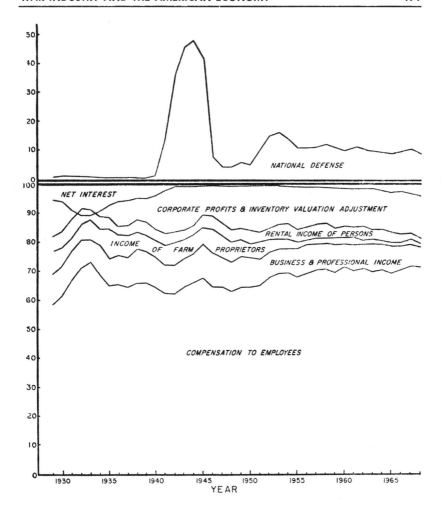

Figure 2.
Components of National Income and National Defense
as a Per Cent of National Income

prietors, Business and Professional Income, and Compensation of Employees. On top of this diagram we have put
National Defense as a proportion of National Income by
way of showing any possible effects. Several items of
interest may be noted. One of the most striking is the
extinction of Corporate Profits in the Great Depression;
in 1932 and 1933 they were negative. This is the combined result of sharp deflation and decline in investment.
The rise in Net Interest in the Depression is a result of the
deflation, for nominal interest payments in dollar terms
stayed up and the price level went down, so that in real
terms interest rose substantially as a proportion of National Income. The relative stability of the distributional
shares is remarkable, apart from the disturbance in the
Great Depression, and we see clearly that the war industry makes very itttle difference. During the Second
World War, indeed, Corporate Profits actually declined as
a share of National Income and Wages rose. The same
phenomenon is noticeable on a smaller scale during the
Korean War. It is not perhaps wholly surprising that labor
unions in this period have been more militaristic than the
business community, though even here the economic effects are quite slight. What this diagram suggests, of
course, is that the distribution of the total income accruing
to the national defense industry, as distributed among
wages, profits, etc., is approximately the same proportion
as income in other industries. There is certainly no evidence that profits in the war industry are in any way
excessive. The decline in the Income of Farm Proprietors,
incidentally, is a result of the remarkable technological
advance in agriculture in this period, with the result of a
sharp decline in the proportion of both the labor force
and the national product derived from agriculture. The
Income of Farm Proprietors is somewhat an anomaly in
the framework of these accounts, and ideally it should
be distributed between, say, labor income and non-labor
income, but unfortunately the accounts do not permit this
breakdown.

It is clear that the facts of the American economy, at
least as recorded in National Income Statistics, give very
little support to two of the great American myths, one of
which is that only a large war industry can give us full
employment, and the other of which is that a large war
industry is good for business, that is, produces high profits.
The first myth, as we have seen, has some basis in history,

but even it is a good example of the fallacies of learning
from experience. There is widespread agreement in the
economics profession today that the American economy
can maintain reasonably full employment at virtually any
level of the war industry. The psychological impact of
the Great Depression, however, still lingers, though it is
declining rapidly now as the generation which was severely traumatized by the thirties begins to die off. The
last twenty years indeed almost deserve the title "The
Great Stability." It is the period in which this whole
generation of students has grown up. The level of unemployment in these years has been higher than I personally care to see, but the whole period could be described as having at least moderately full employment.

We now observe a curious paradox; that full employment
reintroduces scarcity into the economy. As long as we
have unemployment, we can have our cake and eat it
too. We could expand the war industry, for instance, as
in World War II, without very much restriction of consumption. If now we have full employment, then a dollar
on the war industry is a dollar off something else. And
the question is off what? Whose ox is being gored by the
war industry? Over the long-run, the answer is household
consumption. The war industry has gone from practically
nothing to 9 per cent, household consumption has gone
from 72 per cent to 61 per cent of the GCP in the last
thirty-nine years. Remember that in this interval the Gross
National Product was trebled, so that the absolute figure
corresponding to a given percentage is rising all the time.
Proportionally, however, what we have had has been
creeping socialism in the Department of Defense and not
much anywhere else. The private sector, which is the
household consumption and investment, has been mainly
eroded by the rise in defense. Creeping socialism has not
really crept very far, but it has crept far enough so that
the United States Department of Defense is now the
second largest socialist organization—which I am tempted
to call USDOD—or centrally planned economy, in the
world. Its Gross National Product is a little above that
of the People's Republic of China—about 80 billion by
comparison to 70 billion, or whatever it is now. Nobody
knows what the GNP of the People's Republic of China
is now, because they abolished statistics ten years ago, so
it is hard to tell what has happened. Ten years ago it was
under 70 billion dollars, and I would be very much sur-

prised if it is much over 70 today. When, as in China, you turn the country over to people under thirty, it is rather bad for economic development, for it is the people over thirty who do most of the work.

The Soviet Union is much larger than USDOD, something like 250 billion, but the United States Department of Defense is the second largest socially planned economy at any rate, and it stands in the middle of the American economy as an anomaly. If you want to be rude about it, you can think of it as a kind of socialist tumor in the American market economy. It has been contained pretty well in the last twenty years, but this still represents a pretty sizeable proportion of it.

With household consumption and investment as stable as it is, the main victim of the war industry is the civilian public sector, and within the civilian public sector the main victim may well be education, though the long-run growth of education masks the effect. So it is not altogether surprising that the main opposition to the military is rising in the universities. Our ox is being gored! So it is not surprising that people increasingly perceive that a dollar on military is a dollar off something—mainly them! I suspect that this explains a good deal of what has been happening this year. The rising feeling and pressure against the military is precisely because of the fact that the Great Depression is psychologically over. Today, a majority of people in this country do not remember it at all. If you are younger than forty, you don't remember the Great Depression. If you are younger than fifty, you don't remember very much about it. An awful lot of people in this country are under forty so it is not surprising that we are, as it were, at the psychological end of the Great Depression. The labor movement has not reached this point because labor leaders are mainly over seventy, and are still living in the thirties. They have not had many ideas for thirty years! So it is not surprising that the labor movement is still very hawkish. Their leaders remember the great difficulty of getting us out of the Great Depression.

The younger members of our society, however, are not traumatized by the Great Depression at all. They live in a society of scarcity. Thus, things like the Proxmire Committee, the Committee on New Priorities, and this whole movement in Congress to question the enormously high

priority we put on the war industry, are in part a reflection
of the psychological end of the Great Depression. We
now realize that the decline of the war industry means
goodies! Goodies for lots of us, and we want them. This
is not just an American phenomenon. It can be seen also,
for instance, in the abandonment of great power status
by the British. Even though the British got away with
being a great power very cheaply, I don't think they put
much more than 3 or 4 per cent of their Gross National
Product into the war industry all through the nineteenth
century, but once it began to get expensive they quit
because it was not worth it. The plain fact is that from
any kind of economic point of view investment in the war
industry beyond a rather low level has a highly negative
rate of return. This has been true for quite a long time.
War and imperialism may have been profitable in the
eighteenth century when the British got something out of
India, but in the nineteenth century certainly nobody got
much out of empire. I have a graduate student who is
doing a thesis on the exploitation of India by Britain in
the nineteenth century. He discovered that the British
managed to extract half of one per cent of the Indian
Gross National Product out of India, but he cannot find
it in England! It gets lost in the Indian Ocean.

If we look at the relative rates of development of
European countries, who made the highest rate of development from 1860 on? Sweden. Actually the British
and the French empires were very substantial economic
burdens on them. Who has the biggest empire to date?
Portugal, which has the lowest per capita income in
Europe. Economically, empire is clearly for the birds. Certainly if you want to get rich, the way to get rich is to
stay home and mind your own business, like the Swedes.
There is another recipe, which is to stay home and mind
everybody else's business, like the Swiss, but actually the
Swedes did even better than the Swiss. The road to riches
is staying home, taking it cool, being pretty quiet, working hard, and saving a lot.

I have promoted a study of the impact of the war
industry on the Japanese economy, the results of which
are striking.[1] The Japanese empire did not pay off for the

---

[1] Kenneth E. Boulding (with Alan Gleason). "War as an Investment:
The Strange Case of Japan." Peace Research Society (Int'l), Papers, Vol.
III, 1965, Walter Isard and J. Wolpert, eds., Philadelphia, 1965, pp. 1-17.

Japanese. They had quite a lag in development after the Russo-Japanese War, for instance, of 1904. The Japanese did not put very much more than 4 per cent of their GNP into the war industry until about 1936 and 1937, when they were conquered by their own military. After that the war industry in Japan grows astronomically. Even in the middle of the Second World War, the Japanese war industry probably did more economic damage to Japan than the American war industry did! They absorbed about 45 per cent of the GNP, and they got consumption down to 30 per cent, which is absolutely a world's record.

If you really want to know who screws you it is your own military. These are the people who really do you economic damage. I am just talking now as an economist, not as a political scientist. You have to look at the World War Industry as a kind of exercise in mutually induced masochism, that is, how do we all persuade each other to damage ourselves? Who damages the United States? It is the USDOD—the United States Department of Defense—which damages the United States. Nine per cent of the economy is quite a lot. And if you look at it qualitatively, it is much worse than this because there is a very substantial brain drain into the war industry. The 9 per cent here is only the 9 per cent of the GNP, but this represents a much larger percentage of what we might call the "growth resource." The "growth resource" is what we put into growth, and this is largely an intellectual resource. There is a very serious brain drain into the war industry. It is hard to get any estimates of this. One estimate, which perhaps is over done, is about 60 per cent. It could easily be 50 per cent. As a result our civilian industries are all starved of good engineers and good scientists. All you have to do to realize this is go for a ride on a railroad lately. This feels like the decline and fall of the American empire. I am not saying that we should necessarily support the railroads at any cost, but it is clear that the railroads have not made the best of a bad job. Why is this? Anybody who is capable of modernizing a railorad is in the RAND Corporation or in Martin Aircraft, or something of this sort. A large field of American industry—machine tools, shipbuilding, textiles, even a great deal of light manufacturing—is technologically a bit of a scandal. We really have not been putting the intellectual and research resources to work. Perhaps the biggest technological scandal of all is the building industry, which has not developed very much since the time of the Pharoahs—one brick, another brick, another brick, another brick. The building industry is almost as backward as the educational industry, which, of course, is the most backward of industries. Apart from the overhead projector, what I am doing today is exactly what Plato and Aristotle did twenty-nine hundred years ago—getting up and yak, yak, yak.

I am not suggesting that if we divert some of our growth resource into these backward industries that they would necessarily exhibit the spectacular success that we have had in agriculture and in the technology of defense and space. Nevertheless, it is suggestive that the greatest technological development has come in precisely those industries into which we have put a large amount of what might be called the public growth resource. In agriculture, for instance, we have had almost a 6 per cent per annum increase in labor productivity since 1933. This has released a substantial labor force to go into other industries, even if it has polluted all the rivers of the middle West! It may be, of course, that those industries into which we have put our growth resource are precisely those in which the potentialities for growth were greatest. Nevertheless, while a maldistribution of growth resources can never be proved, a strong case can be made that we are now suffering from a severe maldistribution in the growth resource, with disproportionate technological advance in some sectors of the economy and stagnation in others.

This question is likely to be more important in the future than it is today, simply because the decline in agriculture now to something between 6 and 7 per cent of the labor force means that there are no sections of the economy outside of the war industry which have a substantial reserve of labor which could be transferred to other uses. If, therefore, we are to expand other segments of the economy the war industry is the most natural place to look for the resources which other sectors will need if they are to expand. What this means is that the real alternative cost of resources employed in the war industry is likely to increase all the time. The economic gains from disarmament would correspondingly increase.

It is clear that there are no good economic reasons for

having a war industry at all. We must, therefore, get into political science and the theory of international systems if we are to give some explanation as to what determines the size of the war industries of the various countries. My thesis here is that the war industry is primarily a subset of the international system rather than of the economic system and that we must understand the realities of the international system, therefore, if we are to understand what determines the size of the war industry. The international system, however, is not easy to understand. It has strong random elements in it. What we think of as its "realities" very largely consists of perceptions and misperceptions, and even the misperceptions create the realities.

On the whole, the war industry is a cancer in the economy because it does not really belong to the economic sector. It is a result of political and, of course, especially of Congressional decisions. It is a result of Congressional appropriations, and Congressional appropriations are the result of the Congressional image of the international system. We had a very small war industry in the thirties because we did not feel threatened by anybody. These were in the days when the Atlantic and Pacific Oceans still existed as barriers and we felt secure behind them. To some extent, the rise of the war industry is a result of the shrinkage of the planet and the result of technical developments in weaponry which have enormously diminished our security. We were much more secure in the thirties with a 0.7 per cent war industry than we are today with 9 per cent. If we went to 20 per cent we would be still less secure. The war industry produces a negative commodity essentially. The more we spend on it the less security we get. It is part of a self-reinforcing system. It is quite easy to write an interesting system of equations in which we postulate that the size of each country's war industry is the function of the size of every other country's war industry. The reason why we have a war industry this size is that the Russians do, and the reason why the Russians do is that we do. The war industries of the world are what might be called ecologically cooperative. The war industries of the different countries cooperate with each other against the civilians, in order to produce a large absorption of resources into them. How much then depends on the dynamics of the situation. Part of the difficulties in the international system is that the dynamics of the system, largely because of its misperceptions, more easily goes toward a larger war industry than a smaller.

It is easier to have an arms race than a disarmament race, although we have had disarmament races. Disarmament races are not out of the question; they exist as a social phenomenon. They have existed in history. I have always said that Boulding's first law is that anything that exists is possible. It is surprising how many people do not believe this. Disarmament races have existed. We had one with the British beginning about 1817 which was very successful and which resulted in the disarmament of the Canadian frontier. Under given circumstances you can have this and it is extremely important to know under what circumstances this can happen. Disarmament races are less probable than armament races, but they can happen and, of course, we could have a policy to promote them. That is, we could direct national policy deliberately to creating the conditions which would lead into a disarmament race. We may actually be very haphazardly feeling our way towards this. It is significant that we have formally commited ourselves to a long-range national policy of general and complete disarmament. This may be hypocrisy, but never underestimate the power of hypocrisy. Hypocrisy is one of the principal origins of social change. Without hypocrisy, we probably would not have any social change at all. If we were not hypocritical about the race problem in this country, we would not have any movement in this direction of integration. Hypocrisy is a very important social phenomenon and in fact ought to be encouraged, at least up to a point, because it does lead into social change. Even hypocrisy about disarmament is worthwhile, because it means that there is a constant pressure towards the development of realistic systems of disarmament, which is something that is desperately necessary, not only for economic welfare but for human survival.

In the case of the United States, in a sense we can say that we can afford the kind of "9 per cent" war industry we have, in that it does not put an intolerable strain on the economy. Nevertheless, it may diminish our rate of growth perhaps by 1 per cent. This is anybody's guess, but if true, over one hundred years would cost us several trillion dollars. It also introduces an element of extreme danger into the international system. Here we have a very widespread illusion that deterrence can be stable. We have an international system, on the whole, which is based on deterrence rather than on conquest. Conquest is out of date really because there are no more worlds to conquer except the moon and that is a worse desert than Nevada. The critical question is how we transform the international system into one that is livable. One can demonstrate that deterrence cannot be stable in one sentence; if deterrence were stable, it would fail to deter. If the probability of the nuclear weapons going off were zero that would be the same thing as not having them. If you have them, then the probability of their going off must be a positive number, otherwise they would not deter anybody. Now if this probability is a positive number, then if you wait long enough they will eventually go off. If the probability is only 1 per cent per annum, which is only my wild guess, if you accumulate that for one hundred years it looks pretty frightening. If you accumulate for hundred years it is very, very frightening indeed. This is still strictly in historic time. The probability may have been as much as 20 per cent per annum at the time of the Cuban crisis. We got in the 80 per cent, so we were all right; we were lucky.

A nuclear war would produce irreversible ecological changes in the world enormously adverse to man, just to put it mildly. It might not be an irretrievable disaster, but it might be very close to it. Consequently, I resent the war industry very much, and I make no bones about this. As far as the war industry is concerned, 8 per cent is better than 9, 7 per cent is better than 8, 6 per cent is better than 7, 5 per cent is better than 6. I look back on Herbert Hoover with considerable nostalgia, and I am quite sure that 9 per cent is far too large and too dangerous. It has a technological dynamic of its own which is enormously unfriendly to man, enormously unfriendly to the survival and to the welfare of man. Let me give one horrible statistic. We have been spending 350 million dollars a year in this country on preparing chemical and bacteriological warfare. This is approximately equal to the total budget of all the United Nations' agencies put together, all twenty of them. There is a very fundamental principle in social systems which I call the Nino Principle. It stands for nothing in, nothing out. The plain truth is that we put practically nothing into peace, but we put an enormous amount into war, so it is not surprising that we do not have very much peace.

The really surprising thing is that the international system works as well as it does. The surprising thing is that we have not had disaster long ago. The change of disaster is there. I sometimes put it in this way. Every day the hand of fate reaches down into a bag in which there is one red ball among the white. Maybe there is an awful lot of white balls. Day by day there is probably a million white balls and only one red ball, the red ball being nuclear war. But the red ball is still in the bag. As long as it is still in the bag I am not going to rest easy. One of the great tasks of the next generation is to get that red ball out. What this means is a transformation of the international system in the direction of stable peace and general and complete disarmament. This is not a pipe dream. Here again, stable peace is possible because it already exists in certain parts of the international system. It has only developed in the last one hundred and fifty years. Before that nobody had anything like stable peace. We now have unstable peace over most of the international system. But we do have islands of stable peace, as in North America. This was largely an accident. It could have easily gone the other way if it had not been for the Rush-Bagot Agreement, which is the first successful disarmament agreement almost in world history. It was an agreement to disarm the Great Lakes, and it eventually led to the disarmament of the whole frontier of Canada. We have stable peace in Scandinavia, really surprisingly stable. With a little bit of luck, we may get it all through the Temperate Zone. We have got to work for this, and we have got to plan for this. We are not doing this at the moment. We are not putting resources into it. This is, frankly, why I am in the peace research business. Peace research is the attempt to mobilize the resources of the social sciences to work on increasing the probability of stable peace. This is a reasonable and sensible intellectual exercise, but it is astonishingly difficult to mobilize resources for it. I do not suppose there are more than two or three hundred people around the world who are really working on it. I put this up to you students as a challenge, as the most important life work you can have today if you want your children to have a life. Thank you.

FACTORS AFFECTING THE FUTURE DEMAND FOR EDUCATION

Economic Factors Affecting the Financing of Education, R. Johns, et al., eds., National Education Finance Project (1970), pp. 1-29.

Factors Affecting The Future Demand For Education

Economic factors are those which concern the way in which society is organized by exchange and by the transfer of "exchangeables" or commodities. There are a number of commodities, however, which may be called "peculiar" because they are produced, bought, sold, and consumed in a very complex sociological matrix. Labor is one such peculiar commodity and a good deal of rhetoric has been devoted by the labor movement to demonstrate that labor is not a commodity. Nevertheless it is bought and sold and it has a price. Thus it has all the properties of a commodity. But it has other properties besides, which make it peculiar.

Education similarly is a peculiar commodity. It is bought and sold and has something like a price. There is a segment of the economy which can be thought of as the educational industry. In the United States, for instance, Machlup estimated that as of about 1958 the total knowledge industry occupied almost thirty percent of the economy.[1] What we think of as the educational industry, that is schools, colleges, universities, and organizations for formal education, public and private, occupies approximately 7 percent of the gross national product and this proportion is rising very steadily. Formal education is now an "industry" which occupies a larger proportion of total economic activity in the United States than agriculture.

CONCEPTS OF SUPPLY AND DEMAND APPLIED TO EDUCATION

If education is a commodity and schools are an industry, it should be useful for us to ask ourselves how far the economist's concepts of demand and supply can be applied to it, and how far changes in both the price and quantity of education can be interpreted in terms of movements of demand and supply.

Relationship of Price and Quantity to Demand

What the economist means by demand is a functional relationship between the price of a commodity and the quantity which will be purchased. Similarly, supply is a functional relationship between the price and the quantity which will be offered for sale. This is illustrated in Figure 1-1. Here we plot the quantity of education horizontally and the price of education vertically. We postulate a supply curve S'S. This has been drawn with a positive slope indicating that in order to have an increase in quantity of education, we have to pay a higher price for it. The demand curve D'D is drawn with a negative slope indicating that the lower the price of education the more of it will be purchased. If education were left entirely to the market there would be an equilibrium at E, with a quantity of education OF both supplied and demanded at a price FE. We do not have to assume of course that the functions are linear; they are merely drawn as straight lines in the diagram for convenience.

Relationship of Subsidies to Quantity of Education

Suppose now that the society decides that the quantity of education which would be forthcoming under a completely free market is not sufficient. There may be all sorts of reasons for this decision which we will look at later. Suppose that it is decided that the ideal quantity of education is OF_1; then in order to persuade people to purchase this amount the price would have to be F_1D_1. But in order to persuade people to supply this amount the price to the supplier would have to be F_1S_1. The difference, D_1S_1, is a subsidy per unit of education which would have to be given in order to achieve that expansion of the quantity of education from OF to OF_1. If we wanted to expand the quantity of education to OD the price would have to be zero and the subsidy equal to DS. That is the point at

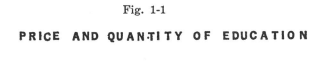

Fig. 1-1

PRICE AND QUANTITY OF EDUCATION

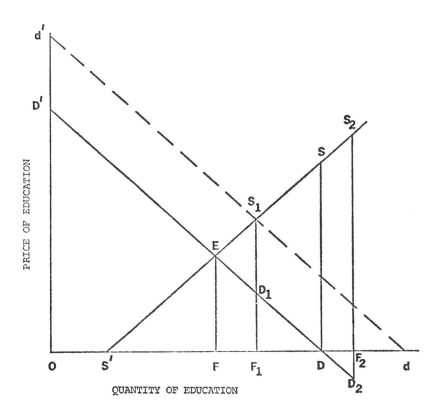

which education becomes completely free to the purchaser. If we wanted still more education than this, say OF_2, we would have to subsidize the purchaser with a negative price of F_2D_2 and subsidize the supplier by an amount equal to F_2S_2 per unit.

Elasticity of Supply and Demand

The discussion above is a textbook analysis. It does, however, point to one important characteristic of the system, that is, the importance of the elasticity of the supply and demand curves. The absolute elasticity is the slope of the curves, or the ratio of the change in quantity to the change in price. If supply or demand is inelastic, this means that a change in price produces only a small change in quantity, and the curves in Figure 1 will be steep. It is clear that the amount of subsidy which is required to achieve any given expansion of quantity depends mainly on the elasticities of supply and demand. If the supply and demand are inelastic so that it takes large changes in price to produce a given change in the quantity, then the subsidies also have to be large. If the supply and demand are elastic the subsidies required will be small. If the functions are linear then the elasticity of subsidy, that is, how much subsidy per unit must be given to produce a unit of expansion of quantity, is equal to the arithmetic sum of the elasticities of demand and supply.

Another useful product of demand and supply analysis is that it separates the concept of demand sharply from the concept of "need." If the demand is a functional relationship between price and quantity purchased it is affected not only by desire and income but also by alternative uses of income. The main reason why demand curves generally have a negative slope is that a high price for one commodity makes the use of income for expenditure on other things look more attractive. The concept of need, on the other hand, is a concept of administrative allocation rather than of market or price allocation. It tends to be thought of in absolute terms without regard to price or alternative opportunities. We could perhaps define need, although this definition might be questioned, as the quantity demanded at a zero price, this representing, as it were, the maximum amount demanded in the absence of consideration of other opportunities and alternatives. This definition however is possibly unacceptable because of the linguistic paradox that we always demand less than we need!

Another useful conclusion of demand and supply analysis is that the effect of an increase in demand depends on the elasticity of supply if the supply function does not change. The effect of an increase in supply similarly depends on elasticity of demand if demand does not change. An increase in demand may mean that the quantity purchased will be larger at each price. That is, it represents a shift to the right in the demand curve. Thus, a rise in the demand for education would be represented by a shift of the demand curve from, say, D'D to d'd, with the equilibrium position moving from E to S_1, with a higher price F_1S_1, and also a higher quantity OF_1. The steeper (more inelastic) the supply curve, the greater will be the rise in the price and the smaller the rise in the quantity for any given change in the demand. As we have been facing a sharp rise in the demand for education in the United States, and indeed in the whole world, the question of the elasticity of supply of education is by no means irrelevant.

Quantity of Education and Price

Supply and demand analysis does give us some qualitative insights into the possible dynamics of any industry or segment of the economy and does enable us to ask some questions which perhaps we may not otherwise have considered. Education however, as a segment of the economy exhibits so many peculiarities that an interpretation of the demand and supply analysis is by no means easy and its results must be interpreted with great care. The first problem is that of the measurement both of the quantity of the education and of its price. These two problems are very closely related, because the price, P, multiplied by the quantity, Q, of any commodity is equal to the total revenue, E, derived from its sale, that is, $E = PQ$. It is fairly easy to get a dollar figure for the total amount E that is spent on education. What is not so easy is to divide this into a price component and a quantity component. Does the rise in the proportion of the economy which is going to education, for instance, represent an increasing quantity of education or merely an increase in its price relative to other things? We can deflate the total dollar revenue of the education industry by some price index to take care of inflation. Even after we have done that, however, the question then arises how much of the real increase is due to price and how much is due to quantity? These are not two questions but one, for if we can define the quantity we will also be able to define the price, which is simply the ratio of the total revenue to the quantity: $P = \dfrac{E}{Q}$.

Any attempt to measure the quantity of education produced forces us back almost embarrassingly on the question of what is the product of the educational industry? Ideally the answer to this question is that education produces a product known as knowledge, which is some kind of restructuring within the human nervous system to produce revised images of the world which are better "maps" of the real world itself. It is odd that we have no word in English to describe "false knowledge," that is a map of reality within the human nervous system which does not correspond to the world outside. Nevertheless it is clearly the business of education to produce true knowledge rather than false knowledge, though we now run into an old philosophical dilemma about how we know that our own or anybody else's knowledge is true. One answer to this question is that we can neither perceive nor measure the truth, or the complexity, of the knowledge structure directly, but that we can detect an *error*, either in our own or in somebody else's knowledge structure. We do this by observing a very specific form of behavior, that is, making predictions by stating an image of the future, and then testing these predictions by observing the future when it becomes the present. Predictions which are falsified produce a "mismatch signal" which, if a rather complicated set of conditions are fulfilled, will correct the knowledge structure, and so move it in the direction of a more accurate map of reality.

The product of education, furthermore, is not merely true knowledge but valuable true knowledge, valuable, that is, to the knower and to the society in which he is embedded. True knowledge about how to find a post office is more valuable to most people than true knowledge about the configuration of the back side of the moon, though to an astronaut who is about to land on the back side of the moon true knowledge about its configuration may be very valuable indeed. In order to measure the quantity of education, therefore, we would have to know not only the amount of true knowledge which has been produced by it in human nervous systems, but we would also have to multiply each item of true knowledge by "shadow price" or evaluation coefficient in order to calculate the aggregate significance of new knowledge.

Part of the difficulty of viewing education as an industry is that to the learner, a very large part of the value of new knowledge, acquired in formal education and in the classroom, arises from its usefulness in passing examinations. Thus the very device which is used to test the value of new knowledge also creates that value. This is a little bit like the problem we face with some commodities, where the evaluation of the commodity itself is a function of its high price. Diamonds are valuable because they are valuable and for no other very good reason. One recalls the old story of the grocer who divides a virtually homogeneous box of tea into three parts, one of which he sells at a low price to the poor, another at a moderate price to the middle class, and another at a high price to the rich, everybody being satisfied that the price he has paid reflects the quality of the tea. One suspects that education is rather similar and that the high reputations and high incomes which are derived from better quality institutions are a function not of the knowledge acquired in these institutions but of the reputation acquired in them.

Here we start out with an innocent question of defining the quantity of education, and we seem to be hovering on a huge morass known as human learning theory. Nevertheless, there is no escape from this. The product of education is the process of learning: that is, the growth of knowledge, and, more than that, the growth of valuable knowledge, the measurement of which presents great difficulties, particularly in the absence of any very good theory of how human beings learn anything at all. It is not surprising, therefore, that the education industry has turned to surrogate measures of the quality of education which, it is hoped, at least bear a moderately linear relationship to the thing we are really trying to measure. An obvious surrogate measure of this kind is time spent in being educated, such as hours of classroom attendance or years of schooling. Knowledge gained, it is hoped, is linearly related to the application of the seat of the pants to the seat of the classroom chair. The defects of this measure are all too easy to state. What many children learn in the classroom is knowledge which, no matter what its truth, has a highly negative value, that is, that they are no good, that they always make mistakes, that they cannot speak good English or do algebra and that they are condemned to the lower class for life. Other children, by contrast, especially those in the more prestigious schools, learn that they are somebody, that they can succeed in almost anything that they really want to apply themselves to, and that if they fail it is because they have chosen to fail rather than because they are failures. Knowledge about personal identity, to which, of course, the whole knowledge industry contributes, is peculiarly significant in formal education. It has a high value either positive or negative for the student and it very rarely gets in any direct way into examination results, accrediting decisions, or even into planned program budgeting systems.

As long as there is any positive correlation, however, between the measure that we are using and the thing that we are trying to measure, I suppose we can say that a bad measure is better than no measure at all. Thus the quantity of education as measured by time spent may be for most students, though not for all, better than nothing. It is the nagging feeling we have that, for some students, classroom hours are negatively correlated with the value of the knowledge acquired that makes us uneasy, but we can hope that these cases are a small minority.

Education and Feedback from Consumer

A further problem of the demand for education, which arises also because of the extreme difficulty of measuring its quantity, is that the demand is made for the most part on behalf of others. All demands are subjective. If I have a demand for tea, it is simply because the consumption of tea gives me some sort of subjective satisfaction, but at least it is my satisfaction. If I buy a tea the flavor of which I do not like, I very soon find this out; there is very rapid feedback in the system and I do not buy that particular kind of tea again. In the case of ordinary commodities, therefore, the market provides a reasonably adequate process for learning about exchange opportunities by the making and testing of predictions, and it provides quite rapid feedback from "purchase error," especially in the case of commodities with a short length of life. The longer the length of life of the commodity, the harder it is to detect purchase error and the less satisfactory the feedback from experience. Though it is easy to learn that one does not buy some particular brand of tea, it is much harder to learn that a particular kind of automobile is a lemon. When purchases are made on behalf of others, the error detecting process of mismatch and feedback is still further eroded. Wedding presents are a notorious case in point where the experience of the recipient is rarely fed back to the giver.

Education is a commodity which suffers from almost every conceivable handicap when it comes to the correction of error and the evaluation of results. Its product has a very long life. All the wrong things we learned in school usually stay with us the rest of our lives. The product of formal education has a life expectancy of some sixty years. Almost the only other commodity with this length of life is housing. It is perhaps no accident that the housing industry, like the educational industry, is notoriously unprogressive, is subject to rather meaningless changes of fashion, and produces an output which seems remarkably difficult to improve. But even houses are frequently bought by the people who live in them, though it is rather rare for them to produce any feedback to the architect about his mistakes. Education, however, is mainly purchased for children and students either by their parents, the church, or the state or some other agency which is acting on their behalf. Under these circumstances the feedback, especially unfavorable evaluations from the student, is regarded as a mark of ingratitude, is discouraged, and very rarely results in much of a learning process on the part of those who pay for the education. Here then is the ultimate paradox that the knowledge industry is precisely the one in which it is hardest to learn anything about success or failure.

Measuring the Educational Product

It is not surprising that under these circumstances the educational industry is remarkably subject to fads and fashions. It is extremely hard to measure the product where the act of measurement of the product distorts it, and the product is enjoyed (or not) by people who do not pay for it. It is not surprising that the practitioners of the industry spend a great deal of time in developing "objectives." Education indeed is almost the only industry in which the measure of success is the achievement of an imaginary product. Schools of education spend a great deal of time inculcating school teachers with the necessity for stating objectives and then measuring their achievement by achieving them. Under the impact of behaviorism, of course, we abandon the notion that anything could be known about knowledge, hence we now go in for "behavioral objectives" on a theory, derived mainly from rat psychology, that learning can only be measured by change in behavior. As long as we include linguistic behavior, treating students as if they were rats is not so dangerous. I am not arguing that the thinking about behavioral objectives is worthless. It can easily, however, become ritual, and there is bound to be a strong tendency for teachers to define as objectives the changes in behavior in the student which they think they can achieve. Here is a wonderful example of the self-fulfilling prophecy in which mismatch signals are utilized to change the information input rather than to change the image of the world.

The Grants Economy and the Exchange Economy

The unfortunate but unavoidable fact that those who pay for education are not usually the ones who receive it, except in the somewhat quantitively minor case of adult education, is reflected also in the fact that the educational industry derives its revenue to a very large extent from the "grants economy." The total economic system can conveniently be divided into two parts. One is the exchange economy which is organized by two-way transfers, in which A gives B something and B gives A something. The other is the grants economy which is organized by one-way transfers, in which A gives B something which is exchangeable but B does not give A anything that is exchangeable, even though he may give A certain psychological satisfactions that are not strictly, however, part of the economy.

Grants are motivated by two principle motivators — benevolence and fear. If A gives a grant and receives nothing tangible in return, this may be, in the first place because A feels benevolent towards B. Benevolence means in technical economic language that the perception of utilities is interdependent; that is, if A perceives that B's welfare is increased, A's welfare is increased by this perception. Benevolence, of course, can be negative, in which case it becomes malevolence. Selfishness or indifference is simply the zero point on the scale of malevolence and benevolence, in which A's perception of a change in B's welfare makes no change in A's evaluation of his own welfare. This, in fact, is rather a rare case. Most relationships have at least a small amount of malevolence or benevolence. A's benevolence towards B may be measured by his *rate of benevolence*, that is, the amount A will sacrifice in order to perceive that B is better off by a dollar. If A's rate of benevolence is anything above .5, and if A by giving B a dollar perceives B to be better off by two dollars, then it is quite rational for A to make a grant of one dollar to B.

There is, we must recognize, a second source of grants. If B threatens A, A may make him a grant in order to prevent him from carrying out the threat. This is *tribute*. It is not always easy to tell in practice where benevolence ends and tribute begins. Grants given for education, whether by parents of the children, which are in the private grants economy, or by the state indirectly to children and students through the state supported schools, in the public grants economy, are mainly the result of benevolence, although the threat of having children around the house all day may not be wholly insignificant in persuading parents to vote for school taxes. The fact that the revenue of the education industry arises mainly in the grants economy introduces some peculiarities which are not found in commodities sold in the exchange economy. The elasticity of demand for a commodity in the exchange economy depends mainly on its substitutability with alternative sources of obtaining similar satisfactions. A rise in the price of a commodity in the exchange economy will usually diminish its purchase mainly because other uses of income for purchase look more attractive. The extent to which the purchase declines depends on whether attractive substitutes can easily be found, assuming the prices of other things to be unchanged. In the grants economy a grant for one purpose competes much more with grants for other purposes than it does for commodities in general. Grants are a part of the total flow of expenditures which in some ways forms an "economy" of its own insofar as the total of grants is the result of the general level of the sense of community or benevolence, so that an increase in a grant for one purpose is likely to lead to a diminution in another grant rather than in the diminution of a purchase in exchange. Thus, the total sum of grants is likely to be more stable than any particular component of it. *The demand for education therefore is likely to depend more on what is happening in other parts of the grants economy*, for instance to other government expenditures, than it is on what is happening to income and expenditures in general.

We do not really know how far this is true in the case of the family. Does the family, for instance, regard the education of its children in private schools as competitive with a new car and other items of conspicuous consumption or does it regard payments for education as competitive with donations to charity or with taxes? A study of family budget response to the surtax of 1968 would be extremely instructive in this regard, yet as

far as I know this has not been done. There is a good deal of
evidence that expenditure on education is highly vulnerable to
major changes in national defense. It is also vulnerable to
severe depression. This is shown in Figure 1-2. Here we take the
Gross Capacity Product as a measure of the total size of the
economy, the Gross Capacity Product being roughly what the
gross national product would have been had there not been

Fig. 1-2

COMPONENTS OF STATE AND LOCAL GOVERNMENT EXPENDITURE
AND

NATIONAL DEFENSE AS A PERCENTAGE OF GROSS CAPACITY PRODUCT

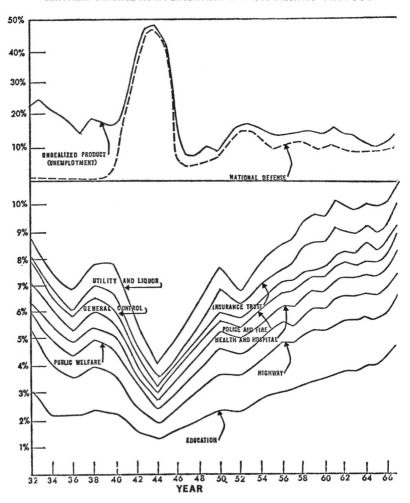

any unemployment. The bottom part of the diagram then shows the various components of state and local expenditure as a percentage of the Gross Capacity Product. The upper part of the diagram shows the proportion of the economy devoted to national defense on the one hand and to what is called unrealized product on the other. Unrealized product is actually equivalent to the proportion of the labor force unemployed, as we have calculated the Gross Capacity Product. The impact made on both local government in general and education in particular by both the depression and the Second World War is very striking. Equally striking, however, is the resilience of education in the face of a large and permanent increase in the proportion of the economy devoted to national defense.

Changes in the Productivity of the Educational Industry

One final point which is relevant to the consideration of the demand and supply of education is that education is still very largely a "craft" industry, the methods of which have not been much touched by the scientific revolution, at least by comparison with an industry such as agriculture. Average productivity in agriculture has increased almost twenty times in the last hundred years. The technology of teaching is still not very different from what it was in the days of Plato. This is particularly true in the universities; in grade schools and high schools unquestionably there is a greater variety and much more use is made of educational tools such as movies, film strips, and other visual aids and there is even a small move into computer-assisted instruction. It is still very doubtful, though, whether much more knowledge-value is being produced per hour of teacher time or per real dollar of total expense than it was a hundred years ago, or even twenty-five hundred years ago. There are very good reasons for this "backwardness" of the educational industry. Its basic field of operation, the human nervous system, is a system of such fantastic complexity that scientific knowledge about it proceeds very slowly and only encompasses a minute fraction of the total system. We know something, by "folk knowledge," about the process by which teaching results in learning, and we must have been doing something right — otherwise we would never have been able to transmit the knowledge stock of mankind to successive generations for thousands of years as we have done. Nevertheless we really do not know *what* we are doing right and we certainly do not know very much about how to do it better. Even the doubling of the efficiency of the educational industry in terms of the knowledge produced per real dollar spent would seem quite beyond our capacity at the moment.

What this means is that the price of education, relative to those commodities being produced under conditions of rapidly increasing productivity, is bound to rise, simply because the relative price structure is so largely a function of relative productivities. Teachers' salaries have to rise at least roughly in proportion to the general rise in incomes and teachers' productivity does not rise in anything like the same proportion. What we have in education, therefore, is not so much an inelastic supply curve, for under given conditions of productivity it is probably not difficult to attract resources into education by a relatively small increase in real incomes obtained from it. What is happening is that the whole supply curve is moving upward and to the right as costs rise. The demand is also probably rising with increased incomes, partly because education is something of a "superior good" which we can afford more of as society gets richer and partly also because with the increase in the stock of knowledge a larger effort is required to transmit it. What we have therefore is something like Figure 1-3. S_0, S_1, S_2 show successive positions of the supply curve of education in successive years, and D_0, D_1, D_2, positions of the corresponding demand curve in these years. The position of equilibrium rises from E_0 to E_1 to E_2 with both the price and quantity of education rising as time goes on. The less the demand rises, of course, the smaller will be the rise in both the price and the quantity. If demand did not rise at all in the face of this increasing real cost we might find the price of education rising and the quantity actually falling as time went on, following the path E_0, E_1', E_2'.

Demand for Different Kinds of Education

Up to now we have assumed implicitly that education was a homogeneous commodity. In practice we know education to be a very heterogeneous commodity indeed. It is not only that the industry is divided into public and private schools, into secular and religious schools, into Catholic, Lutheran, and others, but also that education is divided into vocational and technical edu-

Fig. 1-3

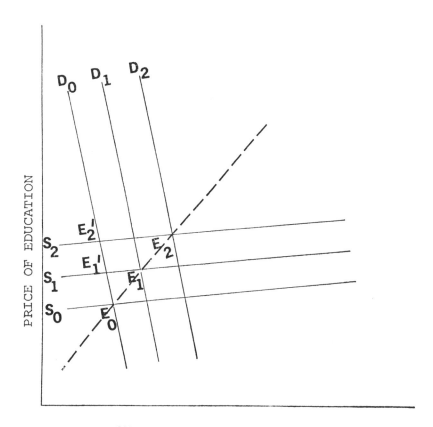

QUANTITY OF EDUCATION

cation of a large number of different kinds as well as general education, also of a number of different kinds. The demand for each of these different kinds of education is different, although all these demands are likely to be related. The demand for private schools, for instance, is going to be related to the quality and cost of the public schools. The dynamic patterns of the interrelationships may be of great importance. We are all familiar with the problem faced by a public school system once it deteriorates to a point where wealthier parents are willing to send their children to private schools and then are unwilling to vote for adequate school taxes. We may find the same phenomenon in communities with strong religious groups where a large private grants economy goes into the parochial schools and therefore the community is unwilling to tax itself for the benefit of public schools which a large proportion of the population does not use.

Some economists, such as E. G. West,[2] have made rather cogent arguments that the existing system of public education prevents the development of variety and competition in the educational industry. They recommend a system by which education would be subsidized by means of vouchers given to all children, and exchangeable for education at any approved school whether public or private. This, it is argued, would permit much greater experimentation and specialization in schools and also permit parents with a particular concern for education of their children to supplement the state subsidy, that is the voucher, by additional payments. The impact of schemes of this kind is not easy to predict. One of the arguments for uniformity in education is, of course, that it is necessary to create a society which is homogeneous enough not to fall apart politically. This presumably is one rationale behind the current pressure for racial integration in education. Educational segregation would create a two-part society which is repugnant to our present sense of social justice and our demand for societal homogeneity. It could be argued, on the other hand, that uniformity is not necessary for political stability, and indeed an enforced uniformity may produce a society which is dull, conformist, and without color and interest. The concept of a "mosaic society" of many different subcultures all living together at peace within some political framework has a great attractiveness as we move towards a world in which the great period of human expansion is over.

Life Experience and Demand for Education

These are very fundamental questions for educational philosophy and are well beyond the scope of supply and demand analysis. But it is important to recognize that they do underlie the apparent simplicities of supply and demand and that we should not be deluded by these simplicities into forgetting that the real world is enormously complex and multivariate. When we introduce the fact that both the demand and supply of education are a result of a long and continuous process of social learning, the situation gets even more complex. The demand for education arises not from its recipients, as we have seen, but from those adult members of society whose decisions determine the supply of funds. Their demand depends in no small measure on the childhood and indeed the total life experience of these same people. People who were deprived of education in their youth and who observed other people benefiting from it are likely to have a very strong demand for education for their own children. People who received education gratuitously and who perhaps took it for granted may not have the same motivation when it comes to making personal sacrifices for the education of their own children. I have heard the observation that the current increasing unwillingness of state legislatures to allocate funds, especially to higher education, as compared to a generation or two ago, is related to the fact that many state legislators, say at the beginning of this century, had not been to college and hence had rather romantic ideas about it and wanted very much to have their children enjoy the privileges of which they had been denied. Today most state legislators have been to college and do not have the same romantic illusions about it; hence they are less willing to make sacrifices for their children than their fathers and grandfathers were. These are learning processes of great complexity. We cannot do much more than note that they exist.

OTHER FACTORS AFFECTING THE DEMAND FOR EDUCATION

With this analysis behind us, let us now take a look at other forces which may affect the demand and supply of education in the next ten or twenty years.

Demographic Factors

The first important factor is, of course, demographic change, especially as reflected in the total numbers of people in each age group in different years. Demographic change is dominated by the principle that anyone who is X years old today will be X + 1 years old this time next year if he is not dead. Consequently, if we have a fair idea of the survival distribution of each cohort, that is, the proportion of all those born in a given year who will die each subsequent year, then we can take the number of births in a given year and follow the cohort through until it finally disappears. Thus in Figure 4 we show the total number of births in the United States from 1940-69. The "bulge" from 1945 to the 1960s is very apparent. It is equally apparent that the bulge is now over. The peak of total births in the United States was 1957, and this cohort is likely to be the largest age group for a good many years to come. The dotted lines show approximately the survival function from each cohort, excluding immigration, so that in 1970, for instance, A shows the number of three year olds, B the number of four year olds, C the number of five year olds, and so on. The top of the bulge is now passing through the high schools. Obstetric wards and kindergartens are beginning to empty and lower grades are declining rapidly. Between the ages of five and fourteen we can

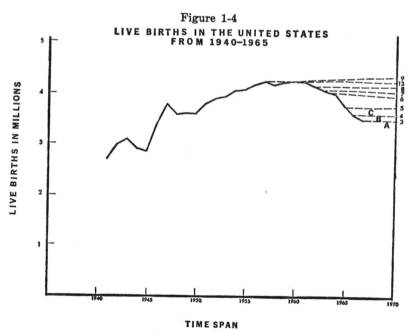

Figure 1-4
**LIVE BIRTHS IN THE UNITED STATES
FROM 1940–1965**

TIME SPAN

(---) APPROXIMATE NUMBER IN EACH AGE GROUP 1970

assume that the proportion of each age group that is in school is very high and is not likely to change much. As we move into the later years of high school, dropouts become important and in college, of course, the proportion of the age group actually attending school is less than 50 percent. At this level changes in the proportion attending school may be as important as the number in each age group. One thing that is certain is that the pressure on the American educational system, which has been intense in the last ten years, will continue to diminish as we move into the future. The 4.3 million babies of 1957 who are now teen-agers will be replaced by only 3.4 million babies in 1969 as teen-agers by 1982. Insofar as the "youth problem" in the United States has been the result of the "bulge" and the unusual numbers of young people, we may expect this problem to diminish in the future. It is hard to say how much is due to the bulge and how much is due to long-run forces in our society resulting, for instance, from the unprecedented segregation of teen-agers in high schools and of young adults in colleges. But we may certainly expect to see amelioration of the unemployment problem among young people simply because labor markets are somewhat age-specific. The high unemployment among young people in the last ten years has reflected in part the very large numbers of them. As the proportion of young people declines, it should be much easier for those who wish to do so to obtain employment.

The implication of the current demographic situation for the colleges is extremely complex. Even if there is no change in the proportion of each age group entering college, freshmen enrollment should increase at least up until about 1974 or 1975. The increase will not be large, and may soon be followed by a substantial decline. There are already signs of severe oversupply of college teachers, especially Ph.D.'s in fields like philosophy, languages, the humanities, and even physics. This is likely to lead to a reduction in graduate school enrollments and thus further reduction in the demand for college teachers. It will not be surprising, therefore, to find an increased number of Ph.D.'s teaching in junior colleges or in high schools. It is a moot point of course, as to whether the conventional Ph.D. is particularly good training for this kind of teaching and it may well be that some retraining programs will be necessary.

One very curious consequence of the "bulge" which may have

some implications for the educational system is that there is now a severe deficiency in marriageable males. The groom in the United States averages two or three years older than the bride. The large cohort of girls in 1947 is going to try to marry the small cohort of men of 1944 or 1945; the deficiency may be as much as half a million. It is not perhaps surprising therefore, than an unusual amount of unrest has appeared among women as reflected in the various women's liberation groups. As the unmarried female is an important labor market source for the educational industry, the next few years may see an unusual number of women entering the teaching profession.

We have not ventured to predict with any certainty the number of births in the future, as it is extremely dangerous to predict linear trends in the birth rate. We would not go very far wrong in assuming that all population predictions are wrong. Even if fertility continues to decline, the "bulge" will begin to marry and presumably have children, so that even with declining fertility (that is, a decline in the number of children per thousand women of childbearing age) we may still have a rise in the total number of births in the next few years. However, in light of the general anxieties about the future and the population-ecology syndrome, it would be somewhat surprising if births increased very sharply. How close we now are to stabilizing the population of the United States may be brought out by reflecting that a stable population of 210 million where the average age of death is 70 would have 3 million births a year. If we achieve this, it would mean that no further expansion of the educational system would be necessary as far as number of students is concerned, at least up to the middle of high school, simply because we are so close to 100 percent of each age group in school now.

Demographic Changes in Older Age Groups

Demographic changes in the older age groups are also of great importance in assessing the demand for education, as it is these age groups that ultimately make the decisions. There is a long-run shift in the overall age distribution from the "triangle" of earlier times to the "rectangle" which we are so rapidly approaching, which has about equal numbers in each age group. The change from 1870 to 1909 is shown dramatically in Figure 5. This means that the proportion of voters of child-

Fig. 1-5

DISTRIBUTION OF THE POPULATION,
BY AGE AND SEX:
1870—1969

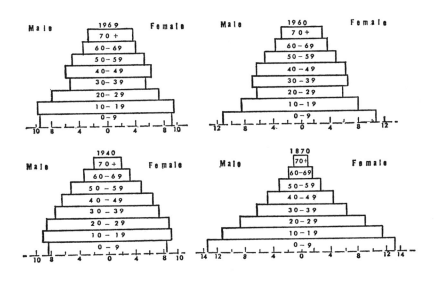

PERCENT OF TOTAL POPULATION

SOURCE: Population Estimates and Projections, U.S.
Department of Commerce, Series P25, No. 441,
May 19, 1970.

bearing age has been declining, which means again that we have
to rely on the much weaker "grandparent motive" rather than
the parent motive for political support of educational expenditures. When the present "bulge" gets to be grandparents in the
early twenty-first century, it will dominate the voting population and the effects on educational expenditures may well be

disastrous. Now, of course, this "grandparent effect" is modified by the fact that the grandparent of 1975-2000 will come out of the low birth cohorts of 1920-45. This also means, however, that there may be some deficiency in the numbers of mature people available for positions of leadership, though this effect is offset by the large proportion of these cohorts surviving into middle age.

One long-run effect of the "rectangular" age distribution has received little attention, but may eventually necessitate a drastic change in the educational system. Hierarchical structures tend to be "triangular" with large numbers in the lower (younger) levels and small numbers in the higher (older) levels. A rectangular age distribution means that older people are increasingly squeezed out of the hierarchial structure and lose status. We have hardly begun to think about how to adapt the educational system to this kind of total life pattern in which the chances of promotion become less and less.

Redistributing Income and Educational Opportunity

A question for the future, which is of course much more difficult to answer, is whether there would be any changes in the structure of the demand for education, especially in the differrent age cohorts. In the lower age groups this is mainly likely to be reflected in the demand for increasing quality rather than quantity though there may be an exception to this in the pre-school years. There is likely to be an increasing demand for kindergarten and pre-kindergarten school experiences. The main changes here may be seen in the bottom 20 percent of the income distribution where it is widely recognized that the educational system is grossly unsatisfactory and has contributed to the perpetuation of the poverty subcultures. This, however, is going to require an extension of the grants system for education from local communities to wider state and national communities simply because this is the only way in which income can be distributed from rich communities to poor ones. Bringing up the expenditure per child of the poor communities and states even to the present median would involve a substantial expansion of the proportion of the economy going to education, even if the total number of children were to remain constant. One possible optimistic consideration in this situation is that as the number of children declines educational expenditures are likely to exhibit a lag, as on the whole it is much harder to get things out of budgets than it is to get them in. There may be a considerable possibility here for improving the quality and distribution of education, with relatively constant total educational budgets but declining numbers of children, unless budgets are tied mechanically to the number of pupils.

The Youth Culture and Education

There seems little doubt that there has been substantial improvement in the quality of American education in the last decade, perhaps due to Sputnik, at least in the upper and middle income groups, in terms of an increase in the rate of acquisition of knowledge. The curriculum reforms of the last decade or so have certainly had some effect though it is hard to measure this. The hardest thing to assess is the "moral culture" of children and young people as this is developed by the sheer fact of segregation. This is the first society in human history that has effectively segregated not only its children but its teenagers and a considerable proportion of its youth in situations where the peer group is the major factor in determining the culture and adults are present in a very small minority and often in a quasi-custodial or even hostile role. The effect of this may be quite incalculable and by no means necessarily desirable. In all previous societies youth cultures have been severely modified by the fact that adolescents and young people especially have begun work at an early age and hence have developed into adults in the midst of an essentially adult society in the work situation. Apprentices, office boys, and so on naturally develop some youth culture of their own, but it is greatly modified by the fact that for a good part of the day they have to conform to the adult culture around them.

Today we have a segregated youth culture which has an enormous dynamic of its own, quite at odds with the adult culture from which it is so sharply separated. Youth cults, however, are likely to be very unsatisfactory as preparations for a total life pattern. Youth, after all, has no future. A culture which idealizes it and models itself on it is likely to get itself into serious trouble, especially in the demographic situation where the familiar pyramidal age distribution with a very small number of old people being replaced by a rectangular age distribution with large numbers of old people. It may be that the learning process which is going on in the present generation of young people in regard to their attitude toward education may be so radical that when they become adults the whole educational system will be revised radically in the interests of developing satisfactory personal identities, satisfactory whole life patterns of behavior, and an integration of youth with the society in which they are embedded. This, however, is a wild speculation and should not be taken too seriously.

The War Industry Versus the Education Industry

Another set of considerations which must be carried in mind in considering the future of the educational segment arises out of the fact that it is so largely financed through the grants economy. Consequently any changes in the overall structure of the grants economy are likely to have disproportionate effects on education. The major factor here of course is the future of the war industry. If we have substantial disarmament, reducing the war industry down to, say, 4 percent rather than the present 8 percent of the economy, this is likely to release a proportionate amount of the public grants economy for other purposes, to which education is an important claimant. On the other hand if the international situation worsens or if we develop still wilder delusions of national grandeur than we now have so that the war industry expands, we can expect one of the major victims to be public expenditures on education. Where the future of the international system is so uncertain we have to be extremely "liquid" in our planning. Educational planning in particular must be prepared for the unexpected. We should be prepared both for good times and for bad.

Effect of Methods of Financing Education on Expenditures

Another possible future set of changes here, which it is at least not absurd to contemplate in the next ten or twenty years, is a radical change in the methods of finance of education which might produce quite large changes in structure. Thus, suppose that we had something like the "Killingsworth plan" as I have been calling it,[3] for setting up educational banks which would lend students the full cost of their education, the loans to be repaid by a surcharge on income tax throughout the subsequent life of the borrower. The surcharge would not need to be large,

perhaps 1 or 2 percent for higher education. The person bene-
fited most in terms of increased income would pay most and we
would at least get education out from under the grants economy
in part into something that looks like the market sector, thus
at least avoiding the stigma of "charity." Unfortunately this
proposal, which seems to be eminently sensible, has run into
severe political opposition especially from the Association of
Land Grant Colleges. It certainly merits serious political consideration. If we run into continued "taxpayers revolt" as we
are all too likely to do, proposals of this kind may be much more
politically acceptable. The proposal, after all, is based on a very
fundamental truth, that for the individual who receives it,
education is an investment and frequently a very good investment, and there seems to be no reason why we should not devise
financial institutions to recognize the fact. Education as an
investment, of course, is not the same as investment in a house,
and obviously cannot be financed by a chattel mortgage. The
fact that it is a peculiar kind of investment, however, does not
eliminate it as an investment, and we should be able to devise
peculiar financial instruments and institutions which could
deal with it.

Technology and the Education Industry

Another element of the current situation which is extremely
hard to appraise is the future interaction between education and
business, particularly in the form of new educational hardware
technology. Beginning about 1965 there was a great flurry of
interest in American business corporations in this problem. A
number of established corporations such as Xerox, Raytheon,
RCA, IBM, Westinghouse, and General Electric allied with
Time, Inc., which established the General Learning Corporation, have all either acquired educational subsidiaries or have
developed divisions in this field. In addition some old established publishing houses, especially McGraw Hill, Appleton-
Century-Crofts, and Crowell-Collier-Macmillan, have been edg-
ing into the business of educational hardware and there are a
considerable number of new and small enterprises any one of
which might conceivably turn out to be an incipient educational
IBM. A considerable controversy has been raging, centering
around Antony Ottinger,[4] around the possible value of all these
new developments, and here again, almost like the future of the

war industry, one simply has to advise a "wait and see" policy. Up to now at any rate there are no signs of the "Model T" among educational hardware and even fewer signs that anyone is capable of driving it. Up to now there is not all that much challenge to the ancient inventions of the book and the teacher— the latter especially being a remarkable nonlinear computer of fantastic capacity which is produced mostly by unskilled labor. Nevertheless in this field, as in many others, one has always to be prepared for the unexpected.[5]

One can express modest confidence, however, that any major change in the educational industry will have to be a combination of financial, organizational, and technical changes. Of these it is quite possible that the financial and organizational changes will have to come first. As long as the near-monopoly of the public school system exists intact, substantial technical changes are unlikely to be forthcoming. A very tantalizing question for the future is the mixture of public and private enterprise in the educational industry. It is easy to underestimate the size of the private sector even now, especially if we include the kind of training programs which go on in industry outside the formal educational system. These fall more in the category of adult education and have a very different set of problems from the education of children and young people. A change in methods of finance to one which subsidizes the student rather than the school might indeed set off drastic changes in the organization of the whole industry. This seems unlikely in the next ten years. About the only conclusion we can safely draw from this discussion is that the future of the educational industry in regard to its structure, if not perhaps in regard to its overall size, is highly uncertain. It may look very different in ten or twenty years or it may look much the same as it is now. This may be a somewhat depressing conclusion, but honesty demands it.

FOOTNOTES

1. Fritz Machlup, *The Production and Distribution of Knowledge in the United States* (Princeton University Press, 1962).
2. E. G. West, *Education and the State: A Study in Political Economy* (London: The Institute of Economic Affairs, 1965).
3. Charles C. Killingsworth, testimony to the United States Senate on Employment of Manpower, September 20, 1963. Also, *How to Pay for Higher Education*, Presidential Address to the Economic Society of Michigan (1967), mimeo.
4. Antony Ottinger and Sema Marks, "Educational Technology: New Myths and Old Realities," *Harvard Educational Review*, 38, 4 (1968).

5. "Expecting the Unexpected: The Uncertain Future of Knowledge and Technology," in *Prospective Changes in Society by 1980 Including Some Implications for Education*, Edgar L. Morphet and Charles O. Ryan, Reports Prepared for the First Area Conference. Designing Education for the Future. An Eight-State Project (Denver, Colorado, July, 1966), pp. 199-215.

THE MISALLOCATION OF INTELLECTUAL RESOURCES IN ECONOMICS

The Use and Abuse of Social Science,
Transaction Books (1971), pp. 34-51.

The Misallocation of Intellectual Resources in Economics

The problem of the misallocation of intellectual resources has the unfortunate property of being clearly important and yet extremely intractable. We hav᷈ an uneasy feeling that failures today, insofar as they are avoidable at all, are always the result of misapplied intellectual resources in the past. If we had thought about things differently or thought about different things or put our energies into the discovery of knowledge that would be relevant to present problems instead of knowledge that is not, we have a strong feeling that things would have been better. It is not easy to be wise after the event and to identify exactly what misallocation in the past prevented us from solving our problems in the present. To be wise before the event is much more difficult, for the judgment as to whether intellectual resources are being misapplied today must depend on our image of the future, and our image of the future itself is subject to serious and inevitable controversy.

Unfortunately, the general theory of allocation of resources as we find it in economics is not very helpful at this point. This theory states that if we are dividing a given quantity of resources among a number of different uses, an amount should be allocated to each use such that the marginal return per unit of resource is the same in all uses. The marginal return in any use is the additional return per additional small unit of resources employed. If the marginal returns are different in different uses, then it clearly pays to transfer resources from the uses in which marginal returns are low to the uses in which the marginal returns are high. Thus, if an extra unit of resources produces eight dollars in one use and ten dollars in another use, then if we transfer a unit of resources from the first to the second, we will lose eight dollars in the first and gain ten dollars in the second. If there is some law of diminishing returns to increasing use of resources, these transfers from uses of low marginal return to uses of high marginal return will raise the returns in the one and lower the returns in the other until they are finally equalized, at which point there is no further gain from shifting resources from among the uses and presumably the allocation is the best possible.

As a purely formal theory, this is fine, but it does not help us if we cannot measure the marginal returns; and in the case of intellectual resources this is extremely difficult, partly because of the uncertainty of the future in which these returns will be manifest and partly because of the extreme difficulty of allocating any specific future product, whatever it may be, to specific intellectual operations at the present. We simply do not know the production functions of most intellectual activity, and without this the calculation of marginal returns is virtually impossible. We have an additional problem of valuation in that many of the products of intellectual activity do not receive any obvious price in the market, so that even if we could define an aggregate of physical products of a specific intellectual activity, it might be quite difficult to calculate an overall valuation of this in terms of some numeraire, such as a dollar.

Attempts have been made to calculate the dollar value of education, for instance, at different levels and in different occupations, and this perhaps is the closest we can get to specific economic evaluations in the market of intellectual activity. There does seem to be a certain long-run tendency for the rates of return on investments in education to equalize themselves among the different occupations, if allowance is made for certain nonmonetary advantages and disadvantages of the occupation itself, such as pleasantness or unpleasantness, the prestige it offers and so on. There may be considerable imperfections in this market. There is lack of knowledge and misinvestment, as for instance when people prepare themselves as obstetricians just before a sharp decline in the birth rate. While the information system in this market could certainly be improved, we do not have a feeling that it constitutes a major social problem. Somehow the educational market does allocate resources among the preparation of doctors, dentists, surveyors, pharmacists and so on, without running into extremely sharp or socially dangerous shortages or surpluses. There is, of course, a shortage of doctors among the poor, but this is because the poor are poor, and reflects the problem of distribution of income rather than the distribution of resources. There is at present a surplus of physicists, but this is because physics has become an unstable government enterprise.

It is when we get into what I have been calling the grants economy, that is, that part of the economic system in which resources are allocated by one-way transfers, that we begin to get into trouble, mainly because of the absence of feedback and the extraordinary difficulties of evaluation. The grants economy now comprises something between 15 and 20 percent of the American economy, and it organizes a much larger proportion of the distribution of intellectual resources, simply because the education and research industries are so dominated by it. Education, which is now 7 percent of the Gross National Product, is for the most part in what might be called the public grants sector, that is, it is financed by one-way transfers of funds from authorities which derive their revenues from the use of the tax power. Even private education is financed to a very large extent by grants from parents, from foundations and from endowments. The profit-making educational institution is so rare that it is regarded as positively disreputable and finds it has difficulties in becoming accredited. Research, especially pure research, likewise is heavily concentrated in the grants economy. Even in the case of industrial research the returns are so uncertain that the research budget has many aspects of a one-way transfer.

There is an allocation problem in the grants economy just as there is in the exchange economy, simply because the total of the grants is not indefinitely expandible, even though at any one time it may have a modest flexibility. If the total of grants is fixed, it is very clear that a grant to A means that there is going to be no grant to B. In this case, the allocation of grants, and therefore the allocation of the resources purchased by them, is very much in the control of the grantor. It is indeed a classic case of Kenneth Galbraith's "revised sequence," in which the initiative comes from the seller, and his decisions are very largely imposed on the buyers, in this case the recipients of the grants. In the exchange economy, there is more tendency to find the "accepted sequence" in which the buyer or consumer originates demands and the producer jumps to satisfy them. In the grants economy, the proposer proposes, but the Ford Foundation disposes.

There is something that begins to simulate the market in the grants economy, insofar as there are a large number of grantors and grantees, for then the grantee can shop around among the grantors and if he is turned down from one he may get accepted from another. Potentially this is a very important check on the arbitrary power of the grantors. How important it is, unfortunately, we do not know, for the one thing that does not get into the information system is failed proposals for grants. A study of these would be extremely illuminating indeed, and would not be impossible to do. It is not self-evident, of course, that the judgment of the grantees is necessarily any better than that of the grantors, and it may well be that a system of extensive interaction between grantors and grantees is most likely to give the best results, though in any system one would have to allow for a fairly large random factor.

In the absence of any accurate feedback or information about rates of return on the use of intellectual resources, one is forced back on considerations of structure; that is, is there anything in the machinery by which intellectual resources are allocated which might lead to serious biases? In the case of research we can look both on the side of the researcher himself, or the producer of knowledge, and on the side of the grantors who are in a sense the purveyors and the users of knowledge.

The main problem in pure research is the power structure within universities where most pure research goes on: old people usually have the power and young people the ideas. Of course the optimum age of creativity varies in different disciplines. It is apparently very low in mathematics and high in philosophy, and it is clearly the result of two factors operating in opposite directions. One is the sheer quantitative deterioration of the human nervous system with age: we lose about a hundred thousand neurons a day all our life. Counteracting this is the learning process which continually rearranges the declining stock of neurons into more and more elegant patterns. It is not surprising, therefore, to find that creativity in mathematics occurs at an early age, where a rich deposit of memory and experience is not so important as the ability to call on large resources in the nervous system. In philosophy and history, however, the accumulating quality of the structure is more important than the declining quantity for a longer period of time. These very physiological facts of aging make it important in all fields to avoid concentrating the granting power too much in the hands of the old and to organize the system so that there are checks and balances and that a young man with an idea who gets a rebuff at one place can find a sympathetic ear at another. It is curious how something like the simulation of the market is almost always the answer to the problem of undesirable concentrations of power.

Another structural problem that may cause misallocation is the phenomenon of fashion. This may be more important among the grantors than among the grantees. Even in the pure sciences there are fashions in research and a spectacular success in some field is likely to attract an unusually large amount of resources. Indeed it is one of the dilemmas of the dynamics of human learning, that whereas in the economics of the intellectual life nothing succeeds like success, in the total learning process what we are most likely to learn from is failure. Here again the only structural remedy for the vagaries of fashion would seem to be the atomization of the society, that is, the development of large numbers of subcultures in which different fashions may prevail in the intellectual life. Thus, the development of "competing schools" may have some effect in preventing the tyranny of fashion, for even though this tyranny may obtain in full force in one place, the person whose insights and information fall outside the rubrics of one school may find another school to go to somewhere else. The graduate student who cannot stand economics at the University of Chicago may find the University of Texas more congenial.

The danger of monopolistic power among the grantors is probably greater than that among the grantees. This is particularly true as national governments increase their importance in the grants economy and become the major sources of funds for research. Here, the accidents of political power or rhetoric have the potential at least of creating very serious misallocations of intellectual resources. If there is any one major source of this misallocation it is the setting up, perhaps for partly accidental reasons, of structures and organizations which then have a strong tendency to perpetuate themselves. We see this in the United States, for instance, in the great attention paid to agriculture, partly because of the structure of Congress, which in earlier days gave excessive weight to agricultural votes, and partly because of the establishment of the Department of Agriculture and of a remarkable tradition within it of the use of intellectual resources, which goes back to the establishment of land grant colleges in 1862. In the building industry, by contrast, there has been no such political pressure group, no such organization in the Executive Branch and no "university of the building trades" to correspond to the land grant colleges. It is not surprising under these circumstances that research in agriculture has been spectacularly successful and that we have had an increase in labor productivity in agriculture of almost 6 percent per year for almost 30 years, whereas the building trades have had a very low rate of development, practically none of which has come out of the building trades themselves. The deplorable condition of our cities is perhaps the main result of this particular misallocation.

One sees a similar distortion in the case of national defense. The fact that national defense is a prime expression of the national community gives it very high priority and so there has been a very serious brain drain into it which not only has very doubtful productivity but also has seriously impaired the quantity and quality of intellectual resources in civilian occupations. Perhaps the most dramatic expression of this misallocation of resources is in the fact that we have been spending yearly in preparations for chemical and bacteriological warfare almost as much as the whole budget of all the United Nations agencies. In the light of this fact, it is hard to believe that there are not strongly pathological processes at work in the structure of world society.

We may perhaps be able to take a small step towards analyzing this problem if we take a single discipline, such as economics, and try to analyze the distribution of intellectual effort within it, in the hope that this may reveal at least gross disparities between the proportion of intellectual effort devoted to a certain theme and its basic importance. In order to do this, we have to scan the *Index of Economic Journals* from 1886, classified according to subject matter; in order to get a total picture of the output of the profession, we should, of course, include books, but this task is beyond our present resources. Besides, articles give a good picture of the distribution of interests of the actively working members of the profession and tend to be more contemporaneous than books, which are often the product of work of previous years. It is reasonable to suppose, therefore, that articles give a good index of the interest of the economics profession in any one year. We have simply counted the number of articles rather than the number of pages, not only because articles tend to be approximately the same length, but also because the presence of an article may tend to be more significant than its length. By a rough check, about 10 percent of the articles are counted more than once, by being cross-classified. We assume, however, that a double or multiple classification increases the significance of the article.

The general growth of the economics profession is shown in Figure 1. The journal articles begin with the foundation of the *Quarterly Journal of Economics* in 1886. The total number of articles reached about 150 by 1892 and fluctuated around this level until about 1909, when growth began again and continued remarkably steadily at about an average of 6.8 percent per annum until the 1940s, doubling about every 11 years. It is curious that even if we take the number of articles, say, in 1886, and compound this at 6.8 percent per annum we arrive very much where we are in the sixties! This rate of growth, incidentally, is somewhat more than that of the Gross National Product, which suggests that economics is occupying a continually larger share of the product. This is not wholly surprising, as economics is, after all, what economists call a "superior good," that is, it is a luxury, the demand for which will tend to increase with increasing incomes. In the light of this consideration, the rate of growth does not seem to be excessive. A rather striking phenomenon is the quite substantial interruption of the growth of economics by the Second World War, from which the profession apparently never really recovered in the sense that, although the old rate of growth was continued, the gap made by the war was not made up. It may

Figure 1. The Total Number of Articles in the *Index of Economic Journals*, (1886-1965)

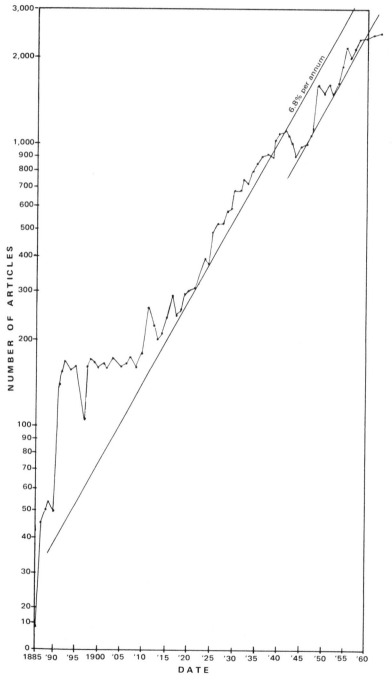

be, of course, that the rate of growth would have slackened anyhow, which would not have been surprising. But the interruption due to the war is surprisingly large and reflects the absorption of intellectuals in the war effort—and also the fact that meetings of the American Economic Association were not held during the war years.

The articles can be divided first into three categories. The first contains articles in which economists are writing to themselves, and about themselves, and about economics. This is a large category. I would put much of economic theory into it, the history of thought, and especially articles about economists, which is a large group. It is clear that economists have a fair amount of narcissism and that they like thinking about themselves and writing to each other about themselves, without a great deal of reference to the world outside. It would be interesting to know whether other scientists do as much of this. One suspects that it is particularly a habit of the social scientists and that physical and biological scientists are less given to it, but we would have to wait for a comparative analysis of other disciplines before we could confirm this hypothesis.

The second category consists of articles about the total economy, rather than about particular sectors of it. It is not always easy to distinguish these from that of the third sector, which consists of articles which refer to particular segments of the economy. The distinction, however, is necessary if we are to look at this third sector with a view to possible misallocation of intellectual resources. A very rough classification of categories gave 22 percent for the narcissistic articles, 33 percent for articles relating to the general economy, and 45 percent for articles relating to segments of the economy.

This breakdown does not seem unreasonable, though we clearly cannot impose any absolute rule on the distribution of the resources of economics among the above mentioned three sectors. We certainly expect to find all three and, while an individual may pass judgment that one of the sectors, especially the first, is excessive, it is hard to justify these judgments in any objective way. The great English economist, A.C. Pigou, is reported to have said, "We do economics because it is fun." Certainly no one would want to deprive economists or anybody else of their fun, and a great deal of the first section is fun of this kind; that is, it satisfies intellectual curiosity, it expresses the passion for order and consistency, and it produces at least some concepts and models that are relevant to the understanding of the economy.

Table 1 and Figure 2 show the breakdown of articles by the 23 categories of the *Index*, by ten-year periods, with the percentage of total articles in each period in each category. Considering what changes have taken place both in economics and in the world in these 80 years, the stability of these proportions is quite striking. There is a slight decline in the proportion in scope and method, a rise in theory, a decline in the history of thought, a rise (though less than might have been expected) in mathematics and statistics, a quite sharp decline in money, which is a little surprising, not much change in public finance, some rise in international economics. The proportion in economic fluctuations not surprisingly bulges in the Great Depression, although it is surprisingly high in the decade before. The proportion in war and defense economics likewise bulges in the period of the two world wars, but tails off very much in periods of peace. There is a rise in the proportion of the firm and a decline in industrial organization. The rise in the proportion in agriculture is quite striking, although it does peak in the thirties. The proportion in natural resources peaks about the same time and has been declining ever since. The proportion in labor economics has been declining and consumer economics has been fairly stationary with some ups and downs. The proportion in health, education and welfare has actually been declining until just recently, and regional planning has been increasing. The overall picture, however, is that of a very stable profession whose interests have not changed radically in 80 years. It is quite responsible to short-run changes in the economy, such as depressions and wars; it seems rather unresponsive to the long-run changes.

When we come to the distribution of effort of economists among segments of the economy, we do at least have something to compare this with in the proportion of the total economy which the particular segment occupies, as measured, for instance, by the proportion of the Gross National Product which each segment contributes. I am not suggesting, of course, that there should be a one-to-one correspondence here; some segments of the economy are intrinsically more interesting than others and have more difficult problems and one would certainly not expect to find the

Table 1
Percentage of Articles in the *Index of Economic Journals* (1886-1965), by Major Categories

	1886-1895	1896-1905	1906-1915	1916-1925	1926-1935	1936-1945	1946-1955	1956-1965	Totals	
Total no. of Articles	950	1,444	1,862	3,112	6,527	9,806	14,863	27,305	65,869	
1. Scope and Method	4.00	2.21	2.63	3.37	1.50	1.87	1.90	1.41	1.78	A
2. Economic Theory	12.21	7.76	8.81	8.26	10.39	12.56	14.45	17.49	14.40	A
3. Econ. Systems Planning	1.68	1.52	0.75	1.48	1.16	1.70	1.44	2.84	2.02	B
4. Hist. of Econ. Thought	7.26	6.03	4.56	3.18	4.19	4.36	3.66	2.99	3.64	A
5. Economic History	1.58	1.52	0.81	1.12	2.59	1.60	1.64	1.79	1.74	B
6. Contemporary Econ. Cond.	2.00	2.77	1.34	1.77	1.76	1.55	2.74	3.46	2.67	A
7. Mathematical Statistics	0.53	0.90	0.81	1.61	2.08	2.48	2.53	2.35	2.25	A
8. Social Accounting	3.26	1.04	1.61	2.60	2.38	2.03	2.78	2.99	2.64	B
9. Money, Credit & Banking	14.00	10.52	10.20	9.06	9.92	6.43	5.87	5.82	6.83	C
10. Public Finance	5.48	6.51	7.68	5.30	4.63	5.22	5.55	4.72	5.13	C
11. International Economics	7.15	8.73	6.45	8.23	8.20	6.14	9.35	9.02	8.44	C
12. Economic Fluctuations	0.21	0.21	0.32	3.21	3.27	1.88	2.20	1.92	2.06	B
13. War and Defense Econ.	0.42	1.18	2.31	7.17	0.25	9.78	2.21	0.51	2.63	C
14. Business Organizations	0.53	1.31	2.31	5.08	3.28	4.50	5.80	6.60	5.38	B
15. Industrial Organizations	13.58	20.85	21.80	14.65	17.42	13.54	11.45	11.61	13.10	B
16. Agriculture	3.37	5.67	5.64	9.54	12.73	9.54	9.91	8.72	9.32	C
17. Natural Resources	1.37	1.67	3.06	2.38	3.52	3.81	2.94	2.19	2.74	C
18. Population	1.89	1.73	1.72	1.06	1.52	0.95	0.95	0.89	1.04	B
19. Labor Economics	12.32	12.39	12.24	8.29	5.47	4.39	8.33	7.19	7.24	C
20. Consumer Economics	1.26	0.84	0.76	1.06	0.73	1.73	1.23	1.36	1.28	C
21. Health, Educ. & Welfare	4.63	2.56	2.90	0.80	1.29	1.66	1.13	1.17	1.36	C
22. Regional Planning	0.95	1.24	0.64	0.61	1.64	2.23	1.89	2.85	2.19	B
23. Unclassified	0.32	0.84	0.65	0.17	0.08	0.05	0.05	0.11	0.12	B

A = Narcissistic (22%), B = General Economics (33%), C = Segments of the Economy (45%).

distribution of intellectual resources among the segments of the economy to correspond exactly to the distribution of the Gross National Product or of National Income among the segments. Nevertheless, where there are large disproportions, questions can be raised as to why they exist. The distribution of intellectual effort, as we have seen, is a mixture of supply factors and demand factors, interest on the part of scientists constituting the demand and the interest on the part of the supporters of research constituting the supply. We can see both of these factors at work in explaining the major gaps between the proportion of resources devoted to study and the proportions of the economy.

Agriculture, as was noted earlier, is quite disproportionately studied, especially as we move towards the present. The very rapid decline in the proportion of the Gross National Product contributed by agriculture is not reflected in an equal decline in the amount of intellectual resources devoted to it. Interestingly, however, the fishing industry is much neglected (0.07 percent of total articles), especially as it presents some extremely interesting problems from the point of view of economists themselves.

At the other end of the scale from agriculture, we see things like education (0.025 percent), health (0.019 percent), and housing (0.051 percent) which have been quite scandalously neglected by economists. Education now represents more than 7 percent of the Gross National Product, by contrast with agriculture's 5 percent, and yet the output of works in the economics of education is still very small in spite of a recent upsurge. Part of the reason for this is again structural; for some reason, schools of education failed to develop departments of educational economics in the way that schools of agriculture developed departments of agricultural economics, perhaps because schools of education do not represent such an important political pressure group and also because educators themselves did not see the payoffs for latching on to the scientific revolution in the way that agriculturalists did. Whatever the reasons, the results are lamentable. One would not want to suggest, of course, that if the same intellectual resources had gone into education as have gone into agriculture in the last hundred years that education would also have developed the fantastic 6 percent per annum increase in labor productivity which we have seen in agriculture in the last 35 years. Still, it is hard to believe

Figure 2. Distribution of Articles in the *Index of Economic Journals*, (1881-1965)

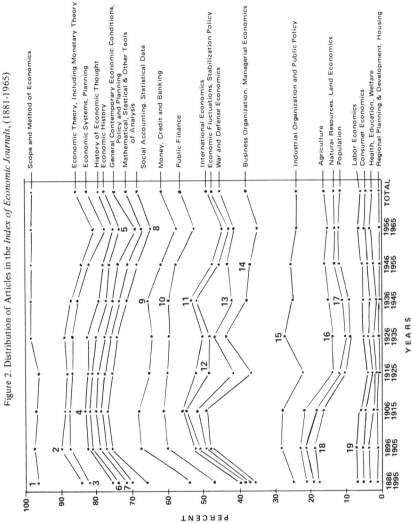

that a little more effort in the economics of education would not have had a high marginal productivity.

One sees a similar effect in medical economics. This is perhaps because these areas have been regarded as not quite worthy of the attention of economists, perhaps because they have been in the "grants sector" of the economy rather than in the market sector, and hence have been relegated to the dark underworld of doing good. Part of the difficulty here may also lie in the difficulties of measurement and the fact that the usual tools of the economists, which apply very well to the production functions of hogs, apply very poorly to the production functions of knowledge or of health.

Housing is an even more scandalous case. We might plead difficulties of measurement in the case of education and health, but housing, after all, is the production of perfectly straight-forward goods and services. Nevertheless, over 80 years there has been a mere 337 articles on housing (0.051 percent of the total) and what is worse, the interest in housing seems to have been declining ever since the 1920s. Economists were more interested in housing at the turn of the century than they are now. Here we see clear evidence of the enormous impact of demand on intellectual activity. The fact that the housing industry, by contrast with agriculture, has been anti-intellectual and anti-research, shows up dramatically in these figures.

Another much neglected area is that of war and defense economics, which rises as we might expect during the two world wars, fell to 0.51 percent of the total in the 1956-1965 decade, in spite of the fact that the war industry constitutes now about 9 percent of the GNP. The small amount of attention paid to consumer economics, only 1.36 percent of the total in 1956-65, in the light of the fact that personal consumption expenditure was 60 percent of the economy, again reflects a certain deficiency.

Table 2 shows the proportion of the total articles in a selected number of the second order classifications in which the time trend, or absence of it, is of particular interest. Thus, it is something of a shock to find that interest in the teaching of economics today is apparently less than it was in the first 50 years of the period, in spite of what seems like a good deal of current effort in the field. In economic theory, we notice the very marked increase in interest in aggregative economics and an equally

Table 2
Percentage of Articles in the *Index of Economic Journals* (1886-1965), by Selected Categories.

		1886-1895	1896-1905	1906-1915	1916-1925	1926-1935	1936-1945	1946-1955	1956-1965	Totals
1.3	Teaching of Economics	0.73	0.48	1.40	1.19	0.40	0.39	0.36	0.33	0.43
2.1	Value, Price, and Allocation Theory	2.73	2.56	3.44	3.12	4.15	4.82	5.28	5.58	4.98
2.2	Factors of Production & Distributive Shares	7.58	3.12	3.22	2.15	2.31	2.34	1.86	2.06	2.22
2.3	Aggregative & Monetary Theory, Cycles, Growth	0.85	1.25	1.13	2.09	3.68	4.85	6.32	8.93	6.38
3.2	Socialist & Communist Systems. Soviet Econ.	0.21	0.14	0.11	0.09	0.13	0.42	0.18	1.52	0.76
3.4	Cooperation. Cooperative Societies	1.26	1.04	0.27	0.77	0.14	0.18	0.17	0.19	0.24
4.8	Individuals (A-Z)	4.52	4.64	4.08	2.48	3.07	3.37	2.71	2.13	2.70
7.2	Statistical and Econometric Methods	0.21	0.90	0.75	1.55	1.88	2.18	1.78	1.55	1.67
9.2	Money. Currency. Monetary Standards	7.27	5.75	1.93	2.21	1.49	1.19	0.58	0.40	1.01
9.6	Prices. Inflation. Deflation	1.15	0.55	1.08	0.77	0.66	0.42	0.42	0.45	0.51
9.9	Monetary Policy. Central Banks	0.84	0.55	2.42	1.64	1.79	1.16	2.07	1.71	1.70
11.3	Balance of Payments. Mechanisms of Adjust.	2.10	0.97	1.18	3.79	3.82	2.95	5.71	4.17	4.09
12.2	Fluctuations. Forecasting	0.21	0.21	0.27	2.86	2.10	0.78	0.67	0.80	0.96
14.2	The Firm. The Businessman	0.43	0.55	1.18	1.45	1.06	0.72	1.21	1.12	1.07
14.5	Marketing	—	0.21	—	1.06	0.75	2.01	1.63	1.99	1.62
15.2	Market Structure and Behavior	0.84	2.14	1.34	1.09	1.10	1.38	1.20	1.66	1.42
15.6	Public Utilities. Electricity. Gas. Water	0.42	0.83	1.23	1.51	3.48	2.09	0.80	0.53	1.18
15.8	Transportation	5.37	5.96	8.54	3.79	3.69	2.13	1.73	1.76	2.43
17.2	Conservation	—	—	0.06	0.03	0.07	0.19	0.10	0.06	0.09
17.3	Land Economics	0.95	1.39	2.31	1.96	3.17	3.23	2.25	1.42	2.09
17.4	Forests	—	0.07	0.16	0.19	0.14	0.14	0.21	0.16	0.16
17.5	Fisheries	—	—	0.16	0.07	0.06	0.03	0.06	0.09	0.07
17.6	Water Resources	0.10	0.14	0.11	0.07	0.05	0.03	0.14	0.21	0.14
17.7	Minerals	0.32	0.07	0.05	0.03	0.01	0.07	0.07	0.11	0.08
20.2	Empirical Studies	1.05	0.70	0.70	1.00	0.62	1.50	1.16	1.21	1.14
21.4	Old Age Economics and Assistance	1.05	0.35	0.38	—	0.06	0.07	0.17	0.06	0.10
21.6	Unemployment Assistance	0.74	0.62	0.43	0.07	0.60	0.31	0.11	0.10	0.22
21.7	Medical Economics	0.31	0.14	0.53	0.06	0.12	0.09	0.24	0.19	0.18
21.8	Economics of Education	0.21	0.07	0.17	0.16	0.09	0.02	0.08	0.48	0.25
22.3	Urban-Metropolitan Studies	0.32	0.14	0.48	0.12	0.51	0.63	0.55	0.93	0.68
22.5	Housing	0.42	1.03	0.11	0.19	0.82	0.83	0.63	0.29	0.51

marked decline in interest in factors of production, with a slight increase, especially in recent years, in concern with socialist and communist systems and a not wholly surprising decline in concern with cooperation. The rise in studies of statistical and econometric methods is, of course, to be expected. Note, however, that these interests seem to have peaked some 30 years ago. The decline of studies of currency and monetary standards is very noticeable. The decline in interest in prices is perhaps more surprising. And it may come as a slight shock to members of the Chicago school to find that interest in monetary policy apparently peaked about 1910.

In international economics, the rise of concern with the balance of payments is rather surprising, and it is a little surprising also to find that interest in economic fluctuations peaked about 1920. We noted earlier the sharp fluctuations in interest in war and defense economics. It is curious that studies of the firm, indeed in business organization in general, which was rather low in the early years, rose sharply in the first decade of the century, and has remained fairly high ever since. It is a little sobering that the peak of interest in market structure was around 1900, long before the development of the theory of imperfect competition. The rise and decline of concern with public utilities is an odd phenomenon, reaching a sharp peak about 1930. Interest in transportation likewise has declined very sharply from its peak in the 1910 decade, which is a little surprising in the light of the fact that we feel such an acute crisis in this field at the moment.

In view of the current excitement about the environment, the very small interest in conservation, which peaked around 1940, and indeed in all the natural resource areas, is a striking comment on how ill-prepared we are to deal with the present environmental crisis. Even population studies were at their height in the first decade of this period and have declined fairly steadily ever since. It is sobering, too, to find that we were almost as much interested in empirical studies in consumer economics in the first decade as we were in the last of this whole period. We have already noted the shocking lack of interest in health, education and welfare, and what is even worse, the declining interest in this section. We were much more concerned with old age economics and unemployment insurance and even in medical economics around 1890 than we are now. The recent upsurge of studies in the economics of education has only brought it to double the minute proportion of the first decade. It is shocking to find that the interest in housing reached its peak about 1900, and that, in spite of the current to-do about urban metropolitan studies, interest has risen quite modestly since the early days.

There are many significant questions, of course, which cannot be answered by an analysis of this kind. It would require much more intricate and intensive analysis, for instance, to answer the question of the interrelation among these various parts of the structure. How far, for instance, did empirical studies modify the theories and the theories direct attention toward new empirical studies? This is perhaps one of the most interesting questions in the theory of epistemology, yet it is a question that is very hard to answer, especially with the rather superficial data of this paper.

One provocative conclusion, however tentative, is that the changes in the methodology of economics in this period did not very much affect its structure. The mathematical revolution in economics, of course, was underway even before the beginning of this period, with W.S. Jevons and Leon Walras coming in 1870, so that the period does not reflect the first transition from the more literary kind of economics and the use of mathematics grows very substantially during this whole period, something which this type of analysis underestimates. A count of the number of lines of mathematical symbols in these journals would, of course, be very interesting, but quite beyond the resources of this study. It would certainly reveal a very rapid increase, especially in the last 30 years. Refinement of mathematical techniques, however, does not seem to have changed very much the overall structure of the subject. It is perhaps too early to assess the impact of the computer, but up to now at any rate, the impact seems fairly small, again in terms of the actual structure of the subject. Up to now one would venture a guess that the impact of the computer has been in the direction of refinement rather than that of fundamental changes. This may not be true in the future.

Economics is one of the few sciences in which the structure of intellectual activity can be tested by any kind of structure in the outside world. However, an analysis of this kind could certainly be performed in the other social sciences and certainly would not be impossible in the field of medical research, where a comparison of the distribution of research effort against, say, the distribution of economic loss to disease, would be quite feasible and enormously interesting. There is room indeed for a large series of studies of this kind, but unfortunately there does not seem to be a great deal of motivation for such studies either on the side of supply or on the side of demand. Scientists, even social scientists, are somewhat averse to self-study, just as the universities are, perhaps because the results might be embarrassing, and these studies, at any rate up to now, have not become fashionable among the dispersers of research funds. An institute for the scientific study of science seems a long way off, yet perhaps there is hardly any other investment in which the granting agencies might indulge that would provide higher returns.

AFTER SAMUELSON,
WHO NEEDS ADAM SMITH?

The History of Political Economy,
3, 2 (Fall, 1971): 225-237.

After Samuelson, Who Needs Adam Smith?

I MUST apologize to my friend, Paul Samuelson, for using his name as a symbol. To have one's name become a symbol, however, is even greater fame than the Nobel Prize, so perhaps he will forgive me. What the symbol stands for in this case is modern economics, of which Samuelson's textbook,[1] and even more perhaps his *Foundations of Economic Analysis*,[2] are widely recognized as outstanding examples. I use Adam Smith, also, partly as a symbol as representing the ancients or the classics, but also as representing something quite unique in himself.

A great debate on the virtues of the ancients versus the moderns took place in Europe around the seventeenth century and indeed in China in the twentieth century, as to whether modern writers should be given inferior, equal, or superior standing with the ancients. There were those who argued that all good things had already been said long ago, and that therefore the modern writers were only feebler repetitions of the ancients. The moderns might be useful for divertissement or perhaps for commentary, but were in no sense a substitute for the writers of antiquity. We see this, of course, in the doctrine widely held in the Christian church, that the canon of the scriptures was irrevocably closed. We saw it also in secular education in the reverence for the Greek and the Latin authors in Europe, and also for the classical writers in China. Reverence for scriptures is by no means confined to Christianity; it is even stronger in Islam, is moderately strong in Hinduism and Buddhism, and, of course, is very strong indeed in Judaism and even in some forms of Marxism. Any-

---

1. Paul Samuelson, *Economics: An Introductory Analysis*, 8th ed. (New York, 1970).
2. Paul Samuelson, *Foundations of Economic Analysis* (New York, 1965).

where, indeed, that the basic revelation is regarded as given in the past and only to be interpreted in the present, we find this attitude.

This first position might well be said to be dominant until the rise of science, which was what really stimulated the great seventeenth-century debate. In literature and the arts the rise of a very high quality of modern art and literature created perhaps the second view that the ancients and moderns should be considered equals, and that Shakespeare, for instance, is neither better nor worse than the great Greek dramatists, for in this field the peak achievement of the human race at all periods has much the same quality. The implication of this view is, of course, that once the full potential of any system has been realized, there can be no long-term trend in its achievement. It may go down from the peaks and return to them, but it cannot transcend them. We may argue that between the Greek dramatists and Shakespeare, there was a long trough, but if the full potential of dramatic and literary creation was realized in the Greeks, the most we can hope to do in the future is to equal them.

The third view, which grew out of the enormous dynamic and success of science, is that man continually transcends his previous achievements and that therefore the moderns exceed the ancients and indeed make them obsolete, so that the moderns include all that the ancients have to say and there is really no reason to read the ancients any more, except for purposes of historical study. Mathematics perhaps is the ideal type of this process. In order to learn mathematics there is really no need to go back to Euclid or to Newton or Leibnitz or Gauss, unless one is specifically interested in the history of mathematical thought. To become a practical mathematician all one needs to do is read the latest textbooks, which embody all that the ancients presumably had to say and usually in a form that is more easily understood. Here indeed we seem to have a cumulative process, even though historically and in particular places there may be certain ups and downs; within it, each present embodies, as it were, all that is really necessary of the past.

There is an implicit assumption in this, however, which is rather startling. It is that there is no need to study the failures of the past, simply because all that we have to learn is embodied in the present scriptures. What we have here, therefore, is a curious reversal of the scriptural approach. The reversal holds that the latest book on the subject is, in fact, the scripture and all that went before it is really in the form of preliminary commentary, a Talmud, as it were, pointed towards future revelation.

Two possible concepts which may be of use in resolving this great debate of the ancients versus the moderns should be mentioned. The first of these is an old one, described by Robert Merton in his inimitable, more than half-serious spoof of scholarship, *On the Shoulders of Giants*,[3] as "Otsogery" (OTSOG for "on the shoulders of giants"). This is the idea that modern man can see further into reality and can achieve more because he stands on the shoulders of the ancients. Thus, the question of the relative intrinsic merit of the ancients versus the moderns is quietly shelved and we can pay all the respects to the ancients we like and still acknowledge that the moderns know more and see further. Merton, incidentally, traces this idea far back into the Middle Ages. It is implied indeed in Christian thought in the idea that the New Testament writers stand on the shoulders of the Old Testament prophets. There is a magnificent stained-glass window in the transept at Chartres which illustrates this point, but we find the same idea in secular writings regarding the achievements of the moderns versus the Greeks and the Romans in European literature. It would be interesting to see if this idea ever occurred to the Indians or the Chinese, for it is perhaps one of the key concepts which legitimated the rise of modern science.

Another concept important in this regard, which I must confess to having made up myself, although it seems so obvious that I can hardly believe that it has not been thought of before,[4] might be called the Principle of the Extended Present. Even in mathematics the present is not a single point in time, but is rather an historical range within which active communication is taking place. In any discipline we find controversy and interaction so that the present has to be defined by the period within which this interaction takes place, as indicated perhaps by the dates of the footnoted references. If the earliest reference in a piece of work, for instance, is to a date ten years ago, then we can suppose that ten years is about the length of its extended present, as this is the period within which intellectual action and

3. Robert K. Merton, *On the Shoulders of Giants* (New York, 1965).
4. This might almost be called the SNOLG, "sticking neck out like giraffe," principle, a companion to OTSOG.

reaction take place. An author whose work is commented on belongs to the extended present, even though he may in fact be dead or may have lived many years ago.

There is a certain difference, of course, between the interactions of living authors, which may be reciprocal, in the sense that A comments on B and B comments on A's comment on B and so on, and the interactions with dead authors, which in a certain sense can only be one-way. Adam Smith says something to me, but unfortunately I cannot say anything to Adam Smith. Even here, however, the dead author may exist as a present subject of debate, that is, A may say something about C, who is dead, and B may answer on C's behalf, saying that A was quite mistaken about C. In this sense, C is in some rather odd sense a part of the conversation, even though he is not participating in it directly.

The length of the extended present differs in different disciplines, and even from different periods, as fashions change. History, indeed, may be regarded as a continuously extended present—continuously extended, that is, into the past, so that the historical present may easily cover thousands of years. In mathematics and the physical sciences, the present may be a relatively short period of time, in the sense that the interaction is only with the world of nature as it exists at the moment, or with work that has been done in the very recent past.

Where then does economics fit into this spectrum of human activity? The question is not so easy to answer as might be thought at first glance, for it raises all sorts of difficult questions about the nature of economic knowledge, about the nature of the learning process in economics, and even perhaps about the teaching of economics. At one extreme we have the scriptural view, that the truths of economics were revealed through Adam Smith and Ricardo, or perhaps through Karl Marx, and that all we have to do now is to find out what these authors really meant. There is a touch of this in nineteenth-century attitudes towards Adam Smith and more than a touch of it in even some quite contemporary attitudes in various parts of the world towards Karl Marx. In Japan, especially, one finds talmudic Marxist scholars who pore over the sacred documents and interpret them page by page and line by line. The astonishing persistence of scripturalism in the world in many different forms indicates that it has a real niche in the ecosystem and that it is one means of resolving uncertainty and establishing legitimacy. In economics, however, the extreme scriptural position is very rarely taken today, even by Marxists, although a strong residue of respect for the ancients may well continue.

At the other extreme we have what might be called the antihistorical school, summed up in the classic words of one economist, whose name I regret I have not been able to trace, that ''he was not interested in the wrong opinions of dead men.'' This presumes that economics is like mathematics in that knowledge about it grows continuously and without loss, so that the moderns contain all that was in the ancients and then some; there is really no point in studying the ancients at all, and therefore, the later the textbook the better. My position, I must confess, occupies a wide Aristotelian mean between these two extremes. I have to confess also to a certain tendency to Otsogery, the belief that we do, in fact, stand on the shoulders of giants.

In terms of sheer human accomplishment, for instance, the achievement of Adam Smith, considering where he started from, is very remarkable. In a certain sense *The Wealth of Nations* is a scripture, simply because in that book economics took shape as a total body of ideas. A large amount of work in economics since then has, in fact, been talmudic, in the sense that it has clarified, expounded, expanded, mathematized, and translated into modern language, ideas which were essentially implicit in *The Wealth of Nations*. The whole of Walrasian, Marshallian, and Hicksian price theory, for instance, is clearly implicit in Adam Smith's concept of natural price, and in this respect one wonders whether any basic new ideas have been added to Adam Smith, in spite of all the elegance and the refinements which the years have brought.

Similarly, in the theory of economic development, one sometimes doubts whether all the modern refinements and mathematical models are much more than talmudic exercises on the fundamental insight of Adam Smith regarding the division of labor, the extent of the market, the impact of accumulation, and the effects of rising knowledge. In monetary theory and macroeconomics it must be confessed that Adam Smith's achievements look less impressive. Living as he did in an age of relative price stability and full employment, it is hardly surprising that he did not appreciate the pathological deviations of which a monetary system is capable and which were really only revealed in the twentieth century. On this score, we clearly have to add Keynes to the classics, although even now Adam Smith's criticism of the liquidity-preference theory of interest at least can make one pause.

Ricardo's achievement is less impressive than Adam Smith's because Ricardo is very clearly standing on the shoulders of a giant. Nevertheless, as a model, particularly of the equilibrium of the price system, he does go beyond Adam Smith and his work represents what might almost be called an aesthetic achievement of remarkable quality. Ricardo, indeed, is Delphic enough to be an admirable subject for talmudic exposition. He did not have Adam Smith's remarkable facility in the English language, and whatever revelation he may have had in his mind comes through a heavy filter of inadequacy of verbal or mathematical expression.

Marx is in another category, simply because for a large part of the world, *Das Kapital* is a scripture, and hence the task of expounding and explaining its revelations is virtually endless. Capitalist economists may feel, of course, that this is a secondary stream or a diversion from the main development of economics. Nevertheless, it can hardly be denied that it is economics and that it is large in quantity.

The question of whether economists who are not primarily historians, but who are practicing their art, trade, science, or whatever it is, need to pay any attention to the classical economists or to any writers of the past depends on one's estimate of the extent to which the evolutionary potential of these past authors has been realized or exhausted. Everything which partakes, however modestly, in the character of scripture inevitably carries with it an element of revelation, which I define in secular terms as the creation of evolutionary potential. A revelation, in other words, whether in biology or in social systems, is an event or cluster of events which gives rise to a "phylum," that is, a tree of genetic change through time which goes back to the original revelation itself. In these terms there seems not the slightest doubt that Adam Smith represents revelation, for a large phylum of thought and intellectual development can be traced directly back to him. Social systems, furthermore, particularly after the invention of writing, possess a property which biological systems do not: the phyla of social systems are capable of direct or genetic interaction with their originator.

Thus, in biological systems there is no possibility of the first vertebrate—whatever it was, it has long since disappeared—mating with one of its innumerable ultimate progeny. In social phyla, however, this is quite possible, simply because the original impulse is embodied in the genetic form of the scripture, which is capable of interacting at any time with the living representatives of the phylum. Thus, the Christian phylum has constantly been renewed and given additional evolutionary vitality because of the constant interaction between the Church and the Bible, the Bible representing, as it were, the original social mutation, or rather a record of that mutation, which produced the phylum in the first place. Similarly, it is not at all fanciful to think of economics as a phylum going back to Adam Smith, who in turn, of course, goes back to Newton and Descartes, and in which, again, the evolutionary impulse may be constantly renewed by "mating," as it were, with the original source.

Thus, a book like *The Wealth of Nations* is "seminal" in almost the literal sense of the word, in that it can easily play the same role in the development of the phylum of economics in the minds of economists, as, shall we say, frozen semen from some distant ancestor which might be used to fertilize a living egg and so produce direct intervention from its original source into the course of the biological phylum. Works like *The Wealth of Nations,* therefore, are inevitably part of an extended present, which shows no signs of coming to an end, in the sense that one can still go back to Adam Smith even after many rereadings and find insights which one has never noticed before and which may have a marked impact on one's own thought. Any writer who is capable of affecting the thought of people who are living and thinking after he is dead may be said to be seminal in this sense and also part of the extended present.

The principle seems to me pretty clear that as long as intellectual evolutionary potential remains yet undeveloped in the early writers, the modern writers are a complement rather than a substitute; that is, we need both Samuelson and Adam Smith. This may not be true, however, of all aspects of economics. If the evolutionary potential of an earlier writer is completely fulfilled in the later, then there is not much point in devoting much time and attention to the earlier one, unless, of course, we are historians. In the accumulation of economic data and the development of statistical methodology we may very well be in an area where evolutionary potential tends to be realized right away, and hence the modern textbook is an almost complete substitute for the study of earlier writers. When it comes, however, to ideas, models, insights, all that which indeed makes the difference between the truly great writer and the mediocre one, we are operating in the field where the extended present is much longer and the modern writers are not substitutes for the earlier ones.

These considerations have considerable applications for the teaching of economics. Here again we find both theories and practices which differ very considerably and which go back to precisely the divergent views about epistemology that we have been outlining above.

At the one extreme there is the ultrahistorical approach which was characteristic, for instance, of the teaching of economics at the University of Edinburgh when I was there as an assistant in the middle thirties. Perhaps this was partly because one passed the tombs of Adam Smith and of David Hume as one walked up to the University, and in the presence of these sacred places, a scriptural approach to economics is hardly surprising. Nevertheless, I thought at the time that the results were little short of catastrophic. The student first learned what was wrong with Adam Smith and all the things in which he was wrong and confused, then he went on to learn what was the matter with Ricardo, then what was the matter with John Stuart Mill, and then what was the matter with Marshall. Many students never learned anything that was right at all, and I think emerged from the course with the impression that economics was a monumental collection of errors.

At the other extreme is the antihistorical school, which is now common in the United States, where the history of thought is regarded as a slightly depraved entertainment, fit only for people who really like medieval Latin, so that one can become a full-fledged, chartered Ph.D. economist without ever reading anything that was published more than ten years ago. If the ultrahistorical method leads to mystified and defeated students who simply abandon economics, the antihistorical method leads to the development of slick technicians who know how to use computers, run massive correlations and regressions, but who do not really know which side of anybody's bread is buttered, who are incredibly ignorant of the details of economic institutions, who have no sense at all of the blood, sweat, and tears that have gone into the making of economics and very little sense of any reality which lies beyond their data. We seem to be producing a generation of economists now whose main preoccupation consists of analyzing data which they have not collected and who have no interest whatever in what might be called a data-reality function, that is, in what extent a set of data corresponds to any significant reality in the world. The antihistorical approach, furthermore, leads to a rejection of any information which cannot easily be fitted onto punched cards or their equivalents, and hence results in a distortion of the information input in the direction of that which can easily be quantified and away from those intangibles and imponderables which may nevertheless be an essential part of reality. The antihistorical school, furthermore, leads into what I have called *Ptolemaic* economics, that is, an endless modification of variables and equations in regions of strongly diminishing returns in the knowledge function, and still sharper diminishing returns in the significance function. We seem to be engaged in finding out more and more numbers which mean less and less, and the parallel with the Ptolemaic epicycles is not difficult to draw.

Here again there is surely a wide Aristotelian mean which includes both Samuelson, with the modern technical economics which he symbolizes and the application of this technical economics to the clearer understanding of what the classical economists are implying, but never quite saying, and also a reading of the past to develop some concepts of an extended present simply because past writers have things to say which no present writer is saying.

There is, of course, a case for history as such, and for the history of thought as such, simply on the grounds that it is interesting, that the record of the struggles and the errors through which man has progressed to a greater understanding of himself and of his world is itself an exciting story which can be enjoyed for its own sake, quite apart from any further utility. We can also argue, however, that the study of history has utility, in that one of the great purposes of formal education is to give the student a sense of an extended present and indeed an extended place beyond his own backyard and his own immediate needs, emotions, and experiences. It is the great message of formal education that experience is a very bad teacher and that, especially as we come to deal with larger and more complex systems, as we do in society, we must develop an organized information input from a long historical present. It is a mark of intellectual poverty to know only one's own time and place.

One of the principal problems in learning indeed is how to destroy the illusions of perspective, the belief that faraway things are in fact small. We do this in the physical world through movement, which soon reveals to us that our own immediate view of the world, if taken literally, would be an illusion, and that far-off things only *seem* small. There is, of course, in social systems a perspective which is not wholly illusion, in the sense that the near are dear and the remote are irrelevant. The call for relevancy, however, cannot avoid the question, "Relevant for what, and for whom?" The society which produces people who have no sense of at least the partial illusion of time perspective is certainly headed for disaster.

Our approach to the seminal writers of the past, however, must be a little different from the conventional history-of-thought approach if we are really to bring them into our own extended present and to make them speak to us directly. The danger with the history-of-thought approach, as I have noted earlier, is that it lays the greatest stress on what was wrong with earlier writers rather than what was right with them. Furthermore, as history, it lays stress quite rightly on the time sequences, that is, who influenced whom and in what way, and also on the environmental connections, that is, how far the current environment, for instance, of Adam Smith or of the English classical economists, was responsible for the particular theories and views of the world which they produced. Both of these are entirely legitimate interests. There is a case, however, for an additional approach to the great writers of the past, which is to treat them quite directly as part of our extended present and study them from the point of view of what they have to say to us today, rather than from the point of view of what their place is in the historical record. I am not suggesting this as a substitute for the history-of-thought approach, but as a complement to it, and indeed as a complement to ordinary textbook teaching of economics.

I have taught for some years now a course called Great Books

of Economics. I am a little uneasy with the title, for there are overtones of undue reverence or bibliolatry in such an approach. Nevertheless, my experience has been that the study of, for instance, Adam
Smith's *The Wealth of Nations,* Ricardo's *Principles of Political
Economy and Taxation,* and Marx's *Capital,* at least in its condensed
version, is of great and continuing interest both for the teacher and,
one hopes, for the student. There are several benefits of such an
approach. One is that the student gets a certain feeling for a peak
achievement of the human mind. The great books are valuable because they give us some inkling of the way in which a really exceptional intellect works. Most of the things which students have to
read in college are after all the product of minds, to put it gently,
which are below the peaks of human experience. A student whose
only acquaintance is with mediocre books and with mediocre minds
has lost something of the sense of potentiality of the human organism,
even though we may only dimly perceive what that potentiality is.

Another great advantage of studying the great books is that they
expose the students to whole areas of thought which have become
unfashionable and hence help him to transcend limitations which are
imposed on him by the fashions of his own time. This is particularly
true with *The Wealth of Nations.* Where, for instance, in modern
economics is there a discussion of the impact of economic development
on the relative price structure? Or where is there a theoretical discussion of the economics of jurisprudence or of religion or of education or imperialism, or all the other delightful things which Adam
Smith discusses in Books IV and V? Reading Book V of *The Wealth
of Nations* can indeed be a revelation to the student who has previously
seen economics only in the narrowest terms of marginal analysis and
commodity markets. Adam Smith may well be considered not merely
the founder of economics as a scientific phylum, but even of social
science in general.

One of the problems of a course of this kind is that the books which
are read have to be reasonably self-contained and understandable
without elaborate antecedents. Fortunately, this is true of *The
Wealth of Nations.* Even though it would no doubt be helpful to have
a thorough knowledge of the mercantilists, the polemic elements in
The Wealth of Nations are in a sense peripheral, and Adam Smith's
own account of the mercantilist doctrines, though biased, is at least

clear enough that the student can understand it. Having read Adam Smith, one can easily go on to Ricardo, who is not really intelligible without Adam Smith, and having read Ricardo one can go on to Marx, so that these three authors provide a remarkably self-contained body of reading.

Unfortunately, not all the great books are equally suitable from this point of view. One year, for instance, in this course we read Keynes's *General Theory,* which was a minor disaster; it simply cannot be understood at all without an extensive knowledge of nineteenth-century economics which the students did not have and which the teacher was hard put to supply.

There are, I am sure, many methods of teaching a course of this kind. One device which I have found particularly useful, however, is to distribute to the students in advance a set of comments and questions on the reading which they are doing. Unless a student is constantly asking himself questions as he reads, he is likely to miss the significance of what he is reading, especially if it is couched in such easy-flowing and delightful language as that of *The Wealth of Nations,* or even when he has to struggle with the crabbed English of Ricardo. The class periods can then be devoted to discussion of the questions which the students have already received and presumably thought about. It is possible, I think, for students who have never had any economics before to get a good deal out of a course of this kind, although, of course, it is very much easier for students who have already had Samuelson or some reasonable equivalent.

The place of the great books in formal education is by no means confined to economics, and this is indeed a very puzzling and important question as we struggle with the expansion of knowledge and the increasing difficulty of transmitting it to the next generation. I am frankly not in favor of a total "great books" approach, except in a few special cases and for exceptional students, simply on the grounds that it takes too much time and that economy in education is one of the most important problems we face. Insofar as the modern is a substitute for the ancient, the modern should be substituted, and there is a continued need for work on condensing the essentials of modern knowledge. Nevertheless, one can see a great many fields in which a limited "great books" approach of the kind I am recommending would be appropriate. In literature, of course, there is very little else. Books about Shakespeare are no substitute for Shakespeare. In the other social sciences, there is a strong case for a modified great books approach, even when there aren't quite so many great books as there are in economics. Nevertheless, a political scientist who had never read Machiavelli or Locke or even John Stuart Mill is surely intellectually impoverished. Even in the biological sciences those who have never read, shall we say, D'Arcy Thompson's *On Growth and Form* or Lotka's *Elements of Mathematical Biology* or even Darwin are again in danger of becoming mere technicians. Even the mathematician's time might not be wholly wasted by reading Euclid. This balance between ancient and modern is hard to achieve and it obviously differs from field to field. Nevertheless, it remains one of the most interesting and important problems within the university curriculum.

ENVIRONMENT AND ECONOMICS

Environment, Resources, Pollution and Society, W. W. Murdock, ed., Sinauer Assoc., Inc., Stamford, Conn. (1971): 359-367.

Environment and Economics

Spaceship Earth and Economic Growth

We are now in a long transitional period in which our image of man's relationship to his environment is changing. We are ridding ourselves of the notion that we live on a physical frontier. But we still have a long way to go in making the moral, political, and psychological adjustments implied in this transition. In particular, economists have not come to grips with the consequences of the transition from an open to a closed system. But the closed earth requires a closed economy — a "spaceman economy" — as opposed to what I have called the open, "cowboy economy."

In an economic system materials flow from mines and so on (leaving a noneconomic reservoir), pass into what one might call the econosphere, and then leave it as effluents into a second noneconomic reservoir. At any one moment the econosphere can be thought of as the total capital stock — all the people, objects, and organizations involved in the system of economic exchange. The cowboy economy typifies the frontier attitudes of recklessness and exploitation. Consumption and production are considered

good things and the success of the economy is measured by the amount of THROUGHPUT deriving in part from reservoirs of raw materials, processed by "factors of production," and passed on in part as output to the sink of pollution reservoirs. The Gross National Product (GNP) roughly measures this throughput.

In the spaceman economy, by contrast, reservoirs of materials are finite — the reservoirs for pollution are finite and cannot accept input too quickly and still remain in equilibrium. Man is seen to be in a circular rather than a linear ecological system. Then throughput is considered something to be minimized rather than maximized; it is the COST of maintaining the capital stock, rather than a measure of economic success. It is with this in mind that I have suggested calling the GNP the GROSS NATIONAL COST.[1] It should be obvious, but does not appear to be generally accepted, that income is not the real measure of economic welfare at all. Economic welfare is measured by the conditions of the person or the society, the extent, quality and complexity of the bodies, minds, and things in the system; income is simply the unfortunate cost of keeping up with decay. Gadgets and clothes wear out, one has to consume food and gasoline, which comsumption is simply decay. It also follows that the bigger the economic system — the capital stock — the more it decays and the more we have to produce simply to maintain it.

When we have developed the economy of the spaceship earth, in which man will persist in equilibrium with his environment, the notion of the GNP will simply disintegrate. We will be less concerned with income-flow concepts and more with capital-stock concepts. Then technological changes that result in the maintenance of the total stock with LESS throughput (less production and consumption) will be a clear gain.

The spaceman economy is some way off in the future. How imminent it is is not clear, though the accumulating evidence of the physical consequences of the closed earth suggest that we should evolve to it soon. There is, indeed, evidence from an analysis of the GNPs of different countries that the very rich countries may approach an equilibrium state naturally, though I would not put too much faith in this natural process! If one plots the logarithm of the RATE OF INCREASE of per capita GNP against the actual per capita GNP itself, for all the countries where information is available, for the period 1900-1960, we find two interesting facts. The first is that most countries in the temperate zone are represented by points lying on a straight line sloping downwards, with Japan at the top left (10 percent annual increase in per capita GNP) and the United States at the bottom right (less than 2 percent annual increase).[2] That is, the richer a country is, the slower it grows economically. If the trend continued into the future, all these countries would stop economic growth when they are two or three times richer per capita than the United States is now. Before then, though, we will surely have been forcibly stopped by our limited environment.

The second fact is that the other group of nations, almost all in the tropics, occupy a roughly circular area in the bottom lefthand corner of the graph. They are poor and they are almost not growing in per capita wealth as fast as the rich countries. They seem to have a sort of Brownian movement. This suggests that there is a "development line" − if you're rich you get richer, but more and more slowly − but if you are in the underdeveloped group you're not going anywhere.

Economics and Environmental Degradation

If the transition to a spaceman economy is some way off in the future, the problems of environmental degradation are of the here and now. The environment of a person consists of all those objects which are relevant to him − the chair he sits in, the clothes he wears, the room he occupies, the meal he is eating, the air he breathes, the sounds he is hearing, and even, we might add, the vast internal environment of his memories and images. The environment of mankind is the sum of the environments of all individuals.

The environment, whether personal or total, can be divided roughly into two subsets − the ECONOMIC ENVIRONMENT and the NONECONOMIC ENVIRONMENT. The economic environment consists of those items which participate in exchange, actually or potentially, or which are valued in some sense in terms of exchangeables and hence appear in somebody's balance sheet. The distinction is not wholly clear because many noneconomic items in the environment affect the value of economic ones and vice versa. Thus, the starry sky is pretty clearly part of the noneconomic environment. Nevertheless, we may be prevented from enjoying it by smog or we may have to pay to go someplace where it can be seen. The economic environment can be divided roughly into private goods and public goods. Private goods are appropriated by individuals; the enjoyment of such a good on the part of one individual precludes its enjoyment by another. Public goods, like roads at low traffic densities, can be enjoyed by one person without excluding anybody else. Goods may be either positive, that is, productive of utilities or welfare, or negative, that is, productive of disutilities or illfare, in which case it is perhaps simpler to call them "bads."

Concern about environmental quality is related closely to the production of bads, both public and private. Bads, in general, are more difficult to deal with than goods and it is not difficult to see why. An individual who owns a private good has strong incentives to administer it wisely and carefully, for any benefits which come from such wise administration accrue directly to him. This is indeed the origin of the "magic of property" which is observable in all societies, even in socialist societies. The peasants' private plots in the Soviet Union are much better cared for and much more productive than the collective farms, simply because of the marginal incentives involved. Bads, however, unless they can be turned into goods, are nobody's business. The private incentive is to get rid of private bads as cheaply and unobtrusively as we can. We make bargains, of course, about both goods and bads. Thus, we pay garbage men to dispose of our garbage, which thus has a negative price. In the exchange of goods, each party is concerned to present his goods in an attractive and well-organized form. There is very little incentive to present garbage in an attractive and well-organized form. If we produce bads, we simply want to get rid of them as quickly and as cheaply as possible.

The difficulty of organizing bads is brought out very clearly when we look at the legal system, a considerable part of which is devoted to establishing property, or at least responsibility, in the production of bads. Thus, the law of torts, which enables us to sue for damages, is in effect a device for making A pay for the bad which he has forced B to accept. If your car runs into my house and so deteriorates the quality of my domestic environment, I can sue you for this and in a great many cases obtain compensation. The identification of the producer of the bad, the setting of its price, and forcing the producer to pay for it is, therefore, a main function of this branch of the law. Nobody, however, is very satisfied with the operation of the system as it stands. Many bads are produced for which the producer is not penalized and the "consumer" is not compensated. The system is extremely expensive, so that the costs of obtaining compensation often eat up a good part of the compensation itself; as a result the system operates better on the side of penalties than it does on the side of compensations. The greatest difficulty of the system, however, arises because of the frequent difficulty in identifying the producer of the bads. In a great many cases we have a system which produces bads fairly randomly, so that it is extremely hard to apportion the blame for their production, as it is a result of the system as a whole rather than of the action of any particular individual within it. Under the simple law of torts, anybody who receives a bad for which nobody else is to blame is not compensated unless he is insured. Insurance, while it helps to spread the risks and is the obvious device for seeing that the person who suffers a bad does in fact get compensated for it, is also costly and where it is not universal may act quite inequitably.

The legal system continues to struggle with these problems. We see, for instance, in the establishment of special laws for workman's compensation a failure of the traditional law of torts in the industrial relationships. An injury to a workman may be part of the inherent risks of the system and may not be the "fault" of his employer. Hence, the system as a whole is assessed for responsibility of the production of these bads, so that suffering can be compensated. Automobile insurance is another area where the allocation of blame is often so difficult that some states, such as New York, are experimenting with a "no fault" insurance plan in which the emphasis is on the compensation of the sufferer rather than the penalization of the guilty. In the criminal law, on the other hand, the shoe seems to be on the other foot. All the emphasis is on the penalization of the guilty, and as a result there are often grave injustices done to the victim. These considerations may seem at first sight a little remote from problems of the environment, but it is important to recognize that a deterioration of the environment, which is the production of a special kind of bads, is part of a much larger problem of the production of bads in general and cannot really be separated from the larger problem.

It is difficult enough to organize society for the proper handling of private bads, but the public bads are still more difficult to deal with, simply because of the high level of political and social organization required. Similarly, public goods are more difficult to deal with than private goods, because they too require a level of political and social organization and even social self-consciousness far beyond what is required for the adequate production of private goods. In the case of public bads, the law of torts is no remedy at all. If a factory pollutes the air which I breathe and induces disease or dirties my clothes so that they have to be cleaned, it is usually not worthwhile for me as a single individual to try to sue the factory owners for so small a part of the total damage. The suppression of public bads, like the provision of public goods, requires political organization. It cannot be done through the market mechanism alone, although the market mechanism can be used as a supplementary device. There must ultimately be an invocation of the police power and the legitimated threat system of the law. There is a further question of constitutionality as to how we protect ourselves against bad government, in this case, the failure of government to eliminate public bads or to provide public goods. This is largely a matter of developing a feedback process from those people who are affected by government decisions and by legal enactments, into the process which produces these decisions and enactments. This indeed is the major justification of democratic institutions. The problem is complicated, however, by the fact that government, political, and legal institutions have a certain tendency to produce public bads, as well as to suppress them, and there are very few legal and constitutional remedies for this. If, for instance, my government threatens my life and property through an irresponsible and foolish foreign policy, there is very little I can do about this in the way of legal remedies. Constitutional remedies are supposed to be the answers to problems of this kind, but very often are not.

Before we can be very successful in constructing political and social institutions which will suppress the production of bads, both public and private, we must ask ourselves the more fundamental question as to what subsystems within the general framework of society are in fact productive of bads. The problem is particularly acute in the case of what might be called cumulative bads, in which we have a process that accumulates negative capital goods and which continually increases the total stock of bads in the society. The concern about the environment, for instance, which is so strong at the moment, arises mainly because there is a perception that certain elements of the environment, such as the atmosphere and the oceans, are deteriorating in quality, that is, are becoming structures with more bads and fewer goods in them from the point of view of the welfare of mankind. The environmental question, therefore, resolves itself very largely into the question of the identification of deteriorating dynamic systems, that is, systems within society which go from bad to worse rather than from bad to better. We cannot, of course, judge these systems in terms of simple

market values alone, although market values are a legitimate part of the total valuation process. We are dealing here, however, with the total environment, of which the economic environment is only a part. One of the major difficulties in assessing whether a system is in fact deteriorating is the difficulty of finding some index of value which measures, or at least assesses in some way, the direction in which the system is moving. For most of these cases, we do not really have to have very exact quantitative information. We do, however, need to know "which way is up" and even a question as simple as this is often quite difficult to answer. It is possible, however, to identify a number of subsystems within society which are likely to produce a deteriorating dynamic. Each of these may have different properties and may have to be treated differently. Any system which produces bads is suspect, although, of course, the production of bads in itself does not necessarily mean that the system is a deteriorating one, as the production of bads may be more than counterbalanced by the production of a larger quantity of goods. The following seven systems within society are suggested as good candidates at least for classification as deteriorating systems.

1. MALEVOLENCE. If A is malevolent towards B, the diminution in B's welfare increases A's utility. Hence, A may produce bads for B, that is, A may diminish B's welfare and diminish the quality of B's environment. If B retaliates and produces bads in turn for A, we may get a mutually deteriorating system. Unfortunately, malevolence frequently tends to produce malevolence, so that it does tend to escalate. Benevolence, by contrast, in which A's perception of an increase in B's welfare increases his utility, also tends to escalate and tends to increase the production of goods.

2. TRIBUTE. A may threaten to produce bads for B unless B gives A goods. B's goods are then given to A as tribute. If B fails to come through, A may carry out the threat, and so may increase the production of bads. Tribute does not necessarily imply malevolence, that is, A may not feel malevolent towards B. He simply wants his goods. On the other hand the use of the threat

system to extract tribute frequently creates malevolence in the victim, and malevolence in the victim may easily produce malevolence in the threatener. The deteriorating quality of the slave system and its low horizon of development is probably mainly due to this factor.

3. DETERRENCE. Tribute, which is essentially the threat-submission system, often tends to pass into defiance, or into deterrence if the victim refuses to submit. Deterrence is a system of threat-counterthreat in which each party threatens to produce bads for the other unless the other refrains from producing bads for the first party. Deterrence may be stable in the short-run, though even then it produces implicit bads by withdrawing resources in the production of threat capability. Deterrence furthermore cannot be stable; otherwise it could cease to deter. Hence it is always tending to break down into the production of bads. Submission and tribute may sometimes be less costly to the victim than deterrence, but the situation is complicated by the fact that threat may not merely be to the goods of the persons involved but also to their identities. Deterrence then tends to yield more satisfactory identities than submission. It is a more equalitarian system in the sense that the threat-counterthreat relationship is one of approximate equals, whereas the threat-submission system is a relationship of unequals. Consequently, there is a tendency for deterrence to be preferred even when it is much more costly than tribute. The international system with its constant tendency to break down into war is, of course, the most striking example of a deterrence relationship and is probably the greatest single threat to the environment.

4. EXTERNALITIES. This is the more traditionally "economic" source of production of bads. It occurs when bads are produced in a process of joint production along with goods that do not have to be paid for in accordance with their negative value, that is, the bads do not form part of the COST of the operation. Under circumstances in which the producer has to bear the cost of the bads, too many resources would be devoted to those processes of production which produce these bads. Air and water pollution from business enterprises are a good case in point. If

business had to pay an assessed value for all the bads which they produced, they would very soon tend to move towards processes of production which produced fewer bads and more goods, and processes of production which produced such expensive bads that they were no longer profitable would tend to disappear.

5. INVISIBILITIES. I just made up this term, as it is badly needed. Invisibilities are the production of bads which are so small, in the case of the individual producer, that they are not noticed, but which cumulatively may be very large. Automobile exhaust and DDT are examples. These are very close to being "public bads"; just as a public good is something which I can use without diminishing your enjoyment of it, so a public bad is something from which my withdrawal will not noticeably affect your discomfort. If a single person stops driving a car, this doesn't do much for the smog problem.

6. SELF–GENERATING OR ARTIFICALLY GENERATED DEMANDS. In any realistic appraisal of the social system we must go beyond the conventional assumption of economics that the preferences, especially of private persons, are givens of the system which are not subject to further discussion. In fact, of course, preferences are learned and because of this it is legitimate to examine the learning process with a view to detecting possible perversities in it. Consumption that is addictive, such as tobacco or heroin consumption, and which has adverse physiological effects, obviously comes under this category of perverse degenerative demands, and almost everyone will agree that it should be controlled in some way. A more difficult and touchy case is that of fashion and the perversion of taste through fashion. The demand to be fashionable in itself would seem quite legitimate, as it is an expression of the identity of an individual with a community. A fashion for virtue, however, may satisfy the desire to be fashionable and is obviously to be preferred to a fashion for vice. There are tastes also which have external diseconomies, like the taste for being an alcoholic, which produces a good deal of misery for other people. A very different question is the taste for sensation and nonsense. The sort of taste which produced Hitler with his enormous external disecon-

omies, or even the taste which perverts science into sensationalism, can legitimately be recognized as candidates for inclusion in deteriorating systems.

7. POPULATION. This is the classical Malthusian problem of the pressure of population on the environmental base. The larger the number of people in any given environment, at least beyond a certain point, the more likely is the environment to deteriorate. A crowded one-room shack is more likely to deteriorate than a suburban dwelling. A crowded country produces pollution of all sorts which is hard to control. Population pressure should perhaps be classified more as an underlying condition which makes deteriorating systems of other kinds more likely rather than a deteriorating system itself. Insofar as unrestricted increase in population is a direct producer of deteriorating quality of human life, however, we can perhaps justify classifying this with the others.

Each of these systems requires quite different means for its control. Malevolence control is very little understood. The church and the family try to do something about it, not always very successfully. One grave difficulty here is that a common malevolence towards a particular object is very often a source of a feeling of community, especially in the national state. Consequently, the national state often actively encourages malevolence towards those other states which it regards as its enemies. Any organization indeed which is bound together by a common enmity, whether this is a sect, a political party, a class, or a nation, or even a philosophical school, is apt to develop malevolence towards its enemy and this malevolence is frequently reciprocated. Furthermore, organizations and communities which are built on a common malevolence towards an external enemy frequently find that the malevolence generated creates a frame of mind in which malevolence is easily turned inward in factionalism and personal hatred within a community itself. The problem of control of malevolence, therefore, is doubly difficult because many of the agencies which ought to control it in fact propagate it in the interests of their own community. A critical question here is what elements in the social system encourage the development of personal identities which do not require malevolence towards others in order to establish the personal integrity and community identities which are based on mutual benevolence rather than on mutual malevolence towards an external enemy.

Private tribute, for instance, by bandits, is brought under control by the development of law and the institutions of government. On the other hand, government then begins to extract tribute in the form of taxation on a scale which even the Mafia cannot emulate, so again we must identify tribute control as one of the major unsolved problems of society. Taxation has a peculiar status. At its best it is a kind of "willing tribute." People are prepared to coerce themselves, as it were, as long as everybody is coerced. The provision of public goods on a purely voluntary basis is never successful, mainly because of the "freeloading problem," that is, the individual who enjoys the goods, but who doesn't want to pay for them. A democratic tax system by which people, as it were, vote to tax and hence to coerce themselves is a possible solution to this problem. On the other hand, the tax system, once it is set up, is always subject to abuse, and it is possible to pass by gradual stages from a voluntary tax system into a tyranny in which the only reason why people pay taxes is that they will be shot if they don't.

Deterrence probably holds the greatest threat to mankind today and is also very difficult to control. The only two known methods are the development of a superior hierarchy of threat systems, for instance, in the present case, in world government, or through the development of other systems, such as exchange or integrative systems which gradually weaken and replace the threat system. Here again we know very little about the dynamics of systems of this kind. We do, in fact, get out of deterrence systems as we pass, for instance, from societies of personal violence into civil societies in which deterrence is rarely exercised between individuals except in relatively mild forms. How we make the transition into a world civil society is perhaps the most fundamental problem which faces the human race at the moment, and the solution of all other problems depends upon it. The greatest threat of all to the environment is war.

Of all forms of environmental deterioration, externalities are probably the easiest to control, although in many cases there are severe problems of identification. The ideal method of control consists of a system of legal penalties for producing bads, such as effluent taxes, so that anybody who produces a bad has to pay for it, either to the government or to the injured party. This, of course, has to be imposed politically through political sanctions. This means also that the problem of estimating how large the effluent tax ought to be is not solved by the ecological process of the market, but has to be the result of a political decision, and hence it is quite easy to get it wrong. However, even bad effluent taxes are probably better than no effluent taxes. The penalties for producing bads may also take the form of prohibitions, fines, or criminal sanctions, but these are usually less satisfactory as ways of changing behavior. Bads are often the product of the activities of relatively powerful people against whom prohibitions and legal penalties are almost universally inadequate as deterrents, as witness the antitrust laws. It is probably a wise strategy in this case to lay off the moral invective, avoid malevolence as far as possible, and treat the matter on rather coldly cost-benefit terms (but see also Chapter 18). A real problem here is the backwardness of the physical and biological sciences in measuring pollutants and in providing monitoring equipment which can detect their production. This is one of those rather unusual cases where the economics of the problem is very easy, but the physics and biology is quite difficult. We do not know the physical costs, for instance, in many cases of air and water pollution in terms of health deterioration, medical expenses, cleaning bills, and so on. In the absence of this information, it is very hard to impose effluent taxes which are just. Nevertheless, these items of information are frequently not in the information system precisely because penalties are not imposed and an apparatus for producing effluent taxes would very soon produce strong pressure to produce the requisite information.

Invisible externalities are much more difficult to deal with than visible ones. Effluent taxes are virtually impossible because the effluence cannot be detected. It may be that the only answer is

the development of "counter-institutions," such as government-subsidized consumer research, with some sort of tax powers on manufacturers who are producing products which in turn produce invisible bads. The legal problems here are quite tricky and need much further exploration. The possibility of a constitutional amendment which would give individuals the right to sue on behalf of the environment, as we have a certain parallel in the antitrust laws, might have rather salutory effects, but might also be very disorganizing. There is a real danger that the environmental concern will lead into a prohibition-like activity which would be an oversimple solution to a particularly complex problem.

The control of the production of perverse tastes is an extremely difficult and intractable problem. Even such relatively simple aspects of the problem as control of harmful drugs, in which one should presumably include tobacco, has been notoriously unsuccessful, especially in the United States. Here the prohibitionist state of mind forces drug users into a criminal subculture almost immediately, a subculture which has strong incentives to perpetuate and expand itself. This seems to be a clear case where one should penalize the seller but not the buyer, mainly on the grounds that the demand is induced by the seller. The problem of how to transform the identity of the drug taker and the community of the drug taker is one which has so far baffled society completely. Our experience with alcohol, which quantitatively is probably a much worse pollutant than drugs, and causes much more human misery, has also been a resounding failure, and it is hardly too much to say that all attempts to deal with it have been unsuccessful. The problem here goes very deep into family and religious subcultures, which are usually not particularly accessible to the control mechanisms of the larger society.

Population control has turned out to be a very intractable problem, perhaps because we really understand very little about the totality of the forces, both social and biological, which govern fertility. The problem is one of reducing fertility to correspond with reduced mortality, so that we can achieve a stationary population with a long average length of life. Thus, in an equilibrium population in which the average age of death is

70, the birth and death rate would have to be about 14 per thousand, whereas the biological maximum birth rate for the human population seems to be somewhere between 40 and 50 per thousand. No government policy in regard to the population has been at all successful, and we may need further social inventions even as extreme as my own "green stamp plan" of marketable licenses for children beyond the second child[3] (see also Chapter 2).

One of the most difficult problems in environmental control is its impact on the distribution of income and wealth. Much of the pressure on the environment today arises because the poor, as a result of economic development, are now enjoying things which used to be the privilege of the rich, such as travel, increased protein diets, and high consumption of power. Solutions to environmental problems frequently involve repressing or confining the activities of the poor, while leaving the rich much as they were. There have been at least two previous periods of strong concern about the environment in the United States, one around 1900 involving the first conservation movement, associated especially with the names of Governor Pinchot and Teddy Roosevelt. This produced the Bureau of Reclamation and an extension of the national parks and forests system. These were in many respects highly creditable achievements. Nevertheless, the overall effect may easily have been adverse to the poor. The Bureau of Reclamation, in spite of its somewhat socialist ideology and its emphasis on the family farm, did very little for the very poor farmer, especially for the Indian and the Spanish-American in the West. National parks and national forests, by raising private land values in their environment, have quite effectively kept poor people out of the mountains, so that the mountain West on the whole has not become an Appalachia. The second period of strong interest in the environment was in the 1930s, following the dust bowl phenomenon. This produced the Soil Conservation Service, which again has done an excellent technical job and has certainly transformed the look of the American landscape. It was the richer farmers, however, who were most able to benefit from it, and it is part of a general

agricultural policy which has driven poor farmers off the land into the urban ghettos and has materially subsidized the rich farmers. One is a little afraid that the present excitement will lead to the solution of high taxes on automobiles to subsidize public transportation, which will leave the rich with their automobiles and will force the poor onto subways. Even effluent taxes might easily turn out to be regressive if they force a rise in the price of low-cost housing, domestic power, and processed food, as they well might. Unfortunately, the distributional impact of almost any economic policy is virtually unknown. This is the great desert of economic science.

It may be hard to solve these problems under a market-type society, but there is very little evidence that centrally planned economics do any better. The pressure to fulfill a plan indeed may be more destructive of the environment than pressure from a profit system, and the fact that prices in socialist societies correspond very poorly to social costs means that even the possibility of control through effluent taxes and manipulation of the price system is likely to be quite ineffective. Furthermore, the bias of most socialist societies towards heavy industry, their bias against agriculture, and the tendency of most socialist societies to exploit their working classes in the interest of national power certainly gives very little comfort to those who seek the solutions to the environmental problems simply in slogans of the left.

Another very tricky problem in this connection, which is perhaps even more acute in socialist societies than it is in capitalist societies, is the problem of justice in distribution among the generations. This is the problem of how far the present generation should be sacrificed for the benefit of its posterity. One can hardly help having a sneaky sympathy with a man who says "What has posterity ever done for me?" and only a very strong ethic of intertemporal community can justify the present generation's making large sacrifices for its posterity, especially when these sacrifices are imposed by the state.

Implicit in any environmental program indeed is a rate of time discounting, and also a rate of uncertainty discounting which is even more difficult. Time and uncertainty discounting apply not only to the problem of distribution between the present generation and its posterity. It is of great relevance also in the problem of the rate at which the present generation should use up its exhaustible resources, as this also, of course, will effect the welfare of posterity. The further we look into the future, of course, the more uncertain it becomes. As we use exhaustible resources to produce knowledge, this knowledge in turn produces more resources. It may be indeed that this process cannot go on forever and that we have to regard the present as a peculiar time in human history when we have to transform the exhaustible resources involved in fossil fuels and ores into enough knowledge to enable us to do without them. If we could do that our own interests and the interests of posterity would be served.

It may be indeed that the key word in environmental control is a very unpopular one, that is, "patience." It is impatience that leads to the destruction of the present environment for immediate ends and a neglect of the interests of the future. Impatient young people, therefore, who think that environmental control is something revolutionary and radical, something for which we wave a magic political wand and all our pumpkins turn into effluent-free coaches (and, incidentally, nobody has yet produced an effluent-free horse) are likely to be grieviously disappointed. Environmental control is conservative rather than radical, evolutionary rather than revolutionary. It is more likely to be achieved through capitalistic instruments, like the price system suitably modified, than it is through socialistic planning. Nevertheless, it does require something like a socialist ethic with strong emphasis on the realization of the ability of the individual to identify himself with the world society which stretches forward into the future.

Perhaps one could describe this as a planetary ethic rather than a socialist ethic, but it is an ethic which is based ultimately on man's sense of stewardship for his beautiful blue and white planet with its incalculably precious freight of genetic material. The ethic of the environment indeed is an ethic of the stewardship of the evolutionary process which is falling more and more into man's hands and which he has the power to destroy as well as to foster. When man finds his identity as the steward of his planet, the problems of environmental control will move towards solution, though the institutions by which they are solved may be highly diverse.

References

1. Boulding, K. E. 1970. Fun and games with the gross national product: The role of misleading indicators in social policy. In *The Environmental Crisis* (H. W. Helfrich, ed.). Yale University Press, New Haven, Connecticut.

2. Boulding, K. E. 1970. Gaps between developed and developing nations. In *Toward Century 21: Technology, Society, and Human Values* (C. S. Walling, ed.). Basic Books, New York and London.

3. Boulding, K. E. 1964. *The Meaning of the Twentieth Century*, Chap. VI, The population trap. Harper and Row, New York.

Further Reading

Boulding, K. E. 1966. Environmental quality in a growing economy. In *Essays from the Sixth RFF Forum.* John Hopkins Press, Baltimore, Maryland.

THE NEED FOR REFORM OF NATIONAL INCOME STATISTICS

American Statistical Assoc. Proceedings (1971), pp. 94-97.

There is no doubt that the body of economic indicators known as National Income Statistics has been a fantastic success. From being a somewhat erudite and even rather secondary interest of the National Bureau for Economic Research in the 1920's, its concepts have become standard categories not only of economic argument but also of political discourse. It is hard to believe that magic letters GNP were virtually unknown before 1930. However, one of my favorite anti-proverbs is that nothing fails like success, and the very success of National Income Statistics perhaps has induced a certain complacency among economists, who sit a little too secure in the high prestige of which National Income Statistics have been a considerable part of the purchase price.

This complacency is now being challenged from a number of sources. The ecologists and conservationists have been challenging us quite rightly because the categories of national income accounting do not usually take account of depreciation of the environment and the production of "bads." The worship of the Gross National Product has been attacked as a source of pollution, environmental degradation, and even of future environmental catastrophe. The Gross National Product can be increased by destroying irreplacable natural resources, and a good deal of the activity which it represents may consist of activity necessary to overcome the bads which are produced as a by-product of goods which are otherwise counted in the Gross National Product. We can perhaps defend the Gross National Product on the grounds that it is intended only as a measure of economic activity and says nothing about what that activity is for. This however is not quite adequate as an answer, because the GNP purports to measure the product of economic activity, not merely the activity itself. Hence, if it does not include the production of bads as negative items, it is seriously defective, simply because it is too gross. The failure to include bads, indeed, is a technical defect quite similar to the problem of avoiding double counting in the production of goods, a problem which was worked out in the very early days.

While the theoretical point is easy to make, its practical application is quite difficult, mainly because of severe difficulties which we encounter in the evaluation of bads. In order to get a figure for the GNP we have to add up an enormous heterogeneous list of items of goods, weighting each by some shadow price or valuation coefficient. We would have to do the same thing for the negative commodities, which should appear as negative items in the addition. The price system, however, does not easily create negative prices for negative commodities, so that it is often hard to tell what these negative prices ought to be. We can visualize this by imagining that we go to a complete system of effluent taxes in which everybody who produces a bad is taxed accordingly. The controversies which would arise over the simple word "accordingly" can well be imagined. The difficulty is that there are very poor markets for bads, mainly because we do not cherish them and exchange them, but rather try to push them off onto somebody else without him noticing it.

We may try to wriggle out of this bind by saying that what we are really looking for is a net national product. Even this, however, is not too satisfactory. The Net National Product in the standard accounts is largely an accounting convention, which is largely a function of the accounting habits of last year modified slightly by the impact of the tax system. The Capital Consumption Allowance which is subtracted from the GNP to produce the NNP is about as much an exercise of the fertile human imagination as any statistic can be. If we want to satisfy the ecologists and conservationists, we should certainly add depreciation of the environment to this Capital Consumption Allowance to get a true NNP, although, unless this were also registered in private accounts and in private net worths, this would cause trouble when it came to evaluate the accounts on the income side. Degradation of the environment, unfortunately, frequently turns up as somebody's income, whereas if it were accounted properly it would appear as a deduction from somebody's income.

Exhaustion of resources should also be deducted from GNP to get a true GNP. When we ask ourselves how much to deduct, however, this seems like an even more difficult problem than the problem of evaluating bads. Natural resources are a function of human knowledge. Because of the spectacular rise in the "quantity of science," as Adam Smith calls it, we have probably been increasing natural resources faster than we have been using them up in the last two hundred years. But whether we can continue to do this is a serious question. We may be reaching the point of diminishing returns in the application of increased knowledge to the discovery of new resources. This, however, is a matter for the future which is extremely difficult to estimate now. If, for instance, we solve the problem of fusion power in the next fifty years, we may not have to worry very much about the exhaustion of oil, coal, and gas. If we do not solve it, we may have to worry a great deal. Who is to say, therefore, whether we should be deducting from the Gross National Product all the oil, coal, and gas that we use up, or whether we should be adding the capitalized value of the unknown future knowledge that we are going to have in fifty years? These are problems which can daunt the most skilled account of any kind and we can hardly blame national income accountants for simply pretending that they are not there.

Another problem of "netting" involves the evaluation of public goods. We could take almost any view here between two extremes. One of these would be to assume that public goods, that is, the government sector of the economy, represents simply something that is extorted by superior force from an unwilling citizenry and adds nothing whatever to their welfare. All taxes then are a simple deduction from real income. There are indeed some kleptocracies which may not fall altogether short of this model. At the other extreme, we have the exchange theory of public finance which supposes that people get something for their taxes equivalent to what they pay. Under these circumstances, the public sector of the economy is simply added to the private sector as individual welfare. The truth certainly lies somewhere between these two extremes, but where it is not easy to say. Even on the exchange theory, it is clear that public goods are much more like Christmas presents than they are like purchases, that is, they involve reciprocity rather than exchange, and just as one seldom gets what one wants for Christmas, one seldom gets what one wants from taxes, so that obviously in this sense the public sector has to be deflated in order to get a welfare index, but by how much it has to be deflated is almost anybody's guess. These problems revolving around the relation of National Income Accounts to welfare, either public or private, have been dealt with with great expertise by A. W. Sametz[1] and there is no need to beat this well-beaten bush much further. One or two other complaints, however, are not so often heard and as long as this is a complaining session we might as well try to get all the complaints out in the open.

One important set of complaints relates to the possible use or lack of use of National Income Statistics for the understanding of the problems of distribution in society. The standard National Income Accounts do have a breakdown of national income into distributional components such as Wages and Salaries, Business and Professional Income, Farm Income, Rental Income of Persons and Corporate Profits. How this fantastic hodge podge ever got into the national accounts is something which would be well worth a Ph.D. thesis. In the first place, the national income concept itself is an absurdity. It is surely one of the least defensible of all the aggregates. It is net of indirect taxes and gross of direct taxes, and there really seems to be no case for it at all, except perhaps on the assumption that only direct taxes measure the real value of the public economy and that indirect taxes represent that part of the public economy which is sheer waste. I doubt, however, if this theory was behind the construction of the accounts in the first place.

We start off, therefore, by distributing a quantity which is absurd to distribute in the first place, and we then proceed to distribute it in the oddest way imaginable. Farm Income, for instance, should surely belong to distribution by the industrial sector of the economy, something which, incidentally, is quite hard to get in any very satisfactory form. Then we have this preposterous aggregate called "Business and Professional" which includes presumably the income of doctors, lawyers, and unincorporated business. I have not been able to get a breakdown of this into business and professional, and one gets an uneasy feeling sometimes that these numbers are simply made up by a little man with a green eyeshade in the attics of the Department of Commerce. It is very peculiar, for instance, that this segment of national income has been declining, relatively, in the last forty years, whereas one would surely have thought that we have been witnessing a considerable expansion of the professions. Another very odd segment is "Rental Income of Persons," which again simply reflects a certain lack of incorporation in the real estate market with, I suppose, a certain amount of literary income. Corporate Profits here are gross of direct taxes and hence are probably overestimated. It would be hard to imagine, indeed, a more preposterous breakdown of a more preposterous total.

What then do we want? In the first place, we want distributional breakdowns of a number of different totals. For some purposes, the distribution of the Gross National Product itself would be quite interesting--for instance, by industries, by regions, and by various segments of the labor force, such as union versus non-union, corporate versus non-corporate, and so on. For other purposes, a breakdown of the Net National Product or something rather like it--perhaps it might be called the "gross national income," that is, gross income before taxes of all kinds. For other purposes, a breakdown of gross private disposable income, which would roughly be equal to the Gross National Income minus the total government sector, would also be of great interest. There are one or two rather tricky technical problems here of minor items such as the statistical discrepancy, certain items of income which are hard to allocate to individuals and the total government surplus or deficit, which are a little too technical to go into here. However, they are all fairly small items in normal times.

For both of these aggregates it would be extremely interesting to be able to break them down into labor income and non-labor income, which we cannot do in the present accounts, and it would be useful to be able to divide non-labor income into interest, profit, and rent in the good old classical style. These categories, unfortunately, are not as simple as they look and some compromises would have to be made, but it would certainly not be difficult to achieve something more significant than the present breakdowns. On the labor income side, it would be extremely nice to have a breakdown, even if somewhat arbitrary, into, say, unskilled, semi-skilled and highly professional, or something of this sort, which again we do not have now. It surely ought to be easy to answer from National Income Statistics questions such as "Is the economy getting more and more corporatized?" or "Are the service industries really increasing?" or "Is distribution going more towards labor or towards capital?" The plain fact is we simply cannot answer any of these important questions from the information as it is now presented.

Other distributions of national income would also be of enormous interest, but would be harder to get. We have certain distributions by race, although the aggregates here can be extremely misleading, as they are likely to hide certain poverty sectors within all the different racial groups. All blacks are certainly not poor and all whites are not rich. Breakdowns of income by religious preference would be of enormous interest, but very difficult to obtain. A breakdown by years of education would also be of great interest. The ideal here, of course, would be a system of computerized information from individuals which would enable us to get any kind of breakdown that we wanted, but this perhaps is too much to expect, and also raises all the specters of the national data bank, in terms of privacy, manipulation and so on.

Another very fundamental complaint against the national accounts is that they are extremely deficient on the side of capital accounting. There is no annual accounting of the national capital and its distribution. And yet, as I have been arguing, apparently without anybody listening to me for years, when it comes to developing an index of human welfare, capital accounts are much more important than income accounts. Welfare is a condition or state, that is, a stock rather than a flow, although it is not unrelated to certain flow elements. With the recent interest in the environmental deterioration the notion of welfare as a stock variable has suddenly become very fashionable. Yet National Income Accounts pay no attention to this at all. It is very difficult to find out from national accounts anything about the distribution of equity in the total capital stock of the society. It is equally difficult to find out much about the significance of the financial variables. What is the real significance, for instance, from the point of view of the distribution either of capital or income, of an increase in debt, both public and private, or of the significance of a change in the rate of interest? The fact that we cannot tell the distributional impact of almost any act of public policy, either in the distribution of capital or in the distribution of income, is one of the gravest defects in our economic information system. I am not suggesting the national accounts are necessarily the answer to this problem, but they are certainly part of the answer.

One of the great difficulties in interpreting the national accounts as a consumer, that is, as an outsider, is that, in spite of the publications on the subject, one does not really know how these things are actually put together in the shop. Anyone who has had any experience at all with the production of statistics by public bodies knows how much finagling, estimation, compromise, and argumentation has to go on inside the establishment before the beautiful tables appear in print. Any statistics-producing enter-

prise develops in the course of time a subculture of its own, along with a good deal of conventional wisdom and what we might call "private learning from experience," which is seldom subject to any outside test, and very rarely subjected to any formal outside valuation. A thorough, outside valuation of these "statistical subcultures" is something that should surely be done at least once every generation.

May I raise the question, therefore, as to whether the time is not ripe for a substantial reexamination of the whole system of aggregate statistics? I do not intend in any way to deprecate the magnificent work which has been done in the last forty years. Indeed, if one were to apply the overworked term "revolutionary" to any social change of this century, it is surely the development of National Income Statistics and the related improvements in the whole apparatus of social indicators. This has probably produced a larger change in social policy than any other single change in the institutional structure we can name, and the influence on the whole has been markedly beneficial. I have often pointed to the contrast between the twenty years after the First World War and the twenty years after the Second as an example of a fantastic transformation in the economic life of the world, a considerable part of which is a result of the change in political and social images which has come about through the use of National Income Statistics, coupled with the development of a macro-economic theoretical system which fitted in with the cumulation of statistical information. The interest which has developed in recent years in the extension of the system of aggregative indicators from National Income Statistics in the field of social indicators[2] is suggestive both of the tremendous impact which National Income Statistics have had and also of a certain sense of inadequacy in regard to them. The corollary of the antiproverb that I quoted at the beginning--that nothing fails like success--is that we only learn from failure, which is why it is so important to identify the right failures and to learn the right things from them. I suggest, therefore, that the time has come when a major research inquiry, not only into National Income Statistics, but also into social indicators in general, is clearly desirable. How this should be financed and organized is of course a question. It should clearly be in some sense independent enough of government to be capable of making sharp criticisms where these are required. On the other hand, it has to be close to government, which is the major provider of the statistical enterprise, and to have the confidence of those who are presently engaged in the business of producing statistics. Perhaps the natural body to sponsor such an enterprise would be the National Academy of Sciences, were it not for the fact that the relations of the National Academy with the social sciences are so marginal and unsatisfactory. Whatever the machinery, however, the need is very clear. Perhaps the preliminary work might be done by a joint committee of the American Economic Association and the American Statistical Association, though this might not have the essential

entrée into government that the enterprise would
really require. Whatever the machinery, it is
important that the enterprise should be well
financed and taken very seriously and that it
should involve the participation of large numbers
of consumers of statistics. It goes without
saying that it should be an interdisciplinary
enterprise, that it should involve all the social
sciences, and it should probably have an element
of collective bargaining in it between the users
and the producers of statistics, so that it might
almost be conceived as a semi-permanent institution after the initial work has been done.

REFERENCES

(1) Sametz, A. W., "Production of Goods and
     Services: The Measurement of Economic
     Growth," in Indicators of Social Change,
     edited by E. B. Sheldon and W. Moore. New
     York: Russell Sage Foundation, 1968.

(2) Toward A Social Report. Washington, D.C.:
     U.S. Department of Health, Education and
     Welfare.

MAN AS A COMMODITY

Human Resources and Economic Welfare,
New York: Columbia Univ. Press (1972), pp. 35-49.

MAN AS A COMMODITY

THE live human body has always occupied a somewhat anomalous position in economics. We can define economics as the study of how society is organized through exchange and through exchangeables, which is at least a workable definition that seems to cover most of the field. The live human body, which we shall refer to simply as a person, occupies a central and yet at the same time a peculiar role both in the capital structure and in the network of transfers of exchangeables. Thus, the person is clearly a capital good in the sense that he is the source of benefits to his owner.

In a slave society, this relationship is extremely clear. Persons who are slaves are domestic animals, as much a part of the assets of their owner as cows or horses. They are bought and sold, they depreciate, they have a cost of upkeep, and presumably they produce a valuable stream of services. Their capital value depends on the discounted sum of the differences between the revenues derived from them and the costs incurred by their ownership. In a slave society, a slave gives off labor just as a cow gives off milk, and this labor presumably results in additions to the assets of his owner, the value of these additions being the gross value of the labor, and the value of these additions minus the cost of maintenance being the net value of the labor.

The total disrepute, both moral and economic, into which slavery has fallen suggests that the person or the capital good at any rate exhibits peculiarities which even a domestic animal does not. The moral attack on slavery rests on the sense of identity of one person with another and on a feeling of community, however fragile, with other members of the human race. "No man is an Island—any man's death diminishes me, because I am involved in Mankinde; And therefore never send to know for whom the bell tolls; it tolls for thee," said John Donne. Empathy, identification, pity, and benevolence are common phenomena in the human race. The man whose sense of identity stops at his own skin indeed is quite likely to end up in the madhouse. We credit these strange two-legged creatures we see around us, in outward appearance so much like what we see in the mirror, as having the same rich and complex inner world that we do ourselves. Therefore, we identify with them.

Slavery has long been morally unstable, although it was not until the scientific revolution made it relatively unprofitable that it became morally intolerable. As processes of production became more complex, requiring intelligence and skill on the part of the human operator and trust between the organizer and the operator, slavery became relatively unprofitable. To put the matter in another way, slavery was a system with a low horizon of development. Free labor, because of the greater richness of relationships which this made possible, had a very much higher horizon of development and productivity, so that the employer could hire free labor at higher and higher wages and still be better off than he would be under a slave system.

Once slavery is abolished, every man becomes, as it were, his own slave. The person is removed as a capital good from the accounting system. There are some apparent exceptions to this principle, in the case, for instance, of compensations for injury or death, and in certain special cases of long-term contracts and services, such as a professional baseball player. The person, however, still receives income by the sale of his services or activities and he exchanges this income for other goods and services. It would seem, therefore, that labor is clearly a commodity, for it is something which is bought, sold, and has a price in either monetary or real terms.

Nevertheless, the constitutions of both the International Labor Office and of the American Federation of Labor solemnly declare that labor is not a commodity. The feeling that some things about a person should not be subject to exchange, which is overwhelmingly strong in the case of regarding the person as a capital good, still clings somewhat to the purchase and sale of activities of the person for short periods, which is what we really mean by labor. It is clear, therefore, that even though labor *is* a commodity, it is a peculiar one; and its peculiarities are related in some degree to the peculiarities of the person considered as a capital good or as a commodity.

The problem here is essentially that of the legitimation of exchange and the exchange relationship where one of the exchangeables is either a person or some activity of a person. The problem of the legitimacy of exchange has been curiously neglected by economists.[1] At least since about 1870, with the rise of the marginalist school, economists outside the Marxist tradition have been unanimous in believing that exchange, if it is uncoerced, is beneficial to both parties. Otherwise, it will not take place, as either party has a veto on it. Consequently, it has been assumed rather generally, though implicitly, that exchange, which is even more clearly twice blessed than mercy, could hardly fail to be legitimate. Nevertheless, the attack on the legitimacy of exchange, especially in the labor market, has been severe and prolonged.

In the socialist countries the legitimation of the labor market has been achieved by the replacement of the private employer by the public employer. The labor market has not in general been abolished. Labor is still bought and sold and has a price, in fact, has different prices depending on the quality of the labor. But the fact that the principal employer is the national state or its creatures and agents sheds, as it were, a warm glow of legitimacy over the whole procedure. Socialism indeed must be regarded as a phenomenon arising out of a prior delegitimation of the market as an instrument of social organization, and the socialist state must be seen, in part, as an attempt to relegitimate it. The market is such an enormously useful beast that we cannot throw it away altogether. Indeed, the only alternative is the slave state in which all persons are slaves of the government. Nevertheless, the market is evidently a beast which is regarded with such hostility and ambivalence that it has to be bridled and tamed before it can be tolerated.

Even in capitalist societies, the same forces of delegitimation and relegitimation of the labor market are at work. Here this takes the form of the rise of the labor movement, resulting in collective bargaining, frequently with governmental encouragement. It also involves direct governmental intervention in the labor market in the shape, for instance, of a minimum wage or through social security taxes, which determine in part the form in which wages shall be paid. Thus, the feeling that a completely unregulated and competitive labor market is illegitimate is almost universal. Even though it is clear that human activities are organized in considerable part by exchange, we have a very strong resistance to any suggestion that they should be organized wholly by exchange.

Relations between persons indeed are organized by at least two other classes of relationships: on the one hand, by threat, and on the other hand, by what I have called integrative relationships, which is a large category that can be broken down again into such things as status, persuasion, identity, and so on. One of the problems in the legitimation of exchange at the level of the person is that exchange is a relatively uncomplicated relationship involving rather sparse uses of information and affect, whereas we have a rather strong feeling that relationships between persons ought to be at least moderately complicated.

It would be an interesting exercise, for instance, to try and find out what people really mean when they complain that something is "impersonal." Exchange indeed can be conducted quite satisfactorily between a person and a vending machine, or with anything else in the environment with which one could have terms of trade, that is, toward which one could direct output and from which one can get input. This is all that is strictly needed for a person to have exchange of money or commodities, especially where the commodity is standardized.

The activity of a human being, labor, however, is hard to standardize; and if it is standardized, the human being is treated as a machine much less complex than in fact he is. The very term "hands" for manual workers—indeed, the very term "manual," which means the same thing—suggests that workers are not really required to have any heads, that there is something undignified in being required to perform an activity which represents only a small part of the potentiality of the human organism. Adam Smith indeed noted this problem in his famous attack on the division of labor as productive of degraded human beings, degraded by the very specialization which made them productive.[2] It is a remarkable tribute to Adam Smith's profound insight that even though he recognized the virtues of specialization and the attendant increased productivity of goods, he also saw clearly that exchange, if left to itself to organize society, might produce a depreciation in the quality of human capital at the same time that it increased the quantity of nonhuman capital.

Another peculiarity of the labor market which may account for difficulties in its legitimation is the fact that the sellers of labor tend to remain sellers and the buyers tend to remain buyers. This in itself would tend to create semi-permanent castes of sellers of labor on the one hand and buyers of labor on the other. Considering also that the buyers of labor tend to be the active organizers of the productive process and the sellers of labor tend to be passive instruments, it is easy to see how a status differential appears, with the buyers of labor having a higher status than the sellers. The buyers and the sellers then become not merely castes but classes. This distinction is in rather sharp contrast, shall we say, to speculative markets, such as the wheat market or the stock market, where the buyer today will become the seller tomorrow, where there is no class or caste of buyers and sellers, and where the relationship between the buyers and the sellers is exactly symmetrical.

These status relationships in exchange are the key to much that is superficially puzzling. There is something still a little paradoxical about exchange. By comparison with either threat or integrative relationships, exchange promotes equality of status. A threat-submission system promotes sharp inequality of status between the one who threatens and the one who submits, of which slave labor is a good example. In order to get equality of status in a threat system we have to develop a threat-counterthreat system (eyeball to eyeball) which tends to be extremely costly and unstable. Equality here is bought at a very high price, for the escalation of such a system tends to ensure that a large amount of resources must be devoted to maintain the threat capability of both parties, which then cannot be used for the production of goods.

Integrative systems, likewise, are frequently built up on the basis of inequality of status. Thus, the relationship between parent and child, or between old and young, or between teacher and student, or between ruler and ruled, all have strong integrative components, but all imply inequality of status. The only integrative relationship, indeed, which implies equality is that of friendship, and this curiously enough is very much like an exchange relationship. If A and B are friends, A does something for B, and B does something for A. If the relationship becomes too one-sided the friendship then tends to break up.

Marriage, likewise, is supposed to be an exchange relationship involving even more division of labor than friendship. We could argue indeed that even the threat-counterthreat relationships also involve exchange, although in this case it is a threat to exchange bads rather than goods. If A does something nasty to B, B will do something nasty to A. In the exchange of goods, the equality of status is still more clear. By contrast, for instance, between the gift relationship, which always implies inequality of status with the giver having a higher status than the recipient, exchange is by its very nature reciprocal and symmetrical. If A gives something to B and B gives something to A, then there seems to be no reason why we should not reverse the statuses of A and B, since it would make no difference to the transaction.

We see this phenomenon in a curiously inverse way in the customs of retail trade, especially in those retail establishments which cater to classes which are higher in status than the retailer himself. Here we observe a traditional pattern of condescension on the part of the customer and servility on the part of the retailer. In the exchange, the retailer's goods and skill have in themselves an equal, or perhaps even a slightly superior status, to the customer's money. This equality implied in the act of exchange then has to be offset by status communications in the conversation, manners, and communications which surround the exchange. In the supermarket we may notice there is no such relationship. The checker at the exit gate is not obsequious, the customer is not condescending, and the very impersonality of the transaction oddly enough makes for equality.

It is at least a plausible hypothesis, therefore, that one source of the difficulties in the labor market is precisely the tension between the exchange itself, which operates as an equalizer, and the status relationships between the employer and the employed, which rise out of the fact that employers are a class who organize the activities of the employed into a process of production. In the utilization of labor, therefore, there has to be a dominance-submission relationship. Here again it is interesting to note that Adam Smith thought that the progress of the American colonies was a result of the fact that the colonists brought with them from Europe what he calls the "habit of subordination," and hence could be organized into political societies and into productive organizations! [3] This dominance-submission relationship which induces the worker to do what he is told rests on a complex set of human interactions. The worker may do what he is told because he respects the superior skill of the employer, or he may do what he is told out of fear of losing his job, in which case it becomes much more like the threat-submission system, with indeed overtones of slavery.

Again, there may develop a rhetoric for legitimating the position of the worker, as we find it, for instance, in the trade union movement, with the rhetoric of "an honest day's work for an honest day's pay." This emphasizes the legitimacy of the relationship, and in a sense the equality of fundamental status as between the employer and the employed. The boss-bossed relationship is seen simply as a convenient division of labor with the boss and the worker each "doing his thing," with each retaining a satisfactory identity in the process. It may indeed well be that the most significant result of the rise of the labor movement in the capitalist countries was the legitimation of the labor market which it fostered. The worker as a member of the union had a dignity as well as a security which the worker as an isolated individual in an atomistic labor market could not possibly enjoy, unless, of course, he had some kind of professional status arising out of some sort of professional mystique.

It is interesting to note incidentally that in the professions there is very little problem of legitimating the labor market —the lawyer, the doctor, the architect, even the professor— feels no threat to his status at all in selling his services to the highest bidder. The problem here indeed has been how to legitimate other arrangements which might be more socially productive than the labor market principle of fee for service. We see this especially in the medical profession, where there has been, and continues to be, very strong resistance to the abolition of the market for particular services and the organization of doctors in organized enterprises on a salaried basis. Among business executives and government bureaucrats, on the other hand, status has gone along with salary rather than with professionalization. This emphasizes once again the principle that where the seller of labor has a status independent of the fact that he sells it, as in the case of the professions, it is very easy to legitimate the labor market. Where, however, the seller is doubtful about his status, then we tend to get salaried workers, whose income is only loosely related to their output and is determined primarily by their position in a role structure. In the case of nonsalaried workers the labor market gets hedged around with organization of both labor and management, resulting in collective bargaining and what might be called industrial jurisprudence.

All this perhaps can be summed up in a question to the

employer: "Are you buying labor or are you hiring a person?"
At one end of this extreme is the person who is hired to do a
single specific task, as on the assembly line, and who is fired
immediately if he does not perform the task precisely as in-
structed. At the other end of the scale, is the professor, or
even the salaried executive, who is hired to "be" rather than
to "do." That is, he is hired to fill a very loosely defined role
and his activity, therefore, depends not on fulfilling instructions from somebody further up the hierarchy but in "doing
his thing," according to his perceived identity. There are always limits, of course, often fairly sharply delimited, on what
the "thing" is that a salaried person is supposed to do, but the
limits are much broader than they are for "hands." The very
distinction between salaried and hourly labor is one of status
in the sense that the salaried person has an identity within
which he has a certain freedom of action and capacity for
originality, whereas originality is the last thing one expects
from a hired hand—in fact, it would be severely frowned
upon.

A considerable portion of the activities of the legal system
arise because there is no market in the capital value of free
persons, yet there has to be in society somewhere a substitute
for this market in the shape of an apparatus which can evaluate the worth of persons, either to themselves or to society,
under circumstances where this valuation is necessary for behavior. These occasions occur mainly at two quite different
levels. On the one hand, the law is frequently called upon to
assess the value of a person when his body has been damaged
by another. Damage suits which seek to assess, and to force
the responsible party to pay, the value of an injury to a person or the cost of his loss in a death to his dependents are a
considerable part of the business of the law. It is a clumsy
apparatus and certainly does not operate with any great justice. Many who are damaged receive no compensation at all
in society and many receive what seems like an overpayment

of their loss. Nevertheless, the very existence of this apparatus testifies to the need for making evaluations, particularly under conditions of loss, of the capital value of the human person. It is a very interesting and difficult question as to whether any reform of this system is feasible, for instance, in the direction of compulsory universal insurance against all losses of capital value of the person, without regard to blame or responsibility. Such a system might, of course, make for irresponsibility and for the production of avoidable damages, though we do not really know how elastic is the demand for doing damage to persons. One hopes that it is highly inelastic, in which case the system of universal human insurance might work pretty well. One would not really expect the problem to be much more serious than the problem of arson in the case of fire insurance.

At the other end of the legal spectrum, we can interpret the criminal law as in very large measure an attempt to assess negative values on persons whom society feels are on balance injurious to it. The criminal indeed is a form of human pollution, that is, as a person he is regarded as a negative good or a "bad" whose removal from society presumably increases the capital value of everybody else. Prisons are then seen as the septic tanks of society into which those persons who are regarded as discommodities are flushed. One can indeed have at least three theories of the operations of the criminal law—deterrent, custodial, or reformist.

Under the theory of deterrence, the justification of the criminal law is that without it more people would have negative capital values from the point of society, and that hence the cost of the criminal law can be offset by the increase in negative capital value of persons which would occur if the criminal law did not exercise its deterrent function. We still know very little about how much in fact the criminal law acts as a deterrent, although there is some considerable evidence that the effect is frequently, though not always, positive.

Whether the effect is large enough, however, to justify the cost of the criminal law itself is another matter and, of course, may vary considerably from one part of the law to the next. We abandoned Prohibition, for instance, because it became clear that the cost of deterrence was in excess of the depreciation of human values which the abandonment of the law would create. We may come to the same conclusion about marijuana. In this sense, the criminal law is supposed to act rather like effluent taxes in the case of pollution, by making the production of "bads," in this case of course bad character or negative capital valued persons, less attractive to the producer.

The reformative aspects of the criminal law, as reflected for instance in the euphemism "reformatory" for prison, is the human equivalent of the reclamation of garbage and sewage. There is no great optimism abroad about the capacity of reformatories to reform, and it is fairly clear that this aspect of the criminal law is very ineffective. It is too much like trying to reclaim the chemicals in smoke after it has left the chimney. The difficulty here perhaps is that the apparatus of the criminal law tends to be symbiotic with the criminal subculture. In many respects indeed the police are a ligitimated branch of the criminal subculture itself. Hence, reform involves a change in the whole subculture, which is very difficult, simply because the processes of transmission and the perpetuation of the culture are so universal and widespread within it that it is extremely difficult to impose other types of communication on it. Certainly the proposition that prisons produce more criminals than they reform is supported by a good deal of evidence. Part of the difficulty here is that deterrence and reformation are often incompatible, so that we have an extremely complicated social production function, the parameters of which are very hard to assess. The whole movement toward juvenile courts, for instance, is an attempt to separate the reformatory and the deterrent aspects of the law to some extent, but it is hard to tell how successful this attempt has been.

The other aspect of the criminal law, the custodial aspect, is unfortunately the easiest, and we continually tend to slip into it. The custodial concept, of course, goes far beyond the confines of the criminal law. We find it in the case of mental disease, old folks' homes, and even the ghettos. The custodial segregation of those whom society regards as having negative value is indeed an ancient institution and pervades all societies. The difficulty lies in the fact that this may be too easy a solution of the problem and hence too stable. If society can segregate those whose capital value is negative so that they will not depreciate the capital value of those who regard themselves as positive, then those who make the decisions for the society, who will of course always regard their own capital value as positive, may find this a very cheap solution, at least in the short run. Septic tanks, however, tend to fill up and overflow and to pollute the whole underground water system, and the same may be true of the social septic tanks implied in the segregation and neglect of the poor, the old, or the mentally and morally ill. A better apparatus for assessing the total capital value of the persons in society therefore is almost essential to any genuine social reform.

It is curious here how we seem to have come full circle. We have rightly rejected the concept of a market in human beings as such, because this perverts the concept of the value of a person, even though it may establish a dollar number on the slave block. Nevertheless, the measurement and assessment of the value of a person and the development of institutions which raise this value rather than lower it is perhaps one of the crucial problems of any society. Institutional reform in society, therefore, frequently takes the form of attempting to find substitutes for the market which perform its function in a more legitimate way. The person indeed is not a commodity, but he has something which commodities have—that is, value—and the study of a simple form of value—that is, commodity value—may throw a great deal of light on the generation, understanding, and even the measurement, of those higher forms by which true value of a person is to be measured either by himself or by society.

In an earlier paper,[4] written at the instigation of Eli Ginzberg for a conference he organized, I attacked the whole concept of "manpower" as implying that there is some single well-defined end of society to which human beings are subordinate. The manpower concept, it seemed to me, implied a political philosophy which made the ends of society or even of the national state transcendent over the multifarious ends of the individuals who composed it. My real objection to the manpower concept which I would make just as strongly now as I did eighteen years ago is that in effect it treats man as an intermediate good, not as an end in himself. I did not mean to imply, of course, that the manpower concept could not be used as a rhetorical device to organize certain aspects of the study of society, as Eli Ginzberg has used it very successfully. My protest was rather against assuming that this abstraction presented some kind of ultimate reality. I am as unfriendly to great societies as I am to great men and my ideal society is one which interferes as little as possible with the ability of little people to have a little fun.

Nevertheless, just as the rejection of the concept of the valuation of the person through the market and the rejection of the notion that man is a commodity does not exempt us from finding other institutions which will value the person in other ways, so the manpower concept, which in its crude form is a sheer affront to the dignity of the person, has its equivalent in the concept of the organization of the human community. The weakness of pure individualism is that there are no pure individuals. The human person finds his significance and his dignity as he finds an identity, and his identity is closely related to the community with which he identifies. To quote John

Donne again, "Every man is a piece of the continent, a part of the maine." It is the existence of this continent of community with which we identify which makes a purely atomistic economics unsatisfactory and hence makes the concept of a single well-defined end, toward which manpower may be directed, expressed in the welfare of community, much more attractive than·it otherwise might be. We reject the concept of man as a commodity pure and simple, but not the concept of a person as a part of the valuable stock of society. We reject the concept of the person as simply a means to some nonpersonal end, but we recognize also that the person *has* nonpersonal ends for which he may willingly regard himself as the means. These distinctions may seem fine, but they are not hairsplitting. They represent indeed a watershed on one side of which society becomes an intolerable tyranny, on the other side of which it becomes a community which enlarges and makes more meaningful the lives of all persons within it. Finding where this watershed lies in practice is perhaps the greatest single task of the social and moral sciences.

NOTES

1. Kenneth E. Boulding, "The Legitimacy of Economics," *Western Economic Journal*, V, 4 (September 1967), 299–307.

2. Adam Smith, *The Wealth of Nations* (New York: Modern Library Edition, 1937), p. 734.

3. *Ibid.*, p. 532.

4. Kenneth E. Boulding, "An Economist's View of the Manpower Concept," in *Proceedings of a Conference on the Utilization of Scientific and Professional Manpower* (New York: Columbia University Press, 1954), pp. 11–26.

INDEX OF NAMES

SUBJECT INDEX